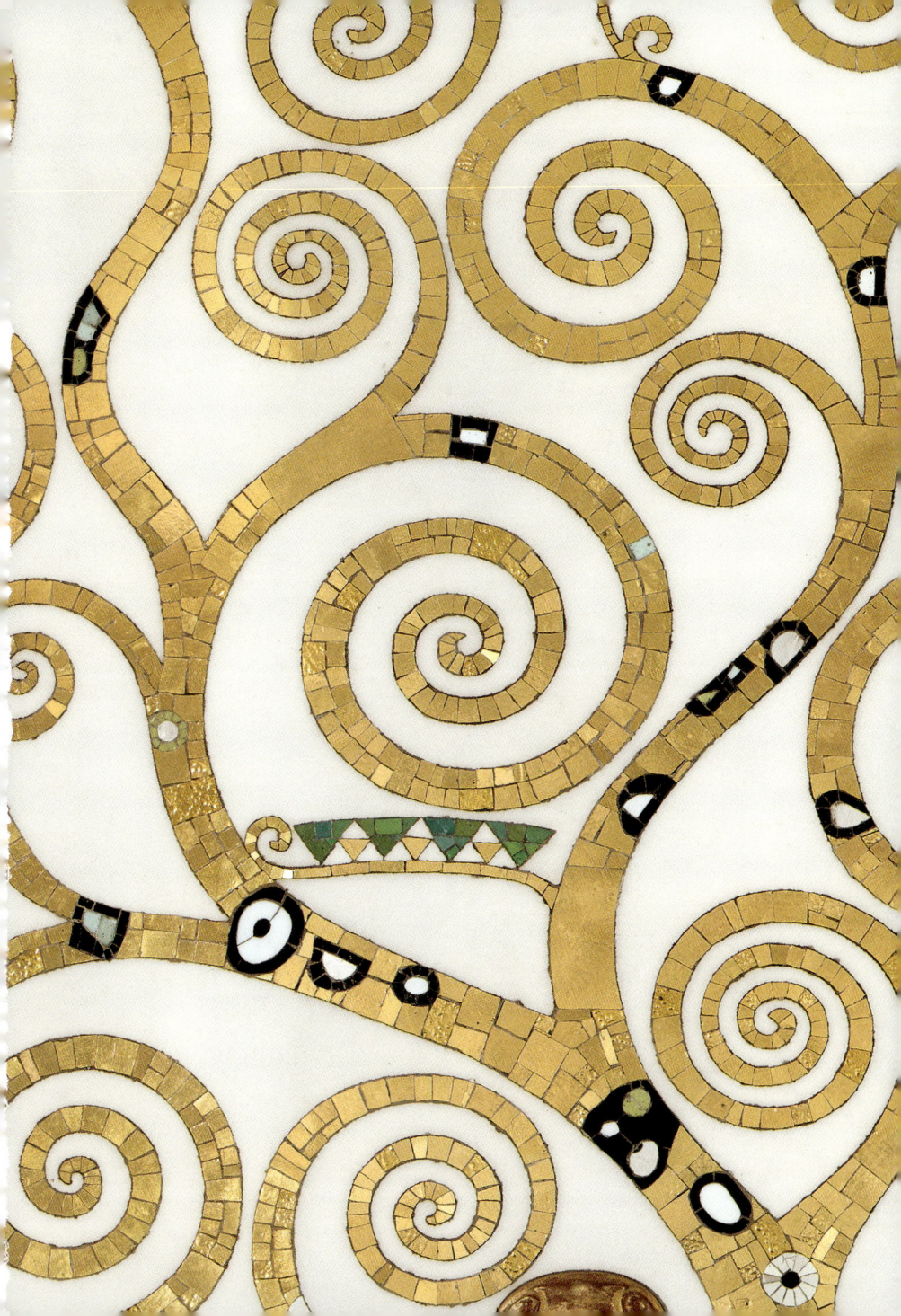

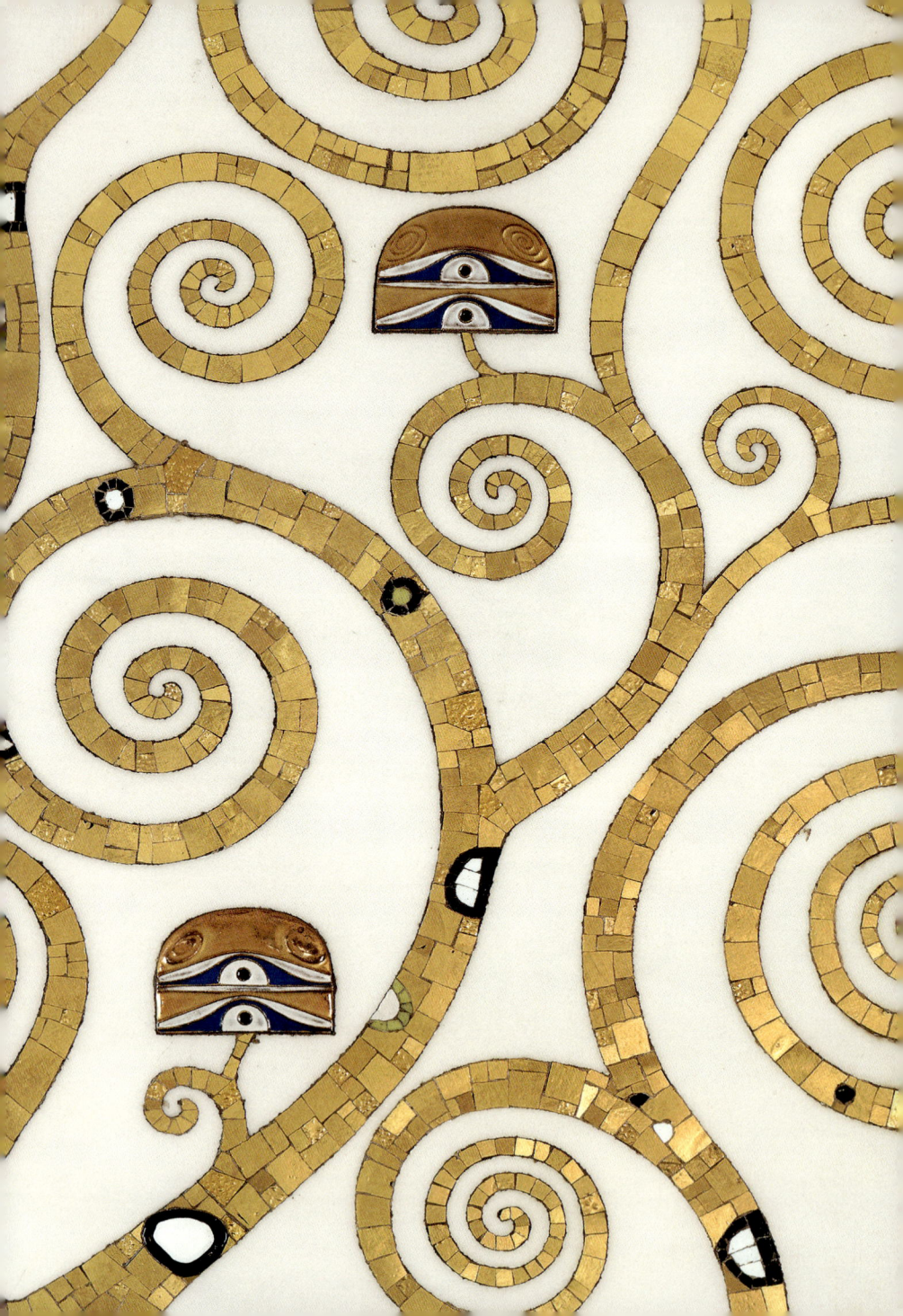

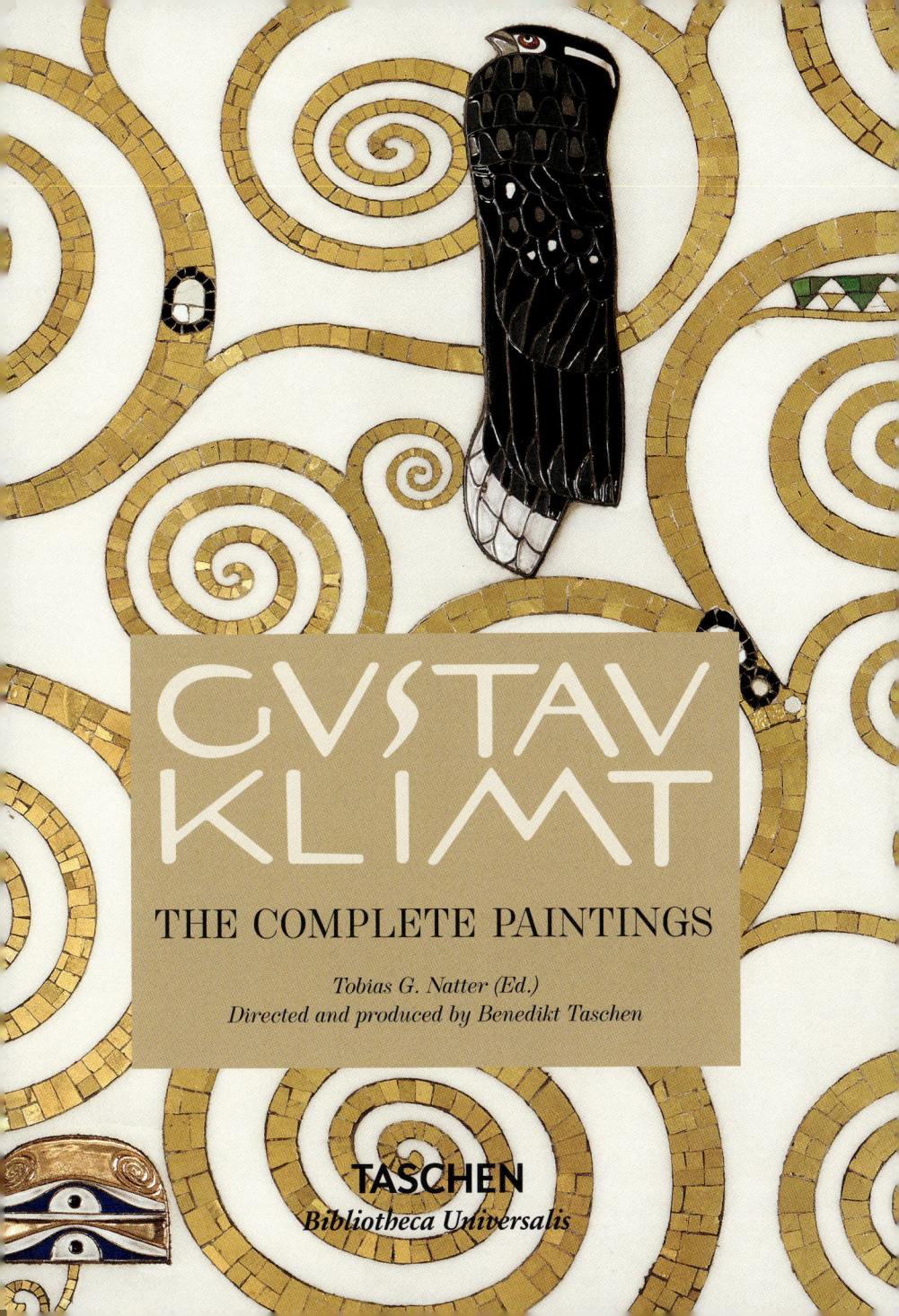

GVSTAV KLIMT

THE COMPLETE PAINTINGS

Tobias G. Natter (Ed.)
Directed and produced by Benedikt Taschen

TASCHEN
Bibliotheca Universalis

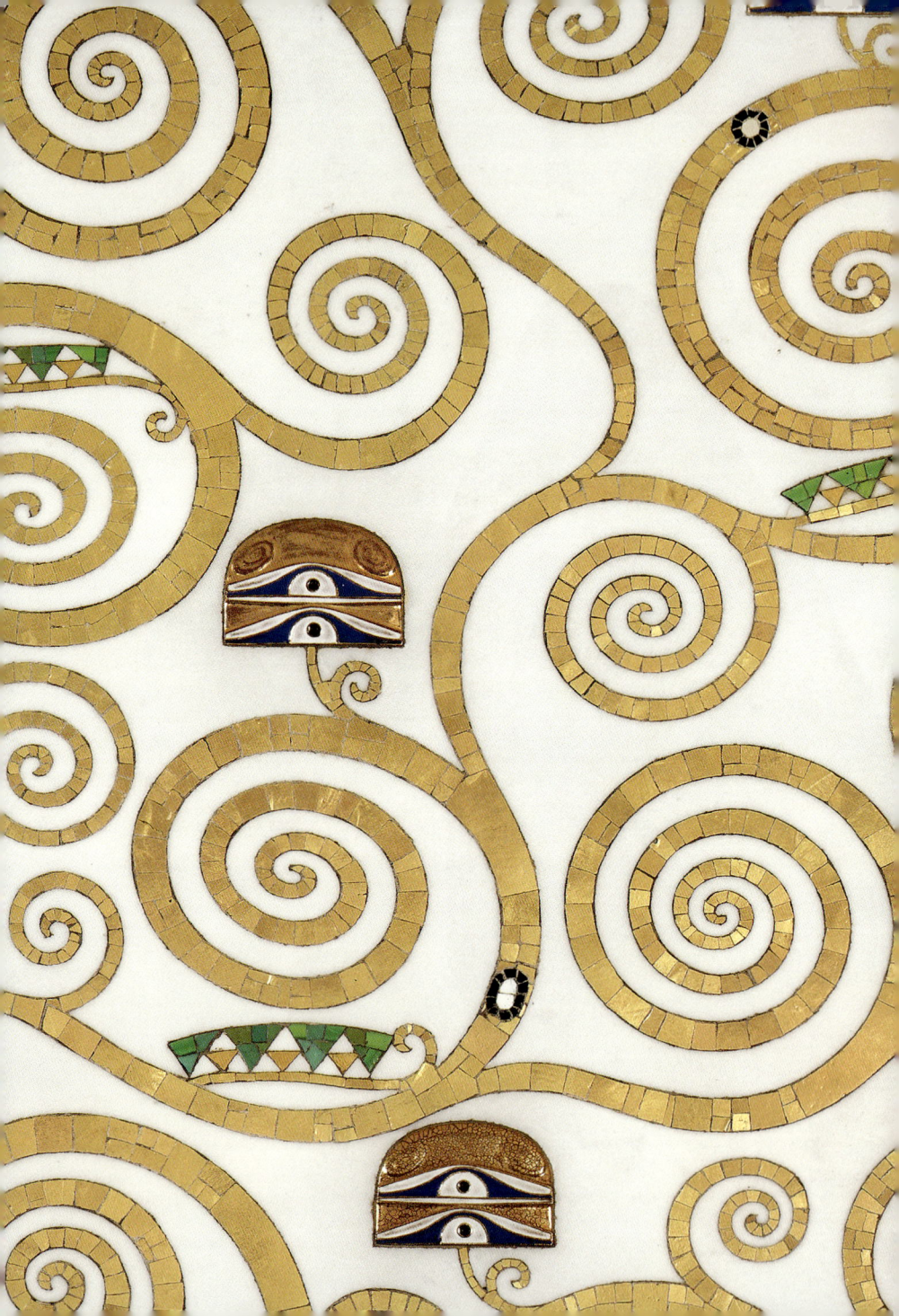

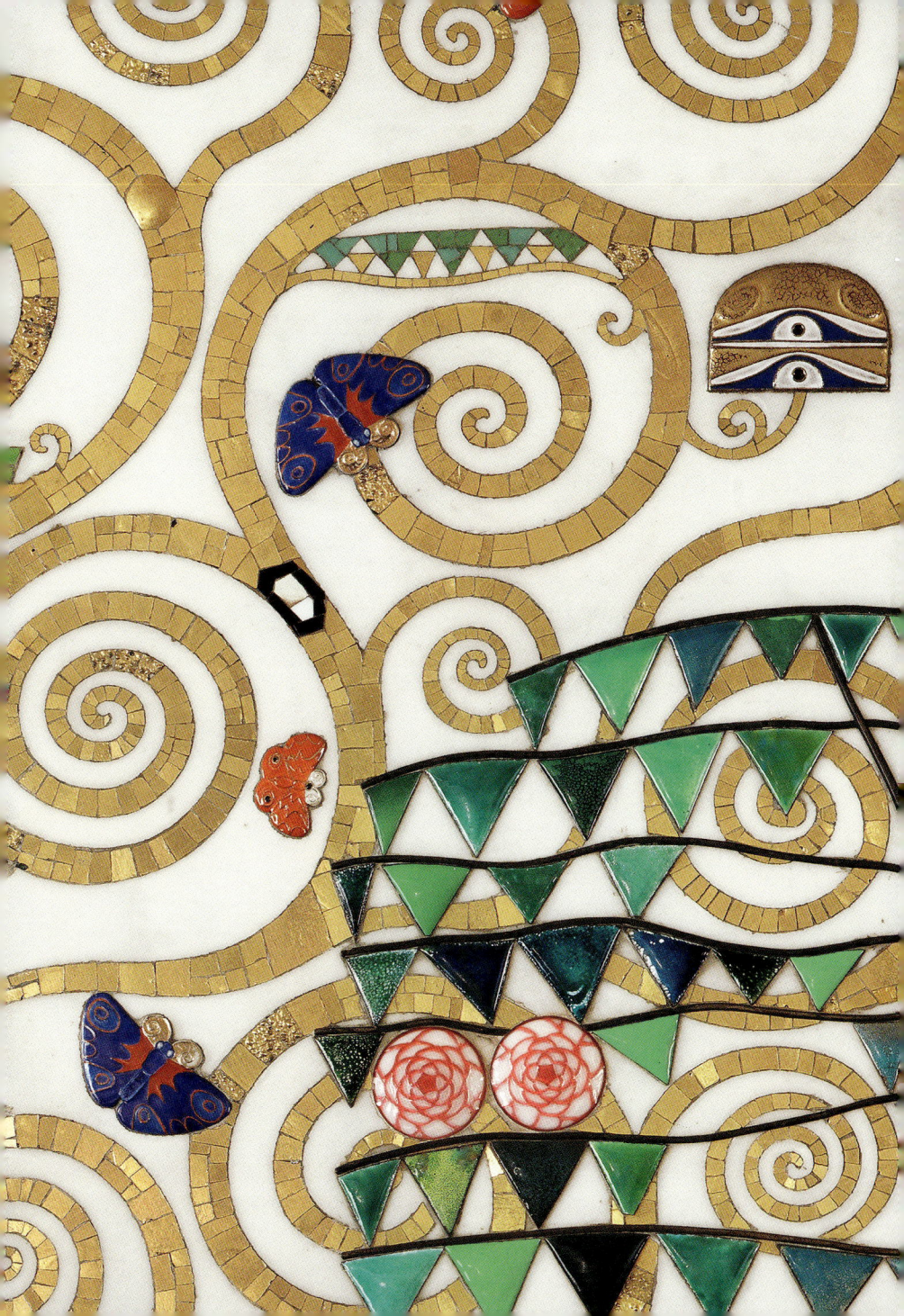

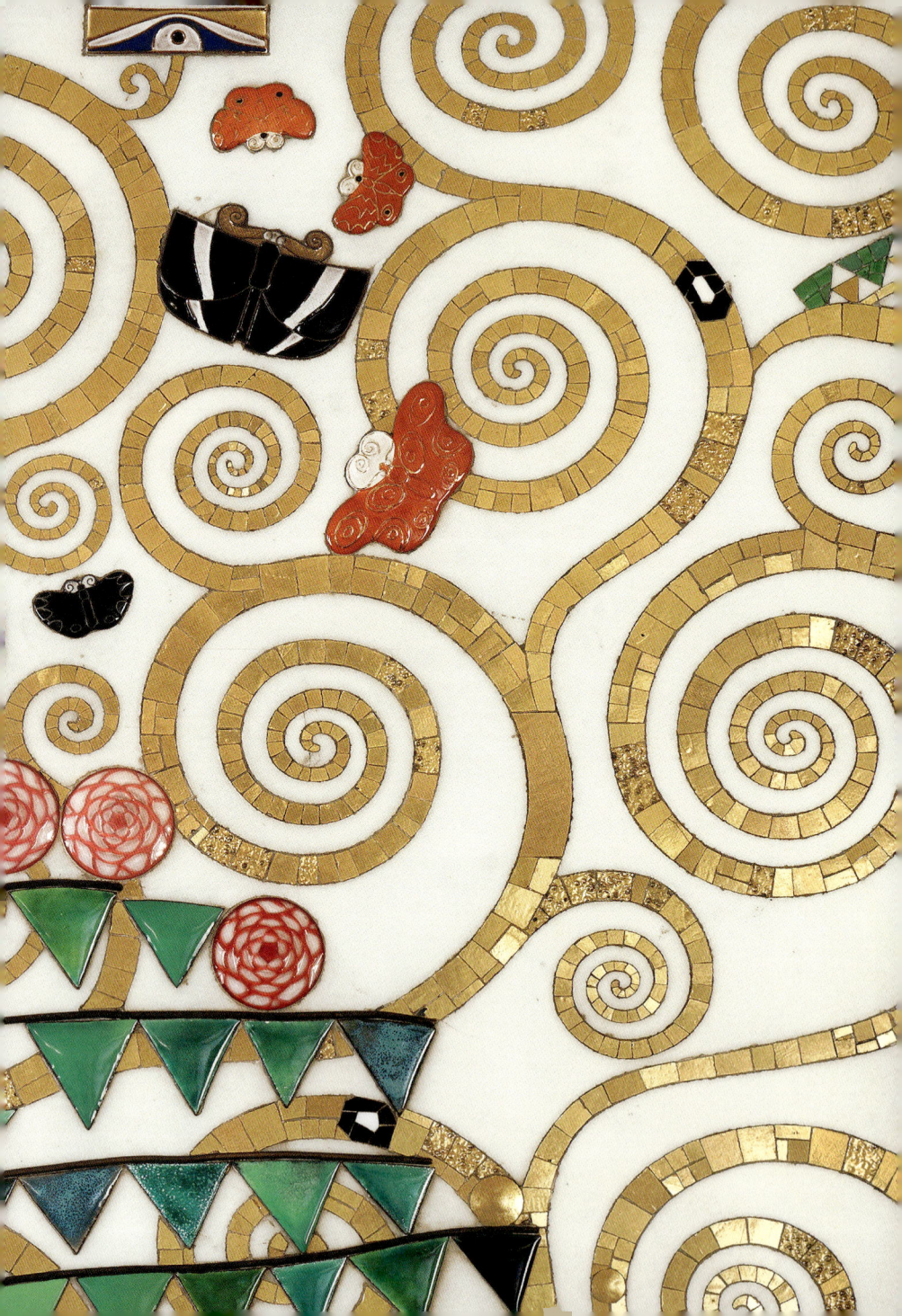

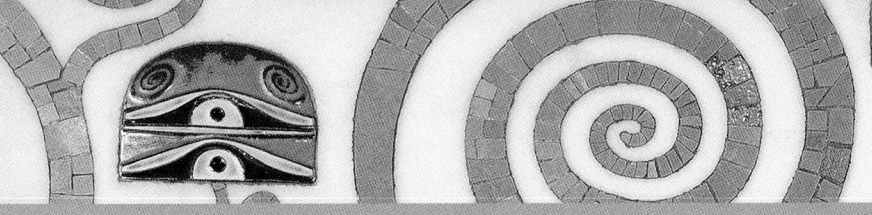

Gustav Klimt:
controversy and topicality

Tobias G. Natter — 8

Gustav Klimt:
controversy and topicality

Tobias G. Natter

When a film about Gustav Klimt, with John Malkovich in the leading role, was released in 2006 and a painting by the artist changed hands for an alleged US$135 million around the same time, Klimt's popularity soared to a new high. In contrast to predictions made back then, however, this interest has not since waned. Instead, it has become once again clear that the work of Gustav Klimt, thanks to its substance, is able to survive the dizzying heights of fame and boundless popularization apparently without difficulty.

In 2012, too, a multitude of museum exhibitions marking the 150th anniversary of Klimt's birth testified to the relevance and topicality of this exceptional artist. Klimt has not always generated public awareness in this way, however, as a brief look back at the past reveals. Klimt was born in 1862 in Vienna, where he rapidly shot to stardom. But his fiftieth birthday in 1912 went by without a semicentennial exhibition. Five decades and two world wars later, the world had dramatically changed: the Austro-Hungarian Empire was now a thing of the past and Klimt was perceived as the representative of a bygone era and at best as a leading practitioner of a Viennese take on Art Nouveau. But that, too, was now passé, dismissed as an isolated development and marginalized with the argument that there were supposedly no paths leading from it to Modernism. As the art scene in the years after the First World War celebrated the triumphal march of abstraction, there seemed to be no place for Klimt.

In multiple respects, therefore, the exhibitions marking the centenary of Klimt's birth in 1962 provided opportunities for rediscovering Klimt and his work. Among the many efforts by public bodies and private individuals, in particular Austrians in exile, to establish Klimt's name beyond the bounds of Austria and to integrate him into the transcontinental discourse, great hopes were pinned on the exhibition mounted at the Guggenheim Museum in New York. The organizers still lacked the confidence to give Klimt a one-man show and so he was presented jointly with Egon Schiele, but it was his first major museum exhibition in the United States and one that indeed proved to be a milestone in the attempt to dissolve the geographical boundaries around Klimt's art.

At the same time, Klimt scholarship in the 1960s was placed on a new footing. With the catalogue raisonné compiled by Fritz Novotny and Johannes Dobai, first published in German in 1967 and followed by an English edition one year later, art-historical research into Klimt's painterly oeuvre was given a solid foundation. This was followed two years later, in 1969, by Christian M. Nebehay's comprehensive documentation of visual and written sources relating to Klimt's life and work. The 1980s saw the appearance of the four-volume catalogue raisonné of Klimt's drawings, the culmination of decades of research by Alice Strobl. These three publications continue to form the pillars of Klimt scholarship. Over the years, meanwhile, new and important insights have been offered into individual facets of Klimt's work, his oeuvre as a whole and, in particular, its interpretation: in the sphere of Klimt's landscape painting, for example, through the recent studies of Alfred Weidinger, Stephan Koja and Anselm Wagner, and in the case of Klimt's female portraits, via the contributions of myself and others. Seminal publications have appeared on the subject of Klimt and women, namely on the topos of the *femme fatale* and its potency, on the artist's position within society, on the individuals who collected his works and their historical milieu, and on provenance research. Experts around the world, above all in the context of the cultural sciences and humanities, have shed new light upon Viennese Modernism and, in particular, upon its relationship to interior design and the concept of the *Gesamtkunstwerk* – a total or unified work of art – that is still so fascinating. A particularly topical area of Klimt scholarship today concerns the analysis of his images from the point of view of gender research. In the area of Klimt's drawings, Marian Bisanz-Prakken is currently working on a fifth volume of Strobl's catalogue raisonné.

On the occasion of the 100th anniversary of his death in 2018, it was evident that Klimt is more than ever firmly anchored both in academia and in the public eye. Meanwhile, Klimt's art can also be observed reaching beyond Europe and North America, to new audiences in Asia. It will be intriguing to see how his presence develops in the future and which aspects of his work will prove particularly relevant.

The collection of six essays building upon the very latest Klimt scholarship opens with the contribution by Rainald Franz and Angelina Pötschner, who examine the artist's early oeuvre. The authors trace the rise of an artist who, as part of the younger generation growing up under Hans Makart, rapidly made a name for himself and was considered Makart's legitimate successor. They present a successful salon painter who won prestigious major commissions such as the ceiling paintings for the staircases of Vienna's newly built Burgtheater and mural decorations for the Kunsthistorisches Museum, and who was thus well on his way to becoming an official State artist. In the 1890s, however, when at the height of this first career, which was crowned by the award of an imperial medal of honour, Klimt suffered an artistic crisis. His work tempo, previously rapid, slowed down and his artistic output dwindled. But after a painful creative crisis, the artist reinvented himself. With the founding of the Vienna Secession in 1897 and his election as its first president, Klimt announced his return as the standard-bearer of Modernism.

The discussion of this new departure and its 'sacred spring' is taken up by Christoph Grunenberg. With the Secession, Klimt and his fellow artists established one of the most prominent avant-garde platforms around 1900. It is not an exaggeration to say that the founding of the Secession marked the start of a new artistic era for Vienna. In the new exhibition building with its distinctive gold cupola, Klimt presented his Faculty paintings one by one – and each time to an ever louder chorus of disapproval. But the Secession was also the setting of the legendary 'Beethoven Exhibition' with Klimt's celebrated *Beethoven Frieze*, an event that saw contemporary efforts to create a unified work of art reach a high point. The idea of the *Gesamtkunstwerk* was translated into a similarly concentrated form one last time in the 1908 Kunstschau, where Klimt showed *The Kiss* in public for the first time. In his opening speech, the artist pointed out that he viewed so-called fine and applied art as one and expressed his conviction that the avant-garde stood shoulder to shoulder with a new society, insofar as he defined artists as "an ideal community of creators and connoisseurs".

In her essay on the mosaic frieze for the Palais Stoclet in Brussels, Anette Freytag discusses the second famous frieze in Gustav Klimt's oeuvre. She complements earlier research, for example, on the genesis of Klimt's preliminary drawings for the frieze and their relationship to the final work, and on the relationship between the frieze and the architecture of the Palais Stoclet, designed by Josef Hoffmann, insofar as she concentrates upon the finished frieze and its position and significance within the Palais Stoclet and proposes an interpretation of the frieze as an artificial garden at the heart of the house.

Susanna Partsch discusses the subject of women in the work of Gustav Klimt, both in his portraiture and in his richly visualized allegories. Paintings of women became the artist's trademark, be they Symbolist-influenced representations of allegorical female figures that revealed manifest and latent gender asymmetries of the day, in particular, in their reinterpretation of biblical figures such as Judith and Salome as *femmes fatales*, or be they classic portrait commissions, starting in 1897 with the portrait of Sonja Knips as the prelude to Klimt's Secessionist works, and leading to the first portrait of Adele Bloch-Bauer with its opulent use of gold, in which many considered the female sitter to have frozen into ornament. Once again, however, we see Klimt reinvent himself and his painting, this time through the power of colour in the female portraits and allegories of his late years. Intimately bound up with the history of these works are the biographies of the women they portray. Klimt's female sitters – members of the assimilated upper bourgeoisie and often with Jewish roots – belonged with their families to the artist's most important patrons and collectors.

Another striking new departure in Gustav Klimt's work is explored by Evelyn Benesch in her essay on Klimt's landscape paintings. Interestingly, this was a genre to which Klimt did not turn until the second half of his life, when he began taking annual summer breaks in the Salzkammergut region, in particular on Lake Attersee. These summer holidays would see Klimt working on four or five landscape paintings at once. Benesch examines the process by which Klimt filtered and transformed seen nature to meet his own artistic requirements. Underpinned by the dates and facts established by Johannes Dobai, Stephan Koja and Alfred Weidinger in their own publications on Klimt's landscapes, Benesch analyses the evolution of the artist's concept of nature from atmospheric paintings hallmarked by Impressionism to abstract 'painted mosaics' and the visual poetry of a natural motif modified by Klimt.

In her essay on the drawings in Klimt's oeuvre, Marian Bisanz-Prakken discusses an area that has attracted intensive study. Drawing was a vital necessity for the artist and his graphic work is considered a particularly fascinating genre, one that was valued by many of his contemporaries above all else in his oeuvre. Bisanz-Prakken shows how Klimt sketched his motifs thousands of times and probed the autonomy and self-sufficiency of drawing, just as he constantly tested the beauty and expressiveness of line. Insofar as she departs from the usual chronological discussion of drawings selected according to strict criteria and instead 'sorts' them typologically, she sheds light on Klimt's elemental feelings and moods, offering new and often surprising insights into his thought processes and working methods.

Klimt found himself in the journalistic spotlight more than any other Austrian artist: surrounded by scandal in his own lifetime, he is today shrouded in myth and misrepresented by clichés. Klimt's paintings, projects and exhibitions were widely reported and discussed in his own lifetime not just in specialist art journals but also in the daily newspapers. He was a controversial star whose works made passions run high; he stood for Modernism but he also embodied tradition. His pictures polarized and divided the art-loving world. Journalists and the general public alike were split over the question: *For or against Klimt?* As Karl Kraus fired off his eloquent attacks in the pages of *Die Fackel*, Hermann Bahr retaliated in the Secession journal *Ver Sacrum*. With his sensitive descriptions, Ludwig Hevesi, more than anyone else, sought to provide the public with a means of understanding Klimt's works. Other notable combatants likewise added their voices to the discussion, amongst them Berta Zuckerkandl, Felix Salten, Franz Servaes, Richard Muther and Eduard Pötzl. Many other articles on the Klimt 'controversy' also appeared in the press, written by journalists who did not always sign themselves by name.

The volume of material and the quality and heatedness of the debate are equally surprising. I find it all the more astounding that this documentary material, so extraordinarily wide-ranging and atmospherically rich, has never before received systematic evaluation. The testimonies by Klimt's contemporaries thereby paint a vibrant picture of the artist and his work. The documentation is rounded off by a biography.

The result is a book that, I hope, will become a standard work of reference. It is a product of the concerted efforts of a great many people. First and foremost, I would like to thank my authors Evelyn Benesch, Marian Bisanz-Prakken, Rainald Franz, Anette Freytag, Christoph Grunenberg, Susanna Partsch, Angelina Pötschner and Michaela Reichel, who have brought their expertise and their passion to this major undertaking. Without their specialist knowledge and their frequently new perspectives on Klimt's work, the voices of Klimt's contemporaries would lack the necessary calibration by the current state of Klimt scholarship. Their essays also provide the framework required to understand the art discussion around 1900. I also owe thanks to my colleagues in the museum world who so willingly supplied me with information about the paintings in their safekeeping. I am likewise indebted to the staff at the Austrian National Library in Vienna, the Institute of Art History at Vienna University, the Art Library in Berlin and the Central Institute of Art History in Munich, for their many different forms of support during the often time-consuming research that was undertaken for this book. At this juncture, I would like to acknowledge, in particular, the private owners of Klimt works who so generously allowed me access to their treasures and to their archives. For their trust, and for the many inspiring conversations with which it was accompanied, I am deeply grateful.

I am continually surprised by the fact that the present book, so exacting in terms of its scope, quality and presentation, could have arisen as the result of a private initiative. Particular interest will be commanded by the magnificent reproductions of the Stoclet frieze, whose details and materials have never before been seen in this form. Thanks to the kindness of the Stoclet family, we were not only granted access to the Palais but were permitted to take a special set of photographs in which Klimt's artistic aims at the interface of painting and applied art are rendered visible with a new immediacy. I would like to express my admiration and great respect for the publisher, Benedikt Taschen. The members of the Taschen team, above all Petra Lamers-Schütze, nursed this book through every stage of its production. From initial idea to final printing, they accompanied its evolution with supreme professionalism and skill and were open to many suggestions along the way. Together, we have made great efforts not just to bring the works of Gustav Klimt vividly to life in outstanding reproductions, but also – and with similar care – to accompany them with visual material documenting the spirit of the age. Visual material that serves to reflect, in particular, Klimt's close association with Josef Hoffmann, the

Wiener Werkstätte and his early collectors and patrons. I would also like to thank Brigitte Beier and the editorial team for their energetic commitment.

The opportunity to write a lavishly illustrated book on Gustav Klimt and to be able to place its scholarly emphasis upon the areas outlined above, proved for me an irresistible temptation to which I willingly succumbed, despite all the pressures it would invariably – although not always predictably – bring with it. It goes without saying that work on this book took a great deal of time and energy, sustained over a long period of time. During this phase, which inevitably lasted much longer than planned, I was able to count on the patience and understanding of the people in my private sphere and to know that they all shared my enthusiasm for Gustav Klimt. To all of them, in particular to Christoph Mai, I owe my warmest thanks.

I.

The salon painter: early works – early career

Rainald Franz, Angelina Pötschner

"*The spandrel pictures [for the main staircase in the Kunsthistorisches Museum, 1890/91] already show the inherent force of his strengthening personality. It is here that Klimt's characteristic female type first appears: this enigmatic being, at once sensual and spiritual. Here, already, is the striving towards purely painterly effect, towards the harmony of the single paint mark and towards the harmony of the colours as a whole.*"

BERTA ZUCKERKANDL, 1908

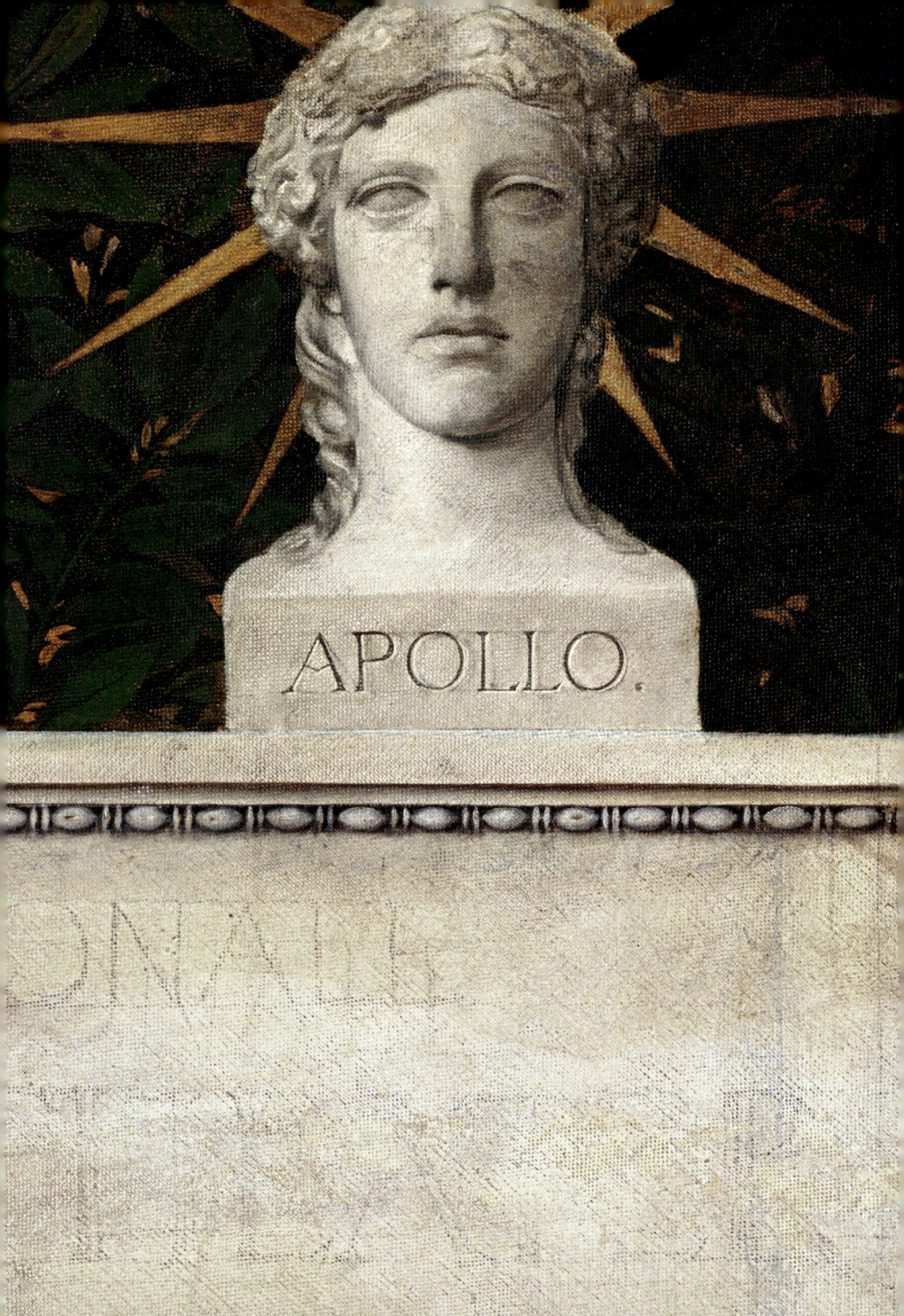

APOLLO.

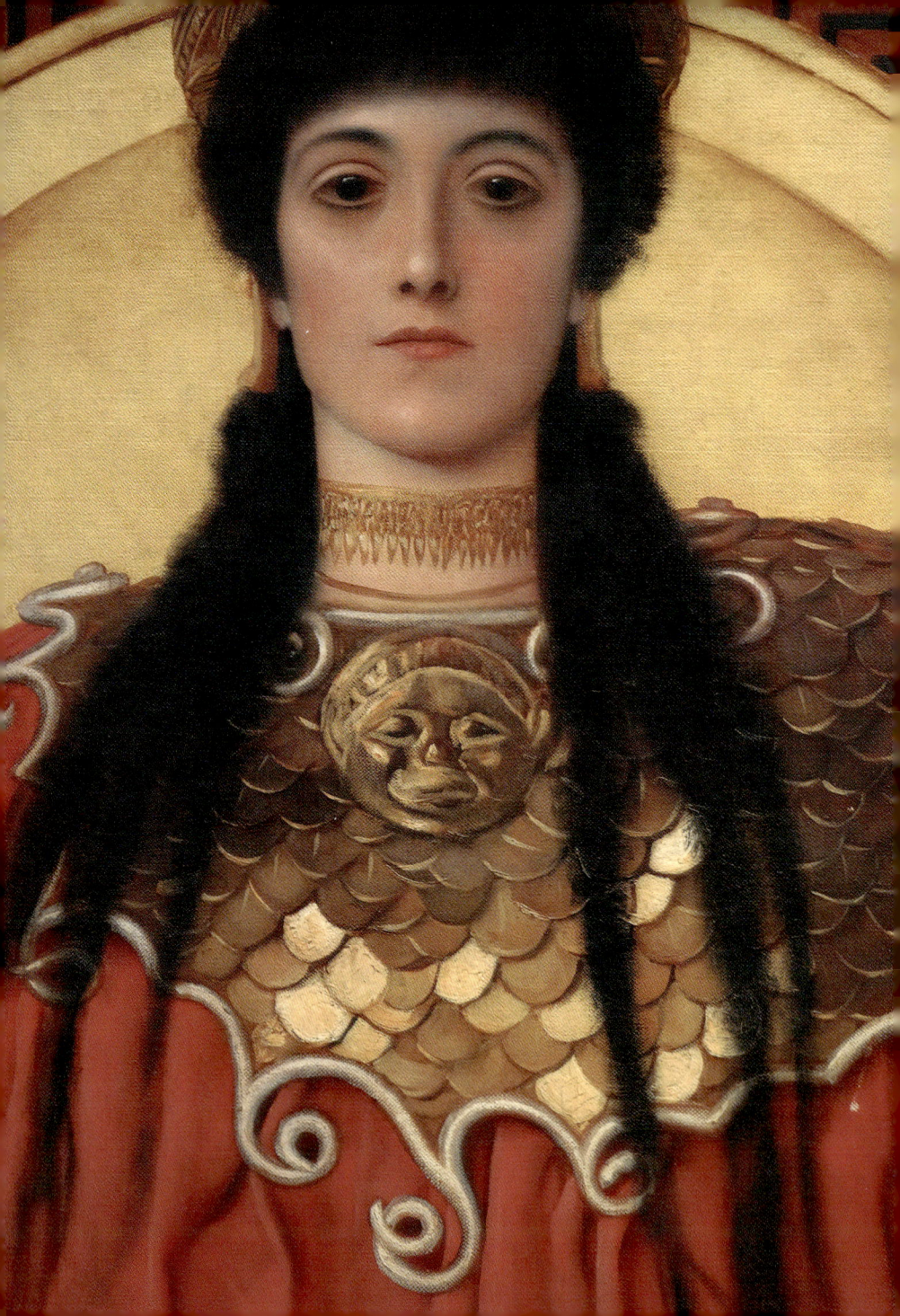

At the School of Applied Arts

Gustav Klimt was six years old when his parents enrolled him at the local elementary school at 61 Lerchenfelderstrasse in Vienna's 7th district in 1868. The young Gustav Klimt displayed a pronounced talent for art even as a pupil, and his teacher suggested to his parents that they should send him to the Kunstgewerbeschule, the School of Applied Arts newly opened in 1867. The fact that his father, Ernst (1834–1892), was an engraver undoubtedly helped foster Gustav's creative leanings. It is a sign of his parents' appreciation of natural talent that they paid for their sons to attend the School of Applied Arts rather than arranging for them to begin an apprenticeship right after elementary school. In October 1876 the fourteen-year-old Gustav passed the entrance examination to the School of Applied Arts – which involved copying an antique head – with top marks. Sitting beside him during that same examination was Franz Matsch (1861–1942), who would become a close friend and colleague for many years (Giese 1976, p. 3). Soon thereafter, Gustav's younger brother Ernst Klimt (1864–1892) also successfully sat the entrance examination to the School of Applied Arts and thus completed the artist trio in 1878.

In comparison to the traditional curriculum taught at the Vienna Academy of Fine Arts, established in 1692, the teaching system at the School of Applied Arts was progressive. The school had evolved out of the Imperial and Royal Austrian Museum of Art and Industry, which had opened its doors in 1864. Just as the Austrian Museum was modelled on the South Kensington Museum (later the Victoria and Albert Museum), founded in London in 1852, one year after the first Great Exhibition, so its School of Applied Arts oriented itself towards the English schools of design, the most modern educational institutes of the day for students wishing to train in the industrial arts. The founder of the two institutions in Vienna, Rudolf von Eitelberger (1817–1885), had inscribed the "elevation of taste" as what we might call a mission statement into the statutes. Eitelberger, himself a professor at the University of Vienna, saw art and applied art as inextricably linked. For this reason, the three major disciplines of architecture, sculpture and painting remained the basis of the education delivered by the School of Applied Arts, "for industrial art consists of nothing other than the application of these three arts to the requirements of everyday life" (Eitelberger 1879, p. 121). When it came to filling the professorial chairs, applicants were informed that consideration would be given to "artists who demonstrate

Page 15
Poster for the Internationale Ausstellung für Musik und Theaterwesen (detail), 1892
Design for the right-hand side. Oil on canvas, 84 x 56 cm / 33 x 22 in. Vienna, Wien Museum

Greek Antiquity (Girl from Tanagra and Athena) (detail), 1890/91
(see ill. p. 54)

thorough proficiency in the particular area of art for which they will have responsibility and at the same time a love of the applied arts as a whole; not artists, however, who are only disposed to work in the sphere of industrial art on an occasional and incidental basis" (Mittheilungen 1868, p. 194 ff.). Rudolf von Eitelberger wanted the School of Applied Arts to educate "skilled forces for the needs of the art industry"; it was to train designers and draughtsmen for factories and craftsmen and teachers for industrial, technical and vocational colleges and for other schools of drawing and design (Eitelberger 1879, p. 118). The School of Applied Arts correspondingly offered a number of different courses, of which the painting and figural drawing classes were taught by Ferdinand Laufberger (1829–1881).

The curriculum followed by Gustav and Ernst led to a qualification as a drawing teacher: two years in the preparatory class and exams in the third year. As a candidate for the teaching profession, Gustav Klimt had to draw plaster casts in the morning, attend lectures in the afternoon and take life classes at night (Giese 1976, p. 3). Our information about Klimt's training at the School of Applied Arts comes to us not only from the institution's own files, but also from the curriculum vitae written by Gustav Klimt himself (Strobl, vol. 4, 1989, pp. 48–52; Krug 2012a, no. 11) and Franz Matsch's *Autobiographical Sketches* (Giese 1976). For the first two years, he attended classes held by three professors: Karl Hrachowina (1845–1896), a practising etcher who joined the teaching staff in 1877 and taught free-hand drawing and historical styles of ornament; Ludwig Minnigerode (1847–1900), a pupil of Eduard von Engerth (1818–1897) at the Vienna Academy and teacher of genre painting and portraiture at the School of Applied Arts from 1876 to 1900; and Michael Rieser (1828–1905), professor of history painting and portraiture from 1868 to 1880. In the case of Franz Matsch, Gustav Klimt and Ernst Klimt, the new teaching methods soon produced results: busy on stained-glass designs for the recently completed Votive Church by Heinrich von Ferstel (1828–1883), Rieser gave his best preparatory-class students, Gustav Klimt and Franz Matsch, the job of enlarging his sketches for some of the windows, as we know from Matsch's writings. The two students were paid for their work, which probably represented their first joint commission (Giese 1976, p. 3). At the start of his career as an artist, Klimt also made a little money by painting chiefly naturalistic portraits, often based on photographs. In her writings, his sister Hermine recollected that, "in his spare time at home, [Gustav] painted portraits from photographs. He did this work to the complete satisfaction of his customers. He was paid 5 gulden apiece" (cit. from Nebehay 1969, p. 60).

In his third year at the School of Applied Arts, when Klimt had already passed the first round of exams and was studying under Michael Rieser for the State examination that would allow him to qualify as a drawing teacher, Rudolf von Eitelberger paid a visit to the school studio. Rieser took the occasion to draw Eitelberger's attention to the work

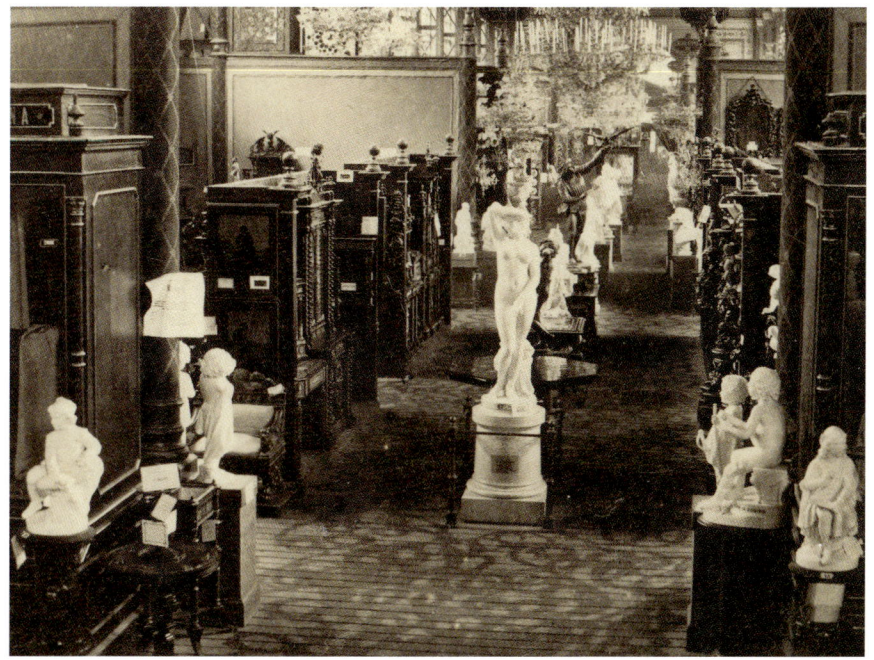

Vienna Photographers' Association
World Exhibition in Vienna, Italian Perspectival Gallery, 1873
Stereoscope, 17.8 x 8.7 cm / 7 x 3 ⅜ in. Vienna, Technisches Museum

of his gifted senior students Gustav Klimt, Ernst Klimt and Franz Matsch. According to Matsch, Eitelberger exclaimed: "Drawing teachers? […] You must become painters!" (Giese 1976, p. 285). Eitelberger decided to award scholarships of twenty gulden a month to all three and invited them to join the painting and decorative-art class for a further two years of study (Giese 1976, p. 4; MAK archives, Akt Zl. 1880–620). "The 'Brothers Klimt and Matsch Company' was financed", as Matsch wrote in his memoirs (Giese 1976, p. 285). Eitelberger recognized the young artists' talent at a point in time when, with Vienna's Ringstrasse in the grip of a construction boom, graduates of the class for painting and decorative art were in enormous demand.

For Gustav and Ernst Klimt and Franz Matsch, their training under Ferdinand Laufberger was decisive for their future careers. Laufberger particularly encouraged the three students and would also procure them their first commissions. He himself had worked as a draughtsman for the Lloyd Austriaco printing house and for Rudolf von Waldheim's

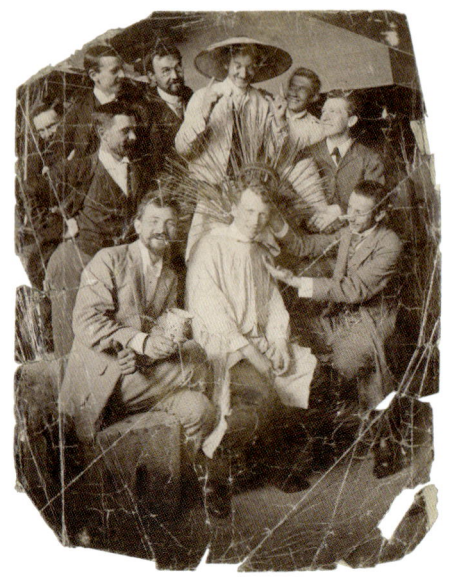

xylographic printers in Vienna, before taking time off from 1862 to 1864 to travel in Europe to further his art education. During this period, he had studied and made drawings in Rome and Paris. In Vienna he was considered a specialist in the revival of historical techniques of mural decoration, such as sgraffito, a technique he also used in his Ringstrasse commissions (Giese 1976, p. 5). A teacher at the School of Applied Arts since 1868, he specialized in decorations for the new buildings on the Ringstrasse. He was responsible for the interior decoration of the Austrian Museum of Art and Industry, including the frescos for the galleries of the covered columned courtyard and the ceilings of the main staircase, and sgraffito decorations for the façade (completed in 1871), as well as the sgraffito decorations for the inner courtyards, of the Kunsthistorisches Museum (Art History Museum; opened in 1891) and the frescos for the crossing of the Votive Church (consecrated in 1879). His most important work is considered *Die leichte Muse* (1866–1869), the second curtain for the Imperial and Royal Opera.

In Laufberger's class, Klimt spent the mornings working first from life models and then from still lifes. He was also set compositional exercises that could vary from a design for an al fresco wall painting for a music room to a subject suitable as an illustration for a book. Here Klimt learned how to work on several commissions at once within a fixed time frame. Laufberger "made comments on all the designs after they had been submitted, mentioning the best works by name […]. Laufberger's motto was: reproduce Nature as accurately as possible, with all her beauties and flaws […]. Laufberger would also often say: there is no boundary between art and applied art" (Giese 1976, p. 6). The academic drawings of male nudes (Natter 2012, Cat. 16–18) that Gustav Klimt produced during Laufberger's classes in 1879/80 show his intelligent absorption of his teacher's ideas. Klimt's

Group photo at the School of Applied Arts, c. 1882/83
Front left Ernst Klimt, Franz Matsch standing behind him, Gustav Klimt in the centre at the back
Vienna, Albertina

enduring endeavour to capture the essence of the human figure in oil sketches, and his life-long practice of working from life models, both find their starting point here.

While in Laufberger's class, Gustav and Ernst Klimt and Franz Matsch also took on extracurricular commissions. In his *Autobiographical Sketches*, Matsch mentions the Klimt brothers painting anatomical models for the ear specialist Adam Pollitzer, for example, and decorating ceramic plates (Giese 1976, p. 285). Laufberger himself employed his talented students: all but the first of the sgraffito festoons in the inner courtyards of the Kunsthistorisches Museum were executed by the Klimt brothers and Matsch, who had already been given their own studio within the School of Applied Arts (Giese 1976, p. 285). The three artists executed this series of *Allegories of the Fine and Applied Arts* (Natter 2012, Cat. 1) on the basis of cartoons by Laufberger. During this same period, the young students also visited the Gusshausstrasse studio of Hans Makart (1840–1884). Their teacher sent them every Sunday to the Upper Belvedere, at that time still home to the Imperial Picture Gallery, so that they could make copies after works by Titian and Rubens. They also visited Schönbrunn zoo, where they made watercolour sketches of the animals as a way of learning how to capture a motif quickly (Giese 1976, p. 7). Gustav Klimt's thorough training with painters who were contributing, with the aid of their assistants, to the interior and exterior decoration of the monumental edifices rising along Vienna's Ringstrasse, cemented his artistic abilities and signposted the way forward for him, his brother Ernst and Franz Matsch.

First works by the Künstler-Compagnie: from pupils to masters

Laufberger's unflagging efforts to further the careers of his pupils also brought the two Klimts and Matsch their first commission as the Künstler-Compagnie, the 'Artists' Company' they formed in 1879. Through the recommendation of their esteemed teacher, they were engaged by Viennese imperial and royal court architect Johann Sturany to execute four paintings for the corners of the ceiling in the salon of his newly built mansion at 21 Schottenring. The three artists completed the project – a cycle of allegories of the performing arts – in 1880. Gustav Klimt was thereby responsible for the *Allegory of Music* (Natter 2012, Cat. 2). The floating figure of the Muse Euterpe, her draperies billowing, is playing a double flute and appears lost in her music. As a female type, she resembles the creations of Makart – we might think of the Allegory of the Five Senses exhibited at the Galerie Miethke in Vienna that same year (today Vienna, Belvedere). Moreover, the commission for Sturany brought the Künstler-Compagnie into contact with executive architects Ferdinand Fellner (1847–1916) and Hermann Helmer (1849–1919), who from 1880 onwards would become the young painters' main source of work. Fellner & Helmer, in partnership since 1873, would become the most important theatre architects in the Habsburg monarchy. Between 1872 and 1915 the duo built no fewer than forty-eight theatres in Austro-Hungary, Germany and the Balkans, including the Deutsches Theater in Prague, the Hamburg Schauspielhaus, the Zurich Stadttheater and the Vienna Volkstheater.

The commission for the Palais Sturany was followed by a project for Fellner & Helmer, under the supervision of Ferdinand Laufberger, to provide ceiling paintings for the concert hall built by the architects in the Bohemian health resort of Carlsbad (Karlovy Vary). The concert hall was demolished in 1966, having fallen into disrepair, and no photographs are known to exist of the decorations supplied by the Künstler-Compagnie. According to Matsch in his *Autobiographical Sketches*, these were paintings in distemper on the subject of music: sacred music, hunting music, dance music and wedding music (Giese 1976, p. 285; Natter 2012, Cat. 7). In his own curriculum vitae, Gustav Klimt mentions simply "ceiling paintings for the Cursalon in Carlsbad" (Giese 1976, p. 7; Seiser 2007c, p. 12).

In 1881 Ferdinand Laufberger died unexpectedly and Julius Victor Berger (1850–1902) took over as professor of decorative painting. Berger, like Minnigerode a pupil of Engerth, had visited Italy in 1877 on an imperial travel scholarship and produced the ceiling painting *Patrons of the Fine Arts in the House of Habsburg* in the Golden Hall in the Kunsthistorisches Museum. The Klimt brothers and Matsch, who had completed their training at the School of Applied Arts, were now themselves offered a travel scholarship to Italy by its director, Josef von Storck. None of the artists accepted the scholarship, however, a decision probably linked with the precarious finances of their families. Like his predecessor, Julius Berger in turn funnelled work towards the three artists and gave them permission to use the School studios for a further two years to be able to carry out their own commissions. In 1881/82 he employed them to execute his designs for the ceiling paintings in the staircase and salon of Palais Zierer in Vienna (25–27 Argentinierstrasse), today housed in the Department of Prints at the Vienna Academy of Fine Art. Of the compositional studies in watercolour that the artists had to submit to the villa's future occupant, the banker Wilhelm Zierer, only those by Franz Matsch have survived. Gustav Klimt's final oil painting, *Putto with Mandolin and Flowers* (Natter 2012, Cat. 8), is a product of the studies of children he had made in Laufberger's class, although still rather clumsy in its proportions.

In May 1881 the Künstler-Compagnie accepted a commission for sgraffito decorations for the new Municipal Theatre (today the National Theatre) designed by Fellner & Helmer in Brünn (Brno). The commission, which probably reached them via the architects, took the three artists back to their student days under Laufberger and their work experience at the Kunsthistorisches Museum. In the frieze zone of the theatre façade,

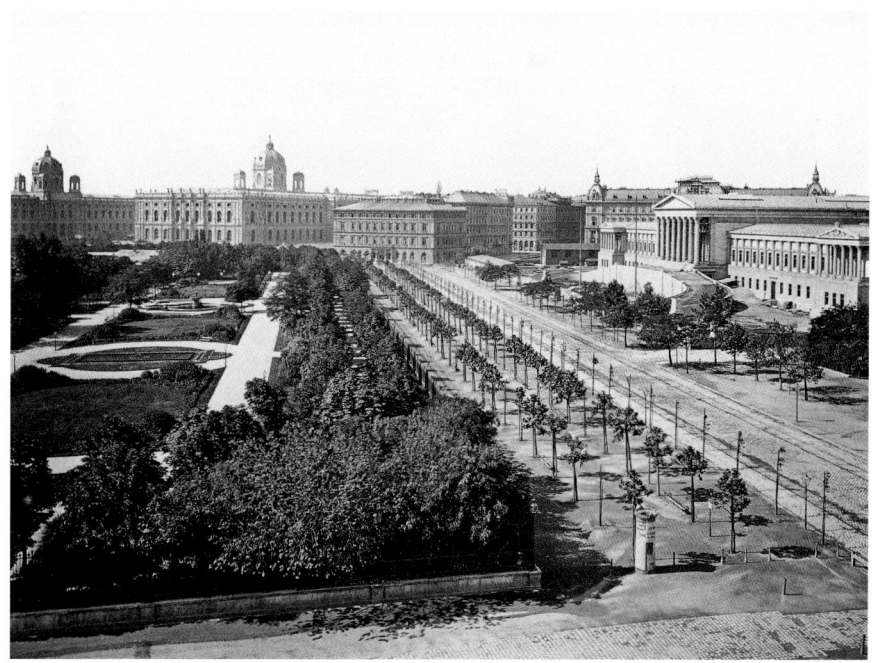

View of the Ringstrasse, c. 1890
Shortly after its completion, with the imperial museums, the Palais Epstein and the Parliament building
Photograph. Imagno/Austrian Archives

subdivided by composite pilasters, they executed a total of four different sgraffiti (Natter 2012, Cat. 12) showing putti with banderoles and cartouches, together with candelabra grotesques. Their designs, whose flatness was dictated by the technique and material, remain wholly indebted to Laufberger's decorative style.

The façade decorations in Brno were directly followed in 1882/83 by another commission, once again awarded via Fellner & Helmer for one of their architectural projects, this time for the stage curtain and ceiling paintings of the newly built theatre in Reichenberg (Liberec). Kitlitschka has pointed out the palpable affinity between the lavish formal vocabulary of Hans Makart and the Künstler-Compagnie's designs in Reichenberg and subsequently their ceiling paintings for the auditorium of the municipal theatre in Carlsbad (Karlovy Vary), with their dynamic compositions, illusionistic depth and sensitive handling of colour (Kitlitschka 1981, p. 168 f.). In Reichenberg, Gustav Klimt executed two ceiling paintings and collaborated with his brother Ernst and Matsch on the stage

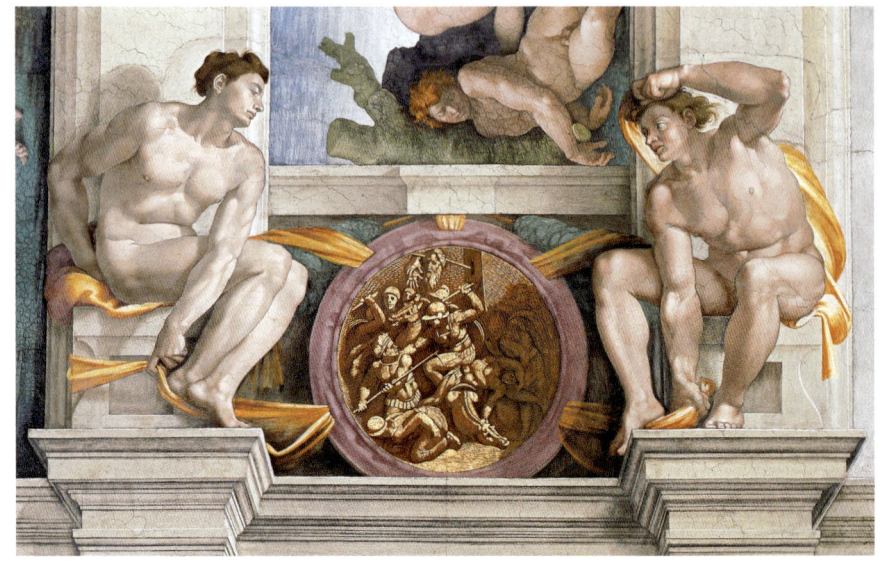

Michelangelo, **Ignudi**, 1509/10
Fresco, 195 x 385 cm / 76 ¾ x 151 ½ in. Rome, Vatican, Sistine Chapel

curtain. At least one surviving sketch documents his contribution to the figure with arms spread wide standing on the prow of the ship in the centre of *Allegory of Merry and Solemn Art* (p. 33; Natter 2012, Cat. 15). Further staffage figures can be attributed to him on stylistic grounds (Seiser 2007c, pp. 21–28). Correspondence relating to the progress of the commission is still preserved in Liberec today and includes a letter written by the Klimt brothers and Matsch containing a detailed description of the composition. In it, they write: "It is also [our] view that, for a municipal theatre in the provinces, where the dramatic repertoire is so broad, the motif on the main curtain must be a general one, so to speak, but one that nevertheless allegorizes the 'merry' and the 'solemn'" (cit. from Seifertová-Korecká 1967, p. 26; Nebehay 1969, p. 82, note 13). The curtain is significant as a combination of clear organization – as learned from Laufberger and seen in the latter's own curtain for the Vienna Opera – with new, dynamic neo-Baroque elements in the composition of the narrative middle section of the wedding scene. The ceiling paintings in the same theatre testify to the different hands of the three artists: Gustav Klimt's *Lute Music* (Natter 2012, Cat. 13) and his *Family with Child Playing the Drum* (Natter 2012, Cat. 14) introduce a diagonal layout creating a sense of depth, whereas Matsch's com-

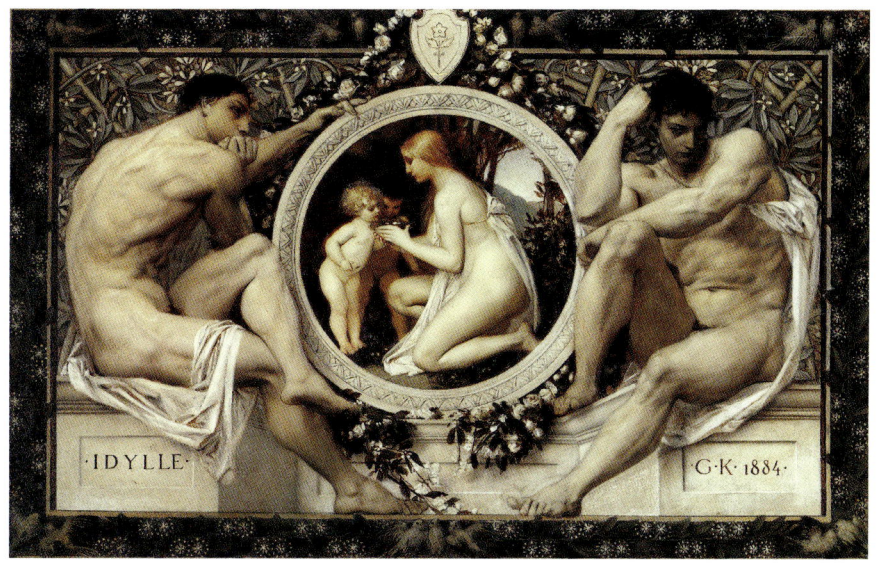

Allegory of Idyll, 1884
Oil on canvas, 49.5 x 73.5 cm / 19 ½ x 29 in. Vienna, Wien Museum

position remains strictly parallel to the pictorial plane. In March 1883, just before their final installation in Reichenberg's new theatre, the paintings by the Künstler-Compagnie were exhibited at the Austrian Museum in Vienna at the specific request of Rudolf von Eitelberger – an indication of just how important they were considered to be.

Their work at Reichenberg served as the *Meisterstück* – traditionally, the work presented by an artist for admission to the rank of master – with which the members of the Künstler-Compagnie graduated from the School of Applied Arts, and paved the way for other commissions. In 1883 the artists accordingly moved into their own studio, on the top floor of 8 Sandwirtgasse in Vienna's 6th district, in rooms placed at their disposal by the house's owner, silverware manufacturer A. Markowitsch. A tondo with a putto blowing a trumpet soon adorned the stairwell in the artist's new quarters.

The Reichenberg commission was followed by decorations for Peleş Castle in Sinaia (pp. 45, 46/47), the summer residence begun by Carl Wilhelm von Doderer (1825–1900) and completed by his assistant, Johannes Schultz, for Carol I (1839–1914), King of Romania. This new commission may have reached the artists either via the agencies of Fellner & Helmer, or at the recommendation of Rudolf von Eitelberger as a leading

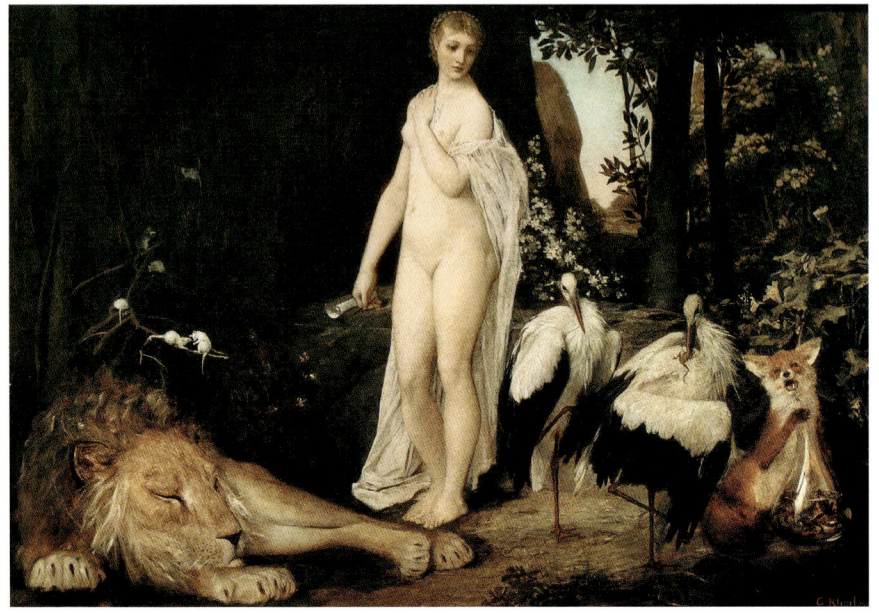

Allegory of Fable, 1883
Oil on canvas, 84.5 x 117 cm / 33 ¼ x 40 in. Vienna, Wien Museum

member of the cultural establishment and patron of the Künstler-Compagnie, or via the Viennese firm of Joseph Kott, which supplied the wood panelling for the interior walls of the new palace. Between 1883 and 1885 the Künstler-Compagnie executed a wide range of decorations for Peleş Castle. Carol I wanted hand-painted reproductions of paintings by Titian, Rembrandt and van Dyck, for example, which were to adhere as faithfully as possible to the originals. In the case of Gustav Klimt's copy of Titian's portrait of Isabella d'Este (Natter 2012, Cat. 35), this even meant trying to locate a damask canvas – something that proved extremely difficult, as Matsch recalled (Giese 1976, p. 286). As well as copies of the Old Masters, Gustav Klimt created portraits – loosely based on historical engravings – for an ancestral gallery of Carol I's forebears (p. 47; Natter 2012, Cat. 28–32). Other tasks included sgraffito decorations for the inner courtyard (Natter 2012, Cat. 27), a "frieze by Gustav Klimt for the Queen's library in the Gobelin technique" (Matsch, cit. from Giese 1976, p. 286) and an allegorical frieze for the queen's music room (Natter 2012, Cat. 33), subsequently assigned to the palace theatre (Natter 2012, Cat. 34). For Gustav Klimt, the breadth and variety of these tasks were an opportunity to demonstrate the mastery and versatility he had now achieved. While the ancestral portraits and copies of Old Masters were shared out individually, in the case of the allegories originally destined for the royal music room, all three artists worked on the same frieze. In the sensually pale flesh of the allegories of Summer and Spring in the shape of two kneeling girls, executed in 1884 for the castle theatre, Klimt comes close to his revered model Hans Makart, for example in the latter's *Japanese Girl* (1875; today Linz, Lentos Kunstmuseum).

Alongside his wide-ranging decorations for Peleş Castle, Klimt also worked on publishing projects. In 1883 he produced the painting *Allegory of Fable* (pp. 26, 42/43; Natter 2012, Cat. 26) for the part-work *Allegorien und Embleme*, a sourcebook of allegories and emblems published by Gerlach & Schenk in instalments from 1882 to 1885. According to the publishers, *Allegorien und Embleme* contained illustrations of original designs by the most outstanding modern artists of the day, copies of guild emblems from the past and modern designs for guild coats of arms in the "character of the Renaissance". Gustav Klimt contributed three examples of allegorical compositions: *Allegory of Fable, Allegory of Idyll* (p. 25; Natter 2012, Cat. 38) and *Allegory of Love* (p. 59; Natter 2012, Cat. 81). *Allegory of Fable*, with its naturalistic portrayals of animals, is reproduced in the sourcebook as number 75A. Publisher Martin Gerlach described the compendium in the following terms: "Not a specimen collection of allegories in the sense of the ancients, it pursues the path of allegorization in a new spirit." Its goal was to arrive at a "new, enchanted garden of modern art" (Gerlach 1882–1885). These allegorical paintings, too, are considered by Klimt scholars to show the artist processing the work of Makart, something that opened the way to new tonalities and – in *Allegory of Idyll* – to a type of anatomy oriented towards masters such as Michelangelo (p. 24). Their architectural framework, meanwhile, also calls to mind the work of the Pre-Raphaelites. With his contributions to *Allegorien und Embleme*, Klimt advanced from being a student and user of specimen designs to becoming a master and author of such designs, which in their printed version served as a resource for other artists and craftsmen. The symbolic content of these allegories also looked forward to Klimt's future work.

The theatre decorations executed by the Künstler-Compagnie in Fiume, Carlsbad and Totis (Natter 2012, Cat. 39–44, Cat. 48–51, Cat. 72) between 1885 and 1893 represent important steps in Klimt's evolution to becoming an autonomous artist. In 1885, prior to their final installation, the ceiling paintings for Fiume (today Rijeka in Croatia) were exhibited in the Austrian Museum in Vienna. The three panels by Klimt (Natter 2012, Cat. 40, 42, 44) included *Orpheus and Eurydice* (Natter 2012, Cat. 40) and show the artist at the height of his day and processing international trends in art, in particular English Pre-Raphaelitism. The influence of Sir Frederic Leighton, for example, can also be seen in Klimt's genre scenes *Delights of the Table* and *Dance* (Natter 2012, Cat. 48, 49), created in 1886 for the municipal theatre in Carlsbad, another Fellner & Helmer project.

First successes in the metropolis: the Künstler-Compagnie as decoration specialists on behalf of the imperial court

Having carried out commissions in various parts of the Austro-Hungarian Empire, the Künstler-Compagnie now sought to gain a foothold in the capital. Their efforts to solicit new commissions are documented by a key letter signed by all three artists, probably composed in February 1884 and today preserved in the Vienna Library, in which they addressed themselves directly to Rudolf von Eitelberger, Director of the Austrian Museum of Art and Industry: "As Your Honour may recall, we carried out more sizeable tasks jointly under the supervision of our unforgotten master, Professor Laufberger. Thus he laid the foundation for our working together, which we also continued later under the supervision of Professor Berger. […] If we, most honoured Counsellor to the Court, are to say what sort of work we really wish to do, may we allow ourselves once again to refer to our late master, Professor Laufberger, whose great achievements in sundry areas of the fine and the decorative arts serve as an incentive to us, and believe that our working together is of crucial advantage because, due to increased productivity, more rapid fulfilment of the commission is effected and the sum of our experiences is augmented. As Your Excellency will surely know, our work up till now has been largely destined for the provinces and abroad. Our most fervent wish is therefore to carry out a larger work in our native city, and perhaps now might be just such an opportunity, since Vienna's new monumental buildings are nearing completion, the painterly decoration of only the most important parts of which will, of course, have been assigned so that the best artists are fully occupied with them; that is why we make so bold as to address this most humble petition to Your Excellency, most graciously to use your benevolent and influential authority in that direction" (cit. from Nebehay 1969, p. 81; Krug 2012a, no. 1).

With this "humble petition", the young artists were hoping to win a lucrative, large-scale commission following the death of salon painter Makart in October 1884. Along with other painters working in a similar style to Makart, they were engaged to complete the decoration of the Villa Hermes in the Lainz game park. The lavish villa complex with its covered riding arena was intended as a private retreat for Empress Elisabeth (1837–1898) – a generous gift by Emperor Franz Joseph I (1830–1916) to his restless wife. Under the supervision of their teacher, Julius Victor Berger, Matsch and the two Klimt brothers executed the decorations for the spandrels of the imperial bedchamber, showing scenes from the empress's favourite play, *A Midsummer Night's Dream* by William Shakespeare (Natter 2012,

Early Italian Art (Female Saint with Cherubin) (detail), 1890/91
Oil on canvas, intercolumnar painting 230 x 80 cm / 90 ½ x 31 ½ in.,
spandrel 230 x 230 cm / 90 ½ x 90 ½ in. Vienna, Kunsthistorisches Museum, main staircase

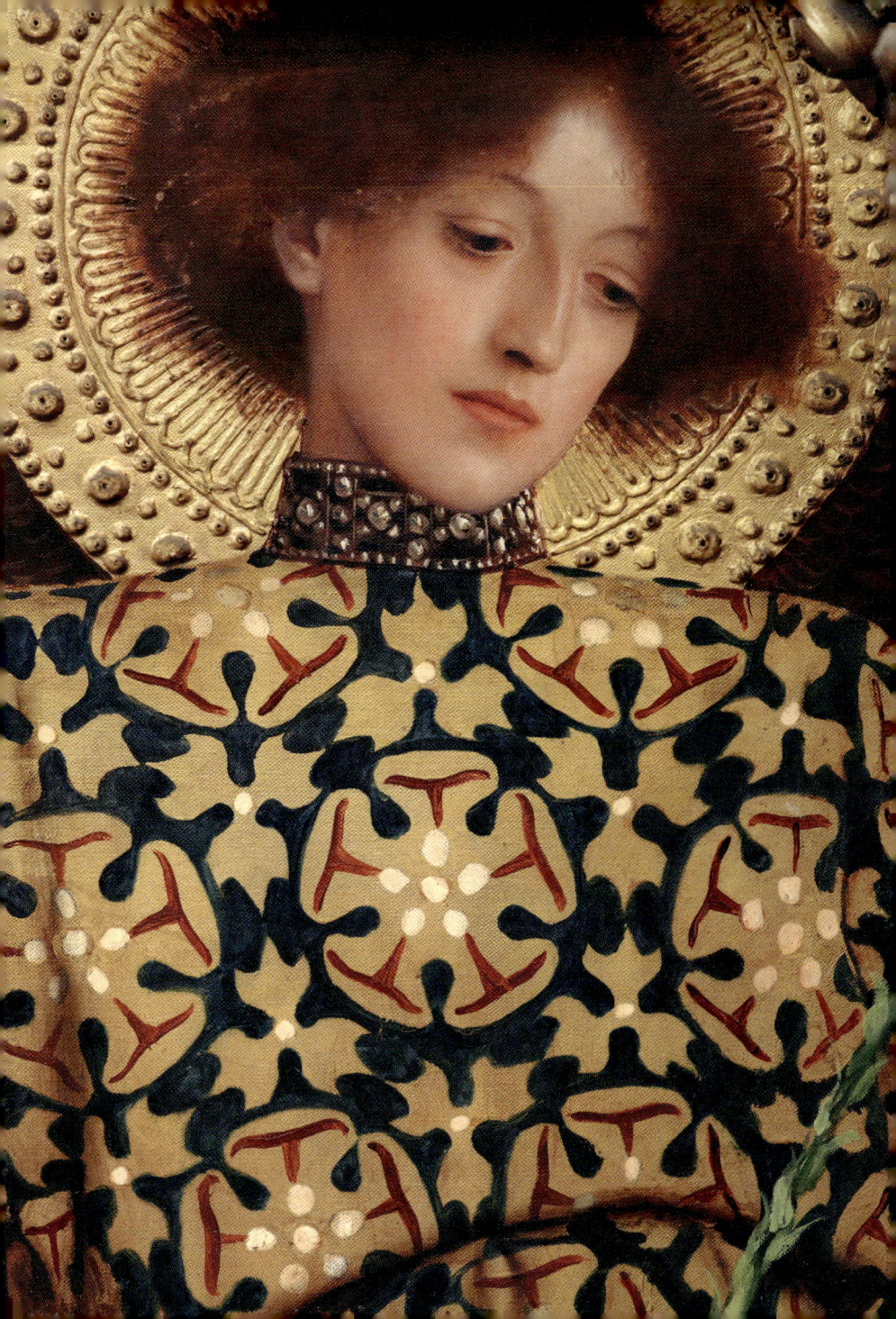

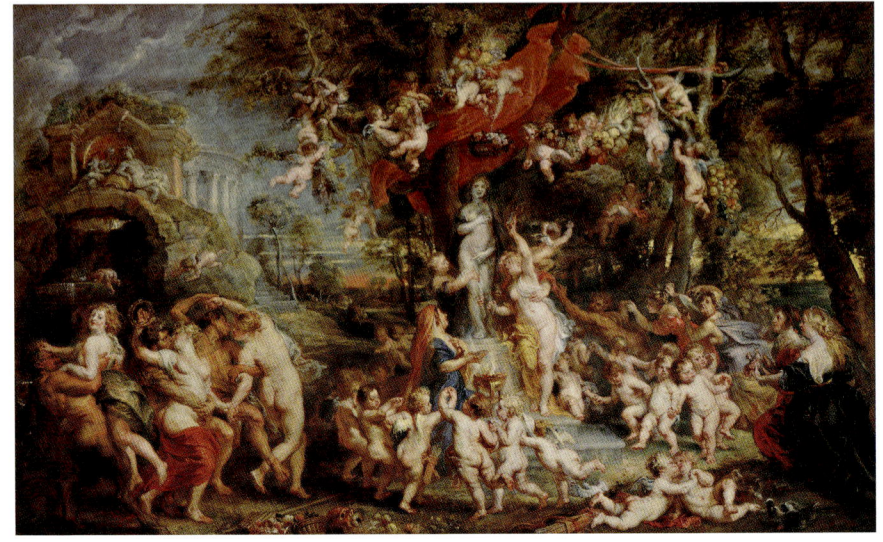

Peter Paul Rubens, **The Festival of Venus**, 1636/37
Oil on canvas, 217 x 350 cm / 85 ½ x 137 ¾ in. Vienna, Kunsthistorisches Museum

Cat. 36). They won the favour of the temperamental empress, however, with *Spring* (Natter 2012, Cat. 45), their ten-metre long ceiling painting for her salon. Executed on the basis of their own designs, with its spacious skies and cool palette, it represents "a clear antithesis to Makart" (Kitlitschka 1981, p. 170). After suffering extensive water damage, Spring's original appearance was further lost behind an amateur restoration (BDA, Vienna XIII, Lainzer Tiergarten, Hermesvilla, Zl. 8450/74, Zl.2240/75). The architect of the Villa Hermes was Karl von Hasenauer (1833–1894), whose attention was thus drawn to the talented trio.

In 1885, while they were still working on their following designs for Carlsbad, Hasenauer awarded the three young artists a highly prestigious commission that would signify their breakthrough. With the words "Lads, I've got another job for you; you can win your spurs with this one", as Franz von Matsch recorded in his memoirs (Giese 1976, p. 13), Hasenauer invited them to supply ten ceiling paintings for the grand staircases in the new Hofburgtheater. With their experience in the sphere of theatre decoration, they responded with paintings fully in keeping with the magnificent architectural setting, which had been designed jointly by Hasenauer and Gottfried Semper (1803–1879). The foundation stone for the new Hofburgtheater had been laid in November 1874 on the site of the Baroque Paradeisgarten park, itself occupying the site of the former Löwelbastei bastion.

The building was supposed to be ready for use by 1882, but due to deep-seated differences between Hasenauer and Semper, the latter resigned in bitterness from the project in 1876, when only the foundations had been laid, leaving Hasenauer to take over the sole running of the project. Semper had designed the ground plan, whereas Hasenauer had been responsible for the detailed design of the exterior architecture and the interior decoration. Hasenauer employed only sculptors and painters hand-picked by himself. On 20 October 1886 the Künstler-Compagnie were awarded an official contract from the Royal Building Committee for ten ceiling paintings. The pictorial programme – the history of theatre from antiquity up to the 18th century – was dictated by the Hofburgtheater's artistic director, Adolf von Wilbrandt (1837–1911), who was also responsible for the iconographical content of the theatre's interior decoration as a whole. The placement, shape and sequence of the pictures were precisely stipulated. Only in the tympana above the entrance doors was the choice of subject left up to the artists. The fee for the whole project was a fabulous 10,000 gulden, some 100,000 euros by today's reckoning. According to the terms of the contract, the paintings had to be ready "at the latest by the end of January 1887" (cit. from Rychlik 2007, p. 39), and in fact most of the work was indeed finished that year. The artists shared out the commission by drawing lots (Giese 1976, p. 55). For the first time in their careers, they renounced allegorical representation in favour of reconstructed history.

In 1915 the small-format oil compositional studies relating to the final ceiling paintings were auctioned from the estate of banker Eduard Palmer (1838–1914), a close friend of the Burgtheater actress Katharina Schratt, herself the emperor's mistress. Most of these oil studies are today lost. The cartoons for the ceiling paintings were discovered in 1996 in an attic room at the Burgtheater (Fillitz 1996, p. 666). They were used by the artists as the template with which to transfer the composition directly onto the sized plaster ceiling (Eyb-Green 2002, p. 106), where the actual painting was then carried out in resin oils. In some pictures, the preparatory coat of size was mixed with fine sand (marble dust). This procedure was evidently omitted in the case of the tympana and the large compositions because its application was not uniformly successful (Krämer 1978, n. p.).

Franz Matsch executed four of the ceiling paintings: the *Altar of Apollo* for the tympanum in the northern staircase (a composition for a long time attributed to Gustav Klimt on the basis of a related sketch by this latter), together with *The Ancient Storyteller, The Medieval Mystery Play* and *A Scene from Antique Theatre*. Ernst Klimt was responsible for *Hanswurst Delivering an Impromptu Performance in Rothenburg* and *Molière's Theatre*. Gustav Klimt produced four ceiling paintings, of which three were situated above the southern grand staircase, on the Volksgarten side of the Burgtheater: *The Cart of Thespis* (pp. 50/51; Natter 2012, Cat. 55), *Shakespeare's Globe Theatre* showing the final scene from *Romeo and Juliet* (pp. 50/51; Natter 2012, Cat. 53, 55) and – in the tympanum – *The Altar of Dionysus* (Natter 2012, Cat. 59). His fourth painting, *The Theatre in Taormina* (p. 49; Natter 2012, Cat. 57), occupies a central position over the northern grand staircase, on the opposite side of the building. Strobl considers that Gustav Klimt painted *Shakespeare's Globe Theatre* first (Strobl, vol. 1, 1980, p. 55). Juliet lies dead, her face as pale as marble, her figure a bright gleam emerging from the shadowy depths of the stage. Romeo is draped lifelessly over the side of her bed and the body of Lord Paris forms a dark patch of colour in the left-hand foreground. Behind the tragic couple, Father Lorenzo recoils in horror from the scene. Sitting and standing in crowded, colourful fashion around the stage are the theatre-goers of the Elizabethan era, staring transfixed at the scene. In his use of dramatic chiaroscuro, Klimt betrays – more clearly here than in any of his other ceiling paintings – the influence of Hans Makart, who had earlier treated this same subject. It is also possible to recognize elements absorbed from contemporary English and French Salon painting, such as the porcelain-smooth female bodies of Alexandre Cabanel (1823–1889). The latter's *Death of Francesca da Rimini and Paolo Malatesta* of 1870 (Paris, Musée d'Orsay) could have provided the inspiration for the central motif of the dead pair of lovers in Klimt's painting.

Klimt used his sisters and colleagues as models for his figures, as attested by a number of carefully staged photographs. His brother Georg Klimt (1867–1931) posed as Romeo, for example, and his sister Hermine Klimt for several of the ladies in the boxes. A remarkable aspect of this central picture is the fact that the only known self-portrait of the artist is concealed amongst the spectators in the Globe Theatre. Gustav Klimt has portrayed himself in the costume of the epoch (with a neck ruff), standing in the box on the right, flanked by his fellow artists Ernst Klimt and Franz Matsch. It is interesting to note, incidentally, that when the preliminary drawing was examined at very close quarters during its restoration in 1977, beneath the somewhat glaze-like layers of paint, it was possible to see the figure of Ernst Klimt depicted leaning casually against a pillar with a cigarette in his right hand (Krämer 1978, n. p.).

In *The Cart of Thespis*, the origins of Greek tragedy are represented by the mythical Thespis, who is said to have used a cart as a mobile stage. The picture is laid out in the manner of a relief against a background of architectural set pieces and stylized greenery. The composition is thereby characterized by an orthogonal emphasis that, with the figures rendered in strict profile on the edge of the scene, reinforces the two-dimensional impression sought by the artist. The formal structure employed here was ultimately one that Vienna, accustomed to the Makart style, had never encountered before, and which pointed to "compositional principles that had already found expression in the rest of Europe" (Rychlik 2007, p. 23) – in the works of the Dutch painter Lawrence Alma-Tadema (1836–1912) and the English Pre-Raphaelites, for example. After moving to London in 1870, Alma-Tadema became the leading exponent of Victorian Neoclassicism. His paintings of scenes from

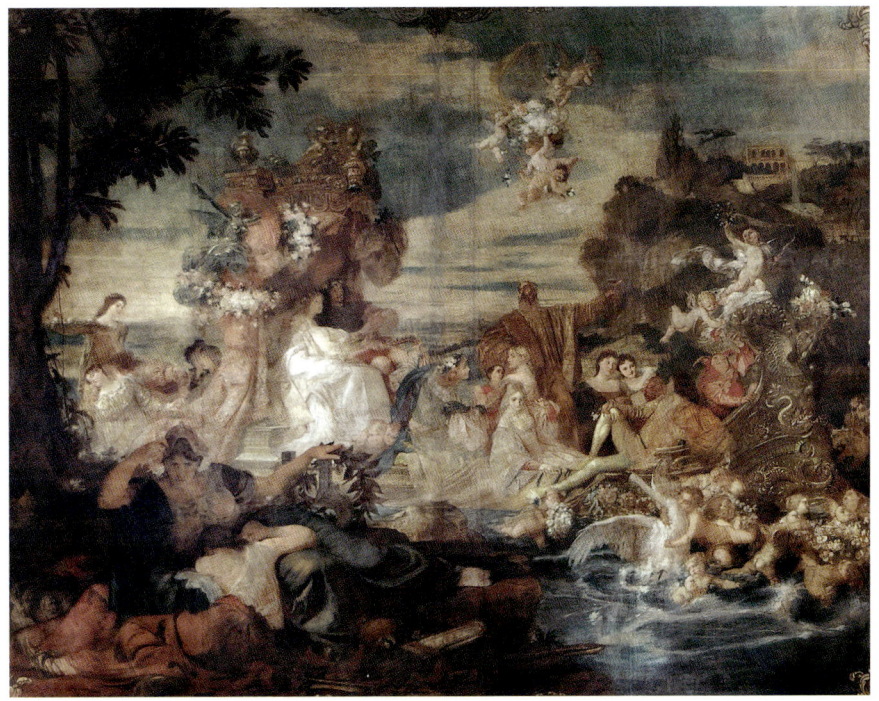

Gustav Klimt with Ernst Klimt and Franz Matsch
Allegory of Merry and Solemn Art, 1882/83
Distemper on canvas, c. 1200 x 600 cm / 39 ft 4 in. x 19 ft 6 in. Reichenberg (Liberec), Municipal Theatre

antiquity are characterized by their detailed archaeological accuracy, achieved with the aid of the artist's personally assembled collection of photographs of ancient sites.

The principles now being employed by Gustav Klimt are even more apparent in his two other ceiling paintings for the Burgtheater. *The Theatre in Taormina*, destined for the northern staircase, shows dance and music in Roman times but relegates the eponymous theatre far into the background. "This private entertainment from the decadent era of the classical world [has] nothing to do with the theatre as such", remarked Josef Bayer, author of the first monograph on the monumental new building, in a critical tone (Bayer 1894, p. 93). The foreground is dominated by pleasure girls dancing and making music in front of an upper-class Roman and his catamite. Despite the view of a spacious Mediterranean landscape behind, Klimt avoids any portrayal of spatial recession through his skilful deployment of architectural elements. Klimt has again allowed himself to be

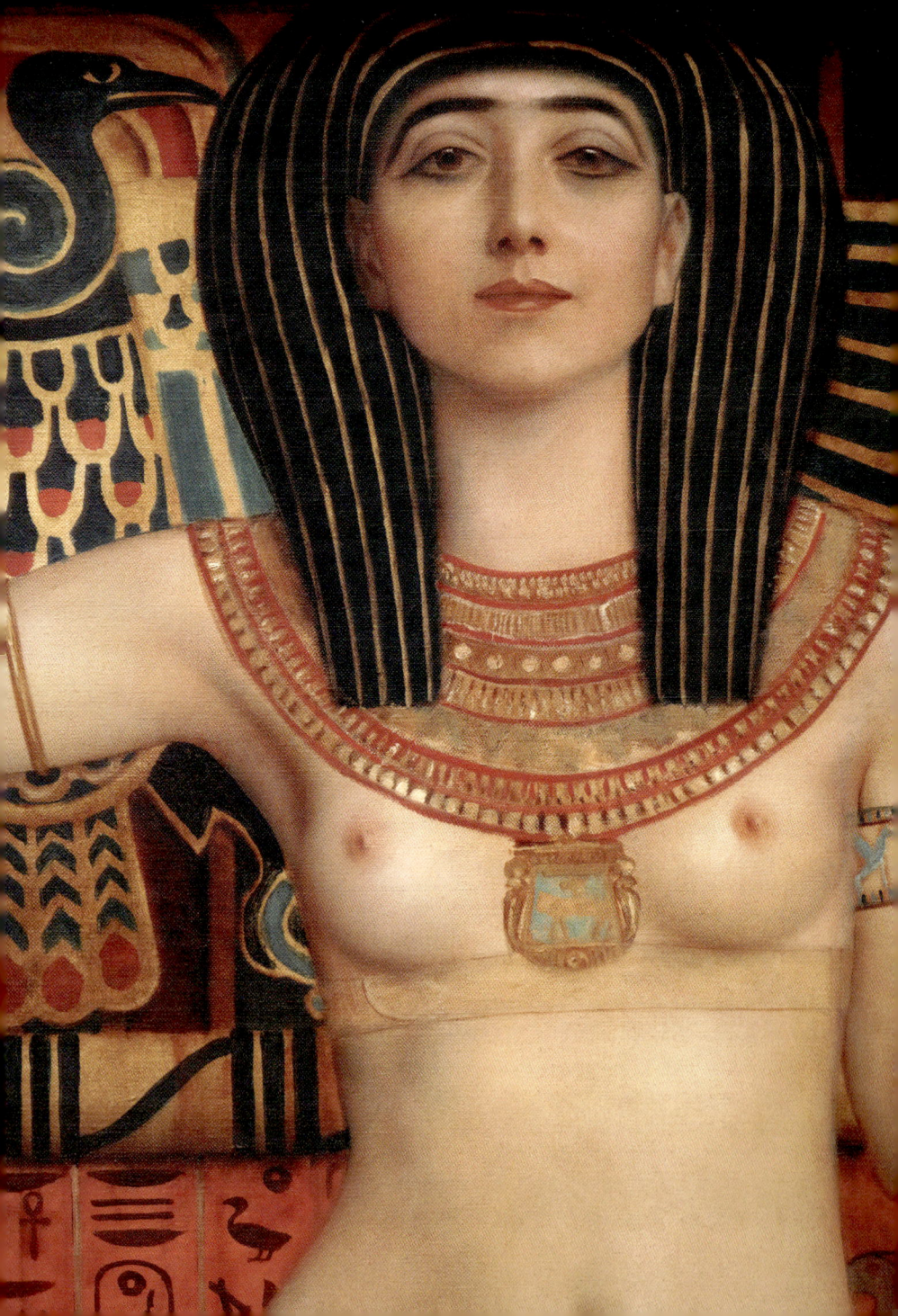

guided by Alma-Tadema in his detailed representation of classical architecture. He may thereby have found a point of departure in Alma-Tadema's *Pompeian Scene (The Siesta)* of 1868 (Madrid, Museo del Prado), in which a female slave seen in strict profile view – as in Klimt's painting – is playing the double flute (*tibia*) in front of two reclining men. The statuette of Venus pudica also appears as an antique set piece in both paintings – in a central position on the table in Alma-Tadema's *Pompeian Scene* and crowning a column bearing the baldachin in Klimt's *Theatre in Taormina*. Klimt's dancers may have been inspired by the female nudes with bodies as smooth as marble found in the work of French Salon painters such as Alexandre Cabanel and William Adolphe Bougereau (1825–1905) – a connection suggested by Bayer at an early date (Bayer 1894, p. 94).

According to Strobl, *The Altar of Dionysus* (Natter 2012, Cat. 59), which shows the veneration of the god of wine and its associated rites as the foundation of theatre, was the last of Klimt's paintings to be completed for the Burgtheater (Strobl, vol. 1, 1980, p. 57). The bust of the god appears on a plinth in the centre of the composition. On the right, a maenad has sunk exhausted to the ground, while on the left, a naked, kneeling maenad presents a votive offering to the god. The composition concludes with a music-making satyr, who is lying naked on an animal skin. This picture, too, is clearly indebted to Alma-Tadema in the light colours of its palette, just as it borrows the motif of the satyr from his 1885 painting *A Reading from Homer* (Philadelphia Museum of Art), as noted by Strobl (Strobl, vol. 1, 1980, p. 56). The exhausted maenad, who represents a development of the allegorical figure of Music in the *Theatre Frieze for Peleş Castle* (Natter 2012, Cat. 34), emphasizes the flatness of the composition. The patent influence of Alma-Tadema was already apparent to Klimt's contemporaries (Ilg 1888, p. 2; Weixlgärtner 1912, p. 52). The Dutch artist's cool aesthetic, which situated naked female bodies of sculptural beauty within the context of a classicizing monumental architecture, was also much admired in Austro-Hungary – so much so that in 1878 Alma-Tadema was made an honorary member of the Imperial and Royal Academy of Fine Arts in Vienna (Wagner 1967, p. 443). Hugo von Hofmannsthal (1874–1929) is said to have taken part in a tableau vivant based on Alma-Tadema (Aurnhammer 2002, p. 295). At the same time, Klimt's *Altar of Dionysus*, "with its ornamental compositional principles" (Rychlik 2007, p. 96), also points most clearly ahead to the artist's outstanding late oeuvre.

When the magnificent new Hofburgtheater was opened on 14 October 1888 in the presence of the uppermost echelons of Viennese society, at the head of which was Emperor Franz Joseph, his daughter-in-law Crown Princess Stephanie (1864–1945) and numerous other members of the imperial household together with illustrious foreign guests such

Egyptian Art (Nekhbet and Sarcophagus with Isis Statuette) (detail), 1890/91
(see ill. p. 55)

as the Prince of Wales, the ceiling paintings by the Künstler-Compagnie also received their fair share of praise. Art historian Albert Ilg (1847–1896) lamented the choice of programme, which had obliged the artists "to supply painted or chiselled textbooks on the subject concerned", but nevertheless praised the "rare talents of these highly gifted young artists" (Ilg 1888, p. 241). In view of its lavish and magnificent decoration and technical innovations such as electric lighting, the building was well received by the Viennese public, but criticism was soon expressed about its poor acoustics. Barely a month after the opening ceremony, Emperor Franz Joseph observed resignedly to his mistress, Burgtheater actress Katharina Schratt: "There is unfortunately much argument, so I hear, over the new Burgtheater." And on an audience with the great tragedienne, Charlotte Wolter, he wrote: "By the way, the interview was short, but long enough to complain about the new Burgtheater" (Hamann 1992, p. 106). Even though Gustav Klimt himself was not satisfied with his achievement, he and his two colleagues received official imperial recognition for their contribution in the shape of the Gold Cross of Merit.

After the successful completion of this major project, the artist trio were now ready for another prominent commission. Vienna's two new imperial court museums of natural history and art history, the Naturhistorisches Museum and Kunsthistorisches Museum, had been under construction since 1872, and by 1881 the main shells were completed. Gottfried Semper was responsible for the design of the exterior architecture, while the interiors were built to plans by Karl von Hasenauer. In 1882 Hans Makart was commissioned to carry out the entire decoration of the ceiling and walls of the grand staircase in the Kunsthistorisches Museum. After the death of the 'Prince of Painters' in 1884, however, the decorative scheme remained only half finished. In February 1890 the Künstler-Compagnie received the prestigious invitation to carry it to completion (pp. 54/55; Natter 2012, Cat. 61–68). It was the last commission the three artists undertook as a team. Whereas the lunettes by Makart show the ten most important painters and sculptors with their models, the pictorial programme he left behind for the intercolumnar fields and the spandrels foresaw only decorative male and female nudes conveying no particular content. According to the terms of the contract now issued to the Künstler-Compagnie, however, these wall zones had to illustrate the leitmotif of the "development of the different styles" using objects housed in the museum's own collections and had to be executed in such a way "that they match their intended purpose, the more exacting demands of art and their titles" (cit. from Kriller/Kugler 1991, p. 221). The contract also stipulated that the works by the three artists had to be tailored, both in their proportions and in their palette, to the lunettes by Makart and to the central ceiling painting, and had to take into account the colour and material of the flanking marble columns. A fee of 14,000 gulden was agreed for the forty spandrel pictures, which were to be executed in

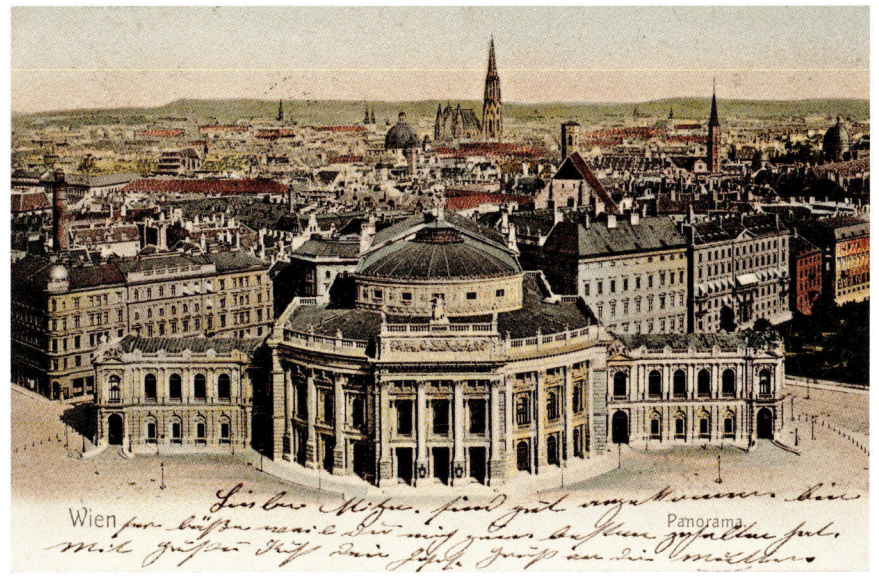

View of the Burgtheater
Postcard. Vienna, private collection

oil on canvas and delivered "at the latest by the end of July 1890" (cit. from Kugler/Kriller 1991, p. 222). They were actually finished and mounted on the wall in 1891, the year in which the museum opened.

It was originally intended that the Künstler-Compagnie should also execute the large ceiling painting over the staircase on the basis of a compositional study bequeathed by Makart entitled *Apotheosis of the Renaissance*. But as Matsch recorded in his memoirs (Giese 1976, p. 18), this task was in fact entrusted to Mihály Munkácsy (1844–1900), an extremely popular history painter of the day, earning him the proud sum of 50,000 gulden. It seems that the art-loving Princess Marie zu Hohenlohe-Schillingsfürst (1837–1920), wife of the Senior Controller of the court museums, Prince Konstantin zu Hohenlohe-Schillingsfürst (1828–1896), and "stepdaughter" of Franz Liszt, used her influence to secure Munkácsy's engagement. The programme for the spandrels and intercolumnar pictures was conceived by Albert Ilg (1847–1896), curator of the collection of applied arts. Ilg did not thereby ask the artists to "aim for archaeological unimpeachability and correctness as their highest ideal" in line with contemporary taste, but to emphasize "individual details, distinctive characteristics in a free, artistic manner" (Ilg 1893, p. 1). The epochs in art are

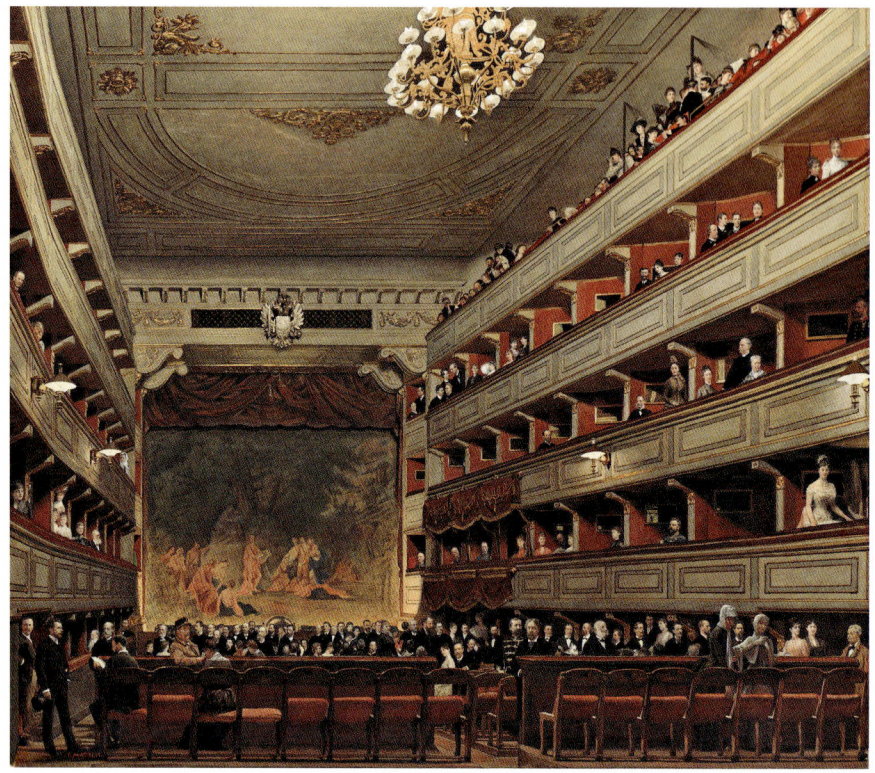

Franz Matsch, **Interior View of the Old Burgtheater**, 1888
Gouache, 90.7 x 102.8 cm / 35 ¾ x 40 ½ in. Vienna, Wien Museum

thus represented in the spandrels in the shape of single figures who conform in their type, clothing and attributes to their respective era. The decoration of the intercolumnar zones makes reference to neighbouring spandrels. The three artists each took responsibility for one whole wall and divided up the fourth wall amongst themselves. Gustav Klimt executed thirteen paintings in total. In Strobl's view, their subjects – the art of Ancient Egypt, Greek Antiquity and the Italian Quattrocento and Cinquecento – would prove "decisive for Klimt's later oeuvre" (Strobl, vol. 1, 1980, p. 83). Some of the figures "resemble paraphrases of existing historical artistic realities" (Hofmann 2008, p. 56).

In their work for the Kunsthistorisches Museum, clear differences start to become visible amongst the three colleagues and their artistic approaches. Gustav Klimt carries the two-dimensional style that he had employed in the Hofburgtheater even further, insofar as he places bright accents in front of large monochrome (or apparently monochrome) surfaces – a tactic plainly visible in *Early Italian Art*, for example, where the naturalistically drawn heads stand out against the ornamental carpet of robes (p. 29; Natter 2012, Cat. 67 and 68). Klimt has here manifestly borrowed from Italian portraiture of the 15th century. The format, in itself unfavourable, suited the artist's tendency towards asymmetry and the isolation of individual details. Within the wall zone devoted to *Greek Antiquity* (pp. 16, 54; Natter 2012, Cat. 65), Klimt's spandrel representation of the statuesque Athena, seen in an archaicizing frontal pose against a golden shield, looks forward to his *Pallas Athene* of 1898 (p. 69; Natter 2012, Cat. 115; Novotny/Dobai 1975, p. 291), whereas the girl from Tanagra peeping out from behind the pillar in the accompanying intercolumnar zone is characterized by an air inspired by the art of the English Pre-Raphaelites and the Symbolists (Dobai 1958, p. 126). Klimt reiterates the subject of his composition in the small bronze Venus standing beside the girl on the parapet, which is modelled on a statuette in the Kunsthistorisches Museum's collection of antiquities (Kugler/Kriller 1991, p. 231). The figure of David appearing in the *Florentine Cinquecento* (Natter 2012, Cat. 61) looks back not just to Michelangelo (1475–1564) but also to other treatments of the David and Goliath story in the art of the Italian Renaissance, for example, the *David* by Donatello (1386–1466) and the self-confident boy with the sword created by Andrea del Verrocchio (1435/36–1488).

Egyptologist Ernst Czerny has recently painstakingly identified the illustrated literature that Klimt consulted for the composition of his *Egyptian Art* (pp. 34, 55; Natter 2012, Cat. 66), upon which he was probably advised by the curator of the Egyptian collection (Czerny 2009, p. 276). Important sources included what were at that time the standard works of reference on Egyptian art, such as Auguste Mariette-Bey's *Album du Musée de Boulaq*, published in French in 1872, and Émile Prisse d'Avennes's *Atlas de l'histoire de l'art égyptien*, which appeared in 1877 in Paris. For Czerny, the two paintings in the spandrel and intercolumnar zone clearly illustrate life in this world and the next, in the contrast between the female nude posing full of life in front of an ornamental frieze in the first, and the accessories such as the sarcophagus belonging to the cult of the dead in the second.

Klimt's own research for his paintings for the Kunsthistorisches Museum, and the assistance provided by the heads of the various collections, evidently introduced him to works of art that would exert a shaping influence upon his future oeuvre. When the new museum was officially opened on 17 October 1891, all three artists were invited to attend the ceremony. At the sight of the staircase, Emperor Franz Joseph paid tribute to their achievement: "That must have been an extraordinarily difficult task. I am always delighted when I see something of yours" (*Neue Freie Presse*, 18 October 1891, p. 6). After the opening, the *Allgemeine Kunst-Chronik* described the grand staircase as "the most magnificent staircase in the world" (Nossig 1891), not just on account of its lavish use of marble but also because of the works by the Künstler-Compagnie, which harmonized "superbly" with Makart's lunettes. For Klimt himself, his paintings for the Kunsthistorisches Museum carried him a major step closer to Symbolism, something reflected in the fact that an article by Ricarda Huch on the 'Symbolist' painting of Romanticism around 1800, published in the Secession journal *Ver Sacrum*, was illustrated by a selection of Klimt's works (Huch 1898). Fernand Khnopff (1858–1921), the most important representative of Belgian Symbolism and an artist whose influence Klimt would continue to absorb in subsequent works, also expressed his admiration for the spandrel pictures (Mahler-Werfel 1997, p. 467).

High point, crisis and new beginnings:
Gustav Klimt on the path towards Modernism

In a work that Klimt produced in 1890, namely the portrait of the composer, conductor and piano teacher Joseph Pembaur (p. 56; Natter 2012, Cat. 60), a new style started to emerge. In the contrast between the photographic accuracy of the likeness and the stylized two-dimensional décor of the background and frame, also painted by Klimt, the artist's orientation towards members of the English avant-garde such as Dante Gabriel Rossetti (1828–1882) can be clearly felt (Novotny/Dobai 1975, p. 295).

Klimt's last project for Fellner & Helmer arose in conjunction with the new theatre commissioned from the architects in 1888 by the Hungarian magnate Count Nikolaus Esterházy (1817–1894) for his summer palace in Totis (Tata Tóváros, about an hour's drive from Budapest). Gustav Klimt, Franz Matsch and the sculptor Ludwig Strictius (1837–1916) were to carry out the interior decoration of the theatre extension, which for unknown reasons was demolished just a few years later in 1913 and of which no photographs appear to have survived. This last collaboration with the theatre architects is noteworthy because it led to another picture destined for Count Nikolaus Esterházy, one that was used to illustrate the above-mentioned article by Ricarda Huch in *Ver Sacrum* in 1898 and which Nebehay described as "the last link in the chain of decorative works" belonging to Klimt's youth (Nebehay 1976, p. 80). A few years after the construction of Totis palace theatre, Klimt was namely commissioned to paint – probably for Count Esterházy – a view of its auditorium similar to the artist's celebrated *Interior View of the Old Burgtheater*,

Greek Antiquity (Girl from Tanagra and Athena) (detail), 1890/91
(see ill. p. 54)

Pages 42/43
Allegory of Fable (detail), 1883
(see ill. p. 26)

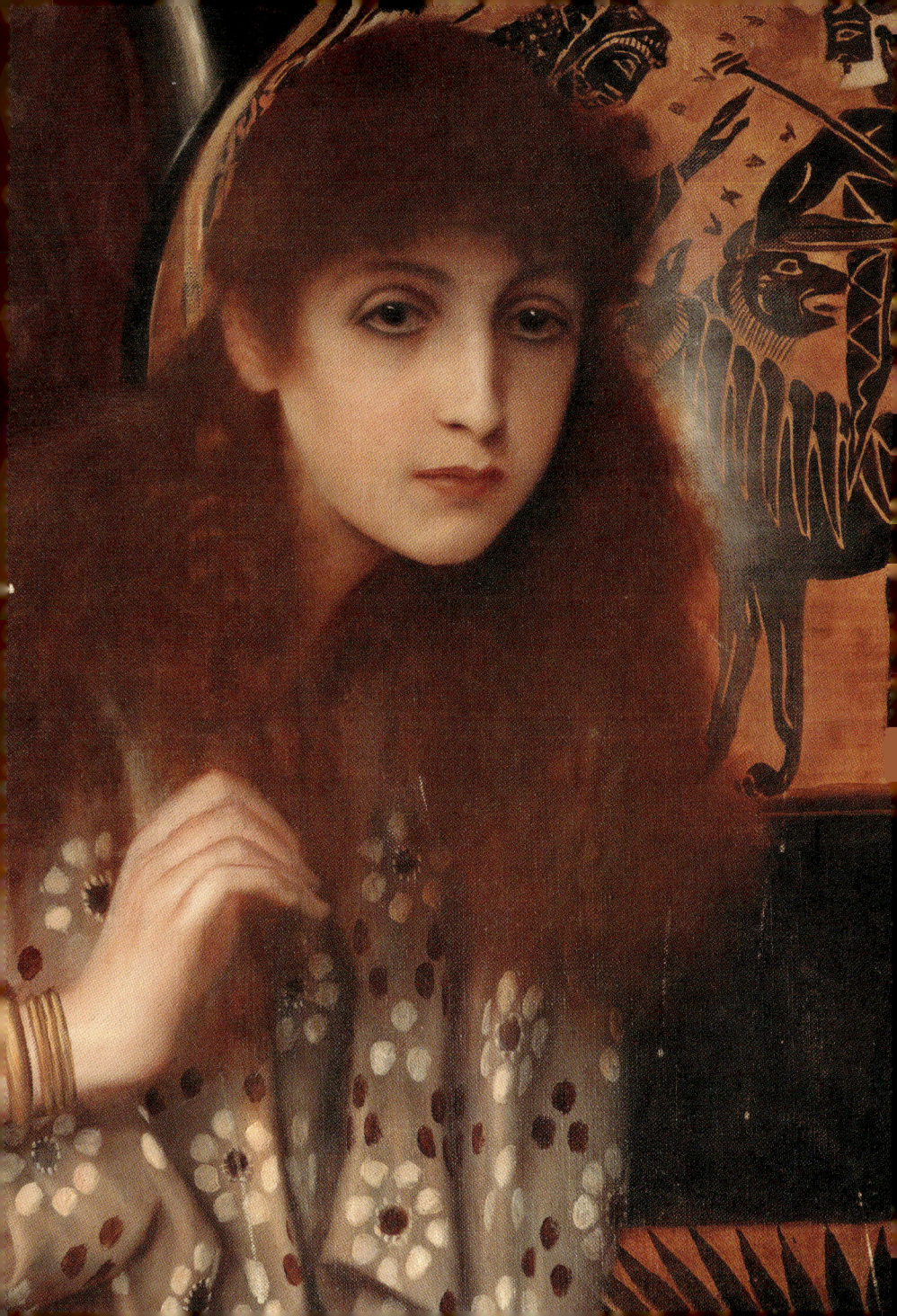

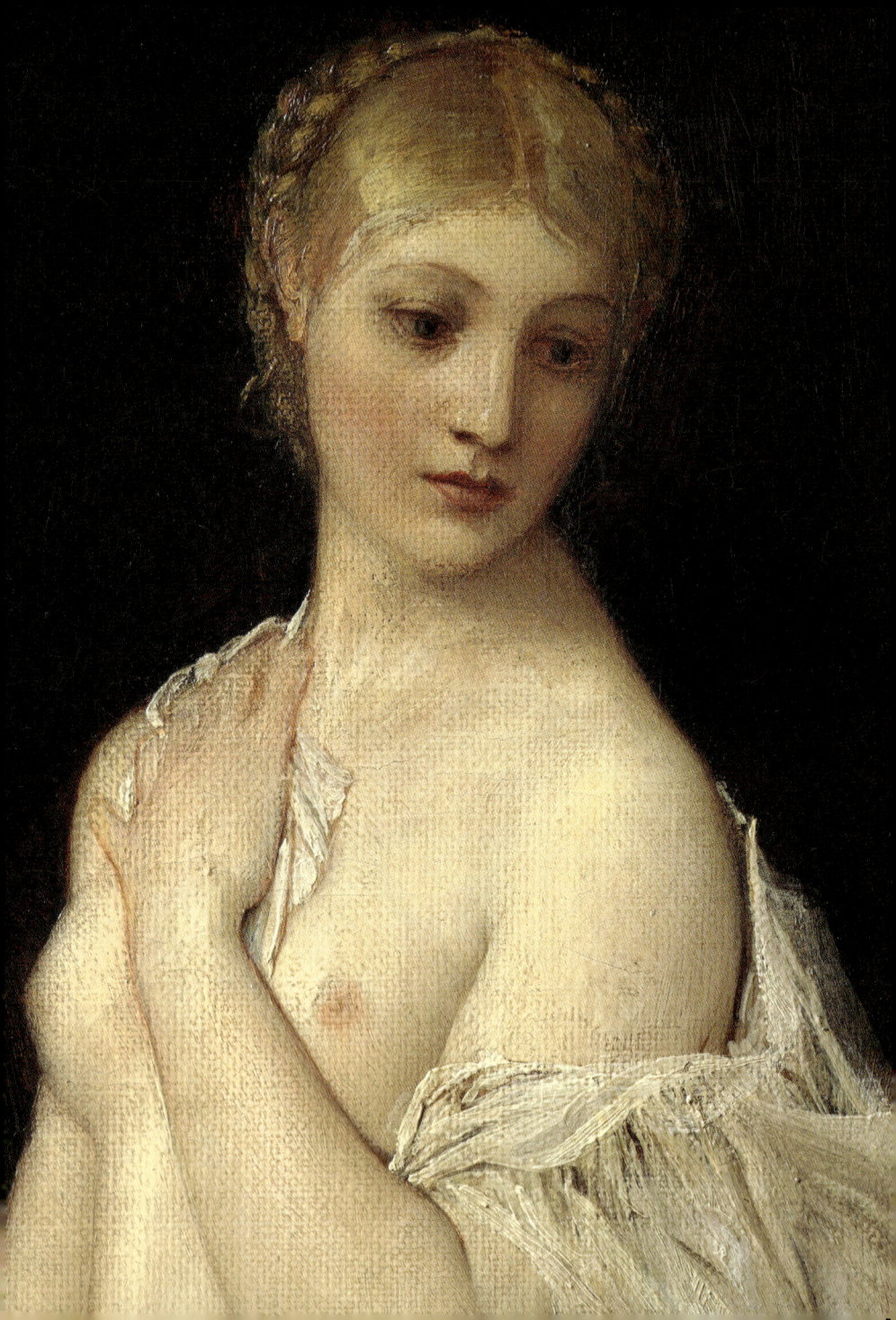

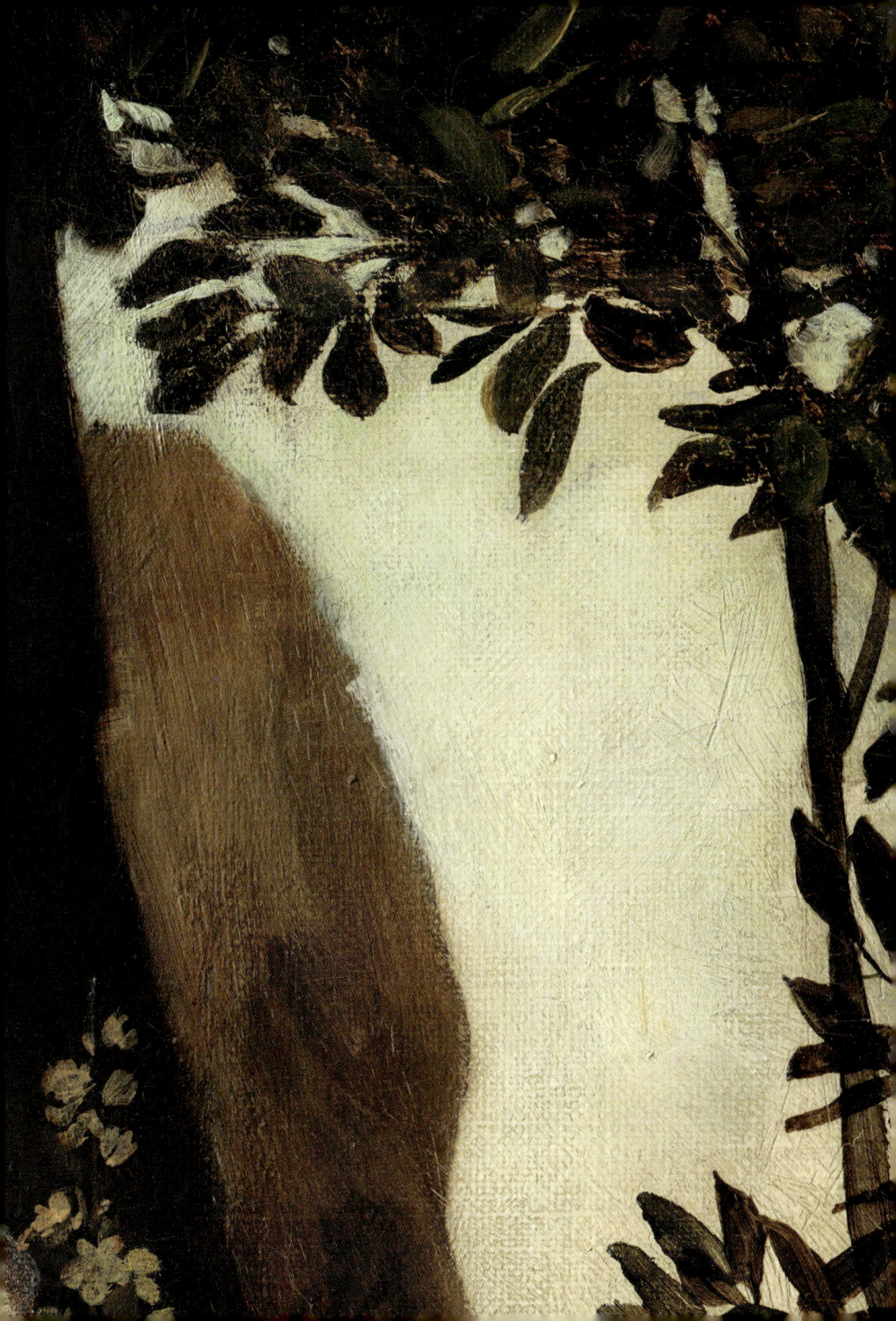

a gouache that had won the Emperor's Prize at the Künstlerhaus in 1890. Klimt wrote about his stay at Totis Palace over New Year 1892/93 and his work on the canvas, which was conceived in a far more painterly way than its forerunner: "That same year I started painting a view of the auditorium of Totis palace theatre for Count Nicolaus Esterházy, with approximately 80 portraits in oils. The picture was shown in its unfinished state at the annual Künstlerhaus exhibition of 1893 and for same I was awarded the Silver State Medal" (cit. from Strobl, vol. 4, 1989; Krug 2012a, no. 11). For this painting – "a task as thankless and torturous from an artistic point of view as the Burgtheater picture" – Klimt subsequently also won the Grand Prix in Antwerp (Weixlgärtner 1912, p. 51 f.).

In 1892 the Künstler-Compagnie were obliged to vacate their studio in Sandwirtgasse because the building had been sold. They moved into a summer house at 21 Josefstädterstrasse in Vienna's 8th district, next door to the house where Matsch was then living. Klimt would continue to use this studio for many years.

Having reached a first high point in his career following the completion of the spandrels for the Kunsthistorisches Museum, Gustav Klimt, now aged thirty, suffered a series of personal and professional blows. First his father, Ernst, passed away following a stroke in July 1892, and in December that same year his brother Ernst died of a cold that went to his chest. The twenty-eight-year-old Ernst left a young widow, Helene, née Flöge, and an infant daughter just a few months old, whose guardian Gustav Klimt now became. He thus came into contact with the Flöge family and Helene's sister Emilie Flöge (1874–1952), who would subsequently become his long-term partner. Then in 1893 Franz Matsch and Gustav Klimt both applied for professorships at Vienna's art schools, but although Matsch was given a post at the School of Applied Arts, where he was appointed Imperial and Royal Professor of Painting on 1 October 1893 (MAK archives, Akt Zl. 1892–0582; 1893–0313), Emperor Franz Joseph chose the artistically conservative Polish painter Kasimir Pochvalski (1855–1940) over Gustav Klimt for the Academy. Matsch made his definitive breakthrough as a court painter with a prominent commission for Empress Elisabeth's recently completed Achilleion Villa on Corfu. In the wake of the fateful commission for Vienna University, Klimt and Matsch broke off their friendship for good. As the representative of the Künstler-Compagnie, Matsch was contacted in 1892 and invited to produce compositional studies for the ceiling of the main hall of the newly built University of Vienna. Without informing his colleagues, Matsch submitted only his own designs. Most embarrassingly for him, these were rejected and the authorities requested that Klimt – having been passed over by Matsch – should also be brought in on the project. When Klimt resigned from the commission in 1905, Matsch declared that Klimt's works were incompatible with his own. In the end, however, his own designs would also be definitively rejected. The socially ambitious Franz Matsch here showed himself to be the expo-

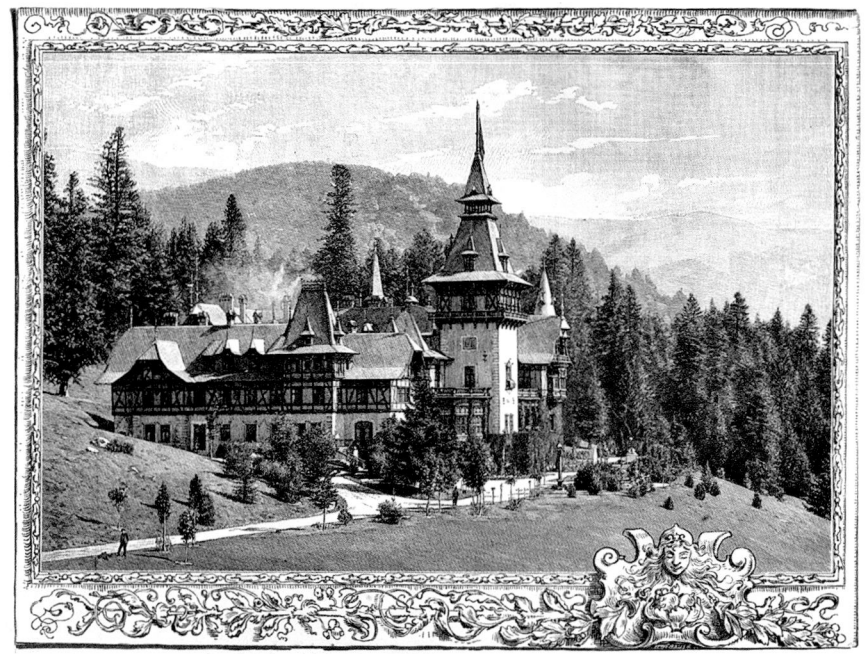

Peleş Castle seen from the south-west, with the domestic wing
From: Jacob von Falke, *Das rumänische Königsschloss Pelesch*, Vienna 1893, fig. 14

nent of a moderate realism tailored to broad public taste; as such, he went on to earn high esteem as an artist and in 1912 was able to crown his career with his long hoped-for elevation to the nobility. Klimt, on the other hand, seems to have lacked the ability to ingratiate himself with society and would never wear "the mask of virtuoso social skills" (Sternthal 2006, p. 44). His primary goal would remain "the ever-increasing permeation of the whole of life with artistic intentions" (Nebehay 1969, preface, n. p.).

After his rupture with Matsch, Klimt moved closer in his art to the works of Belgian Symbolism, whose guiding star was Fernand Khnopff. "Understanding the world in symbols is the prerequisite of a great art", declared Friedrich Nietzsche in his posthumously published essay "The Innocence of Becoming" (Nietzsche/Bäumler 1956, p. 12). The allegorical and symbolic references in the paintings of Alma-Tadema were further developed by Khnopff and Klimt: Alma-Tadema provided the framework into which Klimt and Khnopff poured their own ideas (Becker 1997, p. 79 f.). Belgian Symbolism, primarily directed against naturalism, served as the catalyst for Gustav Klimt and Viennese Jugendstil in their

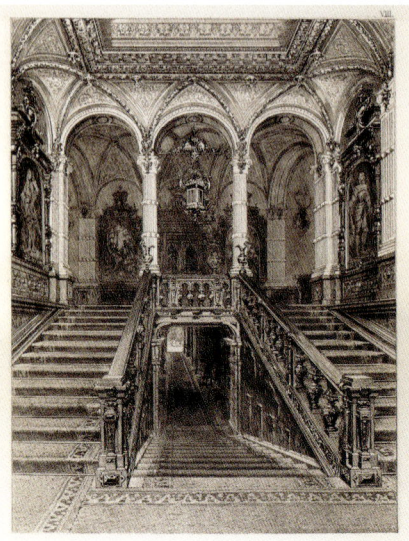

Peleş Castle, the main staircase
From: Jacob von Falke, *Das rumänische Königsschloss Pelesch*, Vienna 1893, plate VIII

View of the staircase at Peleş Castle
On display are the portraits of *Eitel Friedrich VII, Count of Zollern, Johann Georg, Count of Hohenzollern* and *Philipp Friedrich Christoph, Count of Hohenzollern* by Gustav Klimt

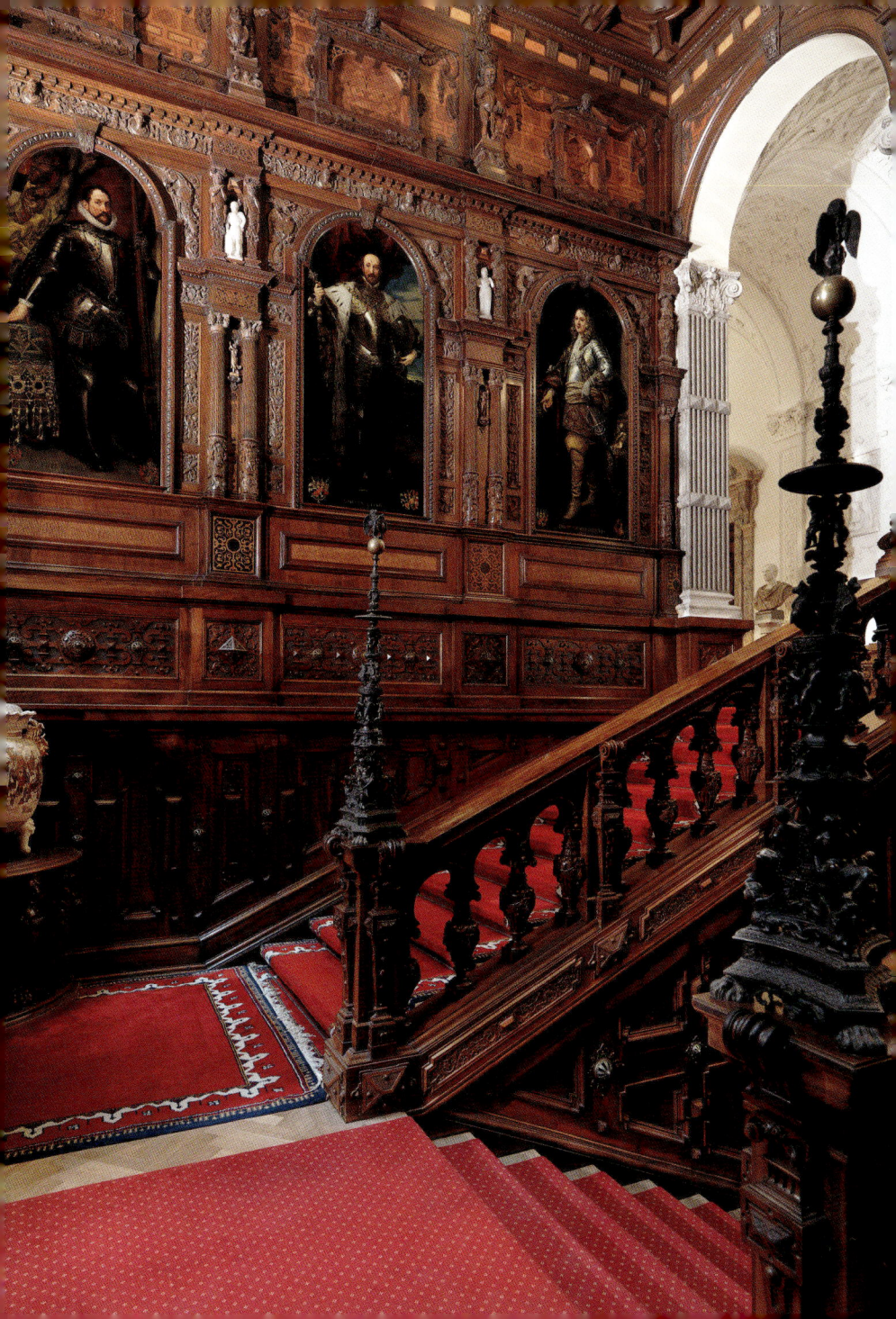

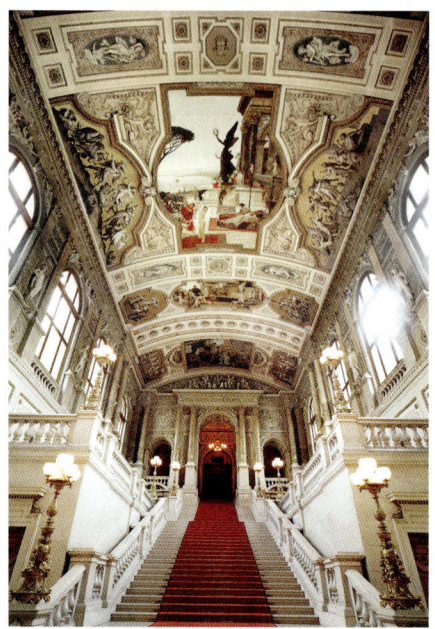

View of the Burgtheater staircase
Vienna, Burgtheater

The Theatre in Taormina, 1886–1888
Oil on marble plaster, c. 750 x 600 cm / 24 ft 6 in. x 19 ft 6 in.
Vienna, Burgtheater, northern staircase

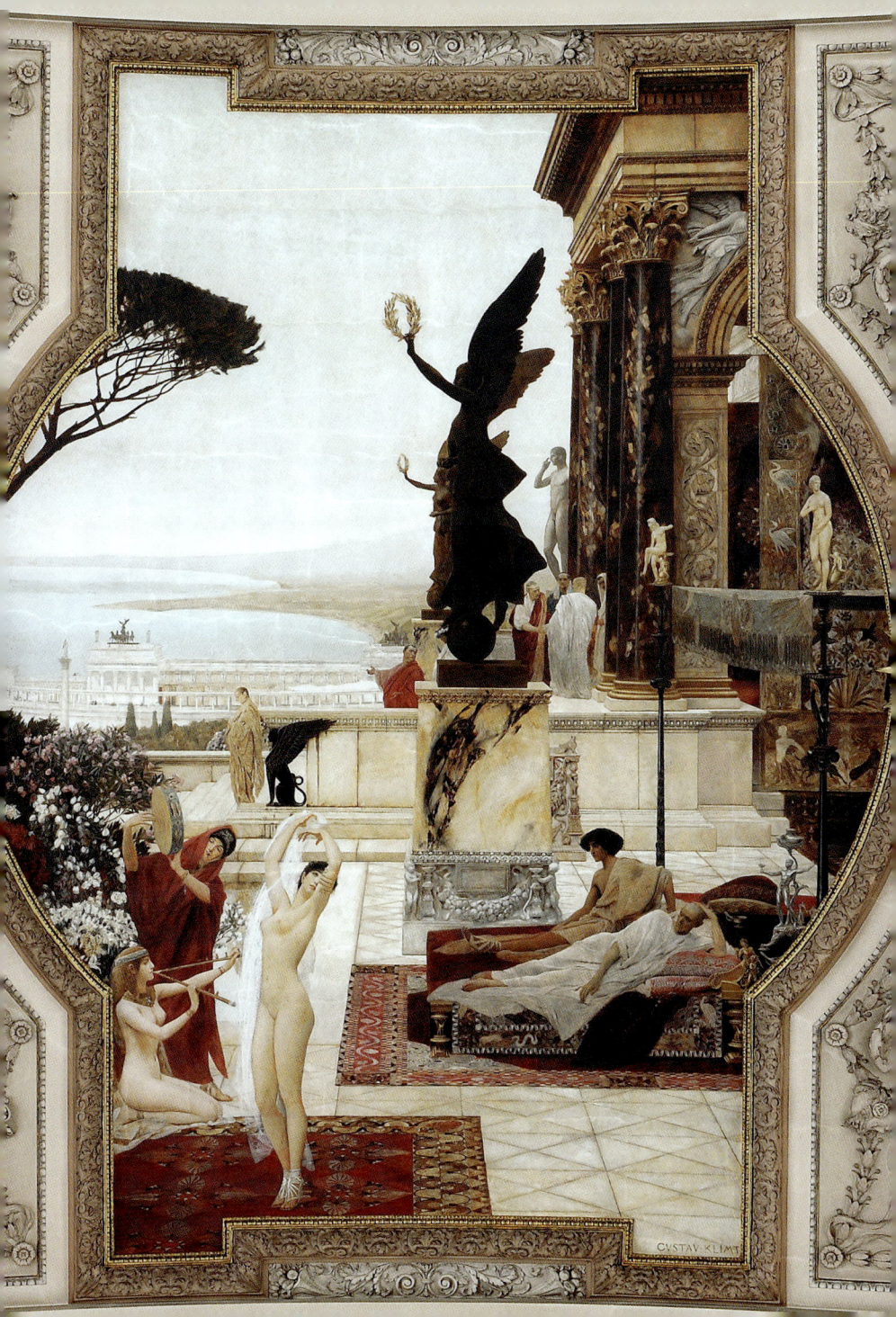

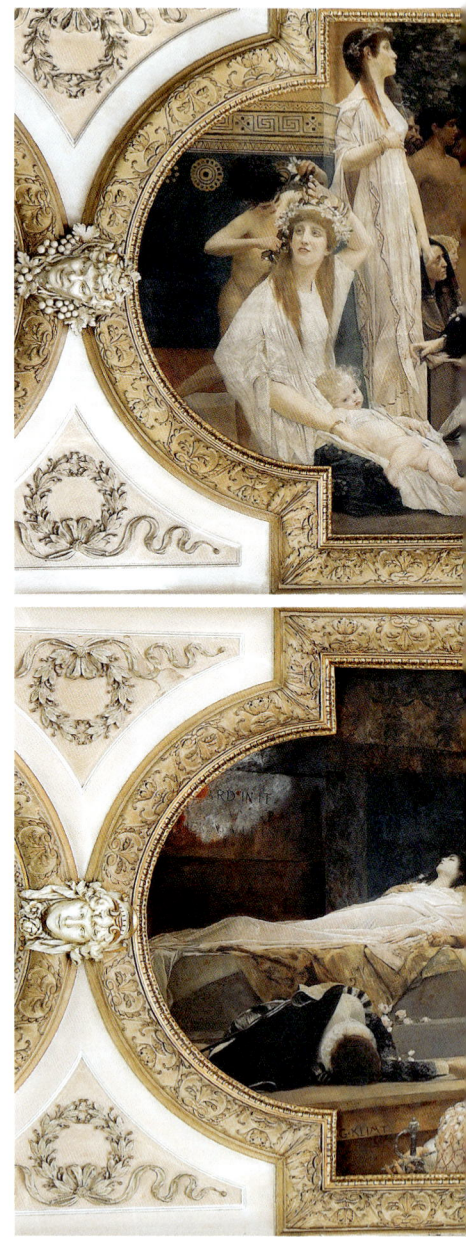

The Cart of Thespis, 1886–1888
Oil on marble plaster, c. 280 x 400 cm /
9 ft 2 in. x 13 ft 2 in.
Vienna, Burgtheater, southern staircase

Shakespeare's Globe Theatre, 1886–1888
Oil on marble plaster, c. 280 x 600 cm /
9 ft 2 in. x 19 ft 6 in.
Vienna, Burgtheater, southern staircase

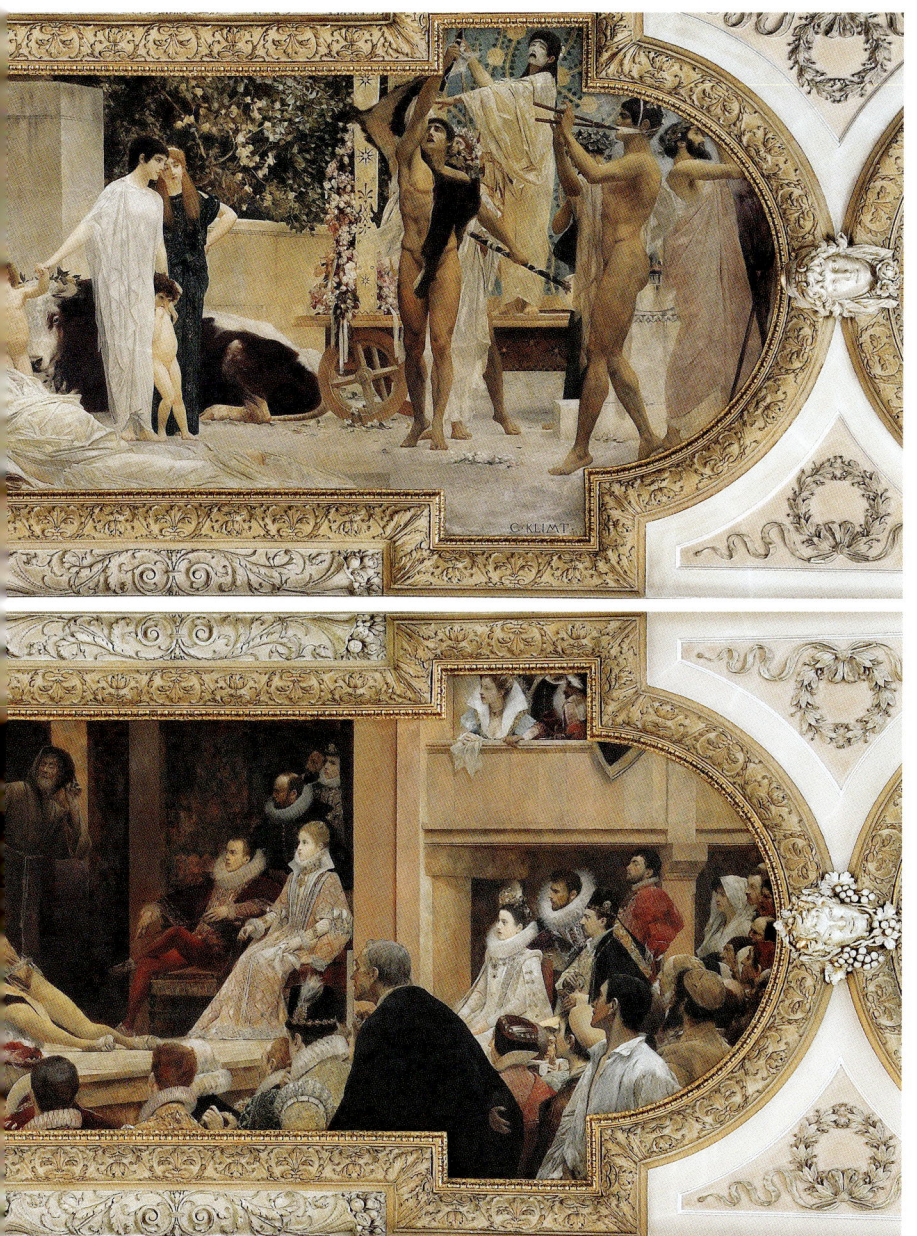

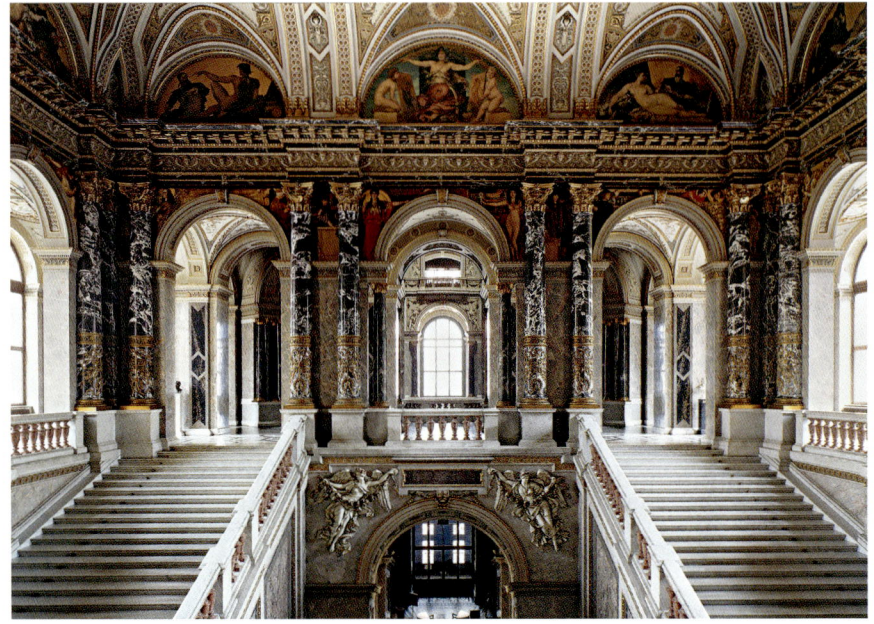

View of the main staircase at the Kunsthistorisches Museum
Vienna, Kunsthistorisches Museum

efforts to overcome historicism (Plakolm-Forsthuber 2007, p. 48). Hans H. Hofstätter speaks in this context of "permutations of historical styles" (Hofstätter 1965, p. 87 f.). Thus the spandrels of the Kunsthistorisches Museum convey a "mood of wistful sinking into a historical dream world". Klimt has "infused the faces of the women with the emotion of the fin-de-siècle mood and thus made them symbols of a sought-after, longed-for past".

In his 1895 study for *Music* (pp. 64/65; Natter 2012, Cat. 82), Klimt takes up a trad-itional motif firmly anchored in art, namely a young woman playing the lyre, but ren-ders her as ornamentalized surface decoration in a manner that documents his interest in antiquity. She is accompanied by a sphinx, a symbol of the enigma of woman and a motif that is also employed by Khnopff, in whose case it is described as "an angel meeting with animalism" (*The Studio*, vol. I, 1894, p. 202). The fundamental shift taking place in Klimt's style can also be discerned in two other paintings that he produced that same year, and with which he made his first public appearance since completing the spandrel pictures for the Kunsthistorisches Museum. His role portrait of senior Burgtheater actor *Josef Lewinsky as Carlos in Clavigo* (p. 57; Natter 2012, Cat. 80) was commissioned by the Gesellschaft für vervielfältigende Kunst publishing company and was executed between May 1894 and autumn 1895 in several sittings. In 1895 Klimt also produced the last of his allegories for Gerlach's *Allegorien und Embleme*, the *Allegory of Love* (p. 59; Natter 2012, Cat. 81). The two paintings exhibit formal similarities: both employ a tall portrait format and present their central motifs bordered on either side by wide pictorial fields in a contrasting colour. Visionary figures emerge out of the mist, taking up their theme in symbolic fashion.

Klimt thereby left behind the last vestiges of 1870s Salon painting and turned toward the atmospheric painting of Symbolism. A first milestone in this new development was the founding of the Secession in 1897 by Klimt, Otto Wagner (1841–1918) and Josef Hoffmann (1870–1956), an association in which the artists could exhibit their "mirror images of the soul" (Fernand Khnopff). In 1899 Klimt presented *Schubert at the Piano* (pp. 62/63; Natter 2012, Cat. 118) at the Secession. Commissioned by Nikolaus Dumba as a sopraporta for his music room, the painting is clearly inspired by Khnopff and marks a key point in Klimt's artistic development. Its importance to Klimt himself is reflected in the fact that he personally led the later artist's muse Alma Mahler-Werfel (1879–1964) – at that time still a young, unmarried girl whom he greatly admired – to the spot where it was hanging, whereupon she commented approvingly: "It is unarguably the best picture in the Secession" (Mahler-Werfel 1997, p. 206). Karl Kraus, founder of the satirical journal *Die Fackel*, delivered a considerably more waspish verdict upon the change of style in Gustav Klimt's work, observing that Dumba had ordered a decoration for his music room from Klimt "at a time when the latter was still working in the worthy manner of the Laufberger School and allowed himself at most a few Makartian extravagances. In the meantime, however, the painter had seen the light" [in "seen the light", Kraus makes an untranslatable pun on the word Knopf ('button') by instead writing Khnopff, in an allusion to the Belgian Symbolist – trans.] (*Die Fackel*, vol. 1, no. 1, early April 1899, p. 28).

The first fifteen years of Gustav Klimt's artistic production were hallmarked by the education he had received at the School of Applied Arts, studying under professors who gave their pupil a solid practical training while remaining conservative and academic in their own approach to art. Under the guidance of Ferdinand Laufberger and Julius Victor Berger and the patronage of Rudolf von Eitelberger, the Künstler-Compagnie gradually evolved from a group of copyists who carried out the designs of their teachers to a professional team of artists who were able to process new influences ranging from the sensual Salon art of painters such as Hans Makart, via the hidden Symbolism in the works of Alma-Tadema, to the English Pre-Raphaelites and the Belgian Symbolists. Gustav Klimt would pursue all his life the study of the human body that he had begun in Laufberger's class, painting and drawing from life models as the basis of his artistic invention. Klimt's path towards Modernism is inconceivable without this foundation.

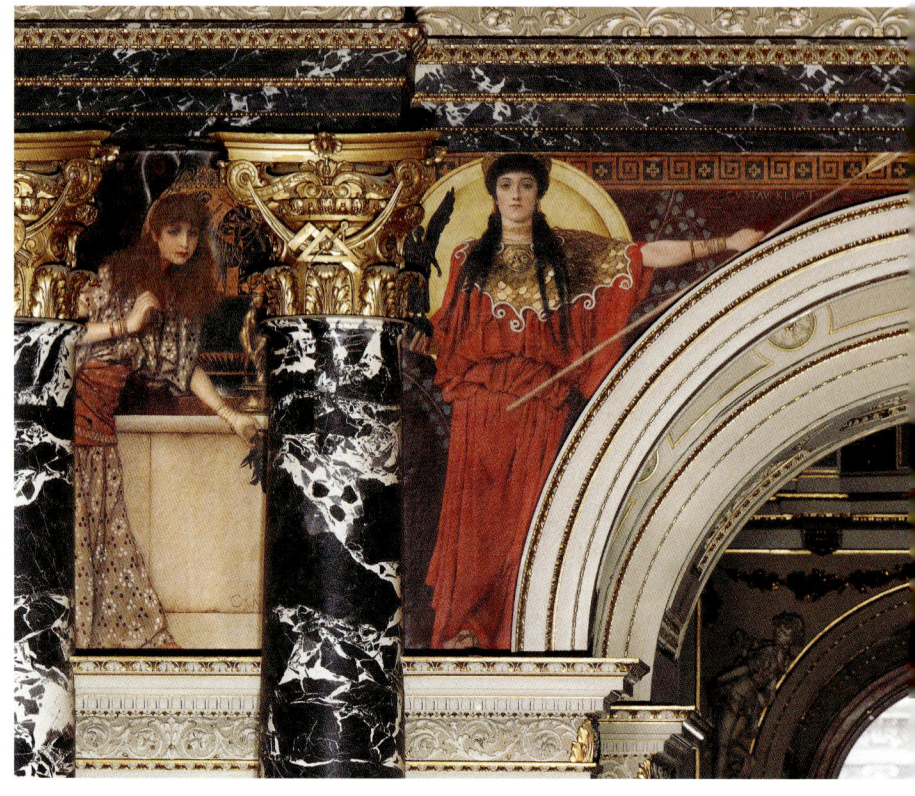

Greek Antiquity (Girl from Tanagra and Athena), 1890/91
Oil on canvas, intercolumnar painting 230 x 80 cm / 90 ½ x 31 ½ in.,
spandrel 230 x 230 cm / 90 ½ x 90 ½ in.
Vienna, Kunsthistorisches Museum, main staircase

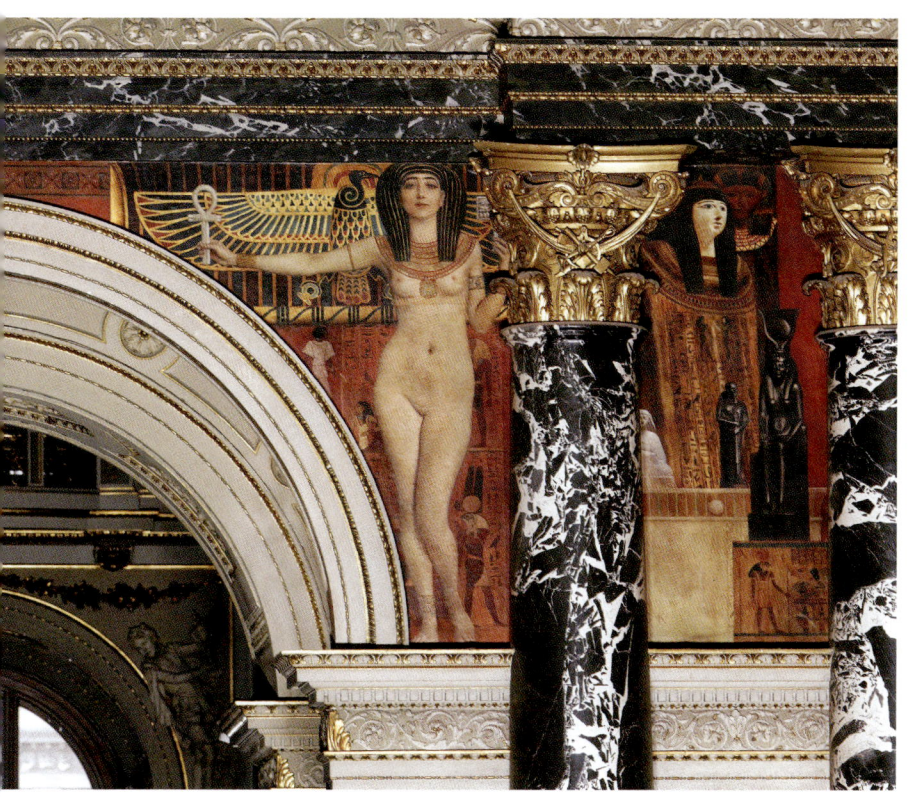

Egyptian Art (Nekhbet and Sarcophagus with Isis Statuette), 1890/91
Oil on canvas, intercolumnar painting 230 x 80 cm / 90 ½ x 31 ½ in.
spandrel 230 x 230 cm / 90 ½ x 90 ½ in.
Vienna, Kunsthistorisches Museum, main staircase

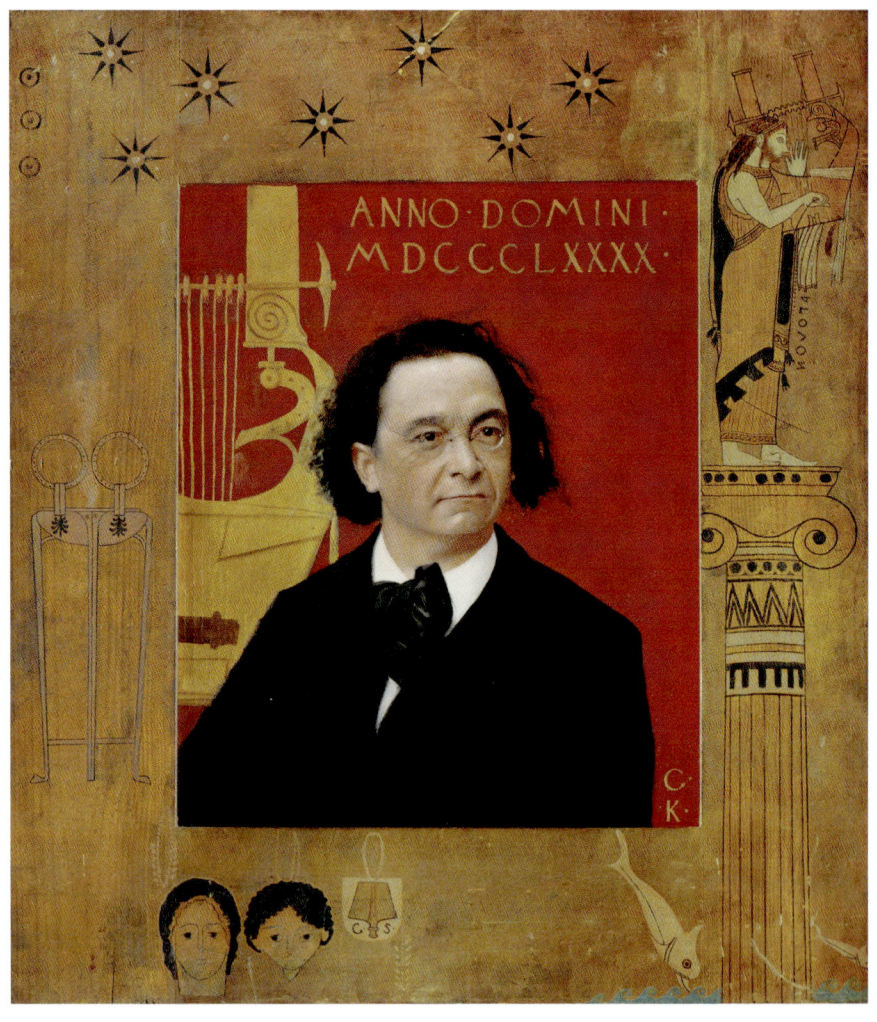

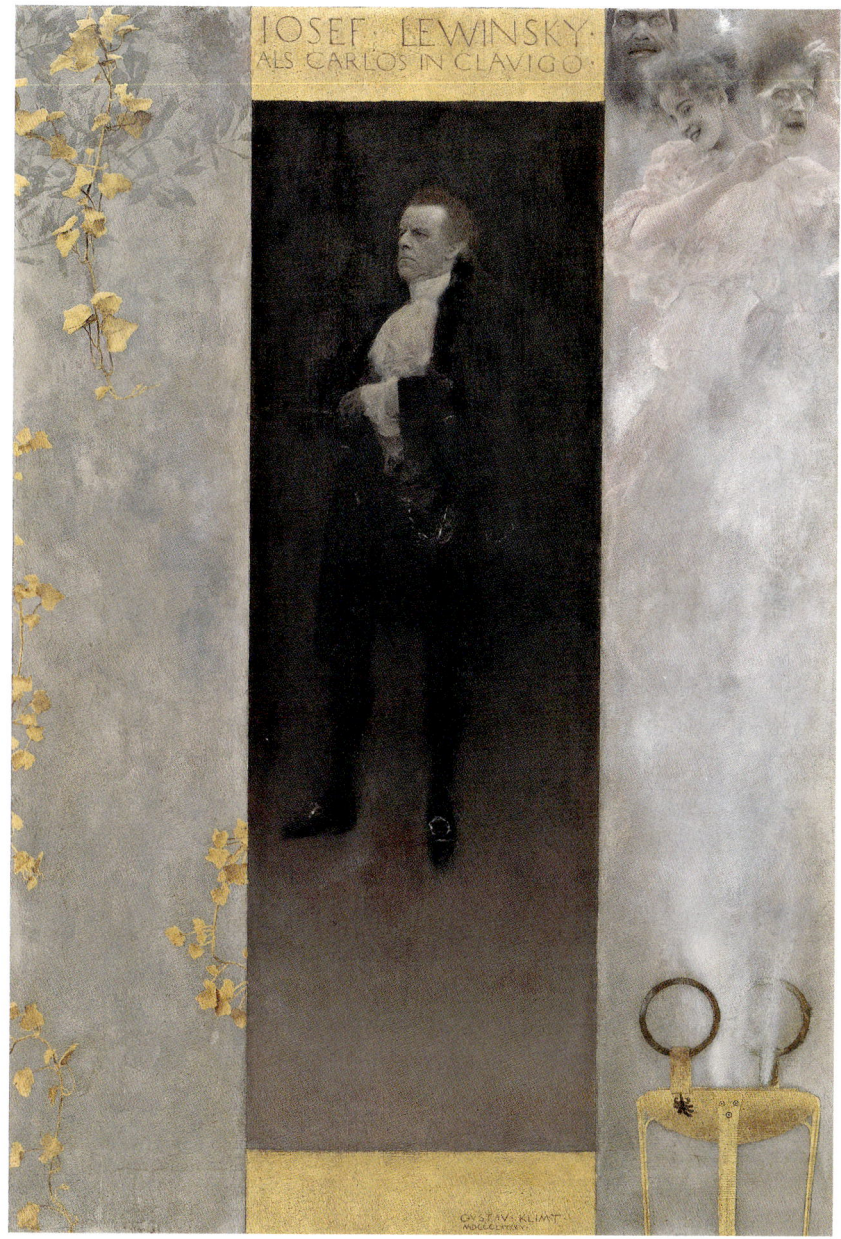

Page 56
Portrait of Joseph Pembaur, 1890
Oil on canvas, 69 x 55 cm / 27 ⅛ x 21 ⅝ in.
Innsbruck, Tiroler Landesmuseen – Ferdinandeum

Page 57
Portrait of Josef Lewinsky as Carlos in *Clavigo*, 1895
Oil on canvas, 60 x 44 cm / 23 ⅝ x 17 ⅜ in. Vienna, Belvedere

Allegory of Love, 1895
Oil on canvas, 60 x 44 cm / 23 ⅝ x 17 ⅜ in. Vienna, Wien Museum

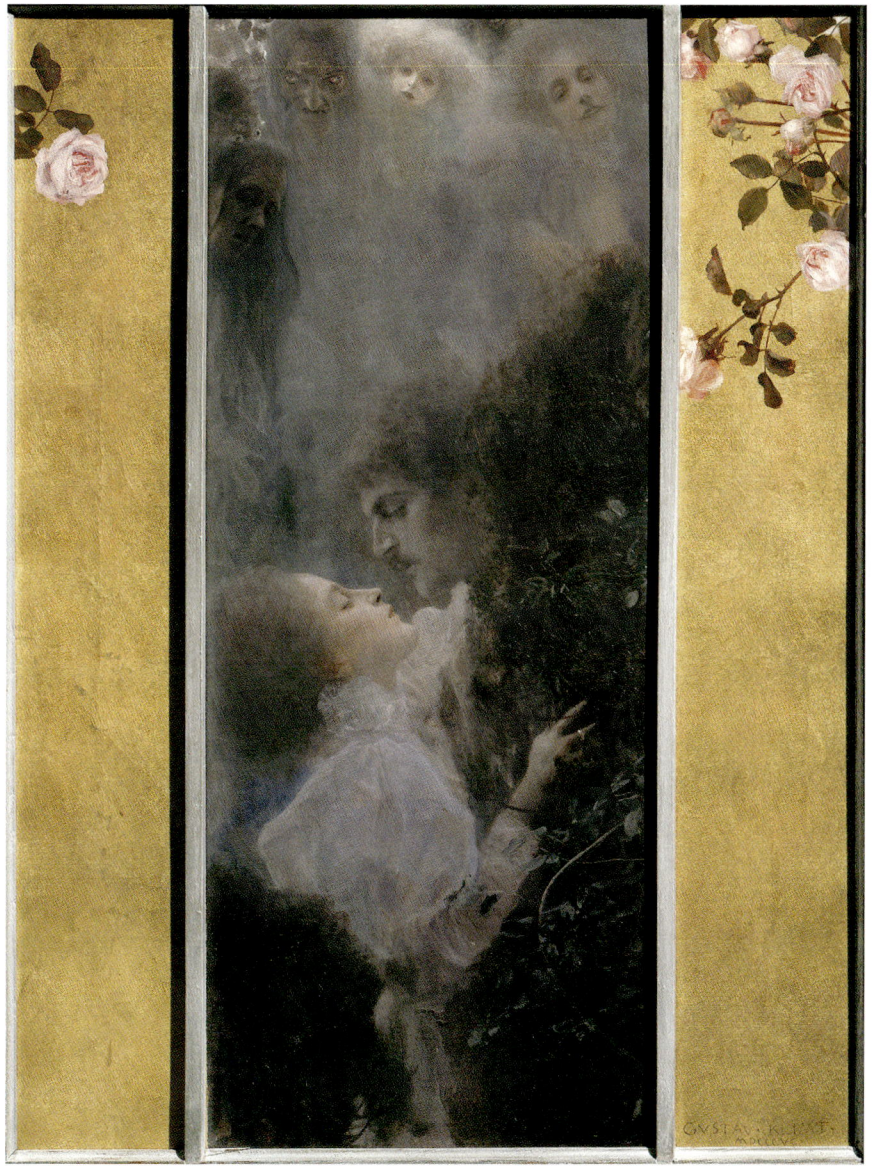

Portrait of a Lady, c. 1894
Oil on canvas, 155 x 75 cm / 61 x 29 ½ in. Vienna, private collection

Pages 62/63
Schubert at the Piano, 1899
Oil on canvas, 150 x 200 cm / 59 x 78 ¾ in.
Destroyed by fire in May 1945 at Immendorf Castle, Lower Austria

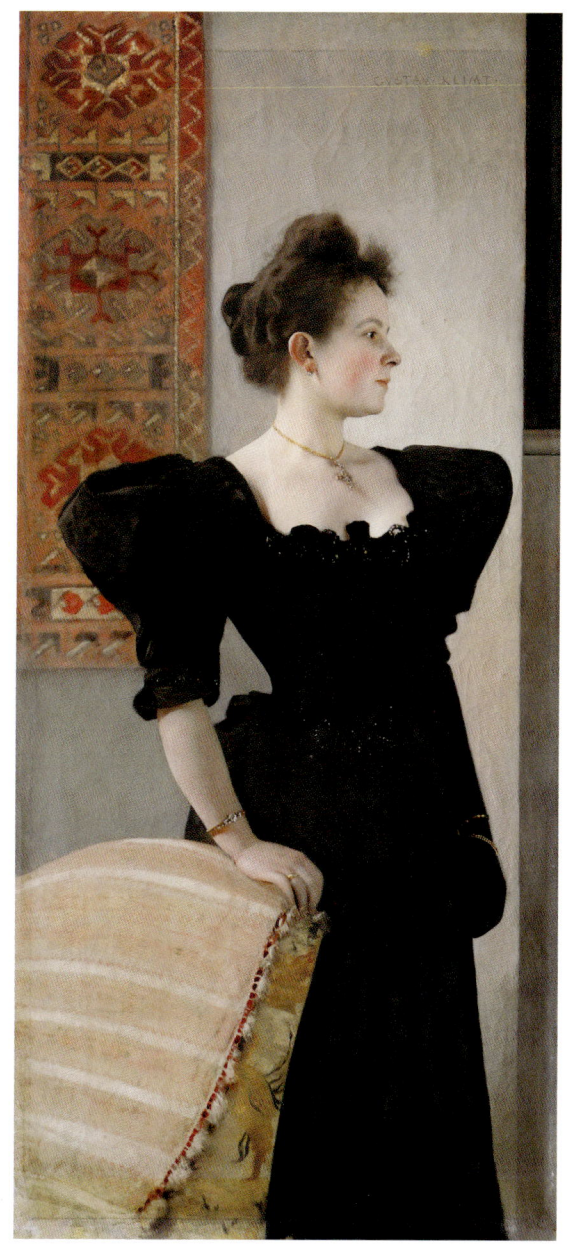

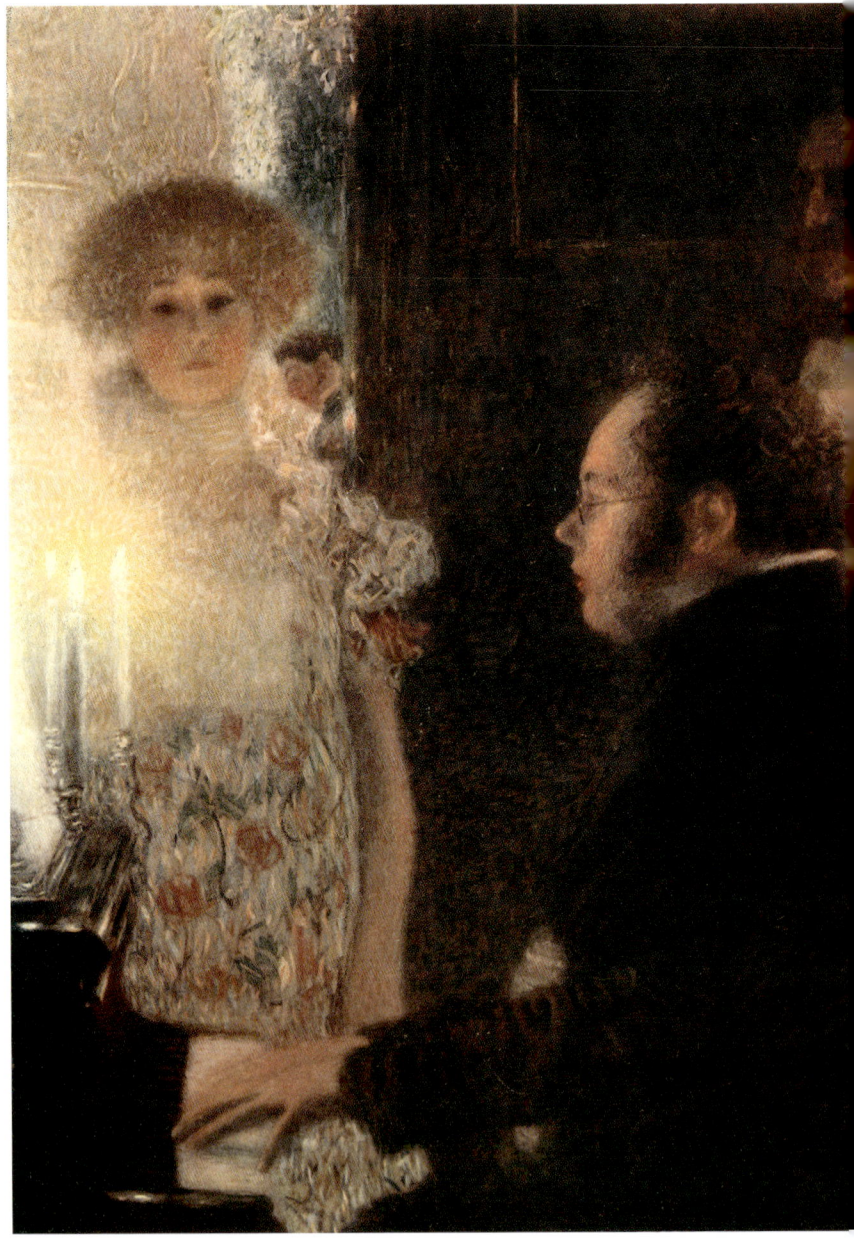

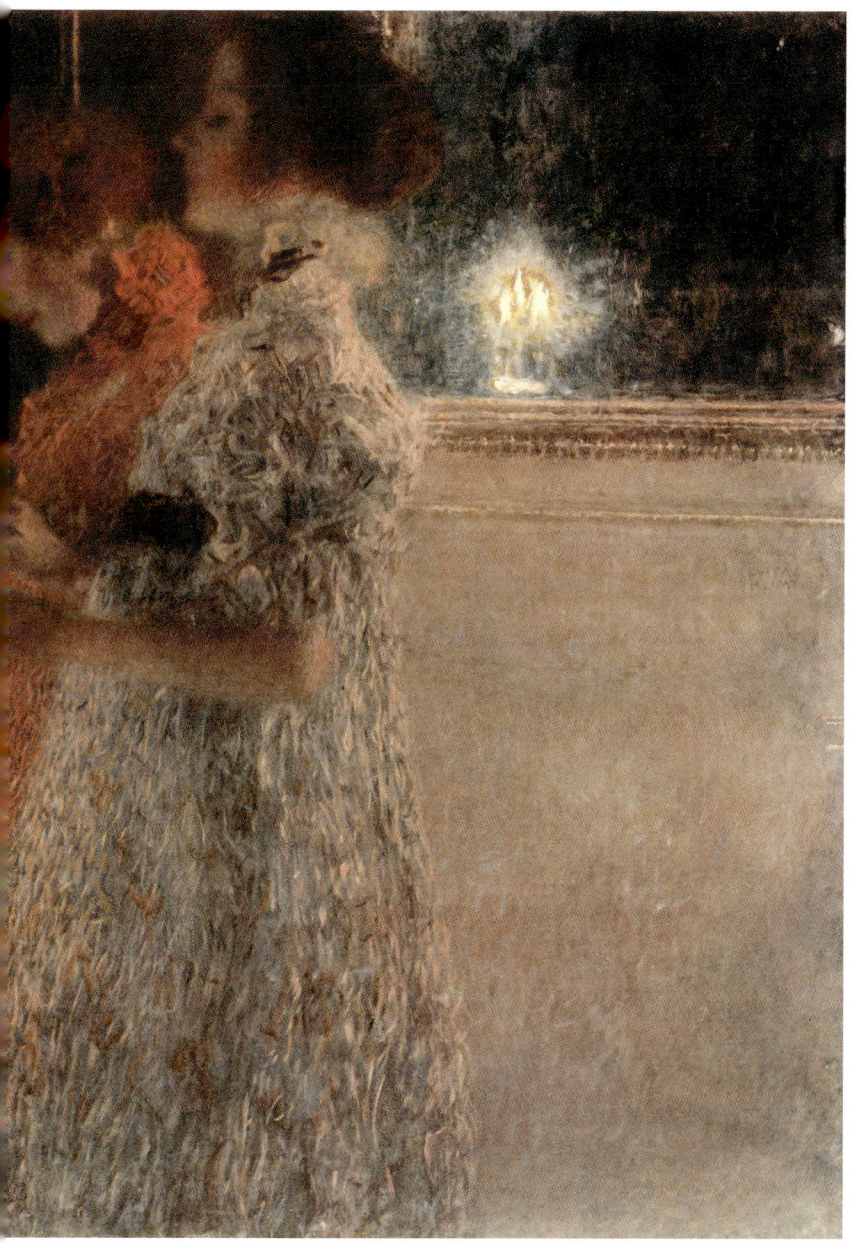

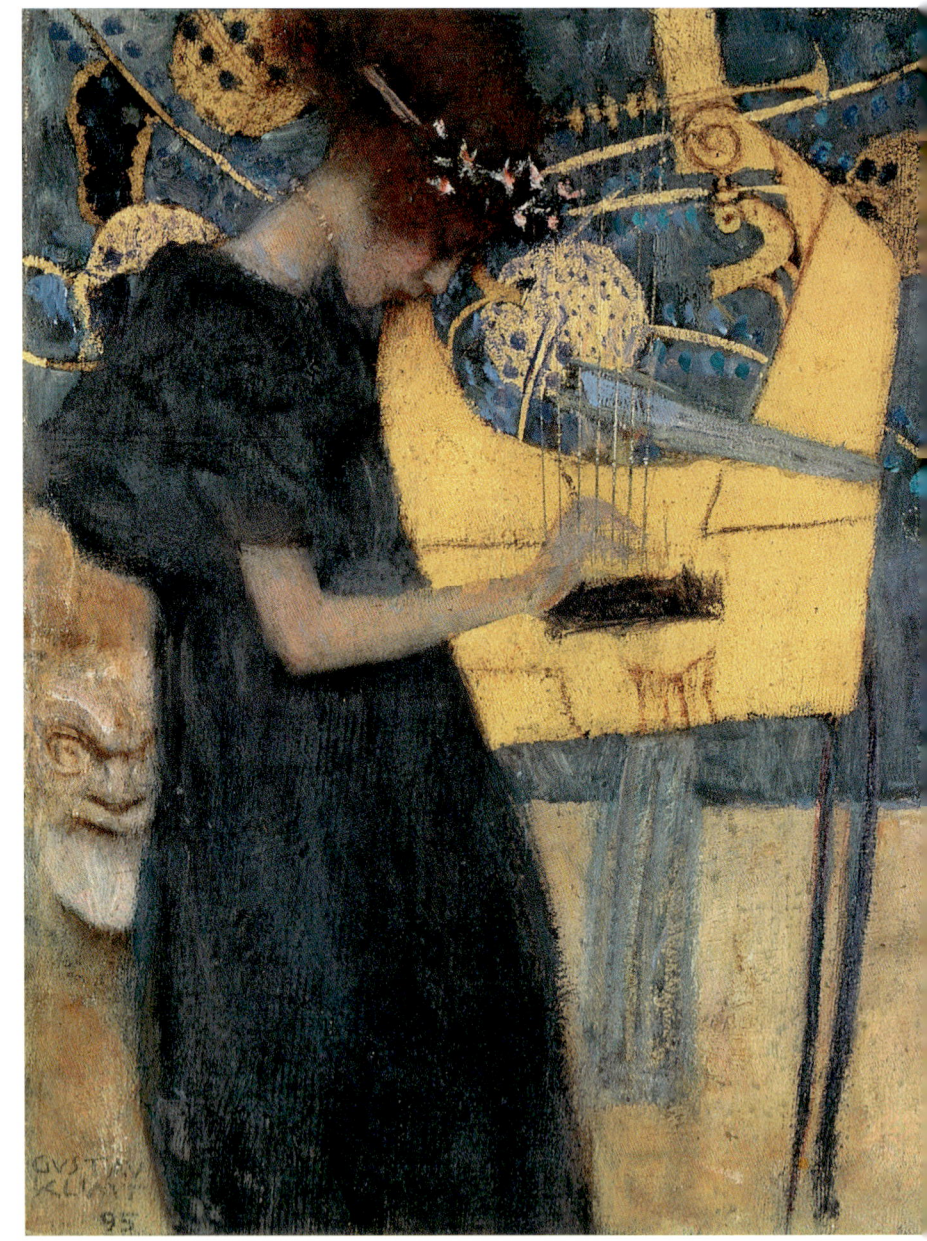

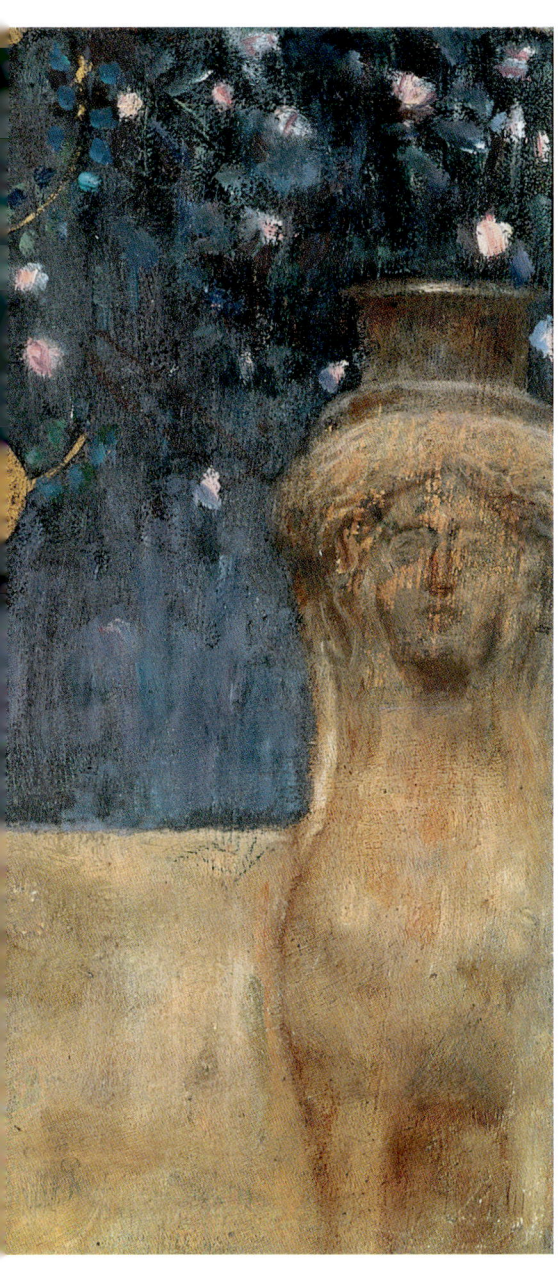

Music (study), 1895
Oil on canvas, 37 x 44.5 cm /
14 ½ x 17 ½ in.
Munich, Bayerische
Staatsgemäldesammlungen –
Neue Pinakothek

Pages 66/67
Fritz Waerndorfer
**Joseph Maria Olbrich (l.), Franz
Hohenberger, Koloman Moser
and Gustav Klimt (r.)**, 1899
In the garden of Fritz Waerndorfer's
villa at 59 Weimarer Strasse in
Vienna's 18th district
Photograph. Imagno/ÖNB

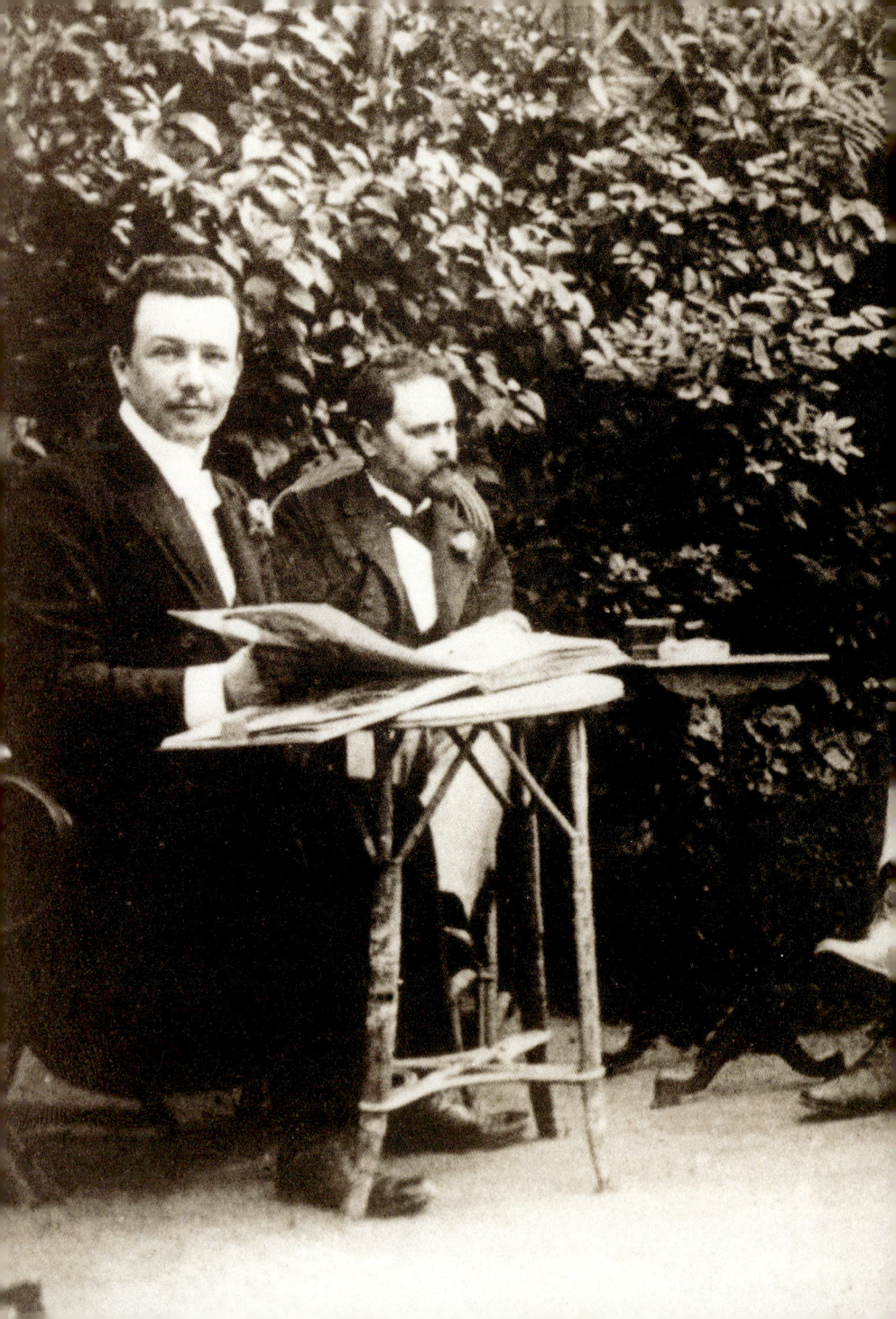

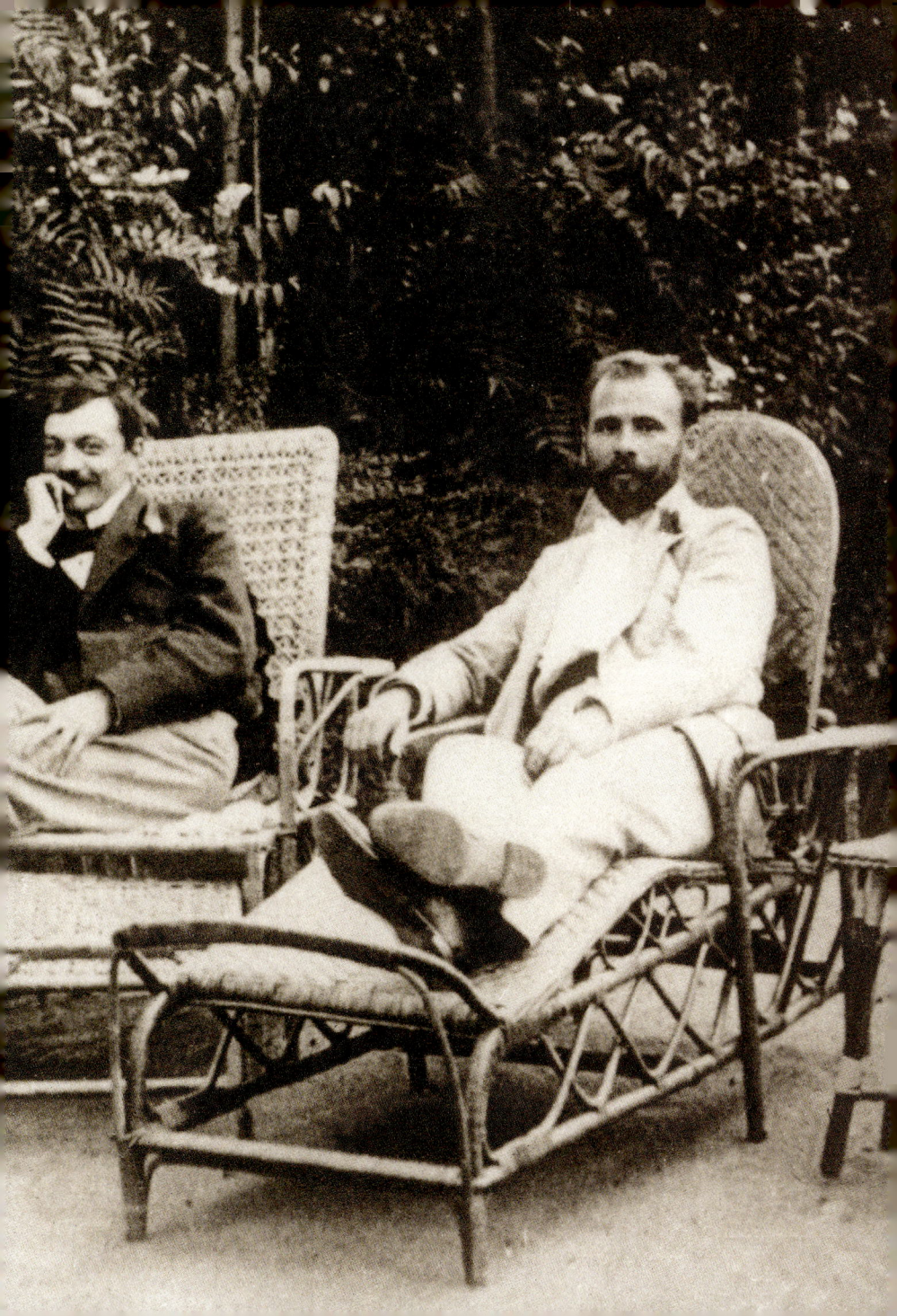

II.

'Sacred spring' and the dawn of a new era: the Vienna Secession

Christoph Grunenberg

*"The Secession –
the birth of a new era"*

KOLOMAN MOSER, 1916/17

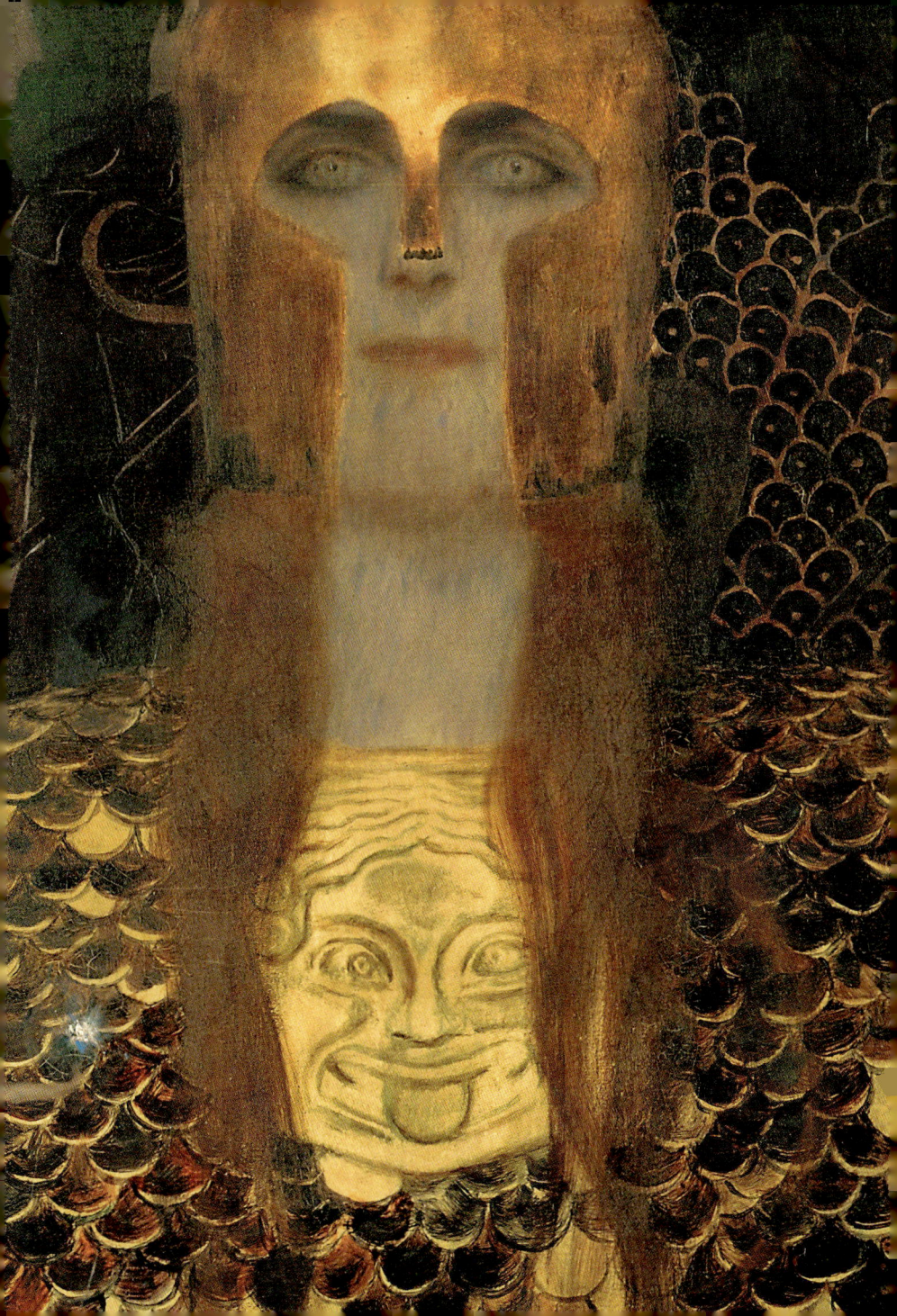

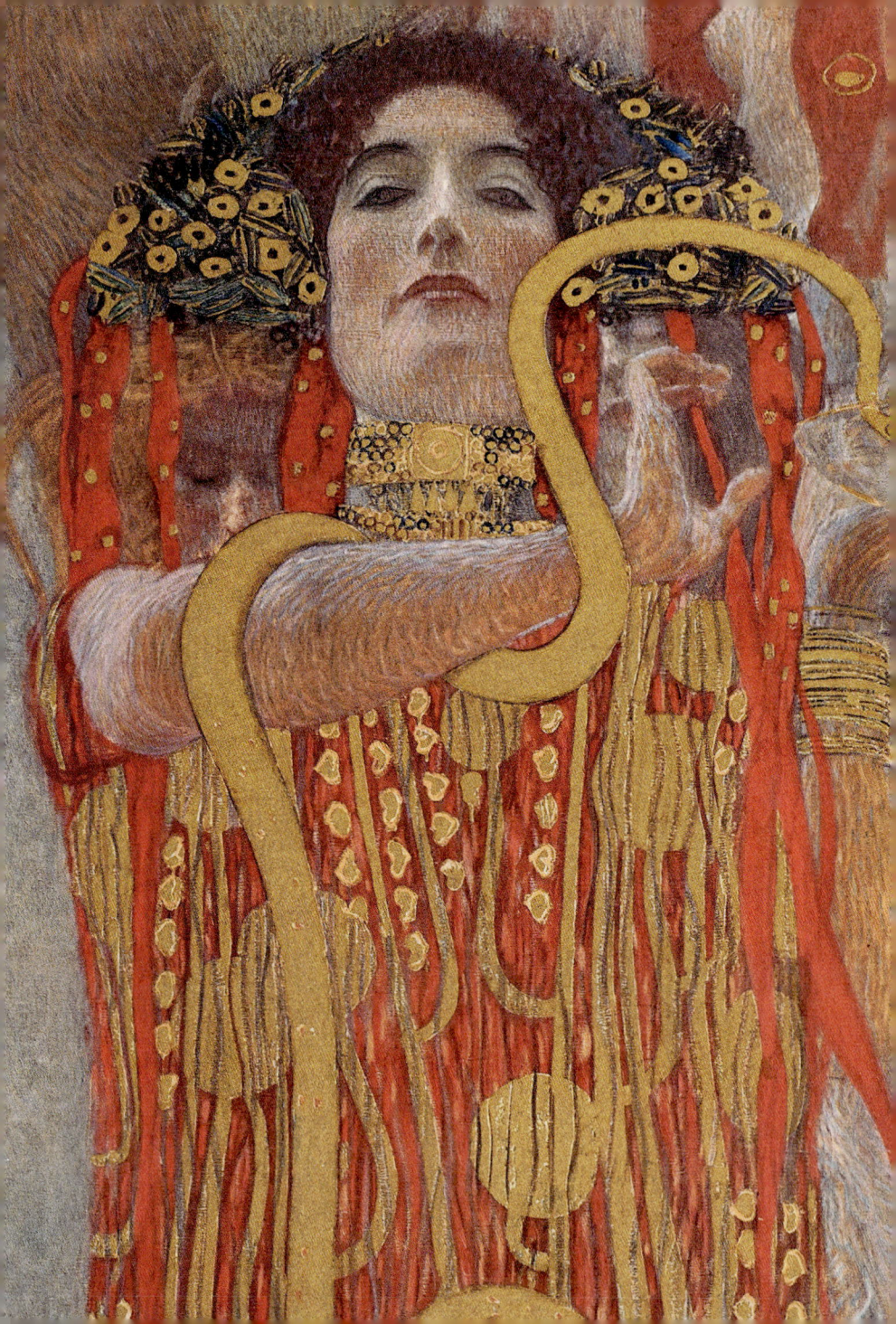

The birth of modern art is often described as a revolution against conservative forces and outmoded styles, the old being swept away by avant-garde artists intent on breaking with the status quo. However, even radical movements need their leaders, manifestos and programmes, rules and regulations, regular platforms and outlets. One of the most prominent avant-garde organizations of the late 19th century was the Vienna Secession, founded in the spring of 1897 in opposition to the established 'Künstlerhaus' association. Gustav Klimt was at the centre of these progressive developments in Imperial Vienna as the Secession's first president, serving not only as a figurehead and kind of elder statesman but also actively determining the direction of the new group, shaping its visual identity and exhibiting regularly in its shows. His involvement with the Secession in Vienna covers the foundation and glory days of the association to the split of the so-called Klimt Group from the Secession in 1905.

The decade following the foundation of the Secession also saw the transformation and invention of the artist Gustav Klimt as we know him today: from a respected and highly skilful, if manifestly academic, painter to a protagonist of one of the most adventurous avant-garde movements in Europe at the turn of the century. Not only did Klimt's style change dramatically during this period to a sumptuous and erotically charged Jugendstil (Art Nouveau) style, but he also became one of the foremost proponents of the so-called *Gesamtkunstwerk* (total work of art), advocating the integration of all arts into a unified whole under the leadership of architecture.

In this period of extraordinary creativity, Gustav Klimt created some of his most significant and stunning works: from the groundbreaking treatment of a classical subject matter in *Pallas Athene* of 1898 to the height of ornamental opulence in the iconic *Kiss* of 1907/08 (pp. 103, 142/43; Natter 2012, Cat. 115, 179). During these years, Klimt was a prominent public figure and, more importantly, executed a number of high-profile commissions for exhibitions, public buildings and private residences. The decorative tendencies in his art found a powerful response in modern environments specifically designed with his art in mind, culminating in the monumental *Beethoven Frieze* of 1901/02 (pp. 114–117, 119–125; Natter 2012, Cat. 141). After the scandal surrounding his so-called Faculty paintings (pp. 126, 129–131; Natter 2012, Cat. 126, 127, 157), which

Page 69
Pallas Athene (detail), 1898
(see ill. p. 112)

Medicine (detail), 1900–1907
This detail is the only part of the painting, destroyed by fire in 1945,
to have come down to us in a colour reproduction.
(see ill. p. 129)

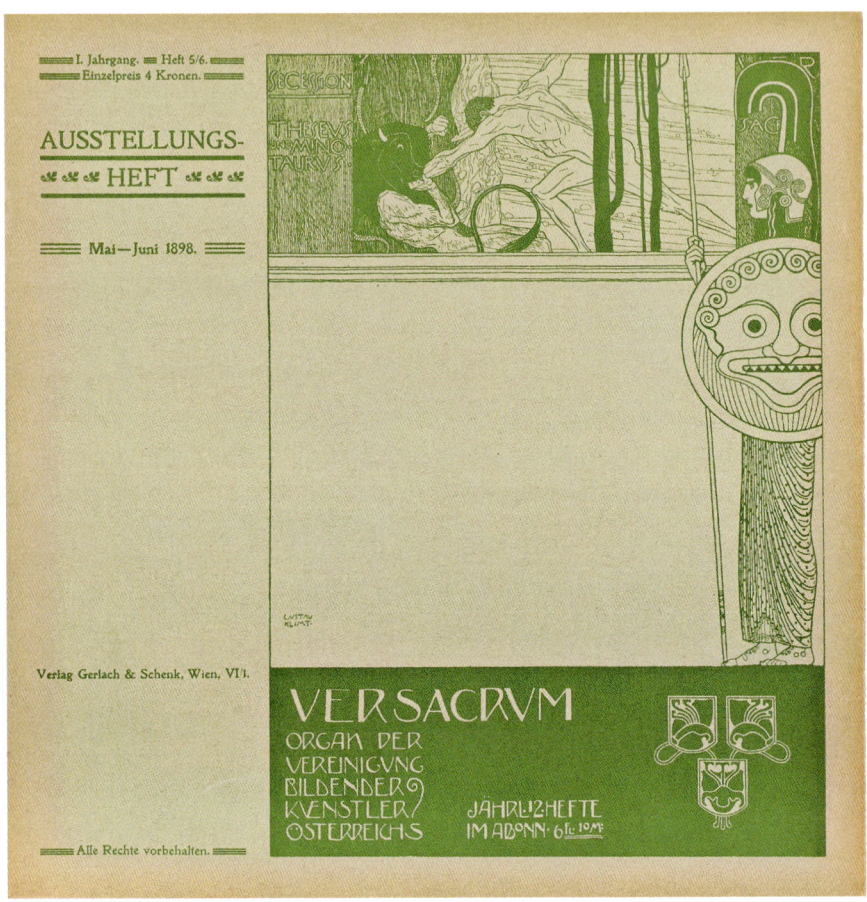

Gustav Klimt, **Cover of *Ver Sacrum***
vol. 1, no. 5/6, May/June 1898. Vienna, private collection

came to a head in 1900/01, and the lukewarm reception of the attempt to return to the public stage with the Kunstschau in 1908, Klimt essentially retreated from public life and increasingly devoted himself to portrait commissions and landscapes. The great era of the Secession as one of the foremost avant-garde movements in Europe had come to an end, overtaken by a new generation of artists and rendered obsolete by the impending Great War and economic crisis.

The birth of the Secession

As in so many European capitals, the intellectual and artistic climate in fin-de-siècle Vienna was ripe for revolution. The city had developed in the 19th century into a major metropolis of two million inhabitants with a grandiose, sometimes bombastic, architecture fitting for the capital of the sprawling, multicultural Austro-Hungarian Empire. Vienna was not only leading in the rich traditions of music, literature and the visual arts but also in science, engineering, medicine, philosophy, psychoanalysis and psychology, producing three generations of exceptional individuals in diverse areas of the arts and science – Sigmund Freud (1856–1939), Adolf Loos (1870–1933), Hugo von Hofmannsthal (1874–1929), Karl Kraus (1874–1936), Arnold Schönberg (1874–1951), Oskar Kokoschka (1886–1980), Ludwig Wittgenstein (1889–1951) and Egon Schiele (1890–1918). However, it was also a culture in crisis, with increasing nationalism and political radicalism putting considerable strains on the multi-ethnic state. The tension between the retrogressive mid-century historicism and the emerging Modernism produced a favourable climate for change in which the creative revolution of the Secession flourished.

The Secession was founded on 25 May 1897 (its constitution was signed on 3 April 1897) in direct opposition to the artistic establishment represented by the Society of Vienna Artists (Genossenschaft bildender Künstler Wien), generally known by its headquarters, the Künstlerhaus ('House of Artists'), on the city's central Karlsplatz. The artistic uprising took the form of youth breaking with the past and proposing a new style and mode of expression commensurate with the realities of the industrial age and modern life in an aspiring metropolis – "the ambiguous combination of collective oedipal revolt and narcissistic search for a new self", as Carl Schorske phrased it (Schorske 1981, p. 209). For the Secession, nothing less than a radical historical departure would suffice in engineering a new dawn through the regenerating force of art – the "sacred spring" evoked in the motto of *Ver Sacrum*, also the programmatic name of its journal (p. 72). The movement was propelled by the "spirit of youth through which the present always becomes 'modern'", as was announced in the inaugural issue of the magazine (Burckhard 1898, pp. 1–3). It thus followed the model of the Munich Secession, which in 1892 had led the way, soon to be joined by the Berlin Secession and many other groupings challenging the artistic establishment across Europe.

Above all, it was the Künstlerhaus's introversion, adherence to academic style, restrictive exhibition policies and old-fashioned presentation methods to which the Secessionists objected. Klimt's poster for the first Secession exhibition, which took place in the spring of 1898, powerfully visualizes the break with the past through the filter of classical myth: the monster Minotaur with its human body and bull's head is slain by the young Theseus, the founder-king of Athens battling against an archaic and outdated order (p. 75). The poster was famously censored, requiring Theseus' genitals to be covered by strategically placed tree trunks. The goddess Pallas Athene in profile guards on the right over the Secession as patron of the arts and crafts. The Secession employed highly effective marketing strategies built around a coherent 'corporate identity', announcing its arrival with a simple graphic design, which also appeared on the cover of the exhibition catalogue and elsewhere (p. 113). The combination of a clean and reduced style with references to classical mythology was employed to state vigorously the 'secession' from the ruling establishment in the tradition of the Roman *secessio plebes* and as the dawn of a new age of creativity. It also indicates the inherent tension of a dynamic movement caught between an ambitious forward thrust and deep attachment to tradition and established authority expressed in an adherence to classical iconography and complicity with the powers that be by, for example, obediently paying homage to the Emperor.

The first Secession exhibition

The Secession's first exhibition was a powerful statement on two levels: firstly, an introduction of the latest tendencies in European modern art to the Viennese public and, secondly, a presentation reflecting the avant-garde spirit of the art shown in environments specially designed by the architects and designers Joseph Maria Olbrich (1867–1908) and Josef Hoffmann (1870–1956), with the assistance of a 'Decoration Committee'. The exhibition brought together for the first time a cross section of internationally leading painters and sculptors, including Arnold Böcklin (1827–1901), Pierre Puvis de Chavannes (1824–1898), Walter Crane (1845–1915), Fernand Khnopff (1858–1921), Max Liebermann (1847–1935), Constantin Meunier (1831–1905), Alphonse Mucha (1860–1939), Auguste Rodin (1840–1917), John Singer Sargent (1856–1925), Giovanni Segantini (1858–1899), Franz von Stuck (1863–1928) and James Abbott McNeill Whistler (1834–1903).

While assembling some of the biggest names in painting and sculpture of the time, it significantly was also a group that reflected the prevalent taste in Vienna for a weighty Symbolism, the Art Nouveau style and proto-Expressionism rather than the latest examples of French Impressionism or post-Impressionism. The foreign masters were juxtaposed with a selection of Secession artists, including Klimt with six works. The prominent literary critic and fervent advocate of the Secession, Hermann Bahr (1863–1934), praised the exhibition in *Ver Sacrum* as absolutely revolutionary for Vienna, "a miracle" in its

Gustav Klimt, **Poster for the first Secession exhibition (uncensored version)**, 1898
Colour lithograph on paper, 97 x 70 cm / 38 ¼ x 27 ½ in.
Vienna, MAK – Österreichisches Museum für angewandte Kunst/Gegenwartskunst

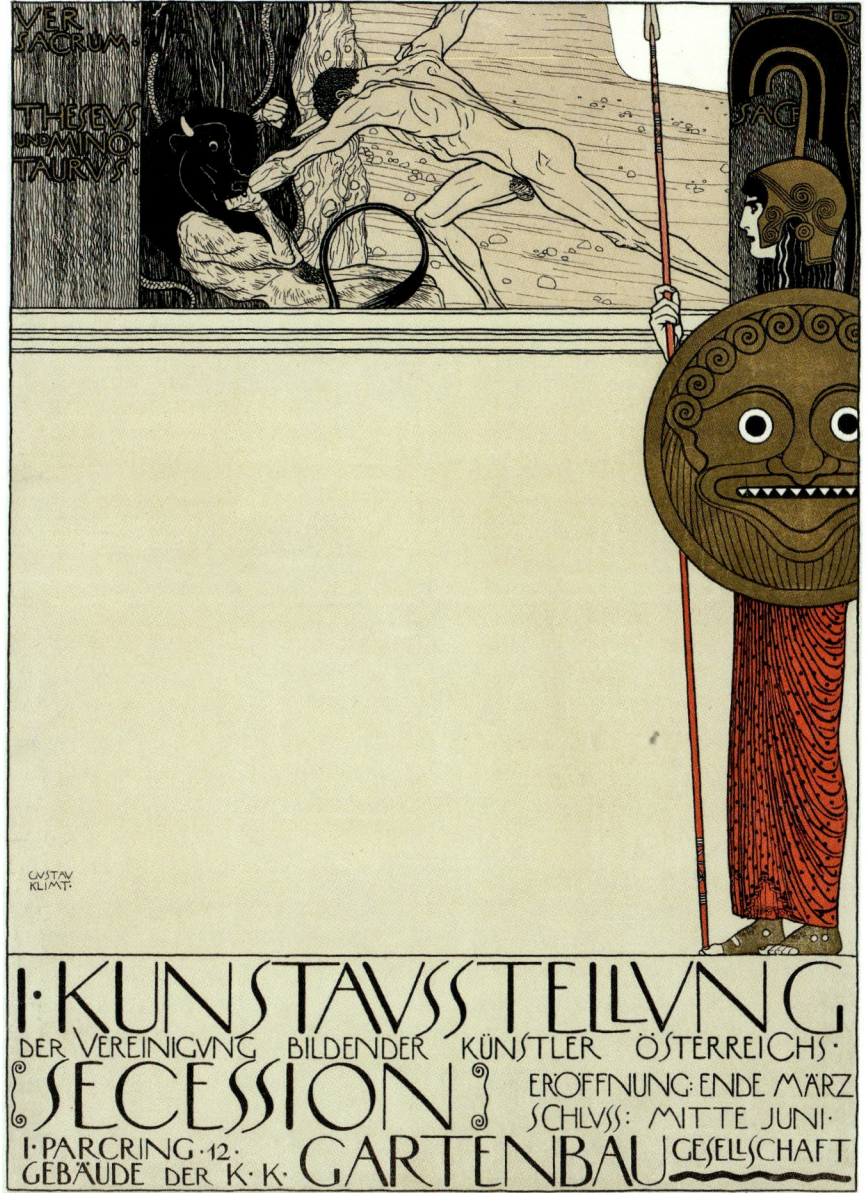

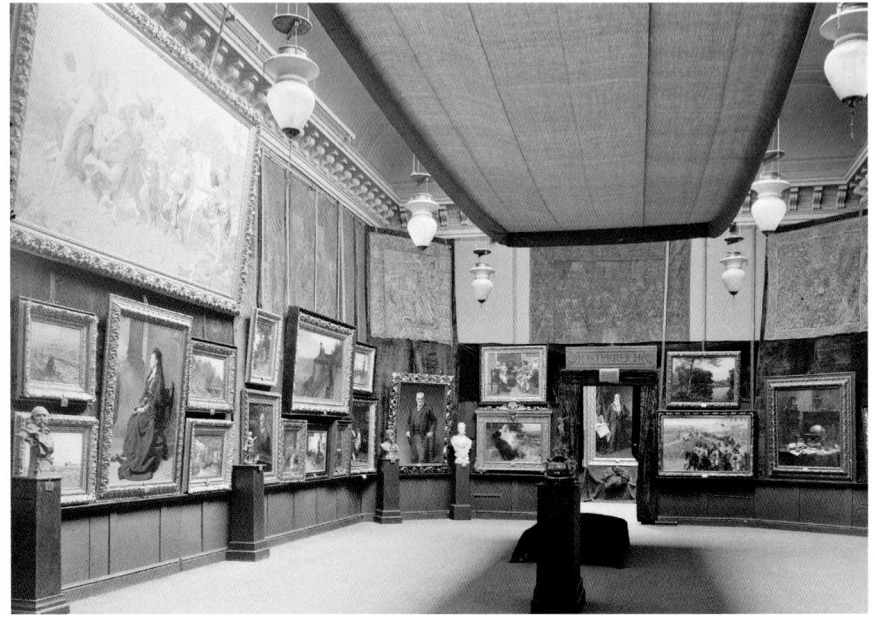

International Art Exhibition at the Künstlerhaus, Vienna, 1894
Vienna, Österreichische Nationalbibliothek

range and quality, presenting "a summary of all of modern painting" and thus fulfilling the organization committee's declared mission to educate the Austrian artistic community and interested audiences (Bahr 1900, p. 15).

The accumulated dust of centuries was blown away by the modern, curvilinear interior architecture and elegantly applied ornamentation. Ludwig Hevesi (1843–1910), one of the principle chroniclers of the Vienna art world around 1900, observed: "The arrangement of the exhibition […] is in itself already a work of art in the modern taste" (Hevesi 1906a, p. 13). "Modern taste" at this time meant a fully developed Jugendstil, which stood in stark contrast to the traditional exhibitions held in historicist interiors with their typical material profusion of draperies, furniture, floral arrangements and penchant for the triple hanging of artworks on dark walls and in dimly lit spaces, as practised in the Künstlerhaus (p. 76).

As the principal architect, Olbrich faced a particular challenge in "artistically" transforming "the vulgar 'Moorish' interiors" of the Horticultural Society where the show was held (Hevesi 1906a, p. 13). The successful makeover of the space owed much to stage design, with a generous wooden arch separating the main exhibition hall, large-scale ornamentation on the walls and flowing wall hangings regulating the lighting and cleverly obscuring the unfashionable architecture. Olbrich skilfully reversed the association of floral arrangements with old-fashioned displays, creating a visual and metaphorical analogy between the rich flowering of modern ornament (originating in the stylization of vegetable forms) and the genesis of a new era; the flowers "specially cultivated in the nursery of the Sophienbad […] bloomed on the day of the opening" (Hevesi 1906a, p. 13).

"To every age its art, to art its freedom": the Secession building

The success of the Vienna Secession was spectacular. Less than a year after the establishment of the association, the first triumphant exhibition had been staged and a luxurious journal, *Ver Sacrum*, was launched as its official publicity organ. Already by 1900 the Secessionists had become the dominant movement in Vienna, its modern style not only accepted by the critics but also embraced by patrons and the general public. The most prominent manifestation of the Secession's success was the move into its own purpose-built home in November 1898, a gleaming white building on the Wienzeile, not far from the central Karlsplatz, only eighteen months after the Secession's constitution had been signed (pp. 80, 492). For the next decade, the Secession was to be the epicentre of art in Vienna, a rapid succession of exhibitions bringing the latest European art to the city as well as providing a showcase for home-grown talent in some of the most significant exhibitions of the period.

The Secession building was erected in a record time of only six months. It was celebrated as a truly modern structure, responding to the contemporary needs of simplicity, adaptability and even lighting: "Here everything is ruled by purpose alone," Hermann Bahr wrote. "This building does not pretend to be a temple or a palace, but a space that allows works of art to develop to their greatest effect" (Bahr 1900, p. 61). The building was designed by Joseph Maria Olbrich, with simplifying input from Klimt, and with the collaboration of the leading architect, designer and painter Koloman Moser (1868–1918) on the decoration and fitting out. Klimt's design is dated early 1897 and seems to coincide with the award of the commission to Olbrich in March of this year, sharing his temple-like structure with flanking wings.

The building's simple "'proto-Cubistic' stereometry" (Karpfinger 2003, p. 47), with its expanded, unadorned white façade, did indeed seem programmatic, announcing a resolute departure from past models by way of preclassical architecture (Egyptian and Assyrian sources were mentioned, one critic describing the building as "the tomb of the

Mahdi"; Hevesi 1906a, p. 63). The gleaming purity of the architectural mass and stark flat surfaces were mitigated by copious, if formally restrained and predominantly linear, ornamental detail in gold with figurative and floral friezes featuring classical masks, snakes and owls. The complex iconographic programme culminated in the golden laurel wreath crowning the central tower, again hinting at the dawn of a new era and spiritual rebirth through art. Modernity here thinly veils an antique symbolism that locates artistic aspiration in an Arcadian utopia of the classical past, promising elevation through spiritual and physical purification.

Olbrich did indeed think of an ancient temple rather than a modern machine for viewing pictures – a sanctuary, however, devoted to the art of its time as the Secession's motto over the entrance forcefully declared: "To every age its art, to art its freedom" (Der Zeit ihre Kunst, der Kunst ihre Freiheit). The architect emphatically described his lofty ambitions: "The walls shall be white, shining, sacred and chaste. Solemn dignity shall pervade everything. Pure dignity as it seized me as I stood alone, shuddering, in front of the unfinished temple in Segesta!" (Olbrich 1899, p. 5). Bahr, who had so enthusiastically praised the pure functionality of the galleries, proposed a similarly reflective method of artistic contemplation. Entering the building was described as a process of "purifying the soul". After the act of artistic worship, "before we return to life, we may dwell pensively in the presence of art's sentiments, to contemplate it, to compose ourselves. We would like here to absorb art's afterglow. Then we may be released" (Bahr 1900, p. 62).

With its building, the Secession was caught in a schism between past and present, looking backwards for inspiration in the simplicity, dignity and elevated spirit of the classical period while yearning for a modern style commensurate with the challenges of the movement's progressive attitude, responding to an age of accelerating change. The artistic reaction to these challenges was astoundingly radical, with the invention of a new symbolic language overcoming the supremacy of the genre of history painting and updating the tired paean of antique gods and myths. The artists of the Secession developed a new painterly expressiveness and an extravagant indulgence in colour and surface materiality while its architects and designers advanced towards an early manifestation of reductive flexibility and functionality in architecture. At the same time, we can also detect a certain hesitancy in the departure from classical myths, from ornament, decoration and other formal and thematic distractions.

Nuda Veritas (detail), 1899
(see ill. p. 111)

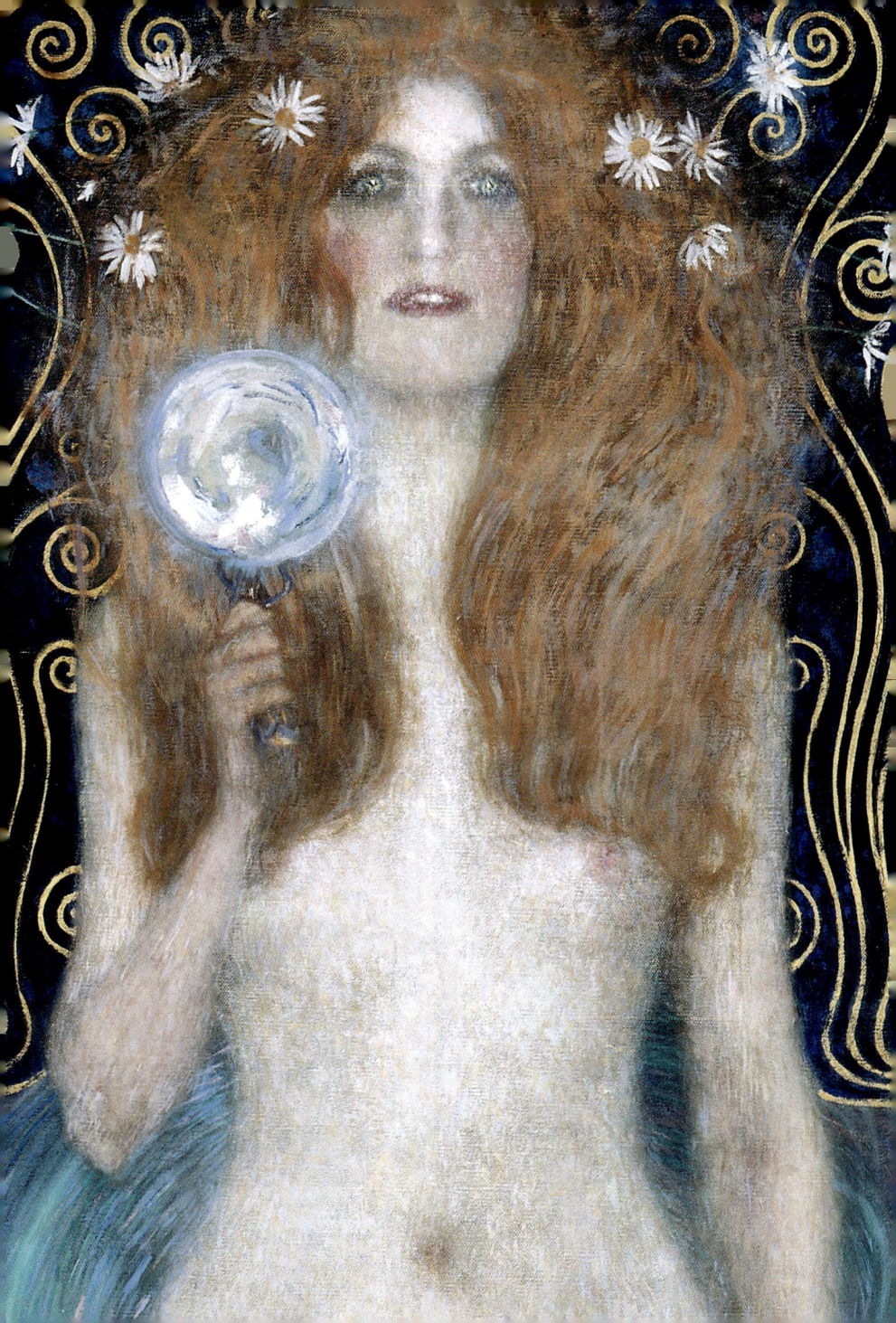

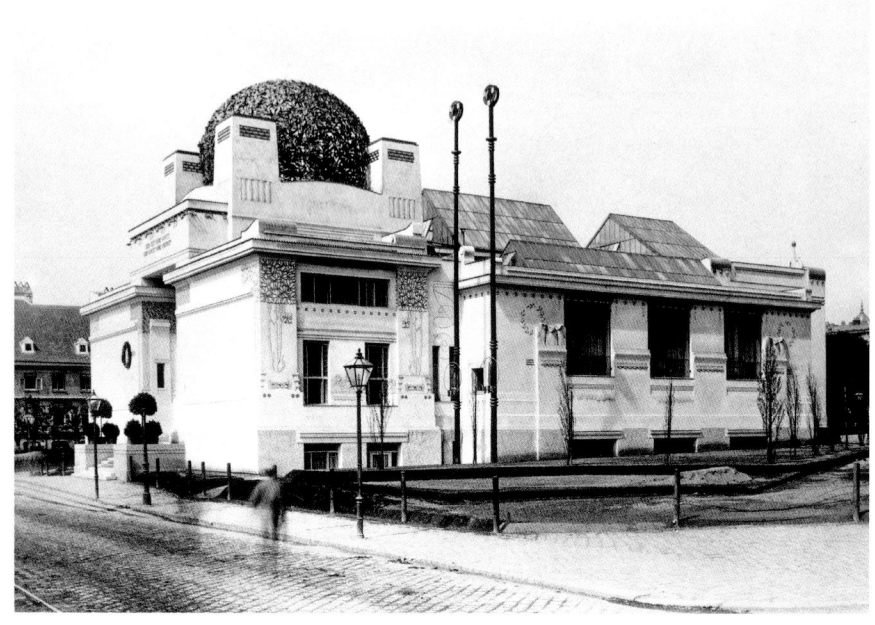

Joseph Maria Olbrich
The Secession building in Vienna, c. 1898
Photograph. Imagno/Austrian Archives

In its most extreme form, this translates into pure escapism with the Secession building functioning as a temple of art, providing a refuge for the modern soul retreating from the pressures of metropolitan life while displaying the creative manifestations of exactly that contemporary hurried spirit the visitor was to escape from. One contemporary critic captured this dilemma of modernity as manifested in the Secession, simultaneously embracing and retreating from the temptations of urban life and the brave new world of consumer capitalism, the dazzling acceleration of transportation and communication and the ever-changing cycle of fashions: "It was to be an exhibition building that reminds us that we are children of our time, restless and of great capacity of absorption. We do not love rapid change and easy pleasures because we have become more superficial, but because we are ourselves the manifestation and the product of our lives, the bustling, rushing, scintillating life that surrounds us, the multiple reflections that we seek in art, in order to find a moment's rest and to commune with our own soul" (Schölermann 1899, pp. 205, 210).

The naked truth of art

For Gustav Klimt, as for the Viennese art world, the year 1897 signified a similar turning point, at which "the process of desublimating art by employing preclassical symbols" was embarked upon (Schorske 1981, p. 220). His paintings continue to feature classical goddesses that, however, increasingly abandon their static postures and come alive, assuming the shocking contemporary appearance of ordinary, vulnerable human figures. *Pallas Athene* (pp. 69, 112; Natter 2012, Cat. 115), presented in the second Secession exhibition, which inaugurated the new building, evokes the ancient guardian of the arts, as Hevesi described, "an obvious Secessionist of today […] as a living Pallas […] of its time, its place, its creator" (Hevesi 1906a, p. 81). The painting is surrounded by an embossed metal frame by his brother Georg Klimt bearing the work's title and linear ornament.

Athena had previously figured in Klimt's work, in the similar context of the decorations for the Kunsthistorisches Museum in Vienna of 1890–91 (pp. 54/55; Natter 2012, Cat. 65). In this early work, we already can detect the beginnings of a fascination with ornament, rich materials and underlying sexual tension as well as an interest in decorative architectural schemes. While the composition shares certain features with the later *Pallas Athene,* the decoration also illustrates the distance travelled as the artist had liberated himself from the limitations of an academic, representational style to a much freer interpretation of the subject with an emphasis on rich patterning and sensuality. *Pallas Athene* of 1898 abandons the full-scale figure and combines dissolution of form in a glistening of gold scales and a decorative frieze in the background with the full-frontal portrait of a powerful goddess, holding a fully naked figurine with outstretched arms.

This small naked figure makes a reappearance in a major related work, *Nuda Veritas* of 1899, this time life-size and in all the glorious nudity of a real human being rather than a diminutive statuette (pp. 79, 111; Natter 2012, Cat. 119). Liberated from her armour and shedding most iconographic attributes, an uncomfortably contemporary female figure meets the viewer. Klimt intended the work as a programmatic statement and forceful answer to his critics, confronting them with the 'naked truth' both in allegorical and real form, holding up the mirror of the blinding light of truth to their faces. Klimt borrowed the words of the German poet Friedrich Schiller as his and the Secession's artistic credo: "If you cannot please everyone by your actions and your art, then please a few. To please many is bad." It is an uncompromising commitment to truth and the highest quality in art but also a decidedly elitist motto, reflecting the escapist tendencies of the Secessionists at the end of the 19th century.

Both *Pallas Athene* and *Nuda Veritas* were attacked by the public at their presentation in the second Secession exhibition of 1898 and the fourth exhibition of 1899, respectively.

The two paintings mark a significant shift in Klimt's art as he continued to build on a familiar repertoire of classical mythology, symbolic figures and emblematic attributes yet gave them a distinctly modern form. *Nuda Veritas* is both an allegory of truth with all the loaded attributes of Symbolist iconography – snakes and blossoming flowers surrounding a seductive nude – and, at the same time, depicts a human being anchored in the present rather than distant classical Greece or Rome. The evocation of vulnerable nakedness in *Nuda Veritas* through transparent skin and flowing red hair mirrored in the budding, golden floral ornament and the pulsating blue background transcend Symbolist allegory and manifest meaning in a new formal language.

The year 1898 also marked the end of Klimt's most active involvement in the Secession, devoting his time from now on predominantly to painting and, in particular, to the commission of the Faculty paintings. He did, however, continue to exhibit at the Secession exhibitions, creating major work cycles and participating actively in promoting the ethos of the *Gesamtkunstwerk* – both through exhibition installations as well as through commissions realized in partnership with Josef Hoffmann and the Wiener Werkstätte ('Viennese Workshop'), which had been founded in 1903 to promote the penetration of modern life by good design and honest craftsmanship.

"Luxury hell": the Faculty paintings

Klimt's trajectory from accomplished historicist painter to a member of one of the most avant-garde movements in Europe can be traced through the most extensive commission he ever received, the series of monumental murals for the Great Hall of the University of Vienna, located on the prestigious Ringstrasse with its many grand buildings. Klimt and his artist friend and long-term collaborator Franz Matsch jointly received this important public assignment in 1894. Eleven years later, and after a series of scandals and vicious attacks, Klimt resigned from the commission in 1905, though the paintings were to preoccupy him until their completion in 1907.

Rather than fashioning distant paraphrases based on the exhausted iconography of classical mythology, Klimt convincingly evoked in the Faculty paintings the merciless cycle of birth, life and death; human misery through disease, war and injustice; and fundamental moral conflicts. Greek and Roman gods and goddesses as well as allegorical representations of abstract concepts, such as Hope and Justice, still figure in his art, but his gods have descended from Mount Olympus and have taken on human form with all

Joseph Maria Olbrich, **Poster for the second Secession exhibition**
12 November–28 December 1898. Colour lithograph, 86 x 51 cm / 33 ¾ x 20 in.
Vienna, MAK – Österreichisches Museum für angewandte Kunst/Gegenwartskunst

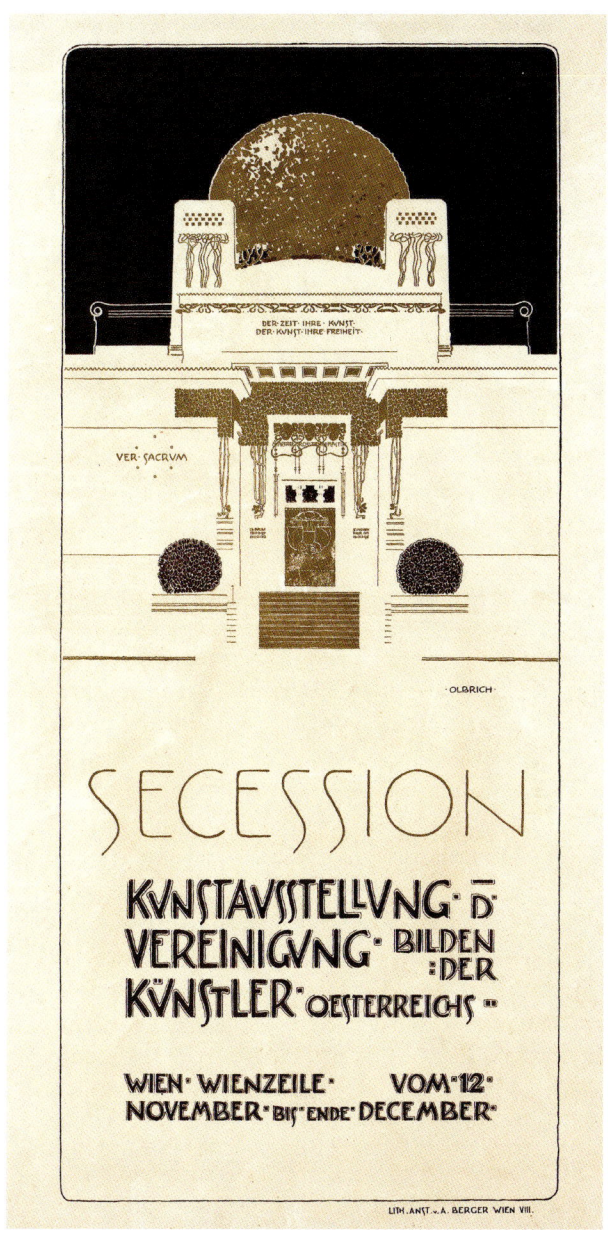

the frailties and blemishes of contemporary beings, cruelly stripped of their divine powers. These are combined with an increasingly potent symbolism of the decorative surface and ornamental patterning that reflect spiritual and sexual awakening. His other innovative device is the empty, almost unstructured field that frames the human figure in an indeterminate space of existential emptiness and hopelessness.

Klimt was commissioned to create allegories of the faculties of *Medicine* (pp. 70, 126, 129; Natter 2012, Cat. 104, 127), *Philosophy* (p. 131; Natter 2012, Cat. 105, 126) and *Jurisprudence* (p. 130; Natter 2012, Cat. 103, 157), which were to surround the central picture of *The Victory of Light over Darkness*. The development from the initial designs to the three completed paintings of 1907 shows a progression from relatively conventional allegories to Klimt's highly individual interpretation of the three disciplines of knowledge. Much of the original compositional scheme remained and it is rather in the explicit rendering of the floating, naked figures and ornamental enrichment that the source and development of the public's consternation lay. Indistinct female figures, for example, are transformed into tempting seductresses with flowing ornamental hair and surrounded by elaborate geometric patterning (pp. 126, 129; Natter 2012, Cat. 104, 127). The artist was unwilling and unable to endorse with his murals the rule of Positivism and the rationalist dictum of science. Rather than glorifying the benefits of science and the independence of justice, his focus is on the cycle of life and the suffering individual. *Medicine* does not conceal the constant presence of death, while the naked and scrawny convict in *Jurisprudence* lowers his head as the personifications of Truth, Justice and Law administer the verdict from afar.

One of Klimt's greatest feats is the almost abstract treatment of space that in each painting conveys a different symbolic meaning. Combined with the vertiginous perspective of Baroque ceiling painting, in which naked figures are positioned at provocative angles, the Faculty paintings are both a revolutionary formal as well as programmatic achievement. In *Philosophy*, this abstract space becomes a visual manifestation of, or, as Bahr phrases it, "a painterly metaphor" for, the emergence of life out of nothingness and the eternal mystery of human existence, illuminated by the desire for knowledge. The critic Ludwig Hevesi praised the painting as "a grandiose vision in which, one has to admit, almost cosmic inspiration reigns. One can detect in the scene the chaos from which it liberated itself, or rather continues to liberate itself, as eternally flowing life is coagulating into forms and then again melts away" (Hevesi 1906a, pp. 333–334). The central figure emerging into "the formlessness of the transcendental is science, or philosophy, or the discerning human spirit" (Bahr 1900, p. 233 f.).

Beethoven Frieze, "Gorgon" (detail), 1901/02
End wall (see ill. p. 119)

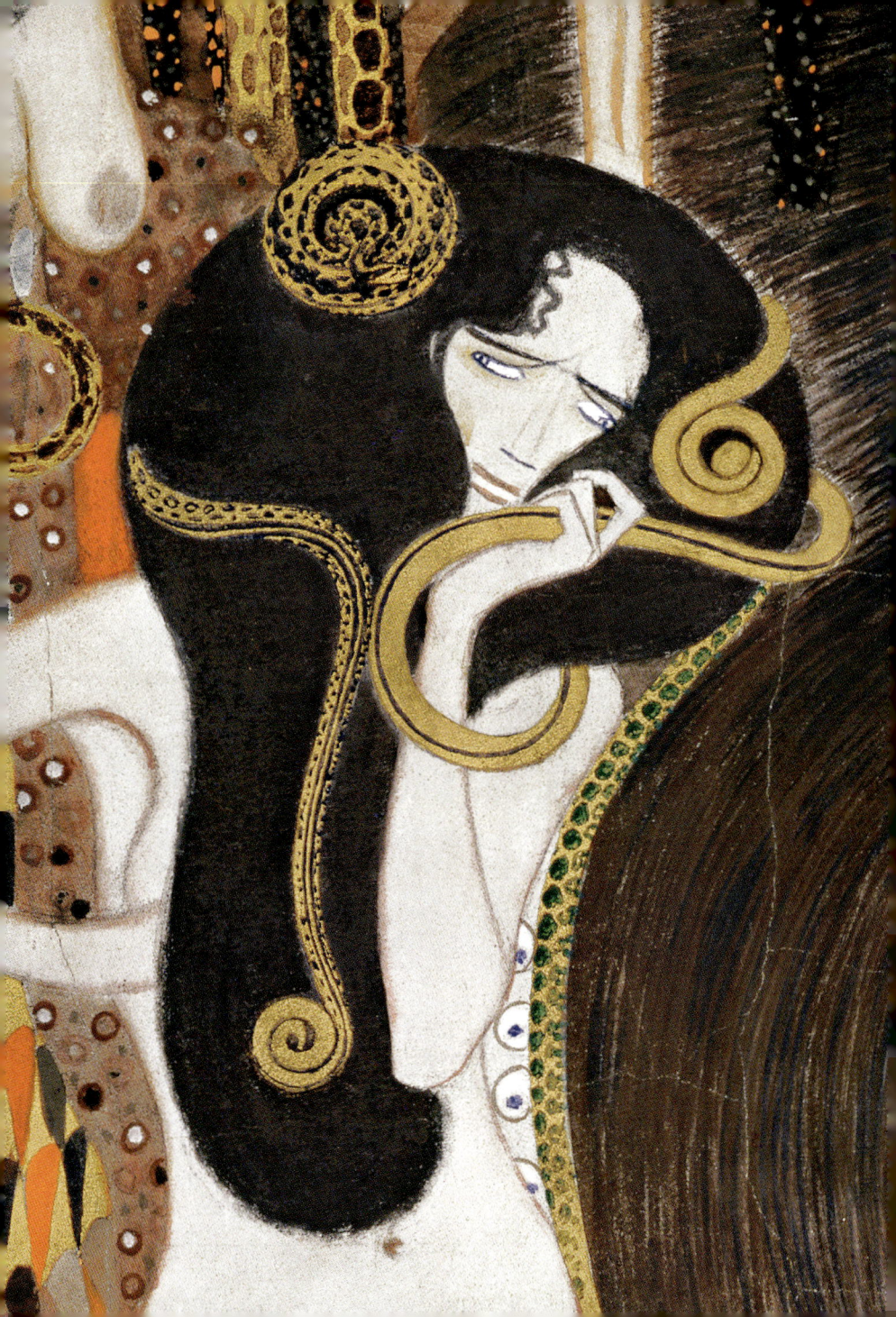

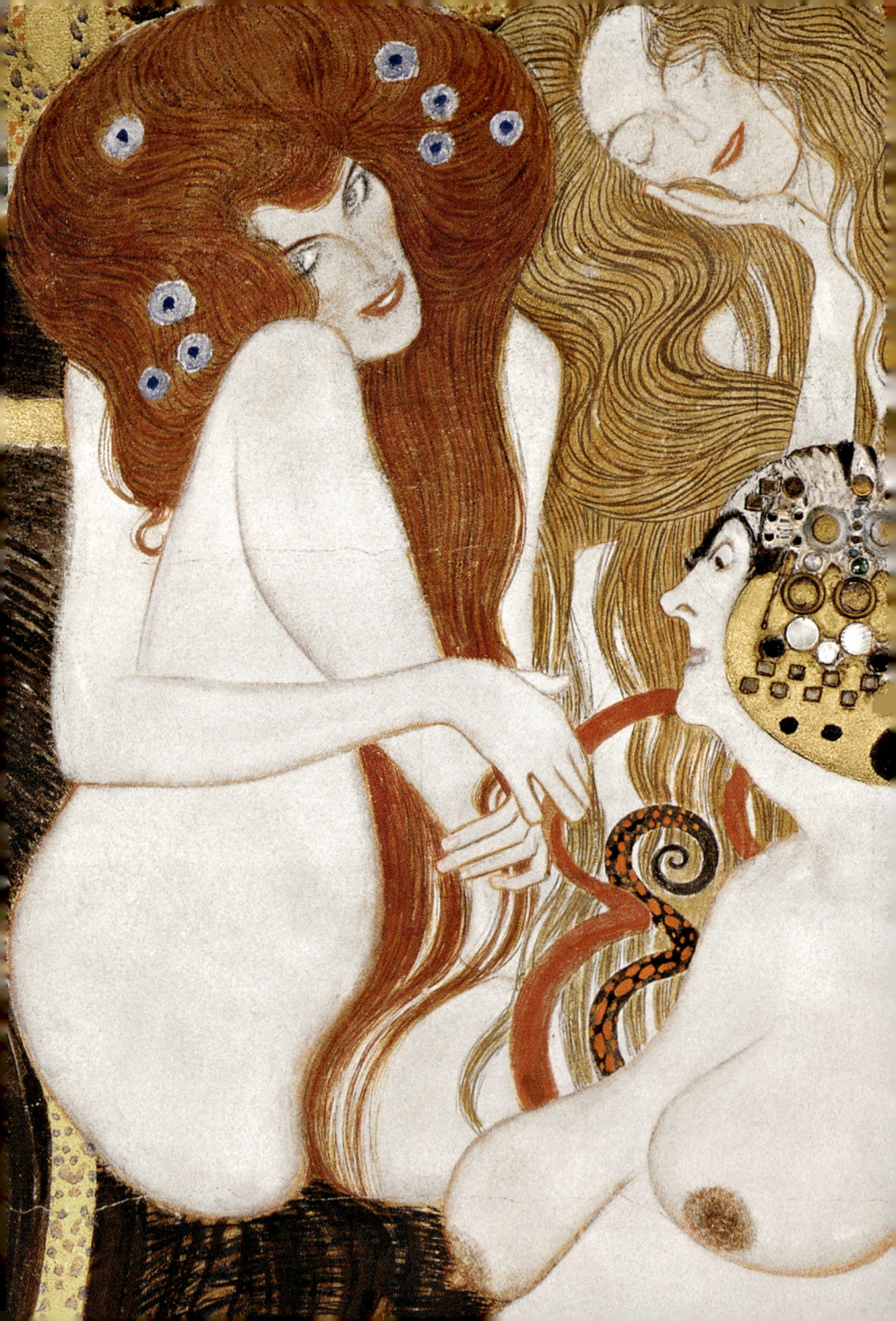

In *Jurisprudence,* it is a threatening and seething dynamic black mass that winds itself like an ominous veil around the three "Furies of the Law", accentuating the *femme fatales'* naked flesh and auburn hair interwoven with golden ornament against a background of expanding darkness. Again, we are confronted with a highly ambiguous interpretation of the subject matter in which the distinction between good and evil, between victim and perpetrator, between the rule of law and despotism are obscured. This tension between the opulent adornment of the three personifications of Truth, Justice and Law and the painting's overall dark mood turns it into what Hevesi called "a luxury hell, where golden instruments of torture are encrusted with diamonds and martyrs bleed rubies" (Hevesi 1909, p. 209).

In his review of the presentation of *Philosophy* at the Secession in 1900, Hermann Bahr acknowledged that the allegory "in the beginning might not be understood, or rather not be sensed", but put his trust in the public, which "in the last three years has expanded the horizon of its capacity for intuition" (Bahr 1900, p. 234). While the audiences streamed to the various exhibitions of the Faculty paintings at the Secession, Bahr had misjudged the enlightened attitude of both the public and the officials. The Faculty paintings caught Klimt in a maelstrom of moral outrage, political reactionism, university intrigue and artistic envy, which eventually led to his bitter retreat from public life and public commissions: "I've had enough of censorship […]," he exclaimed. "I want to break free. I want to be rid of all these unpleasant trivialities holding up my work and regain my freedom. I decline all support from the State, I don't want any of it. […] Above all, I want to take a stand against the way in which art is treated by the Austrian State and at the Ministry of Education. Whenever there's an opportunity, genuine art and artists are under attack. The only thing that's ever protected is feebleness and falsehood. […] The State should not seek to exercise dictatorial control over exhibitions and artistic statements, it should confine its role to that of mediator and commercial agent and should leave the artistic initiative entirely to the artists themselves" (Novotny/Dobai 1967, p. 388).

The Secession's call for the freedom of the arts had fallen on deaf ears. The initial enthusiastic patronage of the State and embrace of the new aesthetic as a powerful reflection of a new Austria did not come to an end but experienced a significant cooling off, in particular at home. The dramatic episode has also been interpreted as a "crisis of the artist's liberal ego" (Schorske 1981, p. 215 ff.), which resulted in Klimt's and his contemporaries' deep suspicion of the political establishment, choosing instead to service their enlightened clients of the Viennese *haute bourgeoisie* with increasingly precious goods.

Beethoven Frieze, "Lasciviousness, Unchastity, Excess" (detail), 1901/02
End wall (see ill. p. 120)

The Faculty paintings had occupied Klimt for a decade and they remain a highlight in the development of his mature style, making their loss even more tragic (during the Second World War, the paintings were sent to Immendorf Castle in Lower Austria for safekeeping, where they, and many other important works of art, were burned by retreating German troops).

The *Beethoven Frieze* as *Gesamtkunstwerk*

The development of the concept of the *Gesamtkunstwerk* – or total work of art – and its realization in a number of exhibitions and architectural schemes can possibly be considered the most significant achievement of the artistic revolution in Vienna around 1900. Artists, architects and designers as well as poets, dramatists and musicians created sophisticated works of art in intense collaboration, attempting to create an artistic and stylistic whole executed to the highest standards of craftsmanship and material authenticity. The pinnacle of the purposeful integration of all arts was the fourteenth Secession exhibition from April to June 1902, the 'Beethoven Exhibition'.

The idea of the *Gesamtkunstwerk*, with its mutual interdependency of art and architectural frame under the aegis of an overall theme, was considered to be most prominently manifested in the musical dramas of the composer Richard Wagner (1813–1883) and found wide currency through his writings *The Art-Work of the Future* and the essay "Art and Revolution", both of 1849. Building on Greek tragedies, Wagner hoped to unite architecture, dance, drama and music in "a communal art form" (Costa Meyer 2008, p. 25) and total spectacle, which would engage and overwhelm all the senses. The ascendancy of the *Gesamtkunstwerk* in the 19th century also reflected an underlying political desire for national unity as well as a more abstract longing for universal harmony transcending the alienated individual.

In Vienna around 1900, the idea of the *Gesamtkunstwerk* had gained currency initially through music theatre, permeating other artistic circles through the campaigns of Jugendstil architects and designers who developed a radical programme of totally unified living environments in which every aspect was to be subjected to strict design and stylistic principles. The influence of the British Arts and Crafts Movement under the leadership of William Morris was critical as was the presence of the pioneering architects and designers Charles Rennie Mackintosh (1868–1928) and Margaret MacDonald Mackintosh (1865–1933) in Vienna through the eighth Secession exhibition in 1900 and commissions from the important patron of Klimt and the Wiener Werkstätte, Fritz Waerndorfer (1868–1939). The integration of so-called fine and applied art was one of the declared principles of the Secession: "We know no difference between 'high art' and 'applied art', between art for the wealthy and art for the poor. Art is common property" (*Ver Sacrum*, vol. 1, no. 1, 1898,

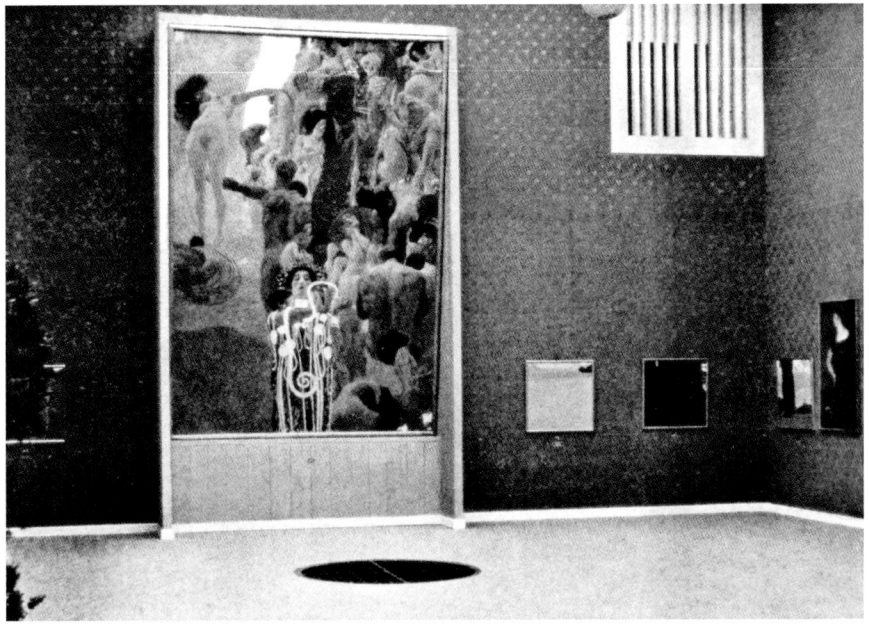

Gustav Klimt, *Medicine*, **exhibited at the tenth Secession exhibition,**
15 March–12 May 1901. Interior design by Koloman Moser
From: *Ver Sacrum*, vol. 4 (1901), p. 159

p. 6). The Secession's founding members significantly included a number of architects and designers – most prominent among them were Josef Hoffmann and Kolo Moser, the latter also an accomplished painter.

The definition of the art forms in Vienna at the turn of the century was fluid, with frequent active collaboration occurring between creative individuals from different disciplines. Many artists of the time also displayed extraordinary talents in multiple art forms, Arnold Schönberg, for example, making a significant contribution in both music and the visual arts while Oskar Kokoschka and Alfred Kubin (1877–1959) also became well known as dramatists and writers. In the Beethoven exhibition, architecture, painting and sculpture came together in a coherent whole around the celebration of the life and music of the composer Ludwig van Beethoven and his Ninth Symphony in particular. Klimt's magnificent *Beethoven Frieze* (pp. 114–117, 119–125; Natter 2012, Cat. 141), the artist's largest surviving integrated scheme, was intended as part of the Secession's homage to the composer, represented by the Leipzig artist Max Klinger's polychrome sculpture, which formed the centrepiece of the show (p. 94).

The Secession deliberately set out to realize an ambitious scheme that fully utilized painting and sculpture in a carefully designed interior space devoted to the worship of the artistic genius of Beethoven, "a sacred space, an ambience with the mood of a temple for one who has become a god", as Hevesi described the experience (Hevesi 1906a, p. 390). It was further intended to honour Klinger himself and his monumental sculpture as well as his pioneering work and writing as an educator in the service of art and the *Gesamtkunstwerk* (his text *Painting and Drawing* [*Malerei und Zeichnung*] was partly reprinted in the catalogue).

The complex scheme was developed by the association's members and, in particular, the architect Josef Hoffmann, who contributed the architectural layout and framework, including the careful staging of Klimt's *Frieze*. The walls of the exhibition architecture throughout the spaces were covered in rough plaster, providing a unifying element. The *Frieze* was located in one of the two wings of the Secession, with a large opening on one side, allowing a view of the statue in the central space. Composed of two long side walls framing the short end wall as the central panel, the *Frieze* was to be read from left to right, illustrating, as the catalogue description suggests, mankind's "yearning for happiness" and its struggle for fulfilment (Max Klinger Beethoven 1922, p. 23).

In episodic chapters, the *Beethoven Frieze* describes humanity's journey and struggle against adversity in its yearning for happiness with the eventual triumphant wish for fulfilment expressed in communal joy. On the left side, the Well-armed Strong One, supported by Ambition and Compassion, responds to the pleas of the Suffering of Frail Humanity – three naked and emaciated figures depicted by Klimt in a state of desperation and with cruel veracity. The short end panel is in many ways the dramatic highlight of the *Frieze*, depicting the Hostile Forces and vices mankind faces in its pursuit of happiness – rather alluring and lascivious female figures tempting weak men and women from the path of virtue.

The giant Typhoeus (pp. 92, 119/20) dominates the scene, accompanied by his three daughters, the gorgon goddesses of fate (pp. 85, 119). The temptations continue with Lasciviousness, Unchastity and Excess (pp. 86, 120), the last depicted by Klimt as a voluptuous female nude wrapped in a gold-embroidered cloth and adorned with rich jewellery. Gnawing Sorrow, a collapsing, angular, naked figure wearing a transparent dark veil,

Beethoven Frieze, "Gorgons"
(in front) with "The Hostile Forces"(detail), 1901/02
End wall (see ill. p. 119)

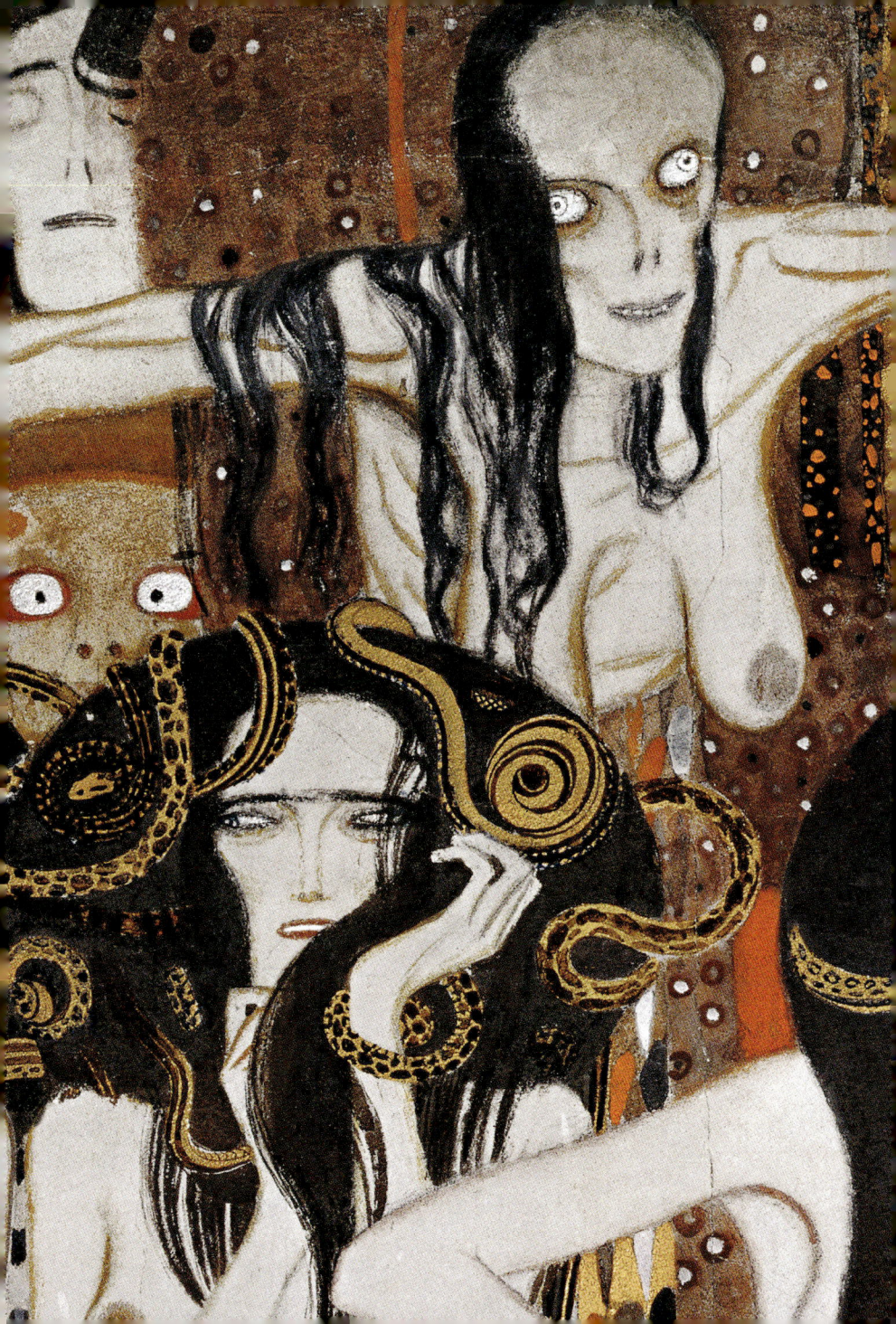

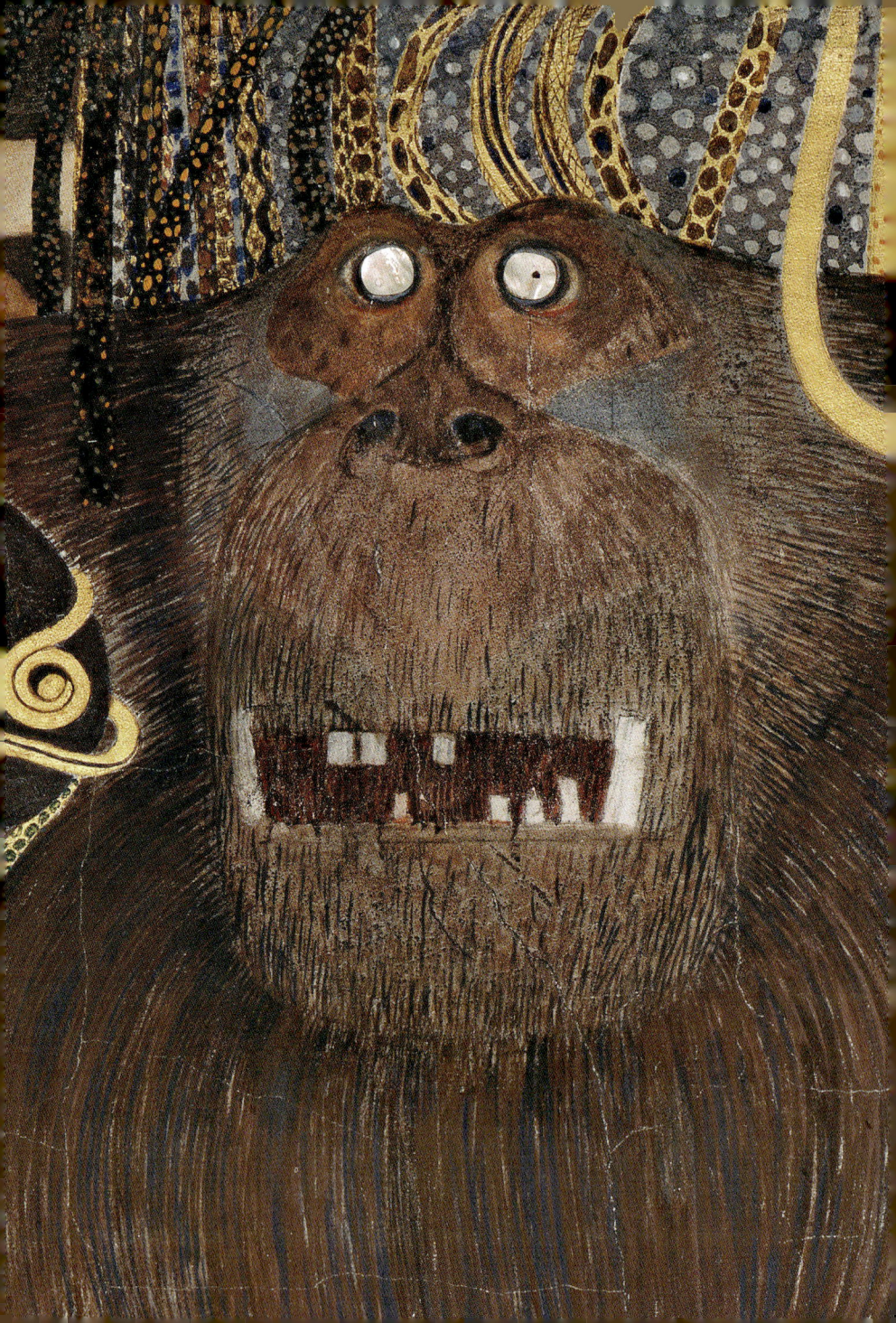

captures the destitution of humanity. The figures with mask-like faces above the gorgons symbolize Disease, Madness and Death.

The Floating Genii overcome adversity and move towards resolution through poetry and the arts: "The arts lead us into the ideal realm, where alone we can find pure joy, pure happiness, pure love. Choir of Heavenly Angels" (Max Klinger Beethoven 1902, p. 26; pp. 124/25). The final section most closely follows Beethoven's *Ninth Symphony* and Friedrich Schiller's "Ode to Joy": "Joy, fair spark of divinity." "A kiss for all the world" (p. 125). The Choir of Heavenly Angels almost seems to float in spiritual jubilation in the background of the "Kiss". At the same time, the embracing couple seems isolated in erotic consummation, contradicting the political undertones of Schiller's original "Kiss of the Brotherhood of Man".

Klimt's *Frieze* represents an idiosyncratic homage to Beethoven's *Ninth Symphony* in which the artist interprets a musical piece through a highly inventive and imaginative visual narrative. Above all, it is a celebration of the power of art and the supremacy of music, in particular in the fulfilment of humanity's destiny. As Peter Vergo has pointed out, it is a reading of Beethoven through the eyes of Richard Wagner and his Schopenhauerian interpretation of music as the leading art form and "pure reflection not only of individual Will, but also of the inner essence of the world" (Vergo 1993, p. 72). As such, the *Frieze* is a programmatic celebration of the fusion of all arts within the context of one of the most successful realizations of the *Gesamtkunstwerk*. Appropriately, the installation found its completion and climax at the private view with a performance of Gustav Mahler's arrangement of the final chorus of Beethoven's *Ninth Symphony*, conducted by Mahler himself.

In the *Beethoven Frieze*, Klimt's unique fusion of rich Jugendstil ornamentalism, charged eroticism, uncompromising, at times brutal realism and classical mythology within a wider thematic and architectural scheme reached its pinnacle. It also remains significant because it points to an abstract future, its extended empty fields and surfaces filled with uniform ornamental patterns hinting at the impending emergence of non-objective art. We thus can demonstrably trace one of the more unlikely sources of abstraction to the devotion to surface decoration and the two-dimensionality of frescos and other decorative schemes in Vienna around 1900, culminating in Klimt's extreme "pure mosaic creations, composed of geometric elements – coloured, golden, silver ones: nonplastic, pure surface" (Hevesi 1909, p. 211).

Beethoven Frieze, "The giant Typhoeus" (detail), 1901/02
End wall (see ill. pp. 119/20)

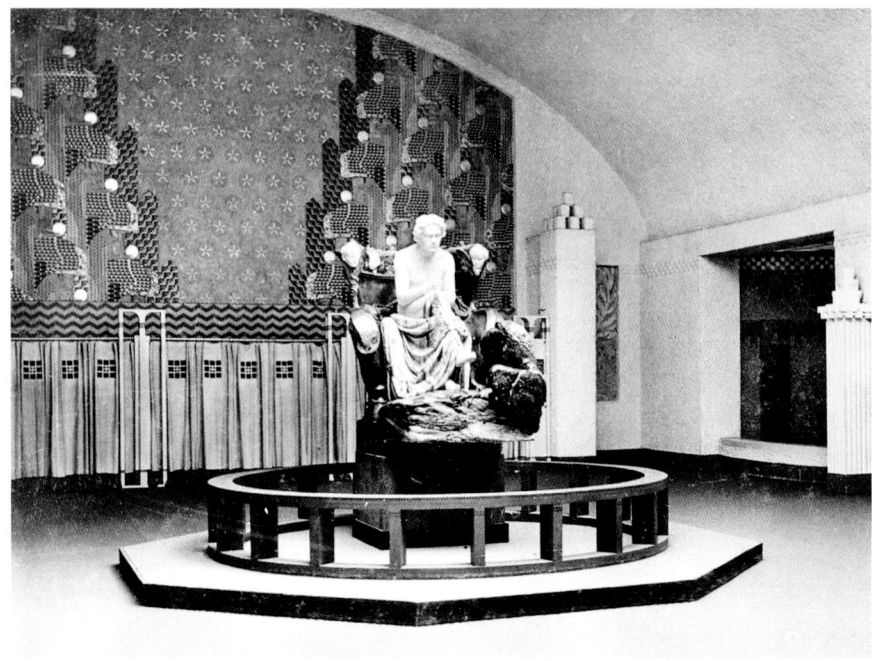

Max Klinger, **Beethoven statue at the fourteenth Secession exhibition
('Beethoven Exhibition')**, 15 April–27 June 1902
Photograph. Imagno/Austrian Archives

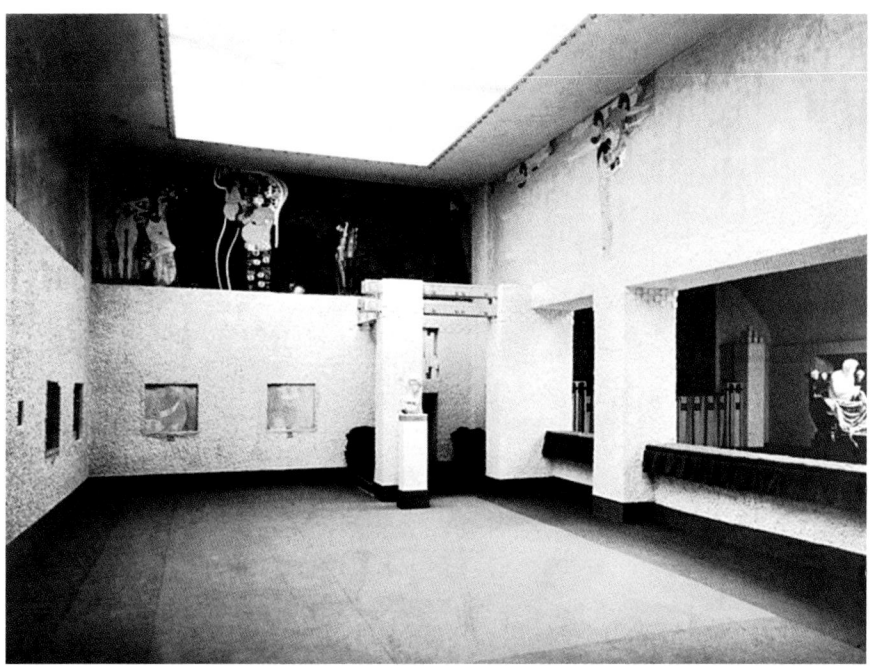

**The Klimt room at the fourteenth Secession exhibition
('Beethoven Exhibition')**, 1902
Photograph. Imagno/Austrian Archives

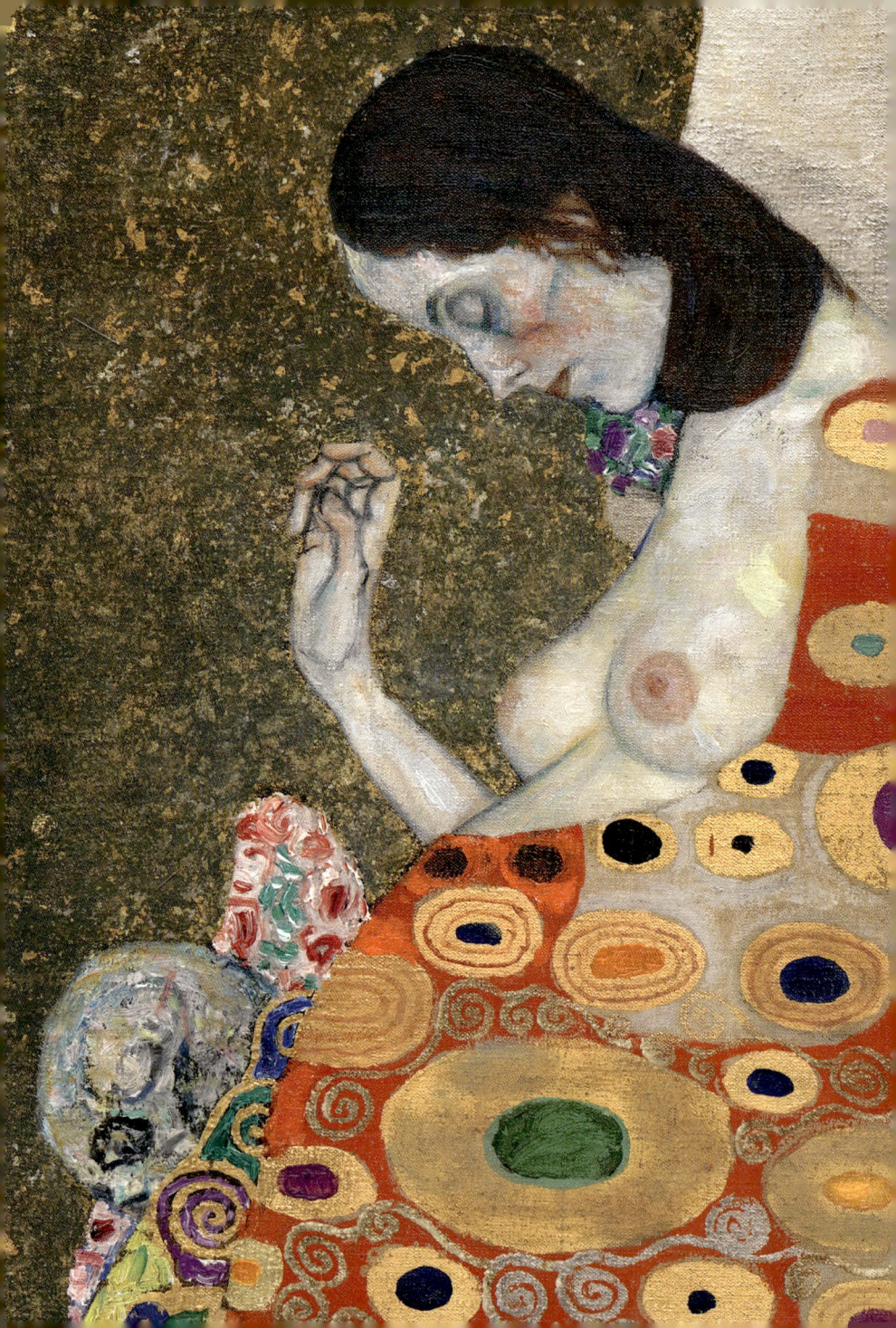

For Klimt and his contemporaries, this approximation of abstraction avant la lettre was only possible to this extreme degree within the perimeters of a temporary decorative scheme (the *Frieze* was originally intended to be destroyed after the exhibition). The transformation of fields of ordered ornament into near abstraction did, however, signify an achievement that Klimt was to pursue over the next decade, leading to a series of intensely rich and opulent paintings.

Human allegories and metaphors of life

The Faculty paintings and the *Beethoven Frieze* signalled the high point but also the end of Klimt's engagement with elaborate allegorical programmes developed for public spaces and thematic exhibitions. In these two major cycles, Klimt had already moved away from traditional iconography based on Christian symbolism and classical mythology to a more abstract programme exploring fundamental human experiences and values. In the remaining years of his life, Klimt was to concentrate his painterly efforts on these human allegories as well as on erotic nudes (similarly extracted from his more ambitious thematic programmes), society portraits and landscapes.

The Three Ages of Woman of 1905 (pp. 140/41; Natter 2012, Cat. 168) is one of his most poignant explorations of the cycle of life, the origins of which can be traced back to the Faculty paintings and the *Beethoven Frieze*. Tender psychologization, rich ornamentalization and radical blankness are combined in what must be one of Klimt's most shockingly realist and at the same time uncompromisingly abstract paintings. The sensitively observed child, young mother and the embodiment of old age are framed and shaped by a rich carpet of Egyptian motifs, angular geometric patterning, biological cell structures and vegetable ornament with transparent veils vigorously winding their way around the mother and child's body.

Ornament here is heavily symbolic, proposing human fate as part of a larger, fundamental cycle of life and death, pointing to the importance Klimt assigned to the "purely biological function of reproduction" (Comini 2000, p. 242). The germinating, vegetative ornament of budding and flourishing life is contrasted with the abstract, microscopic cell structures in the more subdued hues of disease and old age. The phallic shape enveloping the three female figures penetrates a black horizontal band, announcing impending darkness of death. In *The Three Ages of Woman*, Klimt powerfully contrasts ornament as a "metaphor for procreation" (Hofmann 1970, p. 30) with the surrounding two-dimensional

Hope II (Vision) (detail), 1907/08
(see ill. pp. 144/45)

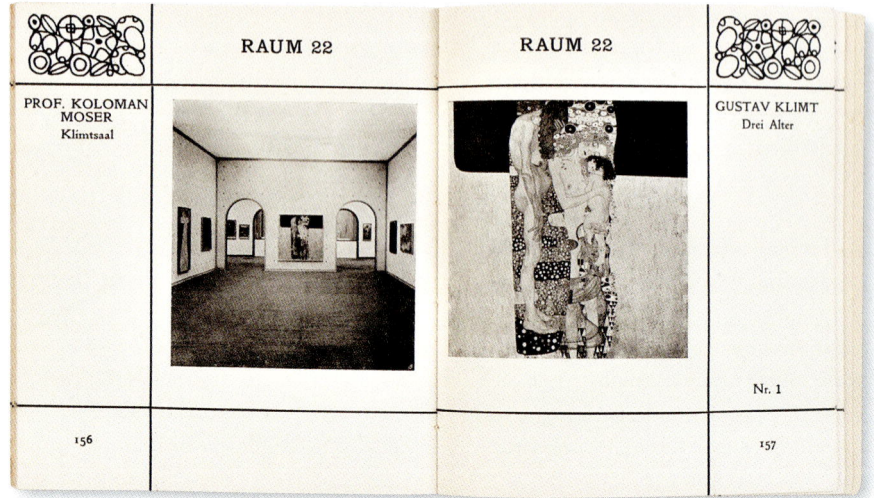

The Klimt room at the Kunstschau
Designed by Koloman Moser, with Klimt's painting *The Three Ages of Woman* (pp. 140/41)
on the right. From: Kunstschau exhibition catalogue, Vienna, 1908, pp. 156/57

field as a metaphor for arrested life – regression and death the ultimate fate shared by all human beings.

In some works of the period, allegory becomes little more than an excuse for the invention of vigorous erotic scenarios with the female figure at its centre, as in the exquisite *Water Snakes I* from 1904–1907 (pp. 104, 137; Natter 2012, Cat. 163). In this perfectly executed incunable on vellum, two mythic mermaids are surrounded by the richly detailed ornament of underwater flora and fauna, evoking the watery world as a dreamlike place of seduction and procreation. *Danaë* of 1907/08 (p. 136; Natter 2012, Cat. 177) also features a sleeping or dreaming nude, transforming the already erotically suggestive myth of Zeus impregnating Danaë in the form of golden rain into a thinly veiled image of sexual ecstasy.

Klimt's pursuit of total environments continued, but these were to be realized in private spaces as exquisite and luxurious environments and domestic interiors fashioned in collaboration with Josef Hoffmann and the Wiener Werkstätte, most spectacularly in the dining room of the Palais Stoclet in Brussels, for which Klimt contributed his frieze (Ch. III). Portrait commissions of his wealthy patrons, which had always been an essential part of his artistic repertoire, became increasingly significant. The retreat into the private sphere coincides with an increasing interiorization and spatial confinement of the female figure within the rigid architecture of their environments, mirroring the extreme aesthetic refinement and stylistic tyranny of Wiener Werkstätte interiors (Klimt's portraits after 1899 were exclusively of women).

In the *Portrait of Fritza Riedler* of 1906 (p. 323; Natter 2012, Cat. 170), the cascading waves of the patron's white dress are contained by a flat geometric panelling, in itself structured with a regular pattern. Only the chair covered with an irregular, undulating Egyptian eye motif destabilizes an otherwise rigid order, contributing to the dynamic tension between the architectonic structured left part of the painting and the more animated and organic right side with the clothed figure and chair. Despite Klimt's increasing indulgence in angular structures and decorative patterns, the face and awkwardly posed hands give Fritza Riedler a fine psychological characterization in this perceptively observed portrait.

The pinnacle of Klimt's Byzantine ornamentalism was reached in the *Portrait of Adele Bloch-Bauer I* of 1907, the sitter disappearing behind a golden screen of intense geometric stylization (pp. 286, 328/29; Natter 2012, Cat. 174). The human figure becomes part of an expanding ornamental design, the subject's pose as artificial as the flat surface decoration covering the interlocking sections, which bears little relation to reality or spatial perspective. It is a golden cage in which the sophisticated patron and member of Vienna's enlightened high society was caught, the hermetic symbolism of abstract ornament substituting for psychological characterization and the expression of real emotions. With the *Portrait of Adele Bloch-Bauer I* an aesthetic and formal endpoint was reached that could only lead to an inevitable impasse of pure ornamental decoration and abandonment to hedonistic luxury. Slowly retreating from this dead end of high aestheticism, Klimt embarked on an alternative route of a more freely expressive style, which found its most productive outlet in the decorative treatment of fabric patterns in exuberant colour, as in the monumental *Death and Life* of 1910/11, which was reworked 1915/16 (pp. 336/37; Natter 2012, Cat. 193).

The end of an era: the Kunstschau of 1908

Between 1903 and 1908 Klimt did not exhibit in Vienna, though important presentations took place abroad, such as in Berlin and Mannheim. In 1905 he had not only rescinded the commission of the Faculty paintings, but this year also saw the end of his long association with the Secession, which he had helped to found eight years earlier, torn apart by a bitter political struggle around the fundamental question about the function of painting. The group of so-called *Nur-Maler* (only painters) viewed with suspicion the close association of the 'Klimt Group' with architects and designers and their expressed objective of the integration of painting into a larger spatial and decorative context. In the spring of 1905 the involvement of the painter Carl Moll (1861–1945), who belonged to the Klimt Group, with the leading Galerie H. O. Miethke (p. 106) led to accusations of commercialization. The Secession split into "a style group and a realistic group. One considers 'art' as a unity, as a great decorative continuity of architectonic, pictorial and applied genres; the others have no interest in the subjugation, the harmonization of the work of art under a totality" (Zuckerkandl 1905b, p. 441).

The ambitious 1908 exhibition Kunstschau was intended as a powerful return of Klimt and his close associates to the public stage and to the forefront of Viennese art with the reassertion of the *Gesamtkunstwerk* as the leading art form. In a sprawling complex designed by Josef Hoffmann with over fifty galleries as well as courtyards and gardens, the Kunstschau brought together Austrian painting and sculpture with the most distinguished manifestations of the decorative arts. The exhibition attempted to realize environments conducive to the group's and the Wiener Werkstätte's expressed desire for a unified and coherent style penetrating all aspects of life (a *'Stilkunst'*), overcoming the separation between the artist and consumer. The contemplation of an artwork was to be an act of creative consumption, as Klimt stated in a rare speech given on the occasion of the opening of the Kunstschau: "And we interpret the term 'artist' just as broadly as the term 'work of art'. Not only those who create art are worthy of this name, all those who are capable of feeling and of valuing artistic creation. In our minds the 'art world' is an ideal community of creators and connoisseurs" (Nebehay 1969, p. 394).

However, in the Kunstschau exhibition, painting and the decorative arts remained largely separated, with displays devoted either to fine or to applied art. The latter took the form of a series of completely styled domestic and public environments devoted to a variety of functions in which paintings featured as decorative additions but not elemental building blocks. It was in the ambitious and sophisticated exhibition of works of art that painting, architecture and ornament came together most successfully, in particular in the large central gallery designed by Kolo Moser and devoted to Klimt. Klimt presented a number of recent and new paintings, including *The Three Ages of Woman*, 1905, the *Portrait of Fritza Riedler*, 1906, *The Kiss*, 1907/08, the rich golden *Portrait of Adele Bloch-Bauer I*, 1907, some allegorical compositions such as *The Water Snakes I*, 1904–1907, and *Danaë*, 1907/08.

The architecture and installation represent a high point of so-called *Raumkunst* ('art of the interior'), as the important discipline of exhibition design was known at the time (p. 98). Klimt's recent work was presented on white walls with a regular background grid of small squares in addition to elaborate geometric soraporta ornaments evolving from the artist's stylized monogram. The walls themselves were framed by thin linear ornament

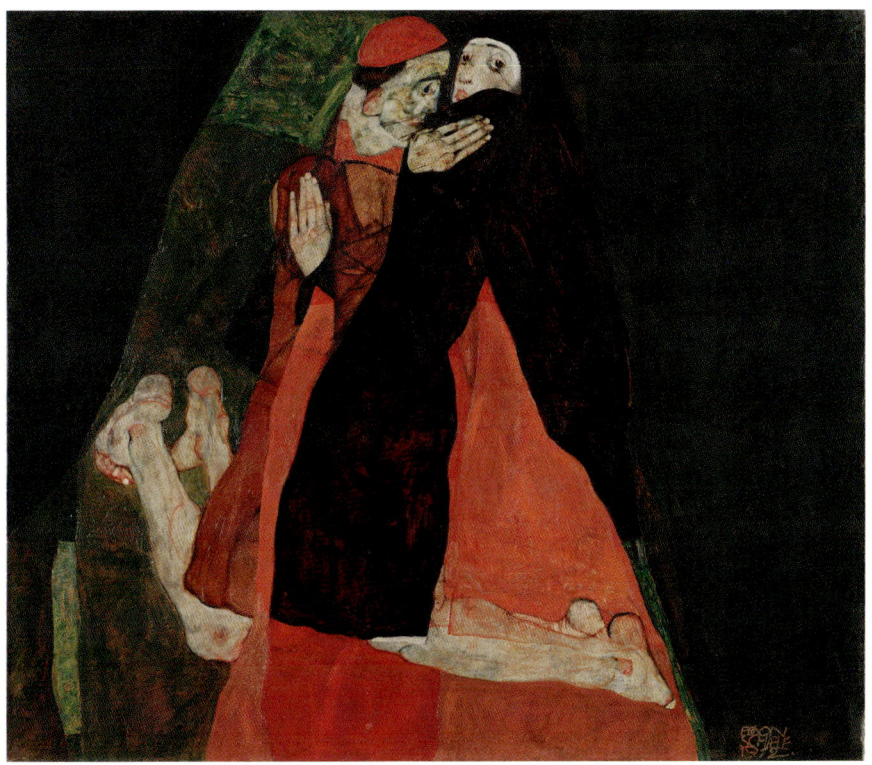

Egon Schiele, **Cardinal and Nun**, 1912
Oil on canvas, 69.8 x 80.1 cm / 27 ½ x 31 ½ in. Vienna, Leopold Museum

in black and white, creating a solid architectural order around the ornamental sumptuousness of his disintegrating surfaces.

The practice of carefully centring single works on a wall or sparsely hanging groups had been introduced only a few years earlier in Secession exhibitions by the architect and painter Kolo Moser. Almost completely white and unstructured walls were also first introduced by Moser in his designs for the seventeenth and, in particular, eighteenth Secession exhibitions, both in 1903. The latter included the magnificent 'Klimt Collective' exhibition featuring forty-eight paintings and thirty drawings. For this presentation, Moser was praised for his "strict economy of the distribution […] if possible with only one picture on a wall and the few works in a room coordinated according to colour harmony. The environment is thus kept as still and discreet as possible" (Zuckerkandl 1903/04b, pp. 341, 344).

The restrained classicism of these installations created a supportive decorative background without competing with the works of art, anchoring the paintings in space while powerfully enhancing the *Flächendekor* (two-dimensional décor) of *The Kiss*, 1907/08, and recent portraits, including *The Portrait of Adele Bloch-Bauer I,* 1907. The opulence of Klimt's art of the period found sympathetic enhancement in the controlled architectonic order set against the "decorative-ornamental sensuality" and the "protean element, the ornamental principle in itself" of his linear ornament (Hevesi 1906a, p. 450 f.).

The Kunstschau did not receive the same attention as earlier exhibitions, its decline in popular appeal being in direct relation to the broad acceptance of that of the achievements of the Secession and the Wiener Werkstätte. The *Gesamtkunstwerk* might not have failed, but it now found its most successful manifestation in sophisticated decorative schemes and interior designs rather than in ambitious artistic visions. In this respect, the exhibition contained the germ, as Carl Schorske argued, for "an explosive reassertion of painting as the medium of instinctual truth", which emerged between the first and second Kunstschau in the following year and coincided with the emergence of the Expressionists Oskar Kokoschka and Egon Schiele (Schorske 1975, p. 41). The Secession had forcefully broken with the past and rung in a new age for art. The next generation followed in their footsteps but, at the same time, felt compelled to replace aesthetic refinement and the penetration of life by exquisite beauty with a more forceful and raw form of creative expression.

Beyond ornament

The birth and triumph of the Secession coincided with the evolution of the artist Gustav Klimt, who was both progenitor and midwife to the most significant period in Austrian art of the 20th century. As a member of a community of kindred spirits and propelled by the exhilaration that came with the artistic insurgence against the old and outdated, he liberated himself from the chains of historicism and a naturalistic style. In the final years of the 19th and first decade of the 20th century, Klimt achieved a unique blend of dark symbolism, human allegory, expressive realism and Jugendstil ornamentation, which resulted in a substantial body of highly moving and intensely ornate paintings, at the centre of which stood the female figure.

The Kiss (detail), 1907/08
(see ill. pp. 142/43)

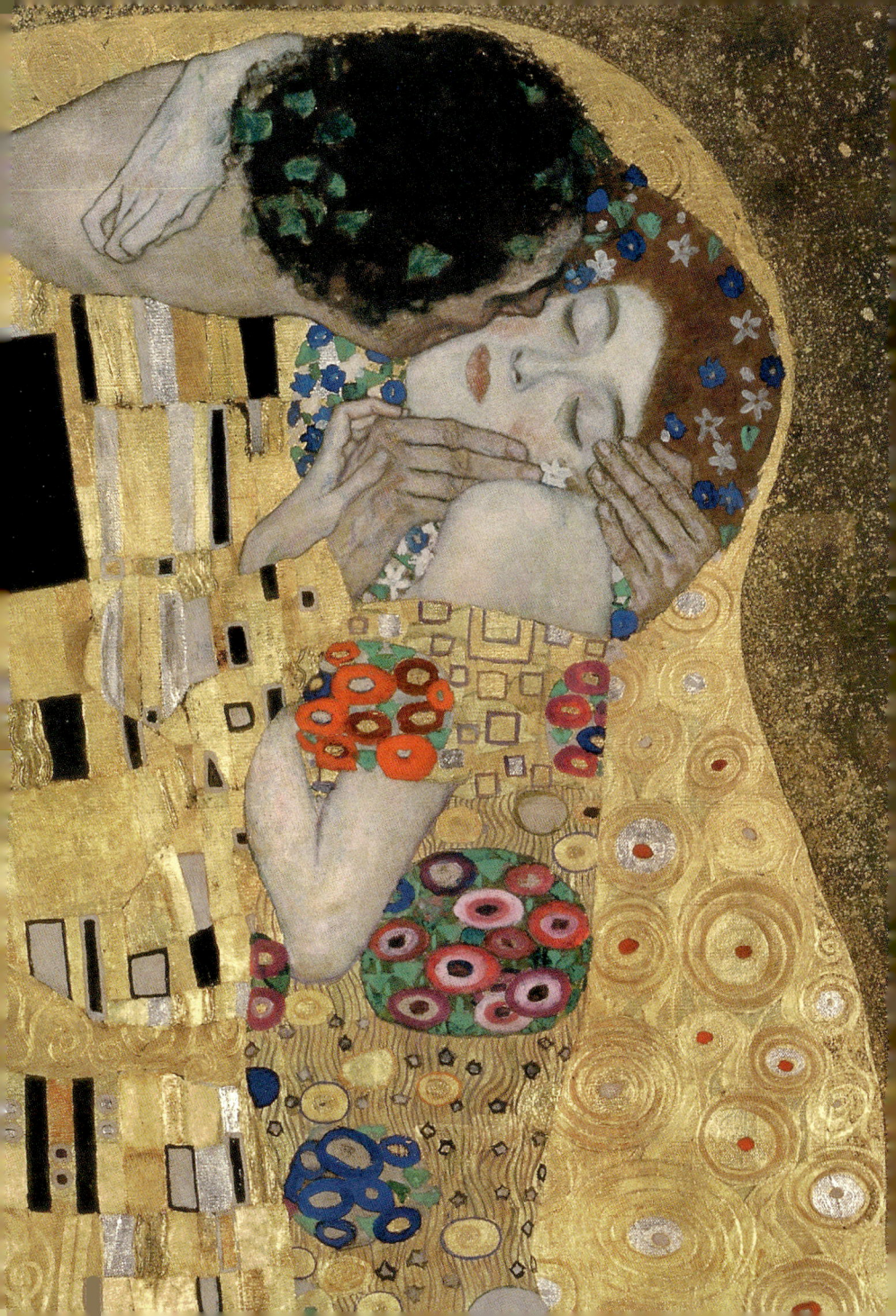

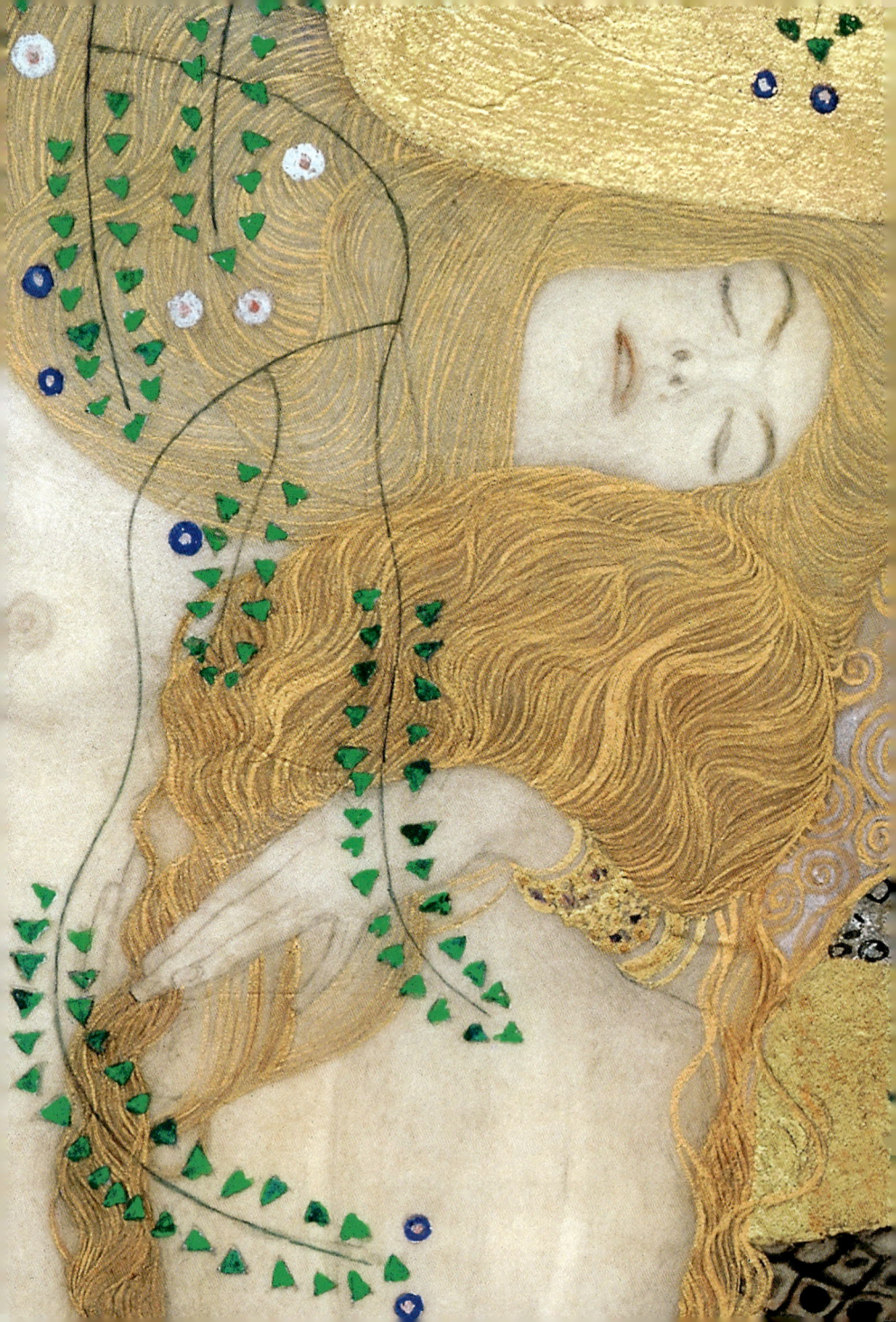

Water Snakes I (detail), 1904–1907
(see ill. p. 137)

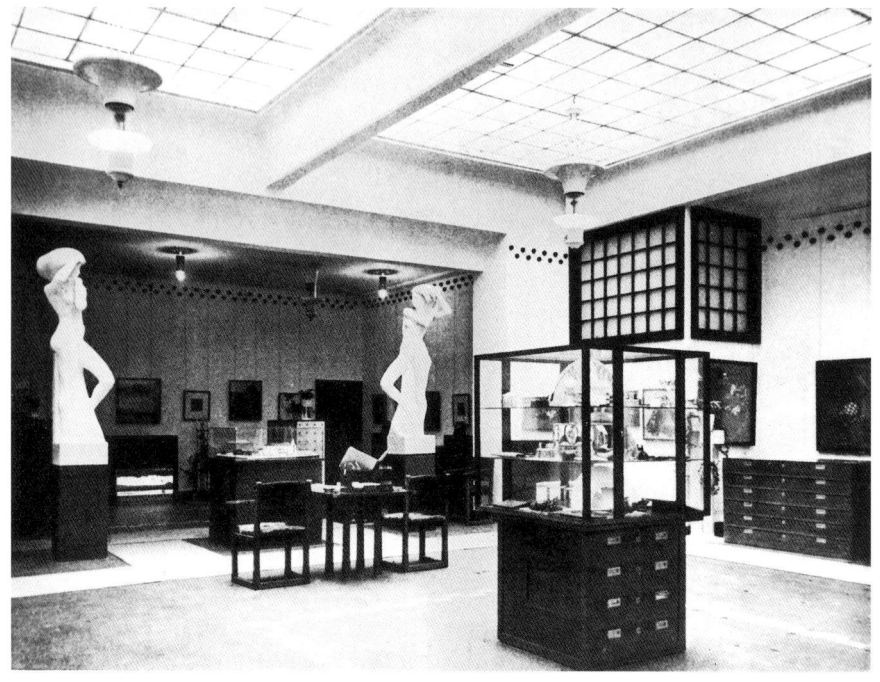

Josef Hoffmann, **Galerie H. O. Miethke at 17 Graben in Vienna's 1st district**
Photograph, 1905. Imagno/Austrian Archives

The artist was most successful when he combined these different and, at times, seemingly conflicting elements, such as in *The Three Ages of Woman* of 1905 (pp. 140/41; Natter 2012, Cat. 168), with its heightened sensuality of animated linear and surface ornament and the merciless depiction of the effects of old age. By 1908 the pendulum had swung far towards the extremes of the decorative-ornamental, almost obliterating the human figure and allegorical schemes under a carpet of gilded ornament and geometric pattern.

This trajectory has often been interpreted as a decline in Klimt's art, a sacrifice of deep psychological insights and expressions of the spiritual torment of a culture in crisis for exquisite craft and superficial "mosaic painting" – a retreat from a grand scheme of unified art to pure beauty and precious decoration in the service of Vienna's *haute monde*. However, the products of Klimt's 'golden period' continue to exert an irresistible attraction that cannot be explained with the pure seduction of glitter and the dazzle of semi-precious stones. Klimt succeeded in transforming extreme stylization and artifice into a meaningful and deeply symbolic mode of visual expression. Ornament, like abstraction, becomes a direct mode of representation, conveying meaning through material form and expressive colour – a living metaphor of creation, growth, exaltation and death. Klimt's paintings seduce with rich visual delights and an overload of aesthetic pleasures while they simultaneously disturb with subtle hints at psychological secrets, moral ambiguities and the debilitating effects of the widespread disease of nervousness and neurotic oversensi-tivity. Behind the dazzling and deeply attractive surfaces loom unexpressed emotions, repressed traumas and unfulfilled sexual urges. It is an art that is symptomatic of a pro-foundly conflicted age in which the inexorable forward progress of science and industry, with its recent discovery and rational analysis of the secrets of the soul and its sexual permissiveness, combated with oppressive authoritarianism, sexual repression, the fear of decadence and escapist tendencies.

Klimt and the Secession's absorption in the *Gesamtkunstwerk* was, in many ways, indicative of this struggle between the dream of the total aestheticization of every aspect of the human environment and extreme interiorization and the retreat from the social and political realities of modern life. In Klimt's art, this dynamic tension between inner worlds and external realities, surface and substance, craft and fine art is not resolved but made manifest in a new and seductive sensibility.

Pages 108/09
Hope I (detail), 1903/04 (see ill. p. 133)

Page 110
Hermann Bahr in front of *Nuda Veritas*, c. 1905
In the study of his villa in Ober Sankt Veit
Gelatin silver print. Vienna, Österreichisches Theatermuseum

Page 111
Nuda Veritas, 1899
Oil on canvas, 252 x 56.2 cm / 99 ¼ x 22 in. Vienna, Österreichisches Theatermuseum

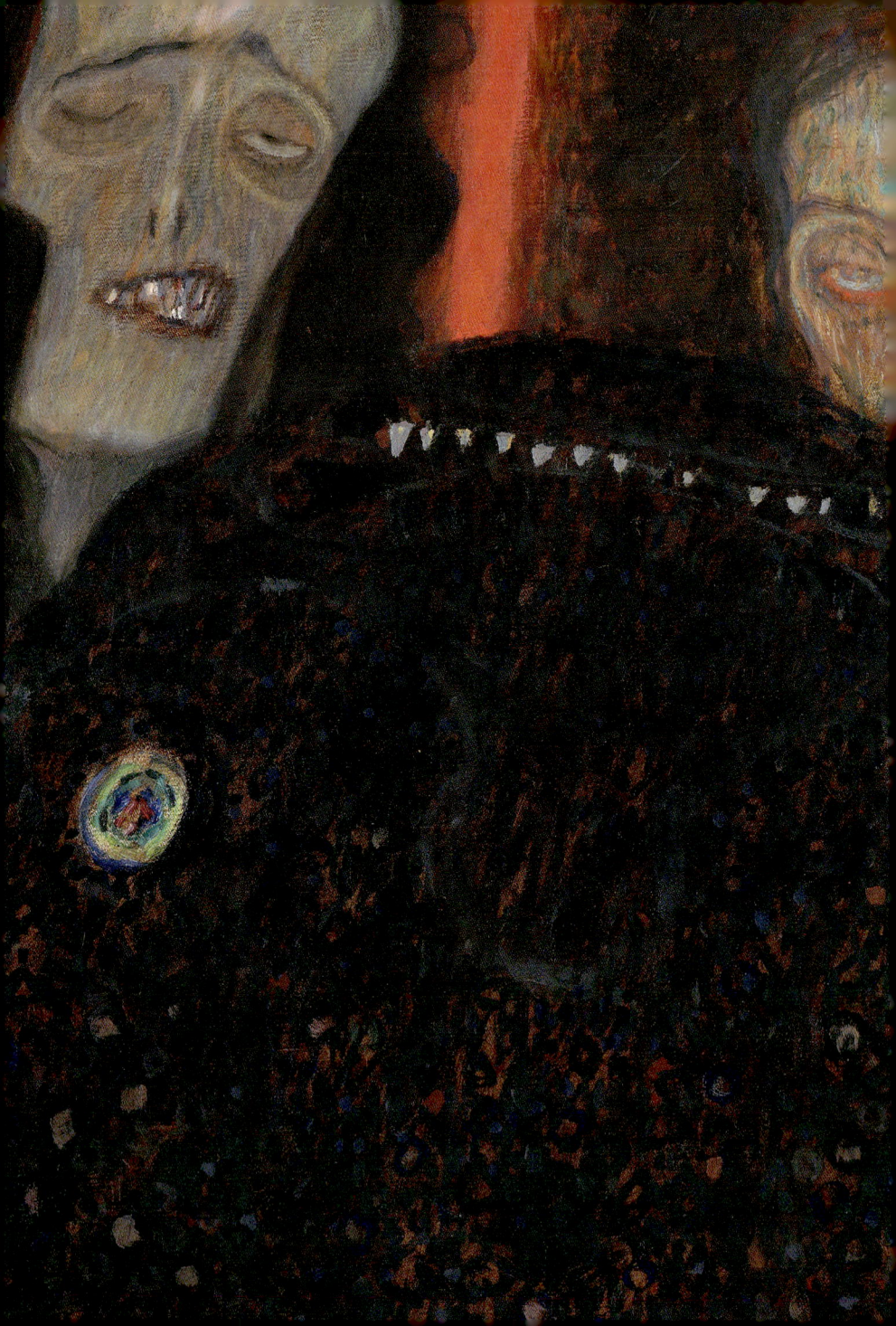

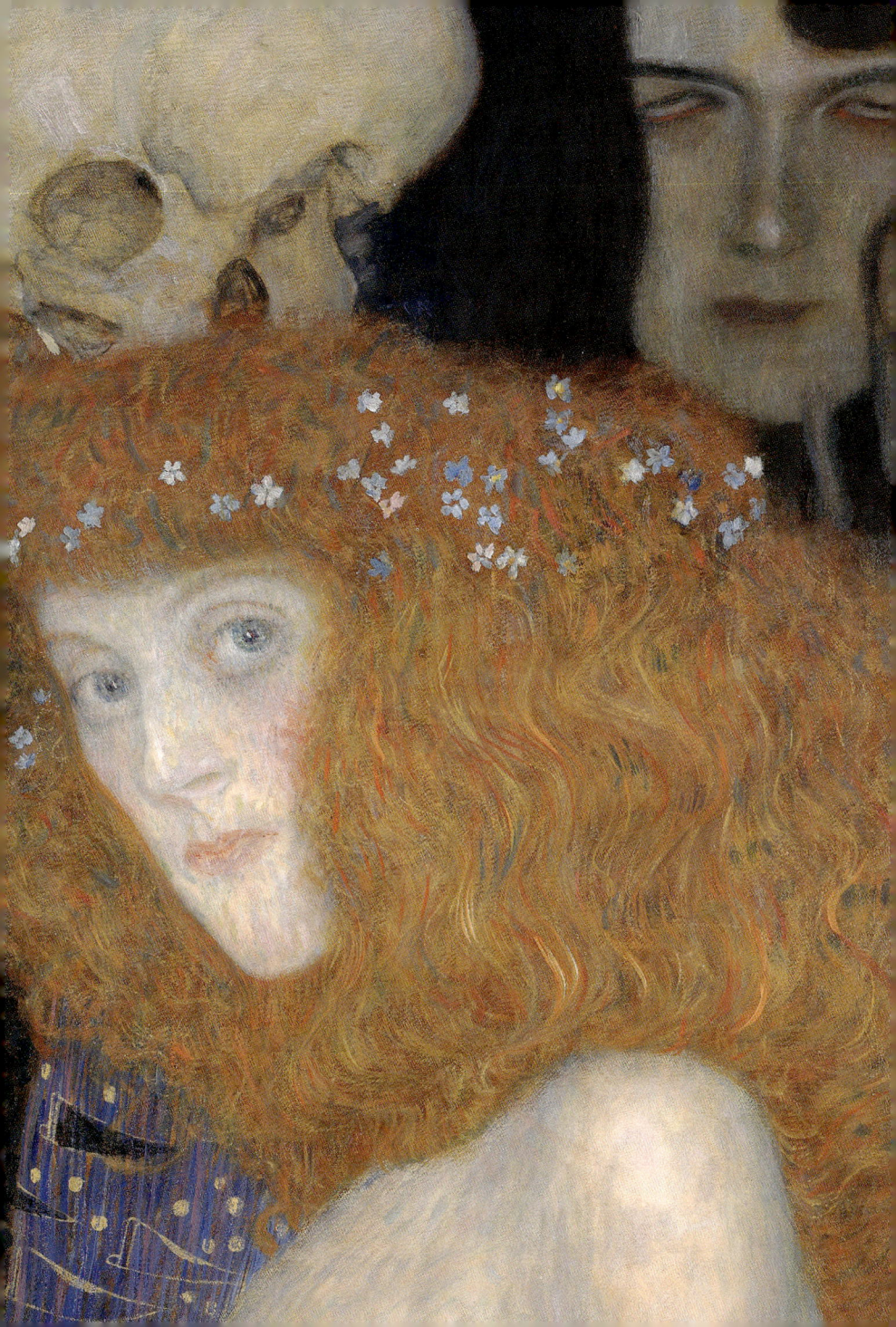

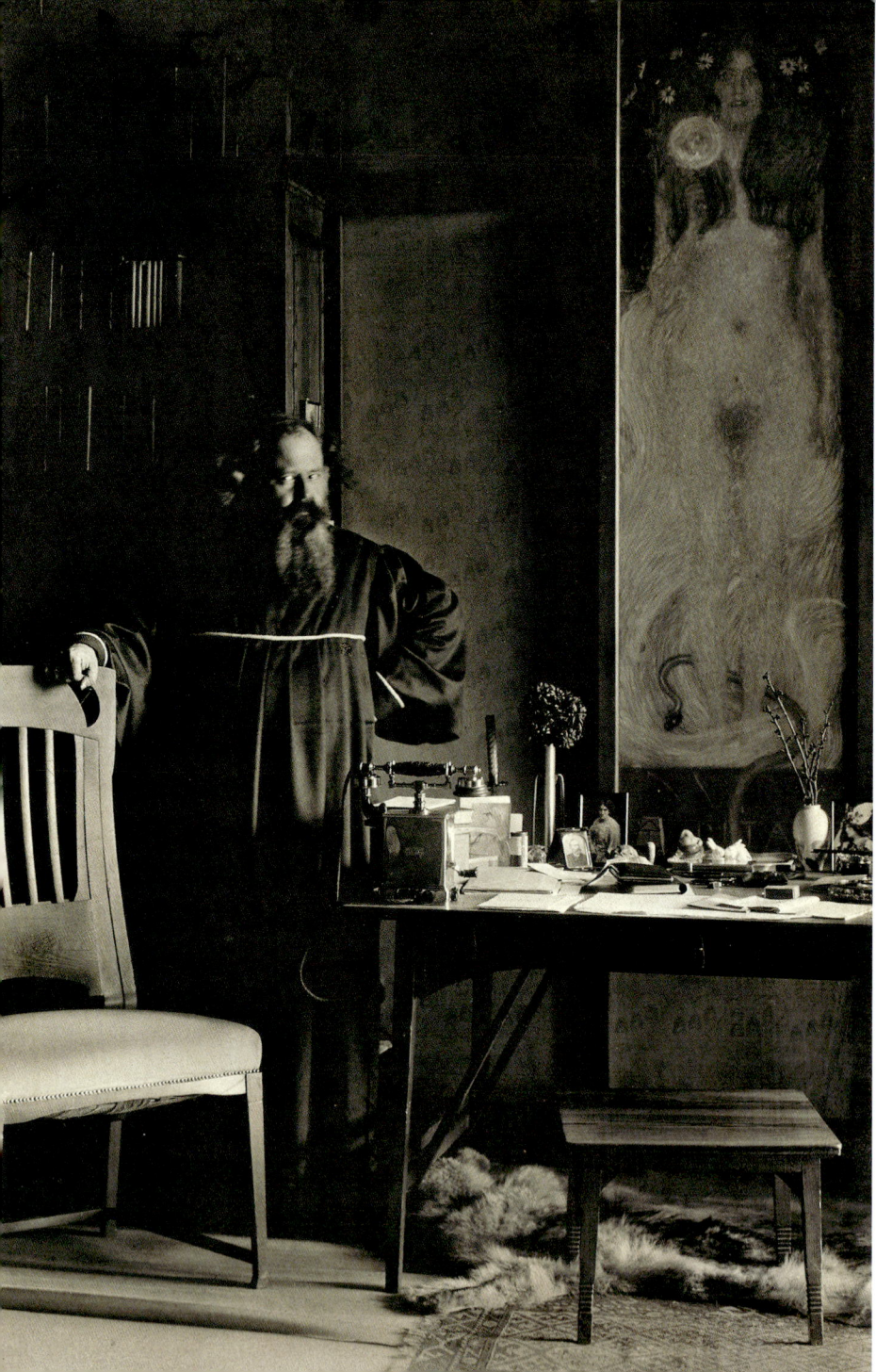

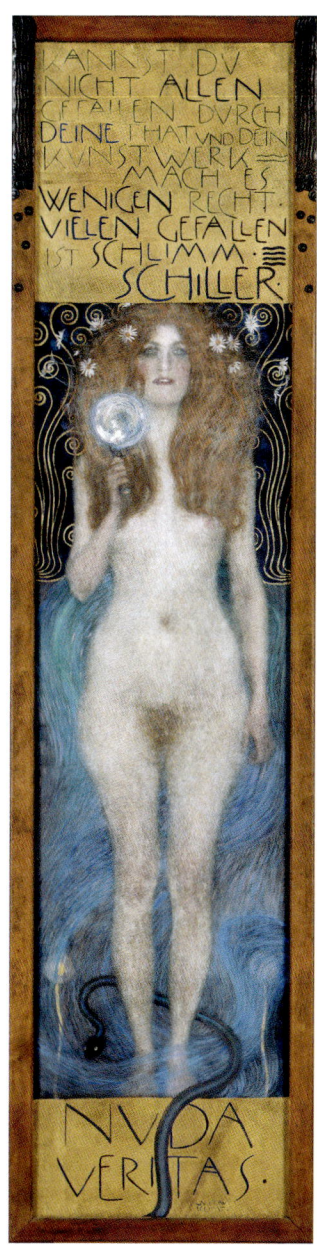

*"When I've finished a picture,
I don't want to lose more months
having to justify it to everyone.
What matters to me is not how
many people it pleases,
but whom it pleases."*

GUSTAV KLIMT, 1901

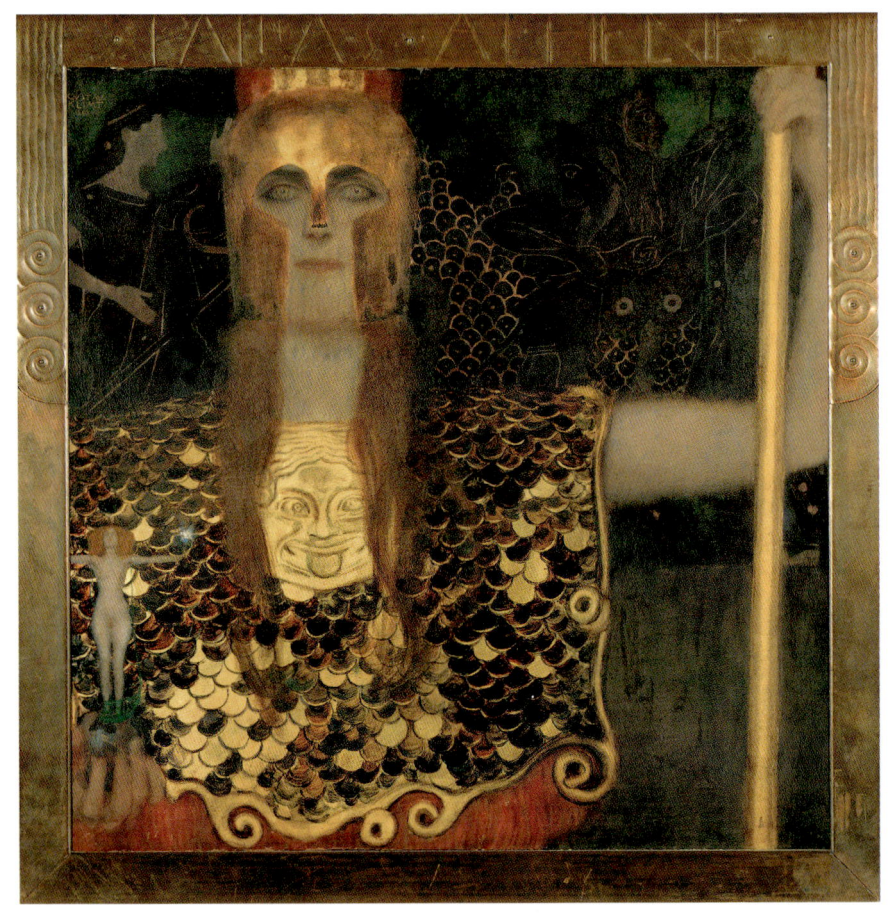

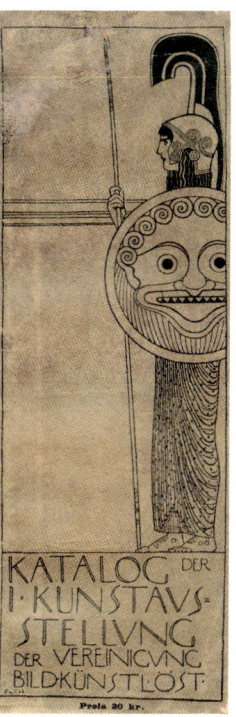

*"Made fascinating by the cool,
clear gaze of the pale grey eyes."*

ARPAD WEIXLGÄRTNER, 1912

Pallas Athene, 1898
Oil on canvas, 75 x 75 cm / 29 ½ x 29 ½ in. Vienna, Wien Museum

Catalogue of the first Secession exhibition, with Gustav Klimt's *Pallas Athene*, 1898
Vienna, MAK – Österreichisches Museum für angewandte Kunst/Gegenwartskunst

Pages 114–117
Details of: **Beethoven Frieze**, 1901/02
"The Well-armed Strong One", left wall
"Poetry", right wall

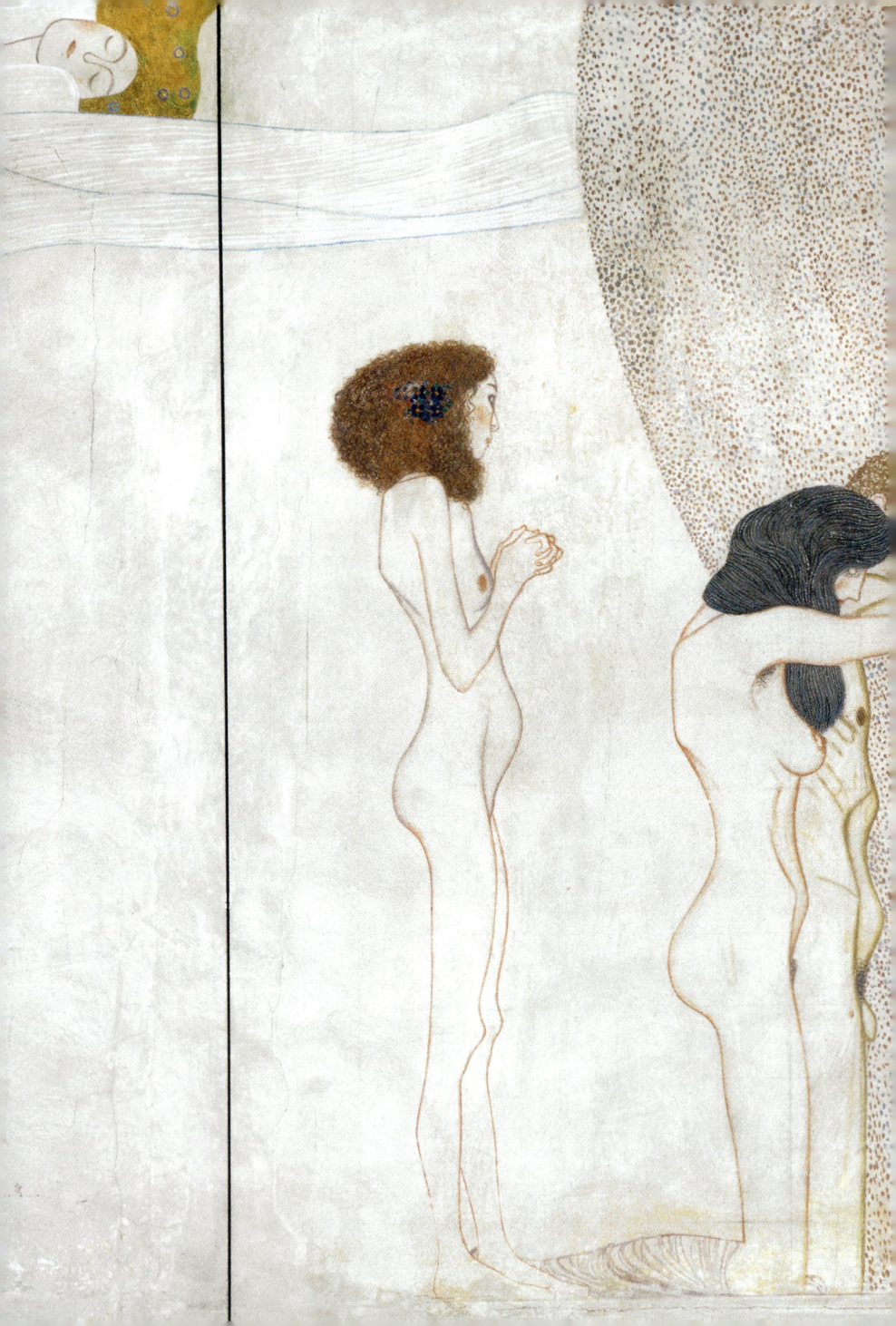

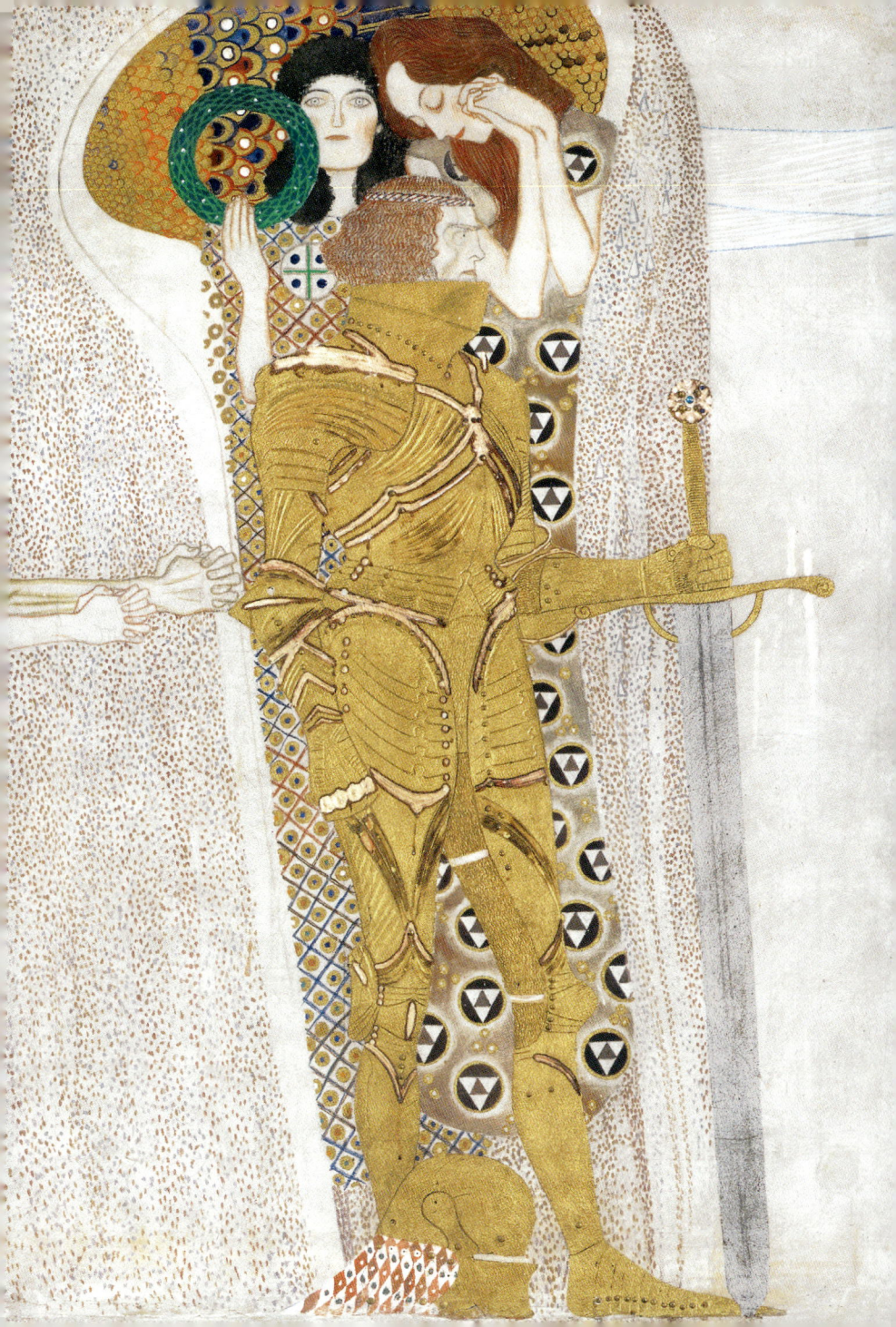

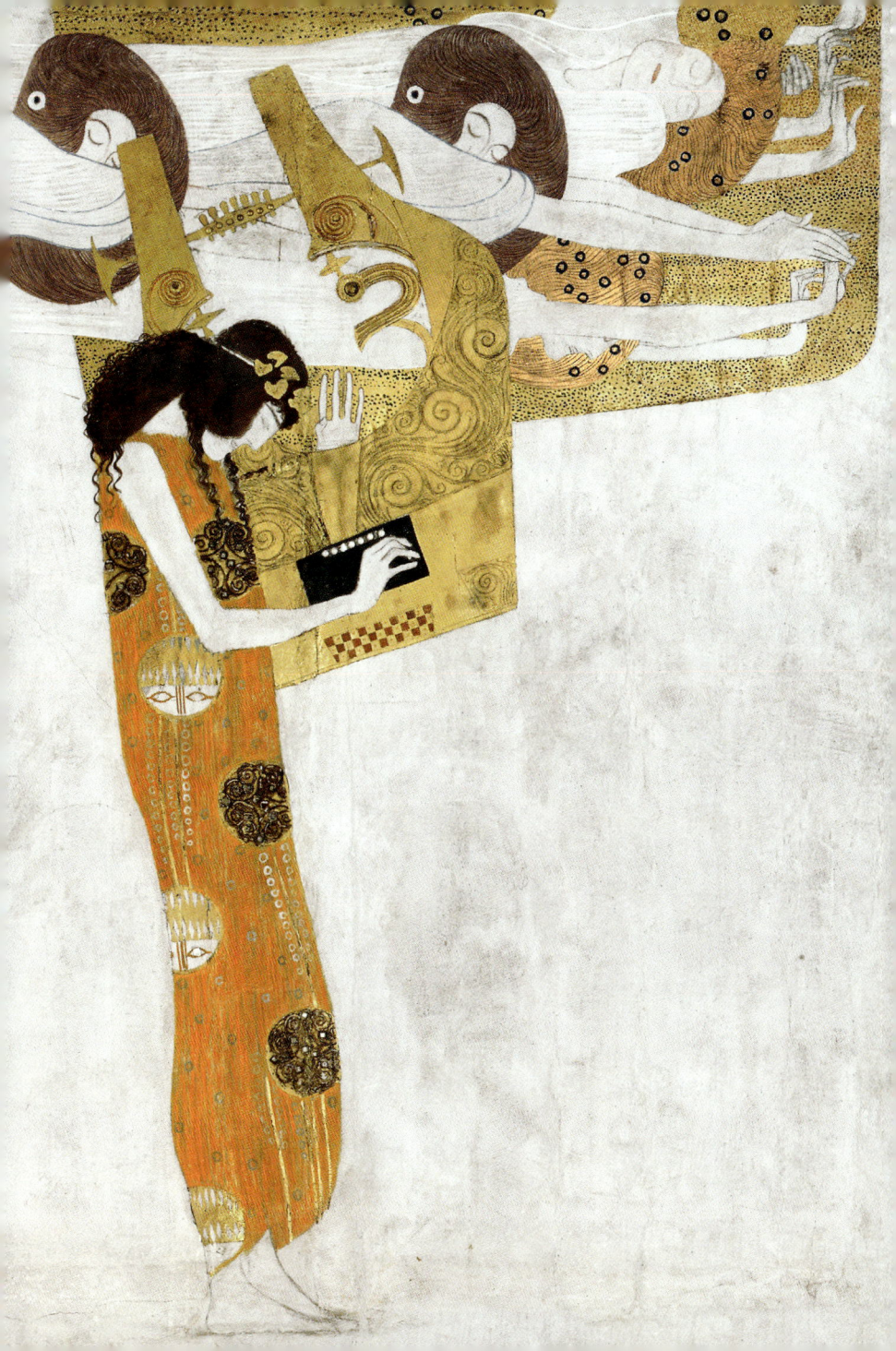

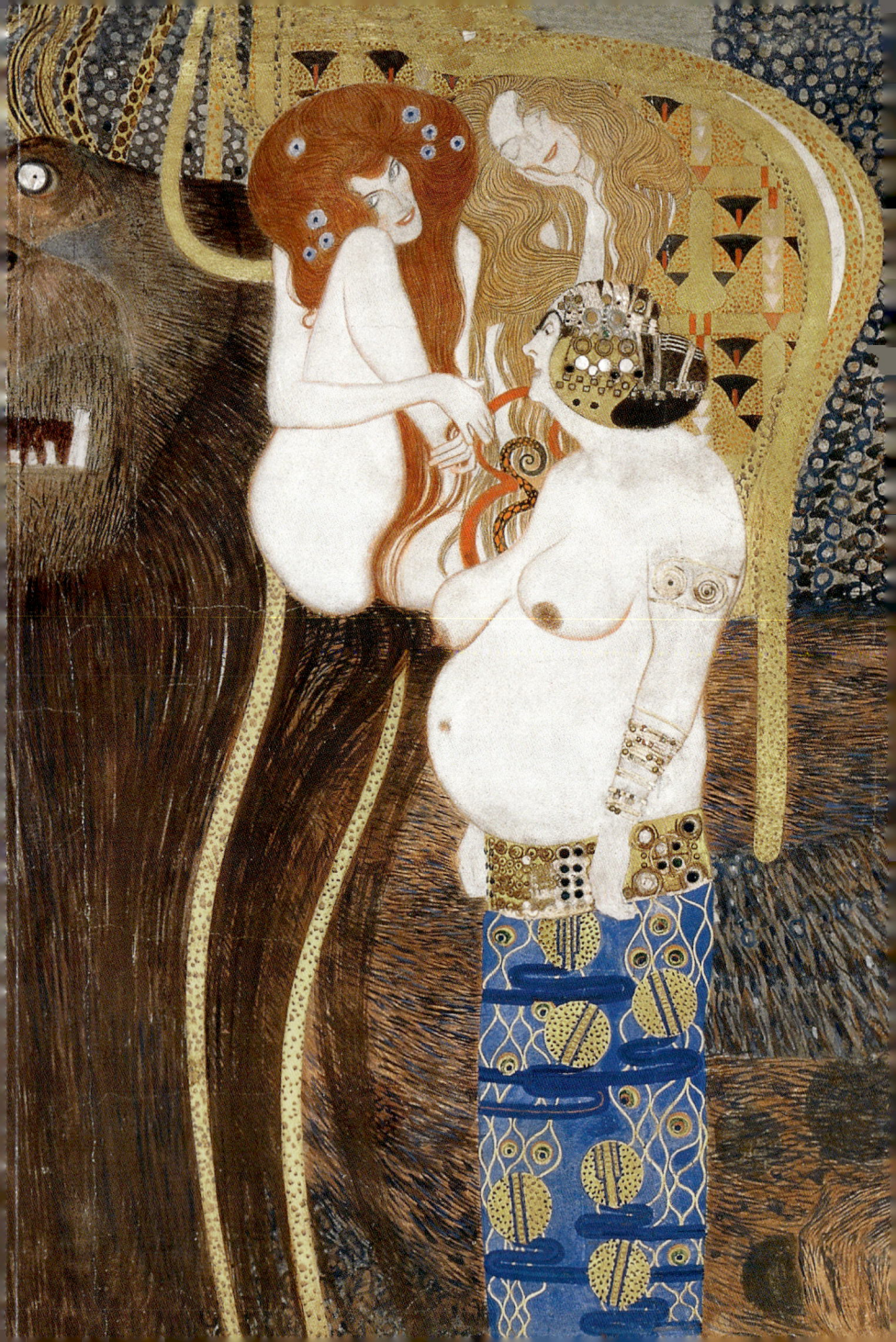

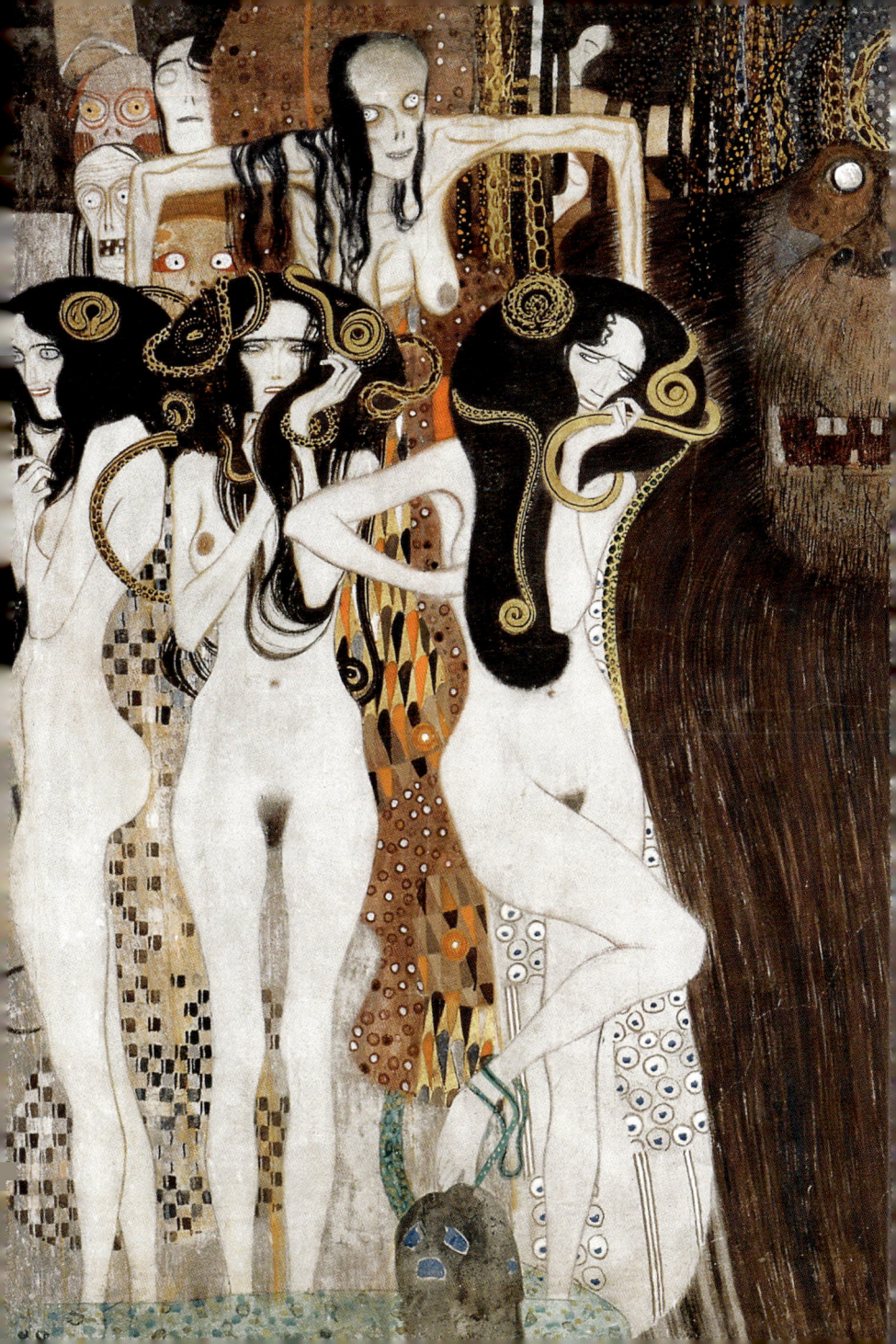

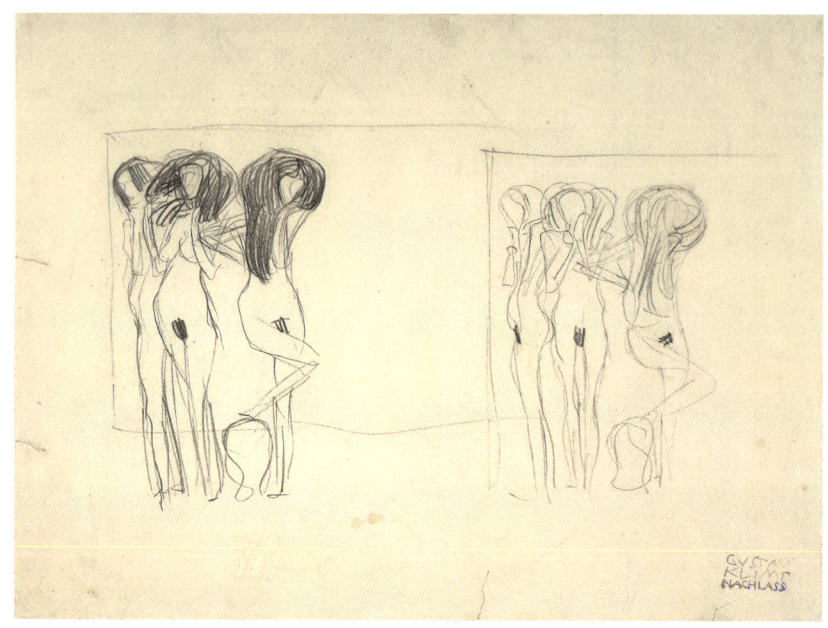

*"At no Viennese exhibition
has nudity ever held such orgies."*

HERMANN BAHR, 1903

**Two compositional sketches for the group
of the "Three Gorgons" in the *Beethoven Frieze*, 1901/02**
Pencil, 29.9 x 39.7 cm / 11 ¾ x 15 ⅝ in. Vienna, Albertina

Pages 119–125
Details of: **Beethoven Frieze**, 1901/02
"The Arts", right wall (p. 123)
"The Hostile Forces", end wall (pp. 119–122)
"'Joy, fair spark of divinity'. 'A kiss for all the world!'", right wall (pp. 124/25)

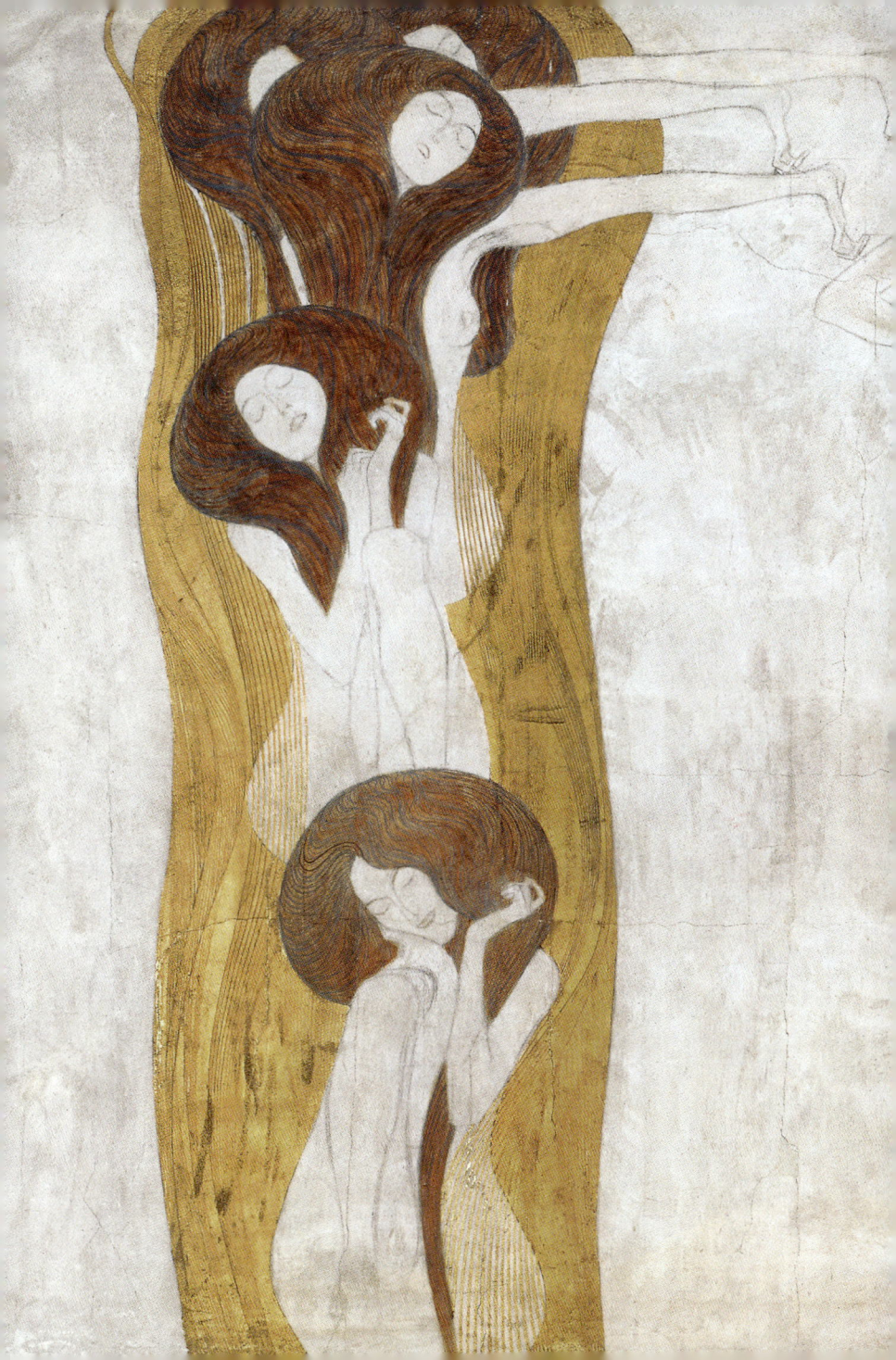

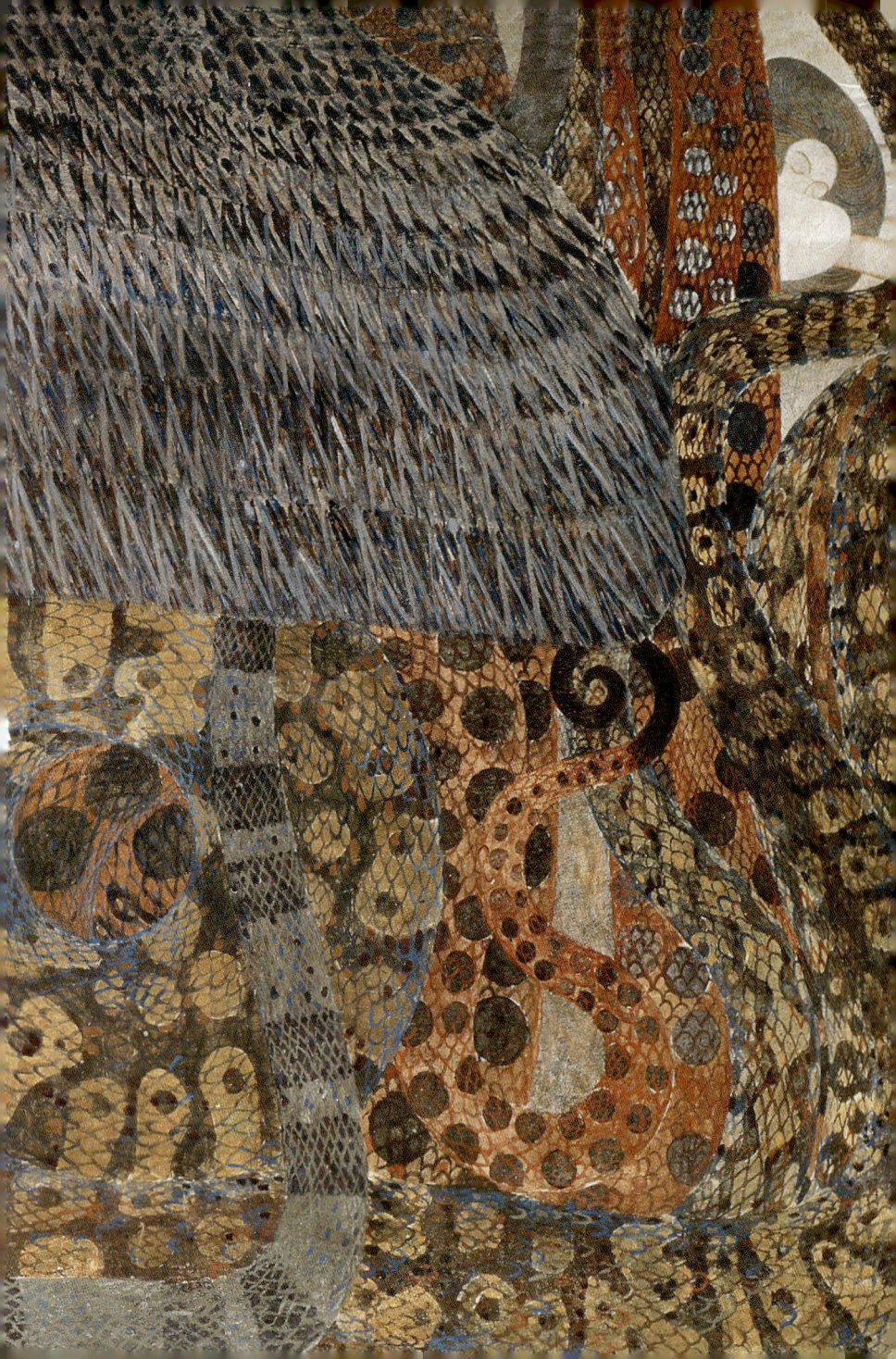

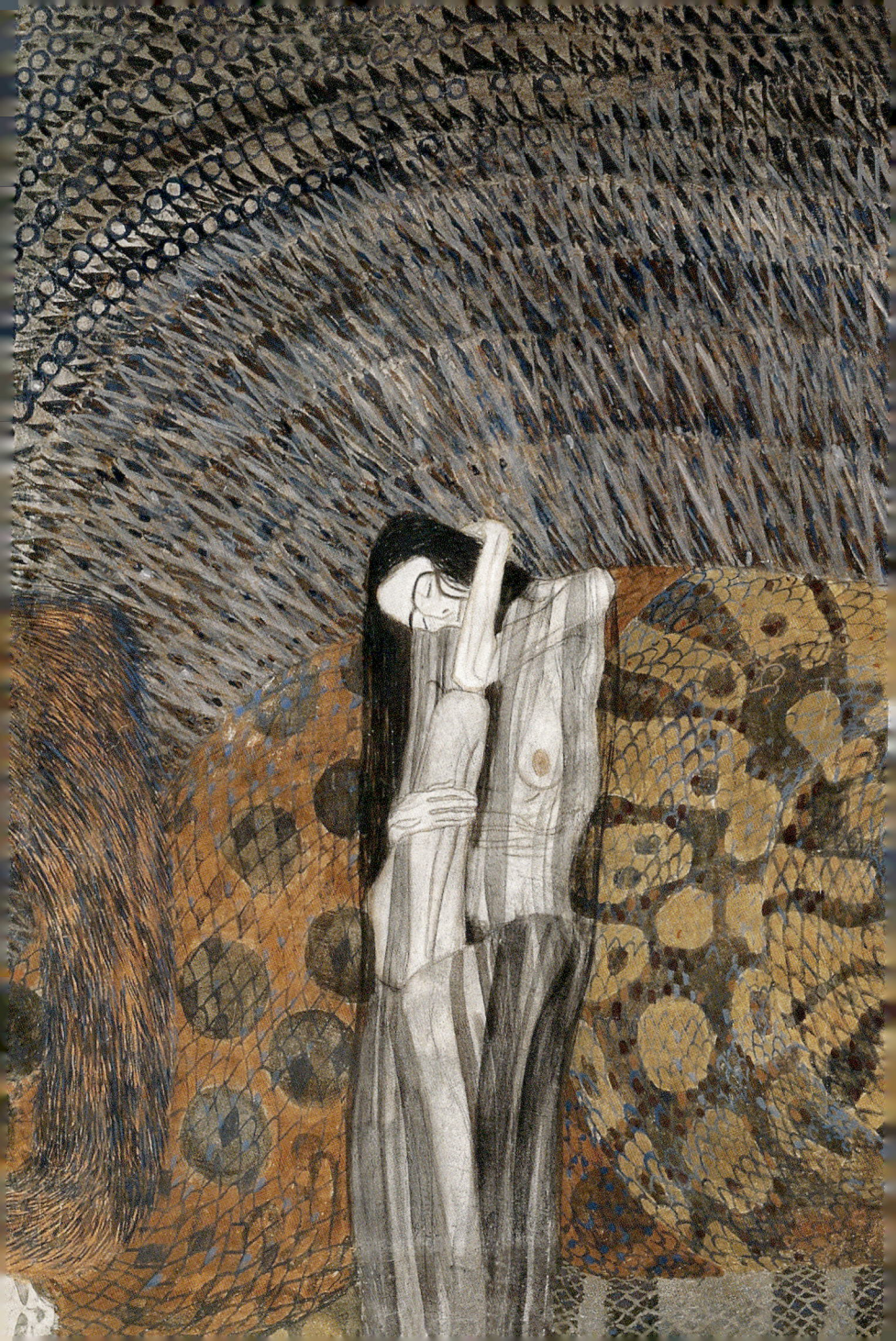

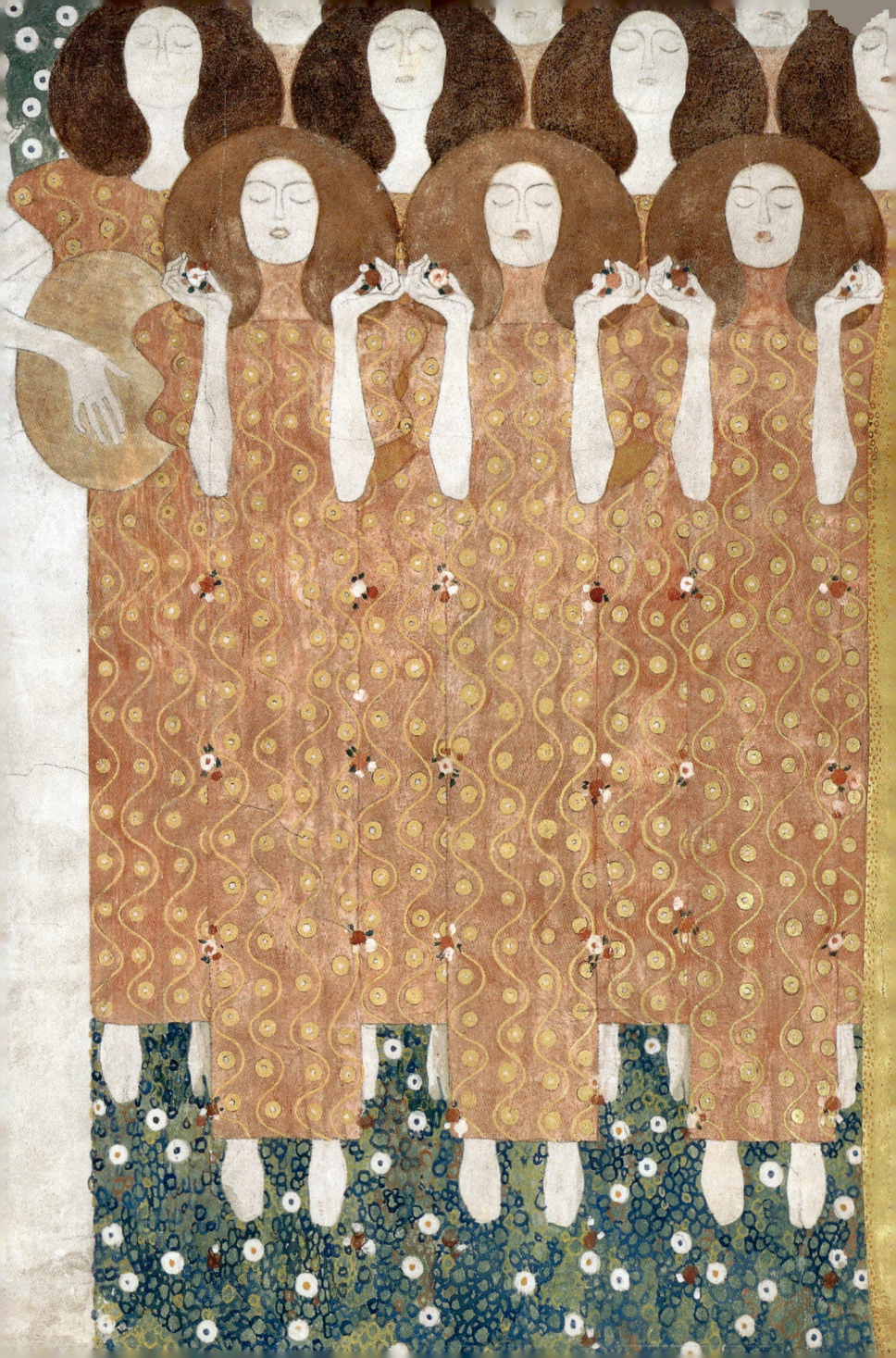

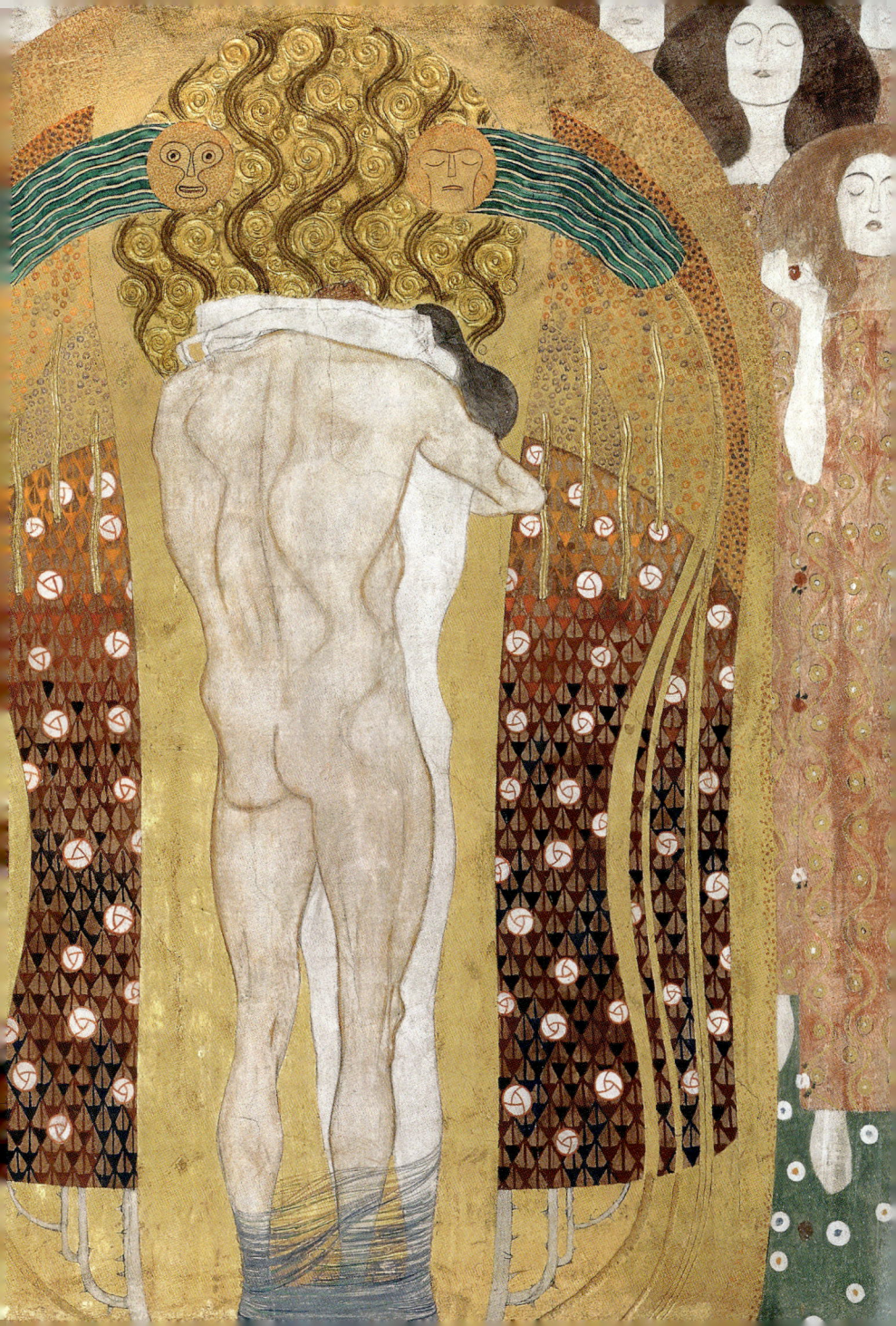

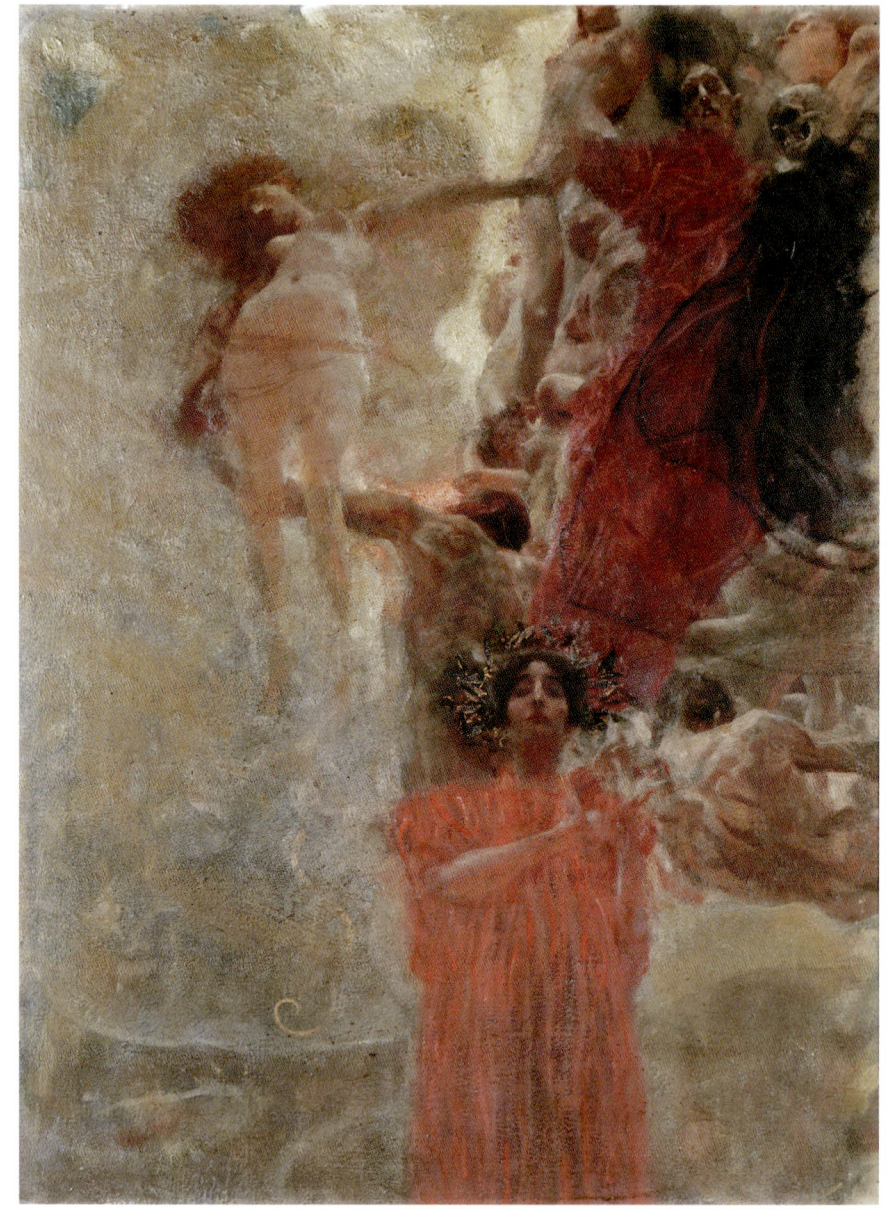

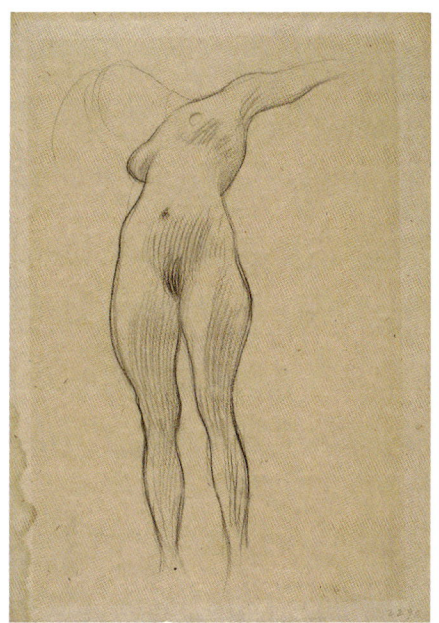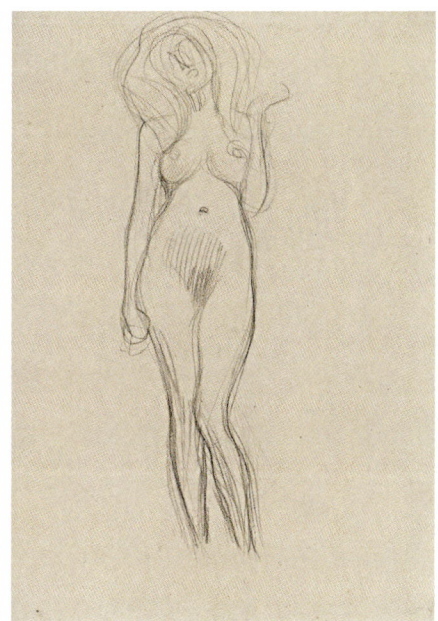

Medicine (compositional study), 1898
Oil on canvas, 72 x 55 cm / 28 ⅜ x 21 ⅝ in. Jerusalem, The Israel Museum

Study for the floating woman in *Medicine*, 1900/01
Black chalk, 41.5 x 27.3 cm / 16 ⅜ x 10 ¾ in. Vienna, Albertina

Study for the figure of "Veritas" in *Jurisprudence*, 1902/03
Black chalk, 42.7 x 30.1 cm / 16 ¾ x 11 ¾ in. Vienna, Leopold Museum

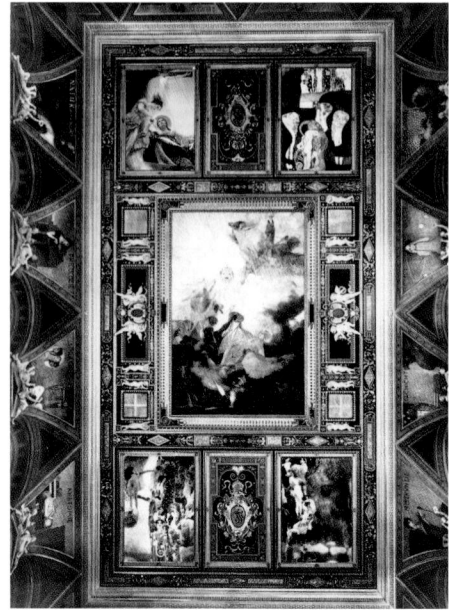

*"Here, we finally have a genuine wall painting.
One full of surface and style, very close to the
ideal of two-dimensionality, covering and
enlivening a wall. Constructed painting
for a constructed wall surface."*

LUDWIG HEVESI, 1907

Reconstruction of the planned layout of the Faculty paintings
Top left: Franz Matsch, *Theology*; top right: Gustav Klimt, *Jurisprudence*; bottom right: Gustav Klimt,
Philosophy; bottom left: Gustav Klimt, *Medicine*; centre: Franz Matsch, *The Victory of Light over Darkness*
The reconstruction stems from Alice Strobl, 1964

Medicine, 1900–1907
Oil on canvas, 430 x 300 cm / 14 ft 1 in. x 9 ft 10 in.
Destroyed by fire in May 1945 at Immendorf Castle, Lower Austria

Page 130
Jurisprudence, 1903, final version 1907
Oil on canvas, 430 x 300 cm / 14 ft 1 in. x 9 ft 10 in.
Destroyed by fire in May 1945 at Immendorf Castle, Lower Austria

Page 131
Philosophy, 1900–1907
Oil on canvas, 430 x 300 cm / 14 ft 1 in. x 9 ft 10 in.
Destroyed by fire in May 1945 at Immendorf Castle, Lower Austria

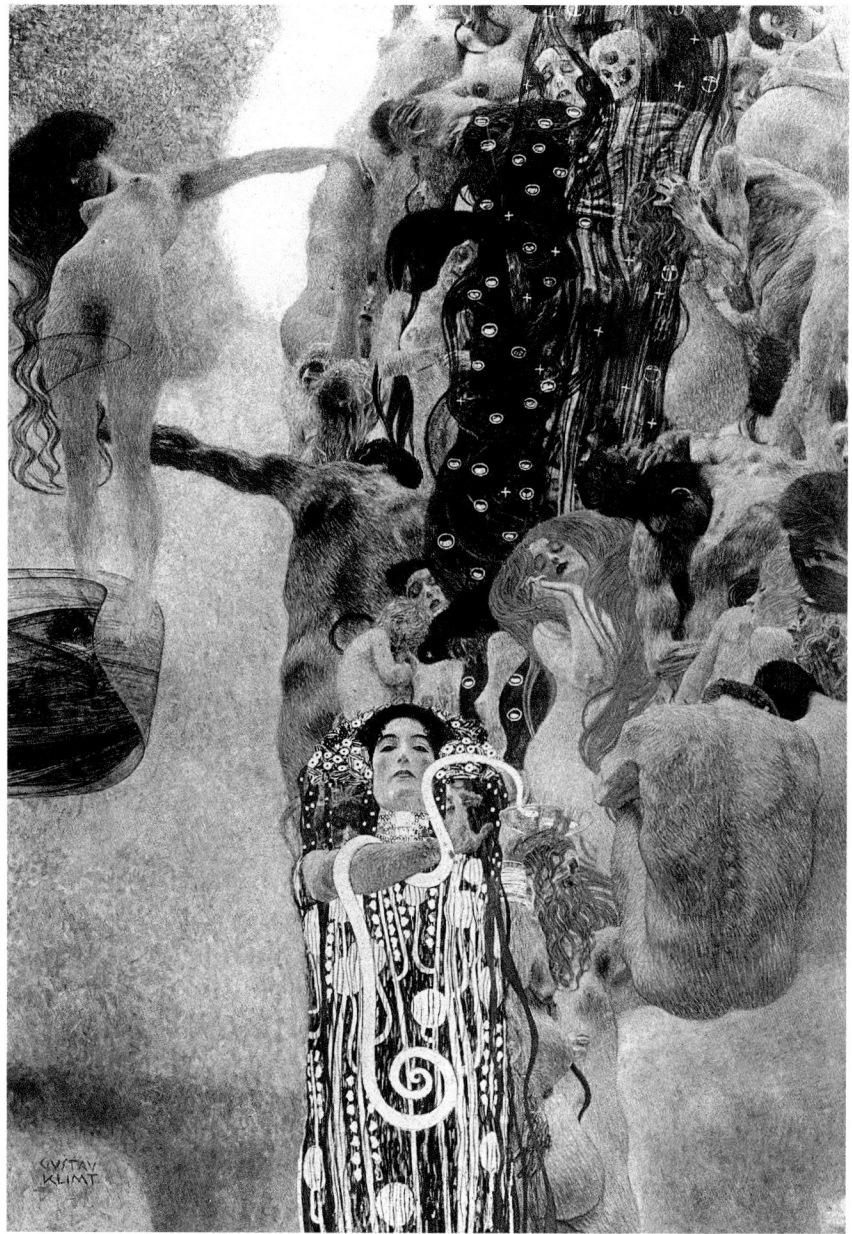

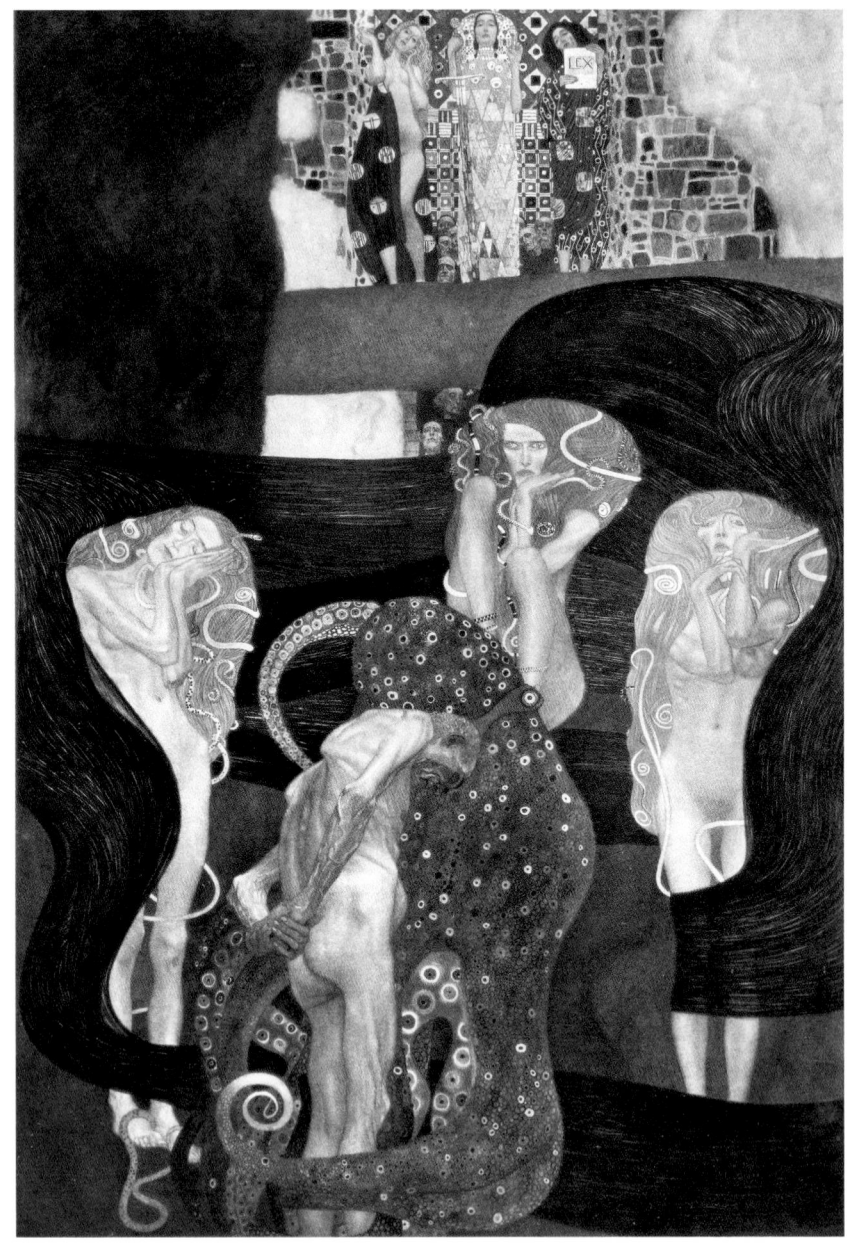

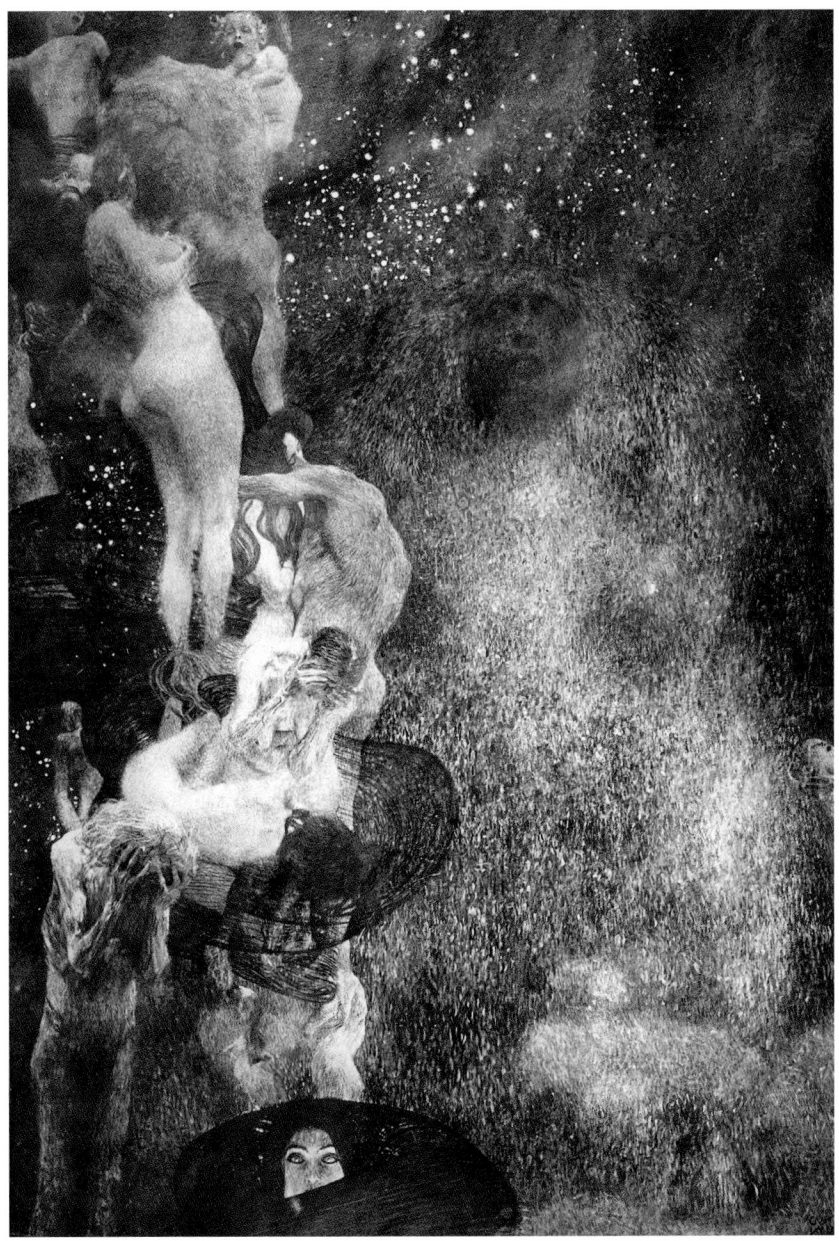

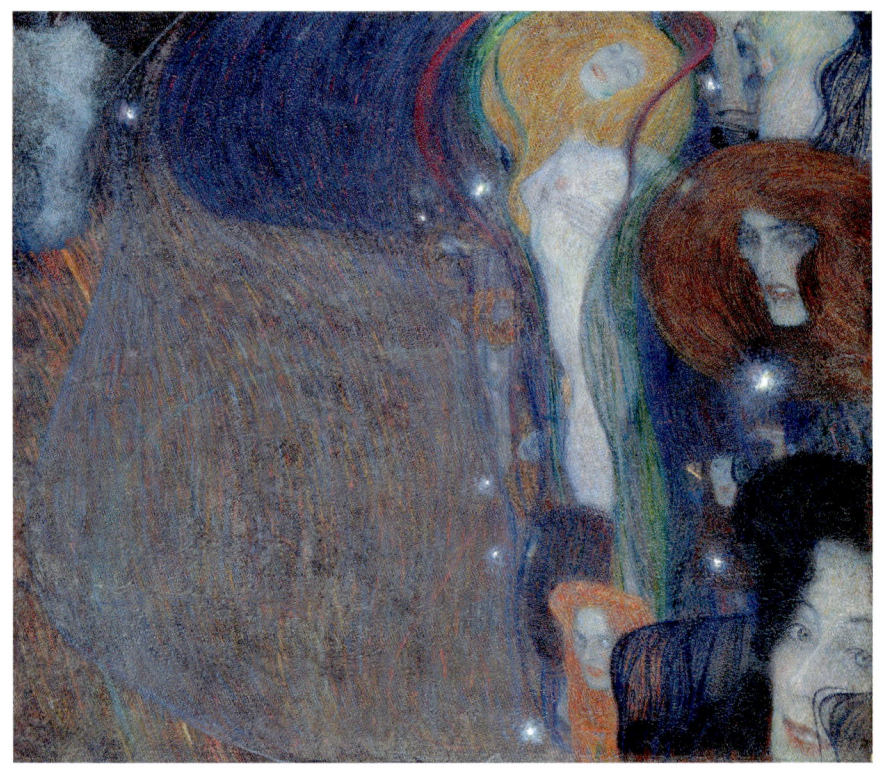

Will-o'-the-Wisp, 1903
Oil on canvas, 52.1 x 59.7 cm / 20 ½ x 23 ½ in. Private collection

Hope I, 1903/04
Oil on canvas, 189.2 x 67 cm / 74 ½ x 26 ⅜ in. Ottawa, National Gallery of Canada

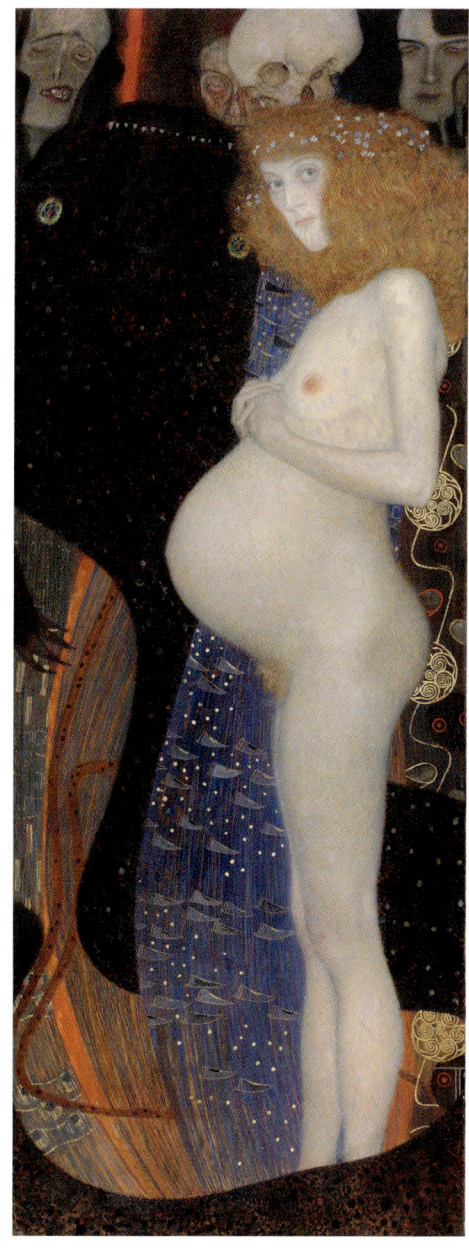

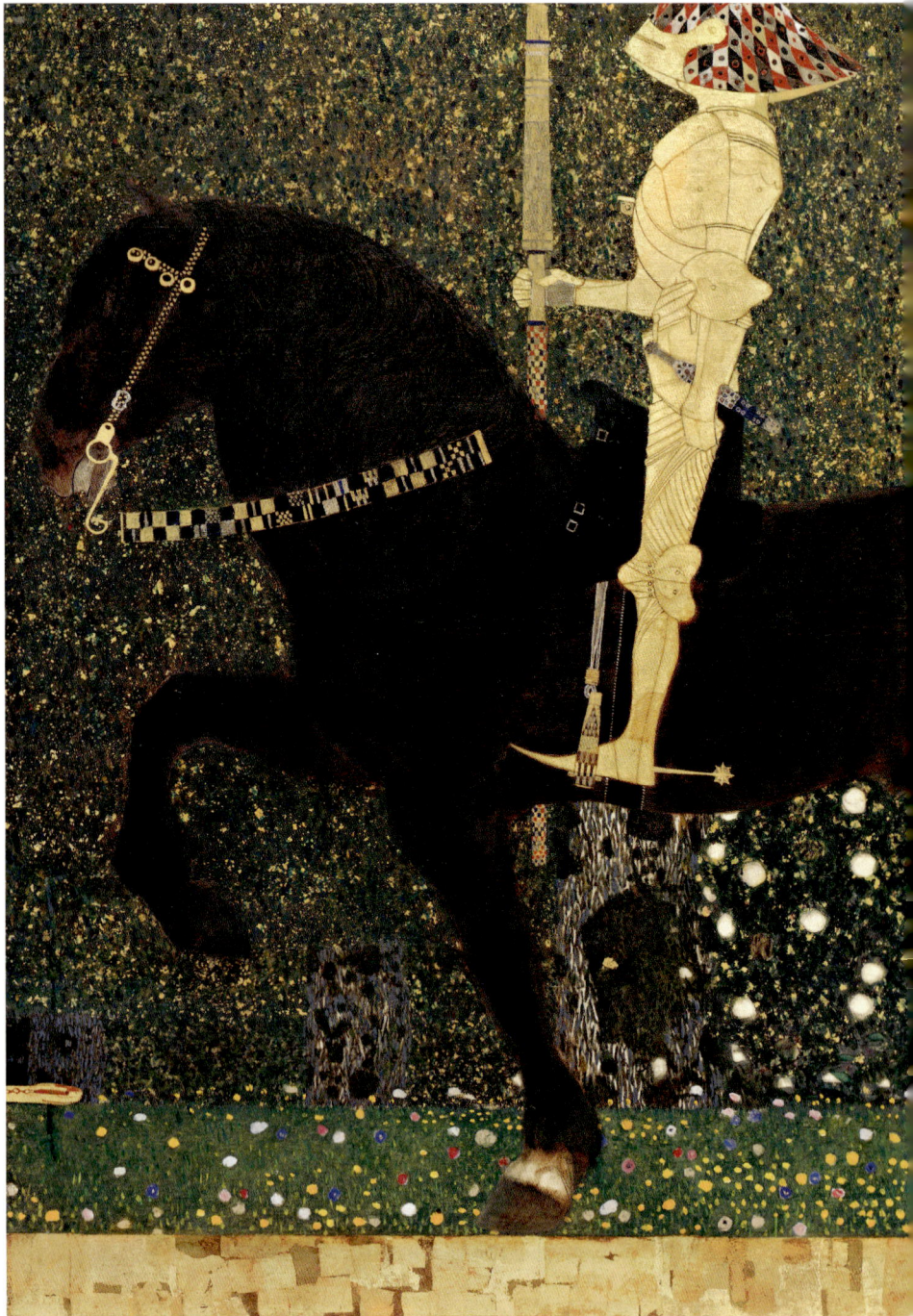

"*The human body really now used solely as raw material for the forms of a fluid imagination. ... A work of unusual tastiness; one is truly obliged to resort to such Lucullan expressions.*"

The Golden Knight (Life Is a Battle), 1903
Oil on canvas, 103.5 x 103.7 cm / 40 ¾ x 40 ⅞ in.
Nagoya, Aichi Prefectural Museum of Art

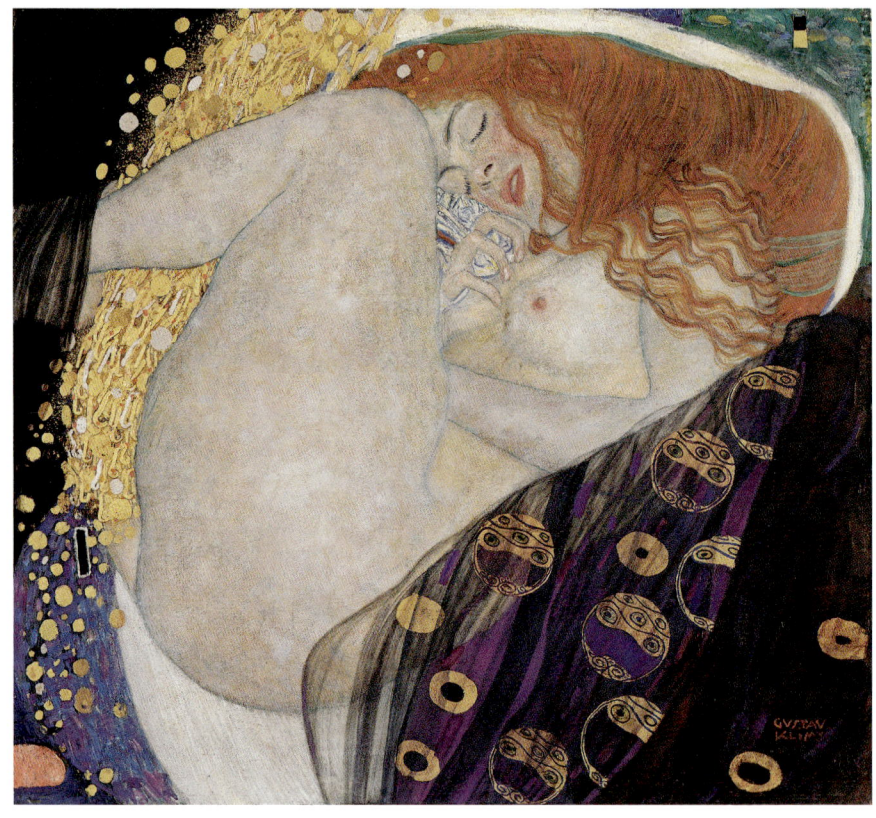

Danaë, 1907/08
Oil on canvas, 77 x 83 cm / 30 ⅜ x 32 ⅜ in. Vienna, Dichand family

Water Snakes I, 1904–1907
Pencil on parchment with watercolour and body colour,
heightened with silver gilt, bronze gilt and gold, 50 x 20 cm / 19 ⅝ x 7 ⅞ in.
Vienna, Belvedere

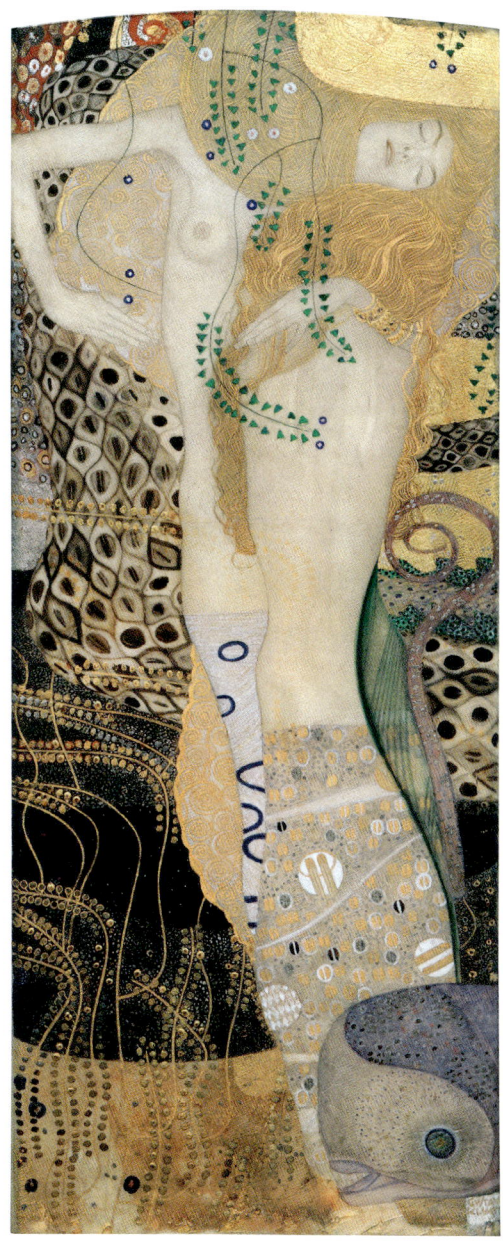

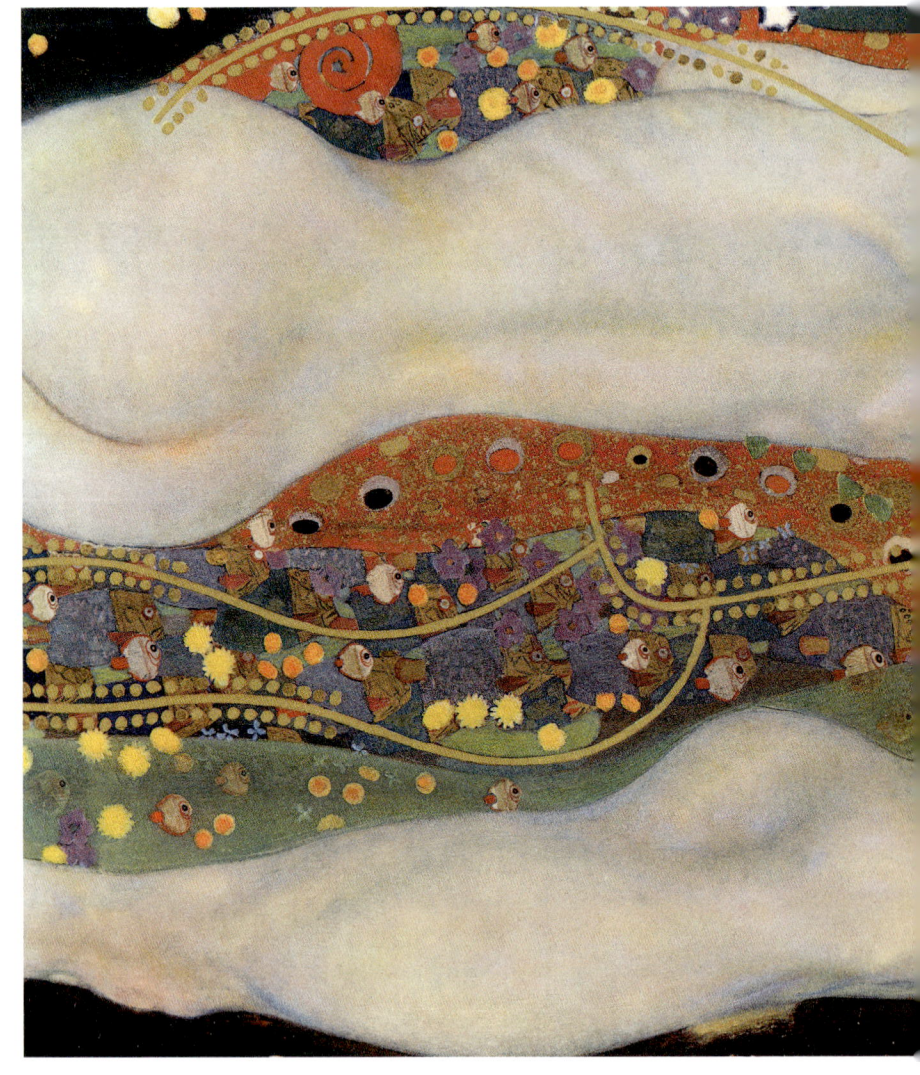

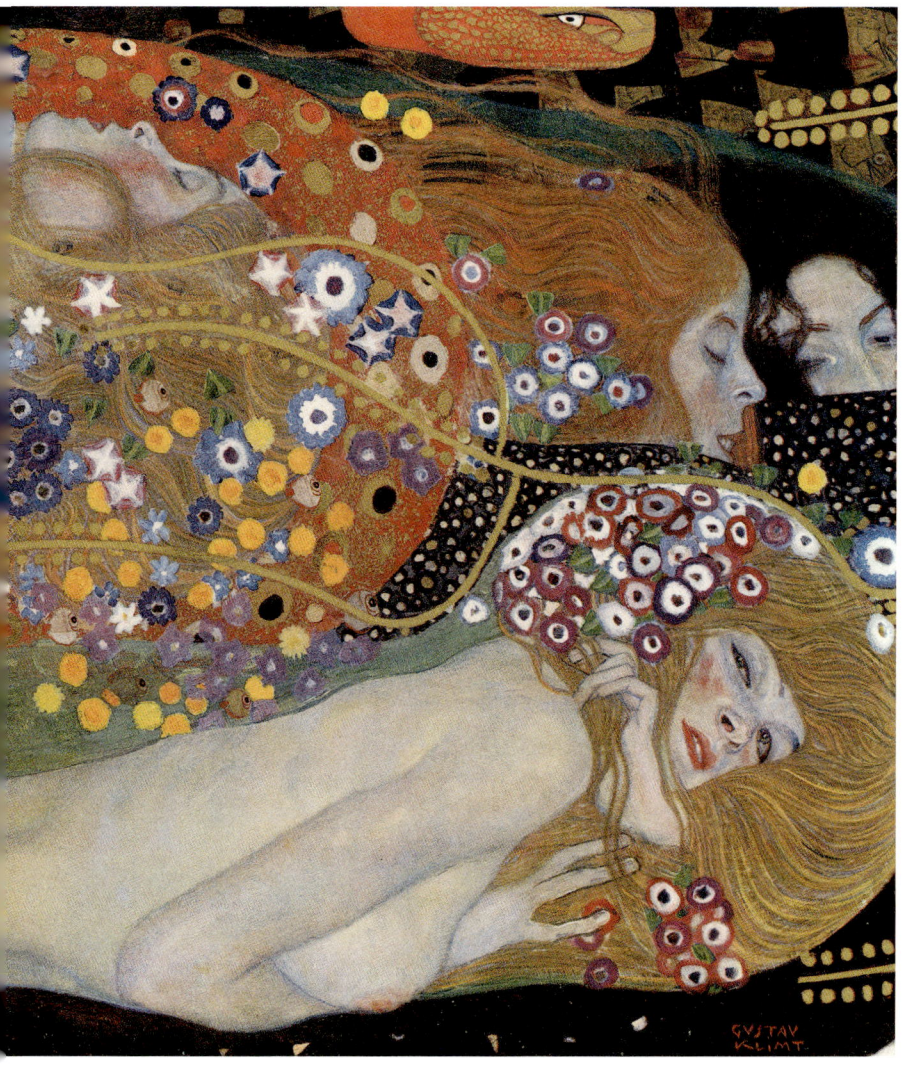

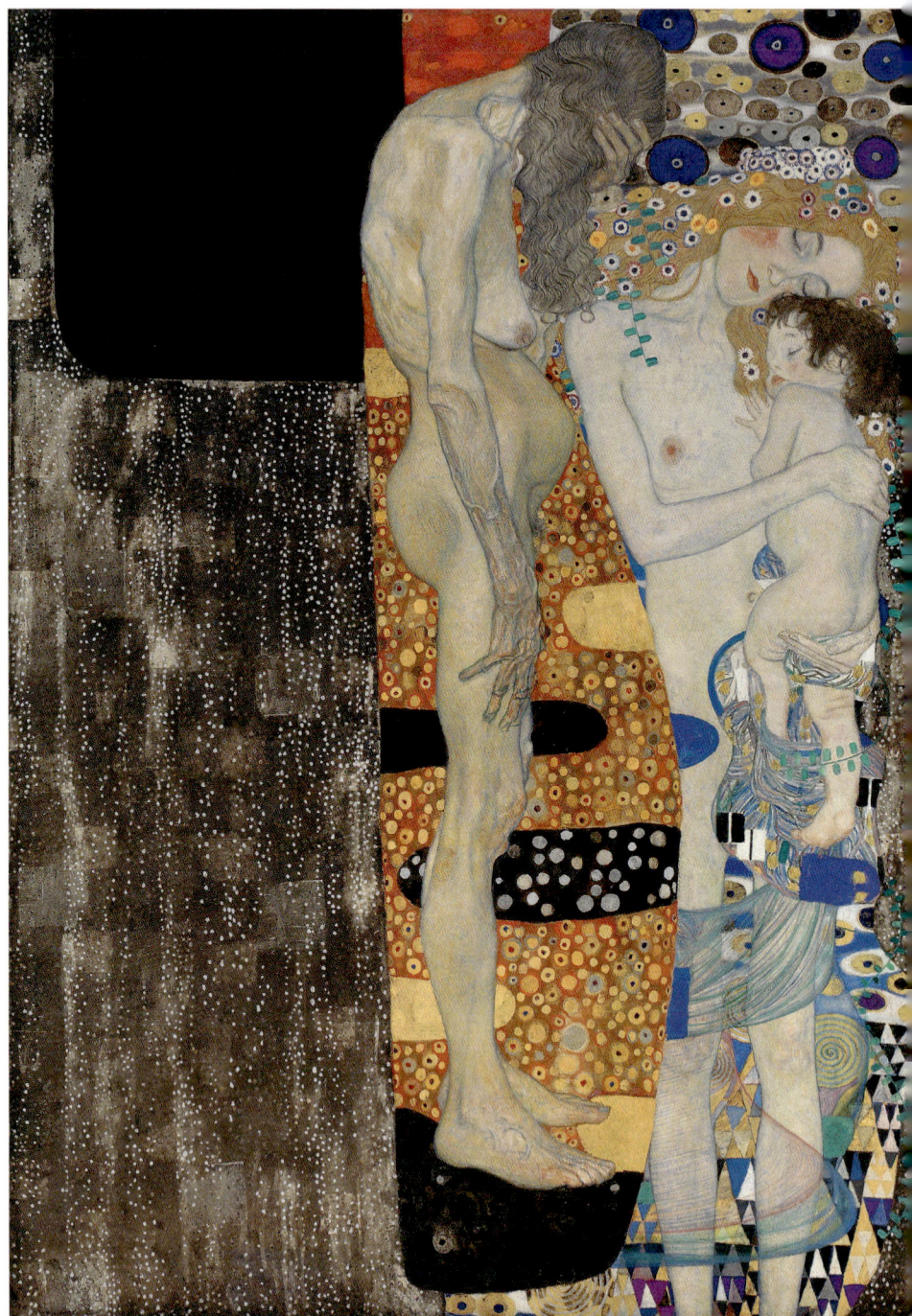

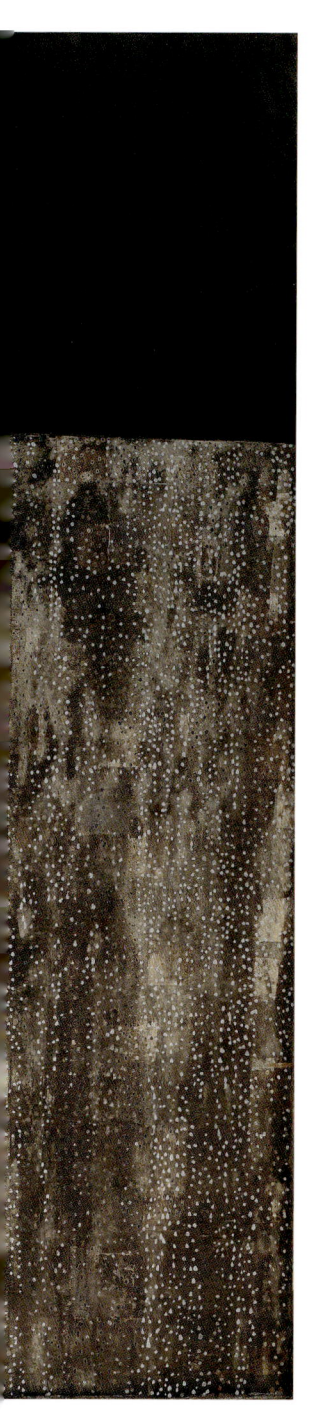

"*Youth and age, blossoming and withering, the entire calamity of desire and suffering known as human life. And the symbolic group intimately surrounded and enveloped by the most exquisite fantasy of mosaic shoots.*"

LUDWIG HEVESI, 1907

Pages 138/39
Water Snakes II, 1904, reworked 1906/07
Oil on canvas, 80 x 145 cm / 31 ½ x 57 in.
Private collection

The Three Ages of Woman, 1905
Oil on canvas, 180 x 180 cm / 70 ⅞ x 70 ⅞ in.
Rome, Galleria Nazionale d'Arte Moderna e Contemporanea

The Kiss, 1907/08
Oil on canvas, 180 x 180 cm / 70 ⅞ x 70 ⅞ in.
Vienna, Belvedere

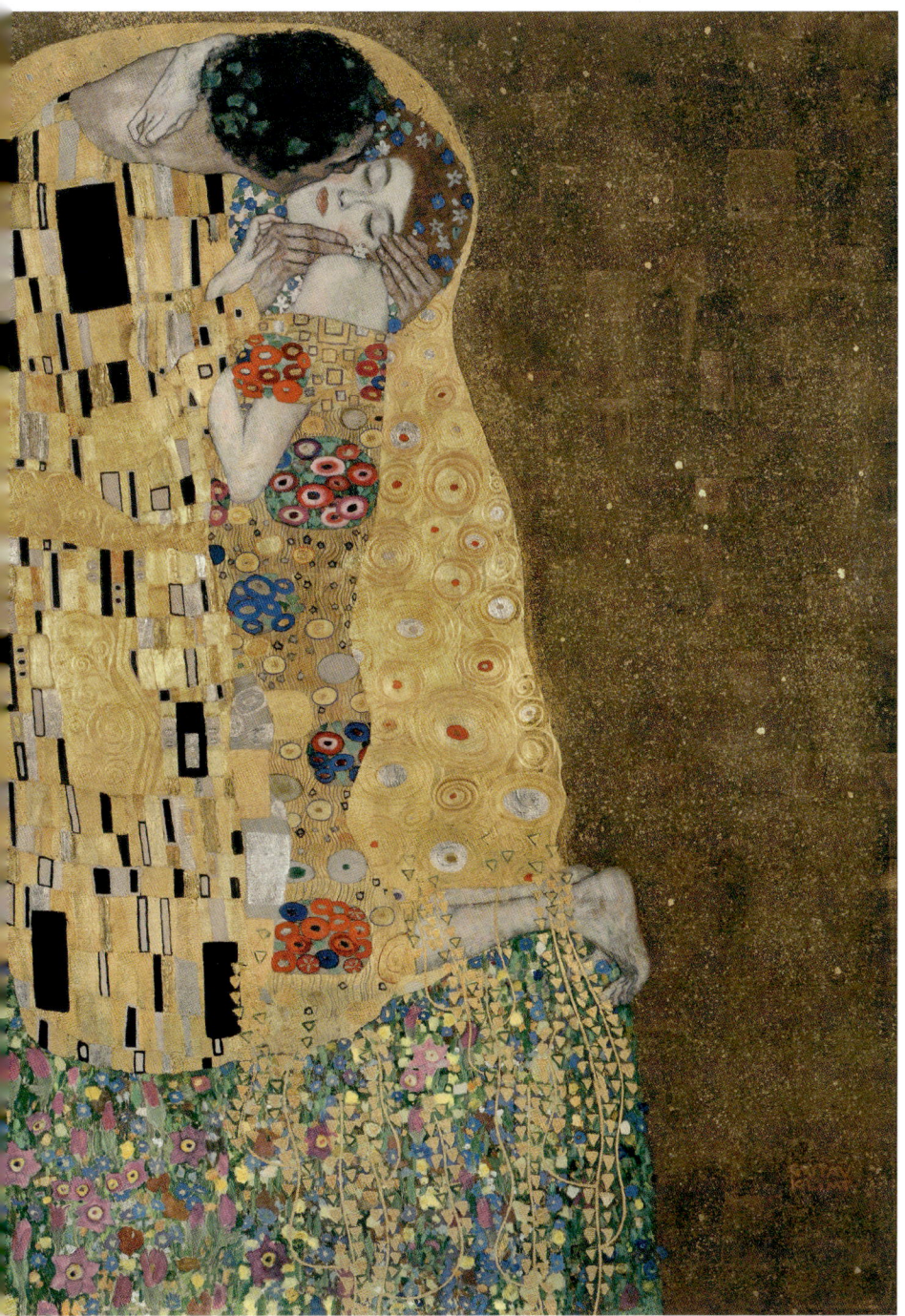

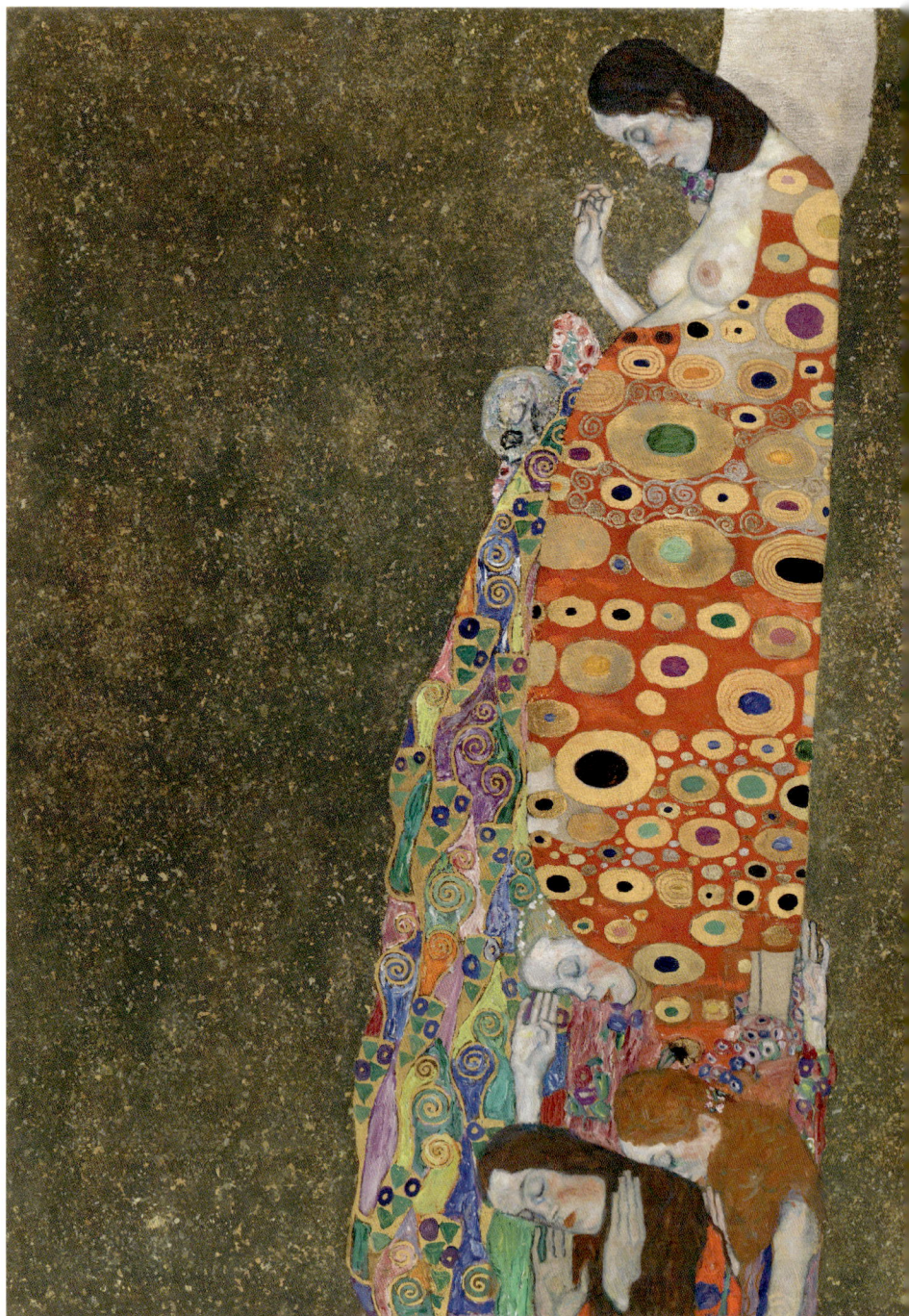

Hope II (Vision), 1907/08
Oil, gold and silver on canvas, 110.5 x 110.5 cm / 43 ½ x 43 ½ in.
New York, The Museum of Modern Art, Jo Carole and Ronald S.
Lauder and Helen Acheson Funds, and Serge Sabarsky

Pages 146/47
Hope II (Vision) (detail), 1907/08

Pages 148/49
Moritz Nähr
**Members of the Vienna Secession at the fourteenth Secession
exhibition ('Beethoven Exhibition')**, 1902
Back row, from l. to r.: Anton Stark, Gustav Klimt, Adolf Böhm,
Wilhelm List, Maximilian Kurzweil, Leopold Stolba, Rudolf Bacher.
Front row: Kolo Moser, Maximilian Lenz, Ernst Stöhr,
Emil Orlik, Carl Moll.
Photograph. Imagno/Austrian Archives

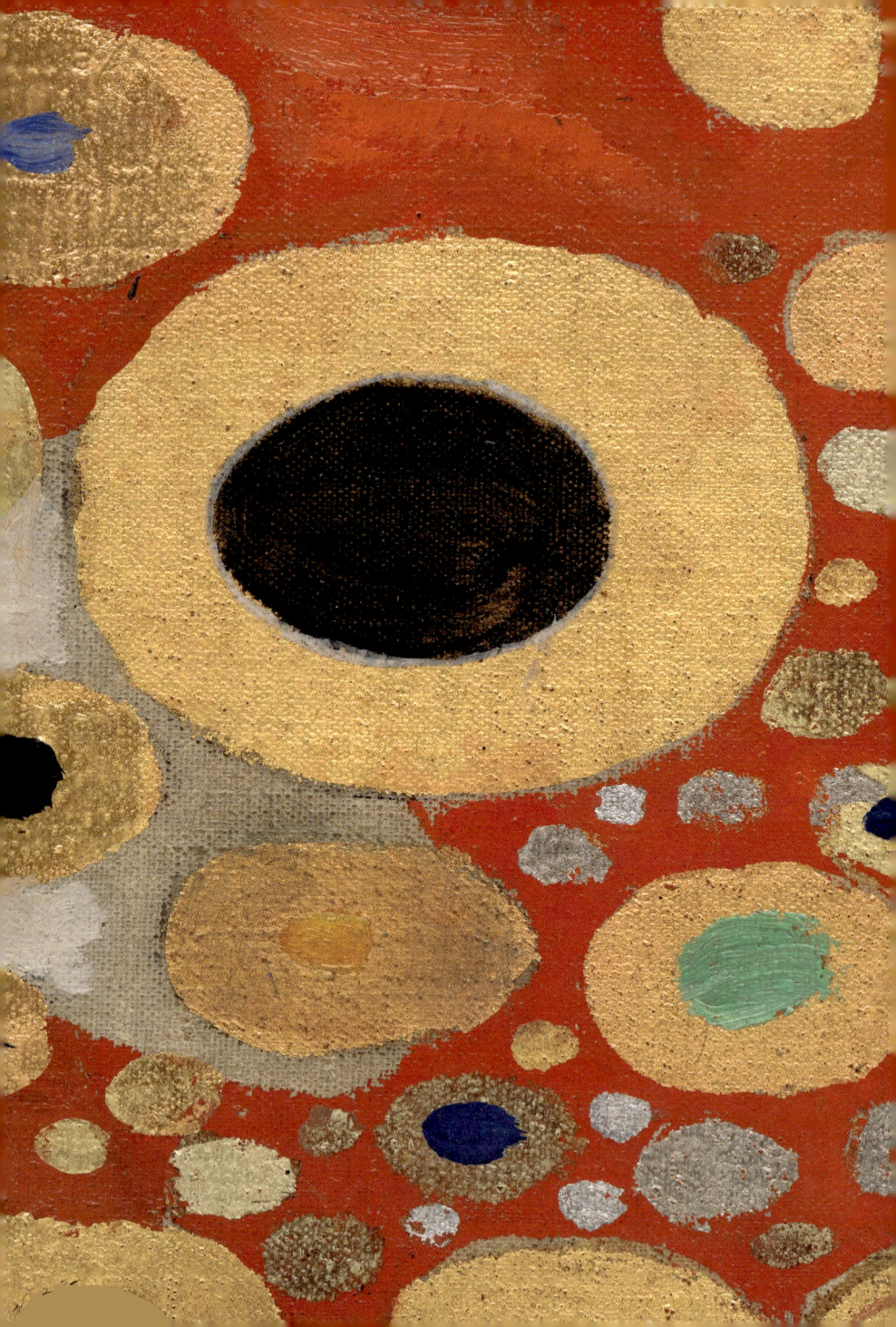

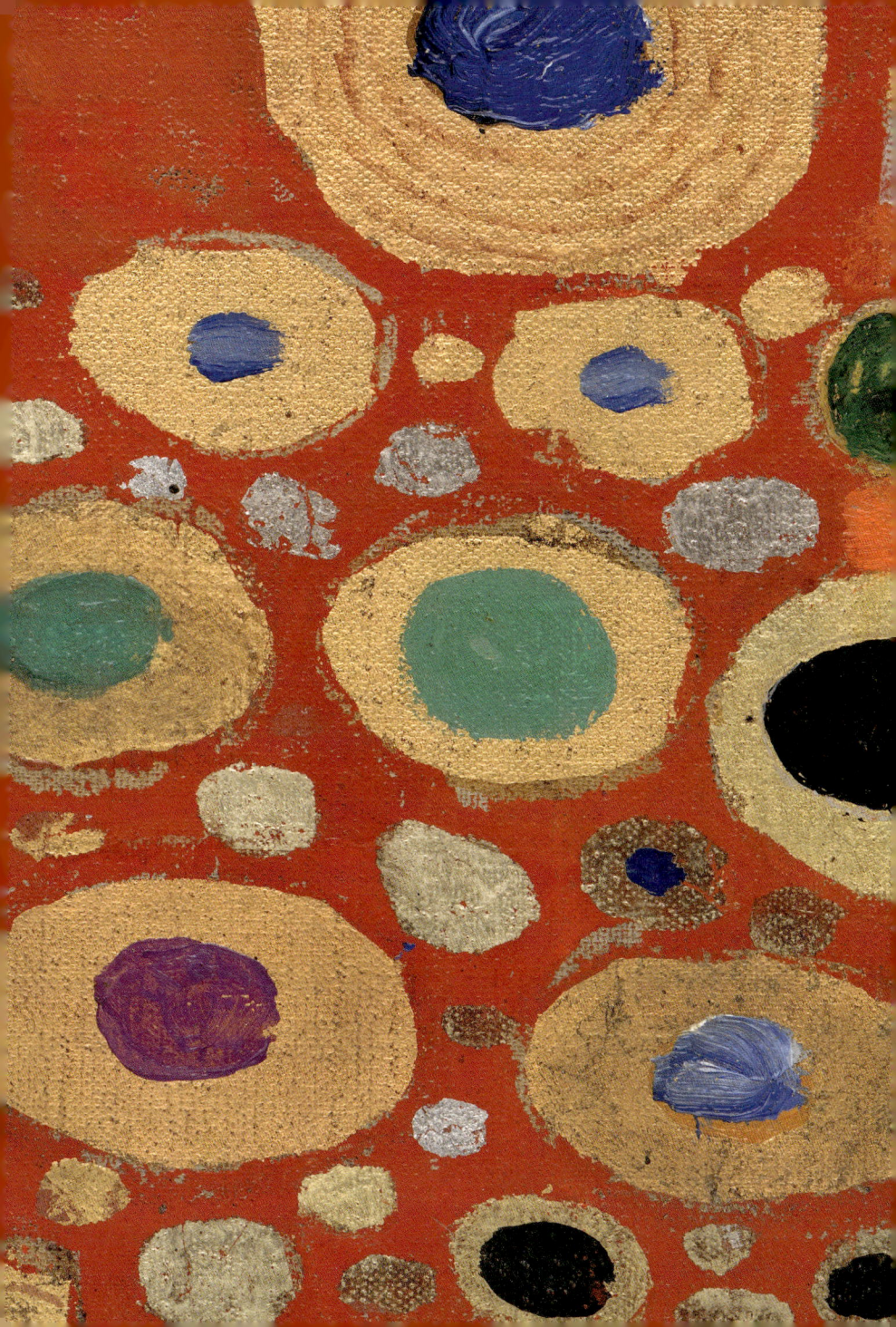

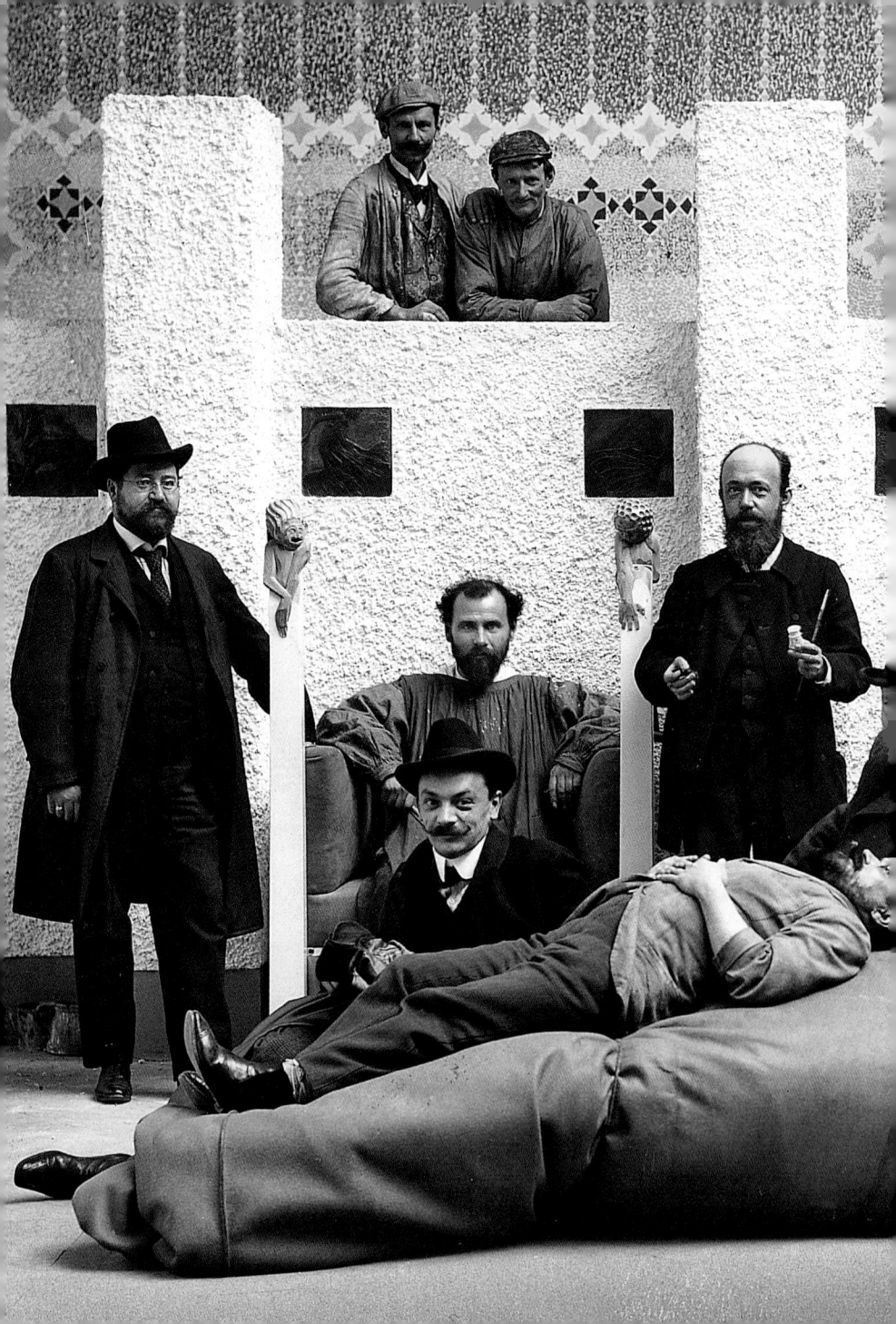

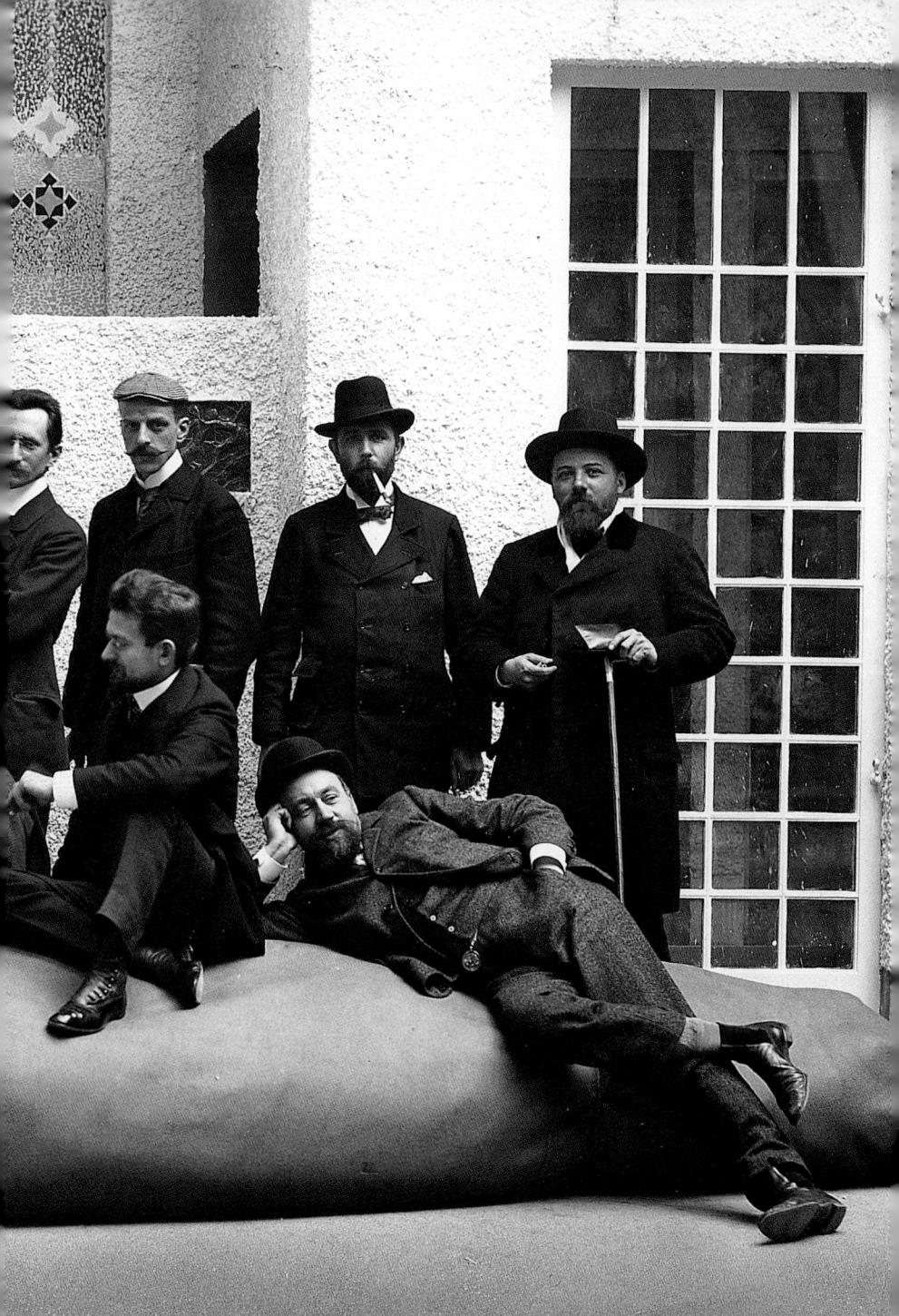

III.

The Stoclet frieze: an artificial garden in the heart of the house

Anette Freytag

"An artist only rarely has the opportunity to execute a work of art in which his imagination takes wing, his ideas become reality and his artistry is able to fully unfold. ... Amongst these houses, the Palais Stoclet gleams like a precious jewel of exquisite beauty amongst stones of lesser value."

A. S. LEVETUS, 1914

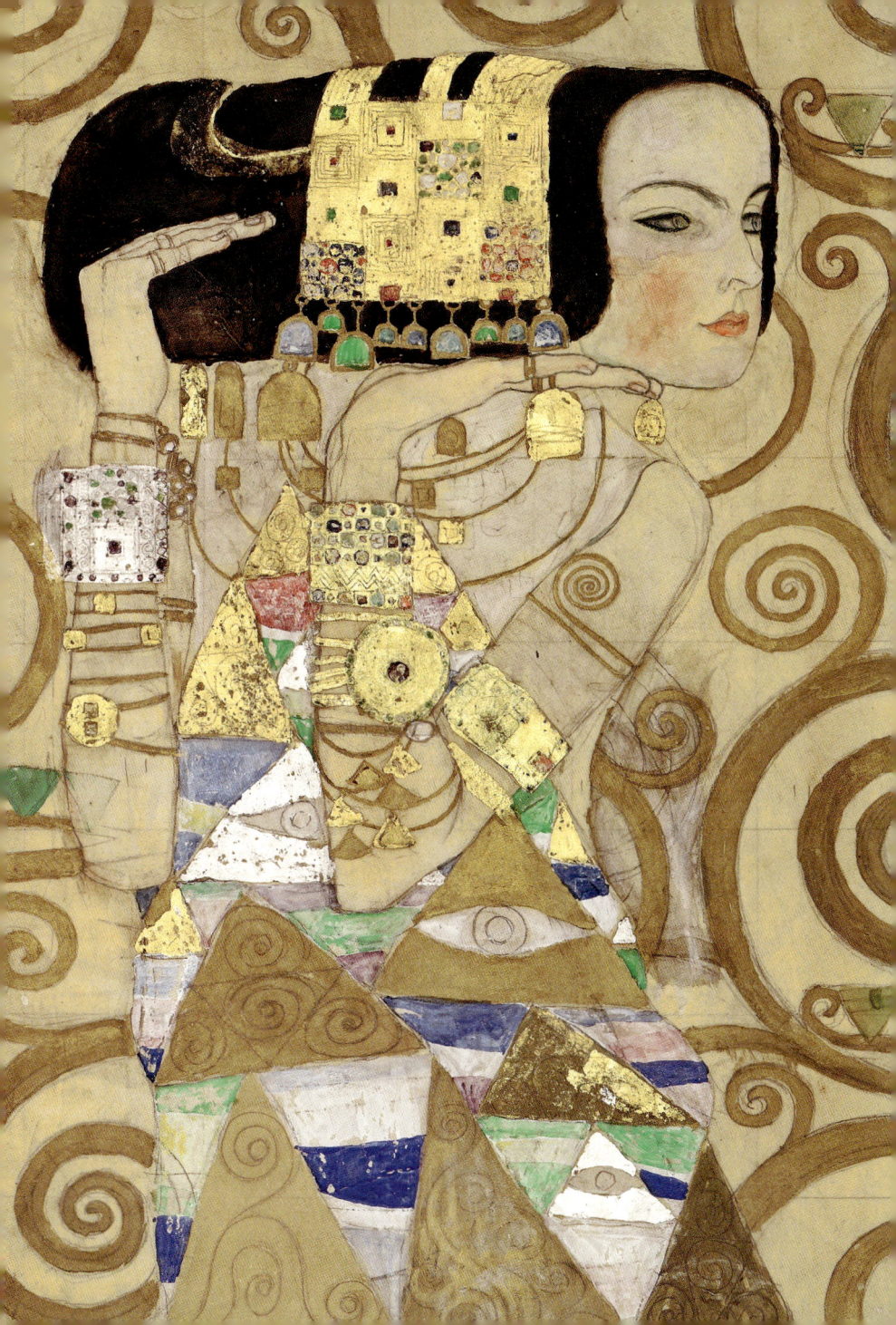

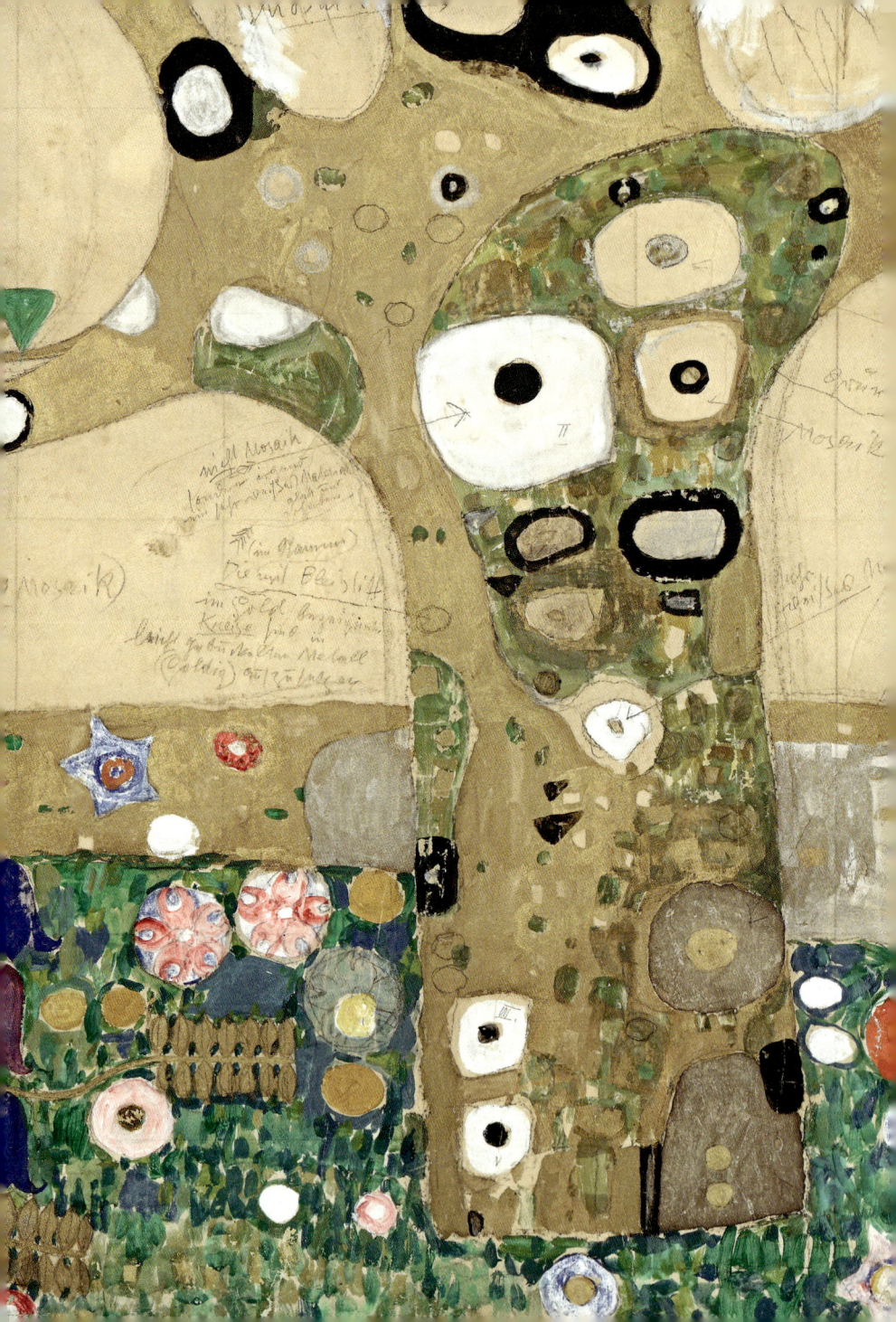

When an official party of Belgian architects visited the Palais Stoclet (1905–1911) in Brussels for the very first time, on 22 September 1912, the excitement amongst its members was great. Everything from the Palais Stoclet's ground plan to its silver spoons had been designed and executed by the Austrian architect Josef Hoffmann and the artists and craftsmen of the Wiener Werkstätte ('Viennese Workshop'). Amidst the historicist façades lining the elegant avenue de Tervuren, the entire ensemble of house, garden and interior – culminating in the dining room with the celebrated *Tree of Life* frieze by Gustav Klimt – struck the Belgian architects as belonging to another world (pp. 254/55). "I think I'm on the planet Mars!" exclaimed one of the architects in disbelief during his visit (Tekhne 1912, p. 802). Owing to the design of its façade, the cubic, fortress-like architecture exhibits a strangely floating character: the house is namely entirely faced in white marble slabs, which to the eye appear to be carried only by the narrow bronze bands surrounding them. The building was conceived by its architect as a stately city mansion – albeit with an unusually modern façade – when seen from the street.

Hoffmann had designed the house as a place to showcase the extensive art collection of its owners, the Belgian engineer and financier Adolphe Stoclet (1871–1949) and his art-loving wife, Suzanne Stevens (1874–1949). Seen from the garden behind the house, the city palace becomes a *villa suburbana* with its rear façade sculpturally modelled by bay windows, balconies and terraces (pp. 156/57). The Palais Stoclet might, therefore, be called a house with two faces, as it was intended to offer the large family all the advantages of a comfortable urban mansion *and* a country house at the same time. Nowhere in his concept for the Palais Stoclet did Josef Hoffmann reference any of the architectural traditions previously established in Belgium. It is not surprising, therefore, that the Belgian architects should view this foreign body with a mixture of scepticism and euphoria: "It's art, obviously, but an intellectual art" (Tekhne 1912, p. 802), as one of them pronounced.

If the building anticipated the sober Modernism of the 1920s in its exterior architecture and in the furnishing of the staff quarters (p. 170), the public rooms were decorated with extreme lavishness and the most expensive materials: "This is what Baudelaire dreamed of! A somewhat austere magnificence, marble and gold, cold and captivating" (Tekhne 1912, p. 802). This exclamation by one of the visitors in 1912 may well have referred directly to the three-part frieze by Gustav Klimt installed one year previously

Pages 151–152
Working drawings for the "Dancing Girl" ("Expectation") and the Stoclet frieze (details), 1910
Black chalk, watercolour and body colour, white body colour, gold leaf, silver and bronze gilt on transparent paper, each 195 x 120 cm / 76 ¾ x 47 ¼ in.
Vienna, MAK – Österreichisches Museum für angewandte Kunst/Gegenwartskunst

in the Palais Stoclet dining room – a work of marble inlay and a masterpiece of applied art that gives the invited guest the impression of dining in the middle of a sparkling, enchanted garden (pp. 188/89).

The interplay of Klimt's frieze, Hoffmann's architecture and the furnishings by the Wiener Werkstätte made this dining room one of the most famous interiors of the 20th century (Sekler 1982, p. 309). In programmatic terms, it expressed the goal of the Klimt faction that had broken away from the Vienna Secession in 1905: to permeate every sphere of human life with art (cf. Rainer 2006, p. 81). In the Palais Stoclet, this programme is omnipresent. The ensemble of house, interior and garden constitutes the most important work by Josef Hoffmann and the Wiener Werkstätte, and is their only work that survives today almost exactly as it was handed over to its patron in 1911. The Stoclet family have kept and lovingly cared for their unique home over four generations and continue to guard it jealously right up to today, so that it is not accessible to the public. The following essay is thereby intended to offer readers a brief glimpse into a world that for the moment remains closed to us in real life.

The *Tree of Life* frieze – a masterpiece by Klimt and the Wiener Werkstätte

Klimt chose for his frieze one of the oldest motifs: humankind's yearning for Paradise. Rising up each of the two long walls of the frieze is a golden tree of life, whose volute-shaped boughs scroll outwards above a colourful meadow of flowers to fill the entire mural field. Black Horus falcons are perched on some of the branches. Together with two rose bushes surrounded by fluttering butterflies, the flowering meadow and the trees of life create an artificial garden. At the north end of the dining room, the Knight – a powerful, abstract figure in a portrait-format mosaic – seems to watch over the scene, while the Dancing Girl, adorned in a lavishly ornamented dress and the finest jewellery, stands in the flowering meadow in front of the tree of life on the west wall, near the south-facing bay windows. Opposite her, on the east wall, a Pair of Lovers are wrapped in an embrace. The man's magnificent coat almost entirely envelops the delicate female figure clasping him in her flowery dress, as if he wished to devour her, something that infuses the garden motif and all its exoticism with an additional erotic note (pp. 214–219, 222, 223).

The frieze numbers amongst the major works of Klimt's 'golden period' and embodies the logical conclusion of his ornamental development (Zuckerkandl 1911), after the influence of the Greco-Spanish painter El Greco (1541–1614) – whose works Klimt had encountered on a trip to Paris and subsequently to Spain in the autumn of 1909 – had wrought a change in his art (Strobl 1991, p. 65). By this stage, Klimt had already produced the first design drawings for the frieze (pp. 200/01, 224/25; Murr 2012), however, and he would remain true to their style – even if reluctantly (Fischer 1987, pp. 178–182) – right up

to the full-scale working drawings completed around 1910 (pp. 151, 152, 159, 160,
167, 168, 177–179). Guided by the many
instructions written in Klimt's own hand
on the tracing paper used for the transfer
drawings, the Wiener Werkstätte began
the task of translating the designs into an
extremely wide var-iety of materials.

Klimt's collaboration with the
Wiener Werkstätte had intensified
following his joint resignation with
Hoffmann from the Vienna Secession.
Franz Blei (1871–1942), writing in the
magazine *Deutsche Kunst und Dekoration*
in 1906, credited Klimt with playing a
leading role in shaping the artistic character of the Wiener Werkstätte: "I believe
I see in Klimt the one who brings the

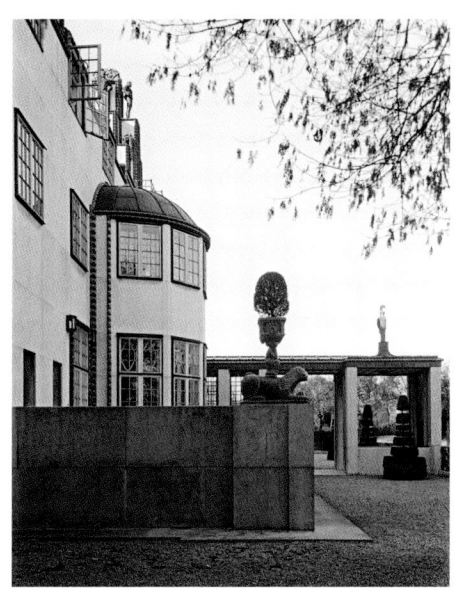

different natures of the Viennese masters into that singular commonality that is called the
Wiener Werkstätte style" (cit. from Sekler 1982, p. 94). Four years later, the critic Franz
Servaes (1862–1947) even pronounced: "Finally, in order to understand the latest Klimt
completely, one needs to know about his close relationship with Moser and Hoffmann's
'Wiener Werkstätte'" (cit. from Sekler 1982, p. 507, note 23).

Contemporaries admired the Oriental influence apparent in the finished frieze and
paid tribute to Vienna's historical role as Europe's portal to the East (Tekhne 1912, p. 802).
The influences of Persian (Tekhne 1912, p. 802), Far Eastern (Strobl 1991, p. 79) and Early
Christian (Weidinger 2007d, p. 132) art have all been identified in the mosaic frieze.
Klimt's fascination with Ancient Egyptian tomb art has also been discussed in the literature, in the analysis of the figure of the Dancing Girl, for example, and with regard to the
monumental mural decorations found in Ancient Egyptian burial chambers, which – it is
suggested – were a source of inspiration for Klimt (Weidinger 2007d, p. 127). Despite all

Josef Hoffmann, **Palais Stoclet, Brussels, view of the street entrance from the east**
Photograph, 1917/18. Bildarchiv Foto Marburg

Pages 156/57
Josef Hoffmann, **View of the garden façade of the Palais Stoclet**
Gelatin silver print, 1910. Bildarchiv Foto Marburg

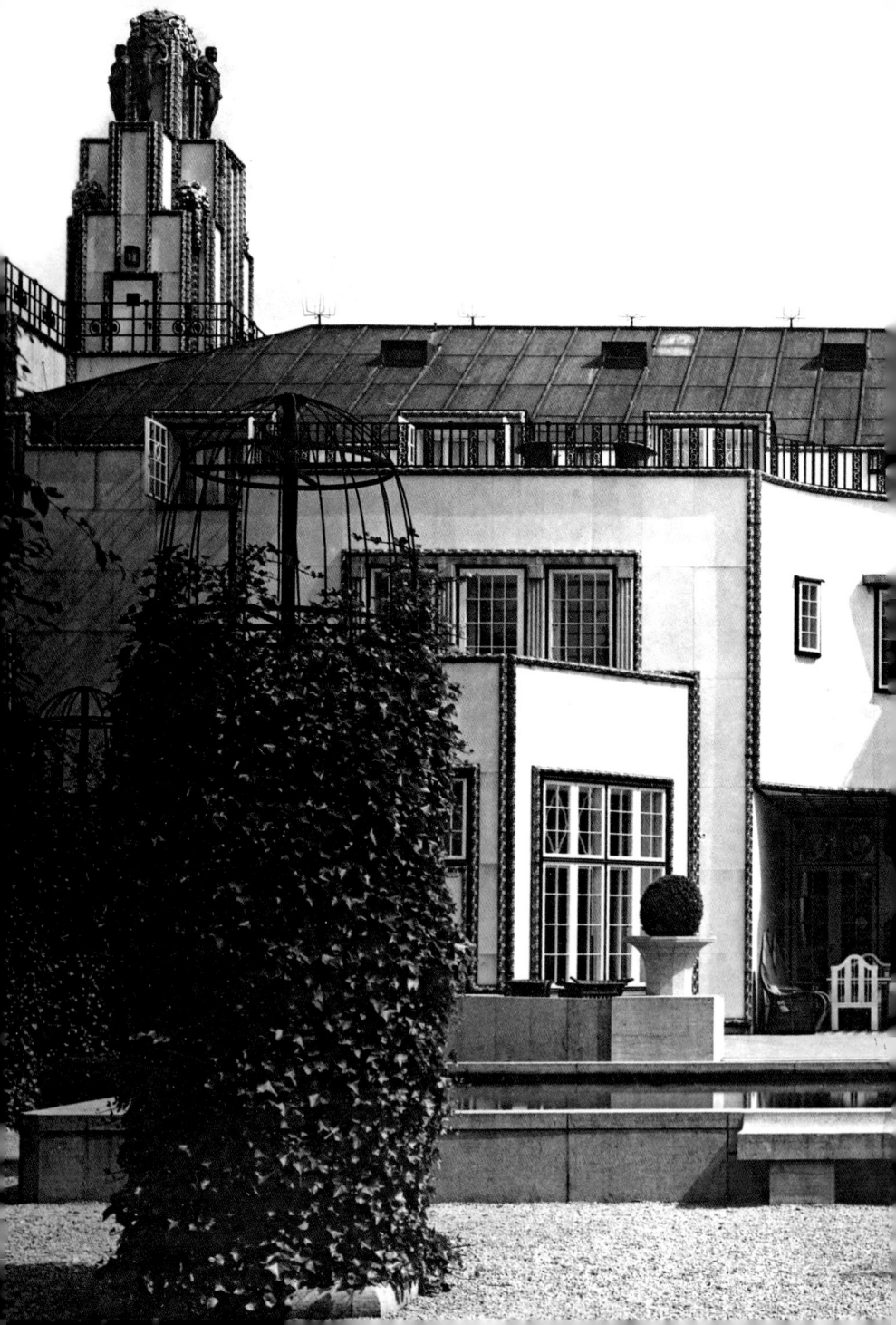

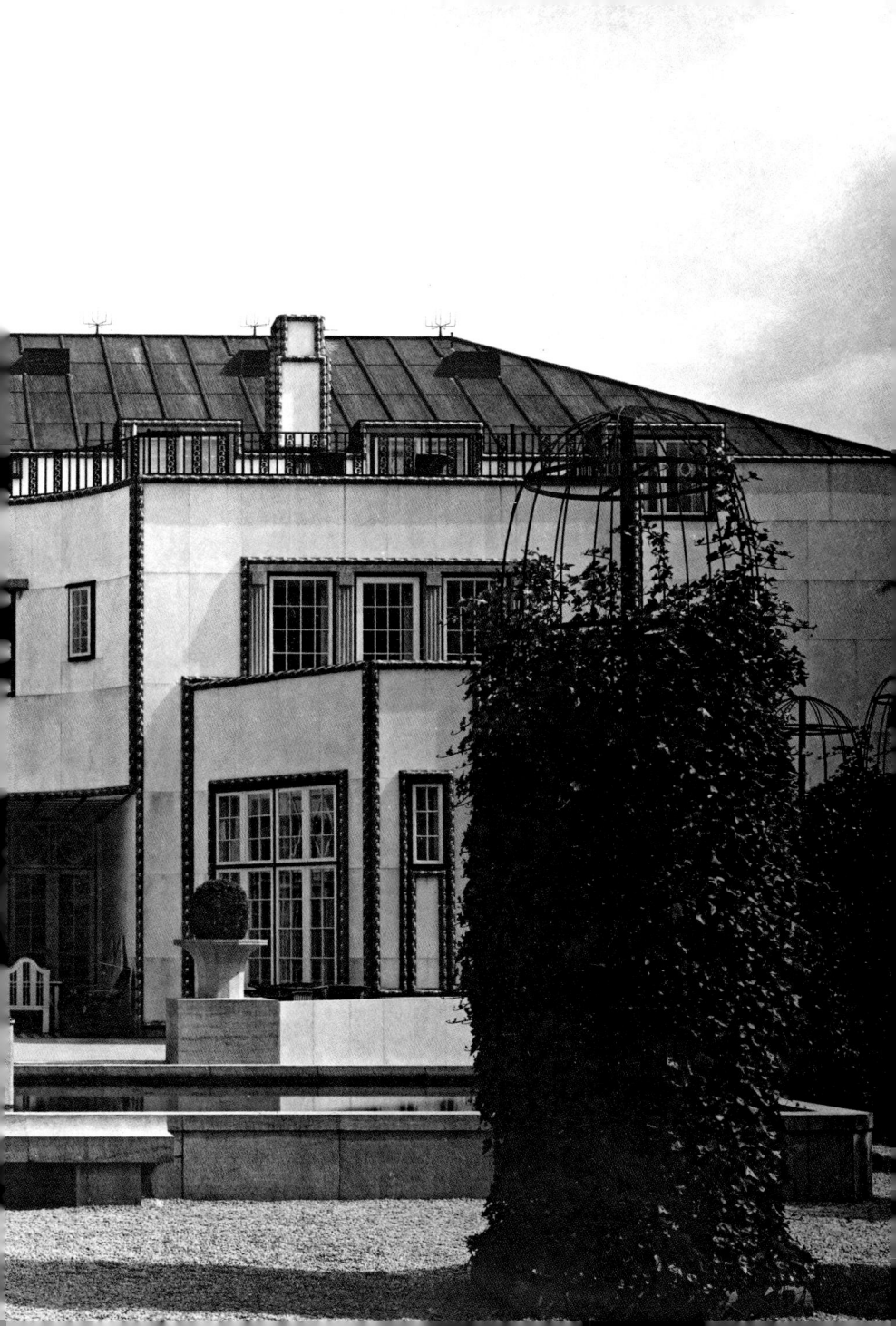

its stylistic, technical and symbolic borrowings, however, the mosaic frieze was admired as a work without compare by Klimt's contemporaries, including the art critic Berta Zuckerkandl (1864–1945), who in an article of 23 October 1911 in the *Wiener Allgemeine Zeitung* reported on the frieze's brief exhibition in front of a select Viennese audience prior to its transportation to Brussels: "Gustav Klimt was exacting in his requests. He demanded of his colleagues the utmost degree of technical perfection and of understanding and skill when it came to transferring his design. And the result may be appreciated all the more highly because nothing like it has ever been created before. Because there is no example, no point of reference for marble inlay work in the past; because the attempt to capture a picture of such unrivalled magnificence, of such a radiant warmth of colour on the wall, using precious items of stone, enamel, goldsmithery and even incrustations of real pearls, has never been ventured before. [...] The materials alone cost over 100,000 crowns, and the work itself took a year and a half to complete" (Zuckerkandl 1911).

The *Tree of Life* frieze for the Palais Stoclet occupies a special place both in Klimt's oeuvre and in the history of the Wiener Werkstätte. The cost of the materials employed in its manufacture amounted to twice the initial capital available to the Wiener Werkstätte at its foundation in 1903 (cf. Hoffmann 1972 [posthumous], p. 11). The three-part frieze consists of fifteen marble slabs, each measuring two metres (6 ft 6 in.) in height and one metre (3 ft 3 in.) in width. Each long wall is made up of seven marble slabs incorporating the tree-of-life motif, with the fifteenth marble slab appearing on the top wall and bearing the mosaic of the Knight. Those involved in the creation of the frieze on the basis of Klimt's drawings included not only the Wiener Werkstätte's own metal and goldsmithery workshop, but also the closely affiliated mosaic workshop of Leopold Forstner (1878–1936) and the Wiener Keramik ('Vienna ceramics') workshop of Bertold Löffler (1874–1960) and Michael Powolny (1871–1954), and the enamellists Adele von Stark (1859–1923) and Leopoldine König from the Vienna School of Applied Art (Zuckerkandl 1911; ÖBL, vol. 13, 2007, p. 105 f.).

The combination of their talents made it possible to translate Klimt's ideas into reality and to grant the mosaic frieze the magnificence that he had imagined for it (pp. 188/89, 190–195). Like the real items of jewellery crafted by the Wiener Werkstätte, the jewellery worn by the Dancing Girl is made of chased gold and other precious metals and set with

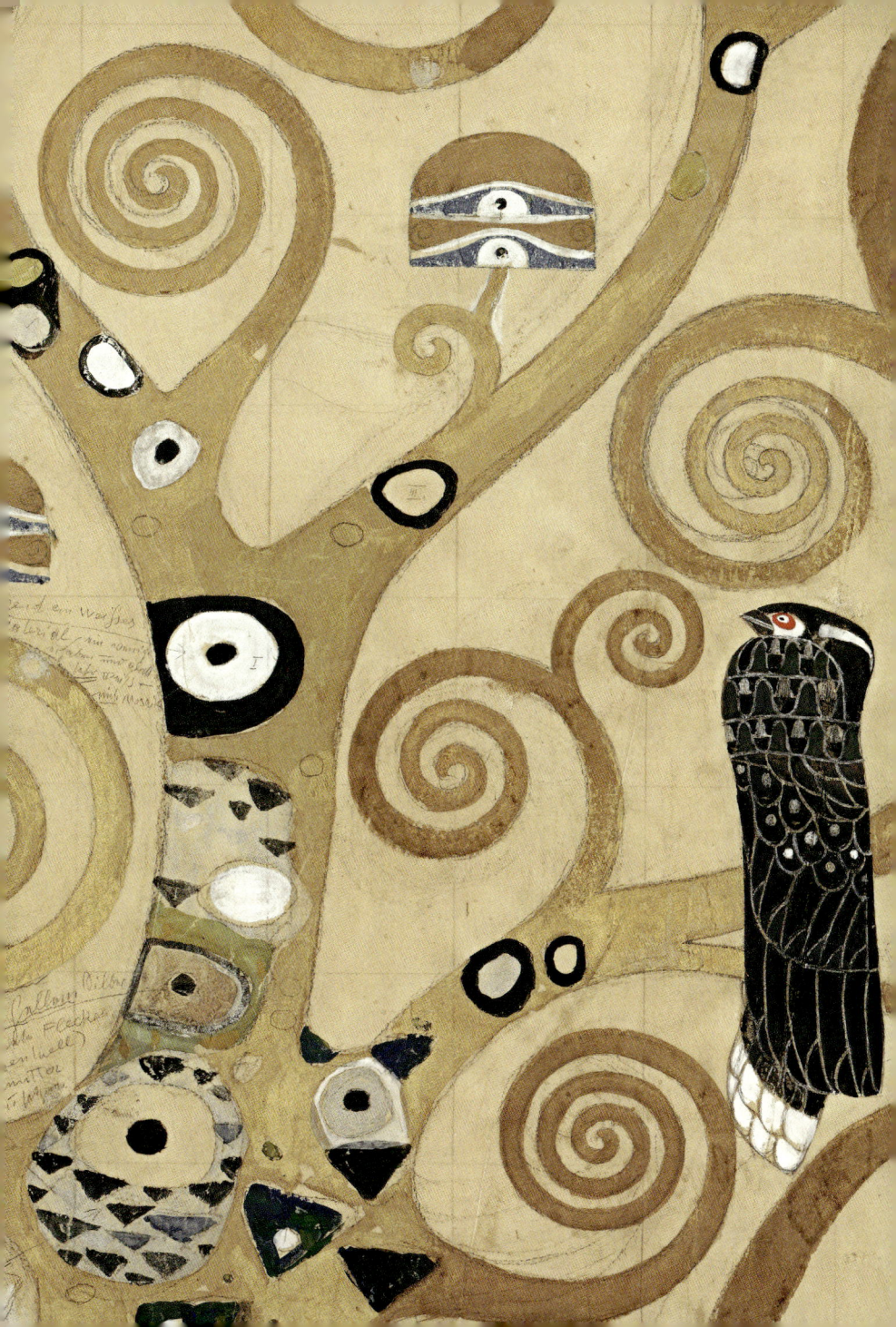

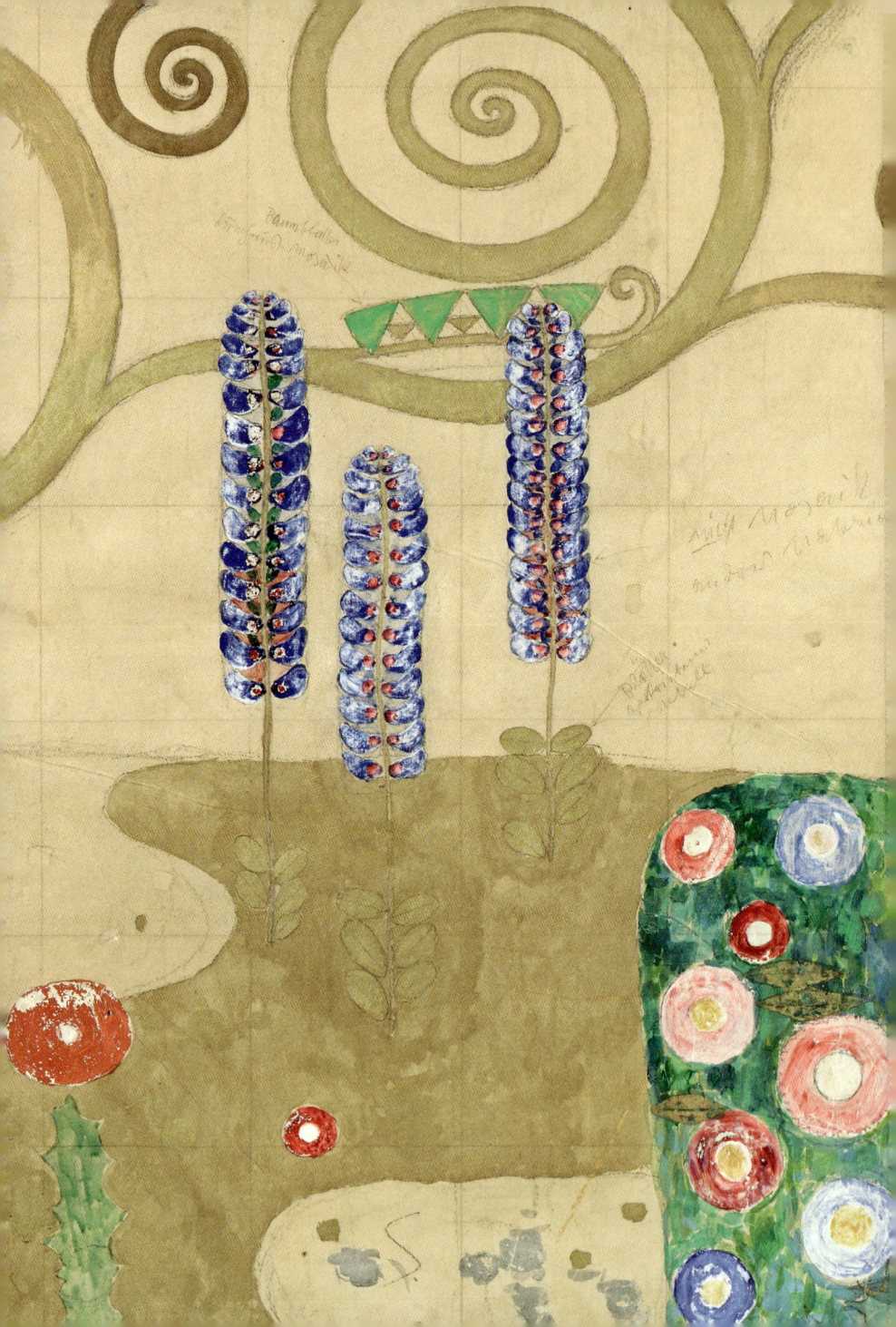

pearls and semi-precious stones (p. 203). The ground of the meadow, which is formed of small gold and silver mosaic pieces, also incorporates hundreds of colourful enamel flowers and blossoms, some of them on slender stems of chased metal. Similar stems also lend structure to the two rose bushes, whose countless green leaves of enamel and flower heads of white glass with petals delicately drawn in red appear to be strung out along metal branches. Like the 'eye flowers' blossoming all over the golden boughs of the trees, the black Horus falcons and the red and blue butterflies are created from ceramic with a colour glaze and are mounted on top of the mosaics inlaid into the marble slabs carrying the frieze as a whole. The surfaces of the mosaic walls are thus not flat but assume a pronounced relief as the materials of which they are composed slightly project or recede (cf. Sekler 1982, p. 92).

On the occasion of the presentation of the frieze in Vienna prior to its installation in Brussels, Berta Zuckerkandl also wrote about the challenges facing the individual workshops and the efforts they invested to live up to Klimt's vision: "Leopold Forstner, in whose mosaic workshop the frieze was created, […] was responsible for obtaining the various shades of gold, for correctly divining the rhythm of light and shade, which of course had to be conveyed completely differently in the actual material than in the coloured drawing. Forstner carried out the most laborious trials […] with eleven gold samples until he achieved the 'Klimtian' effect intended in the original. Miss von Starck also succeeded in producing a work of virtuosity. The rose bush bears some two hundred leaves, and the master's palette had found a different shade of green for each one. To express this in enamel, however, borders on the realm of the seemingly impossible. Particularly when one considers that the individual leaves are placed white-enamelled in the furnace and the process of chemical transformation has to be measured, guessed, intuited in advance. […] The ceramic details by Löffler and Powolny, however, such as the swarm of glittering butterflies and the sharply contoured silhouettes of the birds of prey, recall examples of Japanese art in their strict stylistic adherence to the law of the material, which nevertheless makes the 'skin of things' into surfaces filled with life" (Zuckerkandl 1911).

The collaboration between the various workshops reached one of its high points, lastly, in the colourful garments worn by the frieze's four figures: with their appliqués of coloured enamel and chased precious metal, they offer a dazzling display of inspired ideas for constructing figures out of ornament. Klimt thereby steers the possibilities of representing three-dimensional bodies on a flat surface clearly in the direction of abstraction. This can be plainly seen in the garments that almost entirely cover the bodies of the figures.

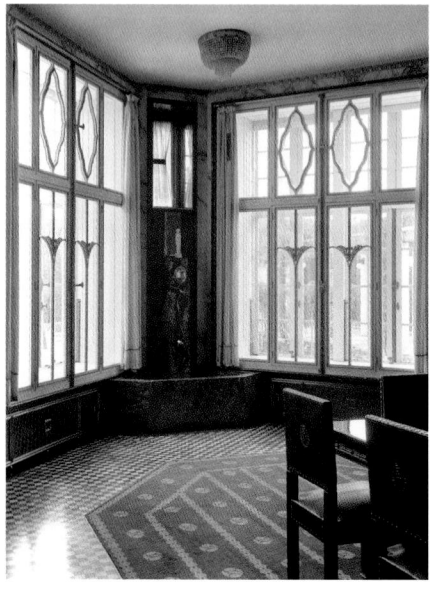

The interplay of frieze, architecture and furnishings

The integration of the frieze within the Stoclet dining room, and the interplay – jointly visualized by Gustav Klimt and the architect Josef Hoffmann – between the architecture of the room and the progression of the frieze, are also exemplary. The interior decoration is complemented by furniture made by the Wiener Werkstätte and by silverware that was specially designed for the dining room and is thereby related both to its architecture and its frieze. This can be seen most clearly of all in the massive silver candelabra, whose shapes take up the staggered geometric forms of the tower that rises above the Palais Stoclet. The candles burning in their holders cause the frieze to sparkle. Here we glimpse a design principle whose validity is confirmed by every closer analysis: in the Palais Stoclet, each element of the interior decoration is related to other architectural or artistic elements. In their interplay, they invariably point towards an overarching system of reference in which the individual elements are subordinated to a larger artistic whole.

This can also be seen in the layout of Klimt's frieze: as visitors, we enter the fourteen-metre (over fifteen-yard)-long dining room through a set of double doors leading from the hall into the top end of the room (pp. 188/89). Our eye moves first of all down the west wall, along Klimt's frieze, and after passing the rose bush and the tree of life arrives at the representation of the Dancing Girl. From here our gaze travels across the bay narrowing to an angle at the south end of the dining room and containing its only windows, and picks up the frieze on the opposite wall, beginning with the representation of the Pair of Lovers. Moving back up past the second tree of life, we arrive at the second rose bush, which – like a mirror image of the first rose bush on the opposite wall – provides the figures situated near the windows with a formal counterweight close to the door. The formal balance of

Josef Hoffmann
The windows of the main dining room; View of the marble fountain in the main hall
Photographs, 1917/18. Bildarchiv Foto Marburg

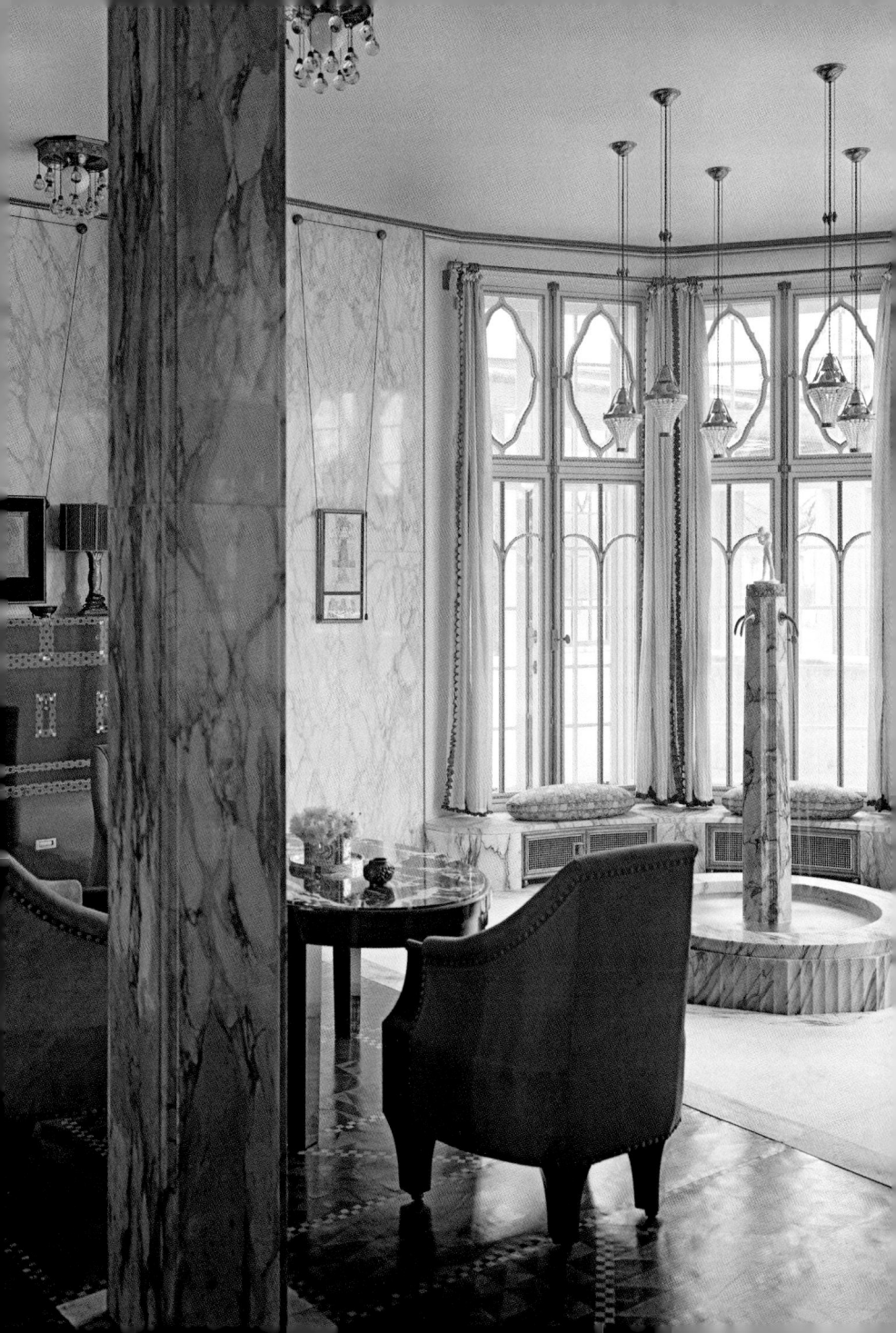

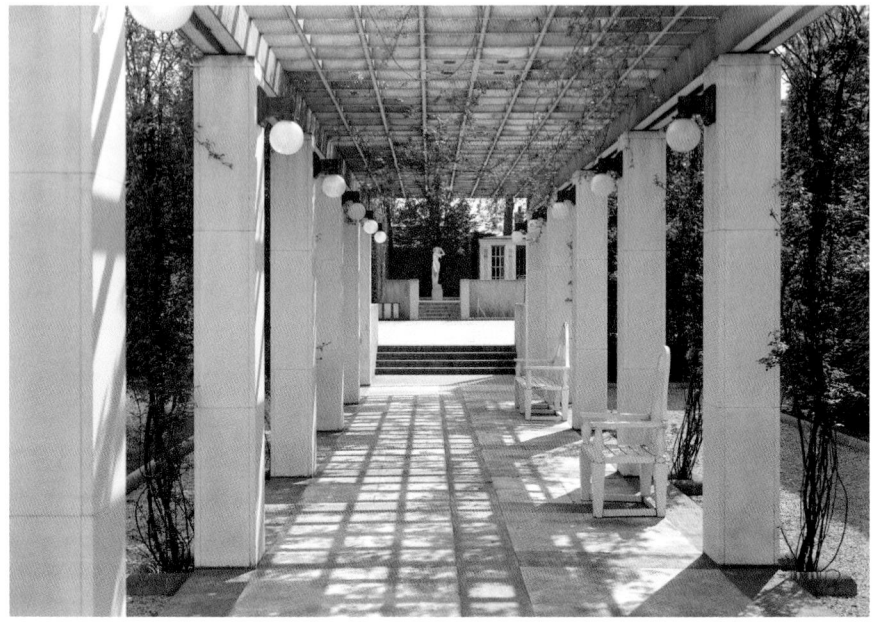

Josef Hoffmann, **Pergola in the Palais Stoclet garden**
Photograph, 1917/18. Bildarchiv Foto Marburg

the frieze with the tree scrolling across the entire mural field is thereby preserved. With their attention drawn first of all to the far end of the room by the long mosaic walls, visitors usually only notice the third mosaic, of the Knight, mounted on the north wall, once they have entered the dining room and turned around (pp. 240/41, 243–253).

Running beneath each of the two tree-of-life sections of the frieze is a strip of wall clad in slightly yellowish, richly veined Paonazzo marble. The individual slabs of marble are mounted in such a way that their veins converge symmetrically, resulting in particularly attractive and harmoniously balanced patterns throughout the room. The frieze – a work itself inlaid in marble – is slightly recessed behind the vertical plane of the wall zones faced in Paonazzo marble. Its appliqué and encrusted elements, on the other hand, project in low relief beyond this plane. The friezes are bounded on either side and underneath by a fine strip of copper beading. The upper edge of the frieze ends directly beneath the ceiling, which is painted white. The transition between wall and ceiling is provided by delicately ornamented, fire-gilt copper moulding (cf. Weidinger 2007d, p. 133), which runs right around the dining room and thereby links all the marble-faced walls and pillars and the windows and doors framed by marble (pp. 188/89, 212/13). This fine detail clearly shows how Hoffmann wanted his architecture to be read: as a self-contained room in which all the walls have the same hierarchy, as found in Baroque church interiors. At the same time, the dining room is divided into three parts by the rhythmic organization of the successive spheres of "entrance zone with stepped walls and Knight mosaic on the short wall – long walls with table in the centre – window niche with marble fountain" (see Sekler 1982, p. 309). The movement of our eyes as we study the frieze, and the actual movement of the visitor inside the room, both trace a circular path: steered by the motifs within the frieze, our eyes travel anticlockwise along the individual mural fields, while the guest walks around the monumental dining table in the centre of the room and back to the entrance area.

The gold border on the ceiling is not the only design detail contributing to the overall impression conveyed by the dining room. Positioned beneath the two long sections of Klimt's mosaic frieze, which are mounted relatively high, are two sideboards of black Portovenere marble with doors of dark Macassar ebony, which thereby serve as a sort of elongated plinth for the pictorial fields above them. Both the marble and the wood are polished to a mirror finish. At Stoclet family banquets, the silverware with its green malachite detailing handcrafted by the Wiener Werkstätte – fruit bowls, silver dishes, trays, food warmers, candelabra and much else besides – is laid out on the marble shelves and buffet tops. All these objects are reflected in the pale and dark marble surfaces and, depending on the fall of the light, seem to double and triple in number.

Alongside such optical tricks, however, the dining room's design also takes account of the practical aspects of modern life. Thus Hoffmann made provision for numerous sockets in the marble walls above the buffet, from where the electric hotplates could draw their current. An electricity supply was by no means a standard feature of a private home in 1911, and no more was a central heating system, which Hoffmann concealed beneath the sills of the dining-room windows (p. 162). The marble panel with the Knight, lastly, is underpinned by an artfully carved table whose diameter was exactly matched to the width of the mosaic (pp. 240/41). Two black leather chairs stand one on either side of the table. This third section of the frieze is framed most clearly of all, however, by the marble panels that clad the mural fields immediately to the right and left of the Knight. These wall zones are stepped twice as they approach the portrait, and for this part of the room, Hoffmann sought out slabs of marble whose veins – when the panels are mounted in symmetrical fashion – form two almost concentric circles. Klimt's Knight appears at the centre of these circles and is thereby set off to particular advantage.

Dramatic effects of this kind are typical of the interplay of architecture, art and furnishings in the dining room. For just as the silverware is mirrored in the marble walls, so Klimt's mosaics are reflected in the highly polished top of the long dining table, which forms the central element in the dining room. The tabletop is inlaid with intarsia employing the most precious woods and its sides feature hand-carved decorative designs. The table legs are crafted with equal artistry from solid ebony. The table is so big that it had to be delivered in pieces and assembled by the Wiener Werkstätte craftsmen *in situ* (Hotermans 2006, p. 379). When all the places are laid, twenty-two people can sit down to dine. As we are told by the Stoclet family, as head of the household, Adolphe Stoclet always sat at the top end of the table, beneath Klimt's mosaic of the Knight. The chairs are upholstered in black leather that is secured by means of gold grooves. The chair legs, like the table legs, are carved from solid ebony and the leather backs of the chairs carry a circular, gold-embossed emblem on both sides. This ornamental motif is taken up within the beige pattern of the aubergine carpet on which the long table and the many chairs stand. The carpet itself lies on top of the dining room's actual floor, namely a mosaic of small, square tiles of black and white marble (pp. 188–190). The square was Hoffmann's most important shape and his architectural module. He drew all his designs on squared paper and established the rhythm of his buildings on this basis (cf. Sekler 1967, p. 229). Black and white squares were at the same time the means by which he sought to develop a form that denied itself all historicist references, and which would thus pave the way to a new modernity for his architecture. Facing the black-and-white mosaic floor from overhead is the dining room's bare white ceiling – the second ultramodern element of this interior. For in Hoffmann's day, leaving the ceiling as a plain white expanse was an unusual and bold aesthetic choice. The dining-room floor and ceiling serve as a foil that heightens the impact of the golden mosaics by Klimt; in the simplicity of their own palette and formal vocabulary, they establish a deliberate contrast to the frieze and offer us, as viewers, a respite from the lavishness of Klimt's pictures and the wealth of their motifs. After refreshing ourselves in the monotony of their white and black-and-white, we can then resume our study of the walls.

The most important element in this interplay of architecture, art and furnishings, however, is light: just as it was for light that mosaics were invented and created in the first place, so every detail of the dining room of the Palais Stoclet took account of light and its possible reflections. This multiplication of light via mosaics has a long tradition that goes right back to the art of Ancient Egypt, Byzantium and Early Christianity. Although mosaics reflect the daylight, their most important function is to reflect candlelight.

Pages 167–168
Working drawings for Stoclet frieze (details), 1910
Black chalk, watercolour and body colour, white body colour, gold leaf, silver
and bronze gilt on transparent paper, 195 x 120 cm / 76 ¾ x 47 ¼ in.
Vienna, MAK – Österreichisches Museum für angewandte Kunst/Gegenwartskunst

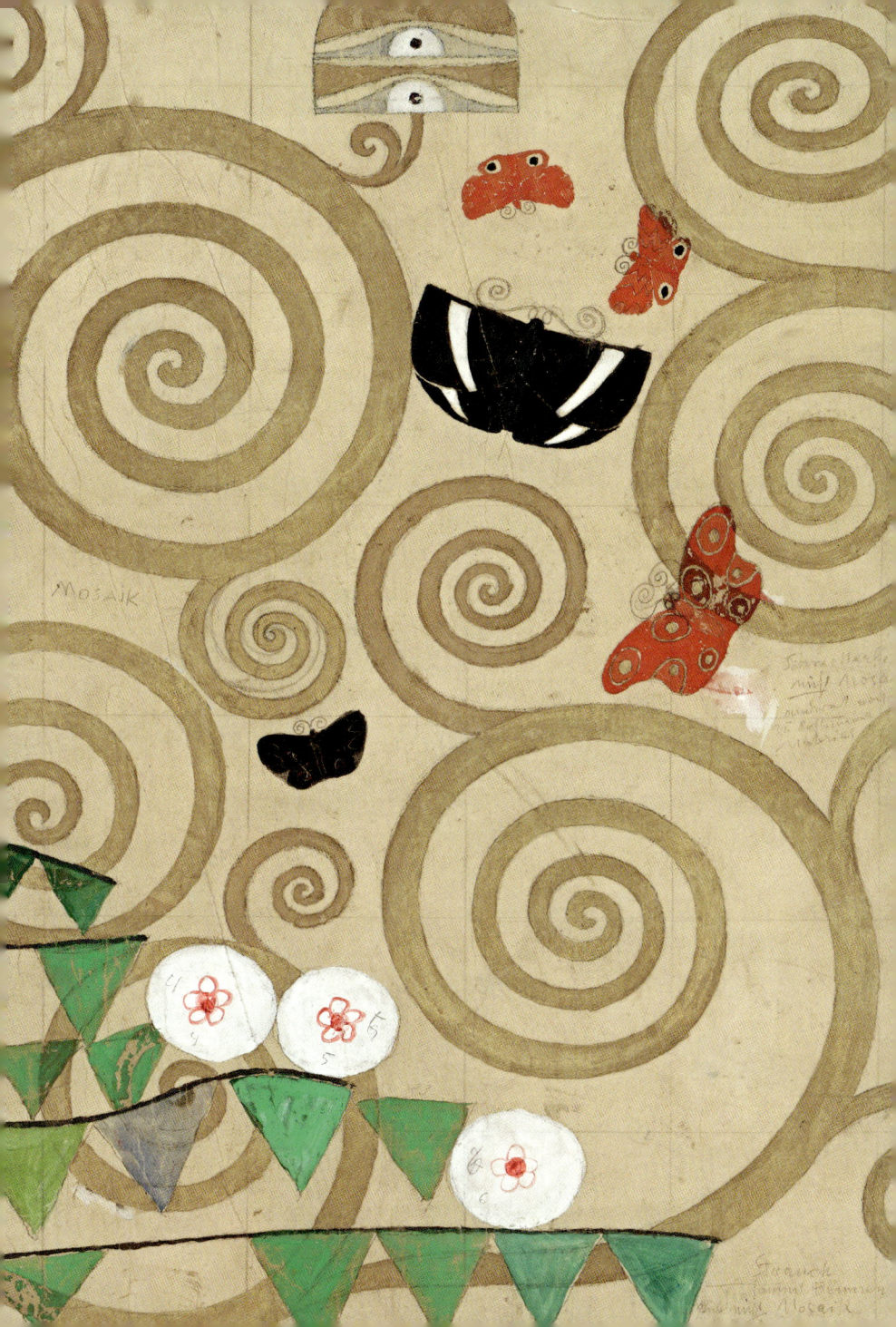

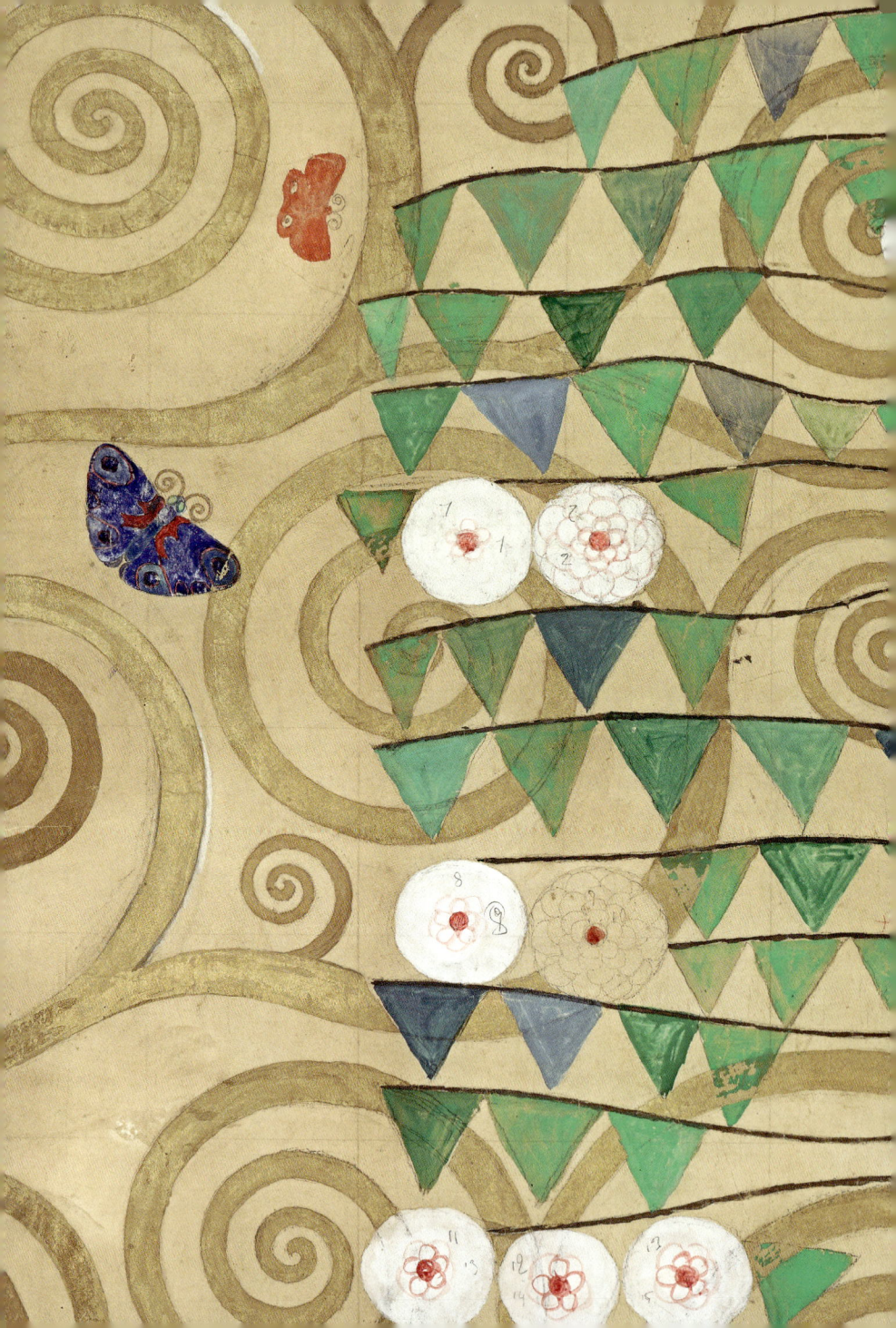

The dining room by day: the artificial garden and the real garden

The dining room, which measures a full fourteen metres (over fifteen yards) in length, has only one source of natural light: the three south-facing bay windows. These windows form part of the rear façade of the Palais Stoclet, with its oriels, balconies and terraces looking onto the garden (pp. 156/57). The two lateral windows catch the morning and evening sun, respectively. Inside the dining room, this means that the Dancing Girl in Klimt's mosaic sparkles in the morning sun and the Pair of Lovers in the evening sun. Leaving aside such magical optical effects, this is interesting from a symbolic point of view, too. By taking account of the fall of the light onto both long walls, Klimt and Hoffmann seem to have wanted to place the interplay of art and architecture in a grander cosmic context. The Dancing Girl is also known in the literature under the epithet of Expectation, and the Pair of Lovers as Fulfilment, whereby the motifs are respectively equated with Yearning and the Pair of Lovers in Klimt's *Beethoven Frieze* (Natter 2012, Cat. 141; cf. Bisanz-Prakken 1977, pp. 47–49); these epithets were not supplied by Klimt himself, however (cf. Strobl 1991, p. 87).

The third window lies directly opposite the portrait of the Knight, but is too far away for the natural light entering through it to produce any light effects in this section of the frieze. The tall rectangular window and the tall rectangular mosaic panel are positioned opposite each other like mirrors, although the frieze panel is much larger than the window. Placing the Knight on the axis of the central window, offering – from the perspective of the Knight – a view straight out onto the Stoclets' real garden, is interesting when we consider the genesis of the work. In Klimt's first design for the frieze, the raiment making up the body of the Knight contains what would later become the rose bush, with black birds of prey perched on its branches (see pp. 196–198). Given that almost all the sketches for the Palais Stoclet frieze were executed in the Villa Oleander on Lake Attersee, this early version of the garment worn by the Knight has recently been interpreted as the view of an imaginary landscape. The lake and its natural surroundings, so it is argued, were thereby profoundly important not just for Klimt's landscape paintings but also for this frieze (Weidinger 2007d, p. 122). The distinctive silhouette of the pollarded lime trees along the shore of Lake Attersee, for example, may have provided Klimt with inspiration for the spreading forms of his tree of life (Strobl 1991, p. 71; Weidinger 2007d, p. 122).

Rather than as a view of a landscape, however, we might also read the rose bush with its black birds of prey in the Knight's garment as a garden motif, because human art plays a much more decisive role in the garden than in the cultural landscape, and because Klimt's Knight – as we shall show below – is a symbol of the artist who ennobles life through art. This reading is supported by the fact that the garden motif formulated in

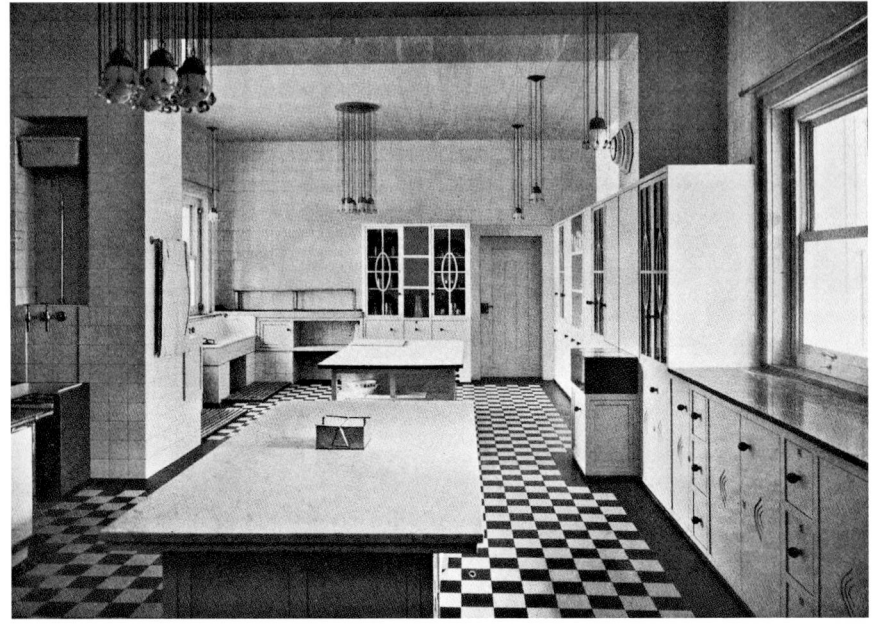

Josef Hoffmann, **View of the kitchen in the Palais Stoclet**
From: *Moderne Bauformen*, vol. 13 (1914), p. 28

this early design is pursued in the newly introduced trees of life in all subsequent design drawings for the frieze. Thus the black Horus falcons now perch in the tree of life, while the rose bush stands alone to one side, an element equally as important as the figures.

This separation of motifs was linked with a change in the layout of the dining room itself, as Hoffmann's plans for the Palais Stoclet evolved. In an unrealized ground-plan design of 1904/05, Hoffmann had visualized the dining room running parallel to the garden façade on an east-west axis. Klimt's frieze was correspondingly destined for the dining room's north wall, facing the south wall with its windows overlooking the garden (cf. Weidinger 2007d, p. 122, fig. 7). Hoffmann's subsequent alignment of the dining room along the north-south axis led Klimt to divide his frieze into three sections. While the garden motif was restated in the long walls via the trees of life and the flowering meadow in which they are rooted, the rose bush disappeared from the raiment of the Knight. This latter now looks directly out towards the Stoclet family's real garden, however, where the flower beds in front of the dining room are home to rose trees and evergreens.

Klimt's artificial garden is linked with the Palais Stoclet's real garden in multiple respects. Hoffmann, who was a great lover of latticework structures covered with tall climbing plants, designed highly distinctive trellises for the Stoclet garden: sixteen cylindrical wire supports, ending in a rounded top like Klimt's mosaic rose bushes and overgrown with ivy, surround the central pond in front of the house (pp. 156/57). Beside them to the left and right are two rose beds with tall rose trees. These are flanked to the east and west by pergolas supported by marble columns and overgrown with climbing roses (p. 164). The tower of the Palais Stoclet is topped, lastly, by a bronze crown of roses and laurel, probably an allusion to the cupola of the Vienna Secession building and a motif that reappears in several sculptures in the garden.

The symbolism of the Garden of Eden and its heathen pendant, the Golden Age, in which it is forever spring, appears regularly throughout the ensemble of house, garden and interior in a variety of ways (cf. Freytag 2010, pp. 362–365). Jugendstil defined itself as a *Ver sacrum*, a "sacred spring" dawning for the art of the young generation. After their split from the Vienna Secession, Gustav Klimt and Josef Hoffmann considered themselves the heralds of this sacred spring and the Stoclet couple wanted to assist their art to blossom – fully in the spirit of a humanistic ideal. The common motifs and forms linking the never-fading artificial garden at the heart of the house and the evergreen garden in front of its windows may be understood only in this context. The figure of Klimt's Knight thereby plays a particular role as it 'watches over' both.

The knight as artist, the artist as saviour

The architectural historian Eduard F. Sekler (1920–2017), who considers the long walls of the dining room to show "a garden of pleasure and love […] with divine Horus falcons", recognized the importance of the portrait of the Knight for deciphering Klimt's artistic programme on the basis of its architectural setting on the end wall: "through its position in a shallow, doubly recessed niche, the feeling is inevitably aroused of finding oneself in a zone of transition between two worlds, as in the case of a fake door in an Egyptian mastaba or the niches of Ancient Mesopotamian sacred buildings. If we should one day succeed in fathoming the meaning of the abstract composition, we shall understand what it was that here, in the most shielded place in the room's interior, Klimt wanted to confront the guests with at their communal meal" (Sekler 1982, p. 94). A clue was provided by Klimt himself in a picture postcard of the dining room that he sent to Emilie Flöge from Brussels on 18 May 1914. In it, he first of all praised the "very, very" beautiful house and then the garden, "much more beautiful than expected", before "fervently" recalling the time he had spent with her in "Kammerl", where he had produced the preliminary drawings for the frieze. He concluded by commenting on the dining room as it appears on the postcard: "This photograph gives a poor picture, too. My poor 'Knight' looks completely black and green. The pattern on his robe is much too 'lumpy' but the alteration in the metal [vis-à-vis the original] is not bad. I should have done some things differently; it would have been better if the Werkstätte had done a lot of things *differently*. The wall could have taken a lot more gold! HEARTIEST greetings, GVS" (ÖNB Bildarchiv inv. no. 800 369B). On the basis of this picture postcard, what Sekler had understood as an "abstract composition", Klimt expert Alice Strobl was able to identify as a further development of the figure of the knight, one that had already been of key importance for the symbolism of the *Beethoven Frieze* of 1902: "In the Beethoven Frieze it was shown how the Knight helps people subjected to the trials of suffering to overcome evil and with the help of art to arrive at pure bliss, whereby we are dealing with a secularized ideology of salvation. […] In the case of the Palais Stoclet, it was first and foremost a question of creating an exceptionally beautiful world permeated by all the arts, a *Gesamtkunstwerk* [total work of art], and thus of turning the Jugendstil ideal into reality. The creator of this paradise was the artist, the knight. That it could only be an earthly paradise, however, is signalled by the apotropaic flowers of the trees of life with their ornament of eyes warding off ill, which are intended to protect against evil, against death, here embodied in the birds of prey" (Strobl 1991, p. 87).

The suggestion that credit for achieving Jugendstil's aim of transcending everyday life belongs to the artist alone, however, is wide of the mark. The Knight in the Palais Stoclet was a product of the Wiener Werkstätte workshops and Klimt's collaboration with them was hallmarked by a common programme. In the renewal of the arts, handicraft was attributed with a particular power. The Wiener Werkstätte's artistic programme was therefore also a socio-political one, in two ways: on the one hand, the Wiener Werkstätte took a stand against the industrial manufacture of goods and against the poor working conditions suffered by factory workers. On the other, it wanted to improve the lives of its customers, in the profound conviction that the quality and beauty of its products would have an impact on those using them on a daily basis (cf. *Arbeitsprogramm der Wiener Werkstätte* 1905, in Noever 2003). The Wiener Werkstätte's unattained goal was to manufacture not just for the privileged, but to allow all strata of society to enjoy these good and beautiful products. The involvement of the Wiener Werkstätte in the Palais Stoclet consequently extended not only to the public and living areas but also to the kitchen and the staff quarters (p. 170). Art historian Werner Hofmann (1928–2013) recognized the profound connection between these two objectives: "This total aestheticization of all spheres of life invoked the authenticity of the past, the not yet corrupted formal language of the craftsman. The consumer was to live conscious of taste. This meant […] that the [Wiener Werkstätte] wished to liberate him from the 'hostile powers' of anonymous mass-produced goods (in which evil had assumed secularized form!). This ambitious, salvationist aim once again

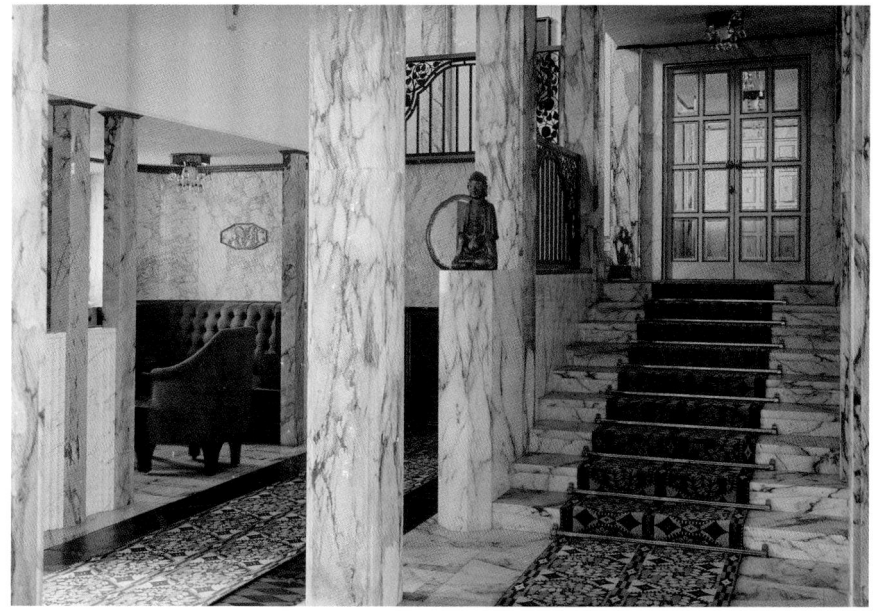

Josef Hoffmann, **View of the main hall with stairs leading up to the first floor**
Photograph, 1917/18. Bildarchiv Foto Marburg

assigned 'comfort' the great importance that the word originally held in English, when it meant consolation for the soul" (Hofmann 1983, p. 88 f.).

A marble wall incorporating electrical sockets, a central heating system to keep guests warm while they ponder the symbolism of the golden mosaics studded with pearls and semi-precious stones: in the Palais Stoclet dining room, the comforts of modern life are linked with the solace that can be provided by an art following bourgeois educational ideals. In the gleam of Gustav Klimt's artificial garden, the Palais Stoclet is transformed into the "dream house" that philosopher and sociologist Walter Benjamin (1892–1940) attributed with the quality of serving as a place of refuge in an alternative world, as a shelter and envelope that protected its inhabitants from the increasingly rapid pace of life in the modern metropolis, while the world outside the façades of such dream houses was arming itself for the First World War (Teyssot 2011). For Benjamin, the "dream house" was a phenomenon of the turn of the century and the opening years of the 20th century. There is little that conjures the atmosphere evoked by Benjamin as accurately as the dining room of the Palais Stoclet by night, when electric light and candlelight mingle.

The dining room by night – the Palais Stoclet as "dream house"

In the artificial light of the Lobmeyr chandeliers hanging from the ceiling and the light issuing from the candles burning in Hoffmann's silver candelabra standing on the marble buffet and in the candleholders by artist Carl Otto Czeschka (1878–1960) mounted on the marble walls in front of gilt reflectors, Klimt's frieze seems to come to life. Each flicker of the light leaves a glittering trail in its reflection in the mosaics. The inlaid squares of gold and silver, the semi-precious stones, mother-of-pearl, ceramics, pearls and chased precious metals sparkle and shine in an enthralling manner. This scintillating effect is reinforced by the silverware, all designed by the Wiener Werkstätte, mirrored in the polished marble wall below the frieze and in the black marble of the buffet. Through these reflections, the silver candelabra, the hotplates and tureens seem to triple in number! The entire scenario becomes an unreal experience.

Adolphe and Suzanne Stoclet's children and grandchildren called the Palais Stoclet "La maison enchantée" – the enchanted house. While the Dancing Girl sparkled in the dining room, real dance performances were staged in the music room with its raised stage on the opposite side of the main hall. Nocturnal offerings such as a performance by the famous Indian dancer Nyota Inyoka in front of a statue of a Khmer dancer from the Stoclet's art collection were unique experiences that one of their granddaughters still remembers vividly (Freytag 2006, p. 360). Around the turn of the century, dance was considered to be the expression of a heightened sense of aliveness, indeed as a symbol of life itself, one that drew force from a blurring of boundaries. "Life is a woman who dances and who would cease divinely to be a woman if she could obey her bound up to the skies." Thus Socrates in an imaginary philosophical dialogue composed in 1923 by the French writer Paul Valéry (1871–1945). "But just as we can go on to infinity neither in dream nor in waking, so she likewise always becomes herself again; ceases to be snowflake, bird, idea; ceases, *in fine*, to be all that it pleases the flute that she should be; for the same Earth which sent her forth calls her back and returns her, all breathless, to her woman's nature and to her friend […]" (Valéry 1923, cit. from English edn. of 1956, p. 31).

To transcend and to alter reality – whether through the sound of a flute, the movements of a dancer, a frieze that appears to come to life under artificial light or through the beautiful gleam of silverware – ranked amongst the primary goals of the Klimt Group. According to Werner Hofmann, where "utility items are handled like works of art, each and every activity [assumes] a ceremonial aura: the whole of everyday life becomes a ritual" (Hofmann 1983, p. 89). Adolphe and Suzanne Stoclet lived such rituals, as their contemporaries remembered: "It goes without saying that the flowers – always in different shades of one colour – on the table and Monsieur Stoclet's tie were always chosen to match Madame's outfit," wrote one friend of the family of their appearance as hosts (de Bruyn

1949, p. 3). The descriptions provided by contemporary witnesses regularly emphasize the unique harmony between the house, its objects and its occupants; it seemed to govern even the smallest details of the décor and the lives of the Stoclets and supposedly extended even to the splashing of the water in the marble fountains (cf. Lion-Goldschmidt 1956, p. XIV).

What was achieved in the Stoclet house and garden, in other words, was a perfect theatrical staging not just of indoor rooms and outdoor spaces, but also of people. Adolphe and Suzanne Stoclet were thereby ideally suited for the leading roles they would play in their own home. Their open-mindedness and their generosity as hosts meant that the Palais Stoclet soon became a meeting point for the most creative personalities of the day: Karl Ernst Osthaus, Serge Diaghilev, Jean Cocteau, Anatole France, Sacha Guitry, Darius Milhaud, Robert Mallet-Stevens, the Pitoëffs and many others were visitors to the house, as we know from their entries in the Stoclets' guestbook.

Adolphe and Suzanne Stoclet were willing to dedicate their lives to the realization of the ideals of the Klimt Group. They had the financial means to do so and disposed, too, of the necessary discipline demanded by daily life in such a "dream house". As was emphasized in an obituary of the couple, who died in 1949, "such puritan magnificence" demanded an "ascetic lifestyle", because the Palais Stoclet as Hoffmann and the Wiener Werkstätte had delivered it to its patrons was complete and would not stand the addition of "family souvenirs, New Year gifts or tombola prizes" (cf. de Bruyn 1949, p. 3).

All these things the family had to do without, at least in the rooms designed for public entertaining. Instead, the Stoclets had to submit to what the architect Adolf Loos (1870–1933) condemned as the dictates of art in his parable *Von einem armen reichen Manne* ('Of a Poor Rich Man') published in 1900. With regard to life in the Palais Stoclet, certain passages in Loos's satire seem almost visionary. In contrast to the Stoclets, who were very happy in their home, Loos believed that anyone who accepted such a house was giving up his own vitality (Loos 1900). Perhaps the Pair of Lovers immortalized in the frieze for the dining room is not, as some authors believe, Klimt and Emilie Flöge (Strobl 1991, p. 81 f.), but Adolphe and Suzanne Stoclet. Their love for one another was legendary: within ten days of Adolphe Stoclet's death in 1949, his wife had followed him.

For both of them, their house – the "last Viennese *Gesamtkunstwerk*" (Hofmann 1983, p. 90) – was the symbol of a successful and fulfilled life. In Paradise, people had the liberty to choose: either to remain living free of care in the Garden of Eden or to taste the fruits of the Tree of Knowledge. The rest is history.

Pages 177–179
Working drawing for "Pair of Lovers" ("Fulfilment") (details), 1910
Black chalk, watercolour and body colour, white body colour, gold leaf, silver
and bronze gilt on transparent paper, 195 x 120 cm / 76 ¾ x 47 ¼ in.
Vienna, MAK – Österreichisches Museum für angewandte Kunst/Gegenwartskunst

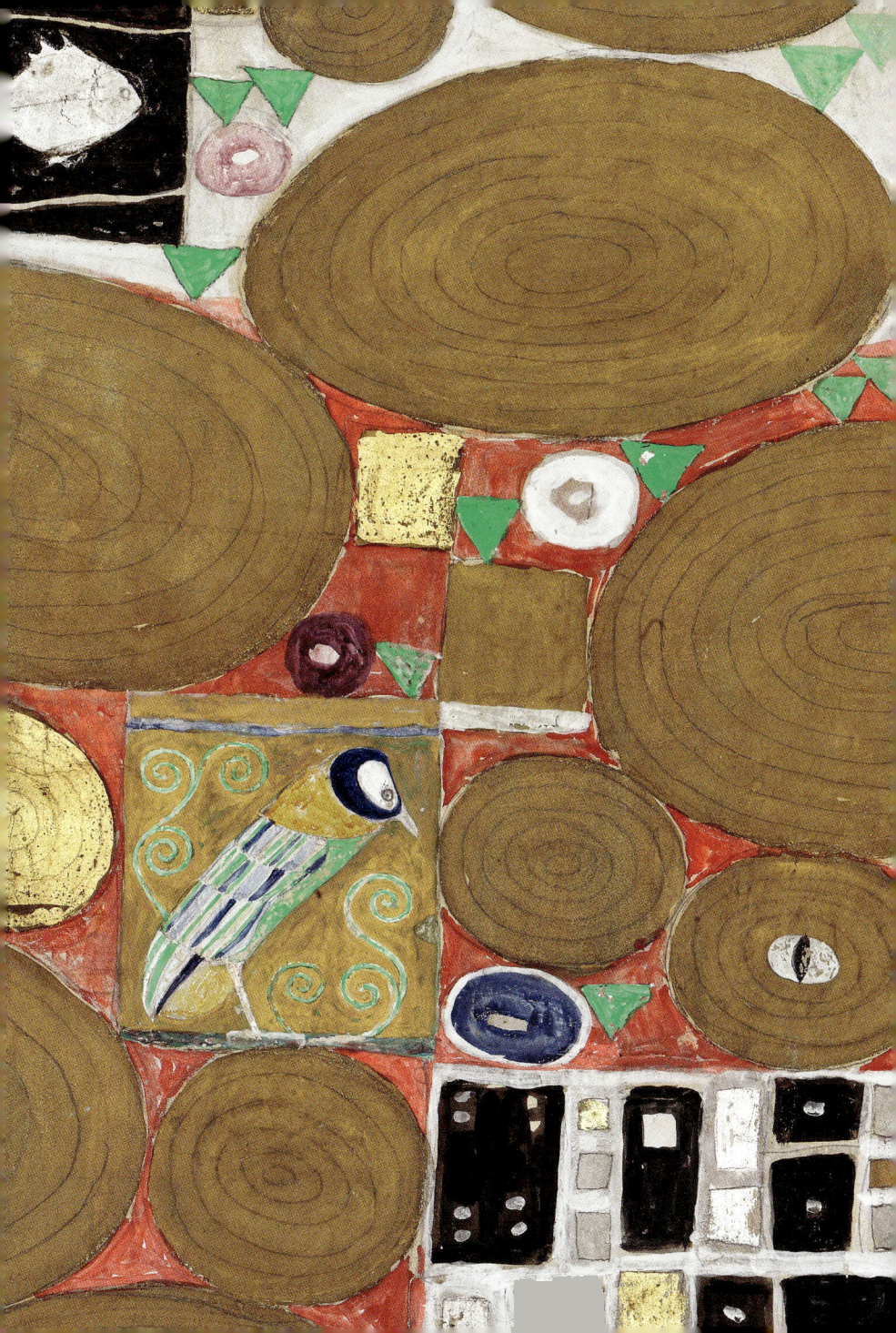

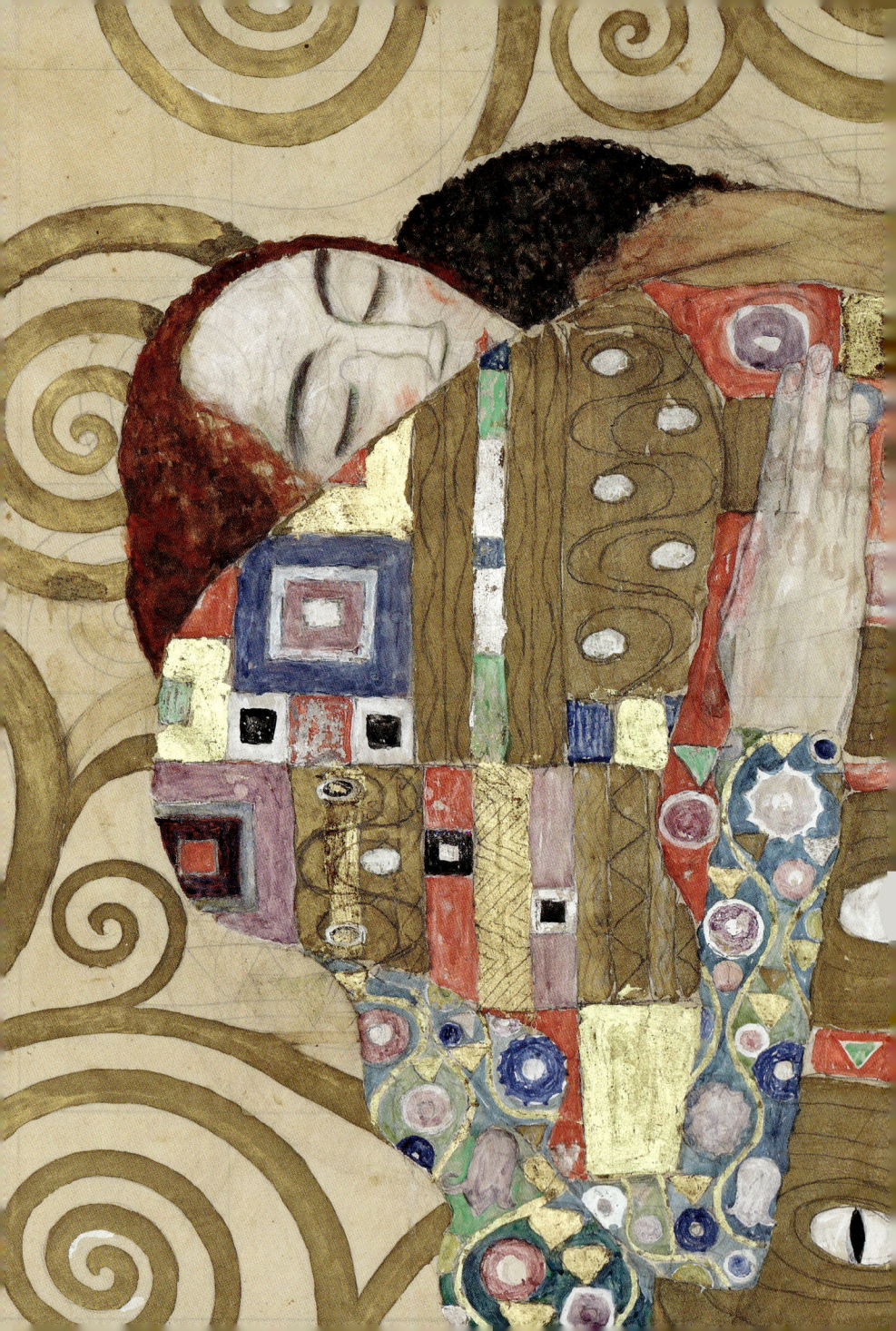

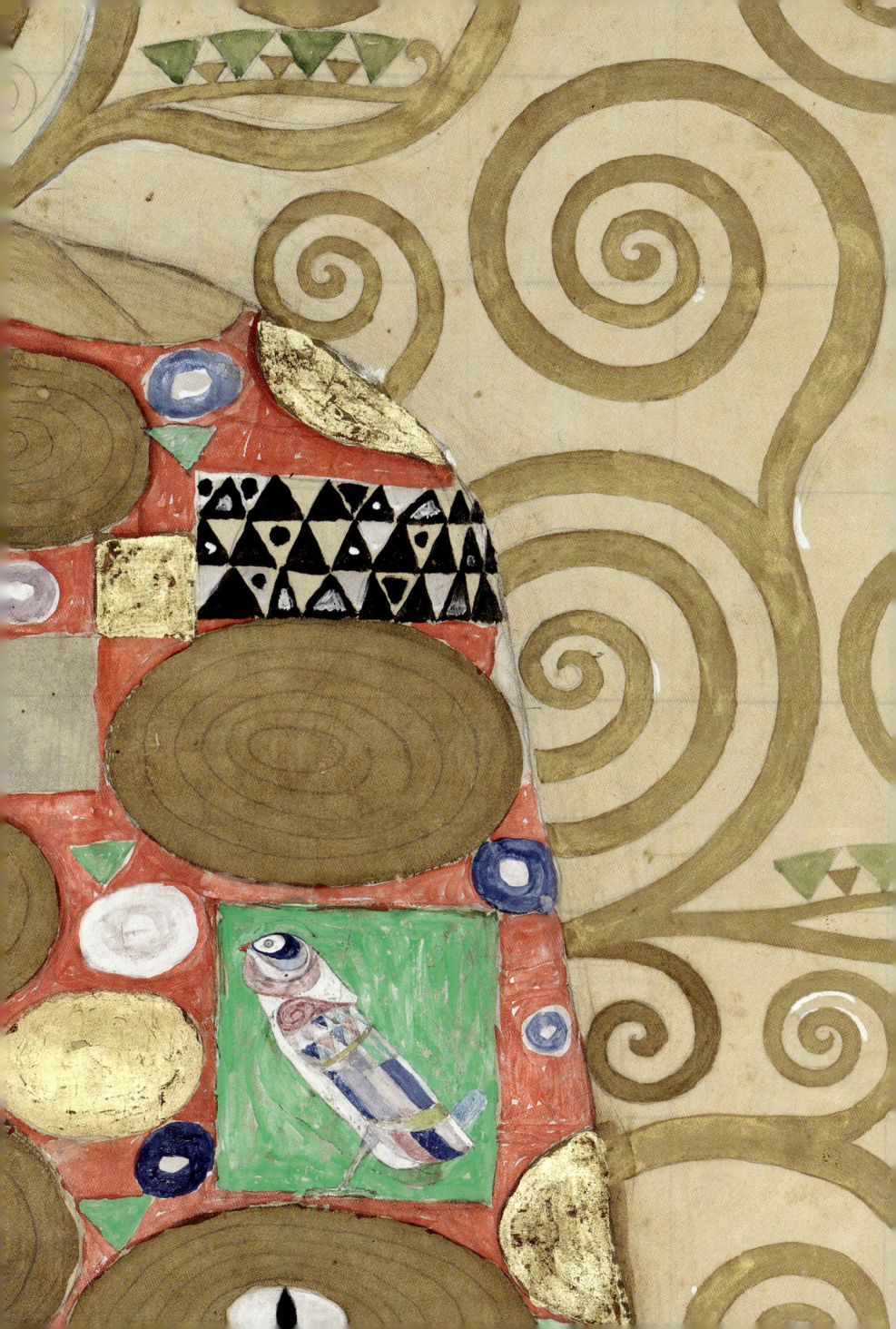

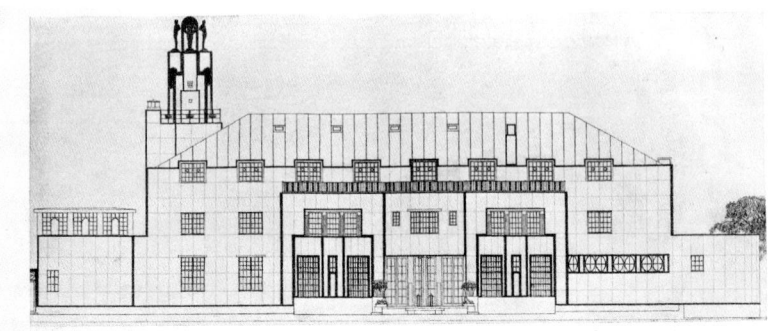

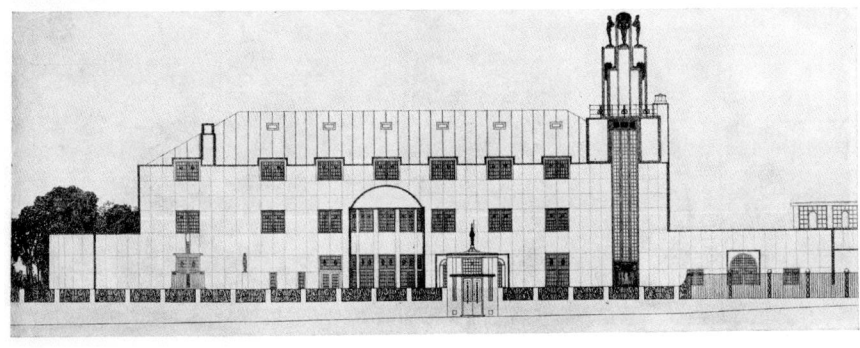

Josef Hoffmann, **Palais Stoclet, elevations of the street and garden façades**
From: *Moderne Bauformen*, vol. 13 (1914), p. 7

Josef Hoffmann, **View of the garden façade of the Palais Stoclet**
Gelatin silver print, 1917/18. Bildarchiv Foto Marburg

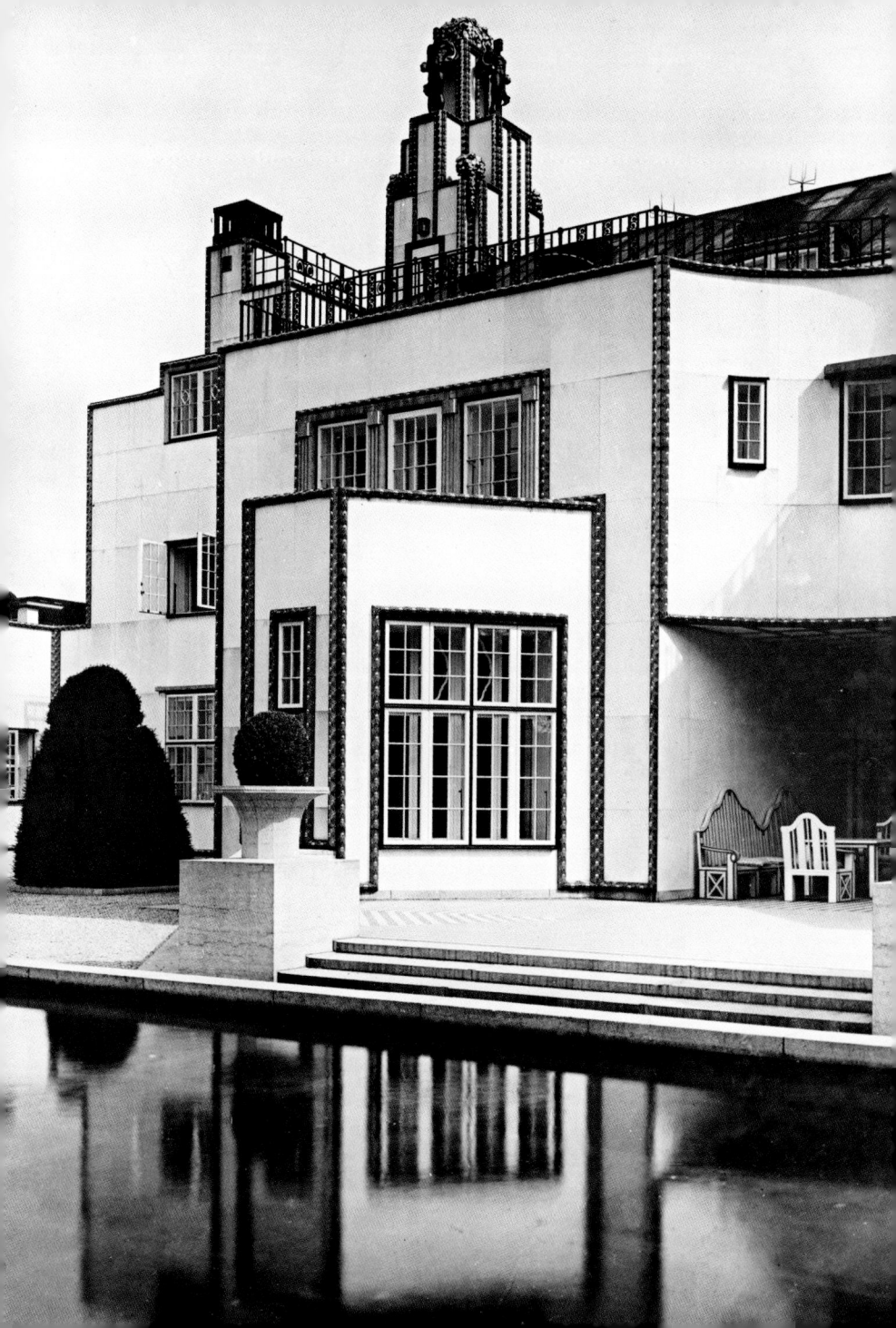

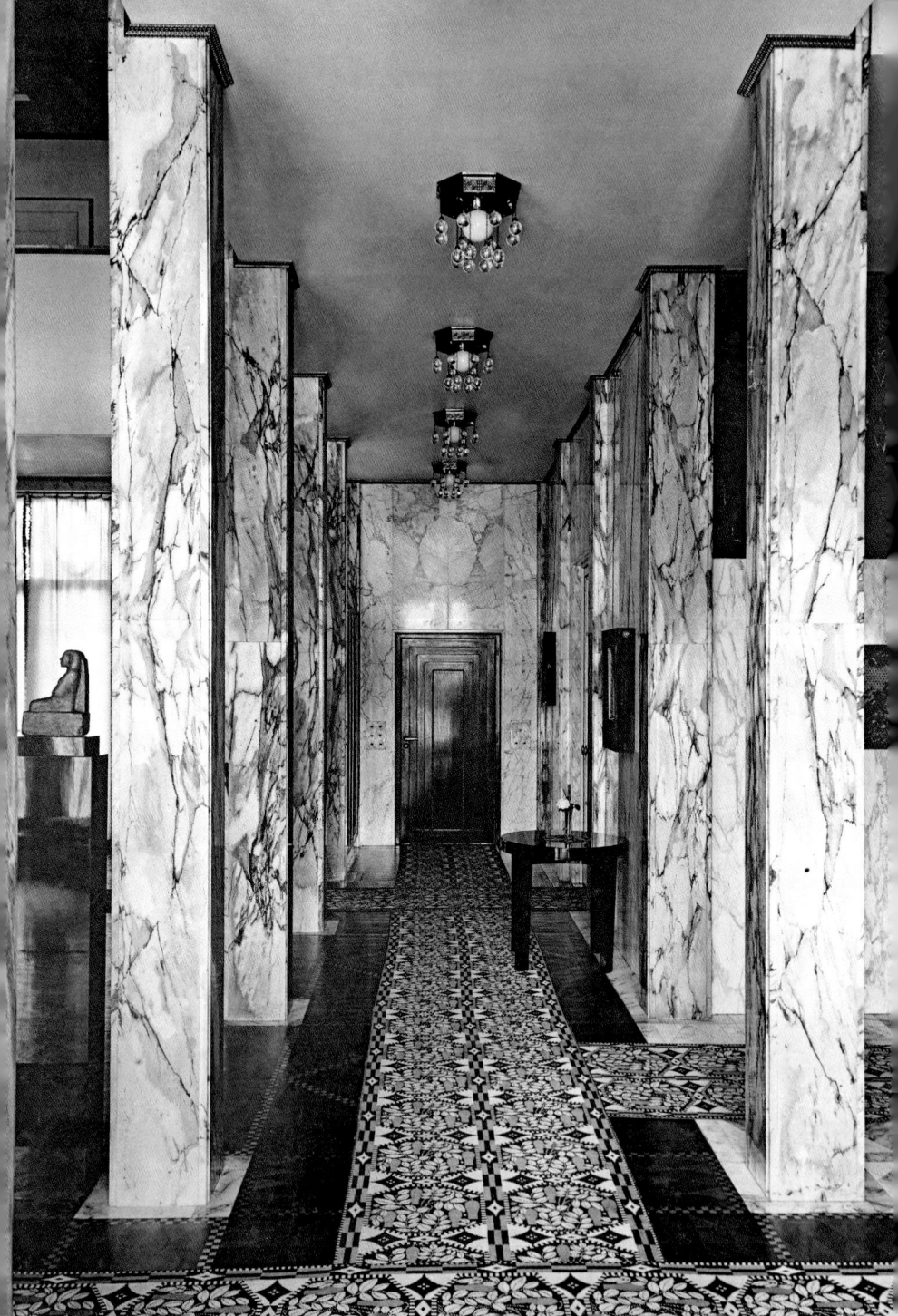

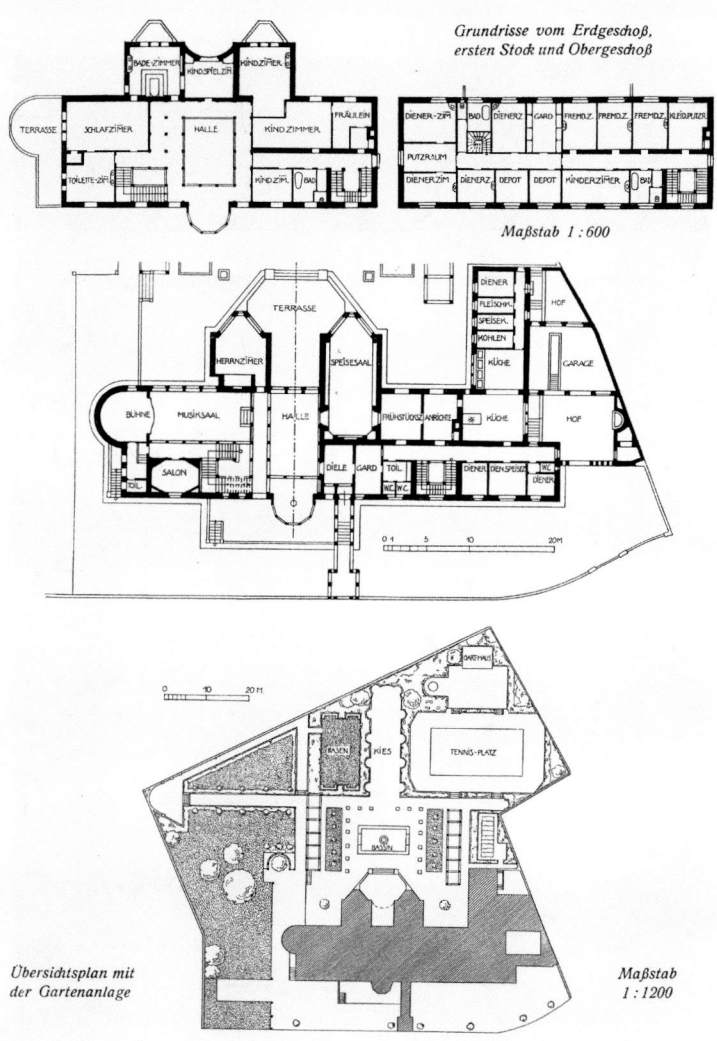

Josef Hoffmann, **View of the hall in the Palais Stoclet**
Gelatin silver print, 1910. Bildarchiv Foto Marburg

Josef Hoffmann, **Palais Stoclet, ground plans of the house and garden**
From: *Moderne Bauformen*, vol. 13 (1914), p. 6

Josef Hoffmann
View of the music room; View of the entrance to the music room
Photographs, 1917/18. Bildarchiv Foto Marburg

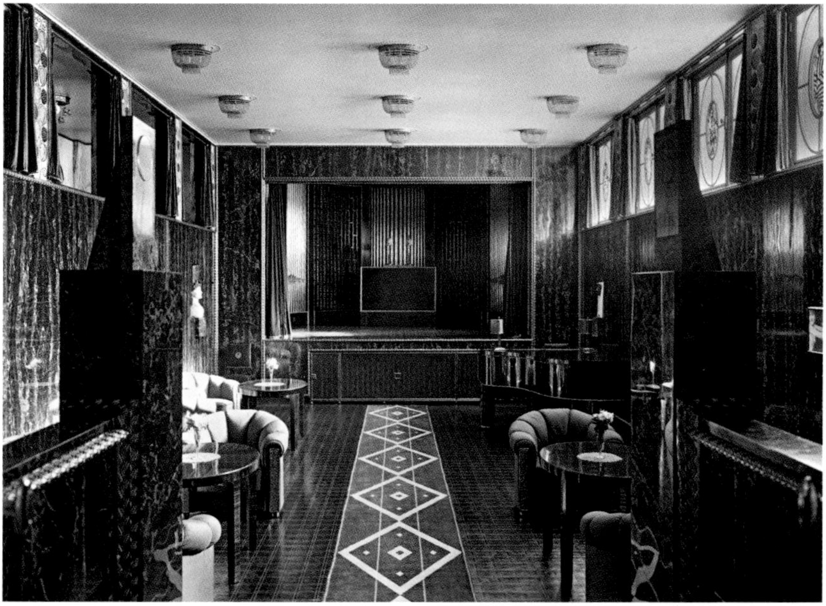

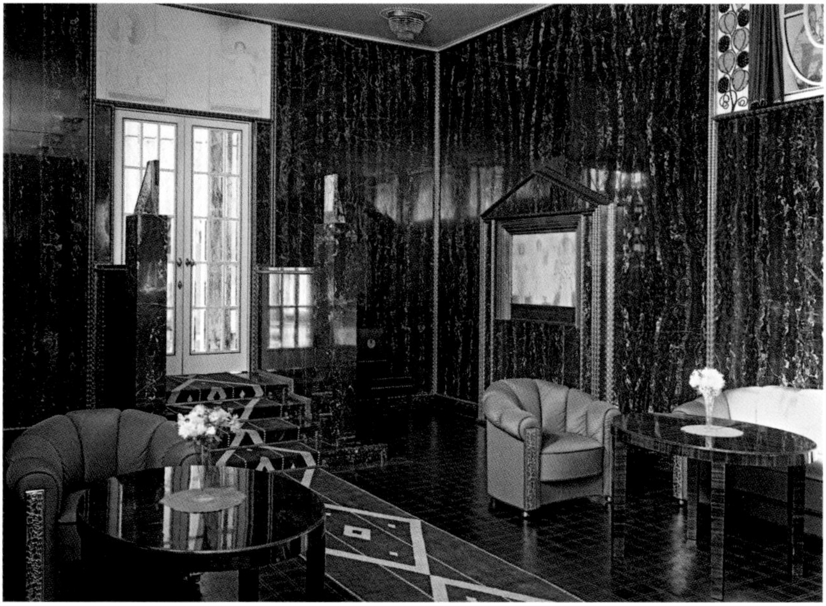

Josef Hoffmann, **View of the main hall, looking towards the street-facing bay window**
Photograph, 1917/18. Bildarchiv Foto Marburg

Pages 188/89
Josef Hoffmann and Gustav Klimt, **View of the main dining room in the Palais Stoclet**
Mosaic frieze: Carrara marble, gold and silver mosaic, coloured mosaic pieces, ceramic, enamel,
mother-of-pearl, paste gems, semi-precious stones, chased gilded and silvered sheet copper
and brass, sheet brass, brass tubing, gold leaf
Long walls each 200 x 738 cm / 78 ¾ x 290 ½ in., end wall 200 x 89 cm / 78 ¾ x 35 in.

Pages 190/95
**View of the side wall with the "Dancing Girl" ("Expectation") above the marble
and Macassar ebony furnishings by Josef Hoffmann**, 1909–1911

Pages 191–194
Mosaic frieze with the "Dancing Girl" ("Expectation"), 1909–1911

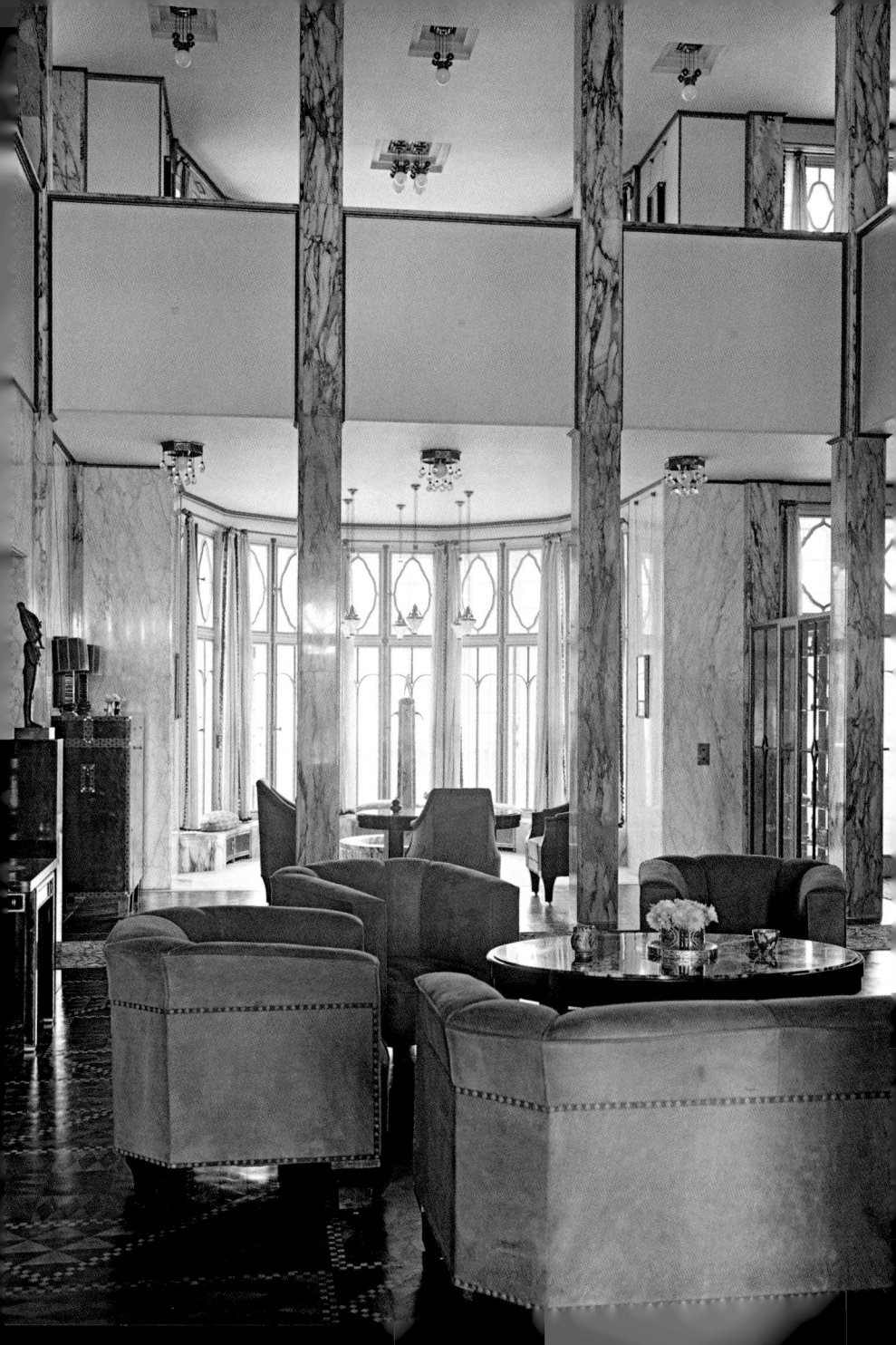

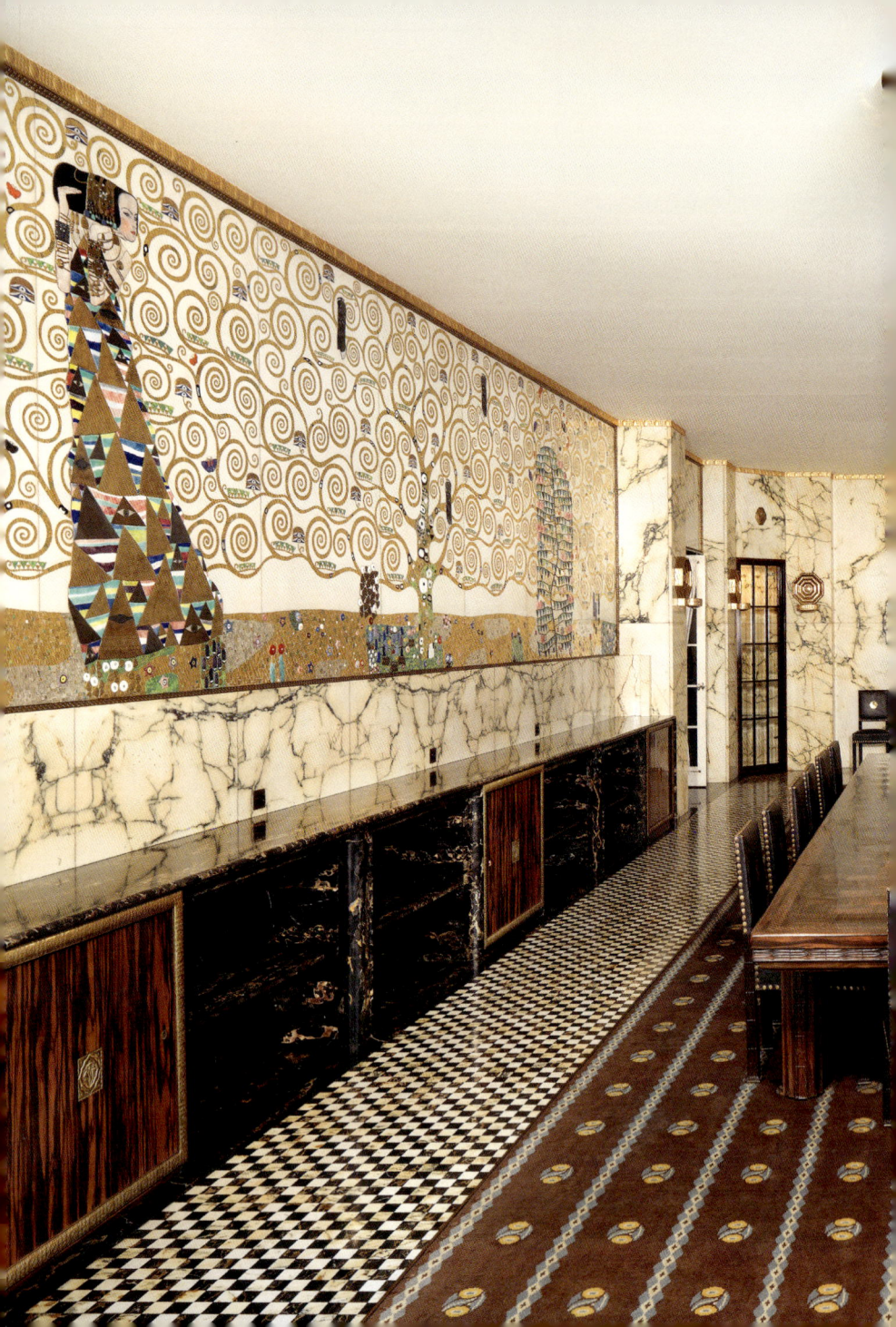

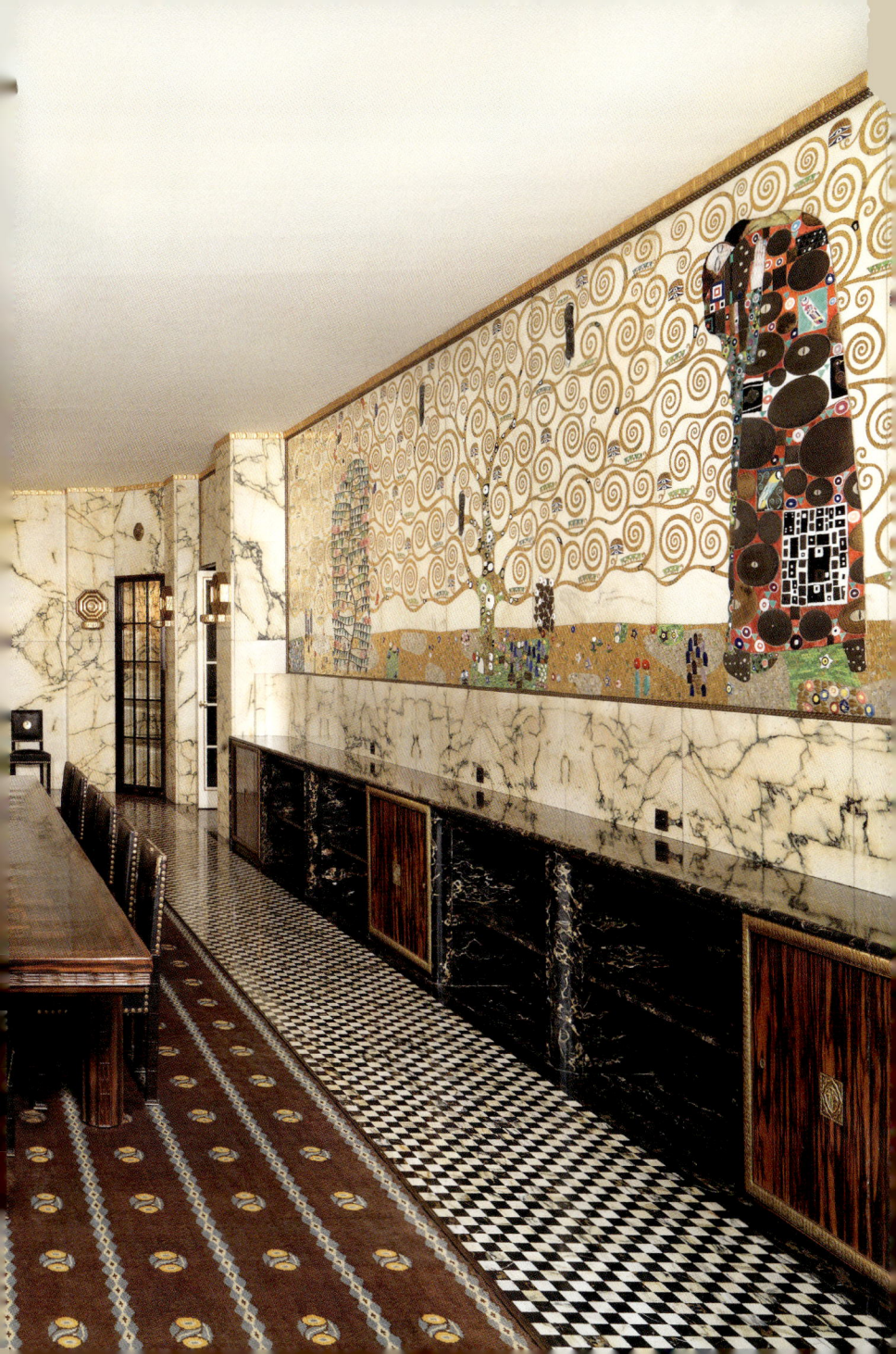

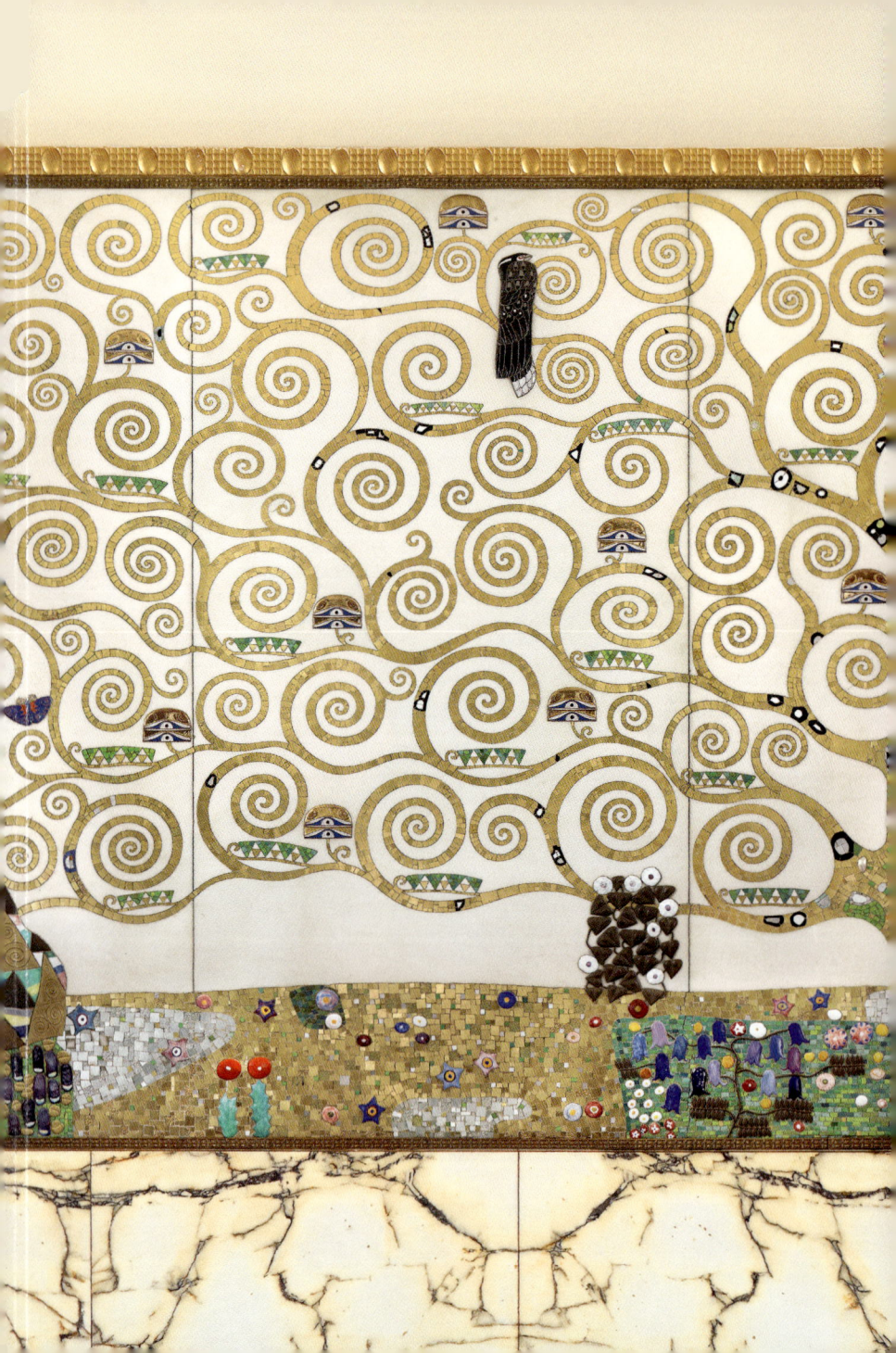

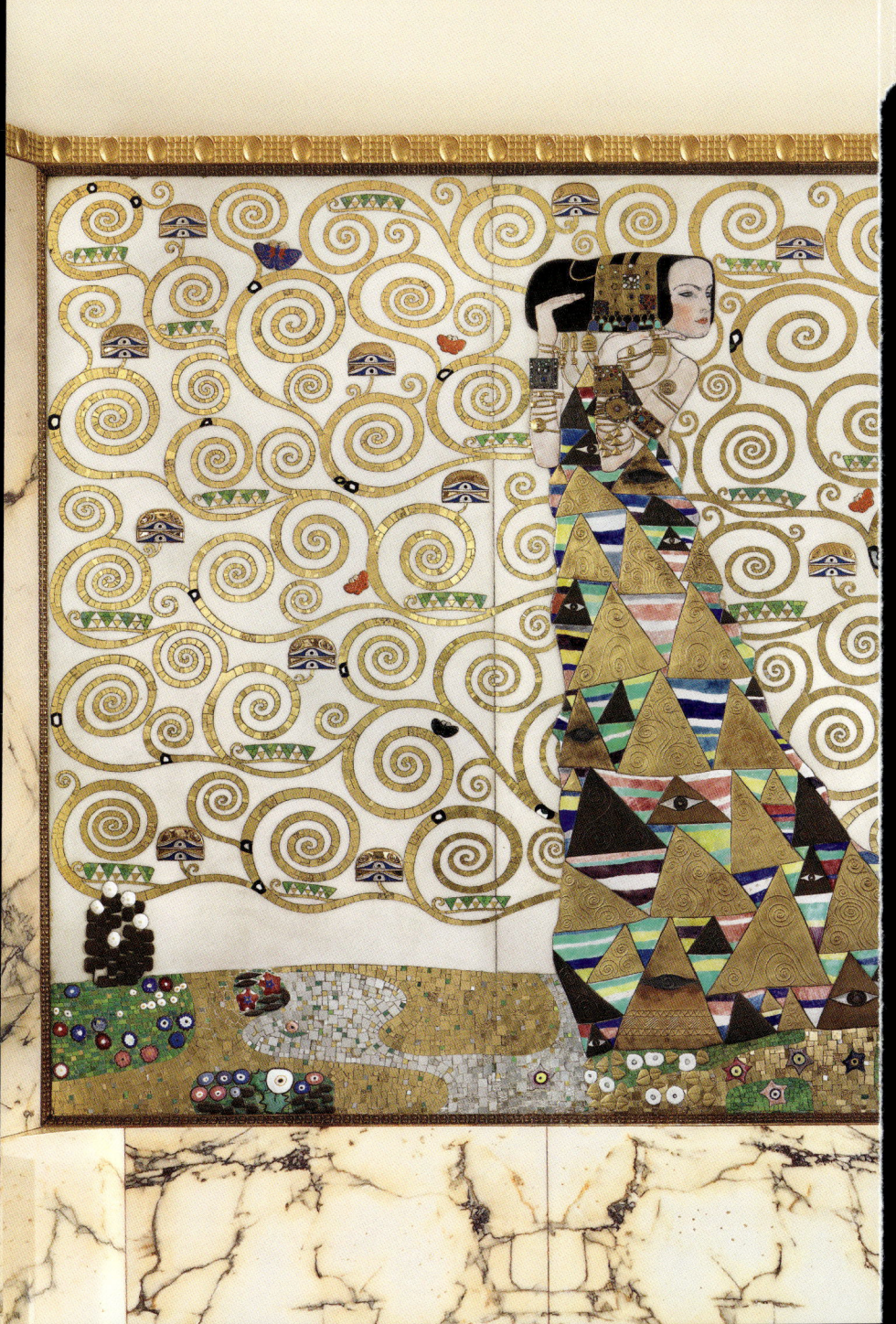

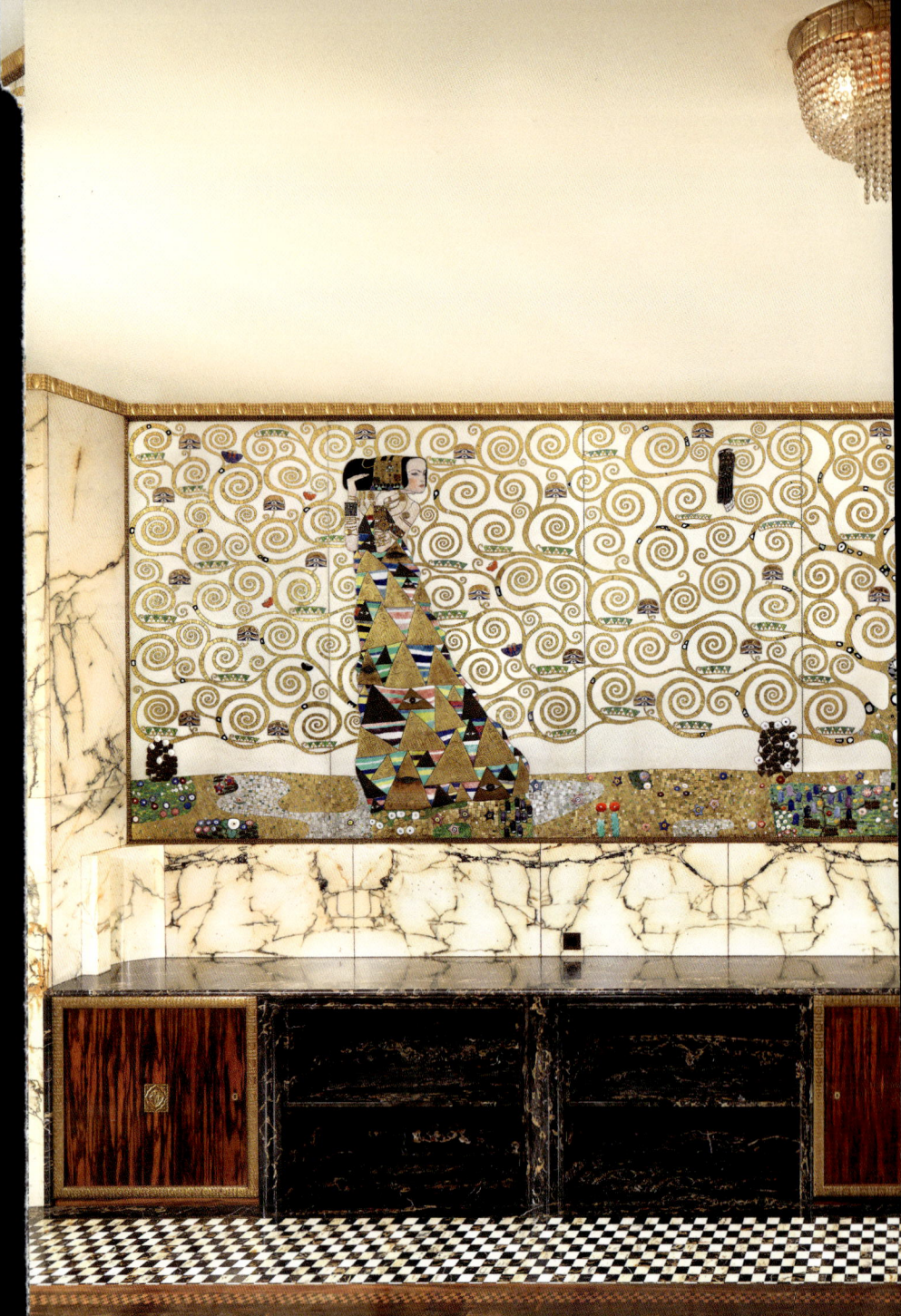

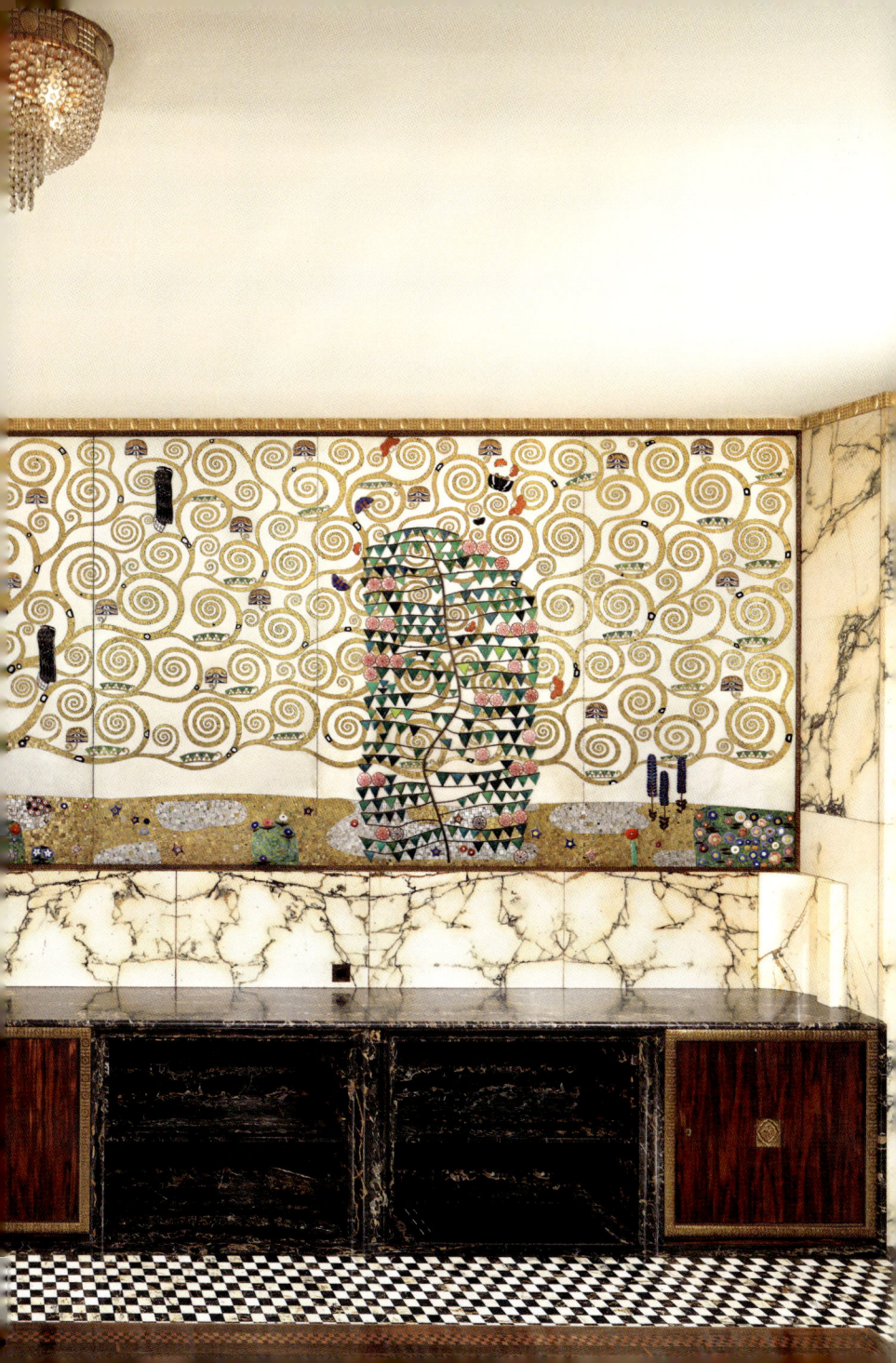

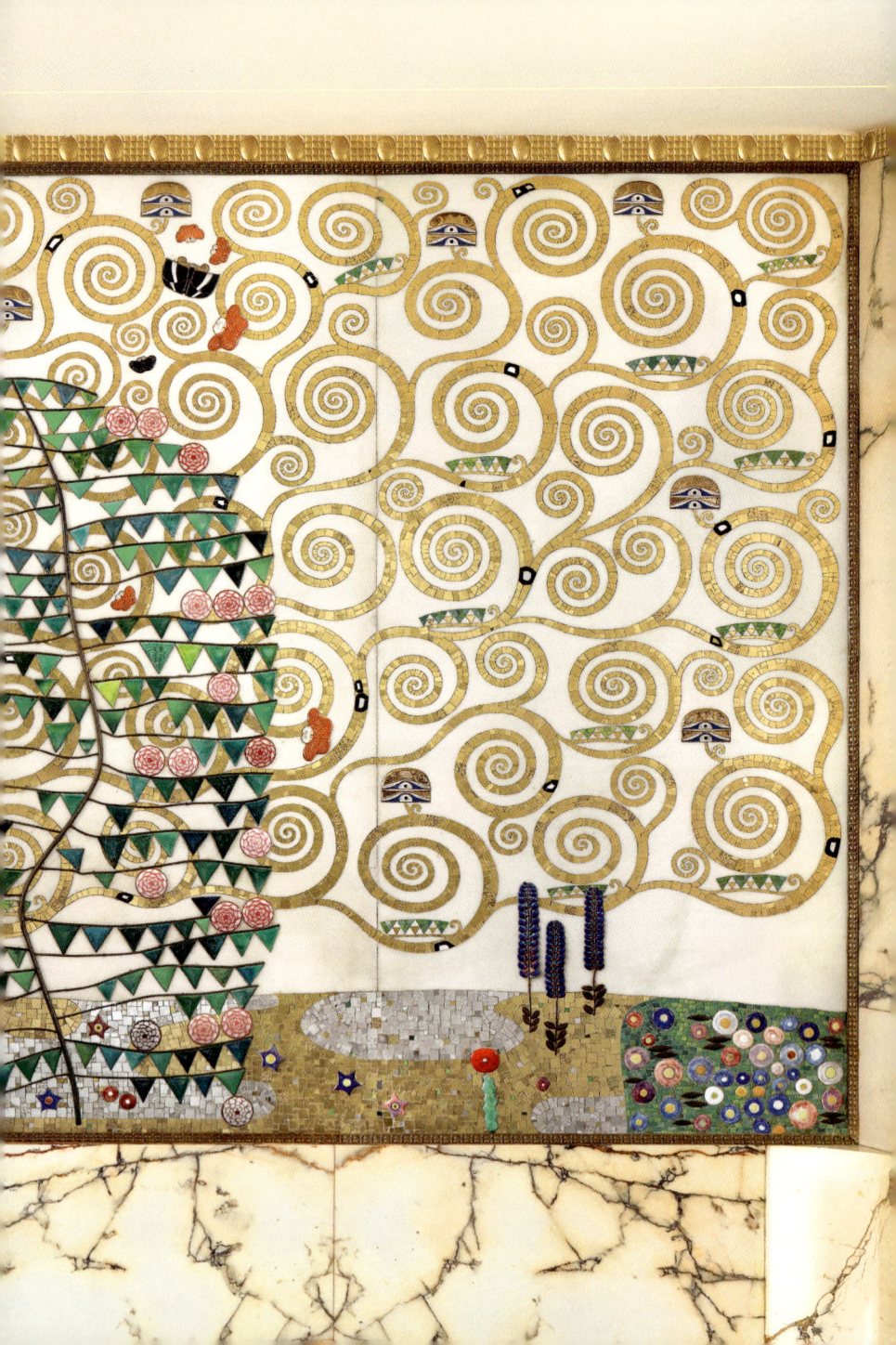

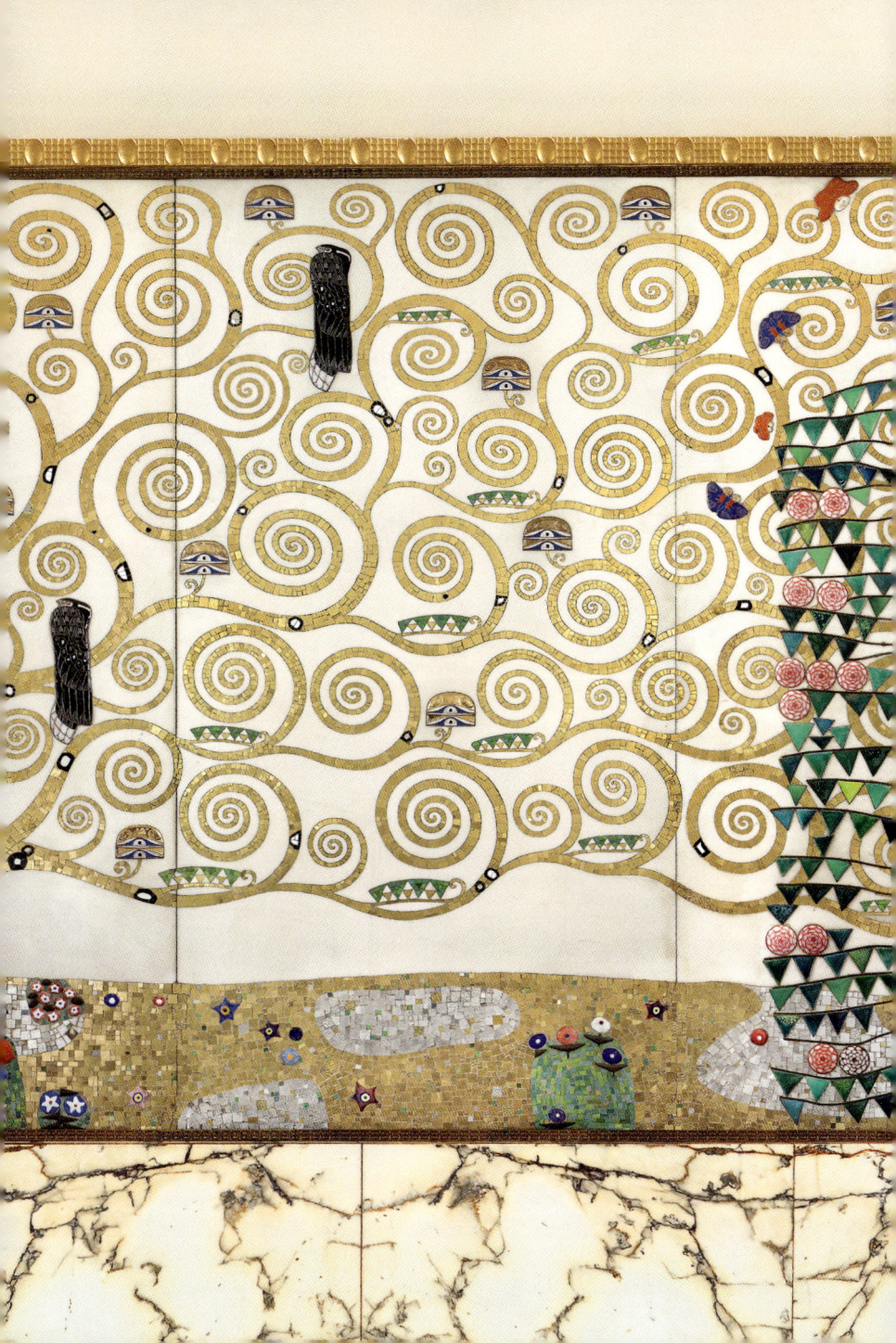

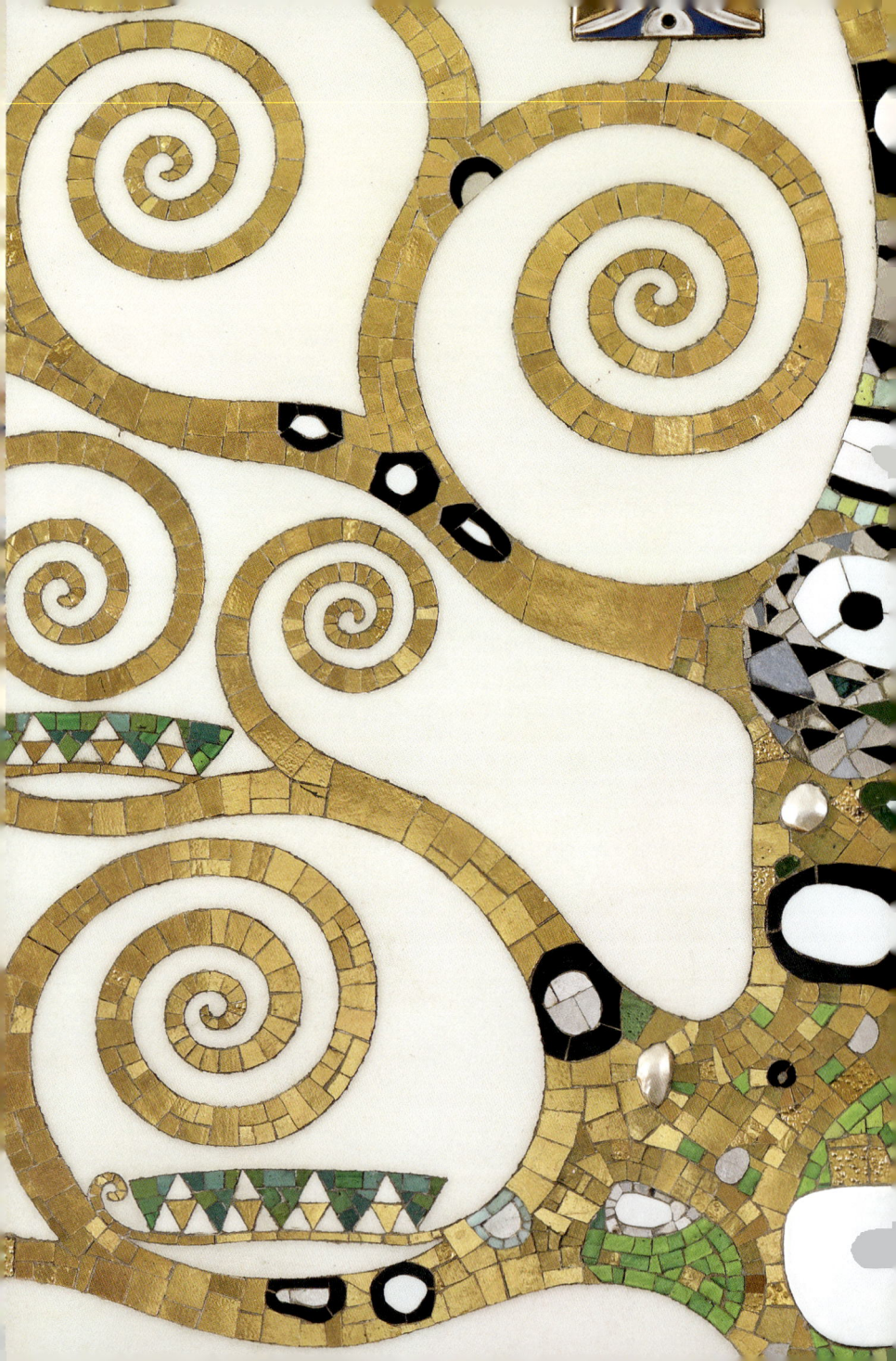

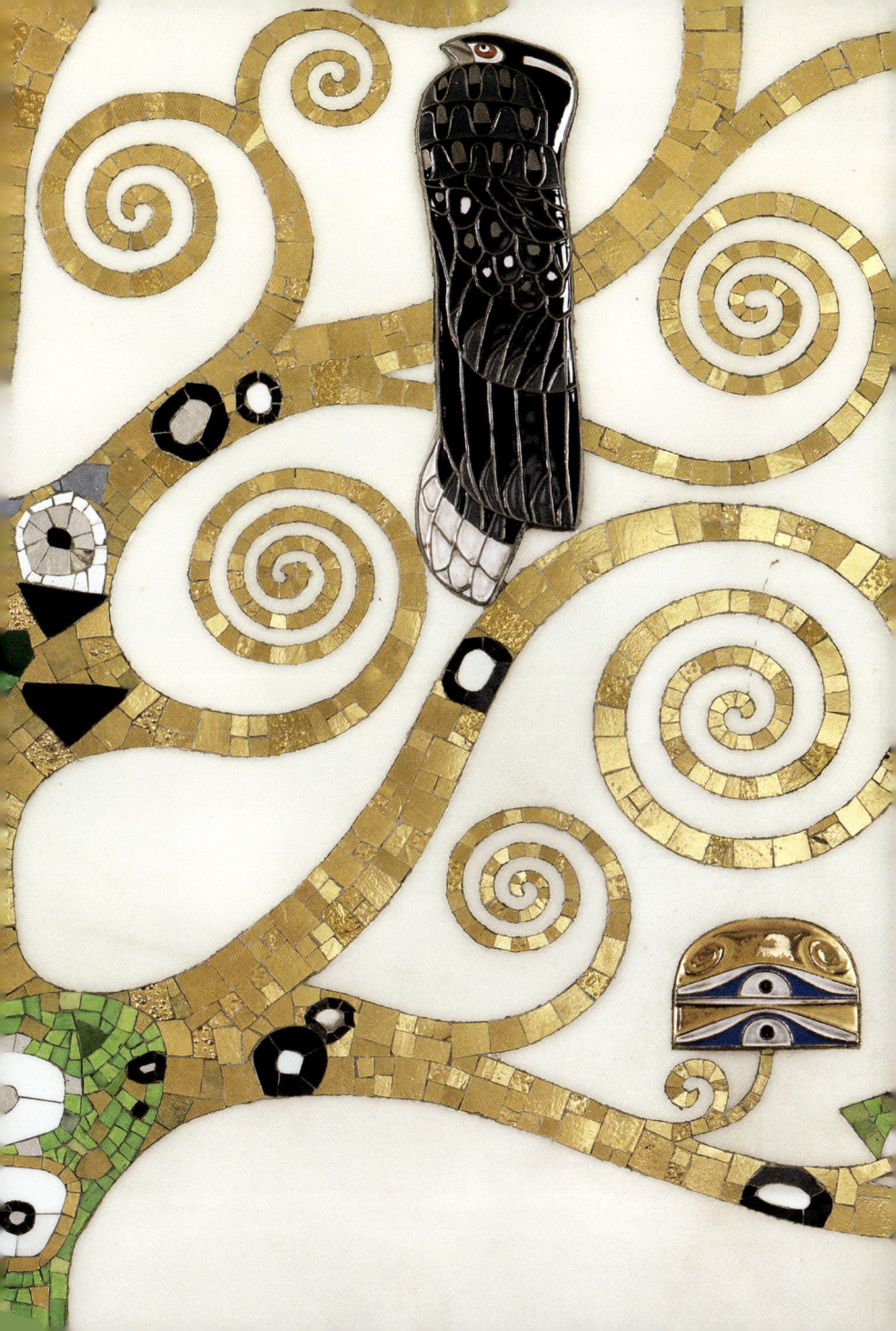

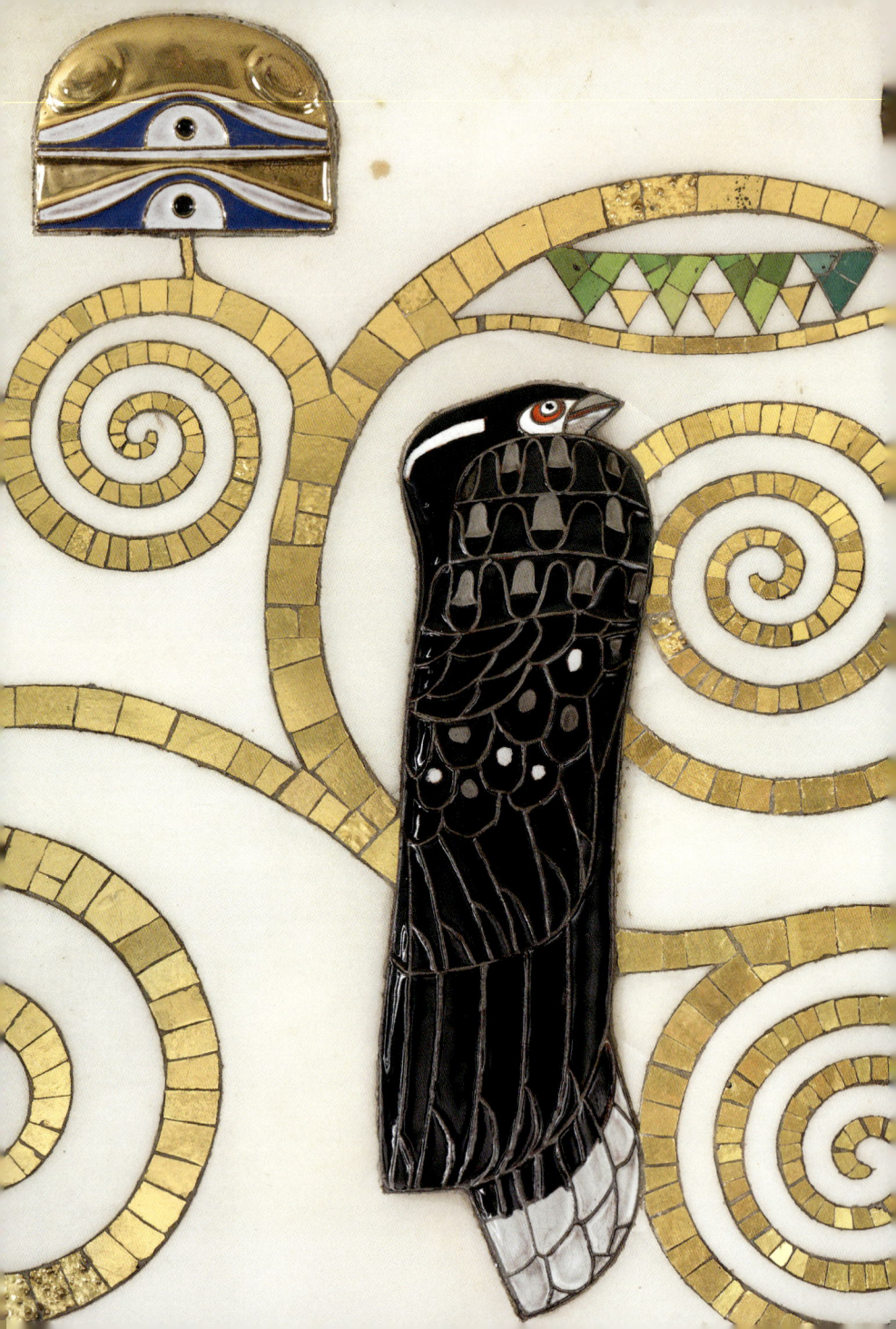

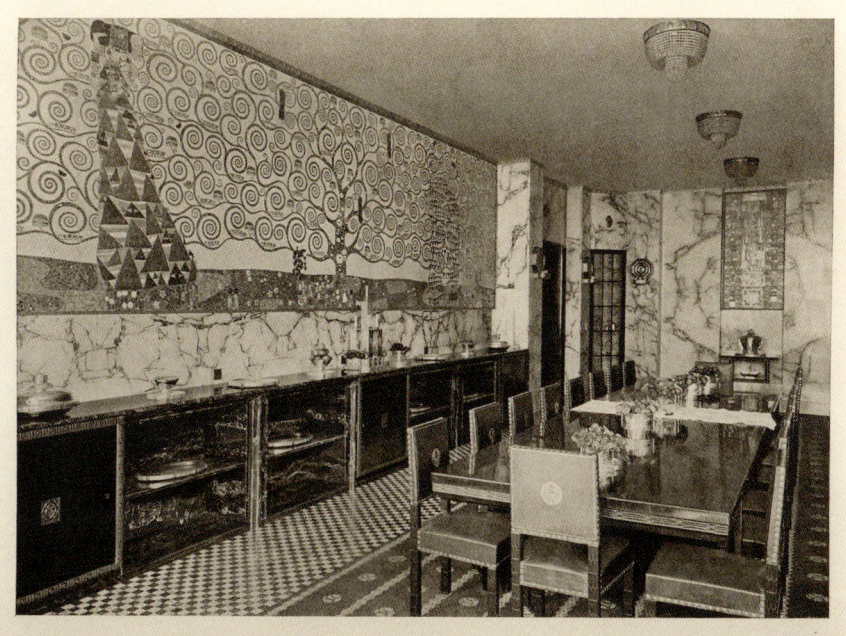

REGIERUNGSRAT PROFESSOR JOSEF HOFFMANN, WIENER WERKSTÄTTE, WIEN
Das Stoclethaus zu Brüssel. — Der große Speisesaal. Fries von Gustav Klimt, Wien

Pages 196–198
Details with Falcons, 1909–1911

The dining room with silverware, candelabra and floral decorations, 1913
From: *Moderne Bauformen*, vol. 13 (1914), pl. 4

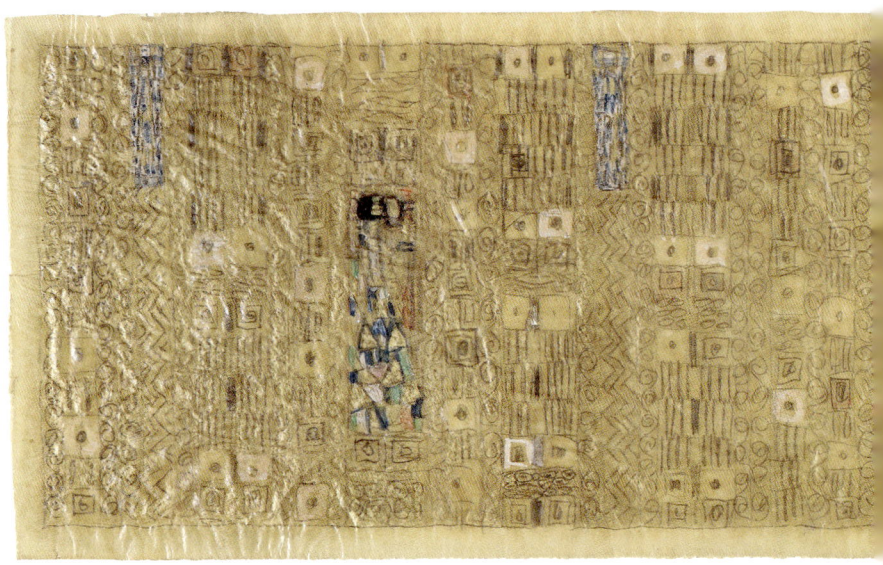

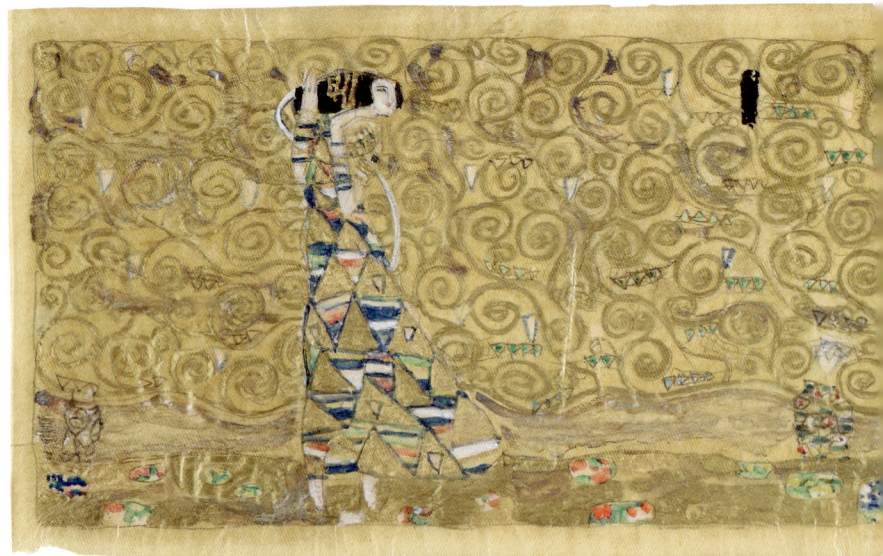

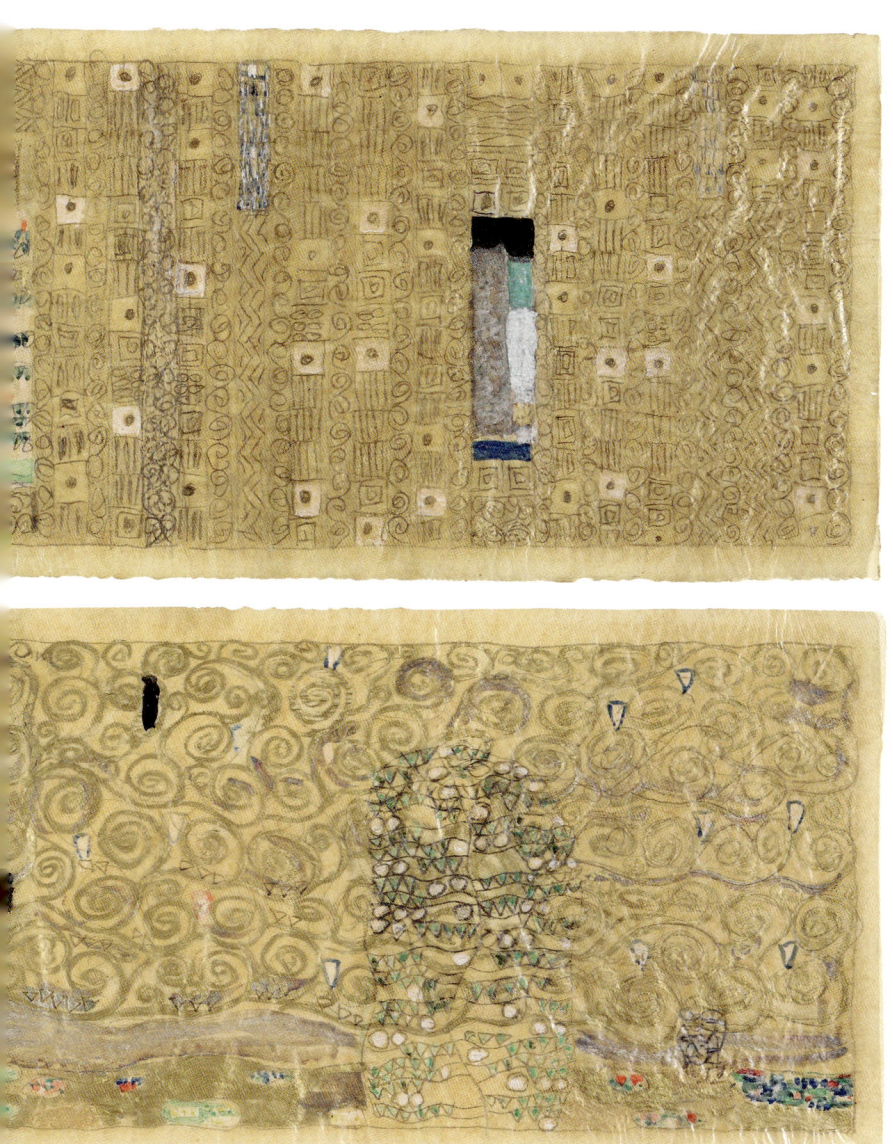

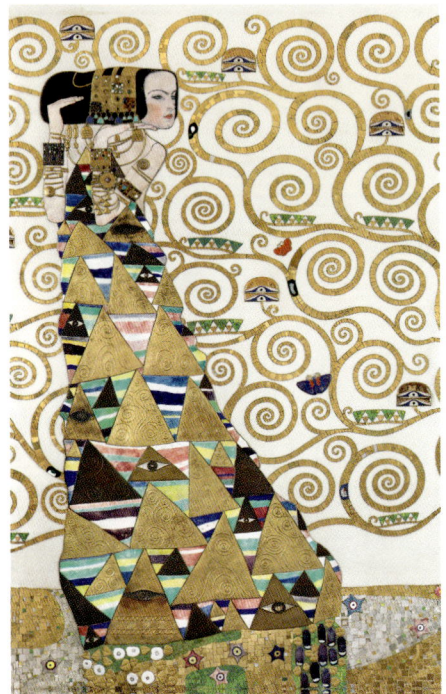

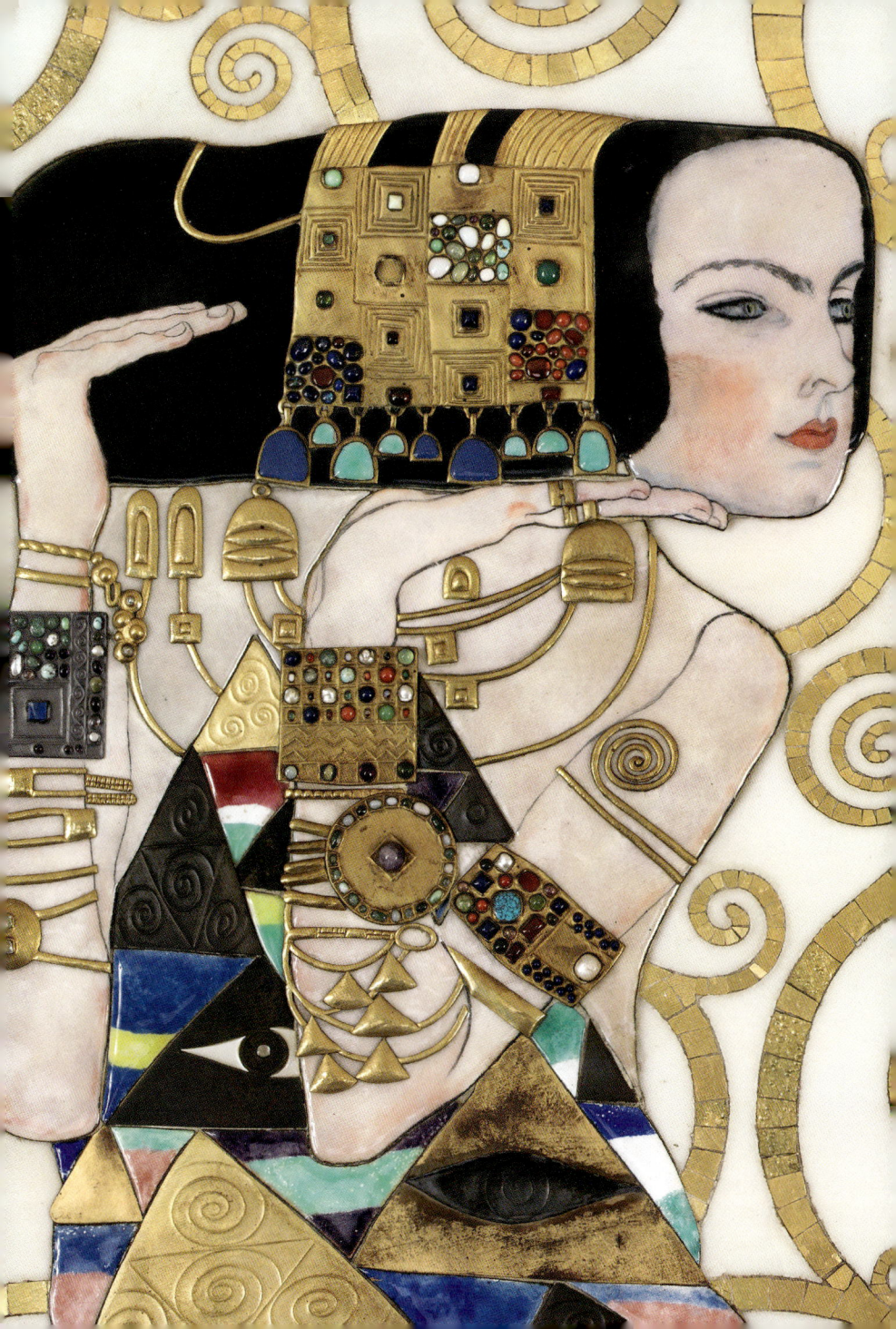

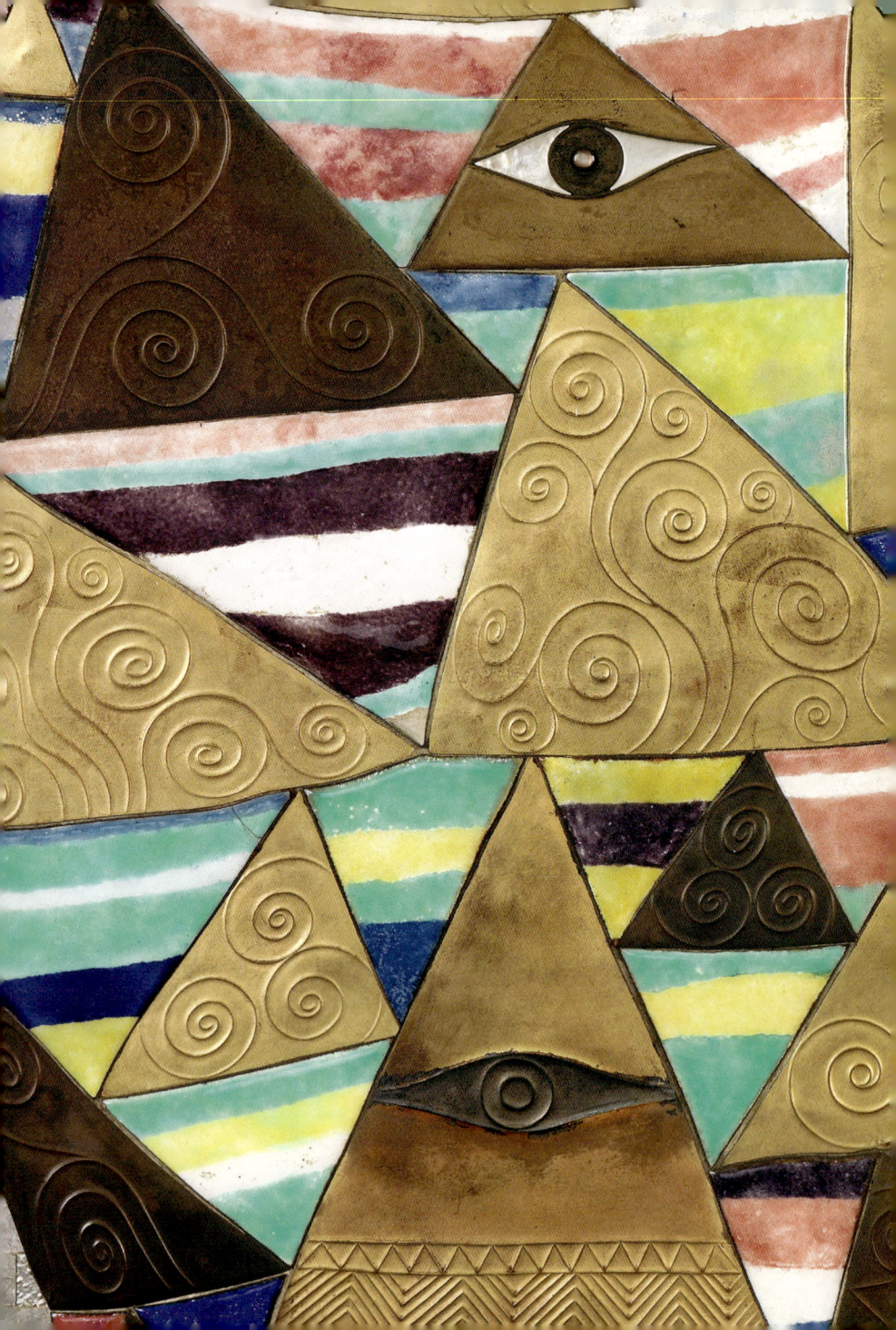

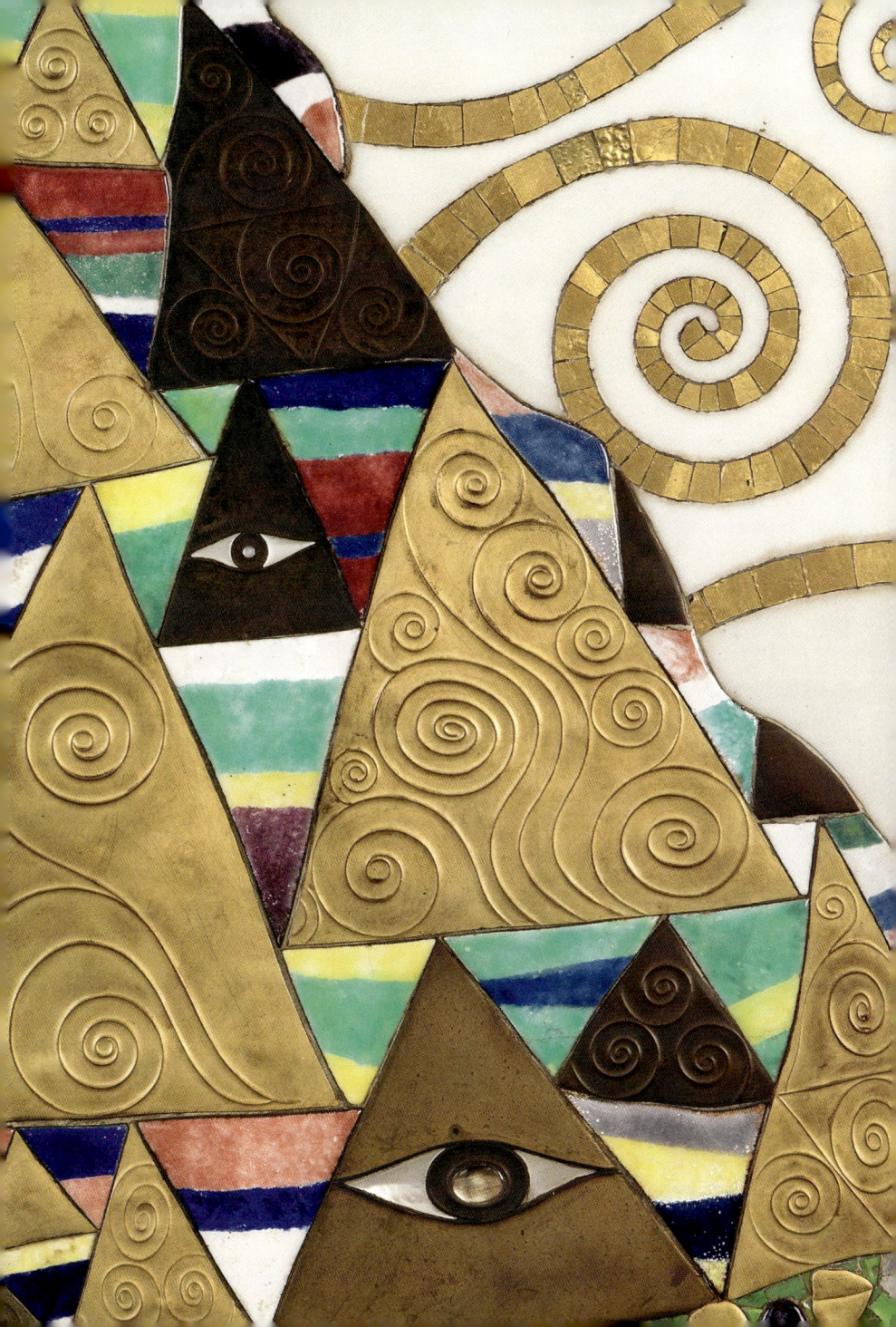

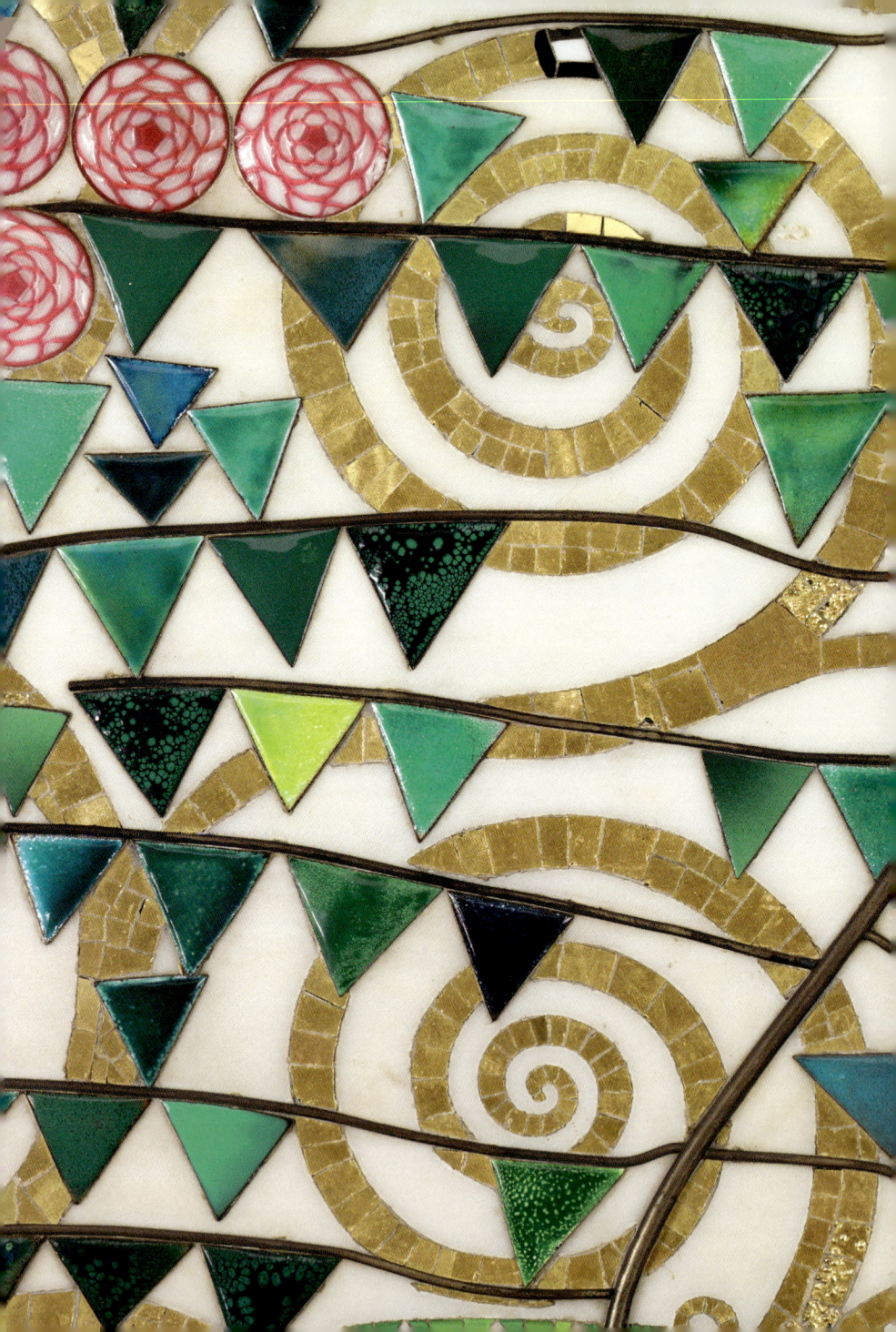

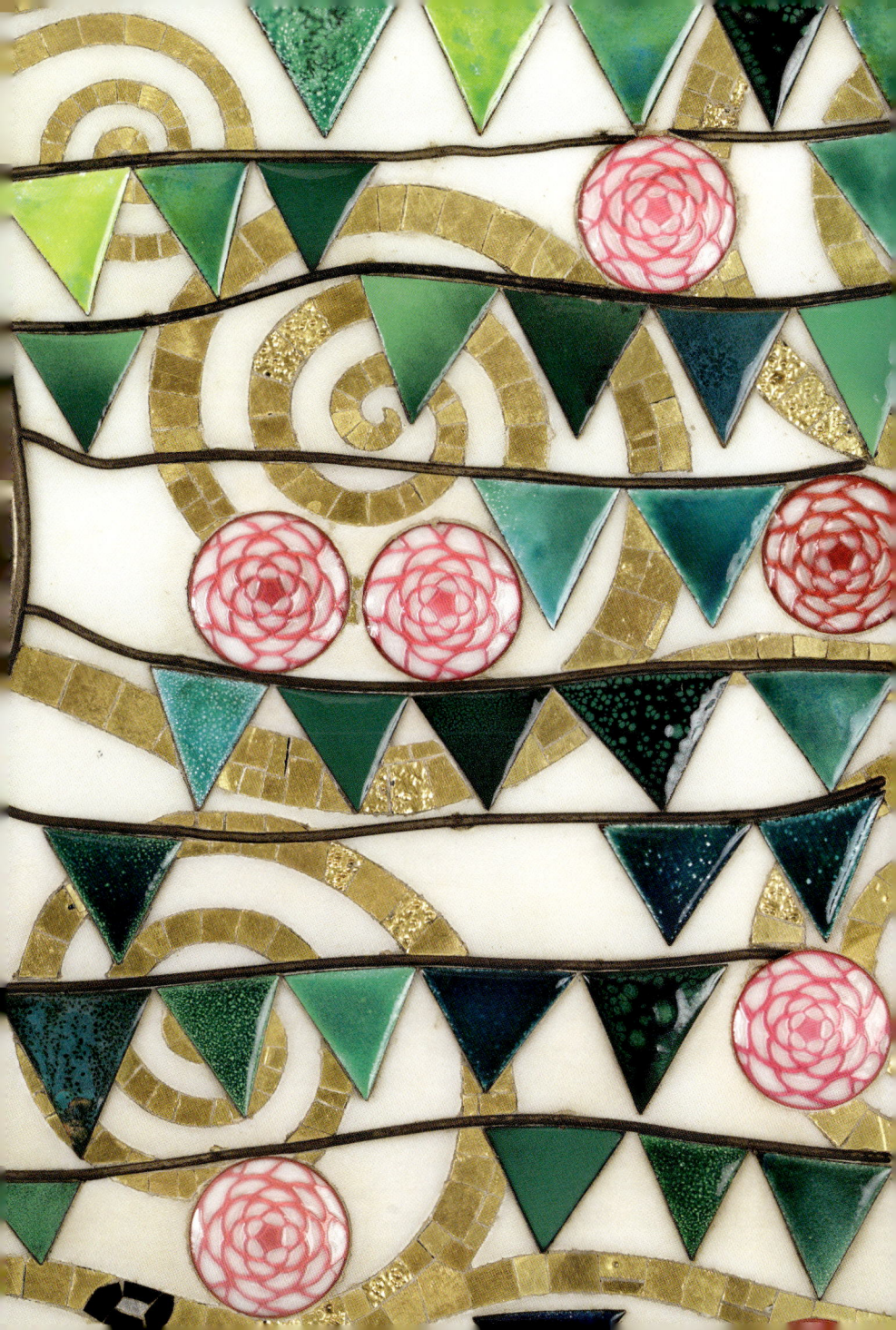

Pages 206/07, 209–211
Details of the right-hand mosaic wall, 1909–1911

Pages 212/13
View of the main dining room with the garden beyond

Pages 214/19
**View of the side wall with the "Pair of Lovers" ("Fulfilment") above the marble
and Macassar ebony furnishings by Josef Hoffmann**, 1909–1911

Pages 215–218
Mosaic frieze with the "Pair of Lovers" ("Fulfilment"), 1909–1911

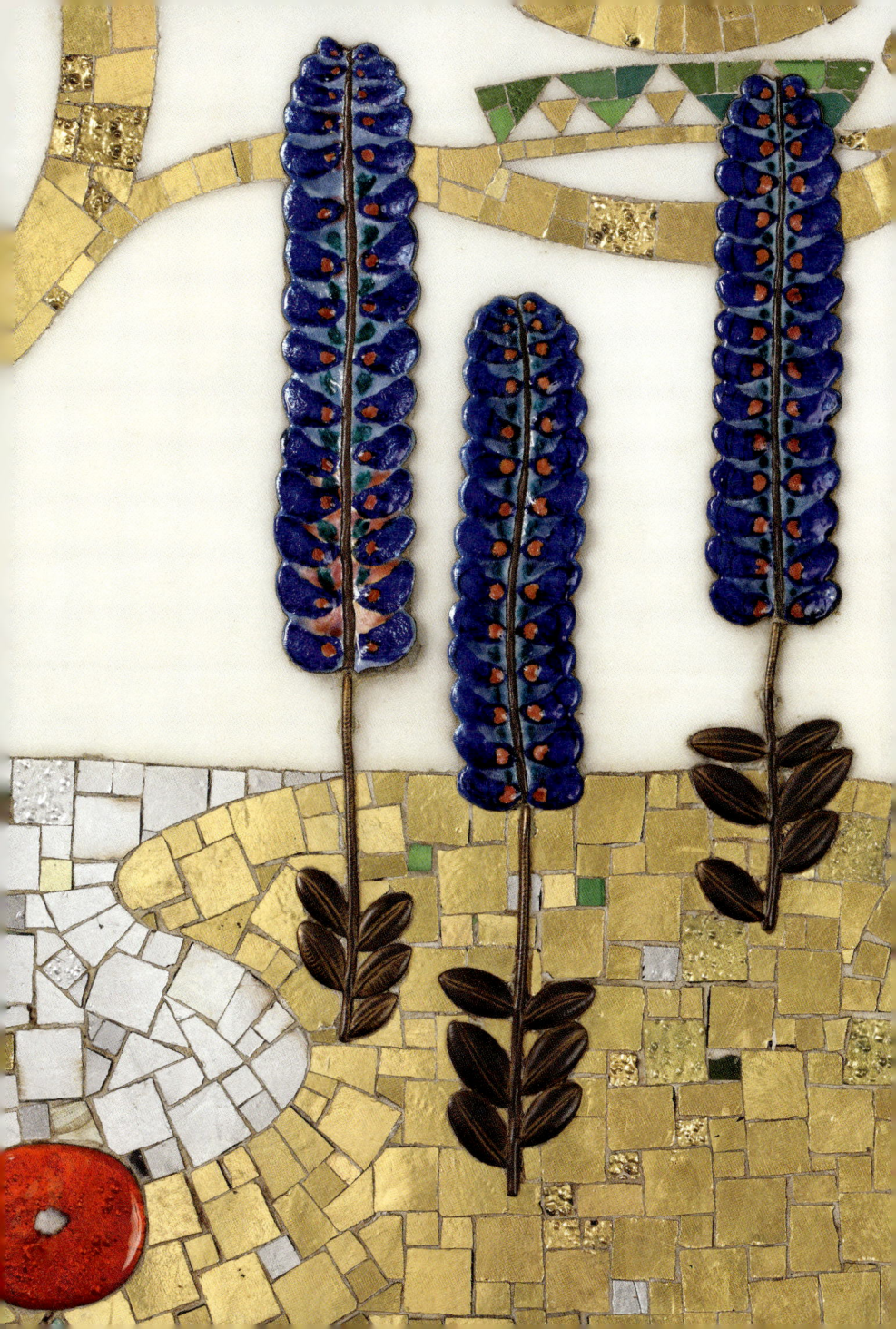

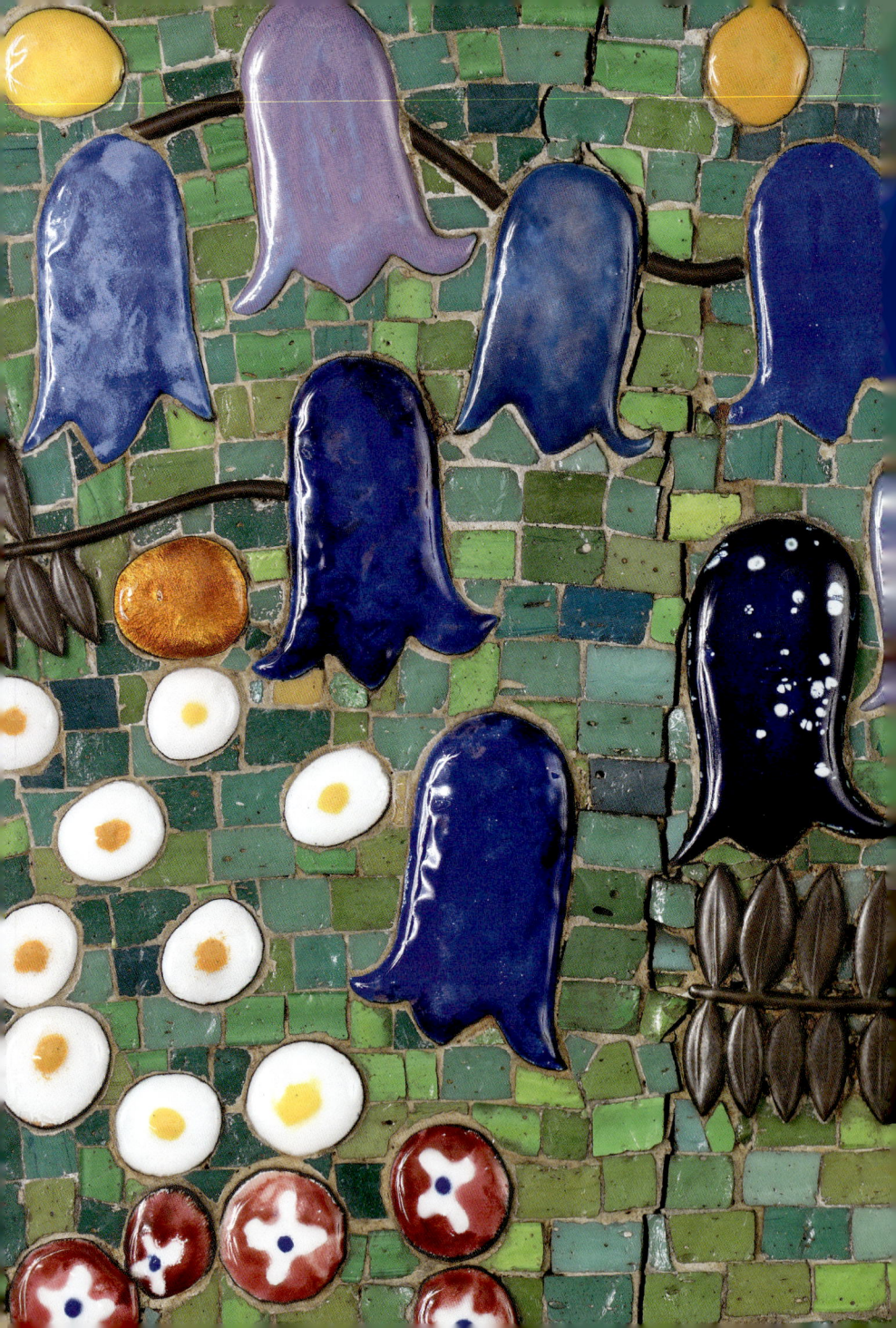

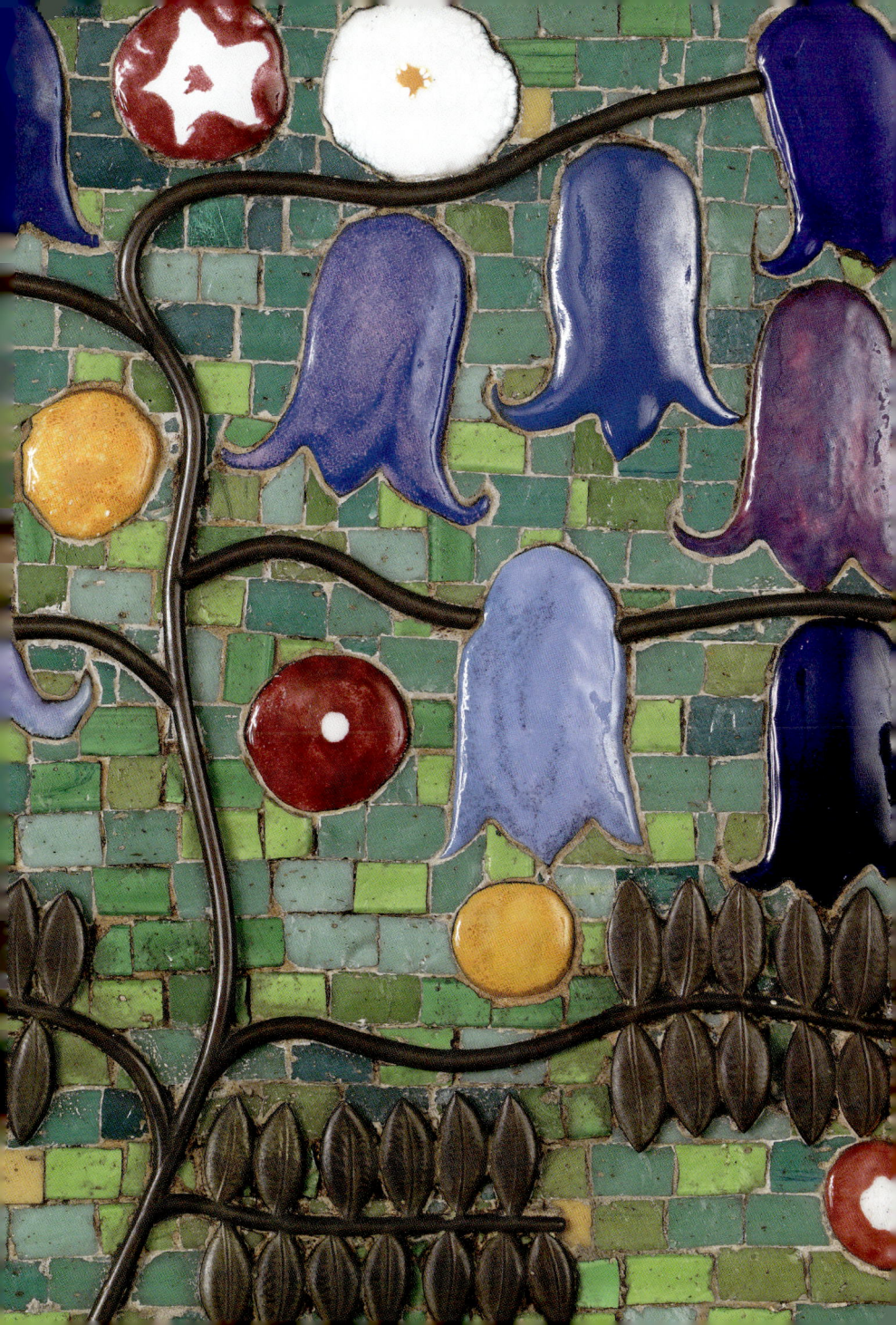

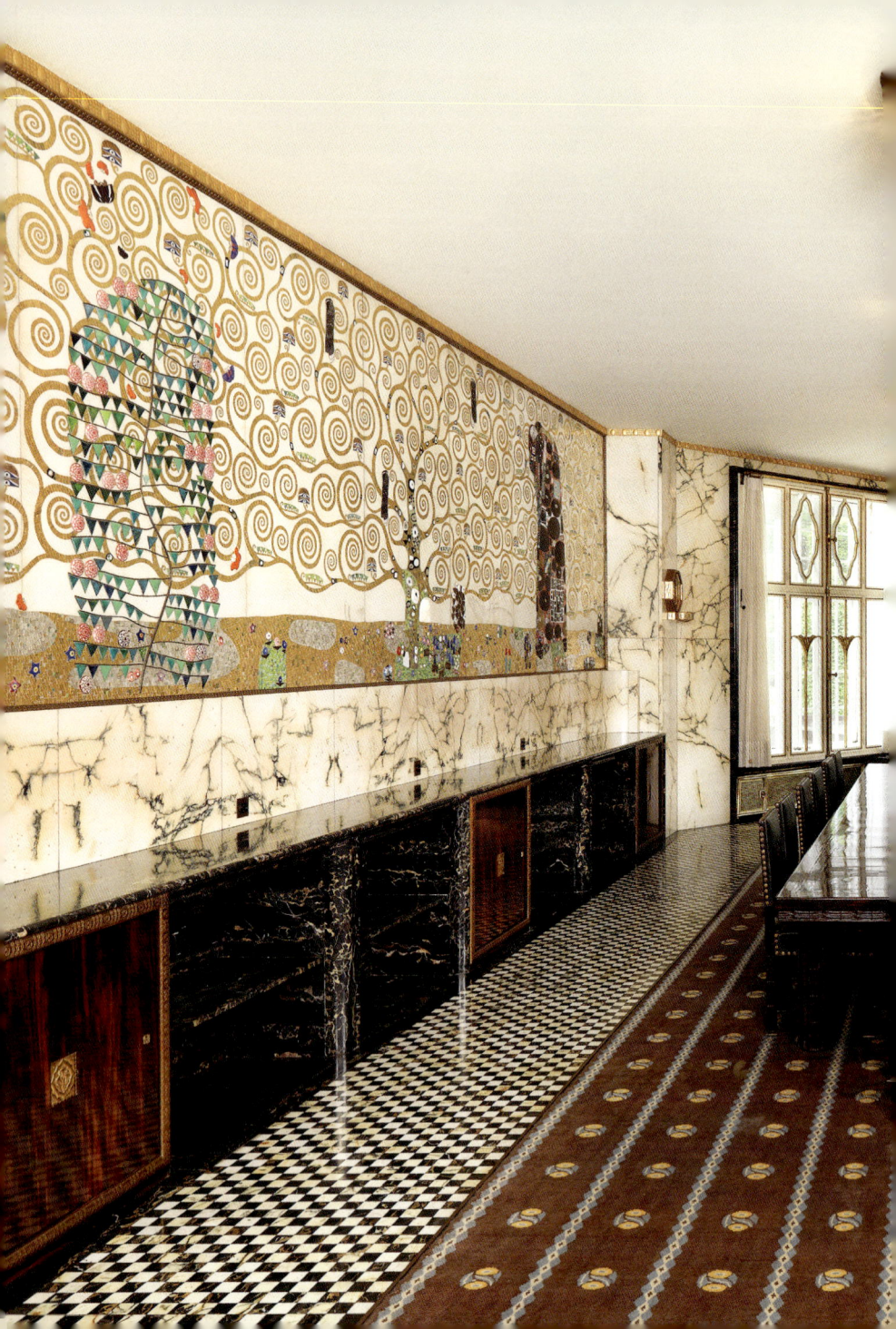

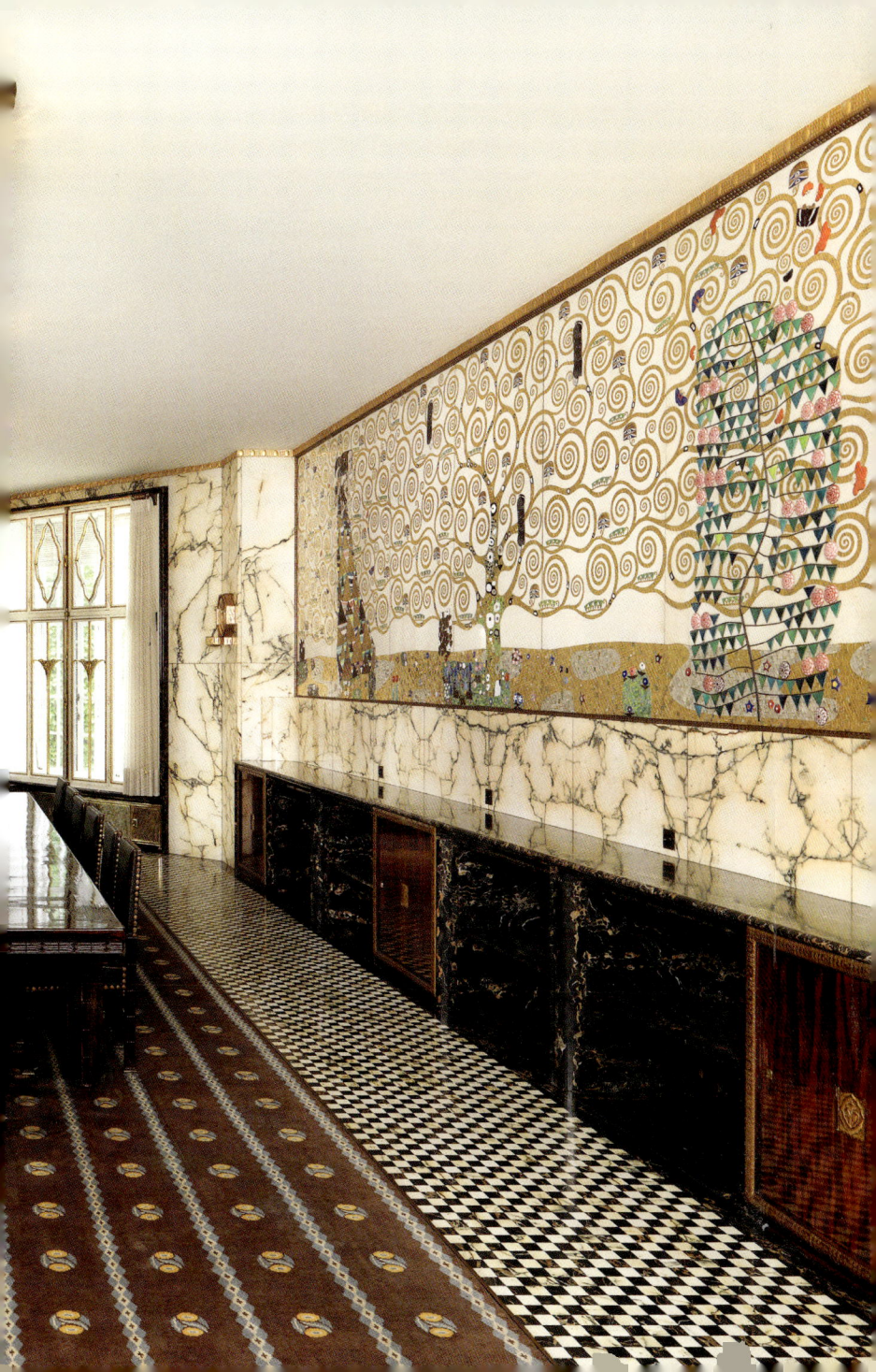

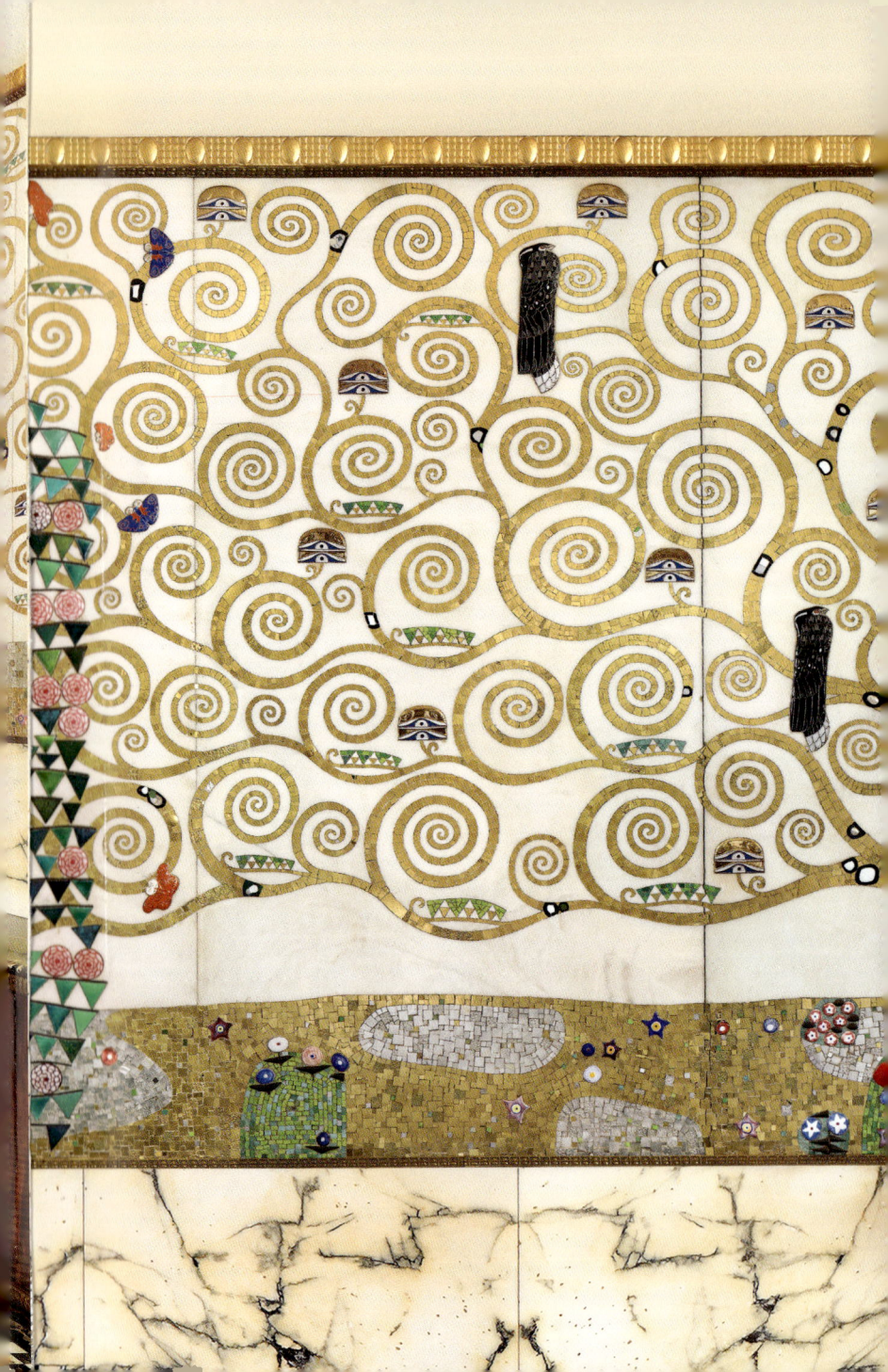

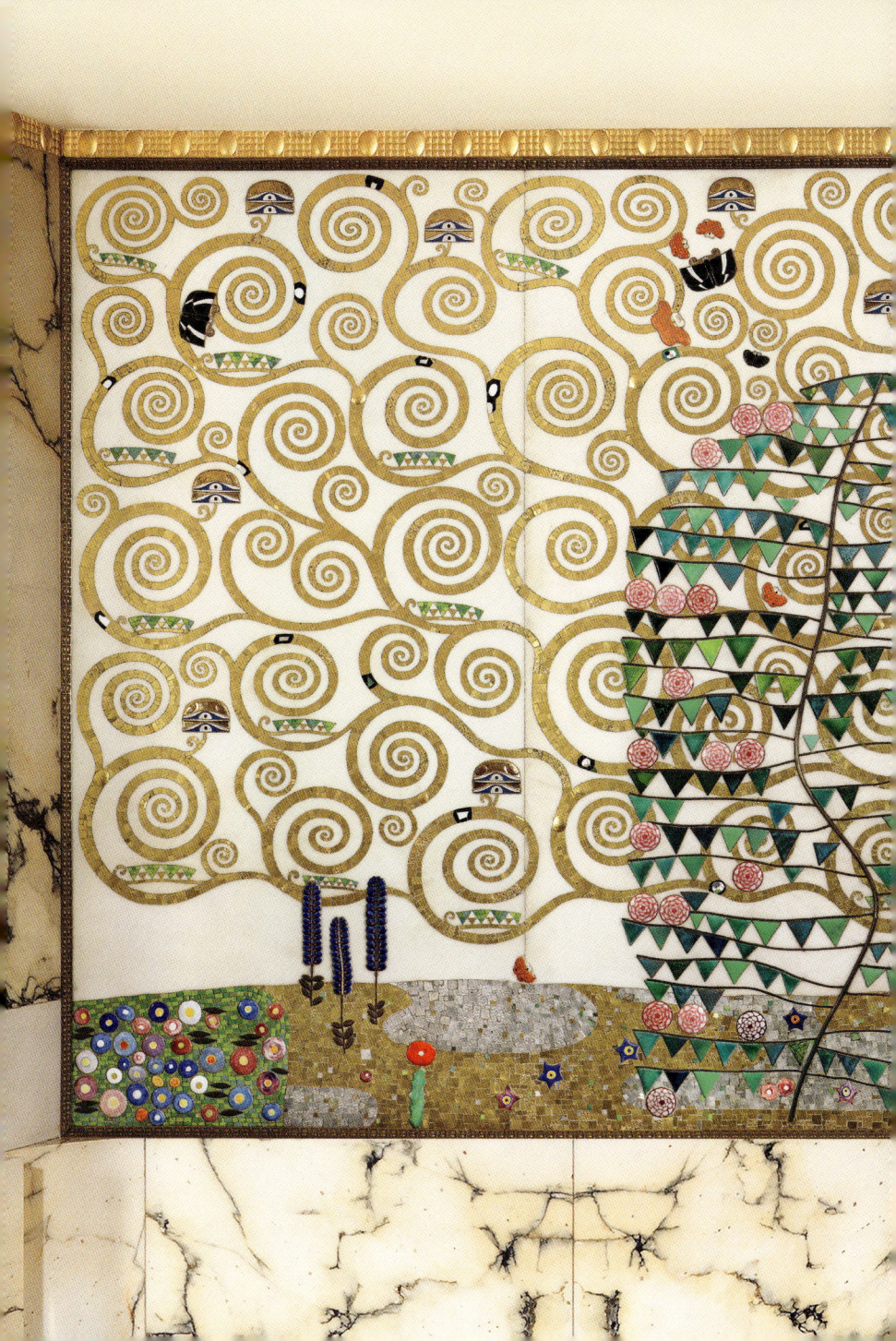

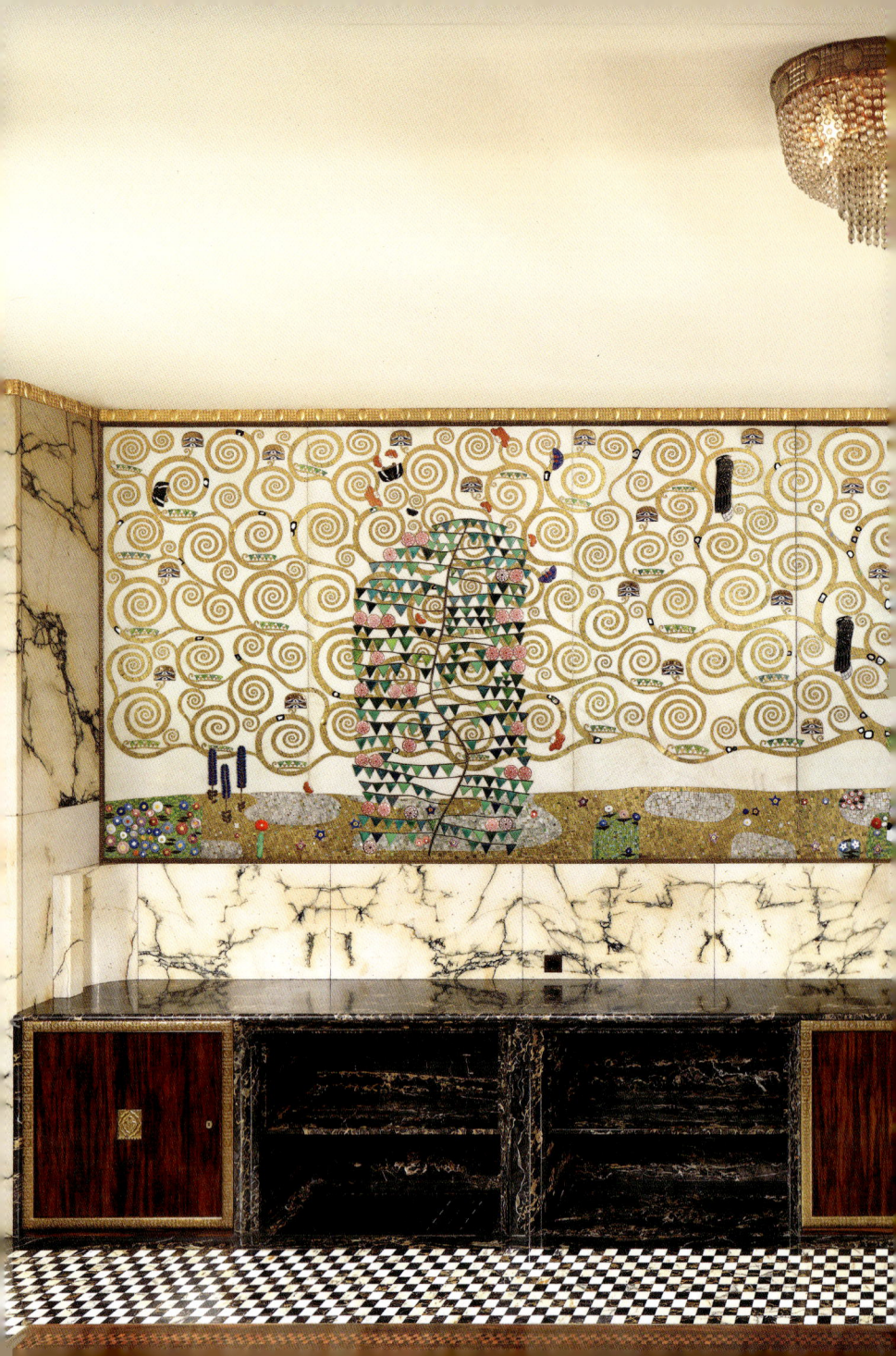

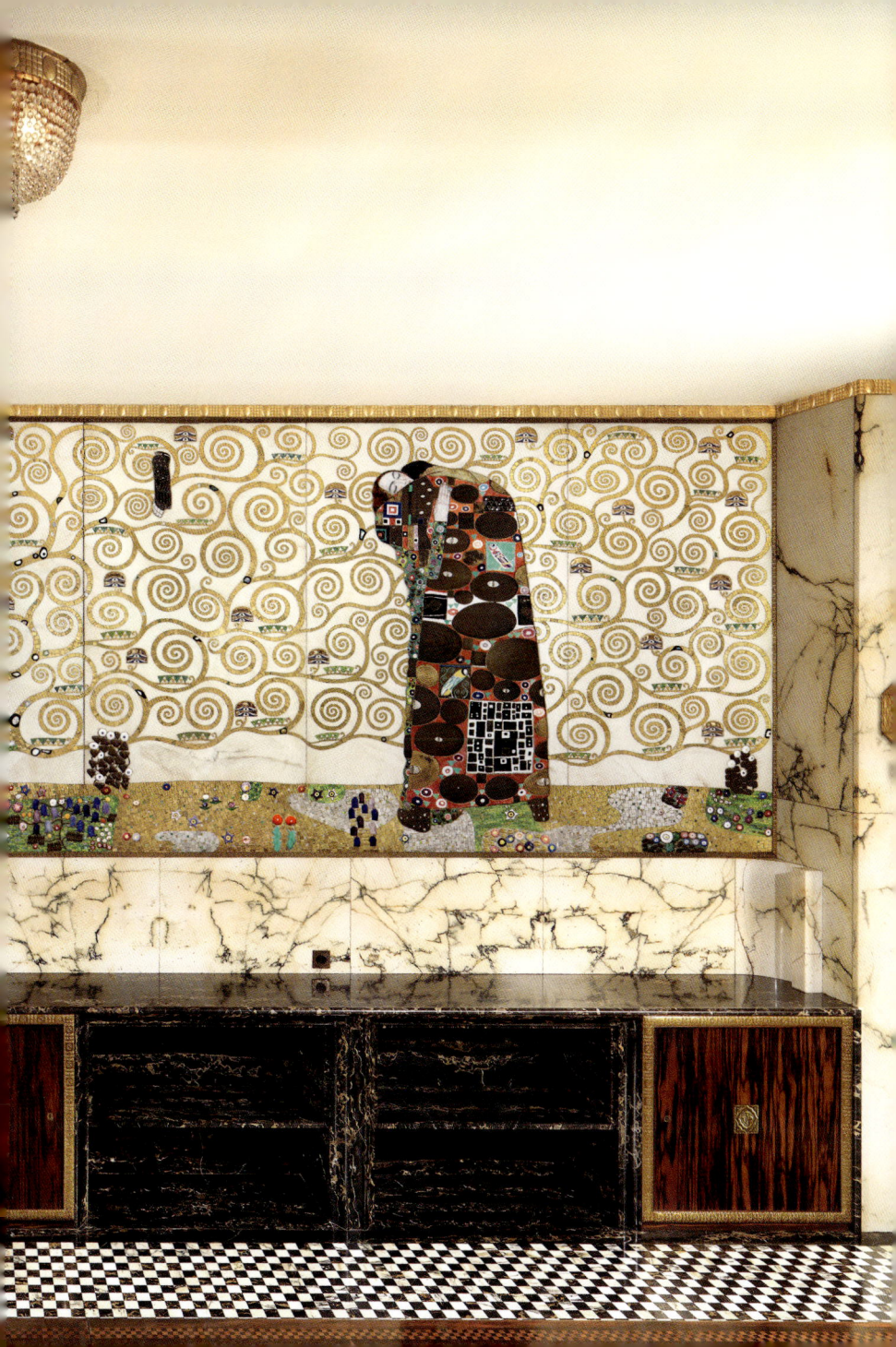

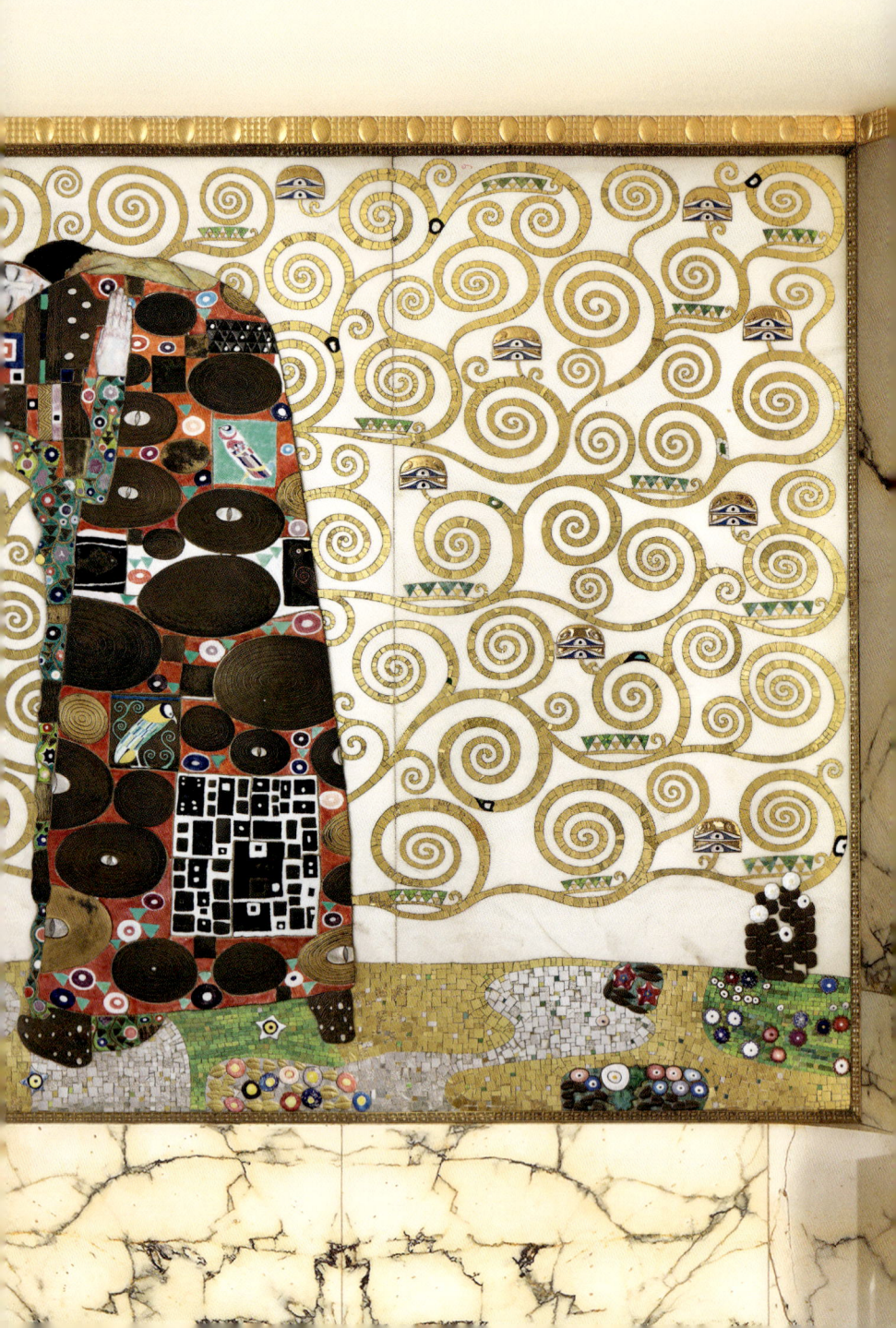

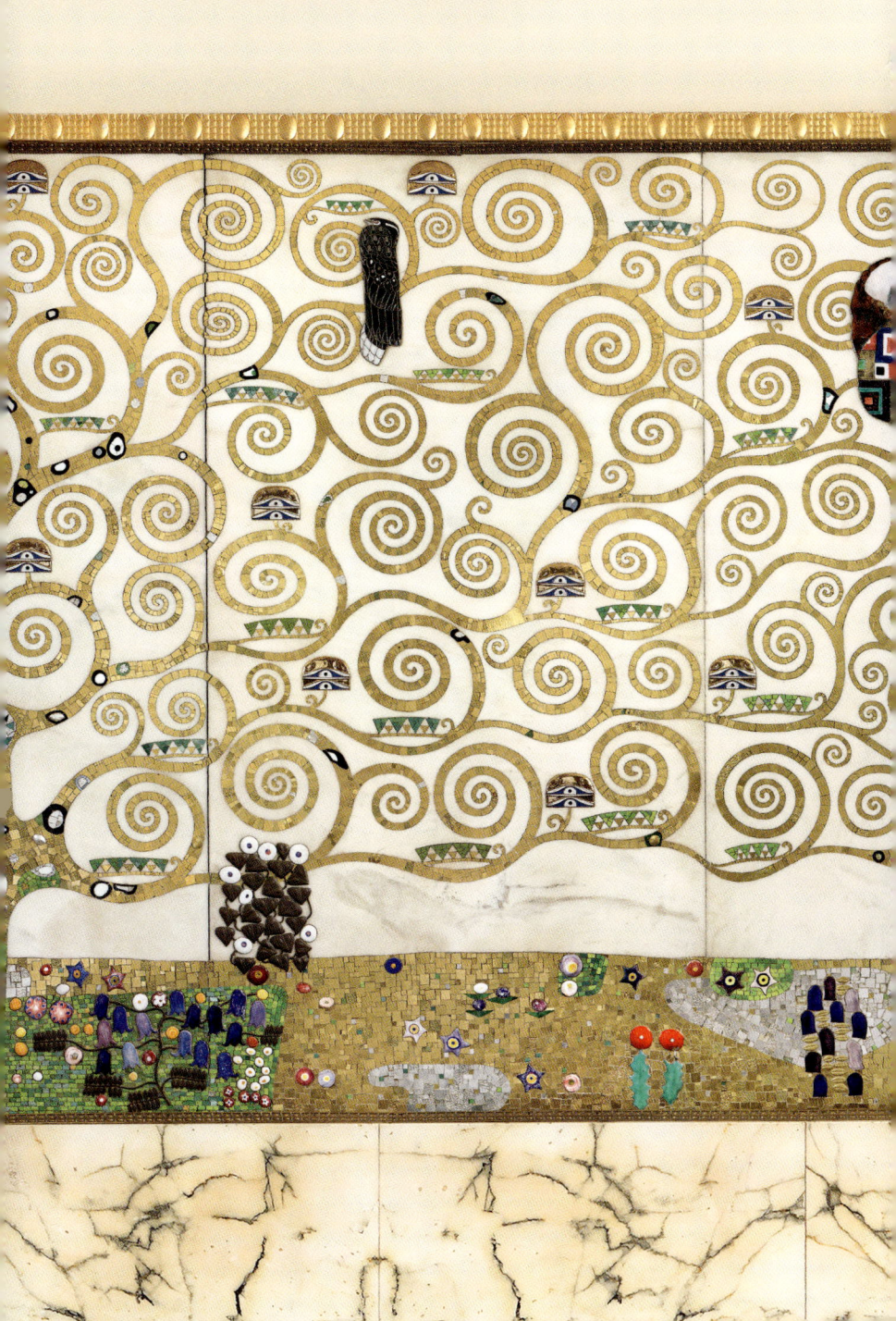

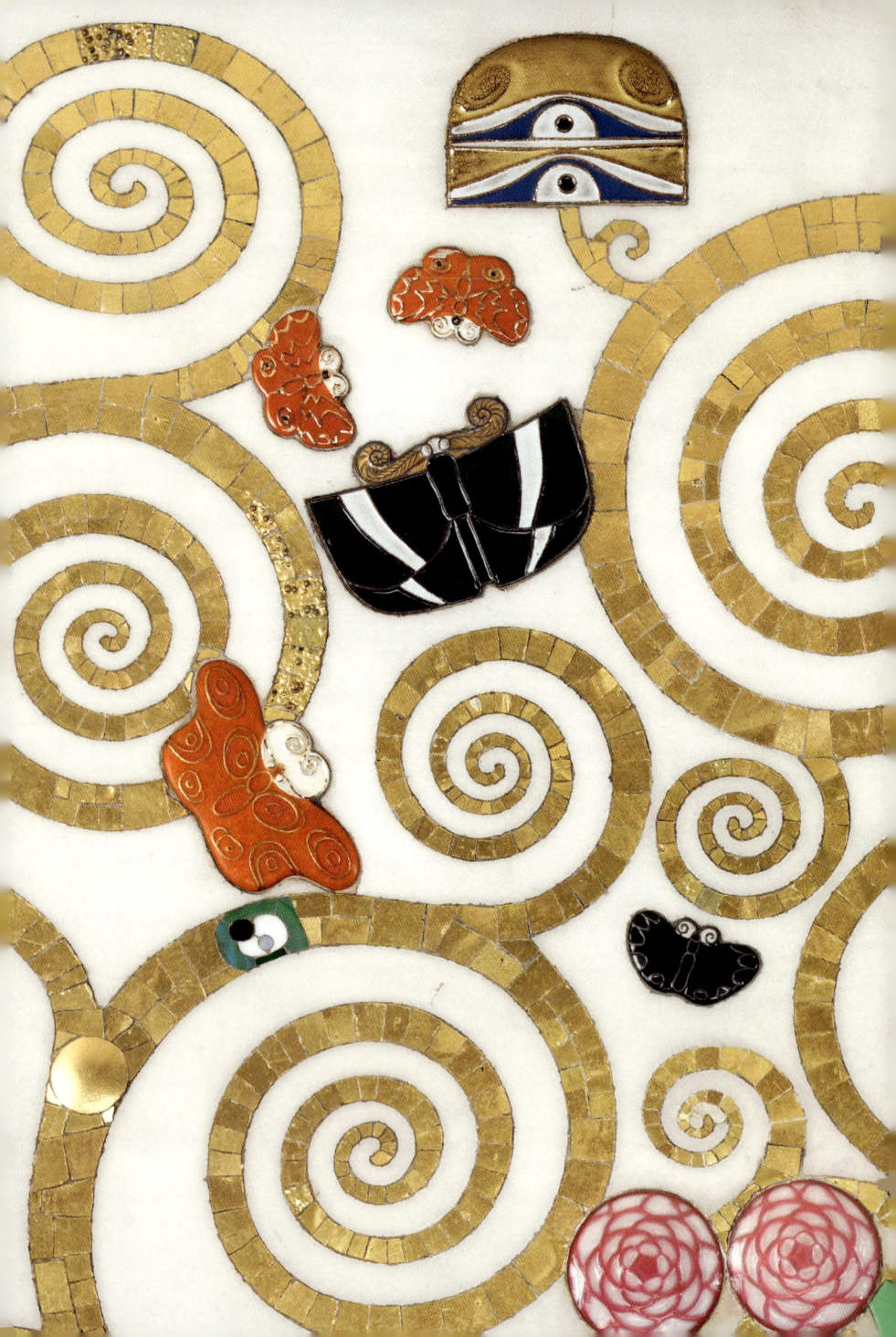

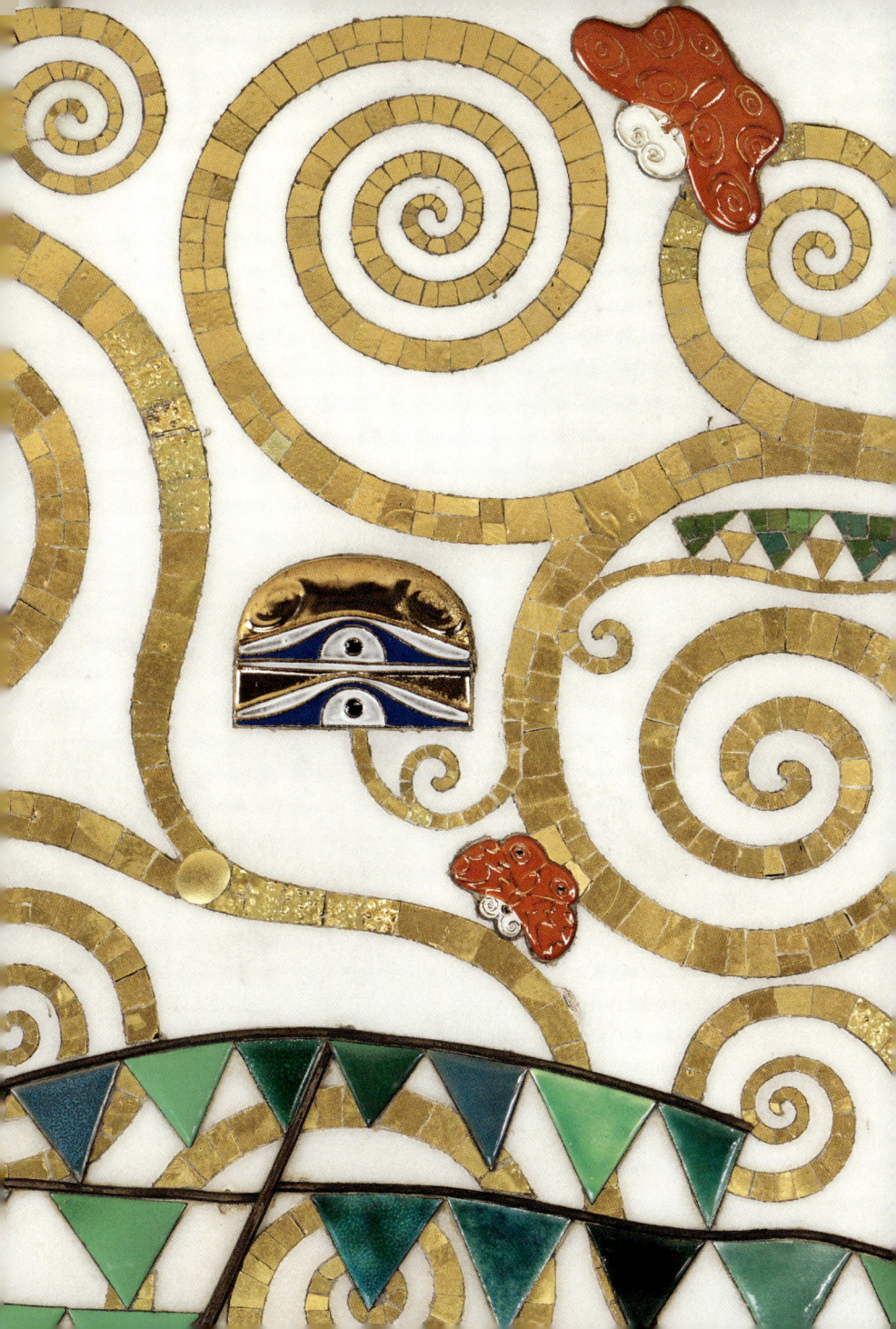

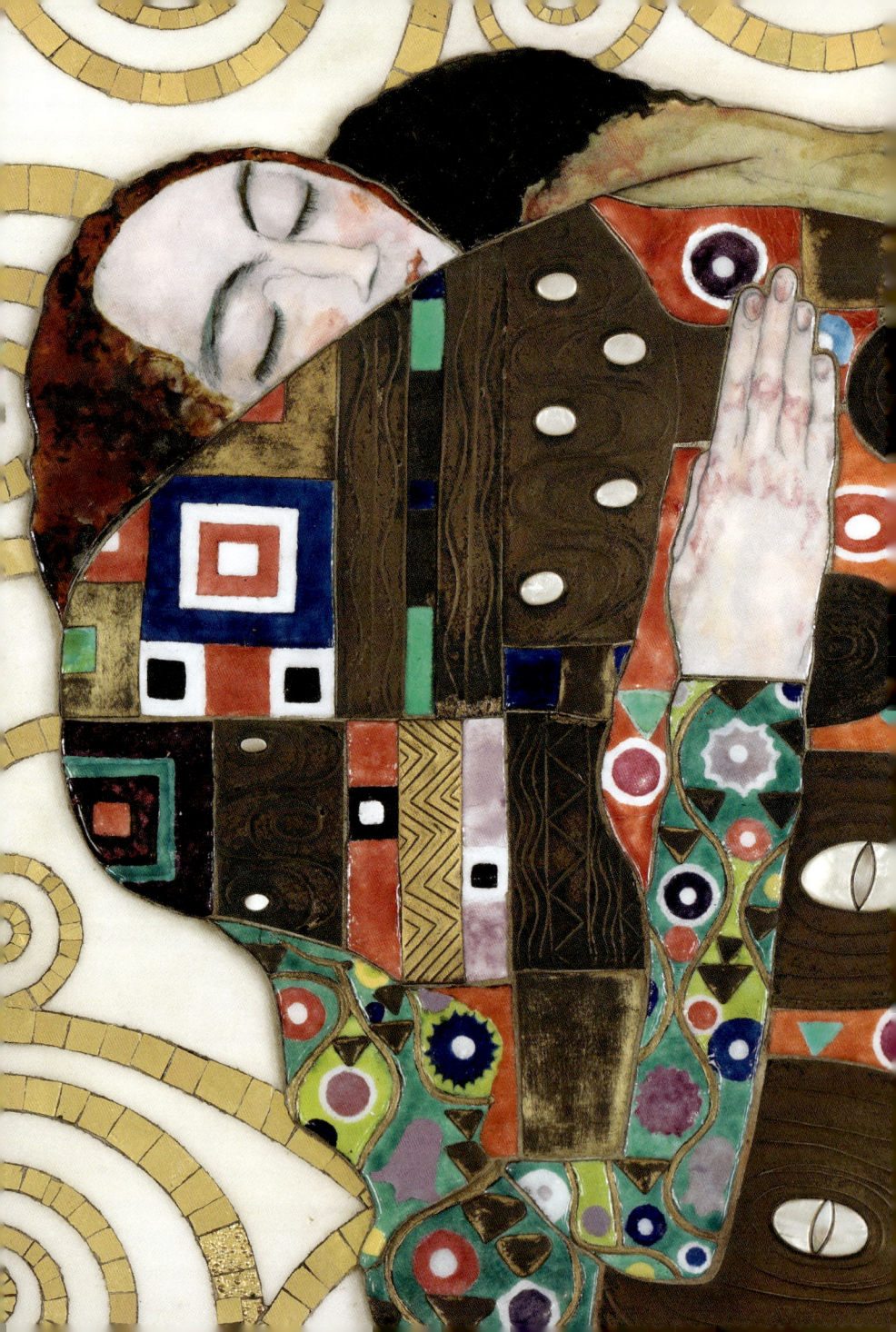

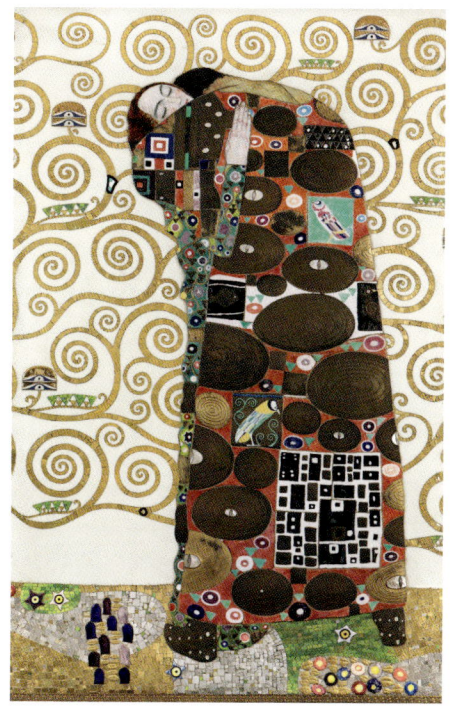

Pages 220/21
Details of the left-hand mosaic wall, 1909–1911

Pages 222–223
The "Pair of Lovers" ("Fulfilment") (details), 1909–1911

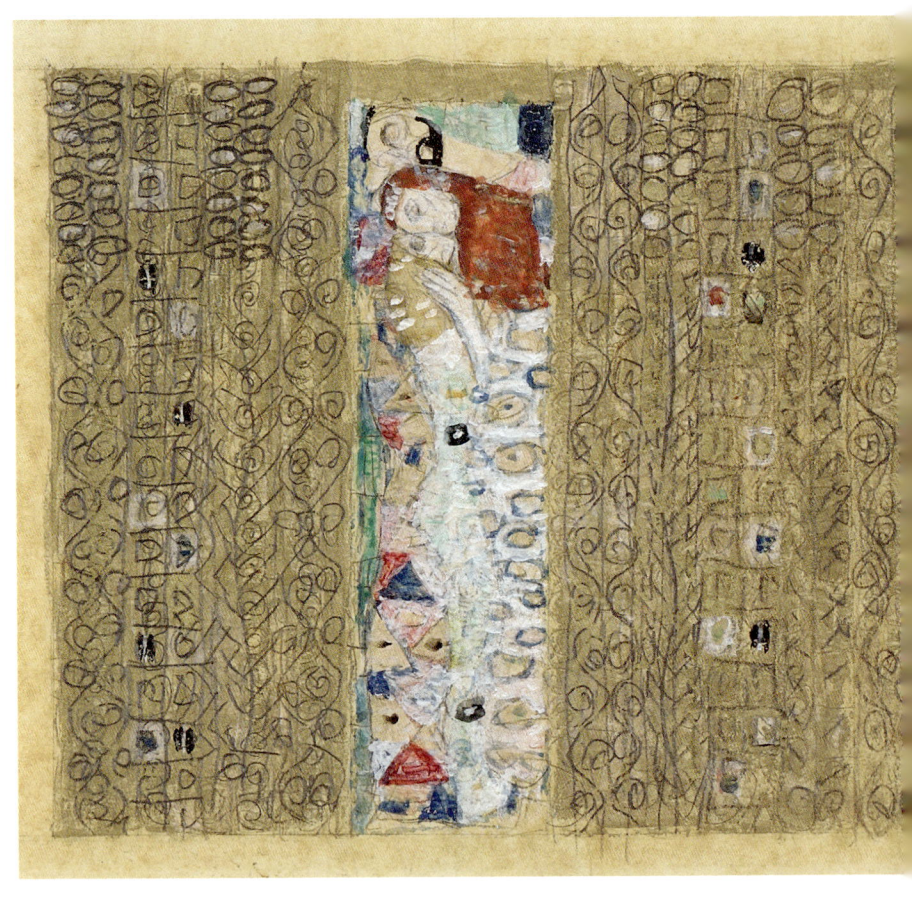

Small design for the "Family" (not executed) (detail), 1907/08
Pencil and watercolour on transparent paper, 22 x 75.3 cm / 8 ⅝ x 29 ⅝ in.
Vienna, MAK – Österreichisches Museum für angewandte Kunst/Gegenwartskunst

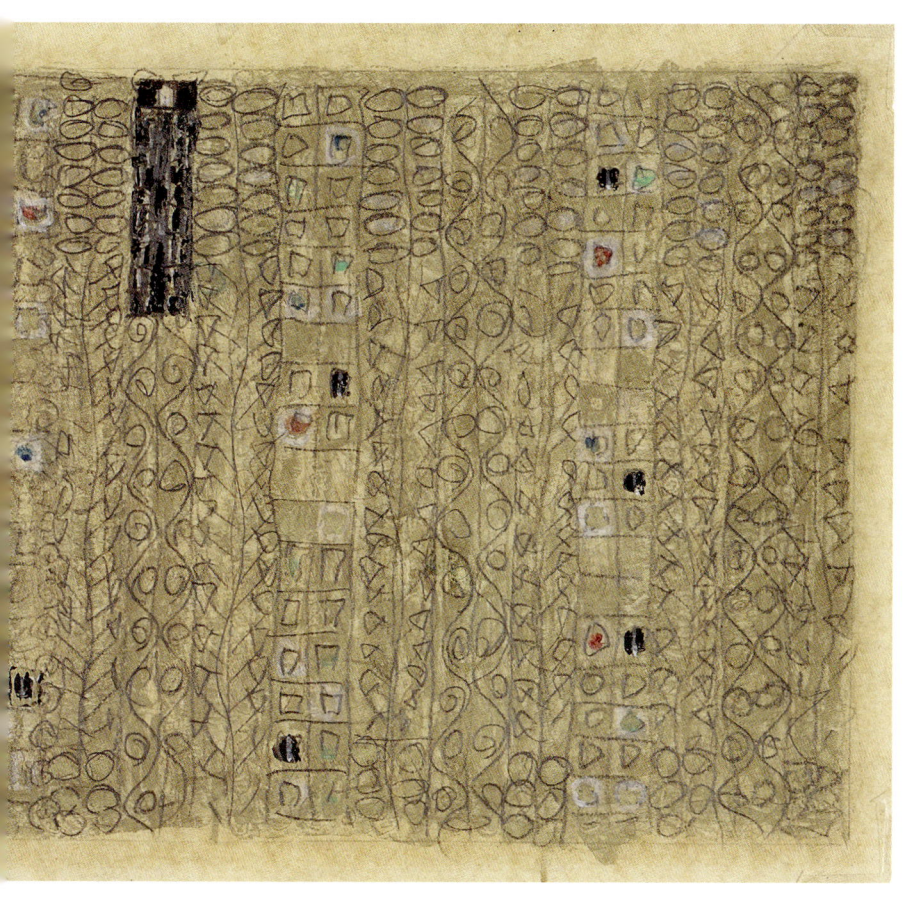

Pages 227–237
Details of the left-hand mosaic wall, 1909–1911

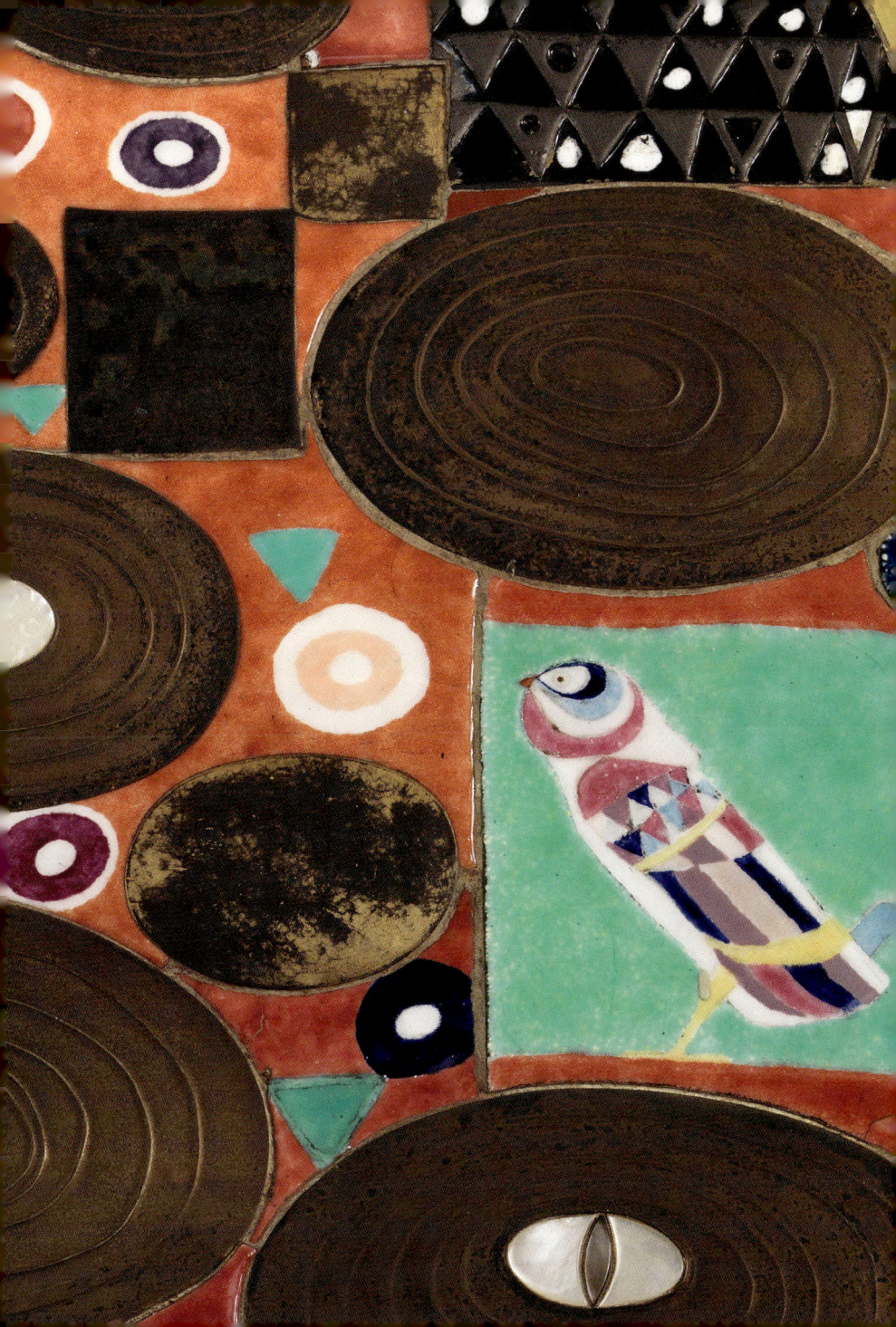

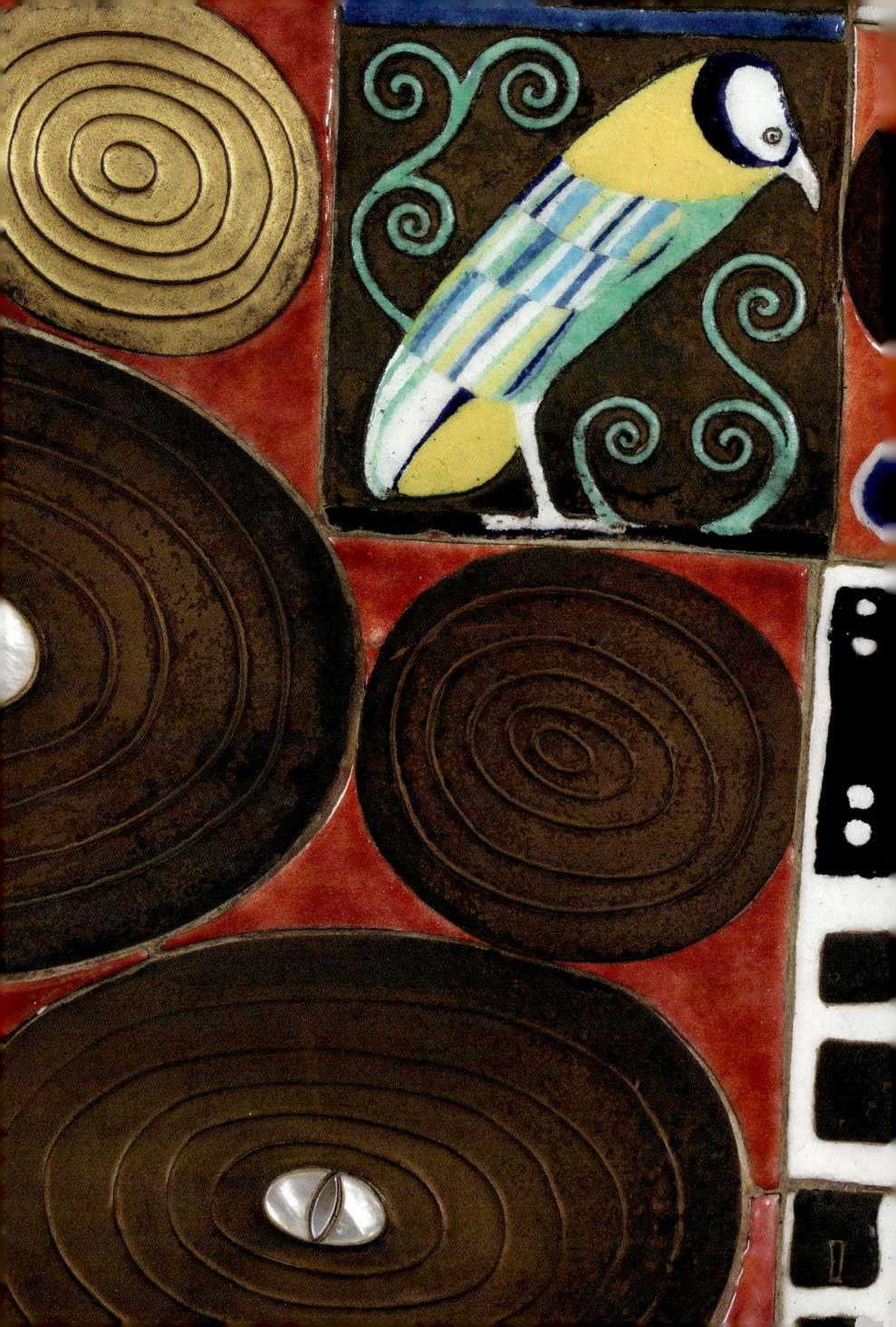

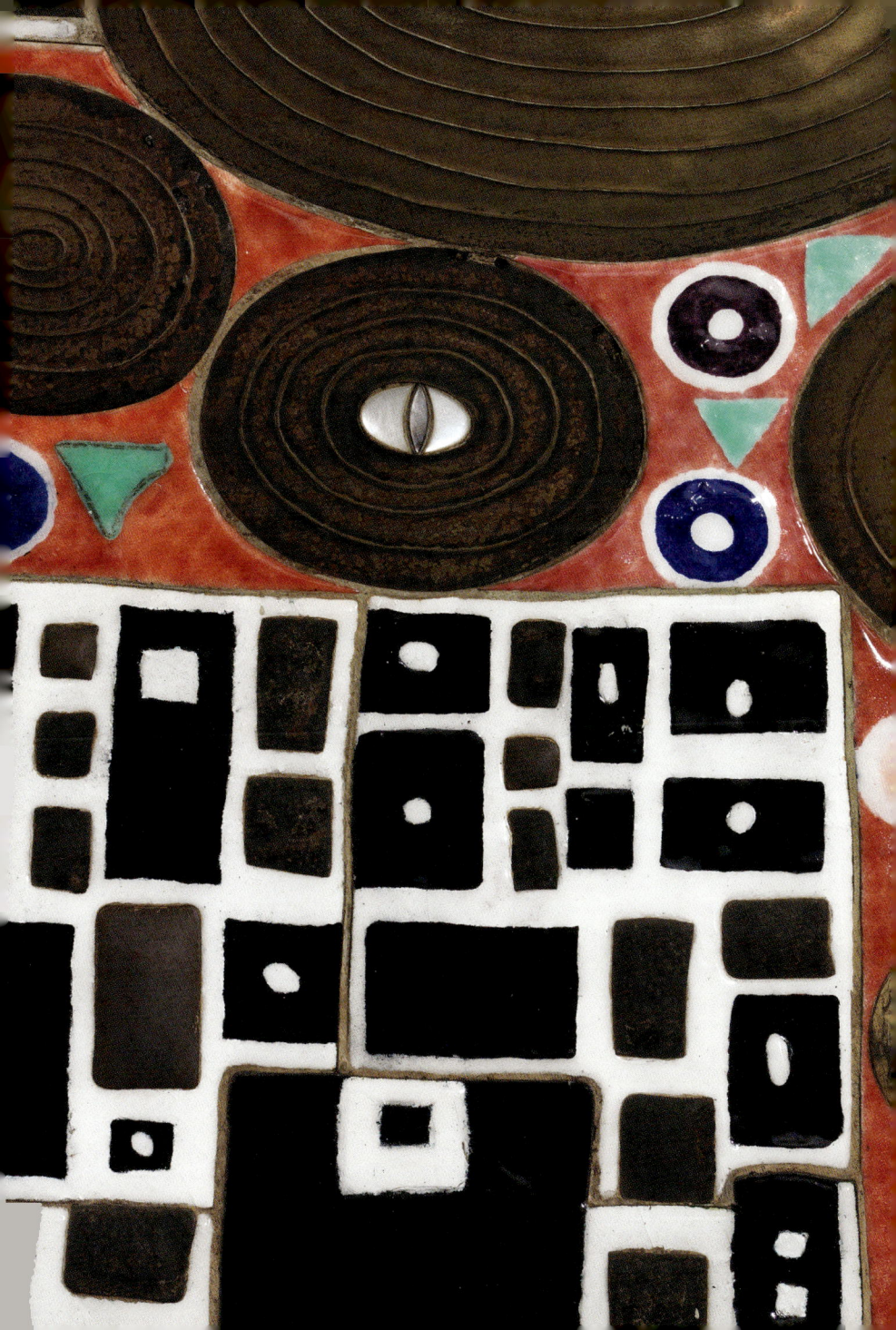

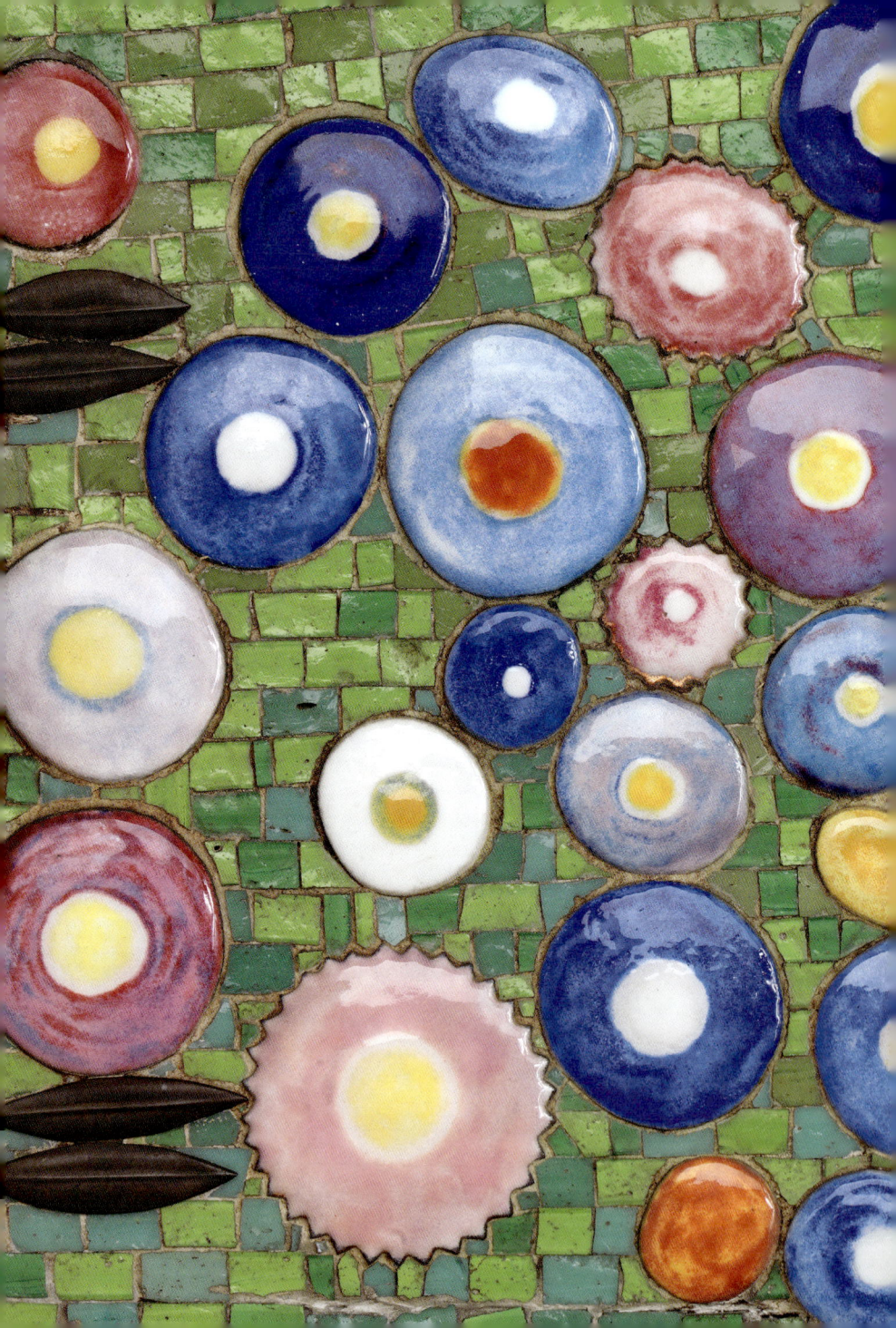

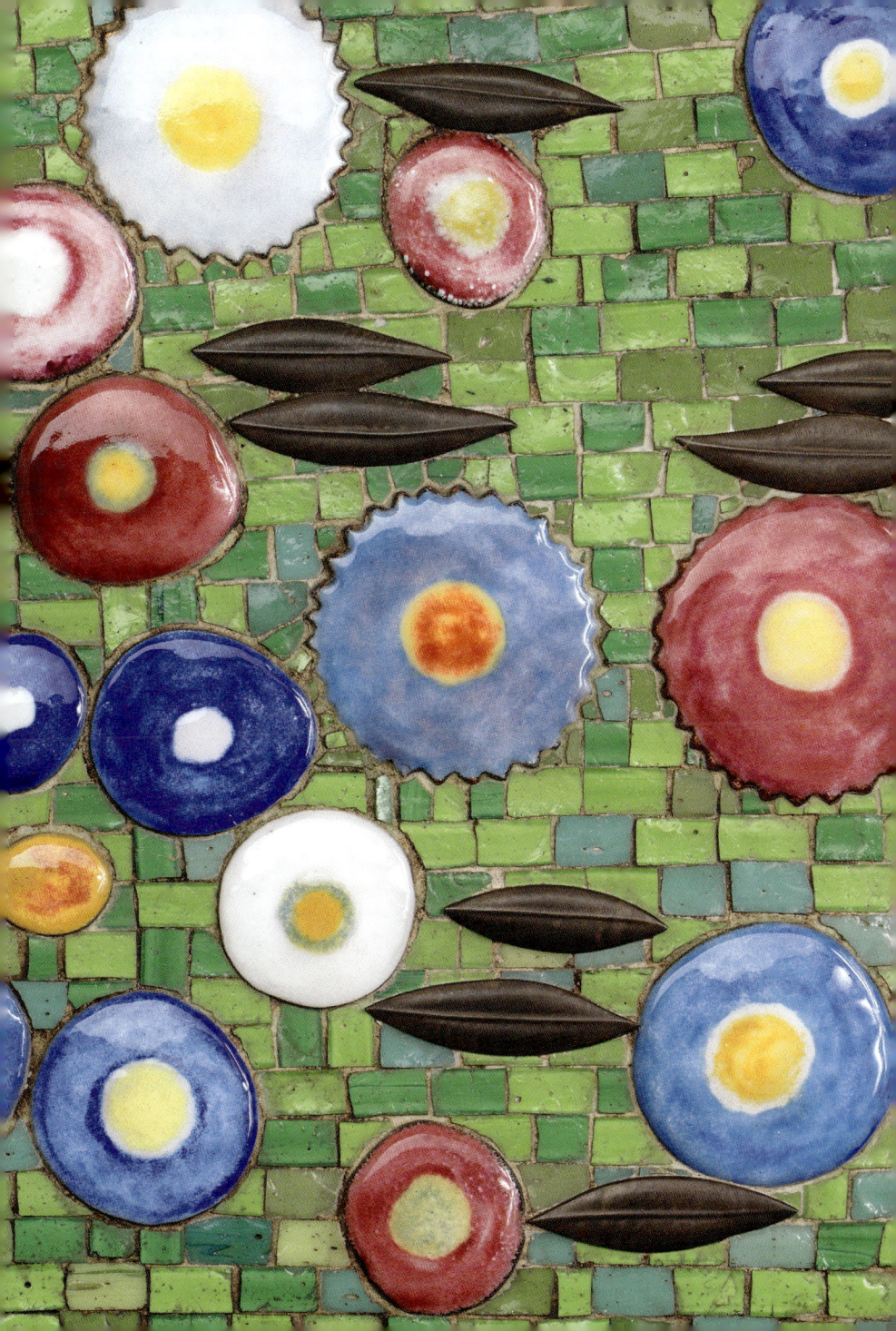

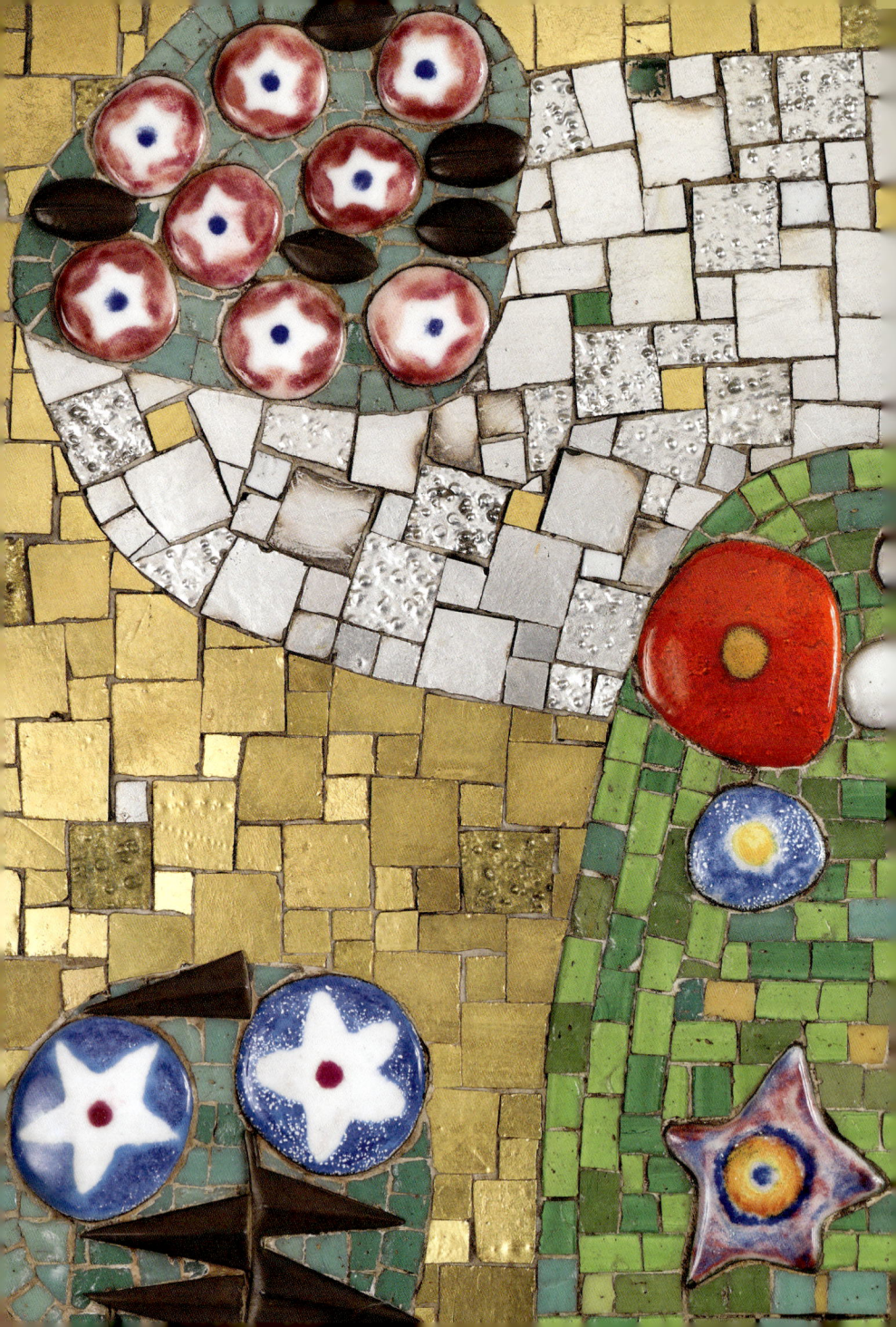

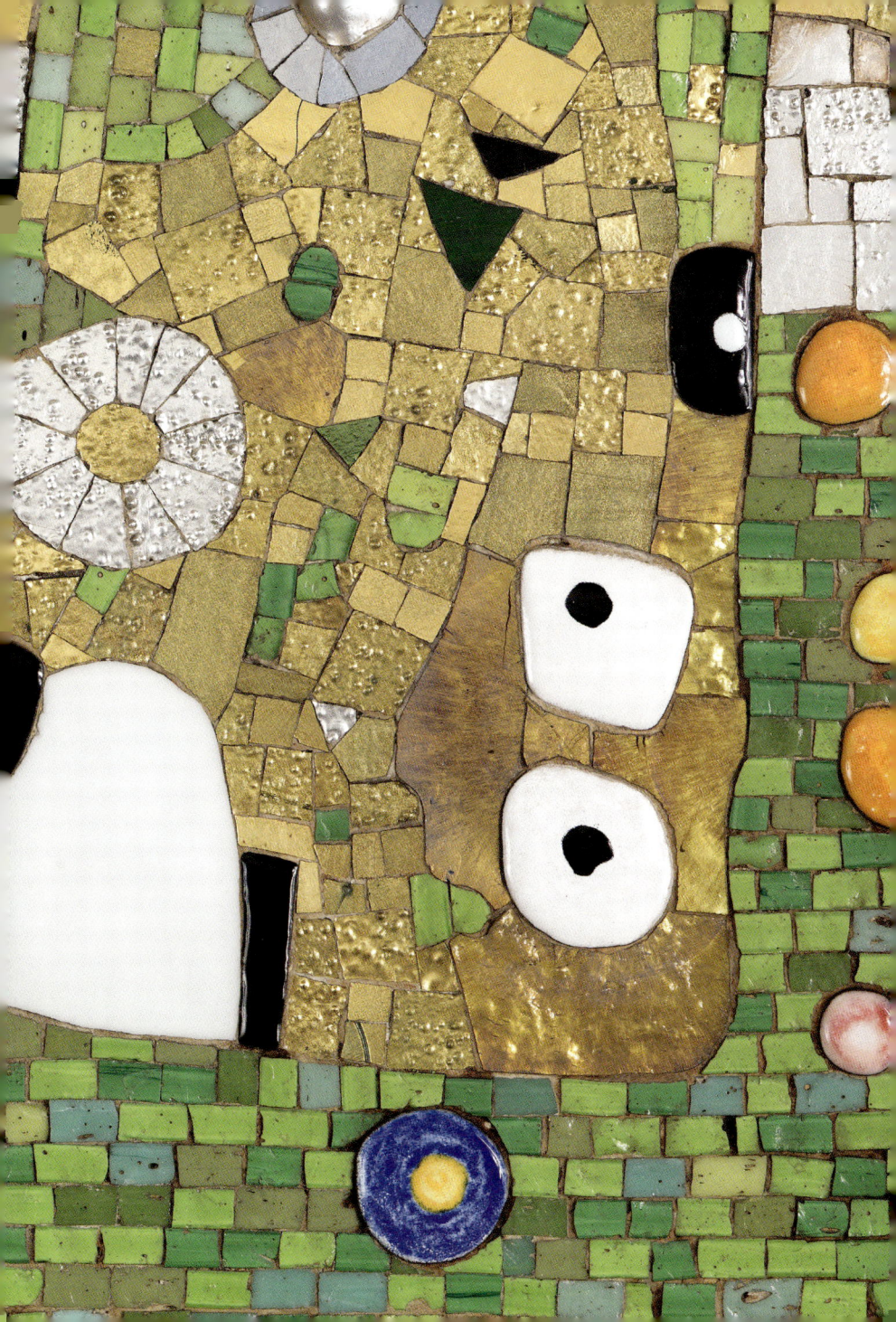

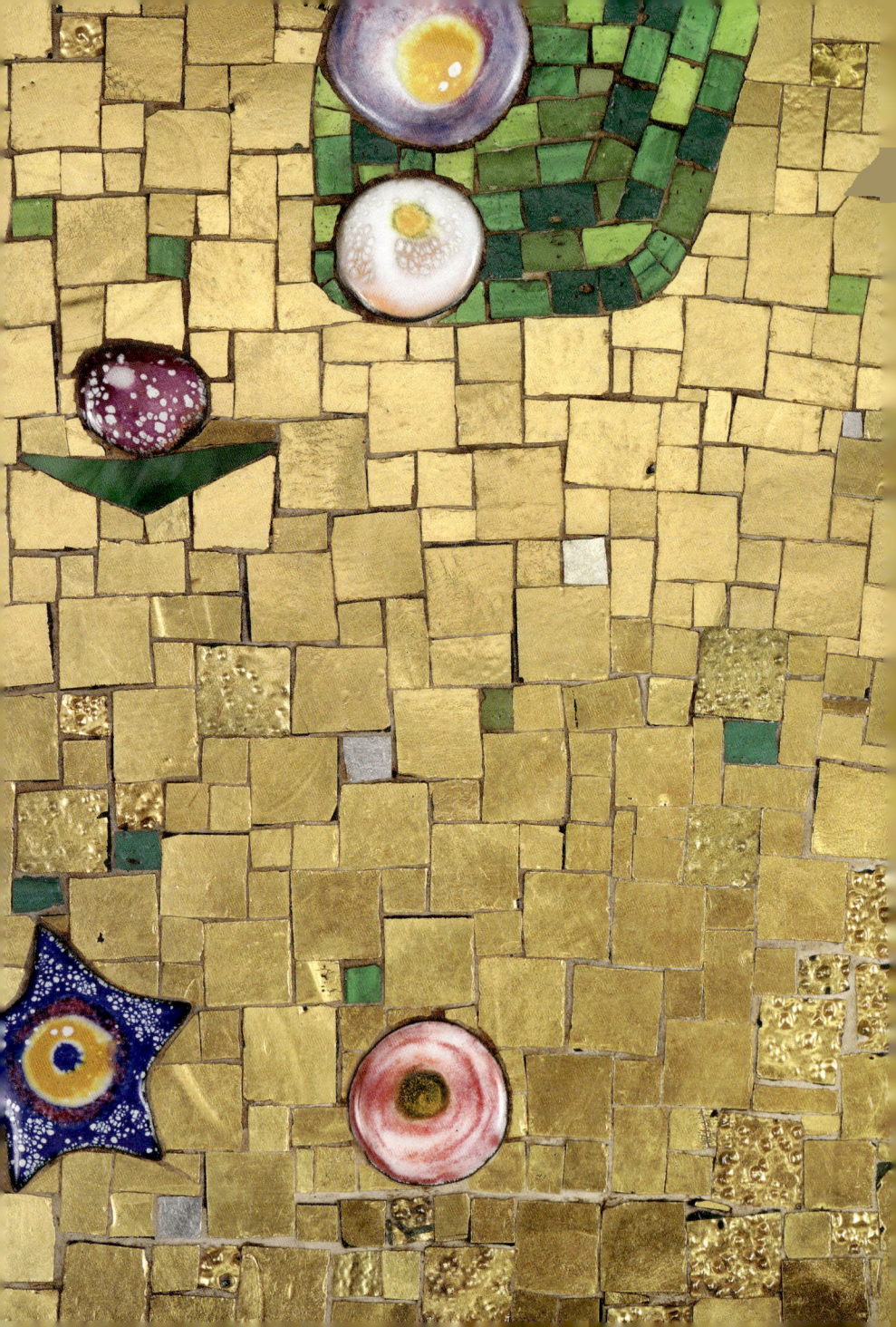

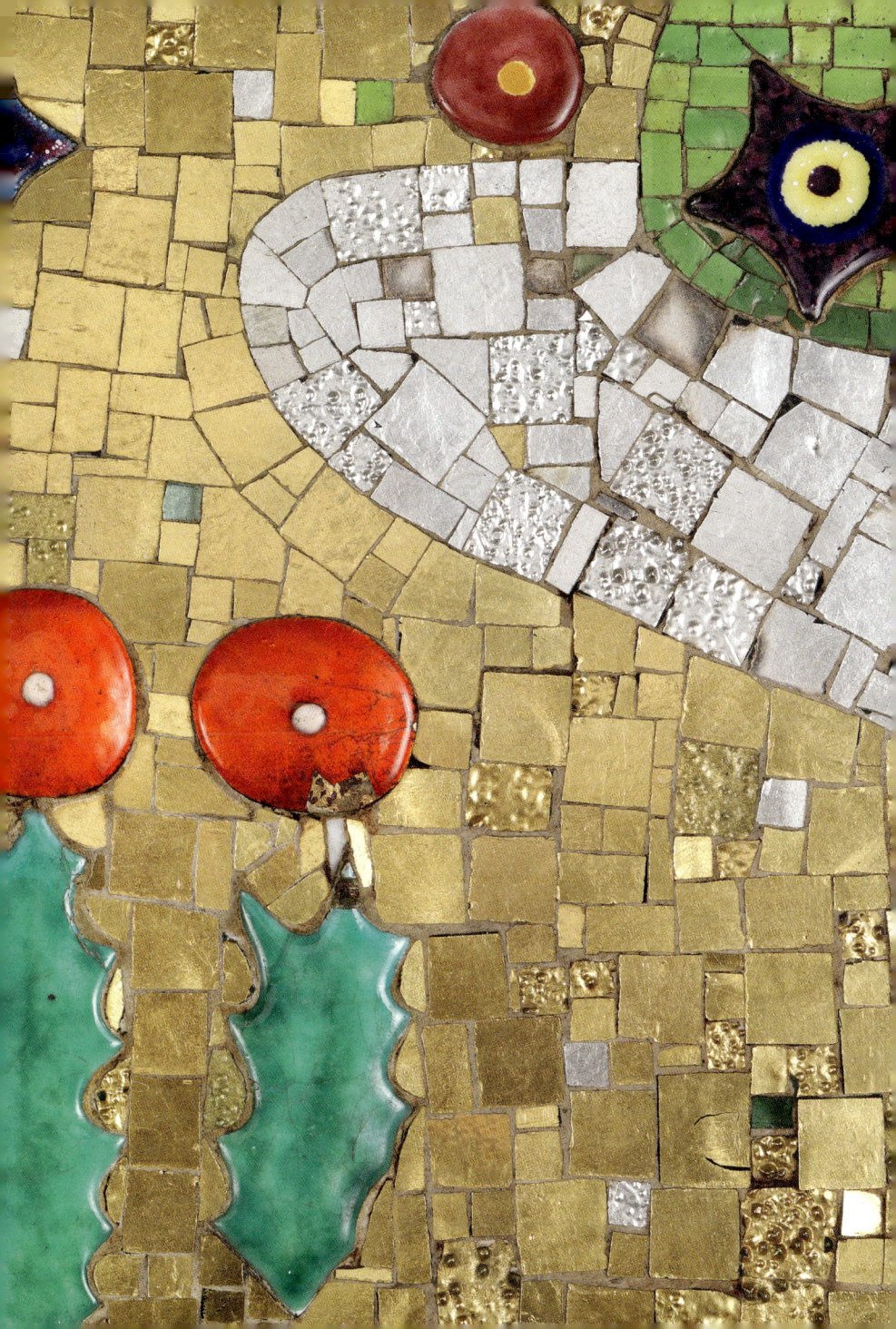

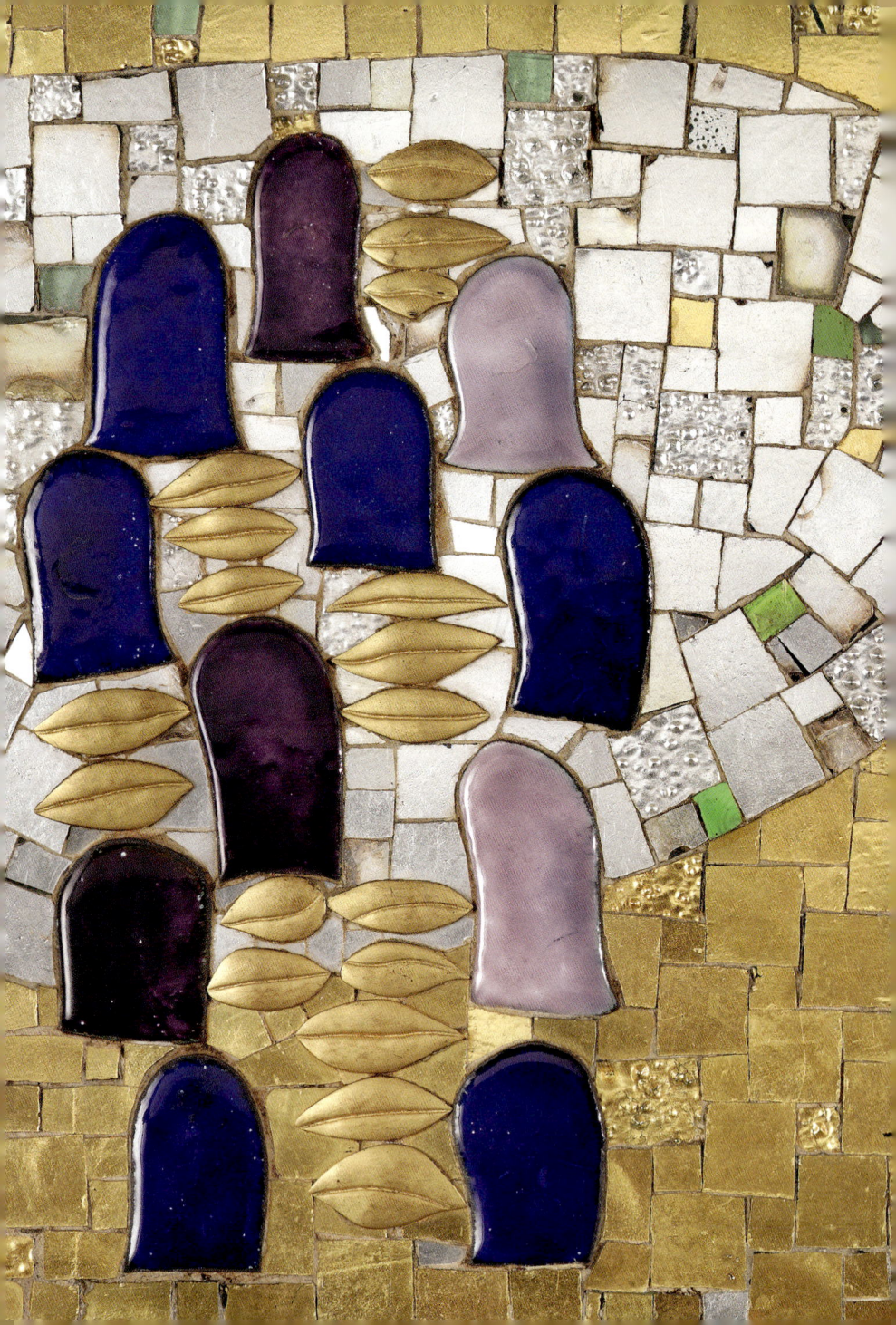

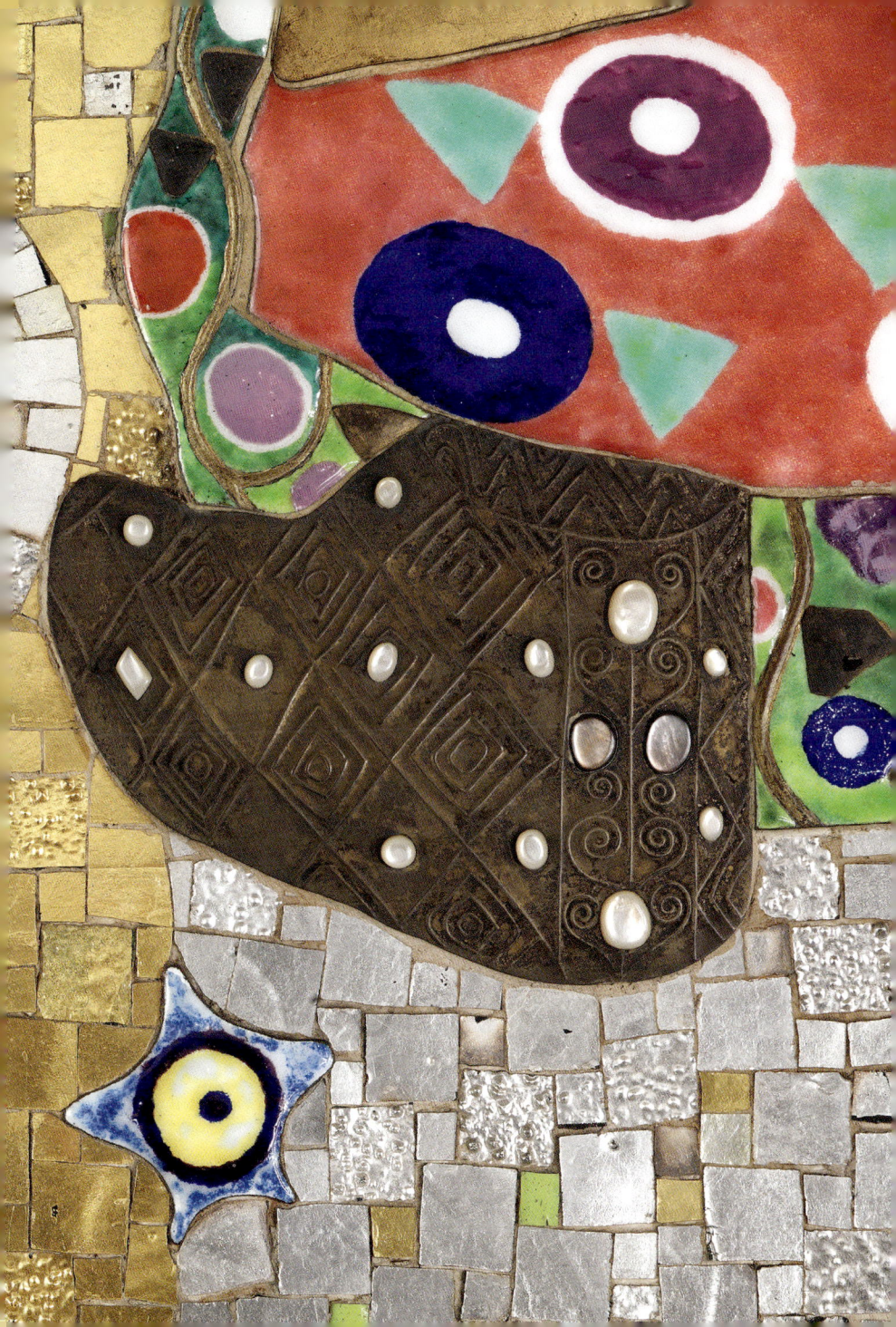

Detail of the left-hand mosaic wall, 1909–1911

Pages 240/41
View of the entrance wall with the "Knight", 1909–1911

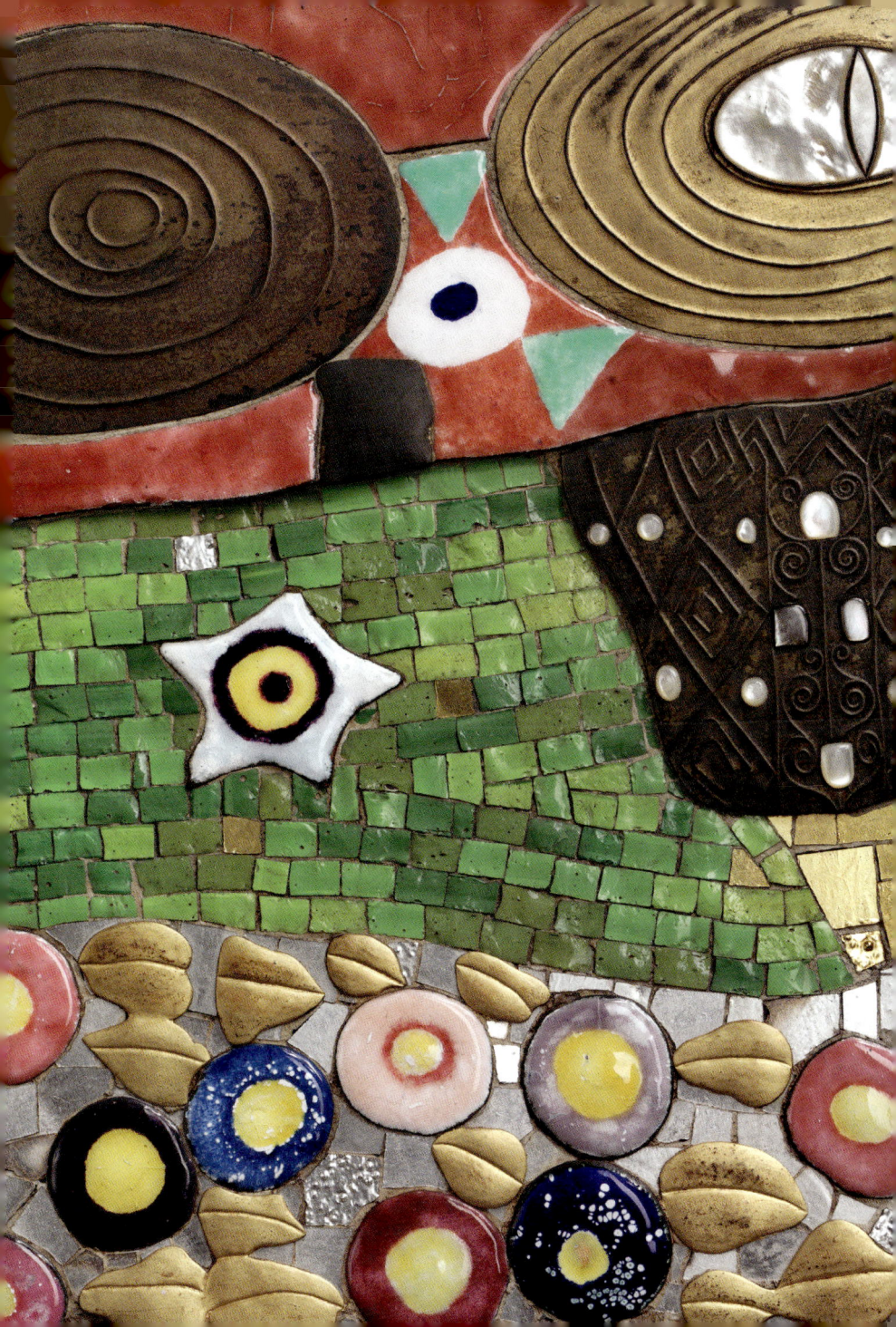

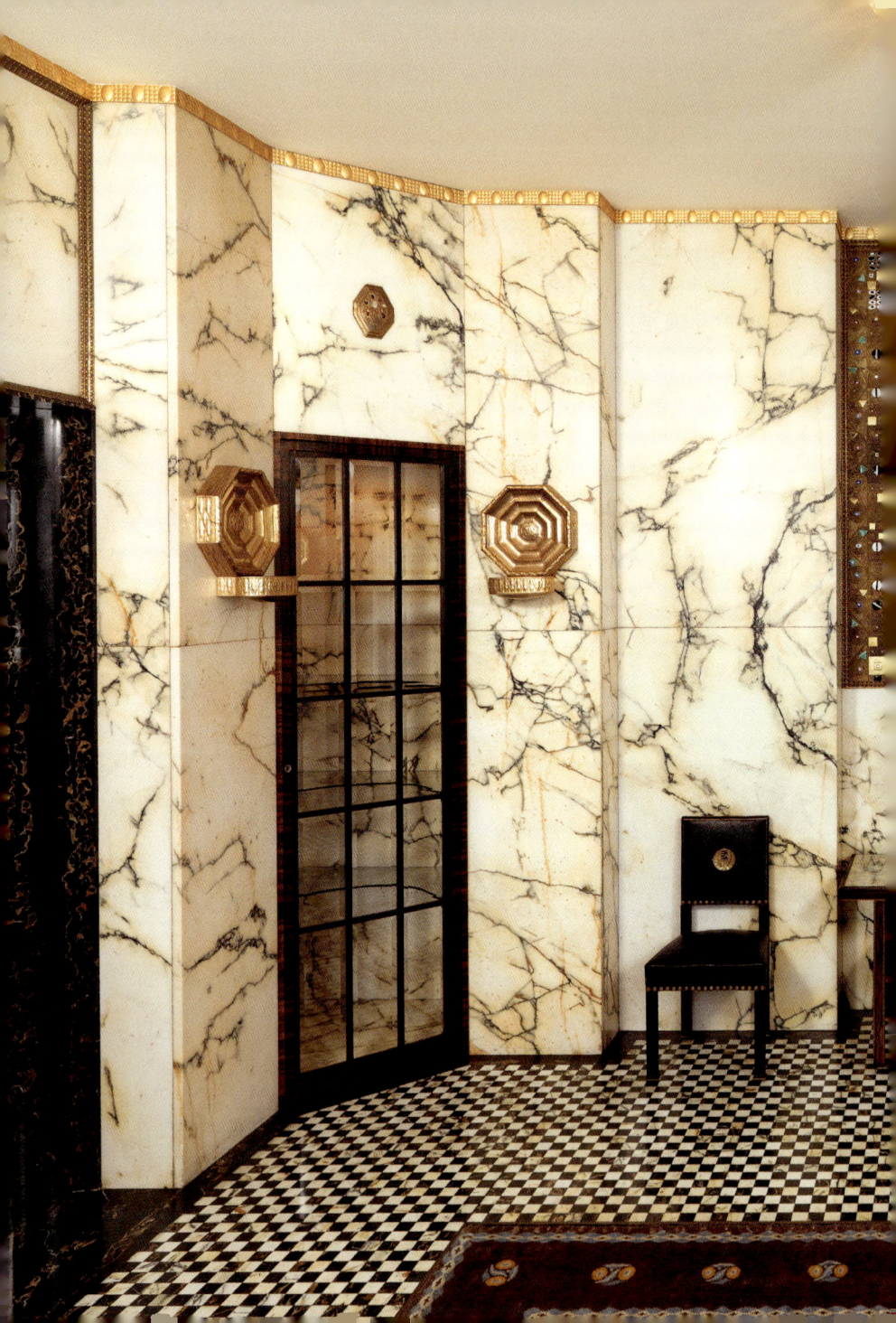

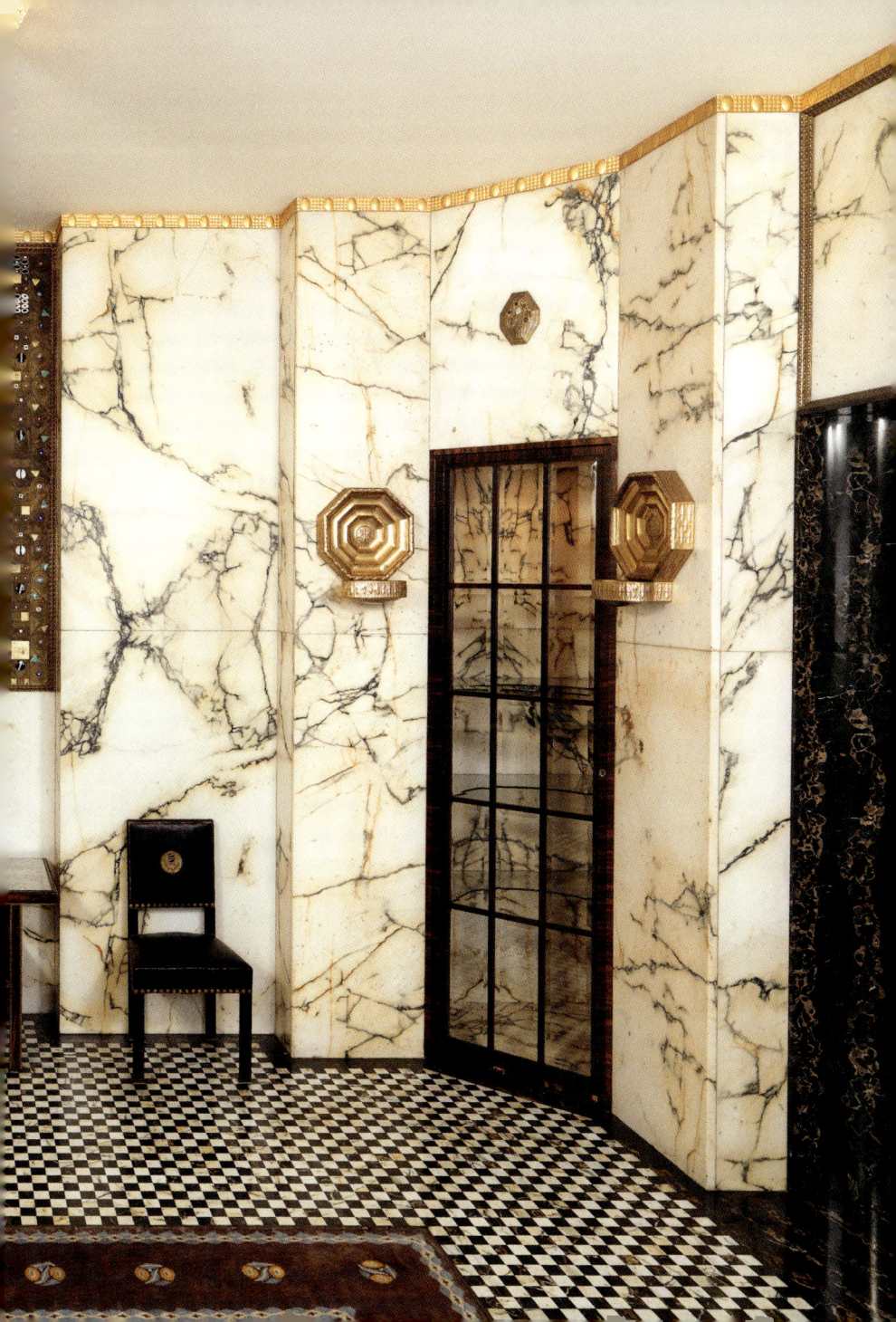

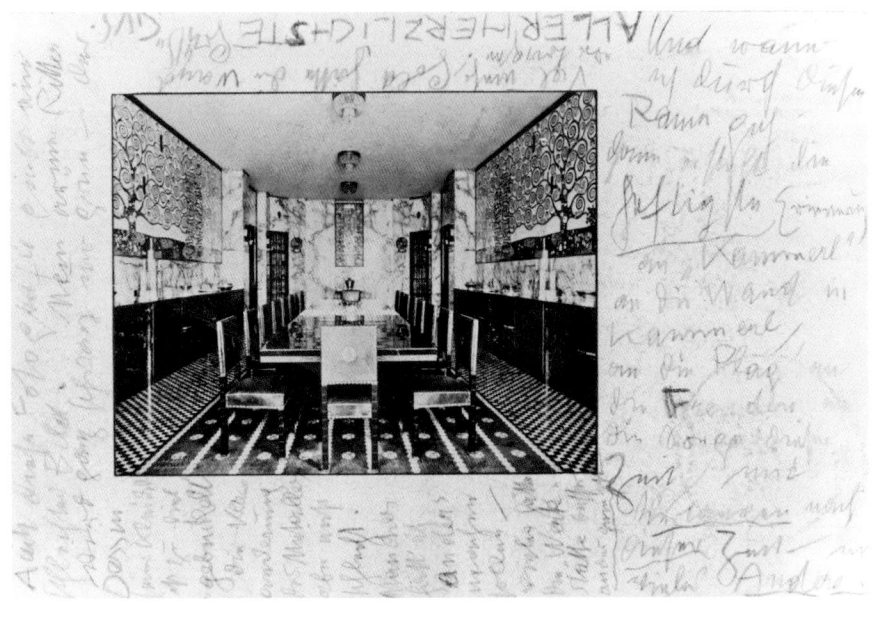

Gustav Klimt, **Postcard to Emilie Flöge with
a view of the Palais Stoclet dining room**, 18.5.1914
Private collection (see also ill. pp. 188/89)

Mosaic of the "Knight", 1909–1911

Pages 244–253
Details of the "Knight", 1909–1911

Pages 254/55
Josef Hoffmann, **street view of the exterior façade of the Palais Stoclet**
Gelatin silver print, 1910. Bildarchiv Foto Marburg

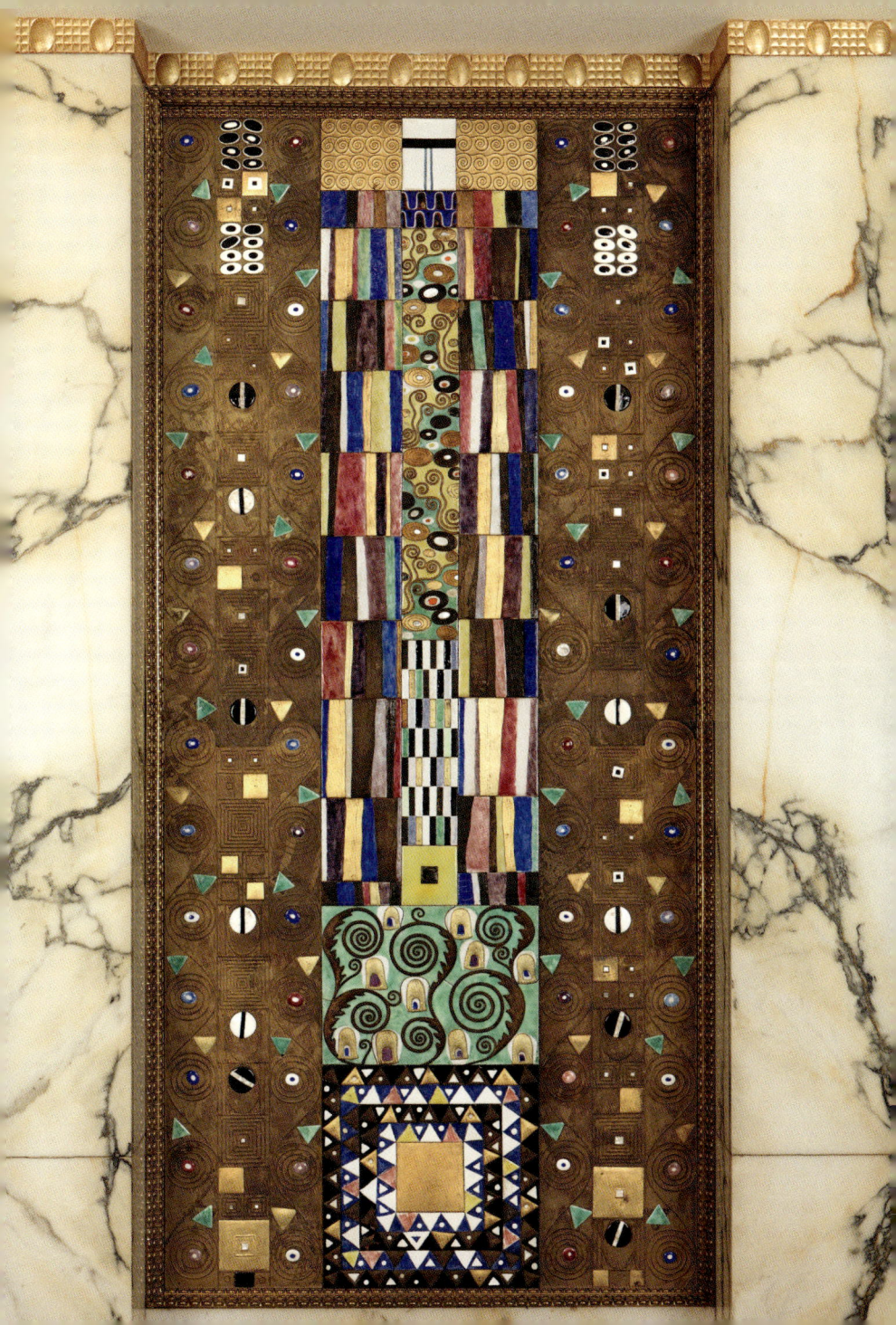

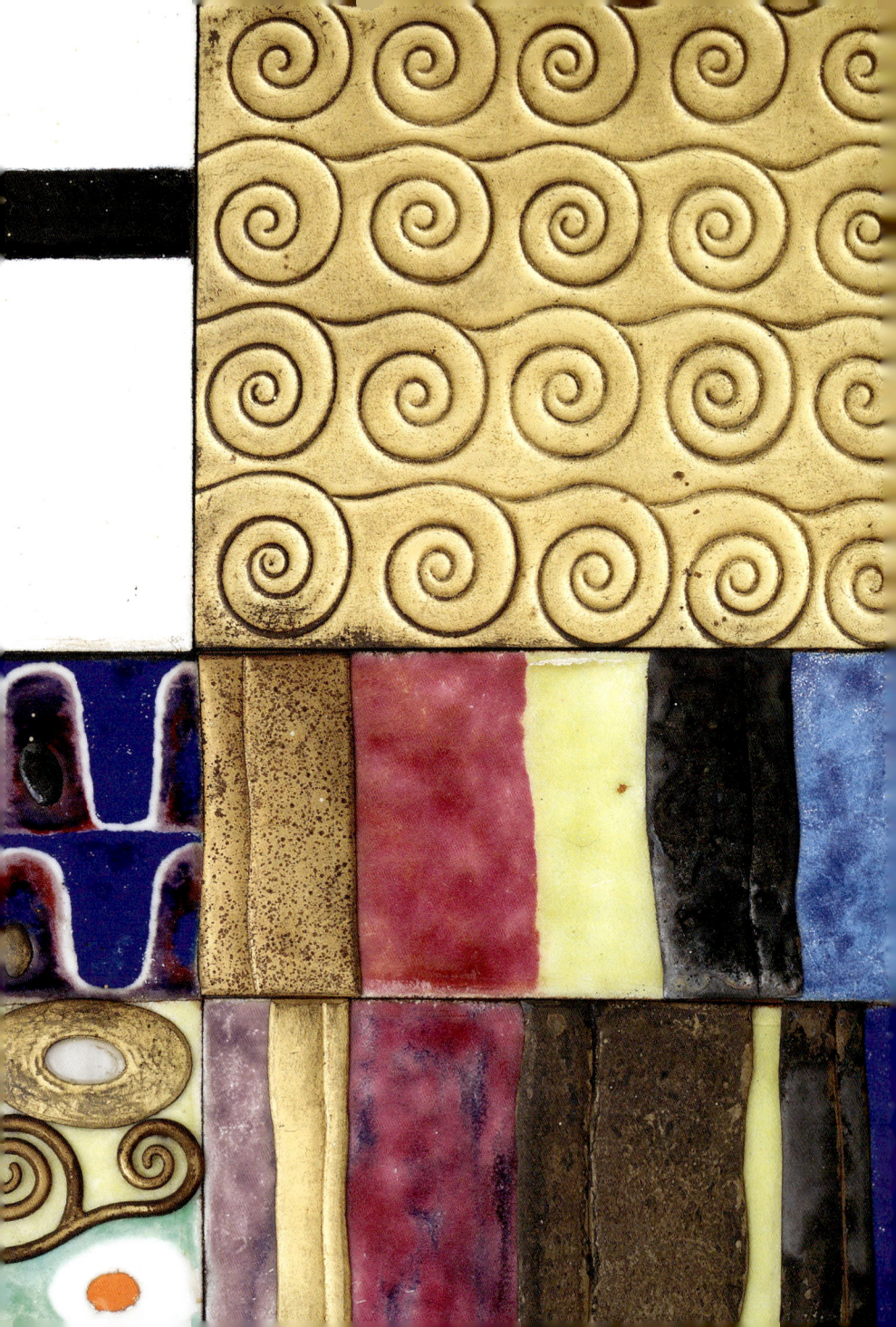

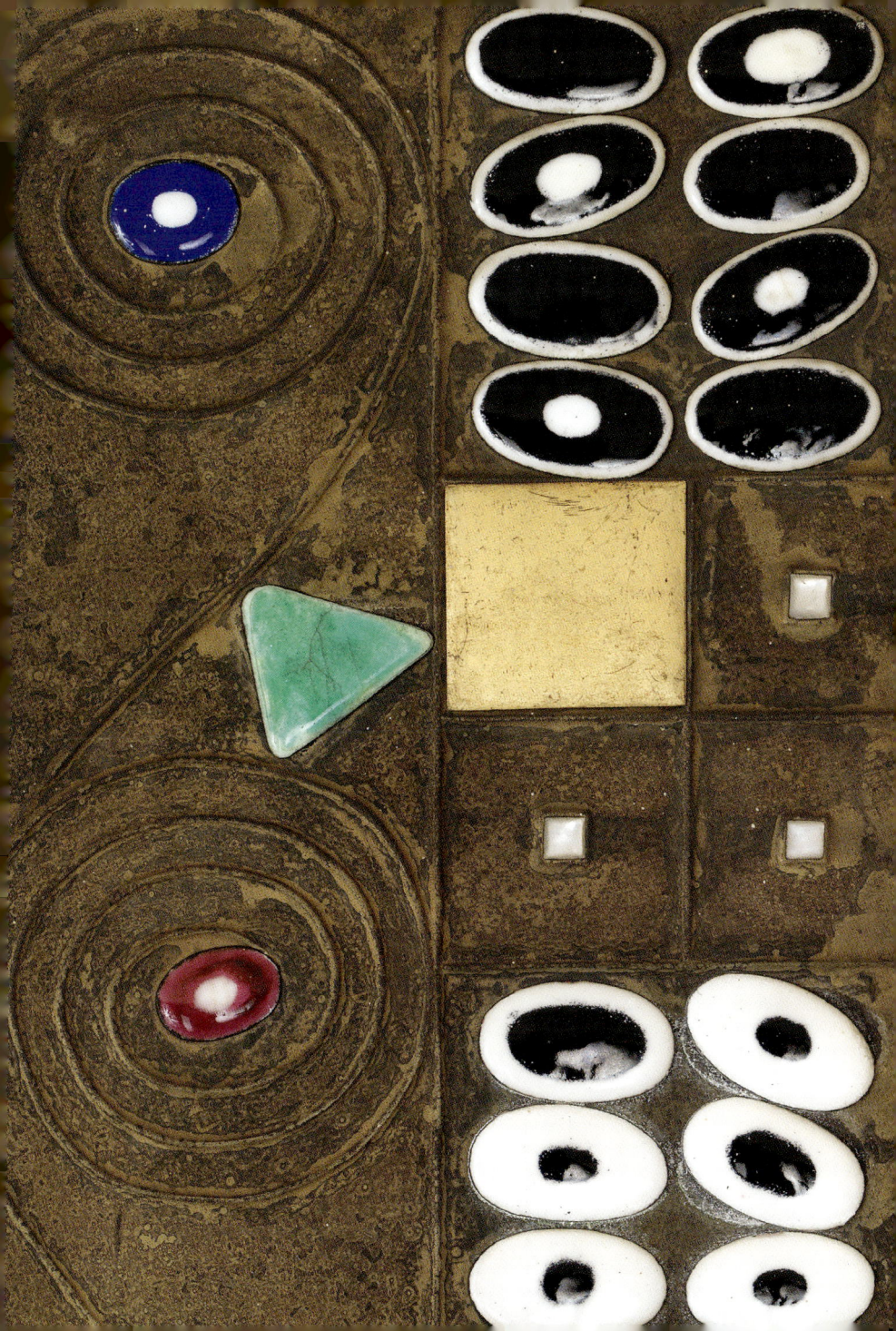

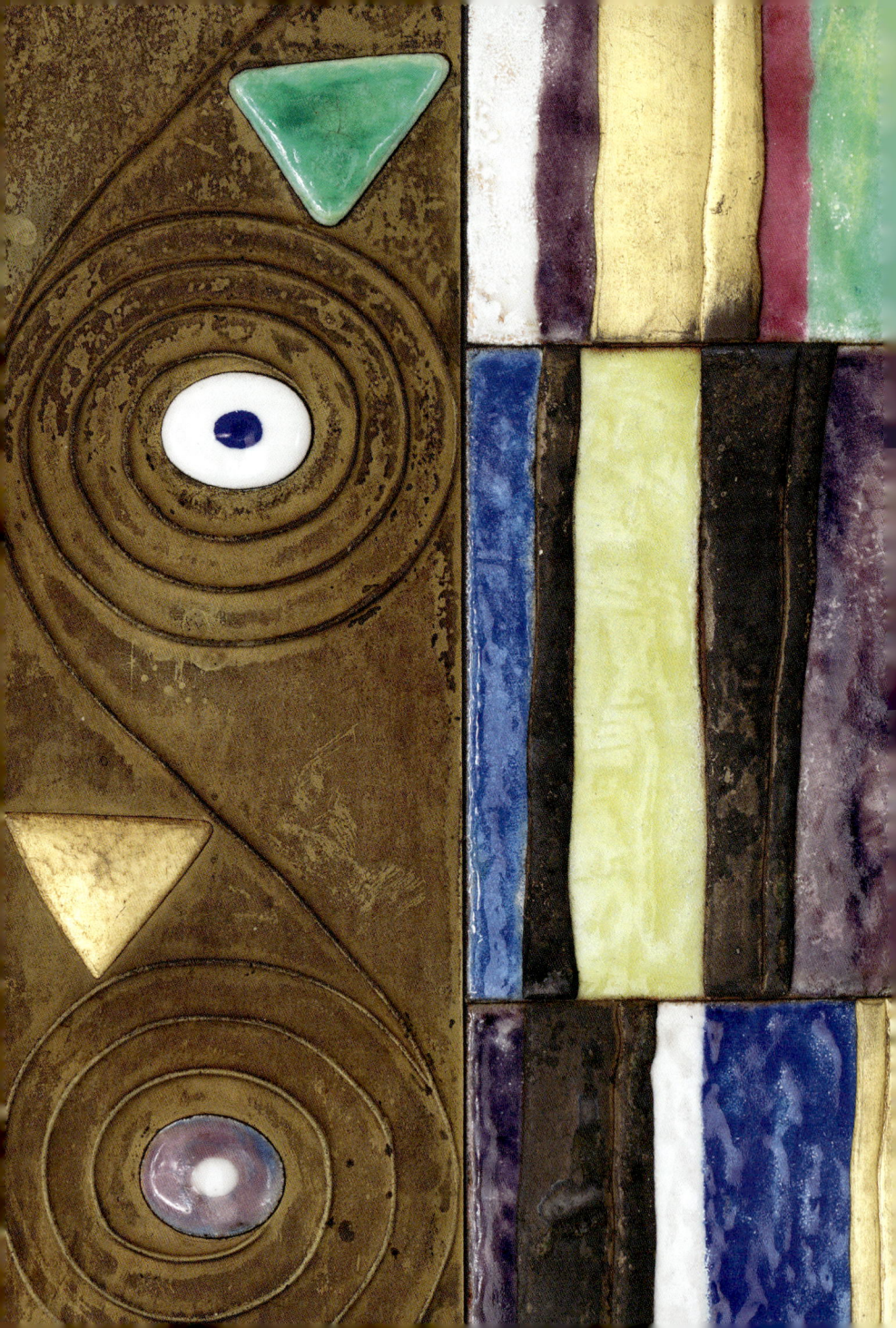

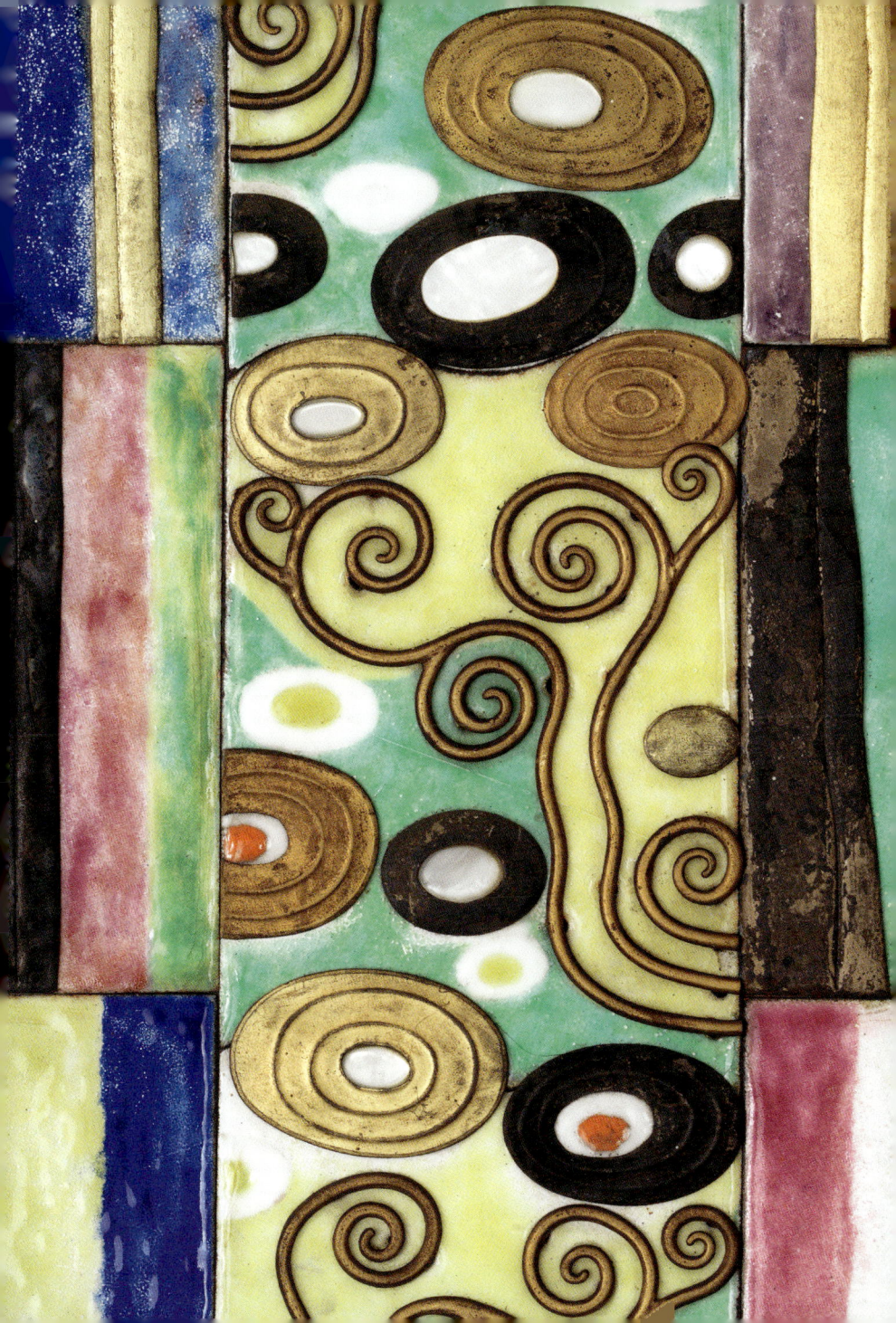

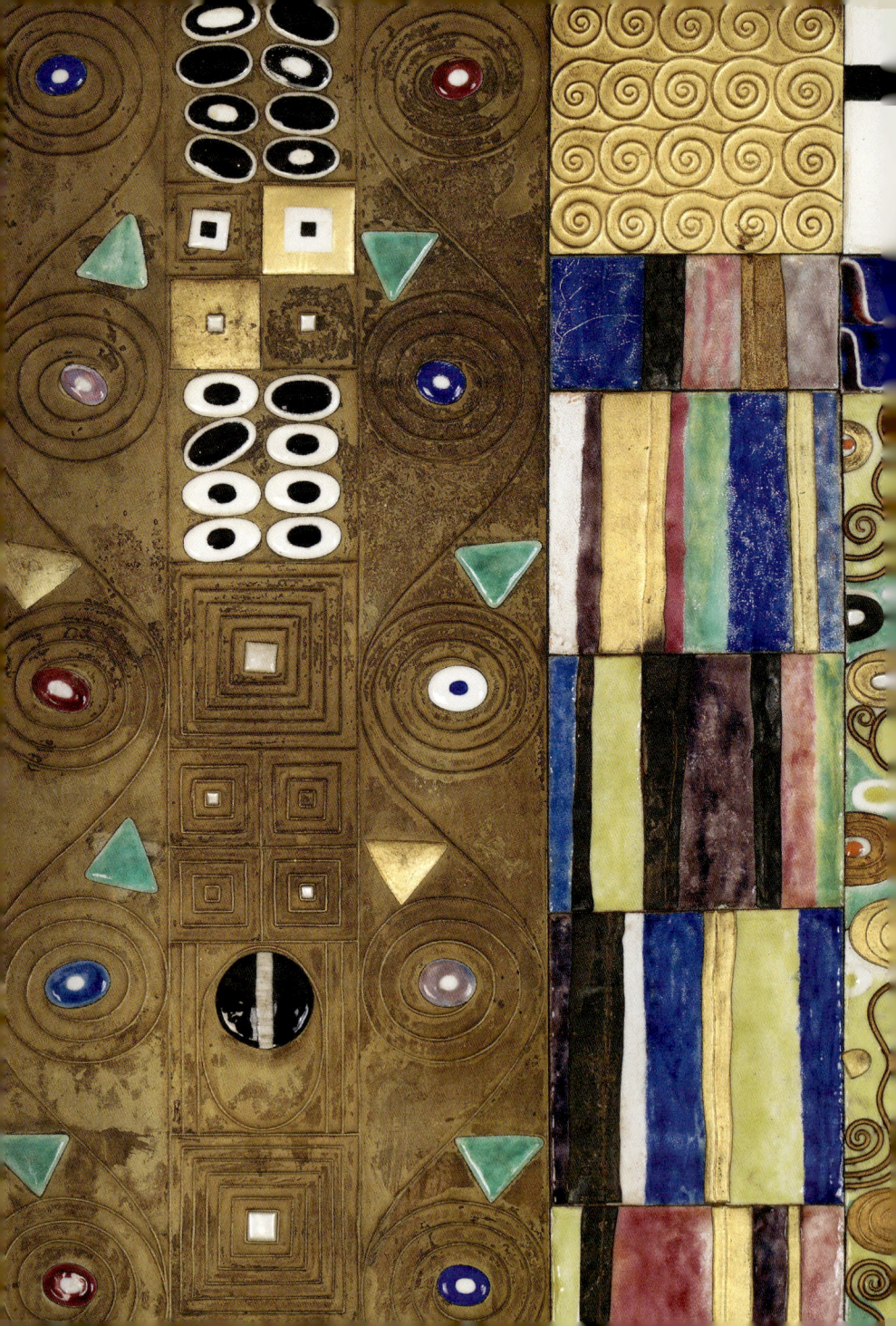

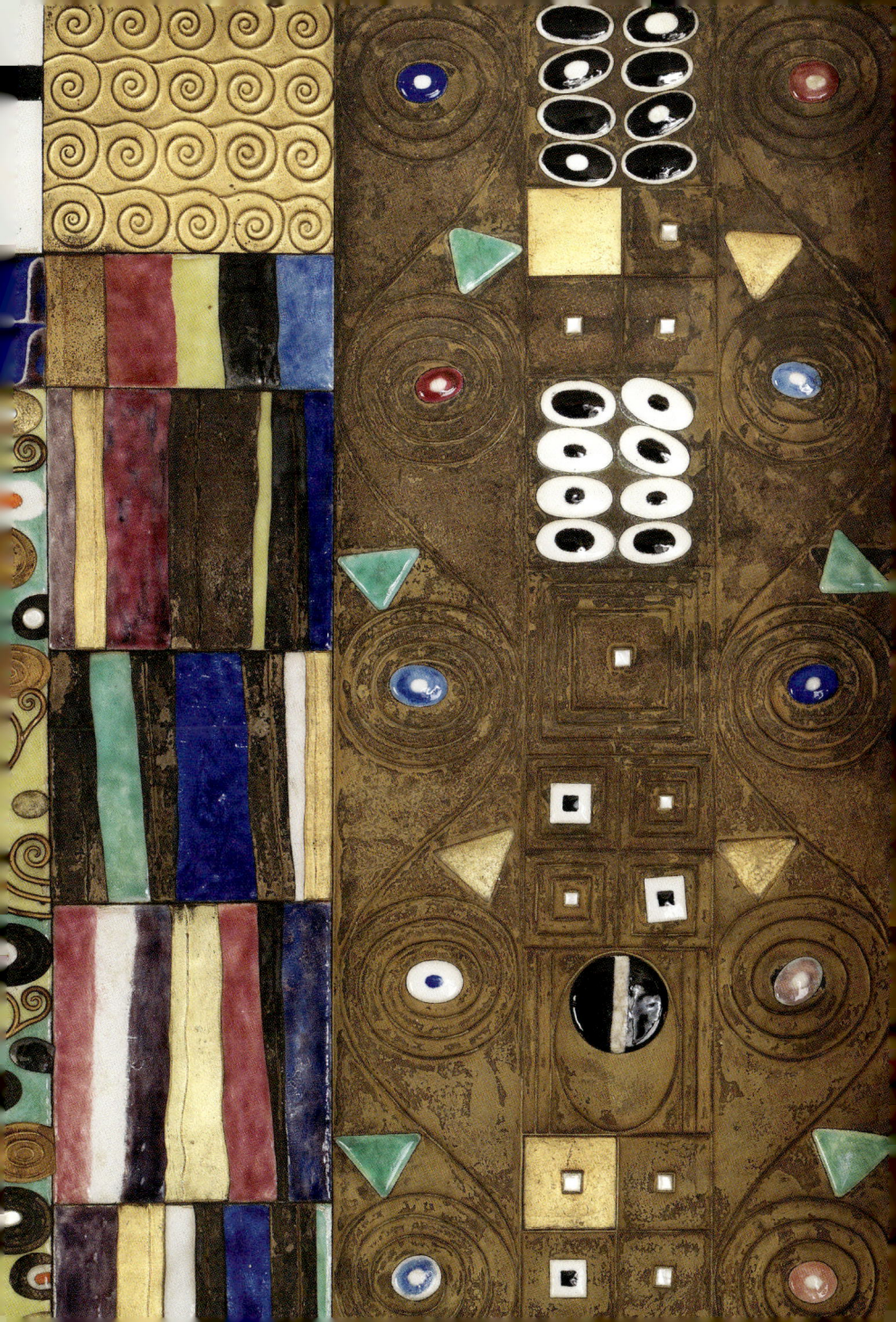

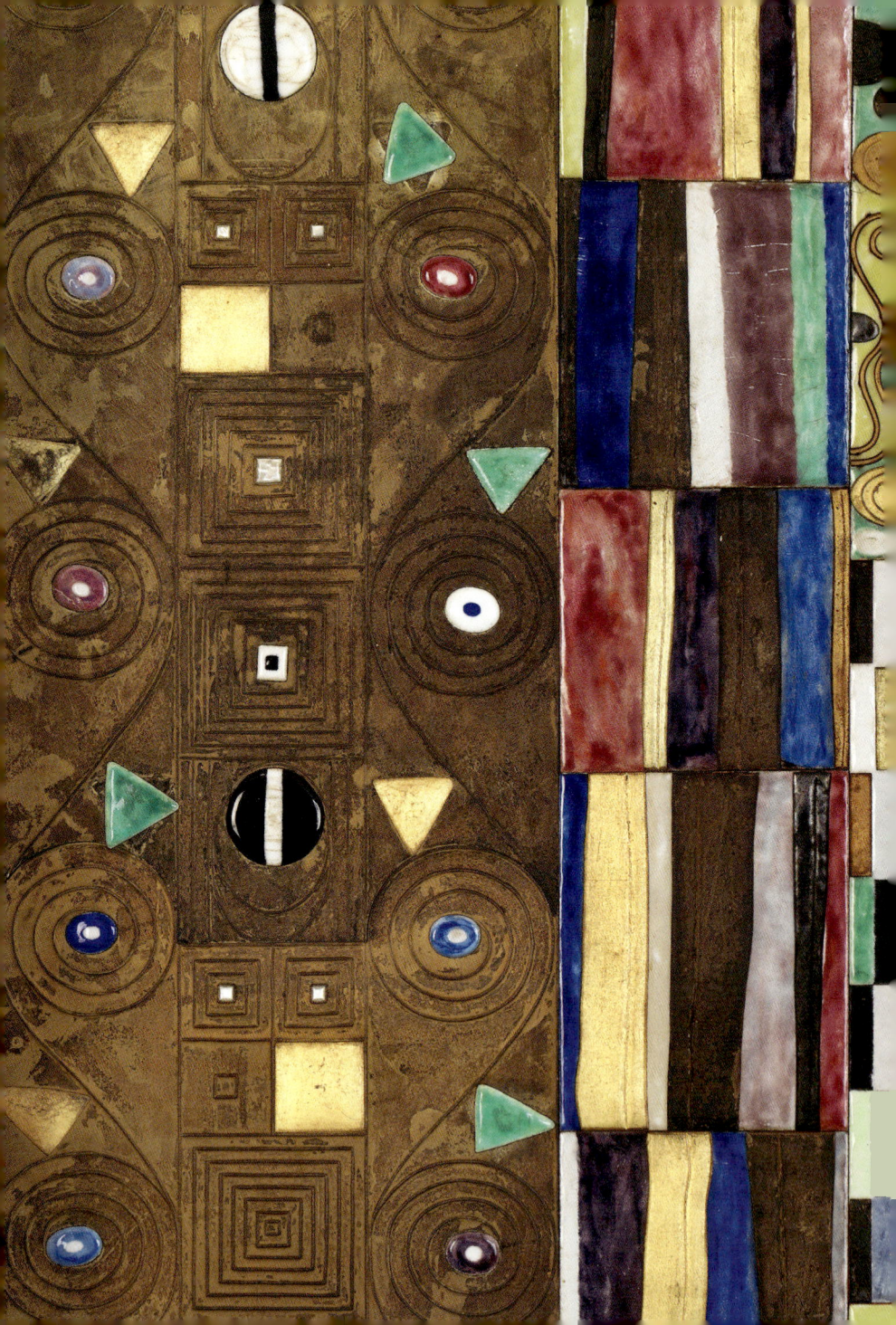

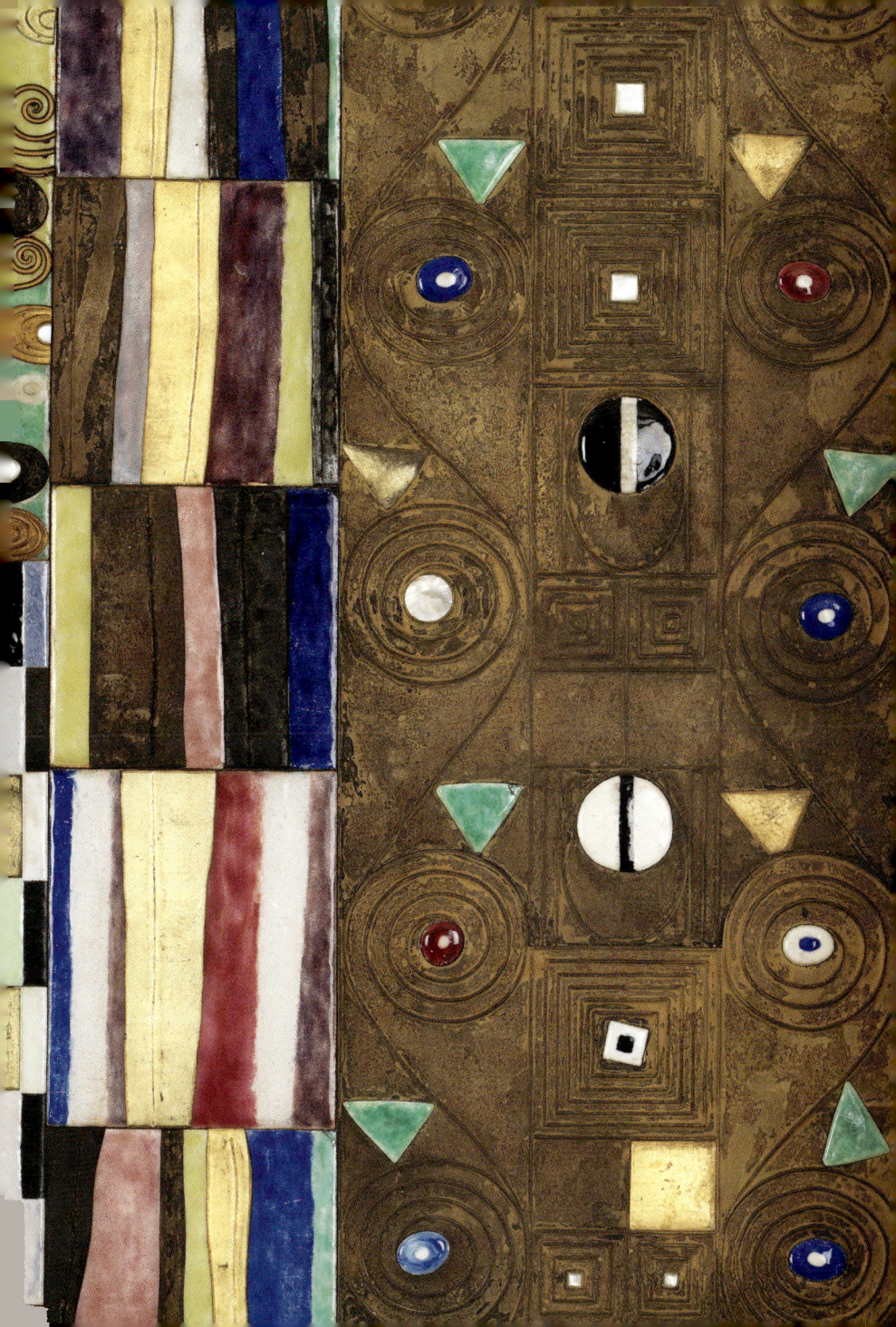

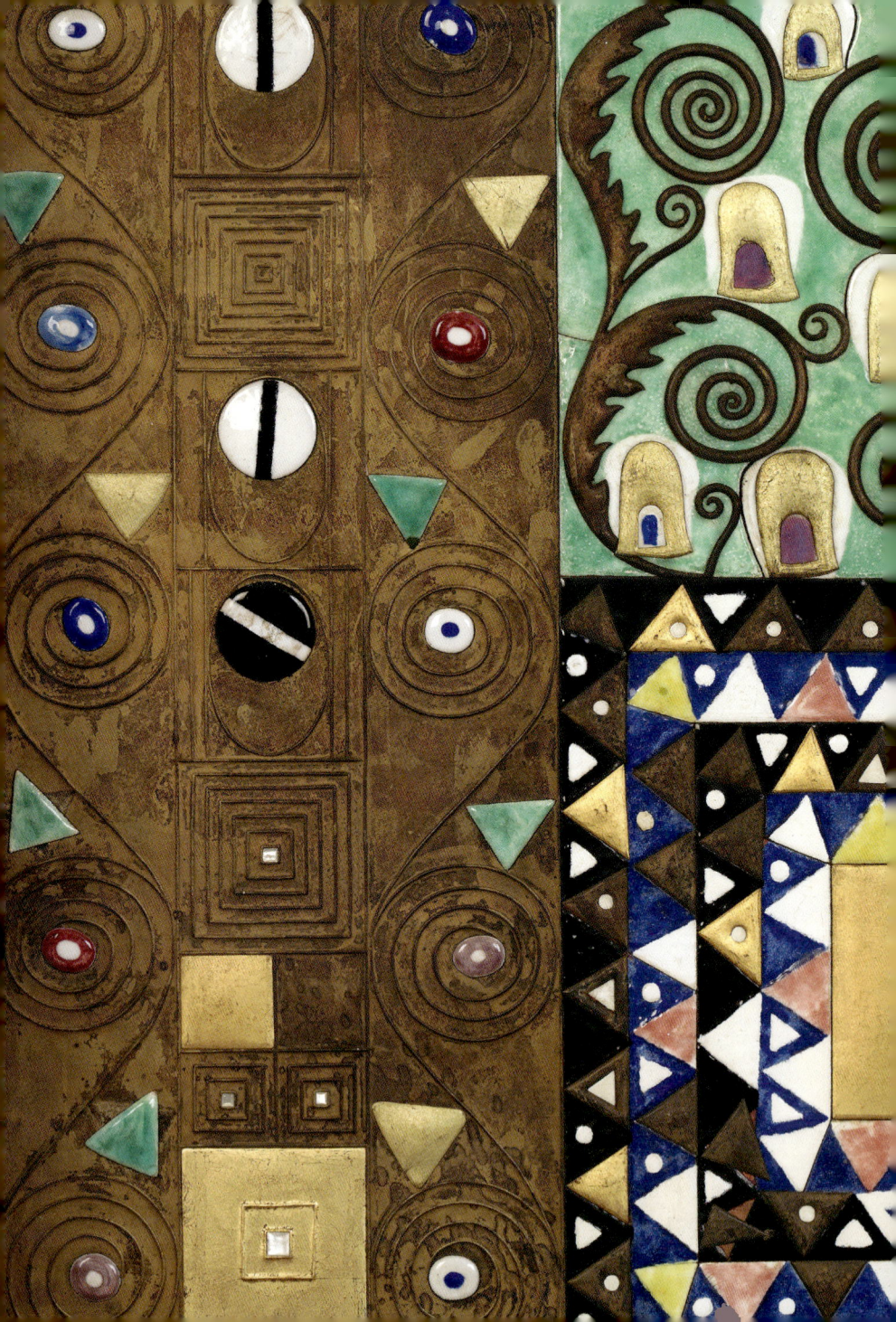

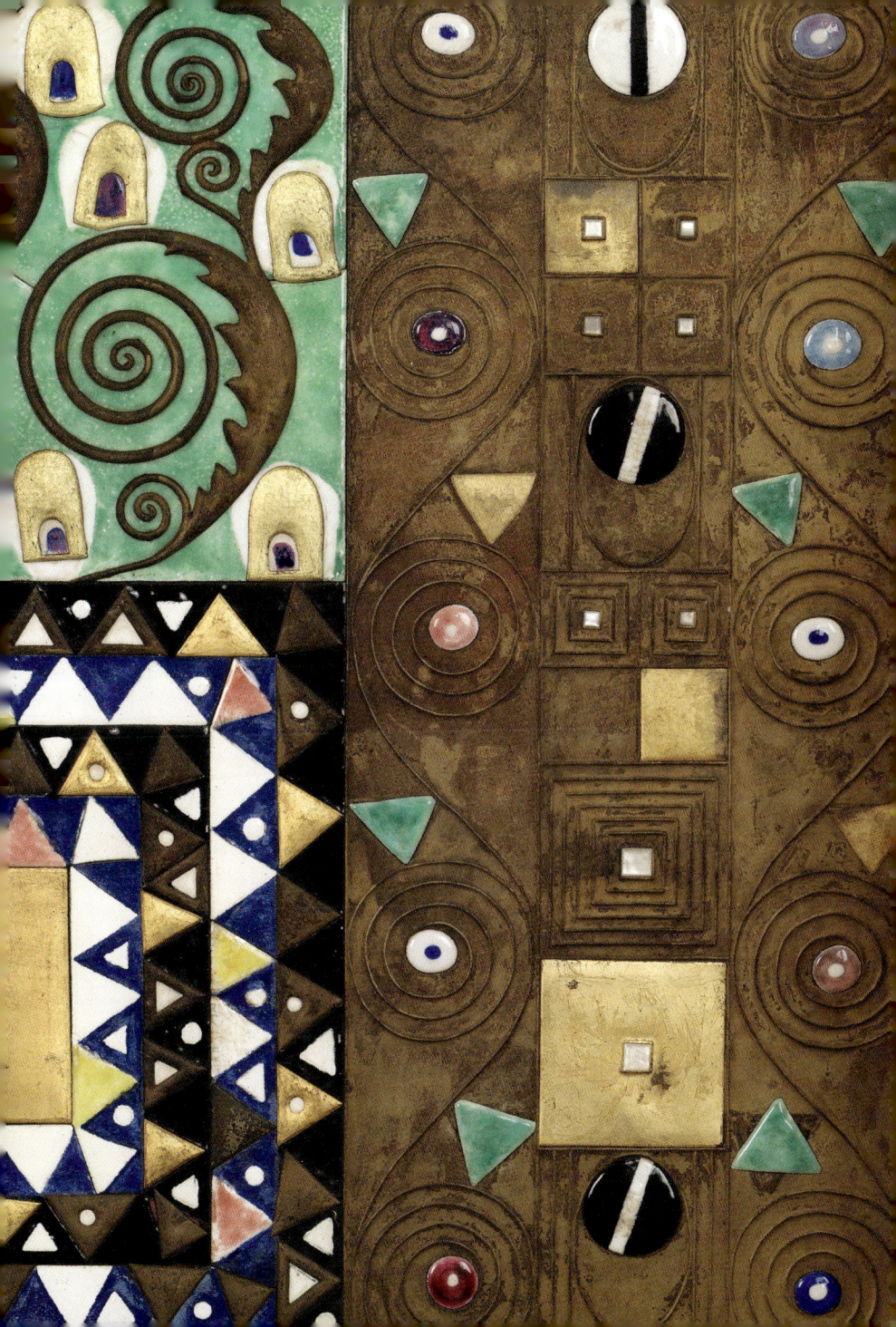

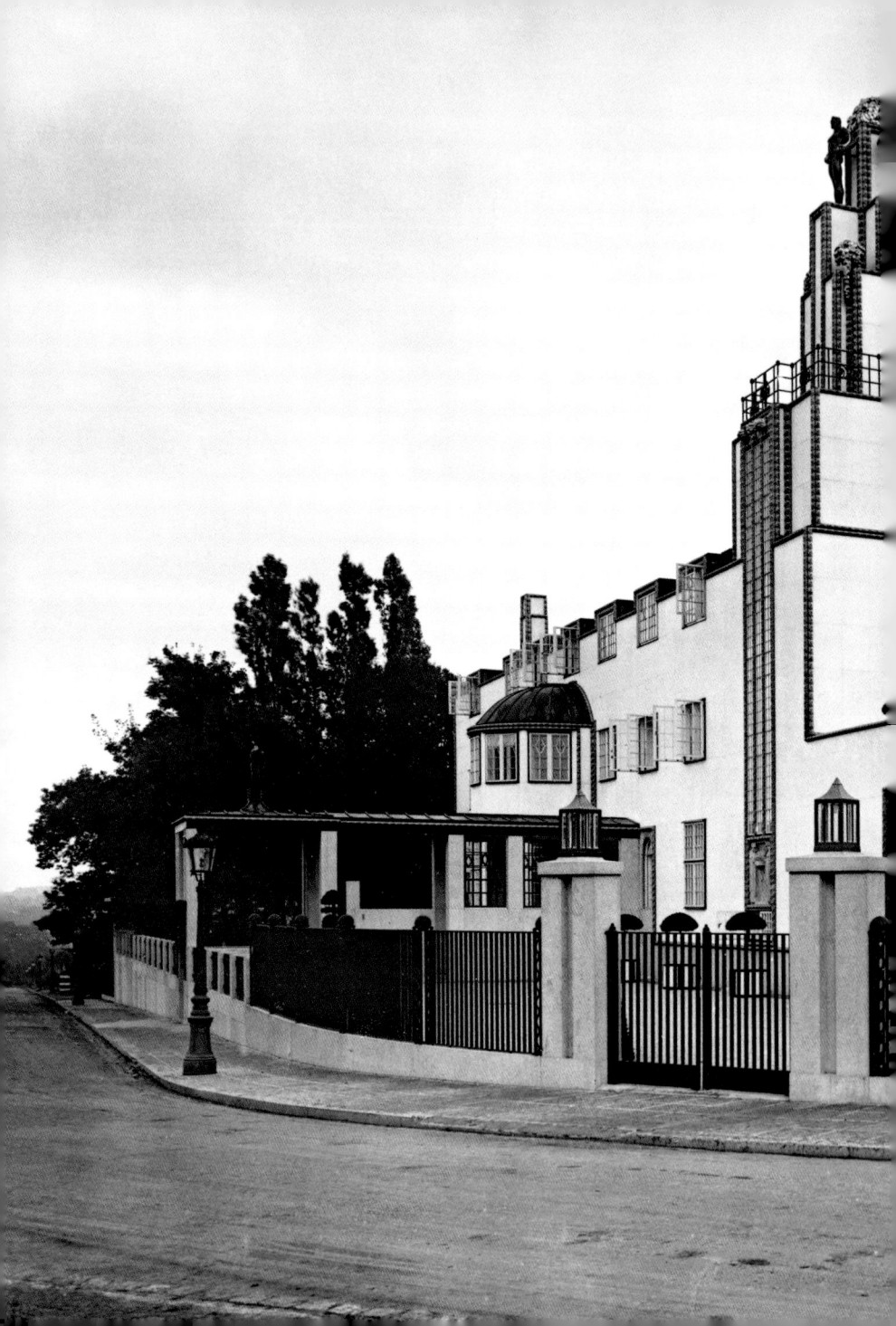

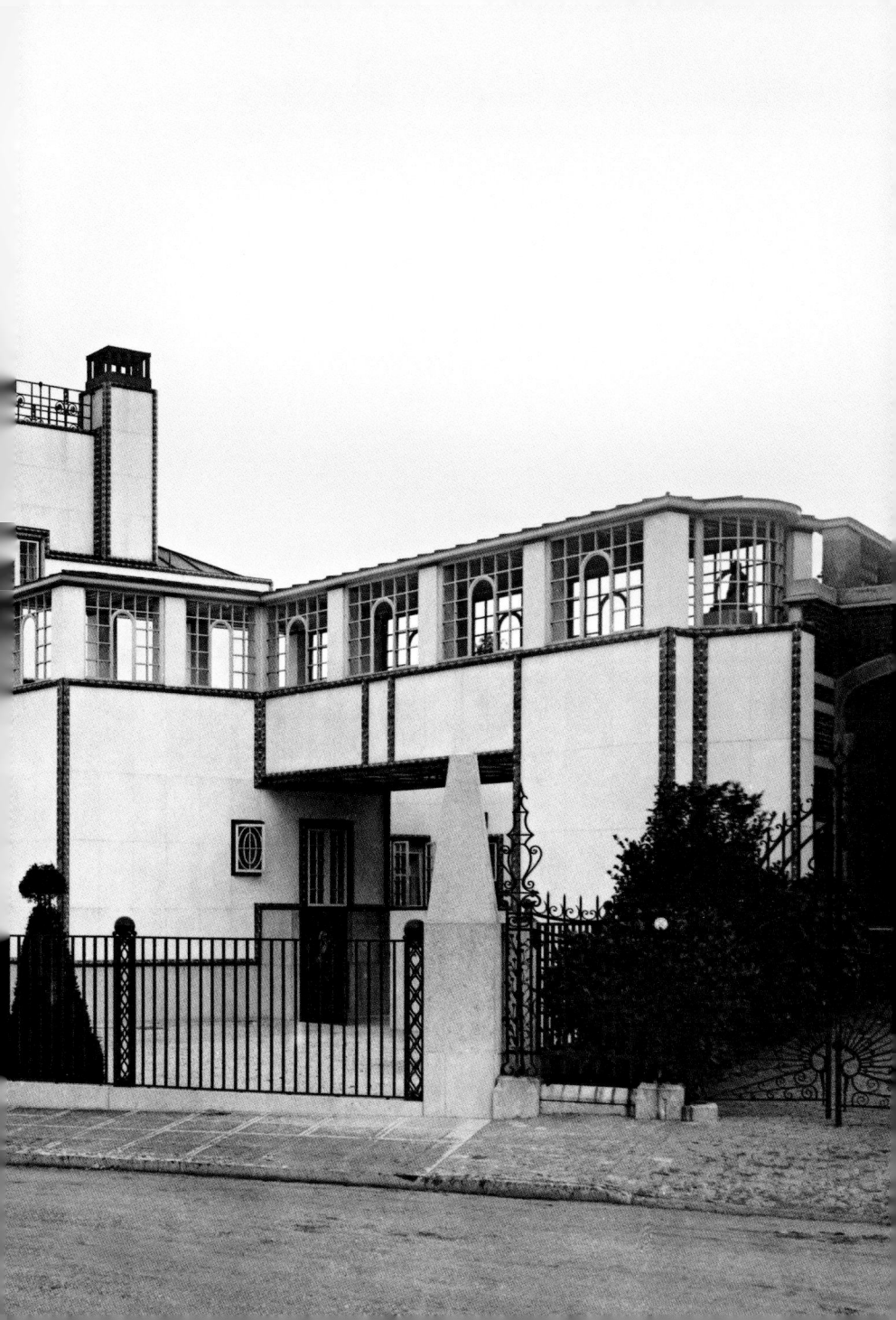

Paintings of women

Susanna Partsch

*"... he let them rigidify to a certain extent
and almost turned them into artificial pieces
of jewellery, just as if – amongst nothing
but jewels – they had been transformed
and forged into jewels themselves."*

FRANZ SERVAES, 1917/18

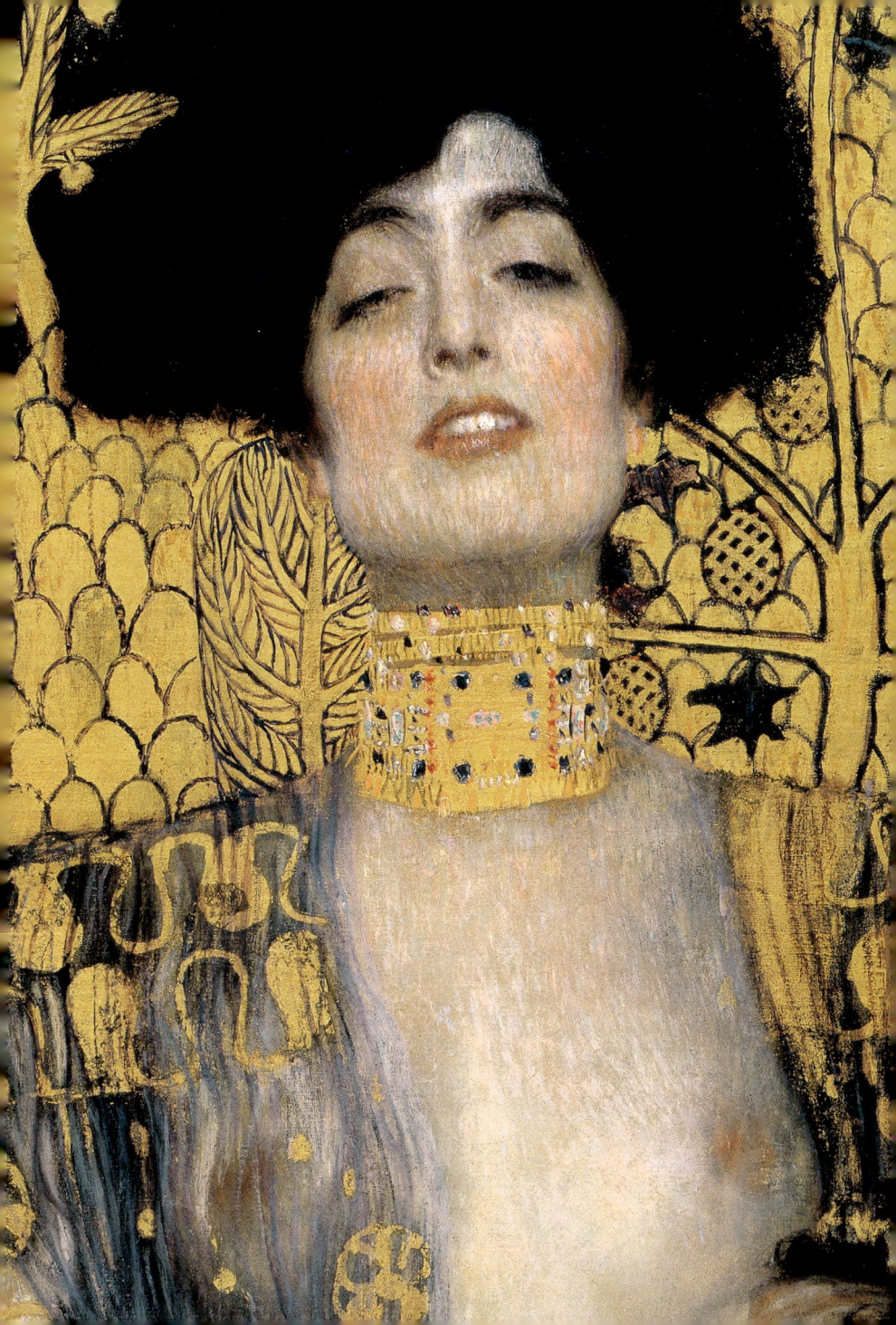

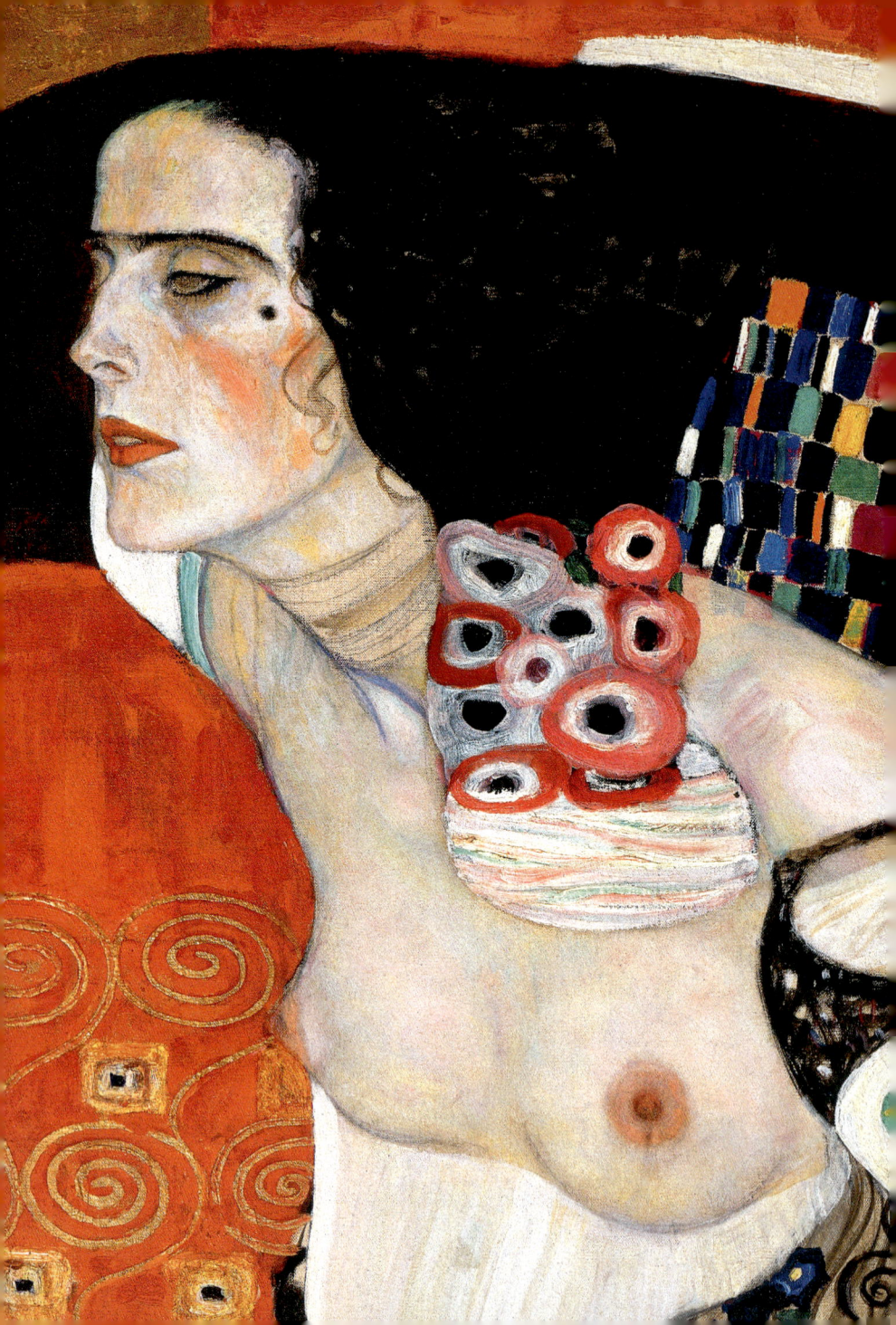

"The portrait of the Viennese lady has here witnessed a new character, or a new stylization. For the first time since Makart. As indeed Vienna is only now seeing, for the first time since that great individual, the triumphant rise of a painter before whom it must yield," wrote the art critic Ludwig Hevesi on 21 November 1903 on the occasion of the eighteenth Secession exhibition, at which – according to Hevesi – some eighty works by Gustav Klimt were shown (Hevesi 1906a, p. 452), including over forty paintings. Amongst these were twelve female portraits and seven female allegorical and mythological figures, adding up to a total of nineteen representations of women. (Disagreement reigns over the actual number of works featured at the 'Klimt Collective' exhibition, as this show was called: Nebehay names forty-eight paintings and thirty drawings in his documentation [Nebehay 1969, p. 311], while Strobl speaks of over fifty drawings spread across several rooms [Strobl, vol. 1, 1980, p. 327].)

Hevesi discussed the 'Klimt Collective' exhibition on several occasions but generally bestowed no more than a few words upon the portraits, making no mention of the sitters' names. This sometimes makes their identification difficult. Klimt's portraits nevertheless drew general praise and the artist would have no cause to complain of a lack of portrait commissions in the years that followed.

His first success as a painter of women lay many years in the past. In 1888, when he was commissioned to record an *Interior View of the Old Burgtheater* with 150 prominent individuals – including the most beautiful women in Vienna – in the auditorium, society ladies are said to have stormed his studio. There were so many of them, indeed, that there supposedly wasn't room in the picture to show them all. But why, then, did Klimt nonetheless include his sisters and their friends amongst the spectators? It seems likely that the number of those willing to be portrayed did not in fact suffice.

The faces of family members and friends had served Klimt right from the start of his artistic career as objects of study. He also worked from photographs. These will have been his starting point, too, for many of the portraits of prominent personalities incorporated within the *Interior View of the Old Burgtheater*. Leading members of Viennese society can be recognized in these likenesses, which are executed in the technique of miniature painting. A lithograph that is housed together with the picture in Vienna's Wien Museum allows us to identify individual personalities even today.

Page 257
Judith I (detail), 1901
(see ill. p. 305)

Judith II (Salome) (detail), 1909
(see ill. p. 331)

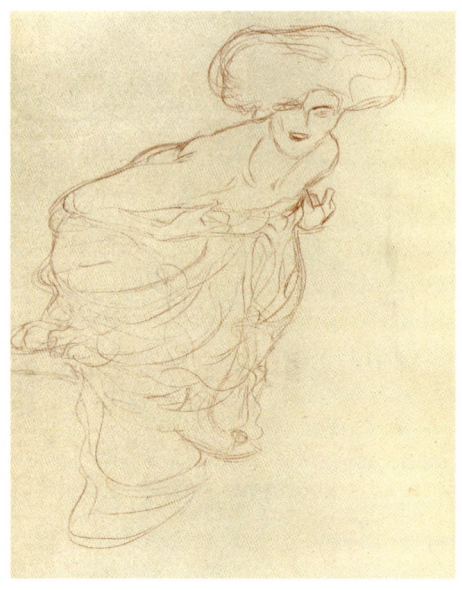

Early portraits of women

First indications of a changing approach to female portraiture can be seen in the portrait of the twenty-year-old Emilie Flöge. There is a possibility that the sitter is not Emily but her sister Helene Klimt, as suspected by Bisanz-Prakken, who also dates the picture for the first time to 1894 (see Ch. VI, p. 595, Bisanz-Prakken in preparation). The picture is executed in pastels on cardboard and thus in a technique similar to that of the *Interior View of the Old Burgtheater*. The face of the young Emilie is painted with great precision and the work is thereby wholly indebted to the Vienna Ringstrasse style. We also have the feeling of being able to identify each individual strand of hair. With its pale, rapidly applied brushstrokes, the tiara in the sitter's dark hair no more matches the Old Masterly painting of the face than the white dress, whose visible brushstrokes and areas of paler colour, suggesting folds and texture, show Klimt turning towards Impressionism. The brownish white background provides a plain foil to the portrait and calls to mind the appearance of a photograph, as noted by Natter (Natter/Frodl 2000, p. 76). Klimt decorated the gilt frame with cherry blossom, grasses and wild flowers. He thereby clearly demonstrated the influence of Japanese art, examples of which had become increasingly widespread in Europe since Impressionism and which subsequently also played a major role in Art Nouveau.

The pastel portrait of Emilie Flöge is not just an early example of a female portrait by Klimt, but indeed one of the very earliest portraits within his oeuvre in which the sitter is identified by name. Four years earlier, in 1890, Klimt had completed the *Portrait of Joseph Pembaur* (p. 56; Natter 2012, Cat. 60), a composer and conductor. No traces of a rapid handling of brush are to be found here: the portrait is still executed throughout in the

Study for the painting *Judith II*
Pencil (Strobl 1695). Private collection

Portrait of Helene Klimt, 1898
Oil on board, 60 x 40 cm / 23 ⅝ x 15 ¾ in. Berne, Kunstmuseum, on loan from a private collection

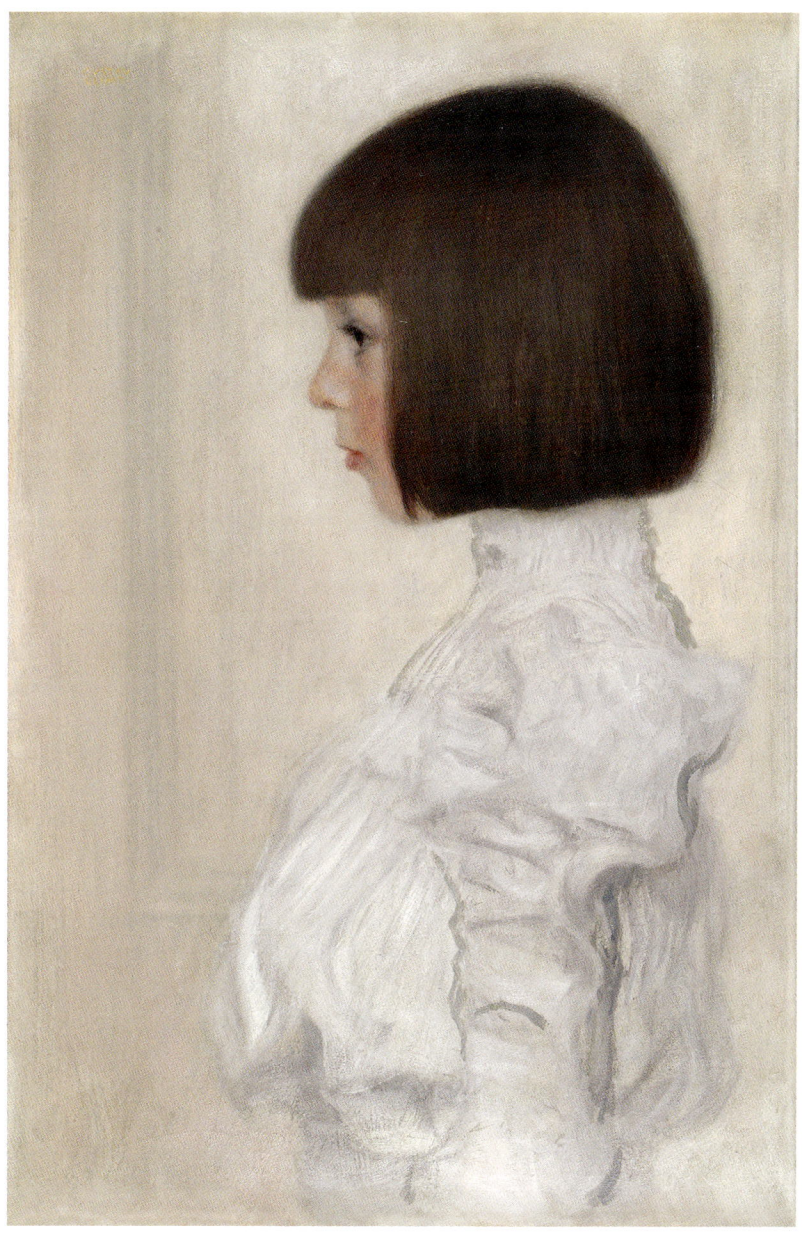

exact manner of painting typical of the Vienna Ringstrasse style. Only the painted frames of the two portraits offer points of comparison.

Klimt's very different painterly treatment of his subject in the Flöge portrait testifies to its experimental character and indicates that it was not produced as an official commission. This would in any case have been unlikely, as Emilie Flöge had been Ernst Klimt's sister-in-law since 1891. The Klimt brothers and the Flöge sisters had probably known each other since 1889. Ernst Klimt is thought to have proposed to Helene Flöge (1871–1936) one year later. They were married in October 1891.

What occasioned Gustav Klimt's pastel portrait of Emilie Flöge is unknown. The artist had already included Emilie and Helene as models in other, commissioned works, for example, when completing the easel painting of *Hanswurst Delivering an Impromptu Performance in Rothenburg* (Natter 2012, Cat. 76), just as he had integrated his own family and friends into pictures such as the *Interior View of the Old Burgtheater*. The full-length study for the *Portrait of Emilie Flöge* shows the model in the clothes she is wearing in the final pastel, standing in front of a wall in an overgrown garden. Her figure is framed on the right by an oleander tree and on the left by a thicket of bushes, trees, grasses and flowers. Her tightly laced outfit emphasizes her waist, and she rests one hand on her hip. She is looking not directly out of the picture but towards the viewer's left. This study has recently been attributed to Ernst Klimt and must therefore have been produced at the latest in 1892 – and not as from 1893 (Weidinger 2007b, p. 112 ff.).

At around the same time as his pastel *Portrait of Emilie Flöge*, Klimt painted a *Portrait of a Lady* (p. 61; Natter 2012, Cat. 79). Its format – a large, upright rectangle – was one that he would employ in many later portraits. The subject is portrayed in almost life size, standing in her elegant black evening gown with one hand resting on the back of an upholstered chair. Part of a tapestry can be seen hanging on the wall behind her. The sitter is looking out of the picture towards the viewer's right, in a similar fashion to Emile Flöge towards the left. No suggestions of Impressionism make themselves felt here, however: the fabric of the dress, the folds, lace, embroidery and jewellery are rendered with the same precision as the sitter's face, her coiffure and the surrounding room.

The painting was not exhibited in public or reproduced in colour for the first time until 2000 (Natter/Frodl 2000, p. 79) and is therefore absent from most analyses of Klimt's female portraiture. Nor was it seen at the 1903 'Klimt Collective' exhibition mentioned above. The earliest portraits on display on that occasion were the private one of his young niece Helene Klimt and the *Portrait of Sonja Knips* (p. 301; Natter 2012, Cat. 114), both of which were completed in 1898. The some twenty portraits that Klimt produced between 1891 and 1898, most of them showing anonymous models, seem to have been finger exercises on the way towards a new style.

A new style

Klimt's portrait of his niece Helene Klimt (p. 261; Natter 2012, Cat. 113), to whom he had become guardian after the death of his brother Ernst, is similar in size to his pastel of the young Emilie painted four years previously. Here, too, the sitter appears against a background that cannot be specifically localized, whereby various nuances lend the white a greater sense of animation. The white dress stands out from the background with an astonishing wealth of contrast, its folds casting blue shadows. Yet despite – or precisely because of – these folds, it is difficult to make out the body. Helene's hair, cut in a neat page-boy style, covers her cheek, so that all we

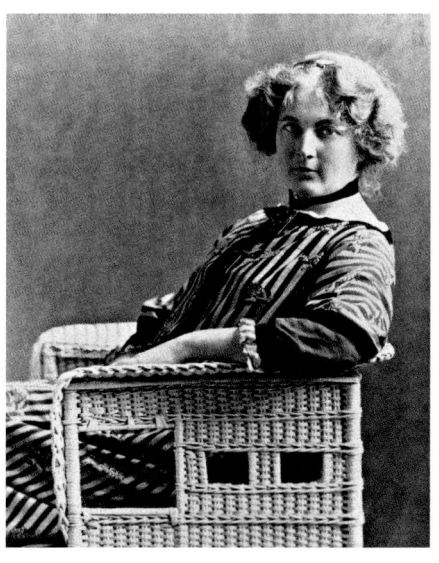

can see of her profile are her eye, nose, mouth and chin, since her forehead is covered by her fringe. The little that we can make out of her face is not executed with the same precision as Klimt's earlier portraits.

This picture was evidently very important to him, since he showed it in public on multiple occasions. At the 'Klimt Collective' exhibition of 1903, Hevesi made no mention of it. Instead, he drew attention to another painting in the same show: "Klimt had begun his characteristic, vibrant rippling in the Schubert picture. Let us also look at the rippling pink of the seated young lady, his first portrait in this deliberately newfangled manner" (Hevesi 1906a, p. 451). Whether Hevesi was here referring to the compositional study for *Schubert at the Piano* of 1896 (Natter 2012, Cat. 83) rather than to the final painting of 1899 (pp. 62/63; Natter 2012, Cat. 118) or had simply got his dates muddled, the "seated young lady" in "rippling pink" can only mean the *Portrait of Sonja Knips*, a painting that had already featured in the second Vienna Secession exhibition from November to December 1898 and which was subsequently shown at the 1900 Exposition Universelle in Paris and at the 1903 'Klimt Collective' at the Secession.

Sonja Knips in a Reform dress designed by Eduard Josef Wimmer-Wisgrill, c. 1911
Photograph. Imagno/Austrian Archives

In his *Portrait of Sonja Knips*, Klimt chose a square format for the first time. The young woman in a pale pink dress is situated on the right-hand side of the composition. She is sitting at the very front of the seat of a generously sized armchair and is leaning on the upholstered arm as if she were about to stand up. In her right hand, she holds a small red book. With her body angled towards the left, she has turned her head so that she is looking straight out of the picture and fixes the viewer with her gaze. The curls of her hair are taken up in the ruffles of her dress, while her head as a whole is framed by a backdrop of flowers – lilies or orchids – that are either growing in a garden or standing in a large vase on the floor. Beyond the top of the canvas, blooms and branches form an invisible arch that descends into the picture in the top left-hand corner in the shape of another flower. This left half of the picture consists of two planes clearly divided by their colour. The area of pale brown, in some places shot with green, in the lower left-hand corner barely distinguishes itself from the tender pink dress and forms a floor of some kind. The dominant field of blackish brown, which provides a foil to the flowers and the female sitter, contains several lighter patches. These have inspired numerous interpretations, with some authors suggesting that Klimt has here painted over what was originally a garden setting. Infrared photography has failed to confirm this theory and it thus remains unclear whether Sonja Knips is situated indoors in a room or outdoors in a garden. The armchair sooner suggests an interior, however, not least since all of Klimt's other female portraits are also located – as far as we can make out – within indoor settings.

As in the portrait of the youthful Emilie Flöge, rapid brushstrokes alternate with a finely detailed manner of painting. The face and the flowers that frame it once again resemble a high-resolution photograph, while the dress, chair and surroundings are out of focus and blurred. In the earlier pastel, Klimt was still exploring the possibilities of this new style; here, he has mastered it in virtuoso fashion and orchestrates an interplay of precision and ambiguity that sows a sense of uncertainty in the viewer.

The difference lies not only in Klimt's greater mastery of this new style, however, but also in the size and shape of the canvas and in Klimt's lack of fear of empty space. The *Portrait of Sonja Knips* has rightly been compared with the work of the American painter James Abbott McNeill Whistler, and in particular with his *Arrangement in Grey and Black No. 1: Portrait of the Artist's Mother* of 1867/71 (Paris, Musée d'Orsay). In Whistler's canvas, however, which is slightly rectangular rather than square, the figure is not positioned quite so close to the right-hand edge of the picture, while the empty background is characterized by a wall and a curtain. The square shape and size of Klimt's *Portrait of Sonja Knips* would

Portrait of Margaret Stonborough-Wittgenstein (detail), 1905
(see ill. p. 321)

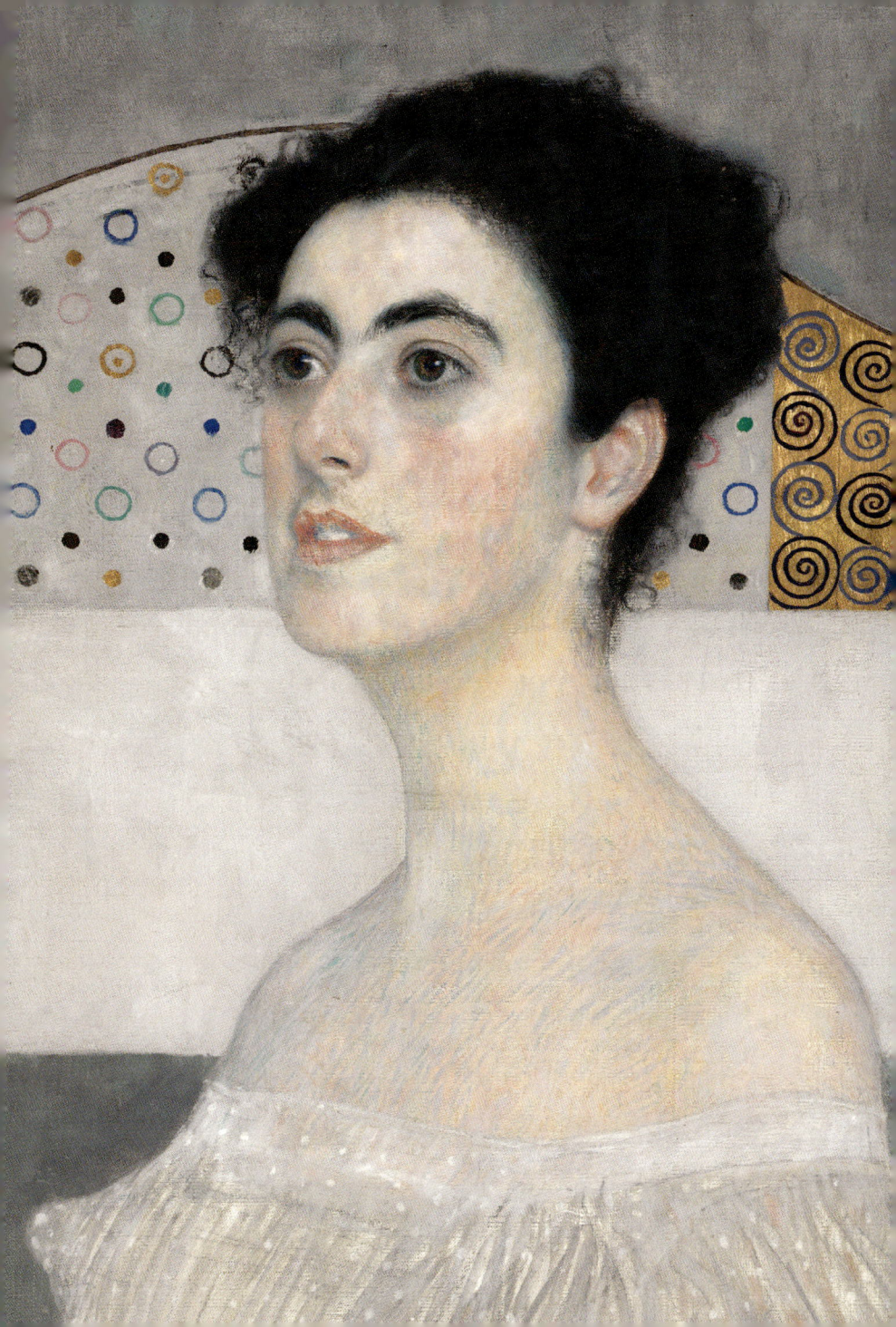

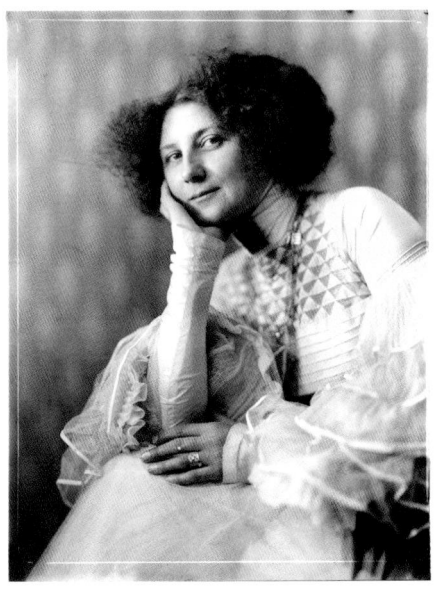

become one of the hallmarks of his works on canvas, albeit less in the portraits of the following years than in his landscapes.

As in the case of most of Klimt's paintings from this period, the metal frame crafted by his brother Georg is an integral aspect of the overall impression presented by the final picture. In comparison with the wide, painted wooden frame surrounding the pastel portrait of Emilie Flöge, the chased decoration within the narrow metal frame around the *Portrait of Sonja Knips* produces a different effect and does not make the picture seem so enclosed.

It is regularly stated that Sonja Knips, née Baroness Potier des Echelles, was one of the very few members of the aristocracy painted by Klimt. In fact, the Potier des Echelles were not long-established members of the nobility but an old and respected family of officers whose ennoblement had only occurred with Sonja's grandfather, in recognition of his military services. Nor was the family wealthy, which explains why Sonja trained and subsequently worked as a lady's companion. In the home of Josefine Krassl von Traissenegg, she met the industrial magnate Anton Knips (1865–1946). The two married on 15 February 1896. Her portrait was probably commissioned in 1897 and completed one year later. It was the first of a series of female portraits commissioned from Klimt by members of the Viennese moneyed social elite.

The fact that Sonja Knips knew Gustav Klimt even before her marriage is evidenced not only by the small red sketchbook that appears in her portrait (see Nebehay 1987, *passim*), but also by a poetry fan that was found amongst her possessions after her death. The front of the fan carries cartouches in which friends and relatives have written a few lines of verse, in a similar fashion to poetry albums. The back of the fan, however, was

Atelier d'Ora, **Emilie Flöge in a Reform dress designed by Eduard Josef Wimmer-Wisgrill**, 1909
Photograph. Imagno/ÖNB

Portrait of Emilie Flöge (detail), 1902/03
(see ill. p. 311)

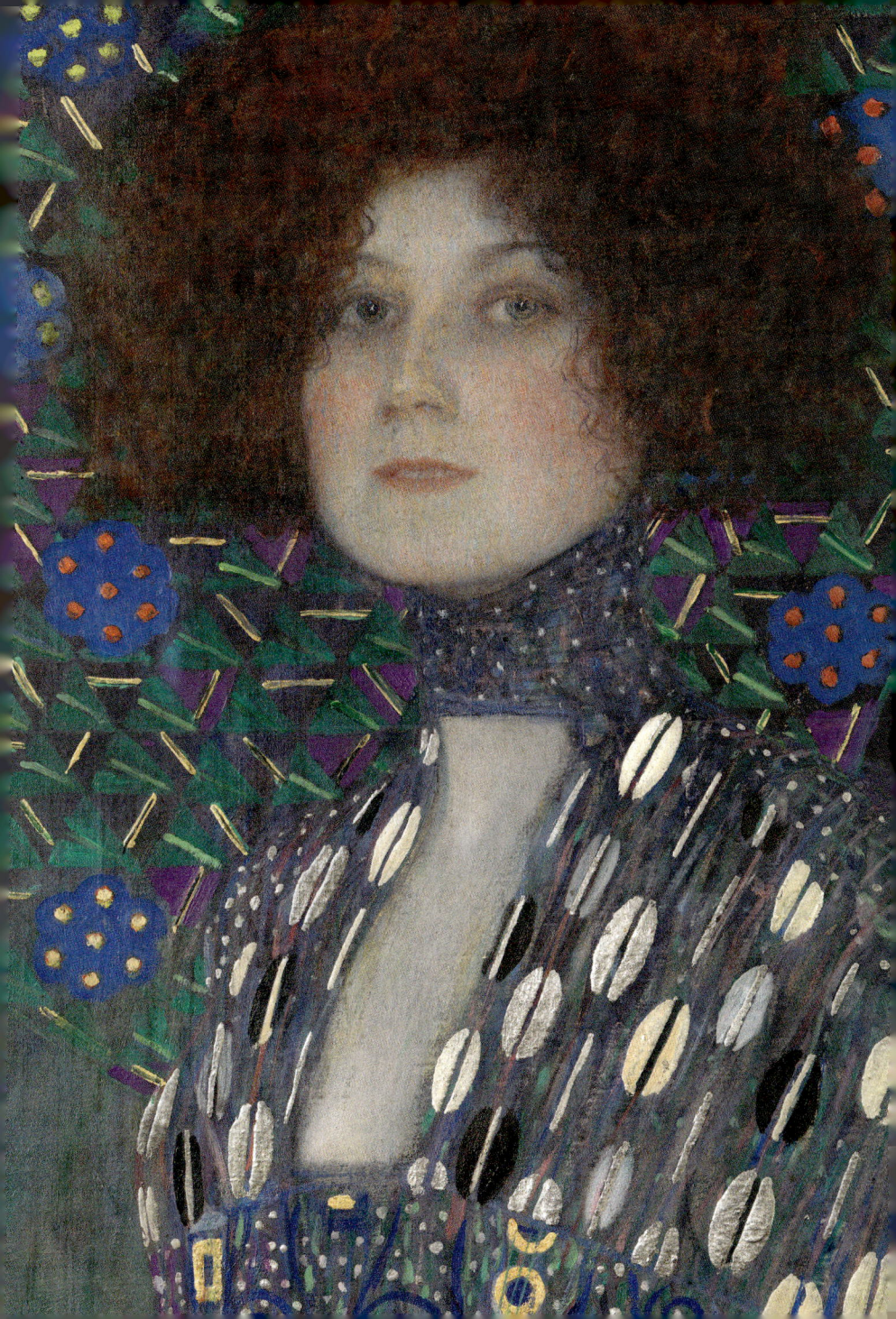

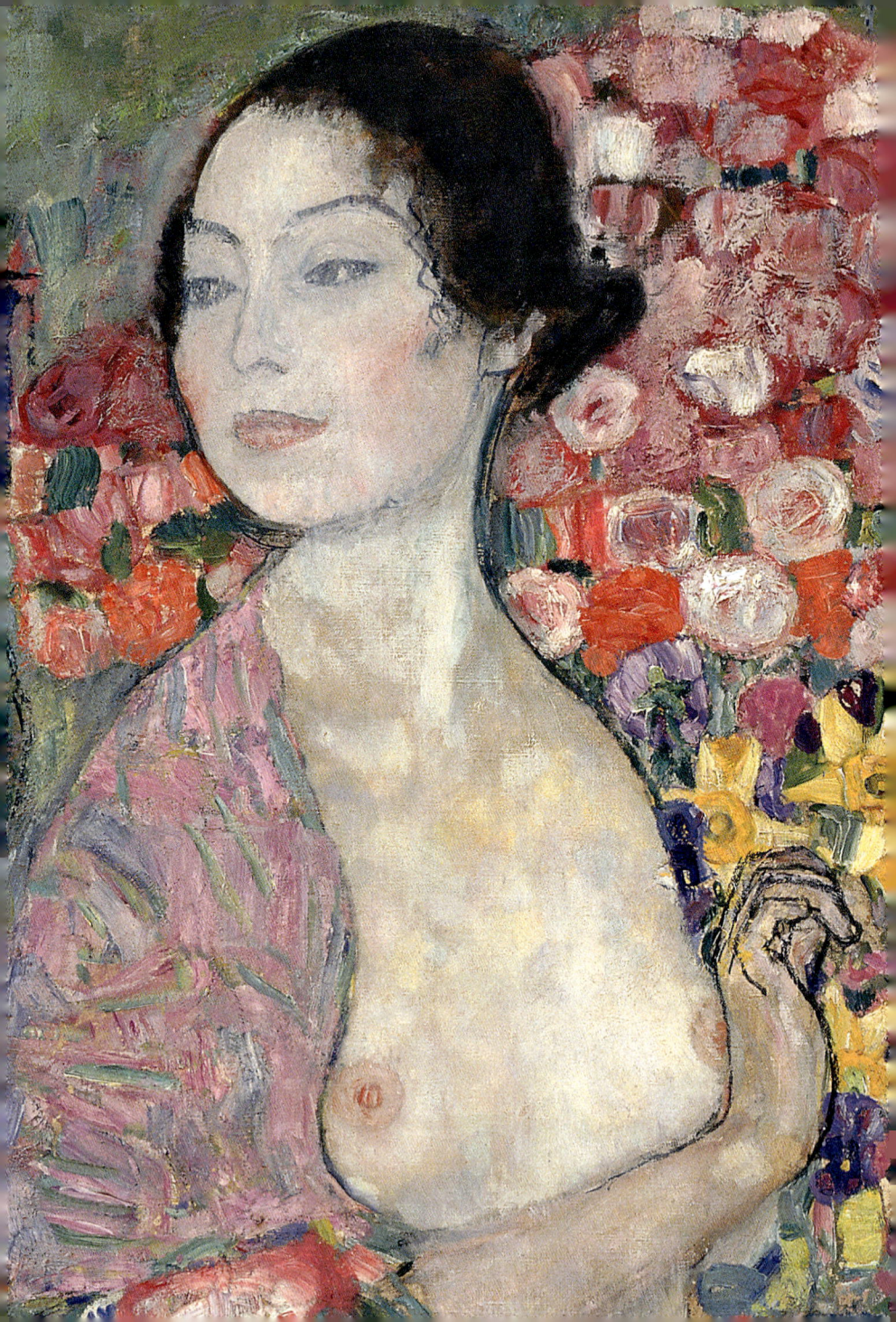

reserved solely for Klimt. It bears a poem by the 14th-century Sufi mystic poet Hafiz about the fisherwoman Love: "Freedom is a sea and its fish hearts; they swim happily to and fro without care. But this pleasure, alas, is of short duration: Love, the fisherwoman, is standing on the shore, waiting to trap them. She fishes with her own rods; she fishes with ambergris tresses. The little purple fish approach without fear. They allow themselves to be lured all too easily by her guile. And one after the other, her cunning wins." To this, Klimt has added the picture of a pretty woman in a white (bridal) dress, fishing in the water with a rod for little white hearts. A winged heart pierced with arrows hovers overhead, with winged heads of cherubs fluttering beneath it. To the right of these heads are a few lines from Goethe: "Love roams every highway and byway; constancy lives alone. Love comes rushing towards us; constancy must be sought" (from Claudine von Villa Bella, 1788, a singspiel based on earlier material from 1775). This quotation is accompanied by Klimt's signature and the date 3 January 1895.

On the basis of this fan and the decoration of its reverse side, Manu von Miller (Miller 2004, p. 21 ff.) reconstructed a love affair between Gustav Klimt and Sonja Knips before her marriage, and proposed that Klimt used the fan as a way of ending their relationship. Miller also suggested that Klimt may have done the same thing in 1899 with the aid of a second fan, destined for an unknown recipient and on that occasion carrying the German proverb "Lieber ein Ende mit Schrecken als ein Schrecken ohne Ende" ("Best to get unpleasant things over and done with"; on this fan, see Strobl, vol. 4, 1989, p. 66, no. 3309). Hansjörg Krug shows on the basis of Klimt's correspondence that the artist painted this second fan for Camilla Sodoma (1874–1953; Krug 2012a, p. 461 f.).

It is my view that the fan belonging to Sonja Knips points neither to a love affair between artist and model nor to a rupture between the two. Rather, it shows Klimt expressing his congratulations to Sonja Knips upon her engagement. Thus the lines from Goethe, for example, can be found on engagement cards dating from around 1900 and remain a standard formula for engagement congratulations amongst German speakers even today – one that is even available as an SMS quote. The poem by Hafiz and the picture of the fisherwoman may have been intended to tease the prospective bride, but were certainly not compromising – or Sonja Knips would never have let anyone else see them. In fact, however, one of the messages on the front of the fan was not written or signed by a certain Adolf Hlaver until 23 April 1895, three months *after* Klimt had decorated the back. The idea that the fan represents a form of engagement congratulations is also supported by Klimt's inclusion of winged heads of cherubs, who wish the bride all the joys of motherhood.

The Dancer (detail), 1916/17
(see ill. p. 353)

Sonja Knips soon afterwards commissioned Josef Hoffmann and the Wiener Werkstätte to redesign her Vienna apartment and in 1924/25 to create an entire house for her. In addition to her own portrait by Klimt, she owned his 1901 painting of *Fruit Trees* (pp. 426/27; Natter 2012, Cat. 136) and purchased the unfinished *Adam and Eve* (p. 362; Natter 2012, Cat. 243) from his posthumous estate. She bought her clothes from the Flöge sisters' fashion salon right up to its closure in 1938 and was thus closely associated with Klimt, his companion Emilie Flöge and the Wiener Werkstätte for many years. The same applied to some of the other women painted by Klimt, for example Serena Lederer (1867–1943), whose portrait Klimt executed one year after that of Sonja Knips.

Serena Lederer, née Pulitzer, had also met Klimt prior to her marriage to the industrialist August Lederer (1857–1936). In 1888 the artist had immortalized Serena, in the company of her uncle Sigmund Pulitzer and his wife, in his gouache *Interior View of the Old Burgtheater*. The Lederers later became Klimt's most important patrons: it was they, for example, who enabled him to buy back the Faculty paintings (pp. 129–131; Natter 2012, Cat. 126, 127, 157). Alongside numerous oil paintings, they also owned one of the largest collections of Klimt's drawings. Klimt was a frequent guest in their home and also gave Serena Lederer painting lessons. He later made portraits of her daughter Elisabeth (married Bachofen-Echt; p. 347; Natter 2012, Cat. 212) and her mother, Charlotte Pulitzer (Natter 2012, Cat. 234).

The *Portrait of Serena Lederer* (p. 302; Natter 2012, Cat. 121), which measures 190.8 x 85.4 cm (75 ⅛ x 33 ⅝ in.), shows the subject in a full-length view, wearing an elegant white dress in the latest 'Reform' fashion, falling in a broad sweep rather than fitted at the waist. The delicate brushstrokes in white and blue suggest a finely pleated fabric. The wall and floor are also white; only the sitter's black hair, dark eyes and red lips provide accents of colour. This picture, too, exhibits points of comparison with a painting by Whistler, namely the latter's *Symphony in White* of 1862 (Washington, DC, National Gallery of Art; Zaunschirm 1987, p. 29), portraying a figure dressed in white standing in front of a white curtain. There, however, the interior is still recognizable as such, whereas in Klimt's canvas, wall and floor become flat surfaces in different shades of white and thereby look forward to the ornament found in his later pictures. Comparisons can also be drawn with two other pictures, namely the studies of *A Figure Outdoors* by Claude Monet (1840–1926). These two paintings (both Paris, Musée d'Orsay), executed in 1886, show a woman with a parasol turned in one case to the right and in the other to the left. Even if Monet was here pursuing different aims, the pose and dress of the female figure in both studies could undoubtedly have served Klimt as a source of inspiration. Echoes of Monet can also be found during this same period in Klimt's landscapes (Weidinger 2007a, p. 145), something that is unsurprising given that Klimt had already been exploring the painting of Impressionism for quite some time.

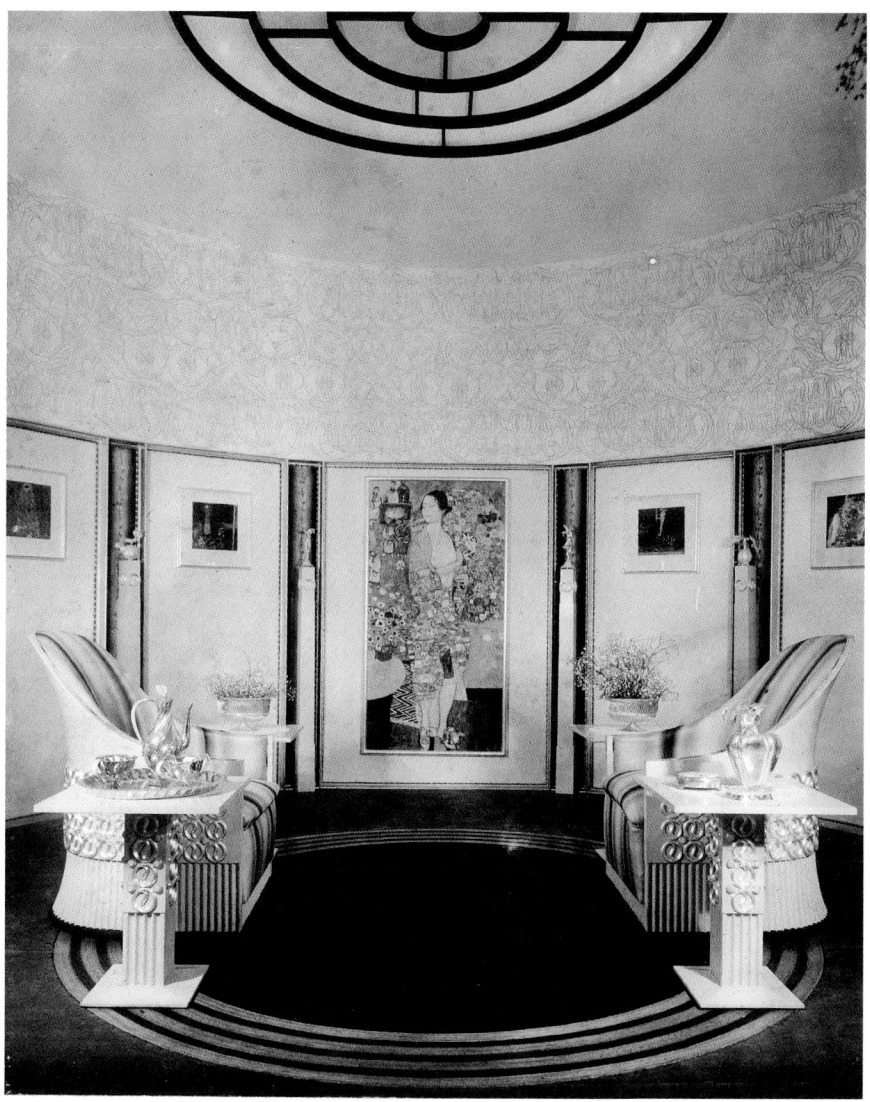

Wiener Werkstätte showroom in New York, 1922
With Gustav Klimt's *The Dancer* in the background
Photograph. Vienna, MAK – Österreichisches Museum für angewandte Kunst/Gegenwartskunst

The relationship between Klimt's sketches and his finished paintings, and the artistic path leading from one to the other, were defined at the latest with the publication of Alice Strobl's catalogue raisonné of Klimt's drawings (Strobl 1980 ff.). The transfer sketch surviving for the *Portrait of Serena Lederer* illustrates Klimt's working method very clearly. Having first of all explored his subject in preparatory sketches, he produced a squared transfer sketch that allowed him to transpose his sitter onto the large canvas (Vienna, Albertina; Strobl 442).

The same dissolving of the background into planes of colour can be seen in the *Portrait of Rose von Rosthorn-Friedmann* painted in 1900/01 (p. 314; Natter 2012, Cat. 133). Once again Klimt has opted for the tall, rectangular format that, as we know, he preferred for his female portraits. Rose von Rosthorn-Friedmann is shown against a blue background, leaning against a red surface that can be interpreted as the back of a red-upholstered chair, something confirmed by the transfer sketch (Vienna, Albertina; Strobl 511). Her right hand is propped on top of the chair back, as if she were about to move off in the direction in which she is looking. She is dressed in a black evening gown fitted at the waist and trimmed with silver paillettes, with a wide pearl choker around her neck and several gold bracelets encircling the wrist of her bare arm. The pale flesh of her décolleté, arm and face stands out from the darker colours surrounding them, while her dark, coiffured hair is barely distinguishable from the blue of the background.

The back of the chair, the sitter's pose and the evening gown trimmed with paillettes recall the *Portrait of a Lady* (p. 61) executed six years earlier. There, however, the accompanying furnishings are still recognizable as such and the pose conveys a sense of formality, with neither the elegance nor the salacious quality characterizing the pose of Rose von Rosthorn-Friedmann. It is nonetheless apparent in this latter portrait, too, that Klimt did not break suddenly with traditions. Just as he took a long time to complete his paintings, so his pictorial types evolved only gradually. The set pieces of chair back, bare expanse of wall and ornament (the tapestry) appearing in his *Portrait of a Lady* may find themselves increasingly reduced, but they nevertheless remain present.

Klimt's portraits seldom reveal the individuality, character or abilities of the women they depict. And so it is with the *Portrait of Rose von Rosthorn-Friedmann*: reduced to a figure of elegance and sensualism, there is nothing to indicate that she was a pioneering female alpinist who became the first woman to climb the East Face of the Watzmann and the Thurwieserspitze in the Ortler Alps. Alma Schindler, later Mahler-Werfel, reported that Rose von Rosthorn-Friedmann had just started an affair with Klimt – a piece of gossip that should be taken with a pinch of salt, especially since Alma was at that time herself still in love with Klimt (Mahler-Werfel 1997, p. 431).

Water sprites and man-eating women

In the 'Klimt Collective' show mounted at the Vienna Secession in 1903, the *Portrait of Rose von Rosthorn-Friedmann* was exhibited under the anonymous title of "Portrait of a Lady". Art critics and reviewers had soon baptized her the "Lady in Black". Rose von Rosthorn-Friedmann was naturally a well-known figure in Vienna. And so the Viennese public also recognized her face and the shape of her body in another picture in the same exhibition, bearing the title *Water Sprites (Silverfish)* (p. 315; Natter 2012, Cat. 148). Opinions differ over the dating of this canvas, which belongs to Klimt's pictures of female figures floating in water, with authors variously arguing for an execution around 1899, around 1901/02 and around 1902/03. In his review of the exhibition cited above, Ludwig Hevesi described the appearance of the two water sprites in detail and compared them – rather unflatteringly – with plaice and tadpoles, whereby he observed: "I declare that one of them is related to one of [Klimt's] best female portraits. The way the painter has inserted these faces so convincingly, giving us natural history specimens with a definite touch of humour" (Hevesi 1906a, p. 451).

In 1980 Alice Strobl convincingly demonstrated that the "Portrait of a Lady" to which Hevesi was referring in his review was in fact the *Portrait of Rose von Rosthorn-Friedmann*, a work at that time believed lost and known only from a photograph (Strobl, vol. 1, 1980, p. 159). Strobl did not at that stage know the name of the sitter, however, whose identity only came to light in 1987, when the portrait was auctioned at Sotheby's. Strobl was then able to link further drawings with the painting (Strobl, vol. 4, 1989, p. 61). In some of them, Klimt shows his sitter holding a rose – an allusion to her name (Strobl 3328a). Whether Rose von Rosthorn-Friedmann recognized her own likeness in *Water Sprites* and felt flattered or insulted, we do not know.

Hanging in the Secession exhibition of 1903 was yet another painting of a woman whose sitter was recognized, even if her name was not mentioned. This was the picture of *Judith I* (p. 305; Natter 2012, Cat. 134), completed in 1901 but already planned in 1899, as evidenced by a preliminary drawing (p. 304). Author Felix Salten (1869–1945) discussed this Judith in his book on Klimt published in 1903: "The modern traits of Klimt's oeuvre can be identified in detail in his *Judith*: how he has taken a figure from the present day, a living creature, the warmth of whose blood has succeeded in intoxicating him, and how he has then transported her back into the magical shadows of distant centuries [...]. We can imagine this Judith dressed in a paillette dress in the latest Vienna Ringstrasse fashion, a beautiful Jewish society lady of the kind one meets everywhere, who, her silk petticoats rustling, attracts the eyes of the men at every première. A slim, lithe and supple woman with a sultry fire in her dark looks, with a cruel mouth and nostrils quivering with passion. [...] The artist slips the fashionable clothes from their bodies, takes one

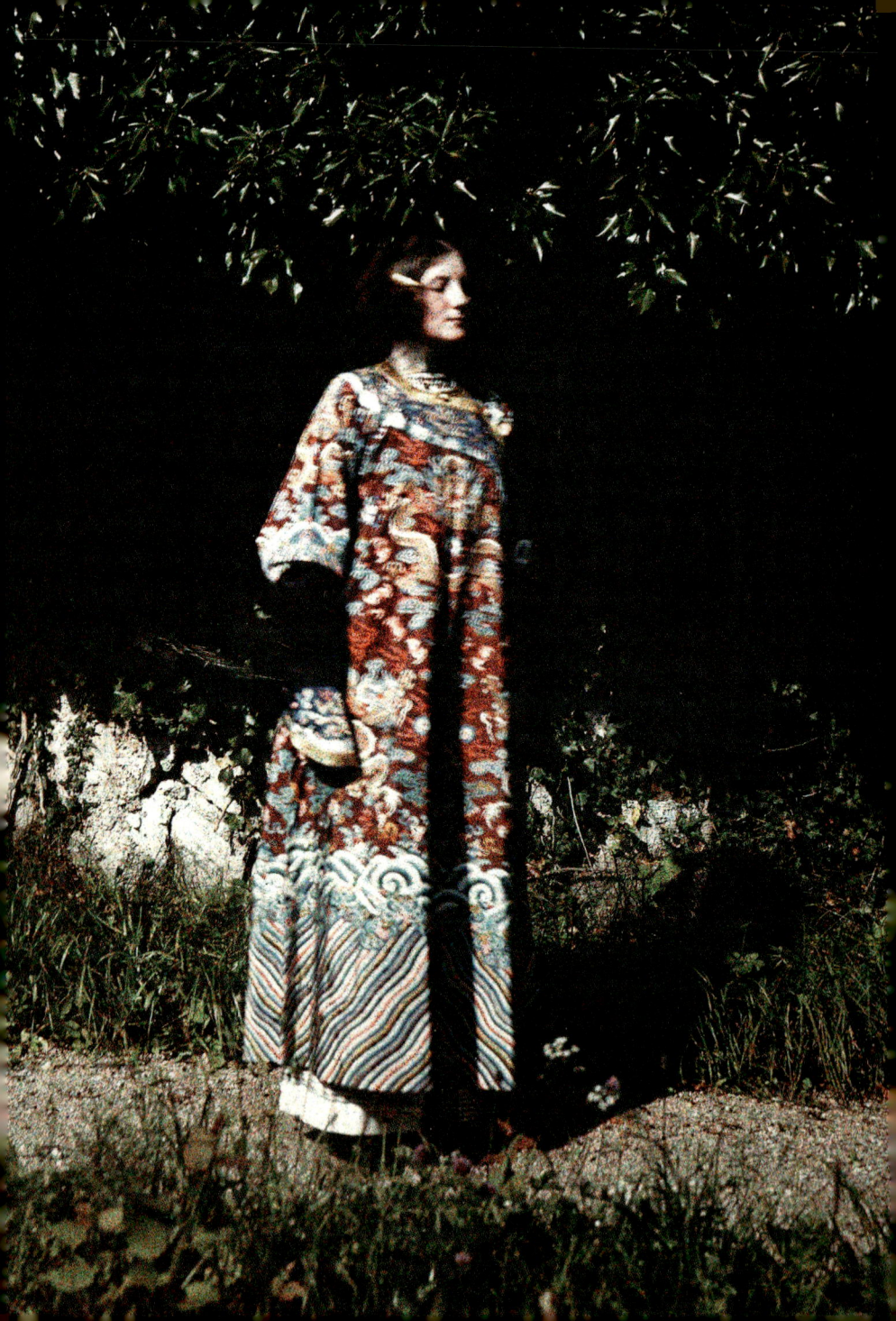

of them and places her before us in the finery of her timeless nakedness [...]" (cit. from Breicha 1978, p. 31).

Arthur Schnitzler (1862–1931) formulated this principle in somewhat more general terms in his *Comedy of Seduction*, published in 1924, in which he created a posthumous literary monument to Klimt in the character of the painter Gysar. At the very start of the play, we learn of Gysar: "Didn't you know that he paints two pictures of every woman who sits for him? One official one, with her clothes on, and then another one" (Schnitzler 1924, p. 19). This Gysar is a ladies' man, who "paints each of his lovers – roughly as Correggio painted Io as the cloud descended to her. And he is always the cloud" (Schnitzler 1924, p. 119). Schnitzler naturally provides no clues in his play to the possible identity of these lovers, and Salten, too, does not name the "Jewish society lady" he has in mind. Many authors have wished to identify her as Adele Bloch-Bauer, whom Klimt subsequently allowed to dissolve completely into gold in 1907. Klimt had previously employed gold primarily in his allegorical paintings and in the *Beethoven Frieze*. These allegorical compositions included *Pallas Athene* (p. 112; Natter 2012, Cat. 115) of 1898, *Nuda Veritas* (p. 111; Natter 2012, Cat. 119) of 1899 and the 1901 painting of *Judith I* under discussion here.

With its dimensions of 84 x 42 cm (33 x 16 ½ in.), *Judith I* is relatively small in comparison with other portraits from this same period. The canvas is housed in a narrow wooden frame with a much broader metal band across the top, once again crafted by Georg Klimt. Between chased ornamentation that spills over onto the sides of the frame, the names "JUDITH UND HOLOFERNES" are written in capital letters (also chased), whereby the emphasis lies upon JUDITH.

This Judith occupies almost the entire pictorial field. Her black, luxuriant hair, clipped by the upper edge of the picture, sits like a helmet on top of her head. Stylized trees and scales in gold recall Assyrian reliefs – an allusion to the Assyrian general Holofernes. The lascivious impression of Judith's gaze from beneath eyes that are half closed is further heightened by her mouth with slightly parted lips. Her only items of clothing are a choker studded with precious stones, a belt in the same style and several bracelets encircling her upper arm. A transparent shawl patterned with a gold print lies draped around her shoulders, but only covers one breast. Her other breast is bare, as is her belly button, visible above her golden belt. Her right hand rests delicately on the hair of Holofernes's head, which is depicted in rudimentary fashion in the lower right-hand corner of the picture.

Friedrich G. Walker, **Emilie Flöge in a Chinese dragon-print dress**, 1913
In the garden of the Villa Paulick in Seewalchen on Lake Attersee
Lumière autochrome plate. Imagno/Austrian Archives

Despite its title, Klimt's *Judith* was frequently interpreted as a representation of Salome, the biblical young woman who, in return for performing a dance for her step-father, demanded the head of St John the Baptist. Judith, by contrast, was a respectable widow who slew Holofernes by her own hand – and with this heroic deed saved the Jews from their imminent defeat at the hands of the Assyrians.

Judith, whose story is assigned to the apocryphal books of the Old Testament, was long considered a positive heroine of Christianity. In the German-speaking world, however, she was downgraded to the status of man-eating *femme fatale* at the latest in the 19th century with the appearance of the tragedy *Judith* by dramatist Friedrich Hebbel (1813–1863). And it is as such that she is portrayed by Gustav Klimt: seductive, armed with the most precious of all metals and thus ready to go to the furthest extremes. Gold already plays a dominant role in this picture – executed even before the artist's 1903 visit to Ravenna, where he was so impressed by the Early Byzantine gold mosaics that subsequently inspired his 'golden style'. Klimt's use of fine, slender brushstrokes – a manner of painting first observed in the *Portrait of Sonja Knips* (p. 301) – nevertheless lends Judith's flesh a certain soft focus and thereby veils her nakedness.

Portrait and ornament

In 1903 *Judith I* already belonged to Dr Anton Loew (d. 1907), who owned Vienna's oldest and largest sanatorium. He had earlier commissioned Klimt to execute a portrait of his daughter, Gertrud Loew (p. 317; Natter 2012, Cat. 145), a painting also on display in 1903 and later known by the alternative title of "Portrait of Gertha Felsöványi", following Loew's second marriage to the industrialist Dr Elémer Baruch von Felsöványi (b. 1882).

In this extremely narrow painting, it is barely possible to identify a background. The overall palette is restricted to white on white, causing the sitter's dark hair, dark eyes and red mouth to stand out in particular, in a similar manner to the *Portrait of Serena Lederer*. Another accent of colour is provided by the four pale blue stripes trimming the vertical seams of the white dress. The fabric of the dress, modulating from white to pale beige, is repeated above as the background behind Gertrud Loew's head and shoulders. Lower down, there follows a white surface, as if the subject were standing in front of a white piece of furniture against a darker wall. The narrow view does not even allow a glimpse of a floor, with the result that the figure fuses all the more strongly with the background and appears "physically dematerialized" (Natter/Frodl 2000, p. 98). The contrast between this figure in virginal white, her hands demurely folded and her entire body concealed behind

Portrait of Ria Munk III (detail), 1917
(unfinished) (see ill. p. 355)

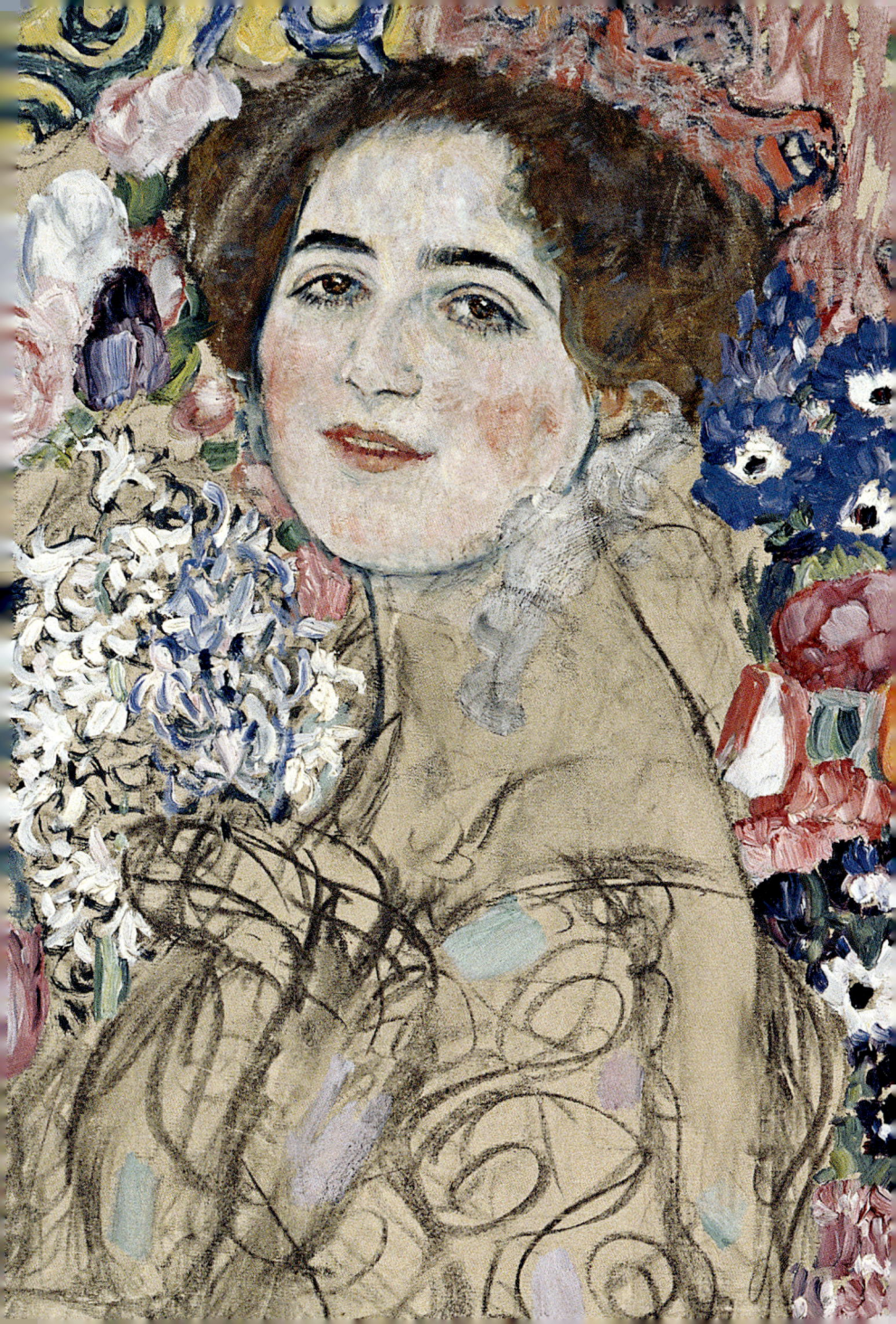

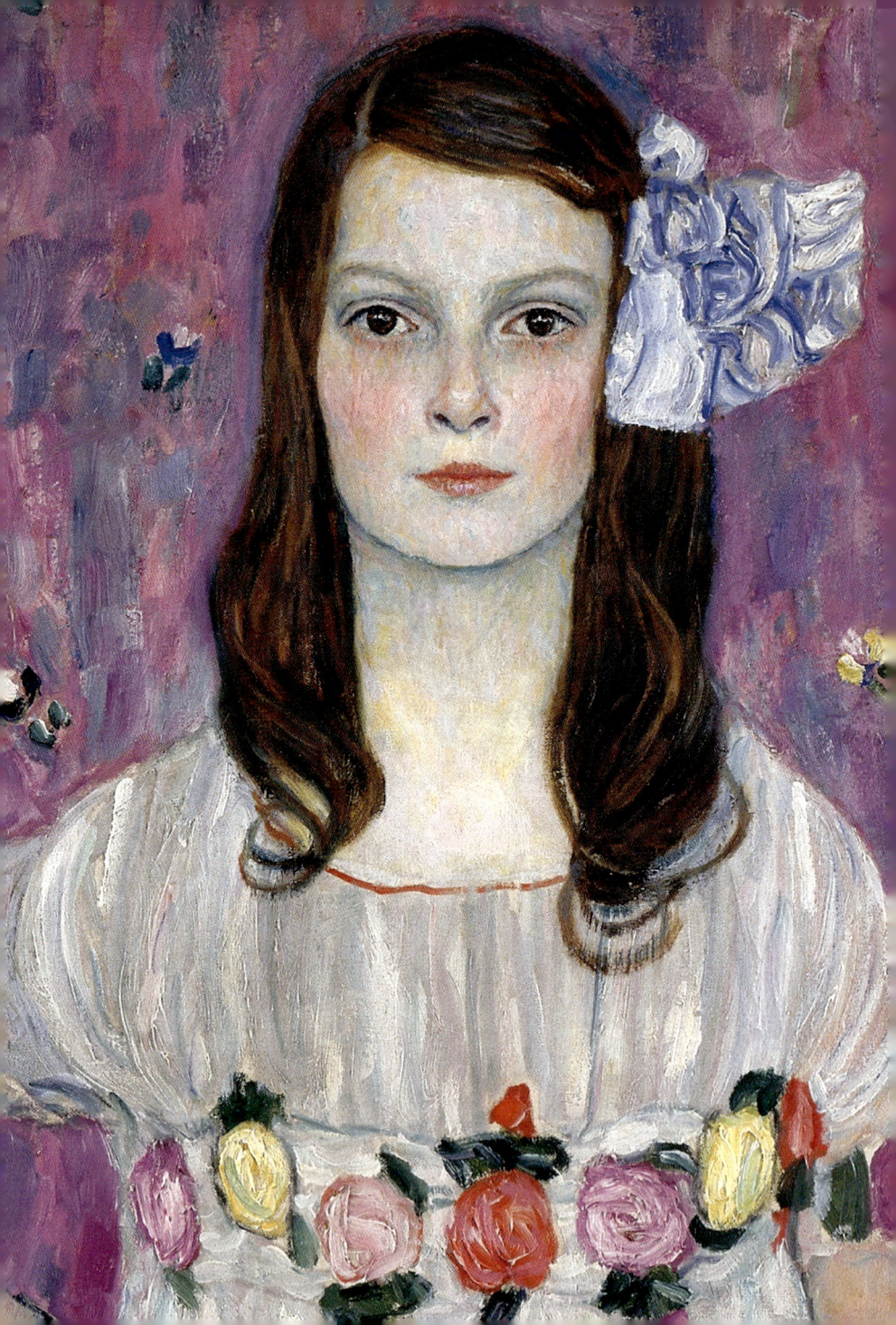

a loose-fitting dress, and *Judith I* could not be greater. Hevesi is struck not by this contrast, however, but by another, namely between *Gertrud Loew* and Klimt's *Portrait of Rose von Rosthorn-Friedmann*: "Take the emphatically sinuous pose of the lady in black of a few years ago and, at the other end of the scale, the very young lady in white from this year, a pure whisper, with the four stripes of pale lilac silk running the length of her gauzy, crumpled dress. Within the shimmering cascade of the fabric, each stripe meanders this way and that, in a random fashion that conceals the most exquisite painterly plan" (Hevesi 1906a, p. 451f.)

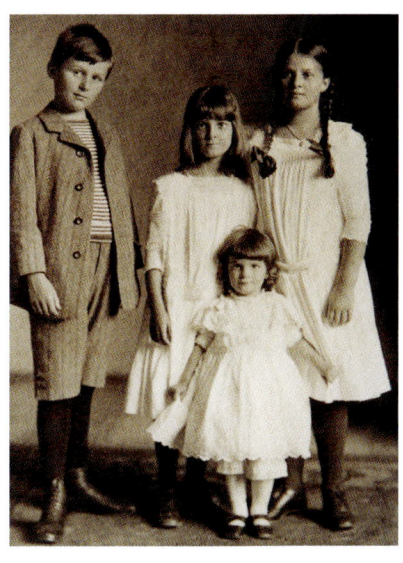

The paintings of women that Klimt showed at his Secession exhibition of 1903 included the powerful goddess *Pallas Athene*, the symbol of the Secession; *Judith I*, the *femme fatale* who in many respects forms an entity with the *Water Sprites*; and *Goldfish* (p. 309; Natter 2012, Cat. 140), dating from 1901/02 – a work that Klimt actually wanted to call "To My Critics" and with which he expressed his fury over the reactions to his Faculty paintings (Natter 2012, Cat. 126, 127, 157). At the same time, however, they also included a very different type of portrait, one in which women become decoration and vanish to an ever greater extent into ornament. This tendency is likewise found in Klimt's large-format portrait of his companion Emilie Flöge (p. 311). Klimt signed and dated the canvas "1902", even though he only actually finished it after 1904. The picture was seen in public before 1904, however, including at the 'Klimt Collective', where it was admired by Hevesi: "Another, unfinished work seems to hail from a colourfully blue world of majolica and mosaic" (Hevesi 1906a, p. 444). On another occasion shortly afterwards, he spoke of "the upright [lady], in blue and green and gold in the Japanese or faience style" (Hevesi 1906a, p. 452).

There is no evidence to support the oft-repeated claim that Emilie and her mother were unanimous in their rejection of the painting. At the end of 1903 or the start of 1904,

Portrait of Mäda Primavesi (detail), 1913
(see ill. p. 340)

The Primavesi siblings, 1910
Photograph. Private collection

however, Klimt was approached by the Austrian authorities, who wished to buy the portrait for the State. It was an offer he could not refuse. In his letter of reply, written in January 1904, he confessed that he had not thought "of selling the portrait of Miss Flöge. Since in the present case it is a question of an eventual acquisition for the State gallery, however, I am willing with the consent of the owner to sell the picture to the Moderne Galerie once it is completely finished" (cit. from Natter/Frodl 2000, p. 100).

In 1908 the portrait was purchased by the Niederösterreichische Landesgalerie for the handsome sum of 12,000 crowns. The mother – whether Klimt's or Flöge's must remain open – protested and demanded that Klimt paint a new one, but he never did. This objection to the sale of Emilie's portrait also argues against the notion that the picture failed to please her immediate family. It seems more likely that, amongst all the hoo-ha surrounding his Faculty paintings, Klimt did not want to miss this opportunity to see one of his newer works from his post-Ringstrasse period pass into a public collection. This suggestion is backed up by the letter cited above. In 1903 Klimt could not have foreseen that the sale would only eventually be concluded in the same year that he also sold *The Kiss* (pp. 142/43; Natter 2012, Cat. 179) to the Österreichische Galerie.

Klimt's *Portrait of Emilie Flöge* represents a further step towards his 'golden style' but at the same time also shows off the sitter to full advantage. The tall, slim woman is standing in a space that is difficult to define. The planes of greys, greens and pinks between which her figure is located recall the upholstered furniture of other pictures and lend the painting an astonishing depth. There is also the suggestion of a floor, upon which Emilie Flöge indeed seems to be standing, even if her dress falls over her feet. The field of blue in the upper half of the composition forms only a weak contrast to the blue dress, comparable to Klimt's use of white on white in the *Portrait of Serena Lederer*. Emilie Flöge dons a dress that, although not gathered at the waist, is nevertheless fitted relatively close to her body. It is sewn from an iridescent blue-green fabric patterned with white dots, gold circles and squares and black spiral-shaped ornament. In the picture she is wearing no jewellery, even though Klimt gave her a number of pieces made by the Wiener Werkstätte (pp. 322, 385).

This gown is described by some fashion historians as a Reform dress, while others insist that it falls into none of the fashion trends of the day but resembles an abstract, incorporeal sheath of ornament (thus Angela Völker in Natter/Frodl 2000, p. 46). We shall never know whether Klimt felt hindered from portraying his partner in a fashionable dress by her thorough knowledge of fashion, whether the costume in which she appears corresponded to her own wishes or whether indeed there were quite different reasons for choosing this outfit, in particular since no preliminary drawings relating to the composition have come down to us.

Emile Flöge is standing with her left hand on her hip and her body angled towards the viewer's left, whereby she has turned her head so that she is looking straight out of the picture at the viewer. Her expression is not salacious, nor is it shy and retiring, but self-confident, which is hardly surprising in the case of a fashion designer with her own fashion salon. Her head is framed by a sort of aureole that takes up the colours of the fabric of her dress but is more geometric in shape and appears to be made of a solid material. The device of emphasizing his sitter's head by placing it against a backdrop of floral motifs was one that Klimt had already employed in his *Portrait of Sonja Knips*. The same device is reinforced with golden ornament in *Judith I* and expressed in more geometric terms in the *Portrait of Emilie Flöge*. This tendency continues in the portraits of *Margaret Stonborough-Wittgenstein* (pp. 265, 321; Natter 2012, Cat. 169) and *Fritza Riedler* (pp. 298/99, 323; Natter 2012, Cat. 170) and reaches its high point, of course, in that of *Adele Bloch-Bauer I* (pp. 286, 328/29; Natter 2012, Cat. 174).

Lady in gold

Adele Bloch-Bauer I is the only portrait by Klimt that can truly be assigned to his 'golden style'. His use of gold in the *Beethoven Frieze* and above all in the Stoclet frieze is found on the same scale in only two easel paintings: *The Kiss* and in the *Portrait of Adele Bloch-Bauer I*. What Klimt had achieved in his other portraits through his choice of colour, he here amplified through the use of gold: the reduction of the female body to ornament. The square picture portrays Adele Bloch-Bauer in a gold dress and seated in a gold chair against a gold background and a green plinth zone. The individual elements are recognizable solely through the fact that Klimt has painted ornaments in other colours – primarily silver and black, but also yellow, orange, blue, grey and brown – on top of the gold. Thus the arms of the chair are decorated with silver spirals, which reappear top left above the sitter's head. This is evidently all we can see of the back of the armchair, which appears to be largely obscured by a form or structure similar to that visible behind the head of Emilie Flöge. It consists of various circular and almond-shaped forms, bounded at the sides by squares, those on the right very much smaller than those on the left. Klimt's preliminary sketches suggest that this form might here be intended as a cushion.

The sitter's head is seen directly in front of it. But if her dark hair, dark eyes and red mouth stand out within her face, her complexion barely distinguishes itself in colour from the surrounding gold. This contrast is even weaker in her décolleté and arms, whose yellowish hue approaches that of gold. Adele Bloch-Bauer is wearing a close-fitting dress that is patterned with eyes inside triangles, which recall both Egyptian hieroglyphs and the Christian eye of God. These are combined with a host of other, smaller triangles, chiefly silver, all pointing towards the left. In Klimt's work, these small triangles embody

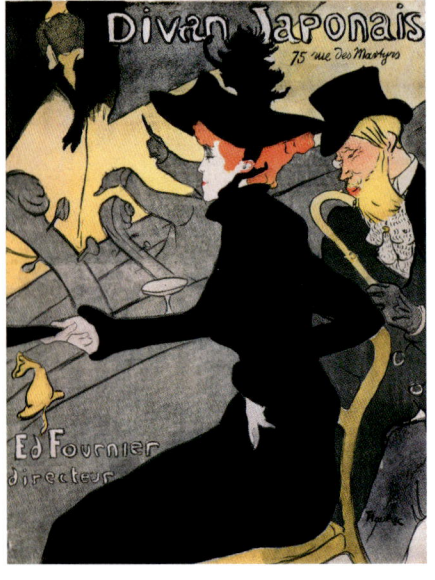

the male principle, following a contemporary convention established above all by the Austrian philosopher Otto Weininger (1880–1903).

The dress allows us to sense the body beneath it, but also suggests that the figure may be standing. It is bounded in turn by fabric sweeping outwards on either side, in a shape that is rigid but which at the same time recalls folds of material through the animated strokes of the brush. The little triangles, this time in gold and straining upwards, are joined by squares containing Japanese ornament as found on the dress worn by Emilie Flöge, along with other symbols that call to mind the signets in the Klimt portfolio issued in instalments as from 1908. The letters A and B, i.e. the initials of Adele Bloch, who did not add her maiden name to her married name until 1917, also make repeated appearances. Klimt's signature and the date 1907 are found in another such square on the right-hand edge of the picture. Whether the fabric represents a cloak (Natter/Frodl 2000, p. 116; Seiser 2007a, p. 286) or part of the sitter's actual dress (Koja/ Kugler 2006, p. 168) is difficult to judge, even with the aid of the preparatory drawings. Alice Strobl lists some one hundred such drawings (Strobl, vol. 1, 1980, nos. 1054–1151, and vol. 4, 1989, nos. 3520–3531c). They show that Klimt drew Adele Bloch-Bauer both seated and standing as he explored ideas for her portrait from 1903 onwards.

Klimt received the commission just after he had seen the Byzantine mosaics in various churches in Ravenna. The resulting portrait has been rightly associated with these mosaics. There the figures are situated in the celestial sphere, which is lent its magnificent expression in gold. The last vestiges of perspective, as (still) known from the art of antiquity, were thereby also eliminated. Klimt also renounced the use of perspective. Just as the *Portrait of Adele Bloch-Bauer I* may legitimately be compared with the imperial portraits in San Vitale in Ravenna, so it should be remembered that in 1907 Pablo Picasso (1881–1973) also banished perspective from his picture of *Les Demoiselles d'Avignon*

Henri de Toulouse-Lautrec, **Divan Japonais**, 1892/93
Lithograph

(New York, The Museum of Modern Art), as did Wassily Kandinsky (1866–1944) in his early Murnau landscapes. Although Klimt, with ornament, took a different path towards abstraction, he was nonetheless in alignment in a certain manner with the spirit of the age. In *Les Demoiselles* and the Cubist works that he produced shortly afterwards, Picasso renounced not only perspective but also strong colour contrasts. Klimt did the same. He furthermore allowed Serena Lederer, Gertrud Loew and Margaret Stonborough-Wittgenstein to 'vanish' into white and Emilie Flöge into blue. In the case of Adele Bloch-Bauer, he chose the material of gold. Perhaps he was thereby fulfilling a wish expressed by his client. Perhaps he could afford the gold for

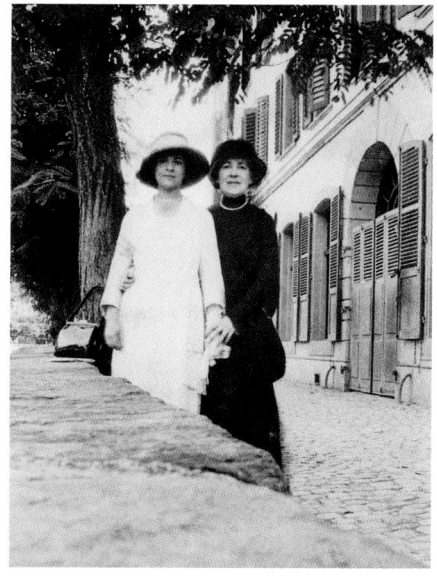

the portrait only because the sugar manufacturer was prepared to pay him such a high fee. The attempt to see echoes of a (past) love affair in Klimt's use of gold seems to me dubious. Whether such a relationship ever existed must remain open.

Anonymous women in hats

Five years later Klimt painted a second portrait of Adele Bloch-Bauer. The paintings of women that he produced during the intervening period were not commissioned portraits but pictures of anonymous female sitters. These, too, testify to the fact that Klimt's 'golden period' had ended with *The Kiss* and the Stoclet frieze. An example is the *Lady with a Hat and Feather Boa* (p. 335; Natter 2012, Cat. 192), executed around 1910, in which Klimt employs an entirely different palette and compositional approach.

The picture, slightly taller than it is wide, employs a dark background, executed in broad brushstrokes that in many places reveal paler streaks reminiscent of points of light. This suggests a metropolitan setting, as does the broad band running horizontally across the centre of the canvas, in which red, green and yellow forms appear to gleam like lights. To interpret them as such would be wrong, however. As Erhard Stöbe, the conservator

Serena Lederer and her daughter Elisabeth, c. 1914
Photograph. Private collection

who restored the painting, was convincingly able to show, they are in fact rapidly drawn Asiatic figures on a chest of drawers (Stöbe 1995). This can be most easily recognized in the yellow metal sculpture on the left-hand side, which represents a figure mounted on an ox. Directly in front of this colourful horizontal strip is the sitter's head, or rather, what can be glimpsed of it: dressed in a wide-brimmed hat and a black feather boa that conceals the lower part of her face, only her half-lowered eyes are visible beneath thin, arching eyebrows, a slender nose and an upper lip lined with red lipstick. The sitter's pale complexion is heightened by two patches of rouge. Her sandy hair corkscrews out from beneath her hat. A white field beneath the feather boa may represent the fur trim of her coat. Her dark hat is decorated with bluish violet trimming that flutters upwards behind her and is cut off by the top of the picture.

Despite the fact that we cannot even make out her coat properly and her face is almost completely hidden, the woman exudes a greater sense of femininity than Klimt's female portraits of the preceding years. This has nothing to do with the model – in this case, probably Hilde Roth (c. 1876/80–1970), who worked in Klimt's studio for some fifteen years and whose face can also be recognized in other pictures (see Partsch 2006) – but is undoubtedly due to the change of direction in Klimt's art. This re-orientation can also be seen in *The Black Feathered Hat* (p. 333; Natter 2012, Cat. 189) dating from 1910.

Only slightly larger than *Lady with a Hat and Feather Boa* and employing a similar portrait format, *The Black Feathered Hat* is a picture in white showing the half-length figure of a woman. Her pose indicates that she is seated: leaning on her elbow and propping her chin on her hand, she gazes towards the left (from the viewer's perspective) with her face tilted slightly downwards. Her contemplative pose does not altogether match her enormous feathered hat, which seems to float on top of the auburn hair she wears pinned up on her head. The outline demarcating her white garment from the white of the background is something that Klimt had not employed in his earlier pictures.

The painting has frequently been compared with the lithographs of Henri de Toulouse-Lautrec (1864–1901; e.g. Natter/Frodl 2000, p. 122), which were exhibited on multiple occasions in Vienna from 1899 onwards. Klimt may furthermore have seen a number of such lithographs on his trip to Paris in 1909 (p. 282). Works by the Fauves, meanwhile, were also featured at the 1909 Vienna Kunstschau. These influences probably played a key role in hastening the end of Klimt's 'golden period' and the start of a new phase in his art, one that first made itself felt in his anonymous paintings of women and subsequently saw him arriving at new solutions in his portraits of Mäda Primavesi and again Adele Bloch-Bauer.

Portrait of Eugenia (Mäda) Primavesi (detail), 1913/14
(see ill. p. 342)

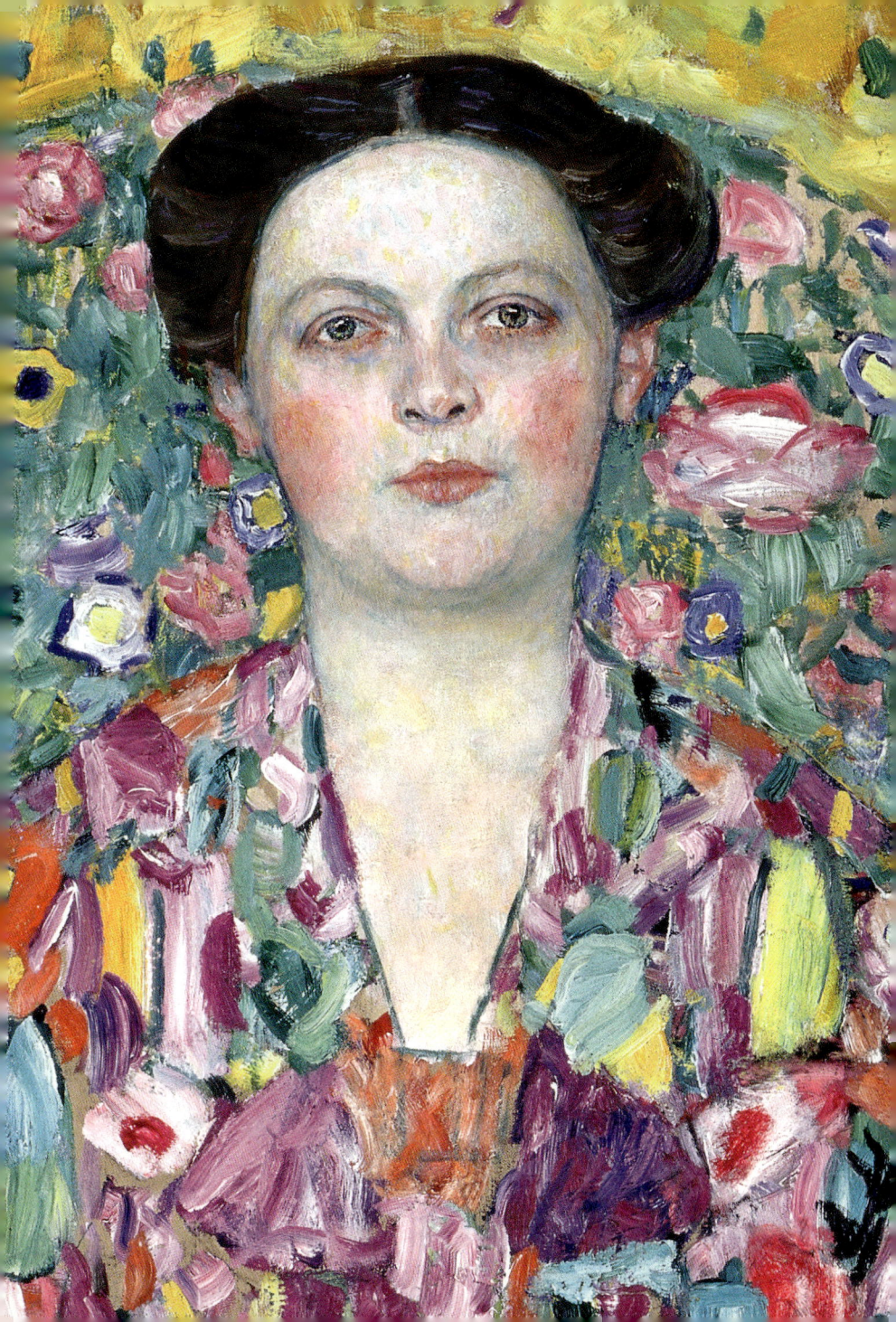

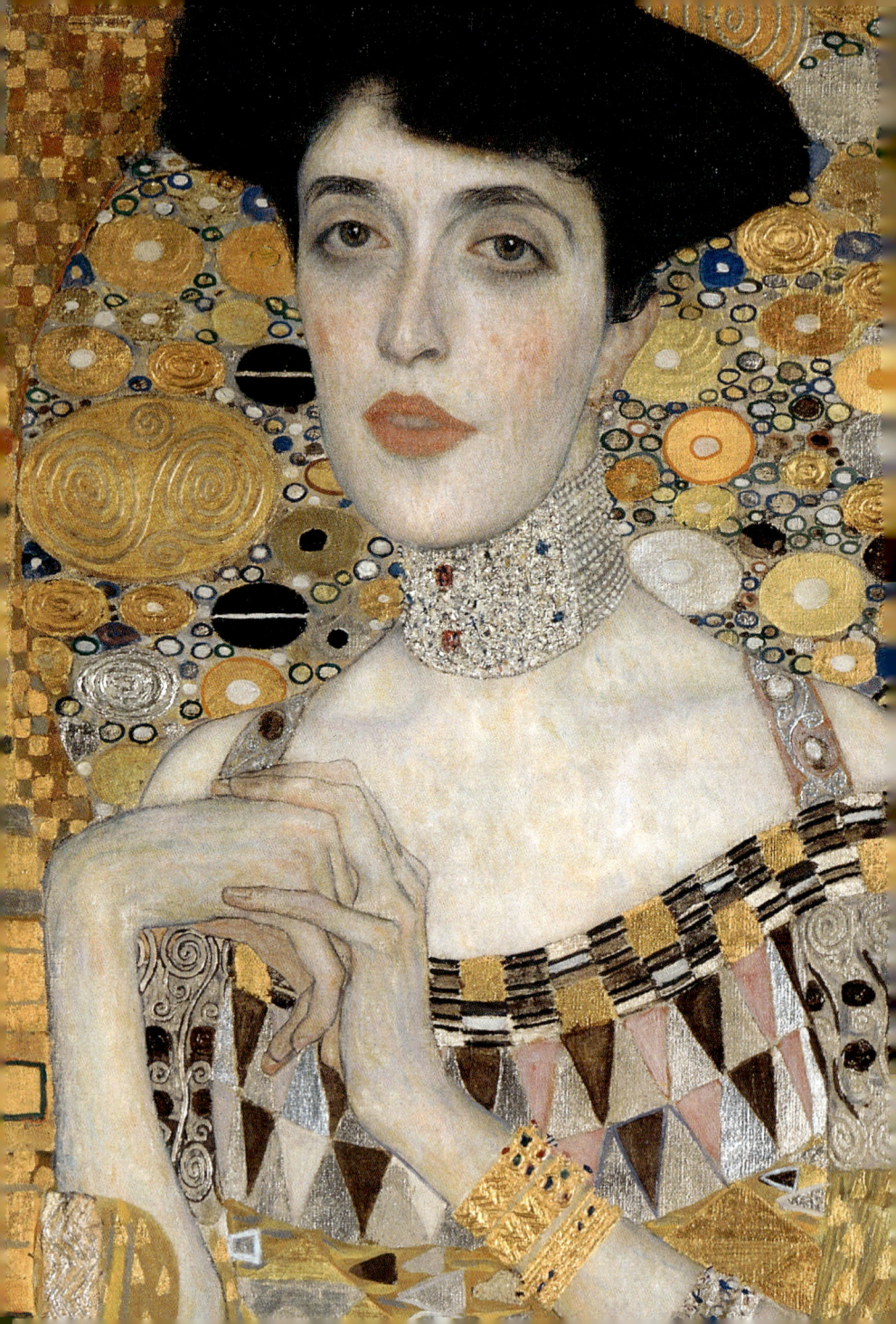

Colourful portraits of Klimt's late period

When Klimt painted the *Portrait of Mäda Primavesi* (pp. 278, 340; Natter 2012, Cat. 202), the latter was not a woman but a child still short of her tenth birthday. Mäda stands at the very front edge of the picture with her feet planted firmly apart. Portrayed in life size, her figure reaches almost all the way to the top of the canvas. Her eyes gaze out of the picture with an alert and searching air. One hand is planted on her hip, the other held behind her back. Her dress, with its yoke of flowers and frilled skirt, reaches to her knees. Her bare legs end in feet that are much too big, clad in ballerina shoes.

Extending behind her is a white surface with clumps of grass and flowers growing on it, and on which a fish, a small dog and a bird are assembled, possibly along with other animals. This white surface is bounded on either side by a sort of carpet, which in its constellation of green, white and red brushstrokes recalls Monet's *Water Lily* paintings. Rising in the background is a purple wall dotted with scattered flowers; these latter might equally well be butterflies carried on the wind. The dominant purple is joined by strokes of other colours, chiefly green. This restless and animated surface nevertheless seems calmer than the 'water-lily carpet' and calmer, too, than the three blue wavy lines in the foreground, which form the floor beneath the girl's feet.

Klimt evidently used different means of representation to distinguish between women bound within ornament (and within their social constraints) and a child still free from such constraints. This manifests itself in a particular fashion in the *Portrait of Adele Bloch-Bauer II* (p. 345; Natter 2012, Cat. 196), which Klimt painted in 1912. Although we can still recognize the sitter's face (p. 293), there are otherwise almost no points of comparison with the golden *Portrait of Adele Bloch-Bauer I*. Klimt has here once again chosen a portrait format. With dimensions of 190 x 120 cm (74 ¾ x 47 ¼ in.), the picture is even taller than the *Portrait of Emilie Flöge* and wider than that of *Margaret Stonborough-Wittgenstein*.

The subject is wearing a high-necked pale dress that starts directly beneath her wide choker, which is this time composed not of gold and precious stones, but of fine chains or small pearls – it is impossible to identify them precisely. The dress with its buttoned bodice is tied beneath the bust with a broad blue sash, from where it falls full length and in a close-fitting cut to the ground. Below the level of the hips, the skirt is made up of horizontal bands of fabric of different widths, most of them vertically striped, the broadest carrying a pattern consisting of frenetic brushstrokes. Draped around the sitter's shoulders is a fur-trimmed stole – in some of the preliminary drawings, still a coat

Portrait of Adele Bloch-Bauer I (detail), 1907
(see ill. pp. 328/29)

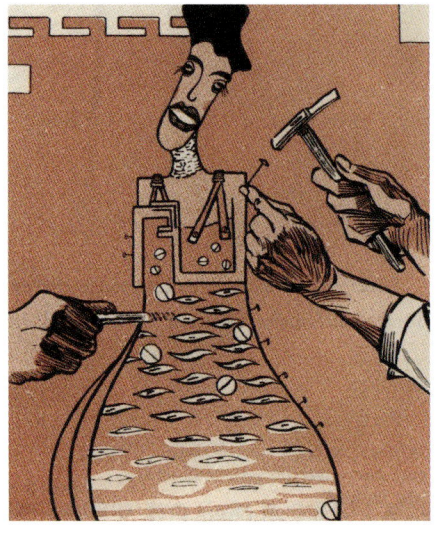

(p. 292) – that reaches almost to the floor. As usual with Klimt, the feet disappear beneath the skirt. The only parts of Adele Bloch-Bauer's body that remain visible are her face and hands. Her hair is hidden beneath a vast hat, of which all we can see is the underside of the wide brim. The glimpse of white around the brim suggests that the hat is trimmed with white feathers.

Adele's face, with its dark, arching eyebrows, heavy lids and large red mouth, looks straight ahead. Neither head nor body are turned even slightly to one side. This frontality makes her figure appear rigid. Just like the women frozen in ornament before her, she lacks animation.

Adele Bloch-Bauer is standing on a patterned carpet. Alongside curlicues and flowers, we can also make out undulating lines that recall the B in the gold portrait, together with a semicircle that likewise seems derived from the semicircles facing each other in the first portrait. Here Klimt transports something of his earlier ornament into this second portrait of Adele Bloch-Bauer.

The remainder of the background, the 'wall', is divided into different zones. Set against a plane of pale purple is a green square, perhaps a sort of tapestry, which is strewn with flowers and thus recalls a meadow. In the red zone above, riders are galloping towards a temple-like house. Other figures are visible as no more than a pair of legs, as if Adele Bloch-Bauer were standing in front of a pictorial frieze that continues upwards.

Klimt had already painted Asiatic figures on either side of his sitter's face in *Lady with a Hat and Feather Boa* (p. 335), even if these are difficult to make out. He returns to this idea in the present composition. He thereby based himself on Asiatic works of art in his

Siegmund Skwirczynski, **Caricature of the *Portrait of Adele Bloch-Bauer I***
From: *Die Muskete*, Vienna, 1908

Pages 290/91
Josef Hoffmann, **The Wiener Werkstätte room
at the International Exhibition in Mannheim**, 1907
From: *Deutsche Kunst und Dekoration*, vol. 20 (1907)

own collection, which he kept in his studio. At the same time, it is evident that Klimt also drew inspiration from the Fauves, and above all from Henri Matisse (1869–1954). This can be seen in the way in which Klimt juxtaposes colour fields and distributes forms and figures across them.

The same colourfulness characterizes the last portraits completed by Klimt before his death. In these, too, the subject is set against a backdrop of Far Eastern figures and thereby 'trapped' in another form of ornament. They include the *Portrait of Elisabeth Lederer* (p. 347), also frequently referred to as the *Portrait of Baroness Elisabeth Bachofen-Echt*. But August and Serena Lederer's daughter did not marry Baron Wolfgang von Bachofen-Echt of the celebrated brewer family until 1921, long after the picture was painted. Elisabeth was already a young woman when her parents commissioned Klimt to paint her portrait in 1914, but was still living at home. She later recounted how her mother regularly argued over the picture with Klimt, who was never satisfied with it. In 1916 Serena Lederer carried off the portrait from Klimt's studio, even though the artist insisted that it was still not finished.

Klimt envelops Elisabeth Lederer in a white dress, just as he had her mother. In this case, however, it is not a loose-fitting gown but a close-fitting top and a skirt, whose styling recalls the *plus fours* that were the latest fashion at the time. Over the top, Elisabeth wears a white chiffon shawl with a floral pattern. Her white outfit makes her pale complexion look even paler, and her hair and eyes even blacker. Only her lips and cheeks are heightened with lipstick and rouge. Beneath her pleated and gathered skirt, her feet are visible in high-heeled white pumps. The placing of one foot just a little in front of the other reinforces the slight angle at which her body is turned.

In a similar fashion to Adele Bloch-Bauer, Elisabeth is standing on a carpet. Here, however, it is a luminous bright red and its ornament is clearly recognizable. The background, on the other hand, is entirely unclear – something that may be due to the fact that Klimt was prevented from finishing the picture. On a surface shot with greys, blues and pinks, Chinese figures are approaching the subject and seem to be paying tribute to her from a respectful distance. Extracted from the context of another picture or indeed several different ones, they resemble figures from a dream. This mood is echoed by the ornamental field rising behind Elisabeth's figure and taken from a dragon kimono, of which Klimt owned an example. The texture of the fabric remains invisible, however, and we see only the figural representations of the blue-red dragon, stylized bats and flowers, all of them symbols of good luck. Together, these form a sort of aureole, albeit one that ends behind her shoulders.

In his *Portrait of Friederike Maria Beer* (p. 349; Natter 2012, Cat. 217), Klimt presented his next customer in a very much less distanced fashion. The tips of her black pumps

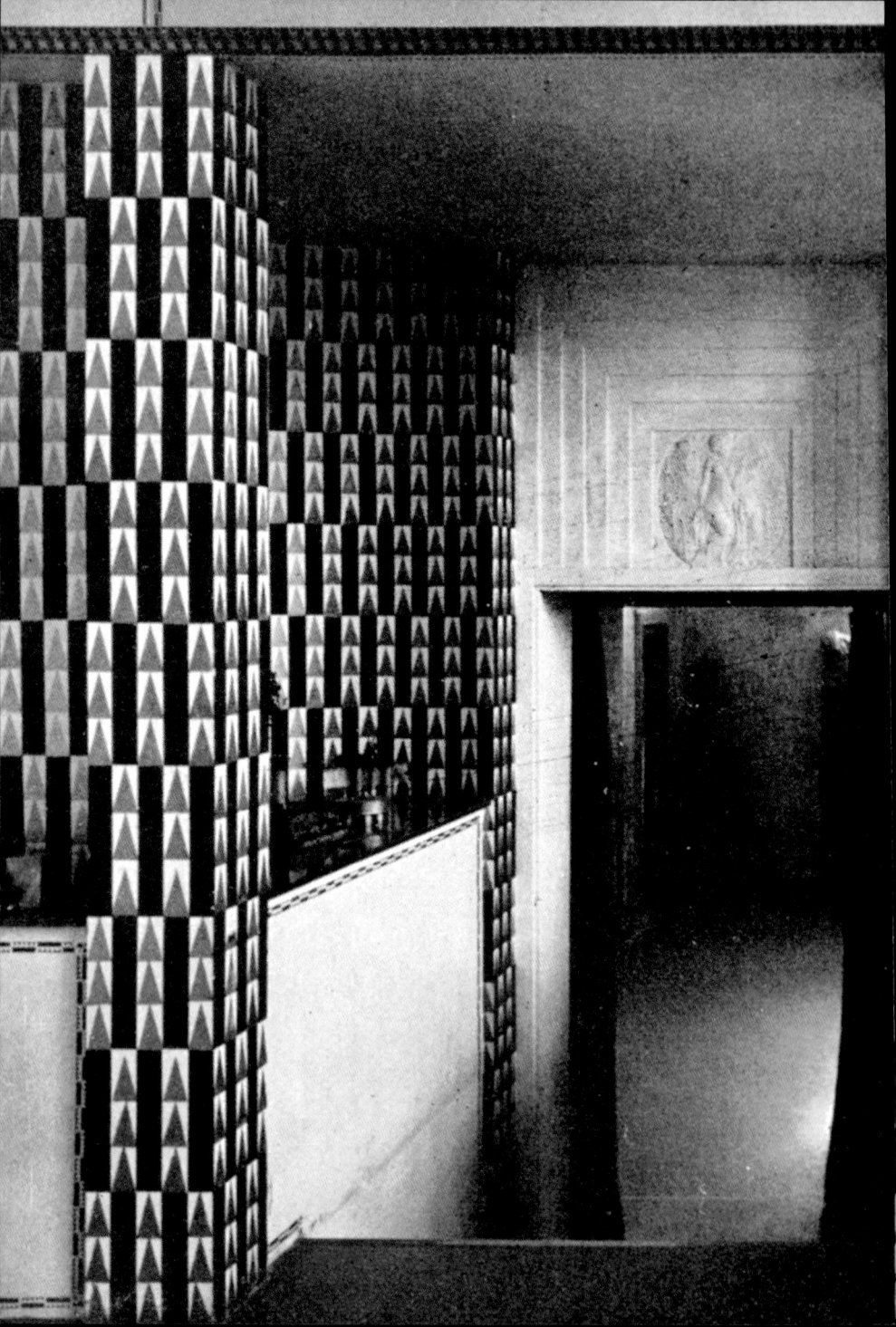

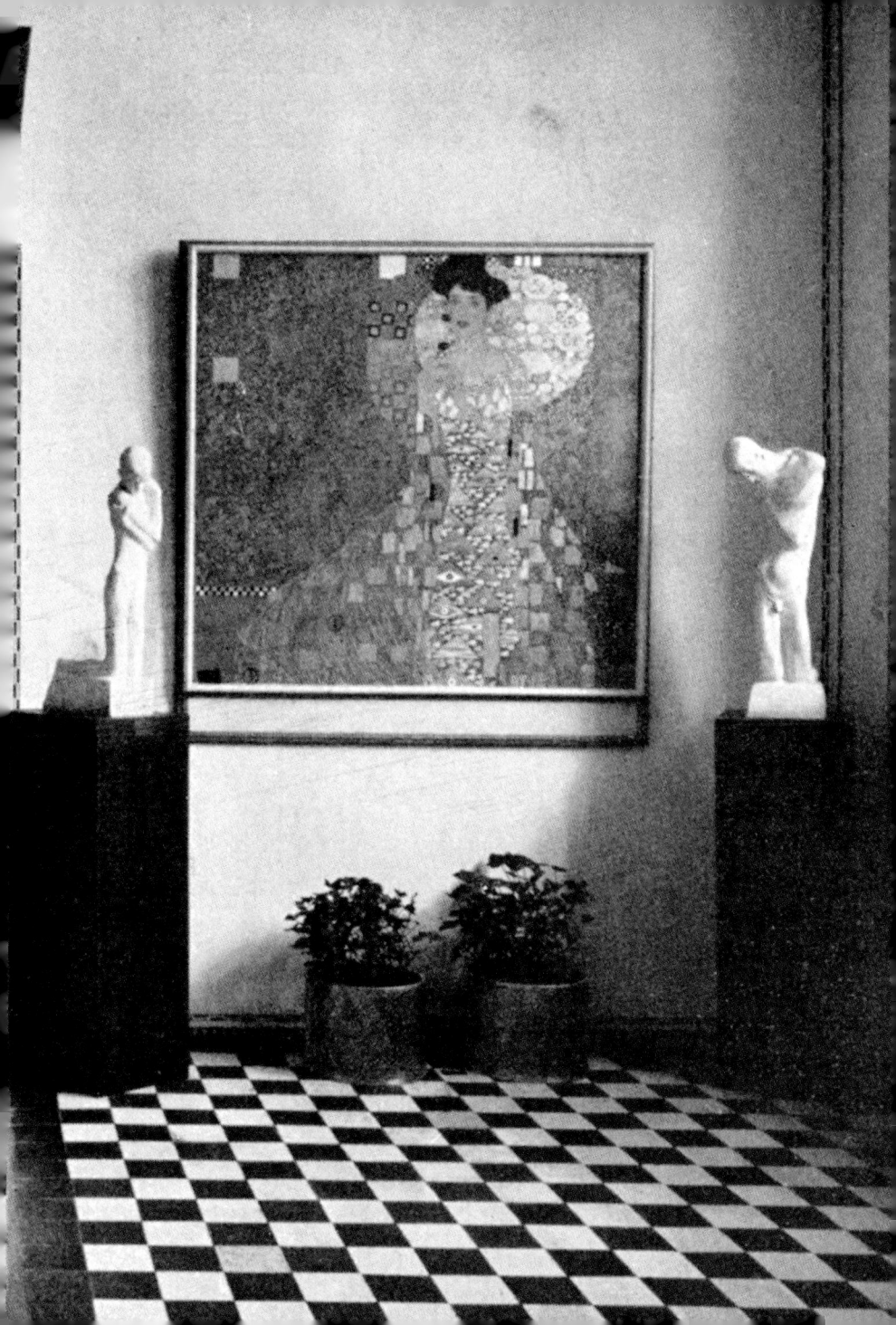

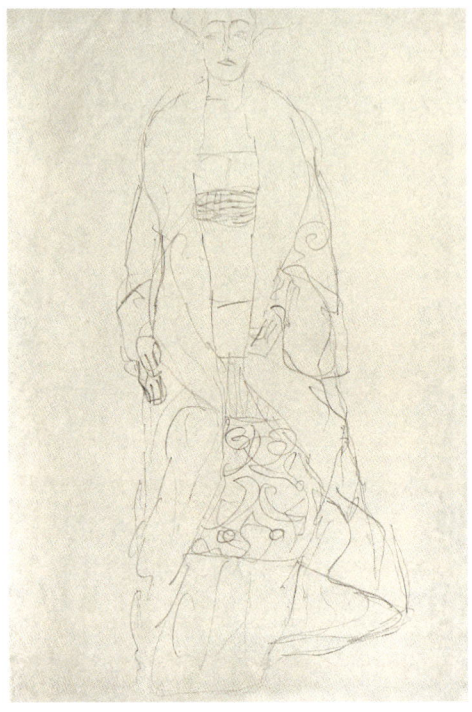

touch the lower edge of the picture. Once again seen in the frontal pose typical of Klimt, the figure rises almost the full height of the canvas. Here, however, the background comprises a ferocious battle scene with large-scale figures. According to the sitter, these scenes were taken from an Asiatic vase in Klimt's possession. Friederike Maria Beer is wearing a Wiener Werkstätte dress with a polecat fur jacket over the top, albeit with the latter turned inside out at Klimt's request, as he was fascinated by the silk lining with its ornamental, in places floral pattern. As a result, dress, jacket and background all compete with one another. The only zones of calm in the entire picture are the green carpet in the foreground and the face beneath the black hair, from where the sitter's dark eyes gaze directly out at the viewer.

Klimt produced fifteen other female portraits up to 1917. One of them, *Friends II* (p. 350; Natter 2012, Cat. 225), passed into the possession of the Lederer family and was destroyed by fire at Immendorf Castle in 1945. Probably square in format, it shows a detail view of two women. The one in the foreground is wrapped in a red garment and wears a turban. The second stands naked beside her, nestling her head against that of her friend. Surrounding the two women on the pink background are birds and flowers. These are neither organized as a group, as in the portrait of Elisabeth Lederer, however, nor thronging the entire surface, as in the case of Friederike Maria Beer, but are distributed in a somewhat more casual manner. Our eye is struck by the two birds on the left and right, recalling a peacock and a swan, respectively – both symbols of beauty, amongst other things. In their pose, the women call to mind Klimt's late allegorical compositions; indeed, they look as if they might just have freed themselves from such a painting.

Adele Bloch-Bauer in a coat and ornamental dress, c. 1912
Pencil, 56.5 x 37 cm / 22 ¼ x 14 ½ in. Vienna, Collection of Monsignore Otto Mauer

Late allegorical representations of women

For alongside his paintings of women, both those that were officially commissioned and those that were not (including his female figures from antique mythology), Klimt continued to paint allegories. The artist thereby pursued the same themes of life and death that he had formulated as early as 1895 in his *Allegory of Love* (p. 59; Natter 2012, Cat. 81), albeit in compositions that registered the changes in his style. The history of *Death and Life* (pp. 336/37; Natter 2012, Cat. 193) – a work also known under the titles "Death", "Death and Love" and "Fear of Death" – allows us to follow these changes

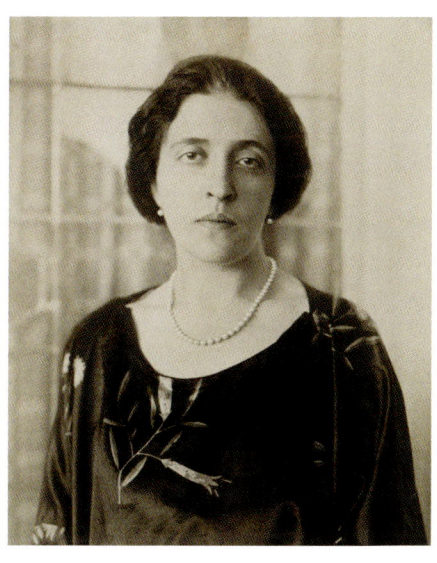

in an exemplary manner, for having painted the picture in 1910/11 and subsequently exhibited it in public, Klimt returned to the canvas 1915/16 and radically altered it.

Almost square in its dimensions of 180.5 x 200.5 cm (71 ⅛ x 78 ⅞ in.), the painting falls into two parts. Standing on the left is Death, arrayed in a blue garment. He is recognizable only from his skull and his bony hands – at least in the version that exists today. Occupying the larger part of the picture on the right is humankind, chiefly represented by women, who are grouped on a flowering meadow.

When the picture was shown for the first time at the 1911 Esposizione internazionale d'arte in Rome, in 1911, Death appeared as a very narrow figure wholly without a body, looking downwards. Even his skull's head half disappeared into his blue robe, which was ornamented first and foremost with heavy black crosses. The gold nimbus behind his head was not only a last reminder of Klimt's 'golden period', but also translated Death into a celestial realm. Opposite him were five people: a mother and child, an older woman and a couple. Their naked bodies were partially covered by fabric (or blankets) strewn with ornament. All had their eyes closed and thus did not look Death in the face, but nor did they appear to be afraid of him. In the version that Klimt then showed at the 1916 Berlin Secession and which we know today, Death has adopted a more menacing pose. The grin-

Portrait of Adele Bloch-Bauer in a Wiener Werkstätte dress, c. 1910
Photograph. Imagno/Austrian Archives

ning skull with the empty eye sockets is looking at the tangle of human bodies. He now holds a red cudgel in his hands. His robe has widened and traces the curves of a human silhouette, as if the body of a woman were concealed beneath a tight-fitting dress. Death has lost his golden nimbus, and the background of the picture is no longer reddish brown but a tone shot with green and blue.

The flowering meadow has also expanded and the original group has been joined by a few more people. At the bottom, the woman of the couple still has her head bowed so that we see only her hair. This no longer tumbles down in long tresses, however, and hence her left arm is now visible. The man behind her enfolds her with his right arm. His left hand, which in the first version clasps her shoulder, is now hidden behind her naked torso. The body of the woman is partially concealed by a section of fabric, ornamented primarily in red. Her pose suggests that she is standing. It would be more logical if she were lying in the lap of the man seated behind her. His upright naked torso is immensely muscular. His skin is astonishingly brown, especially in comparison to the white flesh of the woman. From the waist down, he is draped in a cloth whose pattern recalls the gown worn by the man in *The Kiss*. The old woman is still seated behind him. She wears a blue bonnet and holds her head humbly bowed. Her eyes are closed, as are those of the young mother and her infant, lying behind the old woman. The baby is sprawled on his back; no cloth covers his nakedness and it is clear that he is a boy. His mother clasps him with one hand. His head, turned away from his body, nestles against the face of a girl. Their two heads form a frame around the head of the old woman. Beside them, another head emerges from the sheets, as well as another body, whereby it is not entirely clear how these two are linked. Two more young women can be made out on the other side, facing Death. One of them has her eyes wide open and clutches at her throat, as if sensing the danger close at hand.

A comparison with the Dance of Death, a theme familiar in art since the Middle Ages, seems obvious and has often been drawn. But Klimt chooses to portray neither the representatives of the different social classes [a standard element of medieval Dance of Death compositions, illustrating that all men are equal when facing Death – *trans.*] nor the human fear of Death. For him, "all men" are the ages of (wo)man and the two sexes, whereby in the final version of the composition, youth predominates. Klimt's different presentation of the sexes is also interesting: women – whether young or old – all have a white skin shot with greenish-blues and thus recall the aquatic females whom Klimt so often painted. The skin of the infant boy, on the other hand, is a healthy pink, while the figure of the man with his brown skin and muscular build suggests a sporty individual

Portrait of Friederike Maria Beer (detail), 1916
(see ill. p. 349)

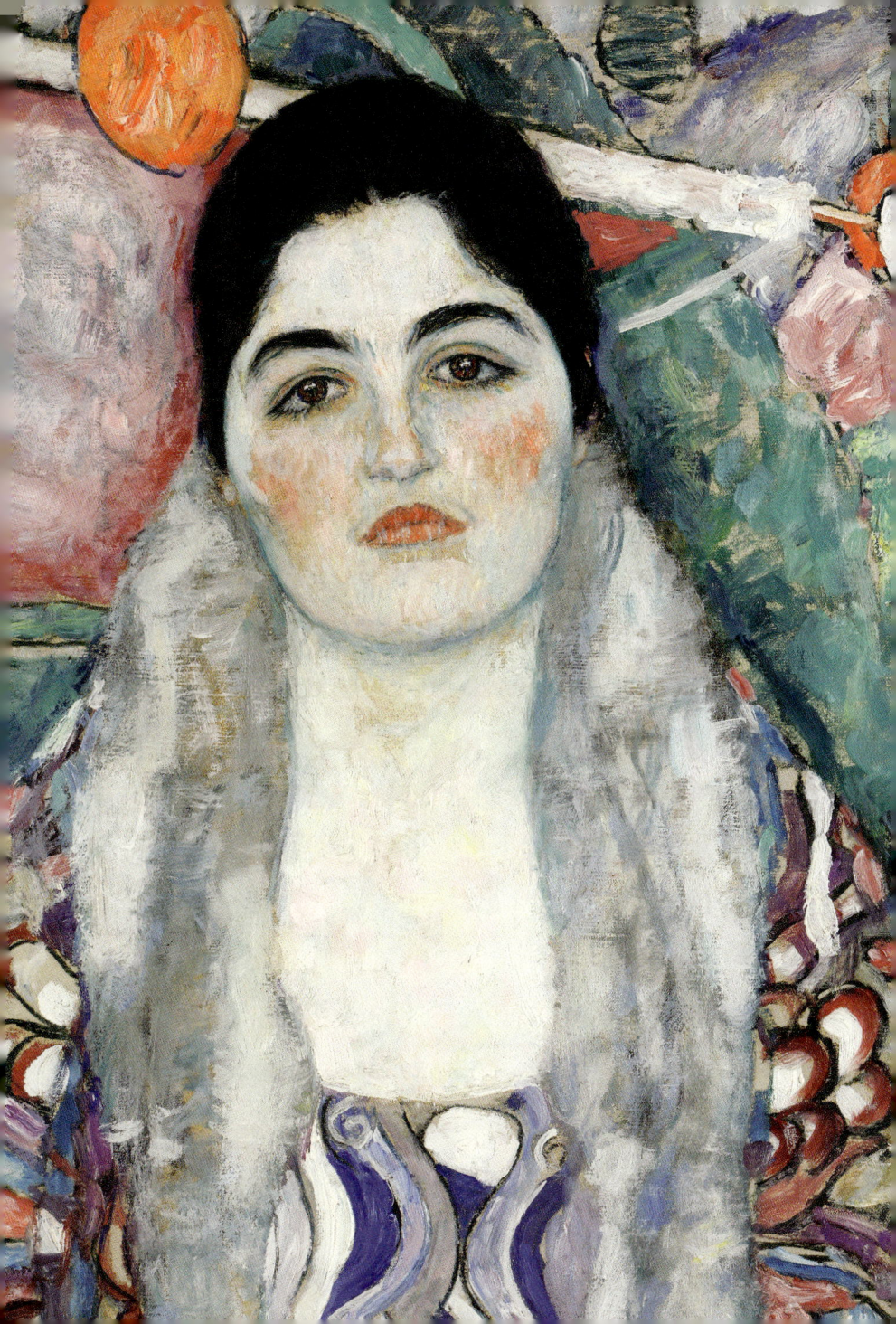

bursting with health, something that does not quite match his simultaneously submissive and protective pose.

The threat presented to life by Death is a theme that runs through the whole of Klimt's oeuvre. It is already present, as mentioned earlier, in his *Allegory of Love* of 1895, but it can subsequently also be found in the *Beethoven Frieze*, the Faculty paintings and many other pictures right up to *The Kiss. Death and Life* equates, as it were, to a combination of *The Kiss* and *The Three Ages of Woman.*

Similar to this latter in terms of its composition, *The Virgin* (pp. 338/39; Natter 2012, Cat. 203), completed in 1913 and hence a possible starting point for Klimt's later changes to *Death and Life*, is entirely devoid of male components and the threat posed by Death. Almost the entire pictorial space is taken up by the flowering meadow upon which the virgin is slumbering. She is chastely covered by a blanket, whose circular ornaments commonly allude to femininity in Klimt's works. She is surrounded by naked women, some younger, some older, innocent children, and women who have already experienced lust and its consequences. The female figure seen from behind on the left-hand side of the picture, lying not on a bed of flowers but on cloth reminiscent of crumpled sheets, is regularly interpreted in this light (cf. Seiser 2007a, p. 297). The parallels between *The Virgin* and the picture *Death and Life* are thus not confined to formal similarities alone. For the virgin and her body are also threatened – albeit in this case by her own sexual desires.

Klimt returns to this theme in one of his final paintings, namely his unfinished canvas of *The Bride* (pp. 366/67; Natter 2012, Cat. 244). The bride in the centre is dressed in a long garment. Her closed eyes, the position of her head and her physiognomy recall the woman in the 'Pair of Lovers' in the Stoclet frieze (Ch. III). She is accompanied on the left by the tangle of people we have already encountered in *Death and Life*, once again made up chiefly of naked women, children and a baby, but this time also including a man, on whose shoulder the bride is resting her head. He is trying to turn towards her. And – most significantly of all – his face is visible. Klimt had painted not a single man with recognizable features since 1900. Further down, a female figure seen in rear view recalls the painting *Goldfish* (p. 309) in her pose. To the right of the bride, on a still unfinished ground, lies a naked women whose head is no more than roughly drawn and whose open thighs are veiled by an ornamental pattern (a skirt?) that does not (yet?) cover them.

How many references to earlier paintings Klimt was planning to assemble in this picture is a question that must remain open. As evidenced by the over 150 drawings relating to the composition, however, he explored the subject in great detail.

Klimt's popularity is founded upon his 'golden style', upon his women in gold. But this reduces the painter to the *Beethoven Frieze* and that in the Palais Stoclet, *The Kiss* and the *Portrait of Adele Bloch-Bauer I*. If we take this last as the high point within Klimt's female portraiture, it becomes apparent that a steady development towards ever more lavish ornament can be observed from Klimt's early *Portrait of Emilie Flöge* onwards. Starting from Whistler, and subsequently absorbing stylistic influences from Jan Toorop (1858–1928) and Fernand Khnopff, not to mention the Impressionists, Klimt arrived at a Jugendstil that incorporated Japonisme and Symbolism and in which he paid homage to ornament. This led him to a certain formal abstraction, one that found its most pronounced expression in the Stoclet frieze. From a stylistic point of view, it is true, Klimt's 'ornamental abstraction' can be compared neither with Picasso and Cubism nor with Kandinsky and Expressionism. But it nevertheless had similar roots. In later paintings, Klimt renounced 'his' 'golden style' in favour of a palette of strong colours. He nevertheless remained faithful to ornament, even if we still feel we can sense the personality of his sitter in certain portraits: an example is the *Lady with a Hat and Feather Boa*, another, the young *Mäda Primavesi*. His lingering Japonisme was now joined by the influence of the Fauves, who were causing a furore in Paris at this same point in time. Klimt's portraits nevertheless led to a dead end. The younger generation took up other influences rather than those of the great practitioner of Viennese *Stilkunst*.

Klimt's specific style and the dominance of ornament are also apparent in the signets that he assigned to the paintings reproduced in *Das Werk von Gustav Klimt*, a portfolio of prints published in five instalments as from 1908. With these signets, he furnished each painting with an ornament, regardless of whether the picture showed a portrait or a landscape. Hence, it does not seem to me that each signet can "definitely be ascribed" to a particular sitter, and that they were individually "tailor-made for the ladies who commissioned his works" (Weidinger 2007e, p. 182). There is nothing to indicate why one signet should have been assigned to a landscape and another to a portrait, and in the case of the portraits, there is also nothing recognizable in the signet that might be deemed characteristic of the sitter, with the exception, perhaps, of the signet accompanying the print of the *Portrait of Adele Bloch-Bauer I*, which uses the letter A. But even the ovals in the signet for the *Portrait of Emilie Flöge* bear no close resemblance to those scattered across her dress. The very fact that these signets shed no obvious light on the personality of the sitter, however, supports the thesis that women in paintings by Gustav Klimt disappear into ornament. Whether this ornament is gold or another colour, a strictly geometrical figure or a flurry of brushstrokes, is thereby irrelevant.

Pages 298/99
Portrait of Fritza Riedler (detail), 1906
(see ill. p. 323)

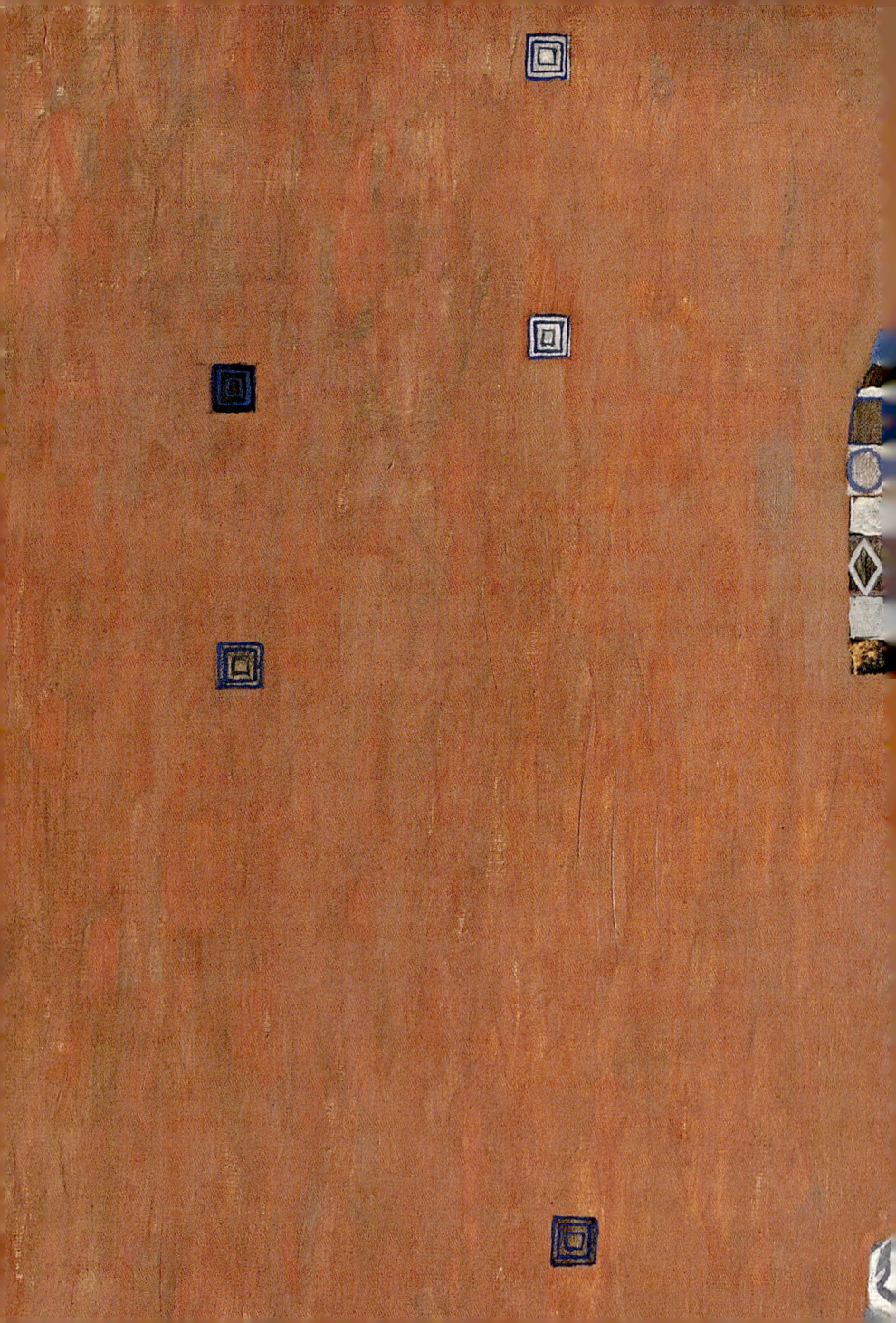

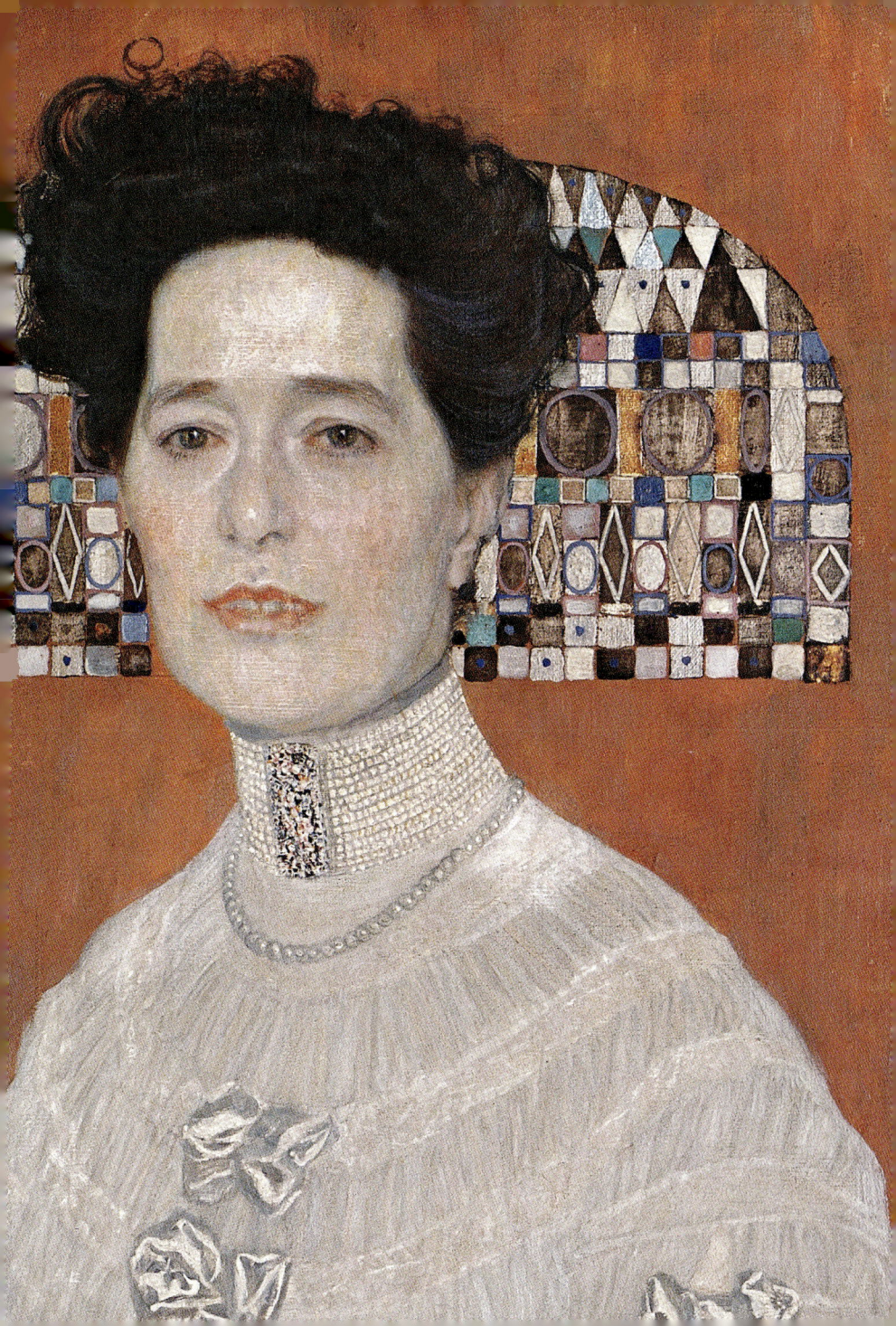

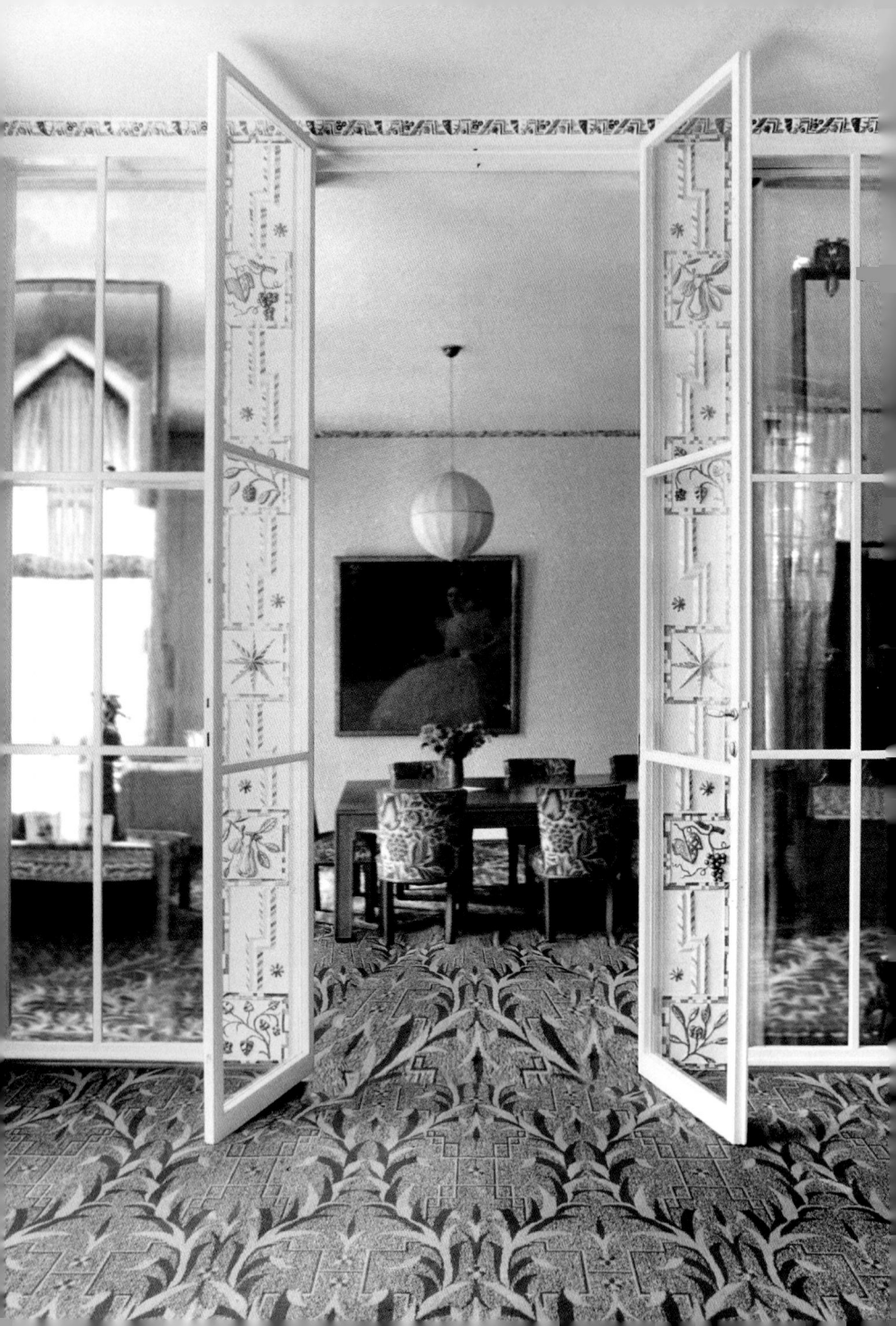

"A scent of sweet femininity wafts towards us.
The brush itself, we are led to think, must have been in love."

FRANZ SERVAES, 1901

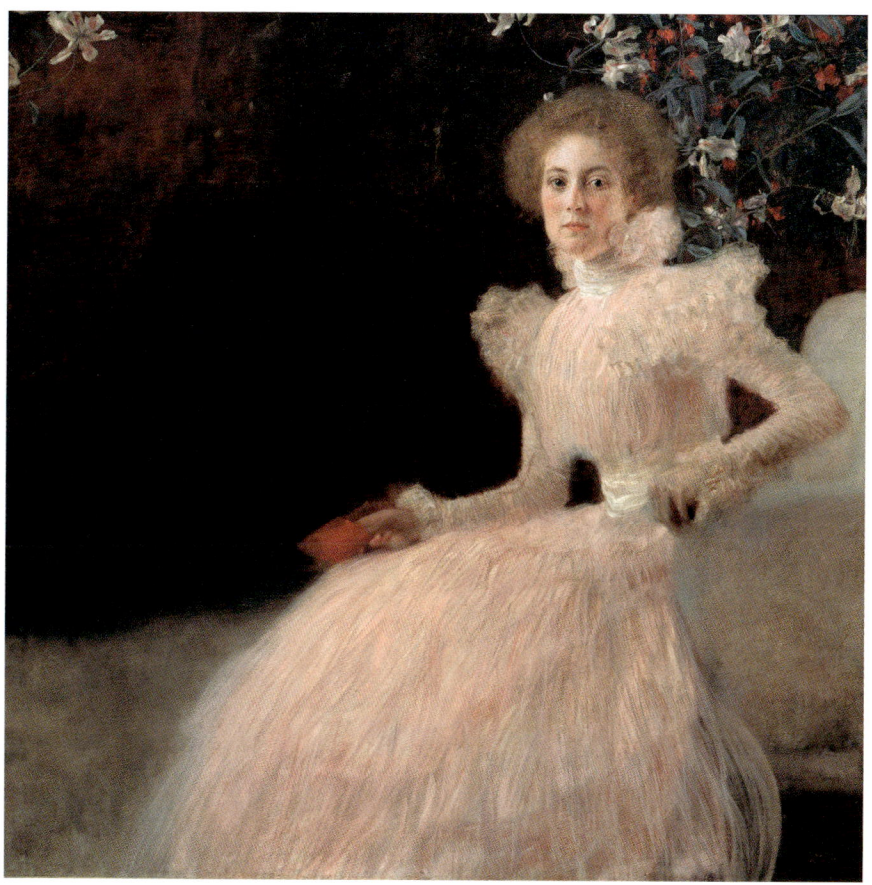

View of the dining room in the Villa Knips in Vienna, 1915
Photograph. Imagno/Austrian Archives

Portrait of Sonja Knips, 1898
Oil on canvas, 145 x 146 cm / 57 x 57 ½ in. Vienna, Belvedere

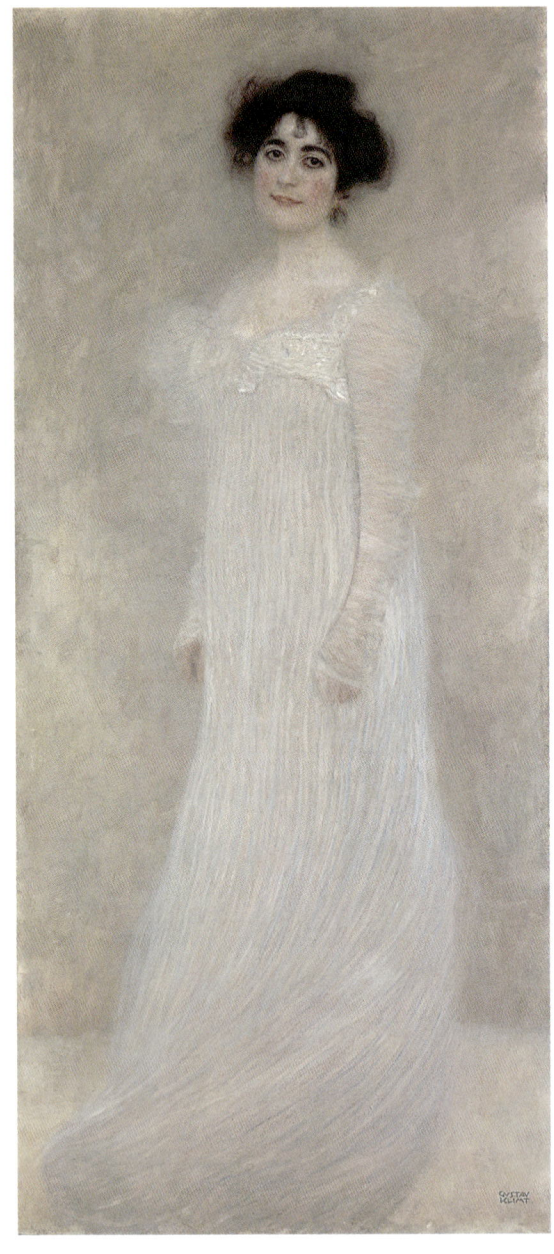

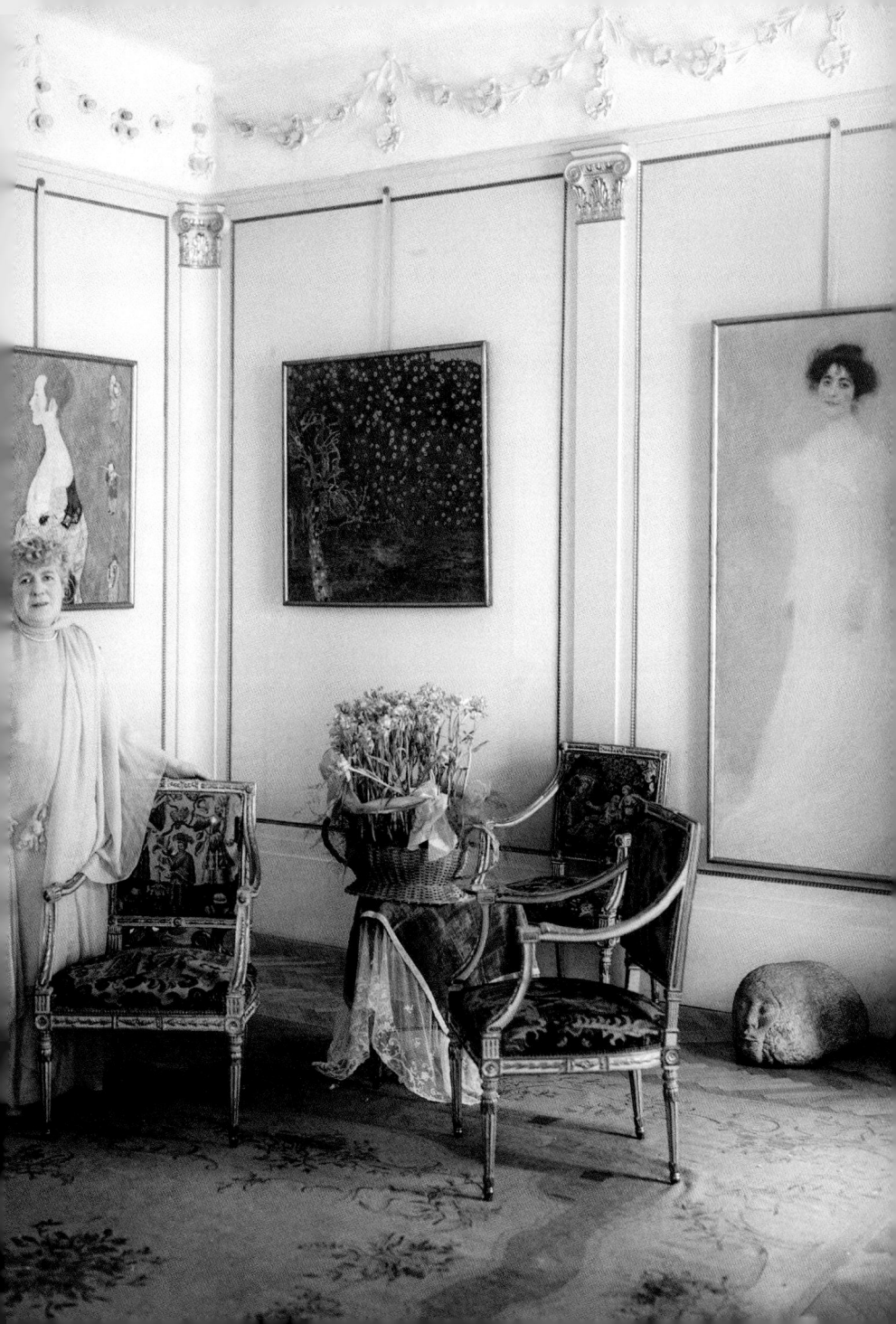

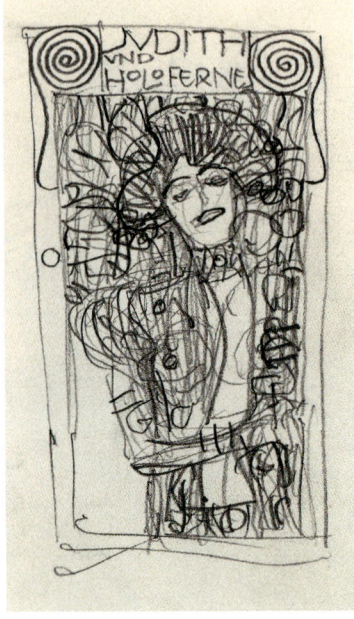

*"Basically, the famous Judith with all her
ancient Oriental magnificence is also
a supremely modern female of perversely
seductive charm, expanded into a symbol."*

FRANZ SERVAES, 1903

Page 302
Portrait of Serena Lederer, 1899
Oil on canvas, 190.8 x 85.4 cm / 75 ⅛ x 33 ⅝ in. New York, The Metropolitan Museum of Art,
inv. no. 1980.412. Purchase, Wolfe Fund, and Rogers and Munsey Funds, Gift of Henry Walters,
and Bequests of Catharine Lorillard Wolfe and Collis P. Huntington, by exchange, 1980

Page 303
Martin Gerlach, **Serena Lederer in her drawing room**, c. 1930
Standing next to the paintings *Wally, Golden Apple Tree* and her own portrait by Klimt
Photograph. Imagno/ÖNB

Sketch for the painting *Judith I*, c. 1899
Pencil, 13.8 x 8.4 cm / 5 ½ x 3 ⅜ in. Vienna, Belvedere, sketchbook of Sonja Knips

Judith I, 1901
Oil on canvas, 84 x 42 cm / 33 x 16 ½ in. Vienna, Belvedere

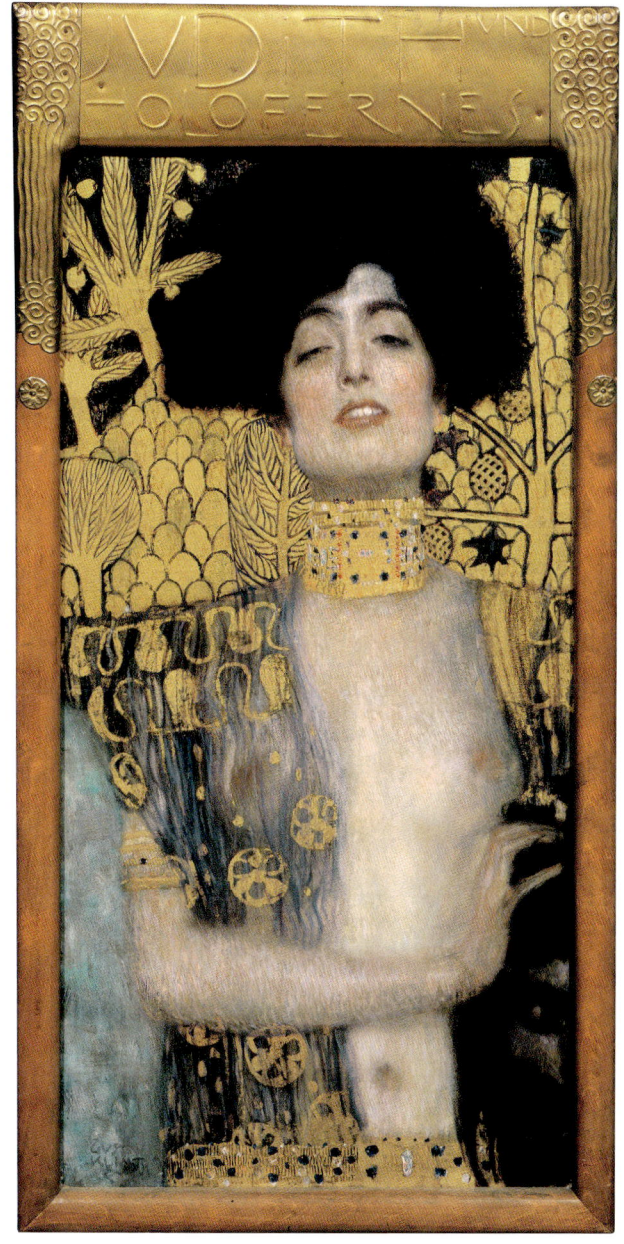

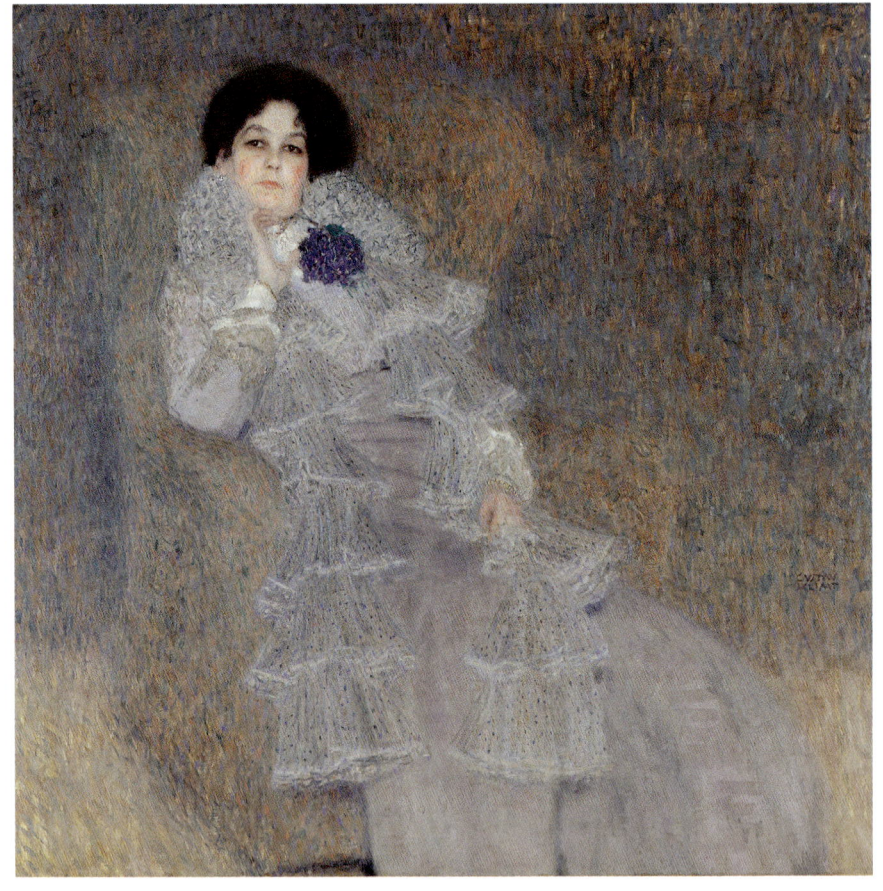

Portrait of Marie Henneberg, 1901/02
Oil on canvas, 140 x 140 cm / 55 ⅛ x 55 ⅛ in.
Halle an der Saale, Staatliche Galerie Moritzburg, Landeskundemuseum Sachsen-Anhalt

Josef Hoffmann, **The hall in the Villa Henneberg at the Hohe Warte artists' colony**, 1900
Photograph. Vienna, MAK – Österreichisches Museum für angewandte Kunst/Gegenwartskunst

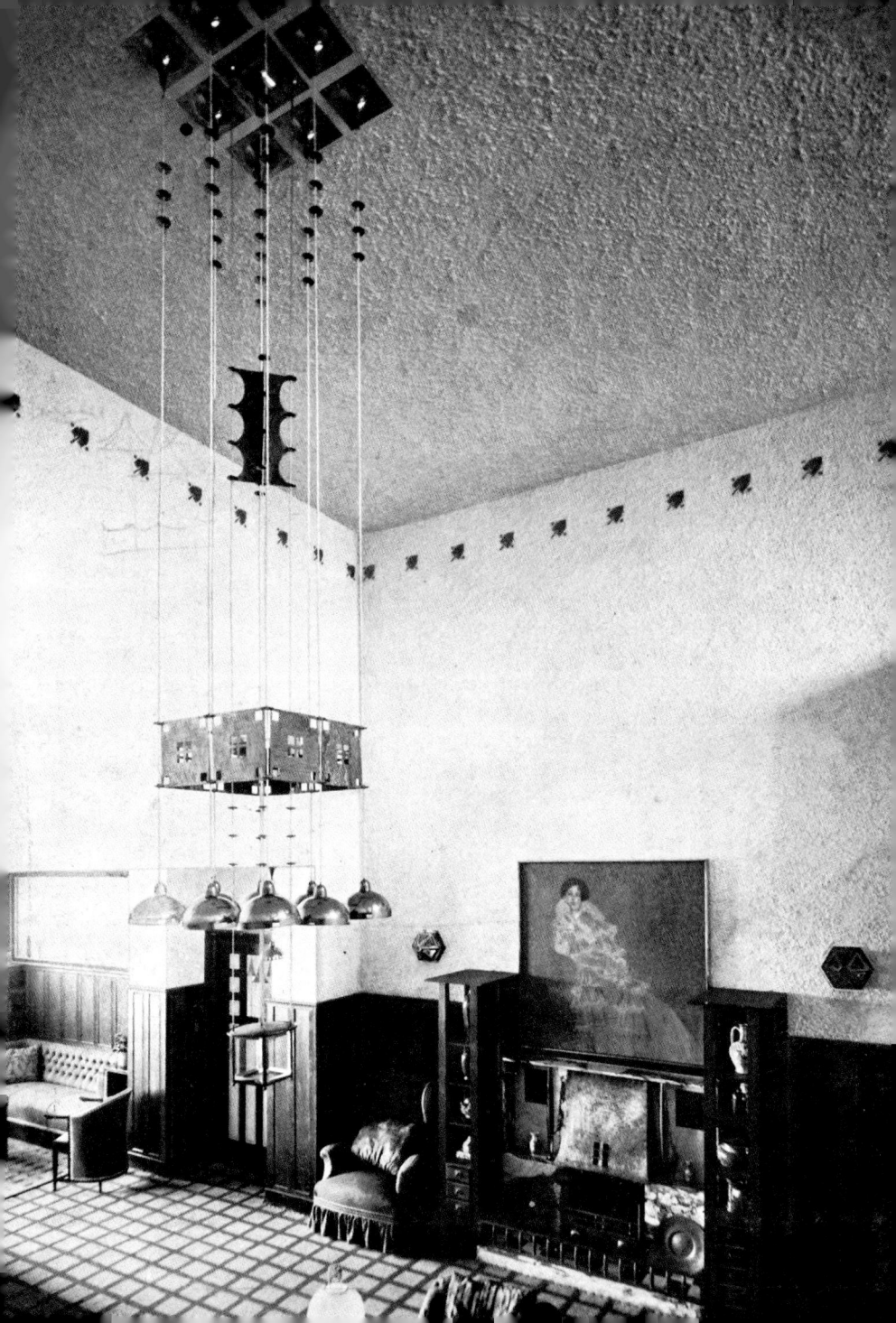

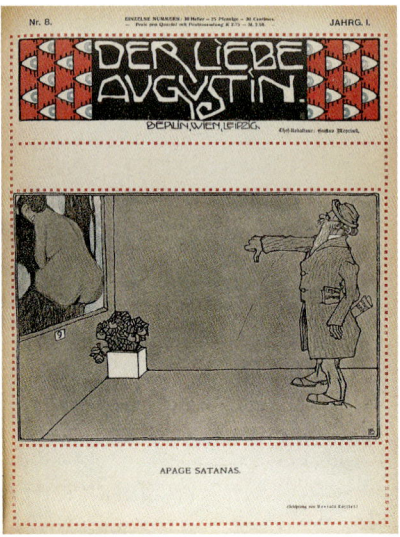

> *"When the storm broke out over his University*
> *pictures, he painted a pithy riposte to all his critics:*
> *a work in which he archly 'turns the other cheek'*
> *to the viewer. He called this rebus 'Goldfish'."*

FELIX SALTEN, 1903

Bertold Löffler
Apage Satanas. **Title page of** *Der liebe Augustin*,
vol. 1 (1904), no. 8

Goldfish, 1901/02
Oil on canvas, 181 x 67 cm / 71 ¼ x 26 ⅜ in.
Solothurn, Kunstmuseum, Dübi-Müller Stiftung

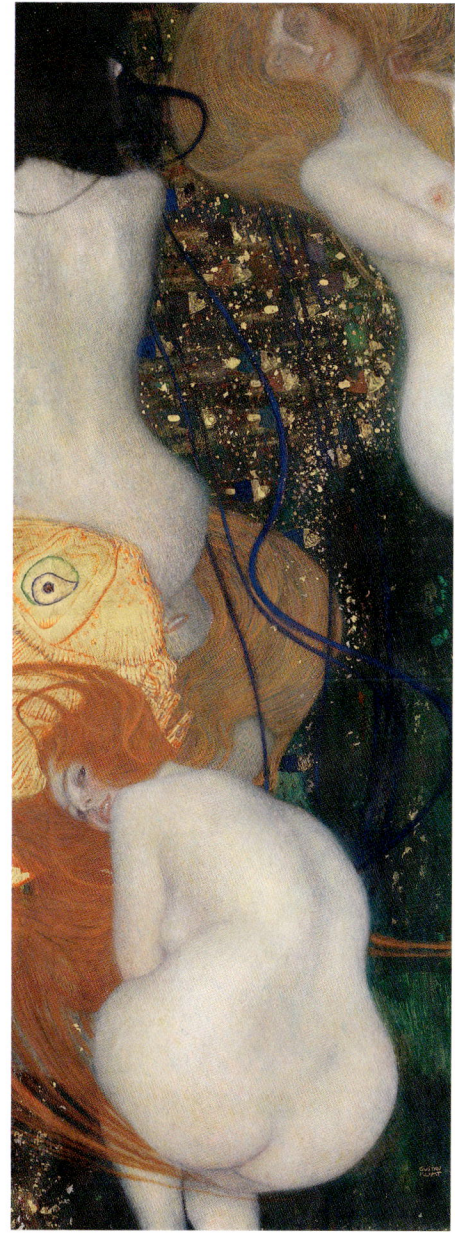

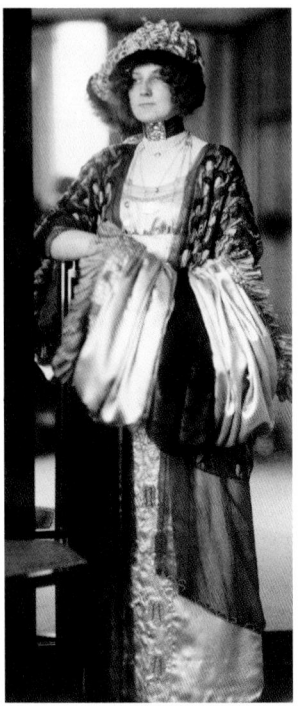

"*A Klimtian colour poem [to] the beauty of Viennese women.
What seems to be shown here is no longer a single individual
but the intoxication and charm of an entire city,
in the shape of a woman gleaming like a jewel and
delighting us like a fluttering butterfly.*"

FRANZ SERVAES, 1903

Atelier d'Ora, **Emilie Flöge in an Art Nouveau dress with muff**, 1910
In the Flöge sisters' fashion salon
Photograph. Imagno/Austrian Archives

Portrait of Emilie Flöge, 1902/03, with later reworkings
Oil on canvas, 181 x 84 cm / 71 ¼ x 33 in. Vienna, Wien Museum

Pages 312/13
Portrait of Emilie Flöge (detail), 1902/03

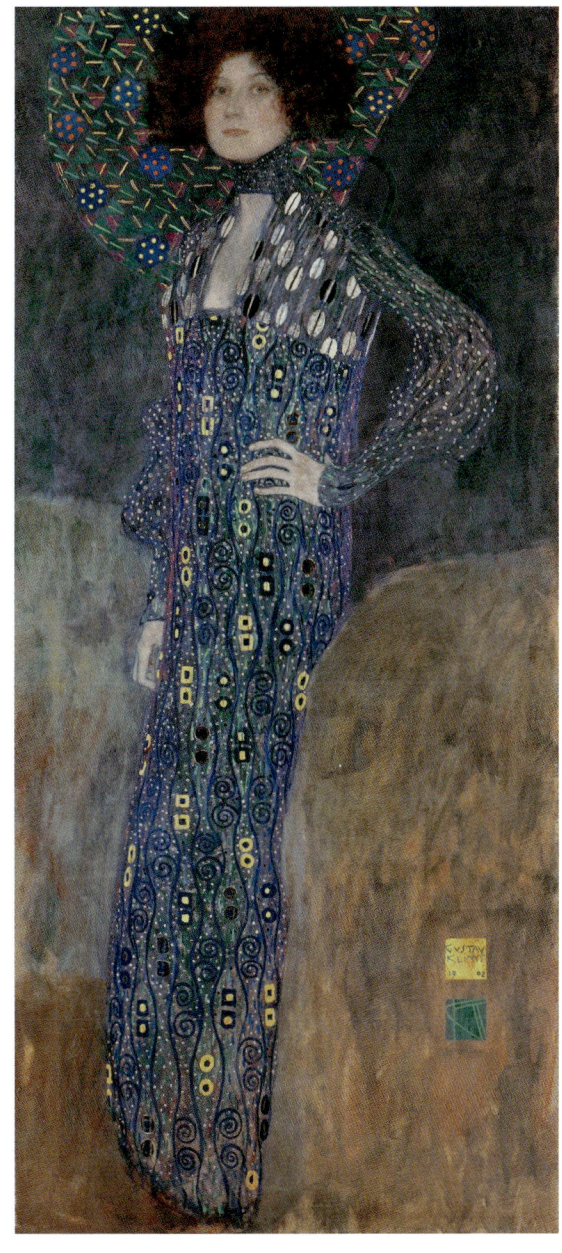

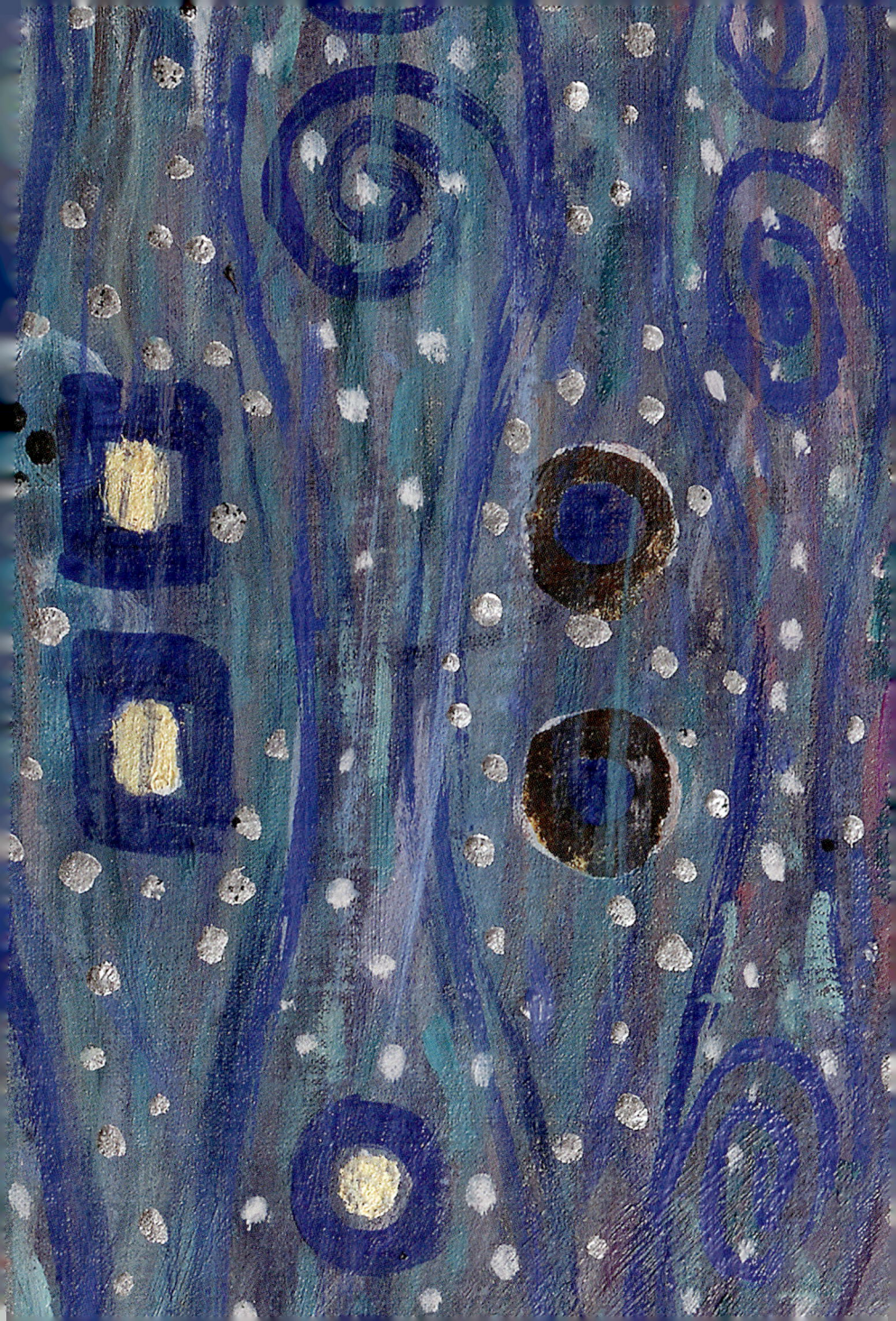

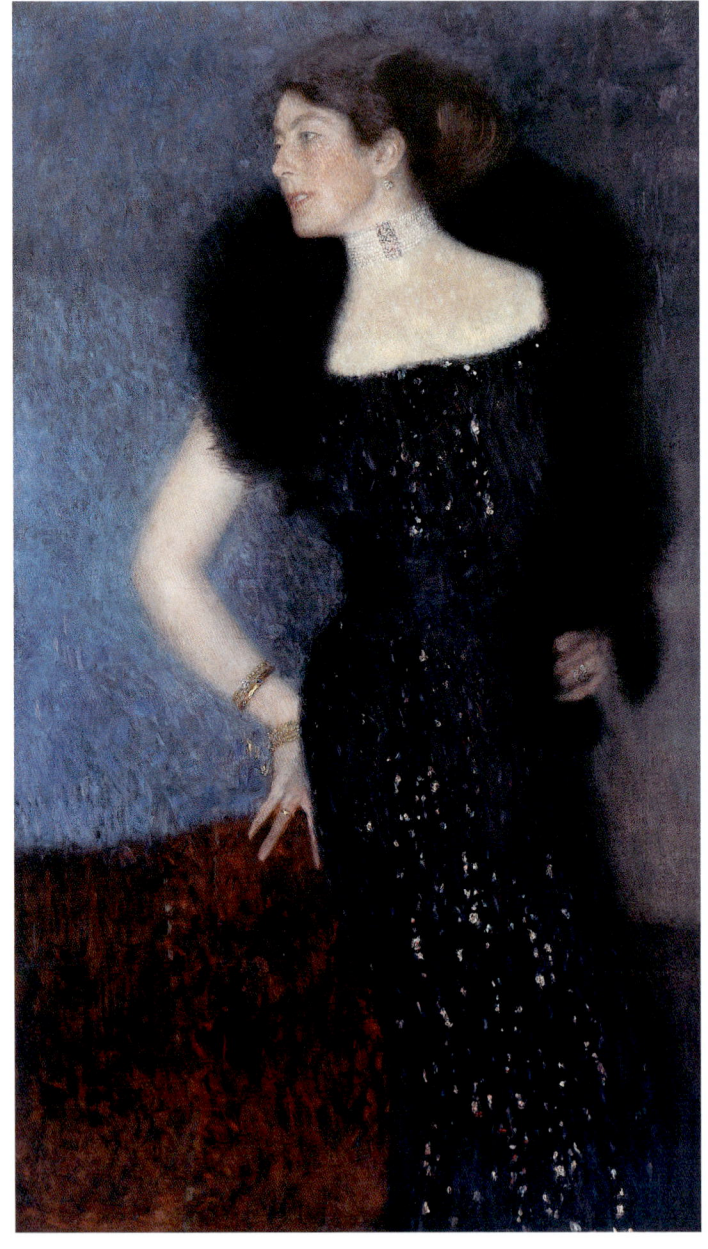

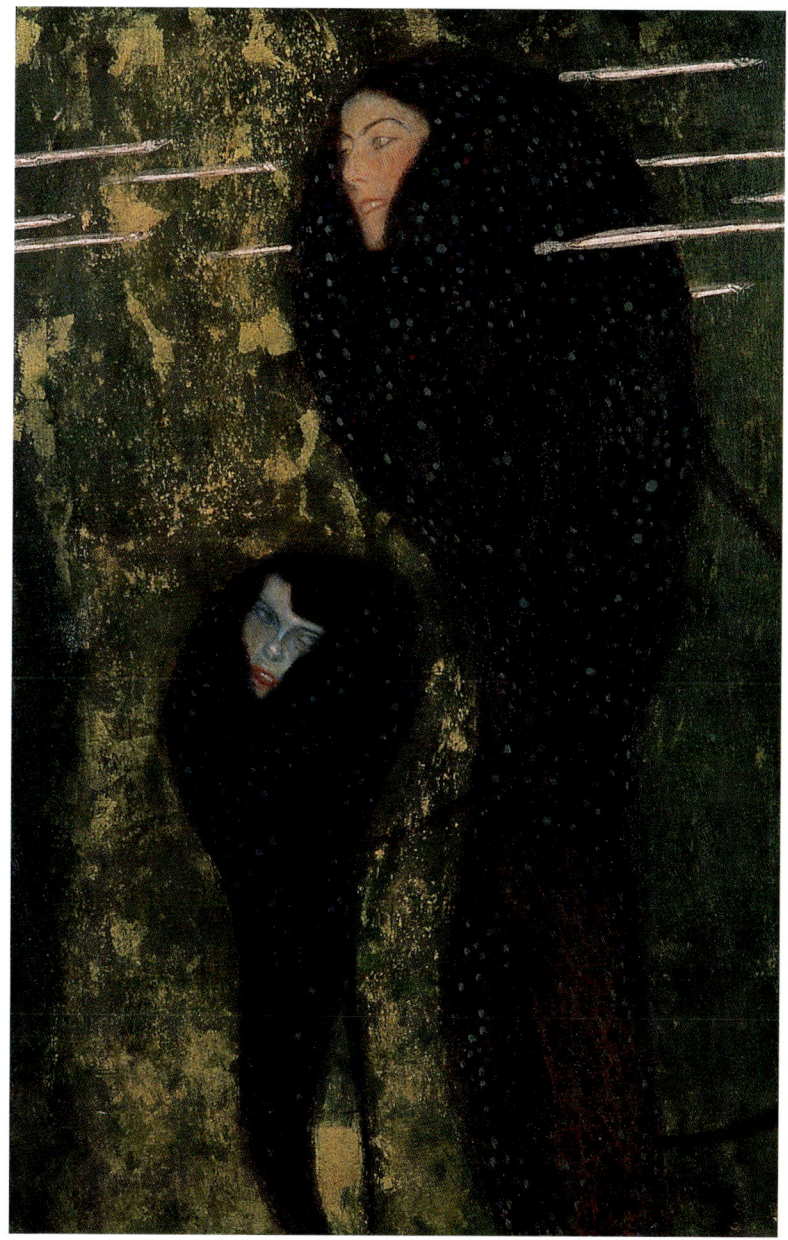

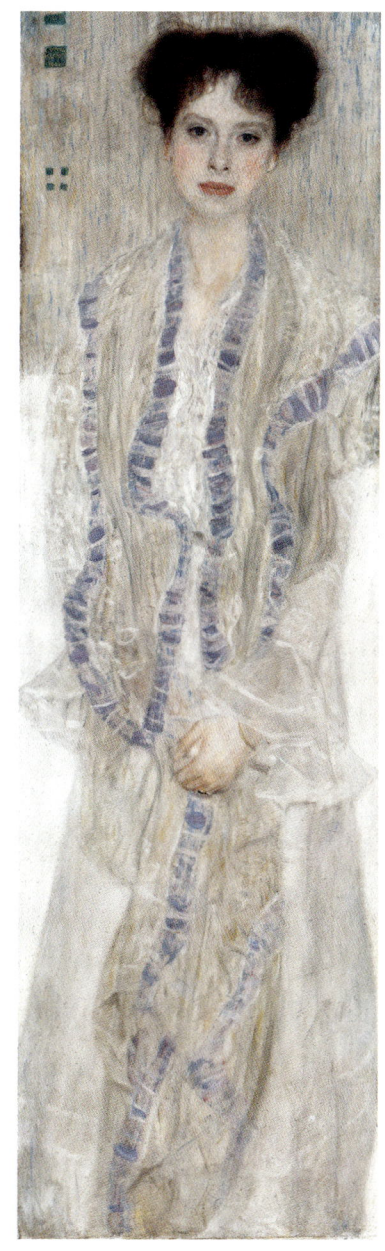

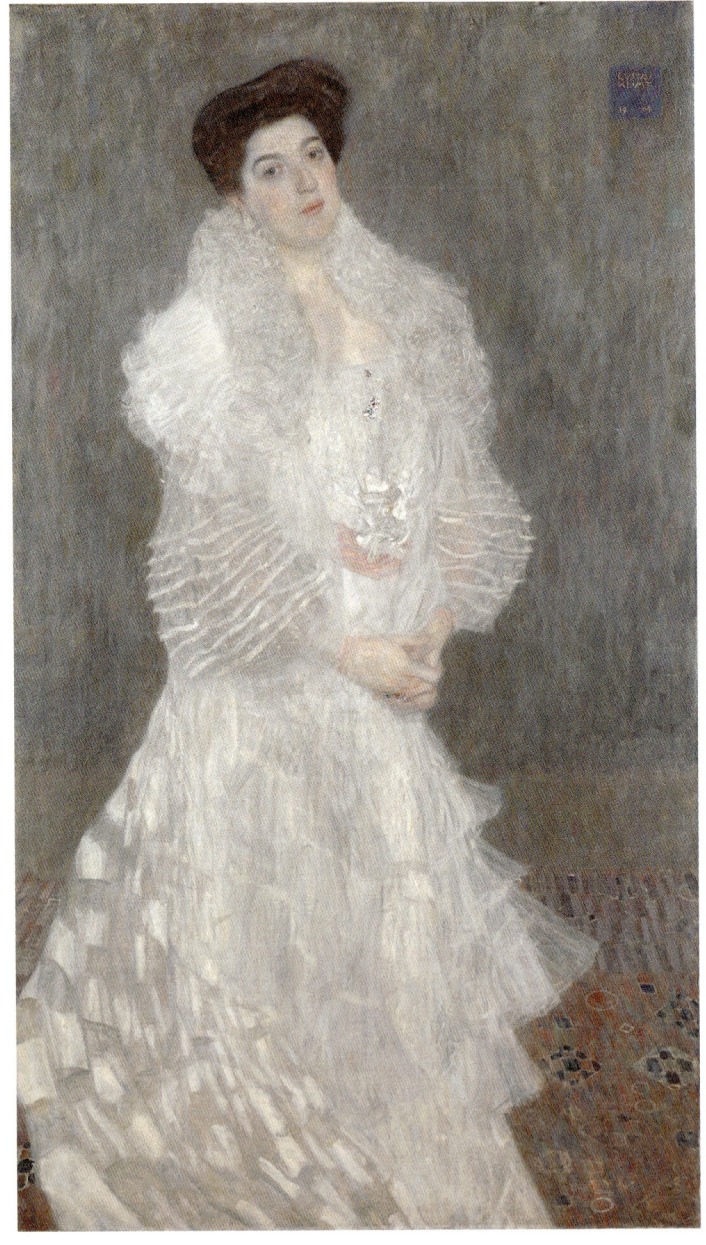

Portrait of Hermine Gallia, 1903, reworked 1904
Oil on canvas, 170.5 x 96.5 cm / 67 ⅛ x 38 in.
London, The National Gallery (on loan to the Tate Modern, London)

Page 320
View of the Klimt room at the International Art Exhibition in Rome, 1911
On the walls: *Portrait of Margaret Stonborough-Wittgenstein* (p. 321), *The Park* (pp. 434/35) and
Jurisprudence (p. 130). From: catalogue of the exhibition, Rome, 1911

Page 321
Portrait of Margaret Stonborough-Wittgenstein, 1905
Oil on canvas, 180 x 90 cm / 70 ⅞ x 35 ½ in.
Munich, Bayerische Staatsgemäldesammlungen – Neue Pinakothek

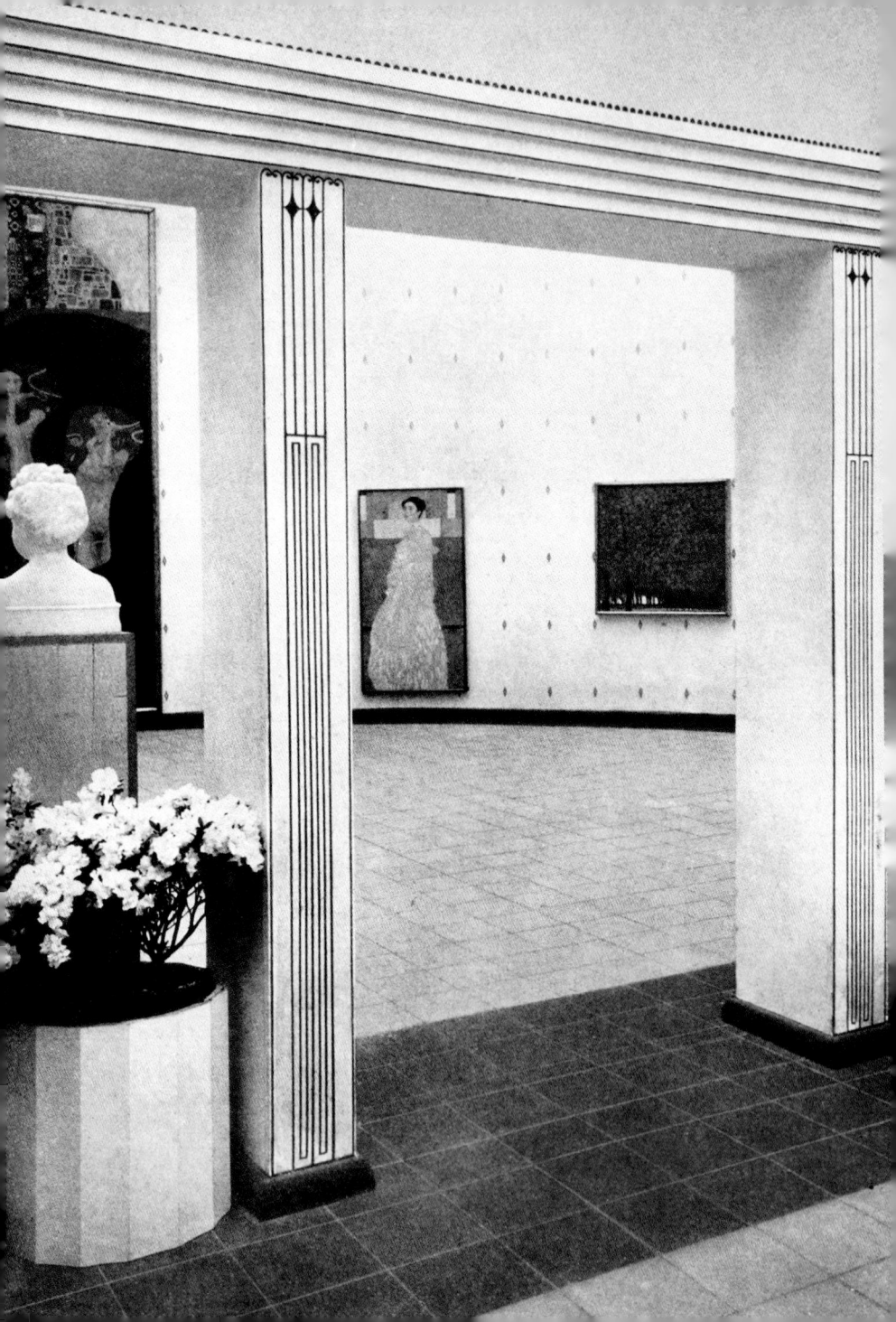

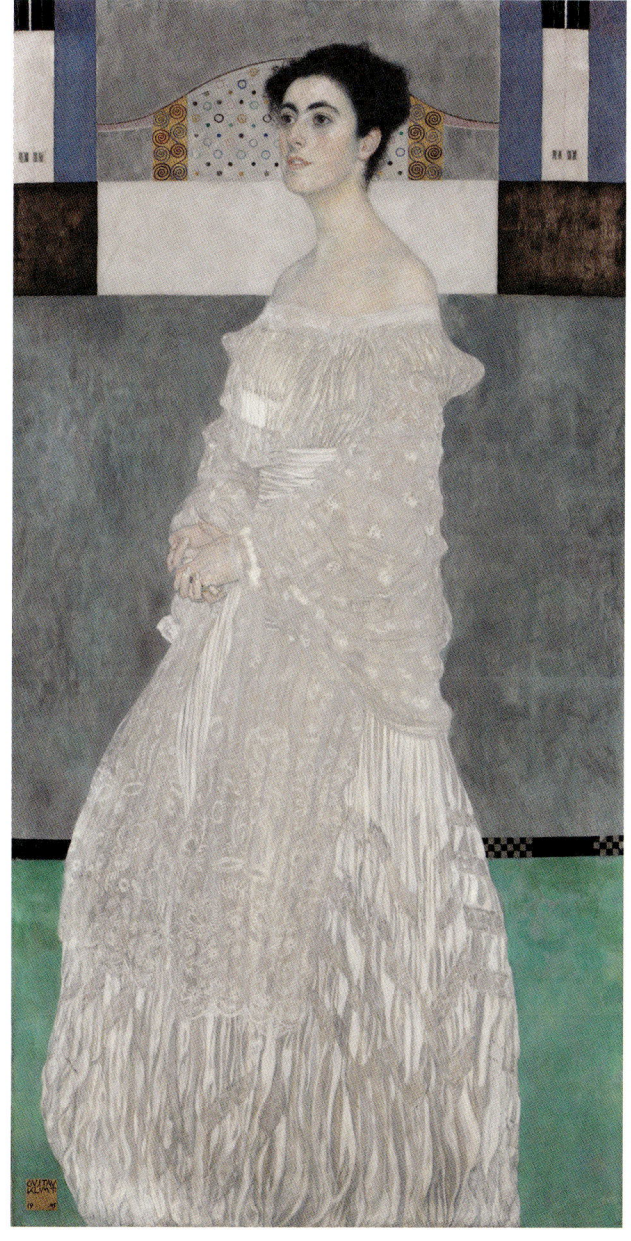

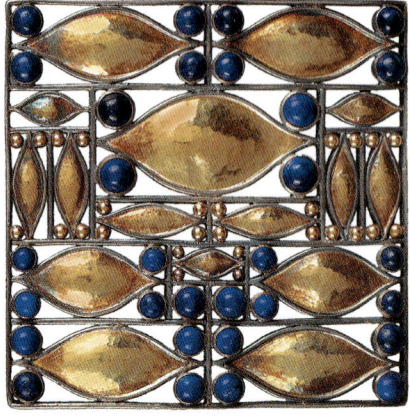

Josef Hoffmann, **Brooch owned by Emilie Flöge**, 1911
Manufacture: Wiener Werkstätte (model no. G 0688). Private collection

Portrait of Fritza Riedler, 1906
Oil on canvas, 153 x 133 cm / 60 ¼ x 52 ⅜ in. Vienna, Belvedere

Pages 324/25
Portrait of Fritza Riedler (detail), 1906

Pages 326/27
Josef Hoffmann, **The Wiener Werkstätte room
at the International Exhibition in Mannheim**, 1907
From: *Deutsche Kunst und Dekoration*, vol. 20 (1907)

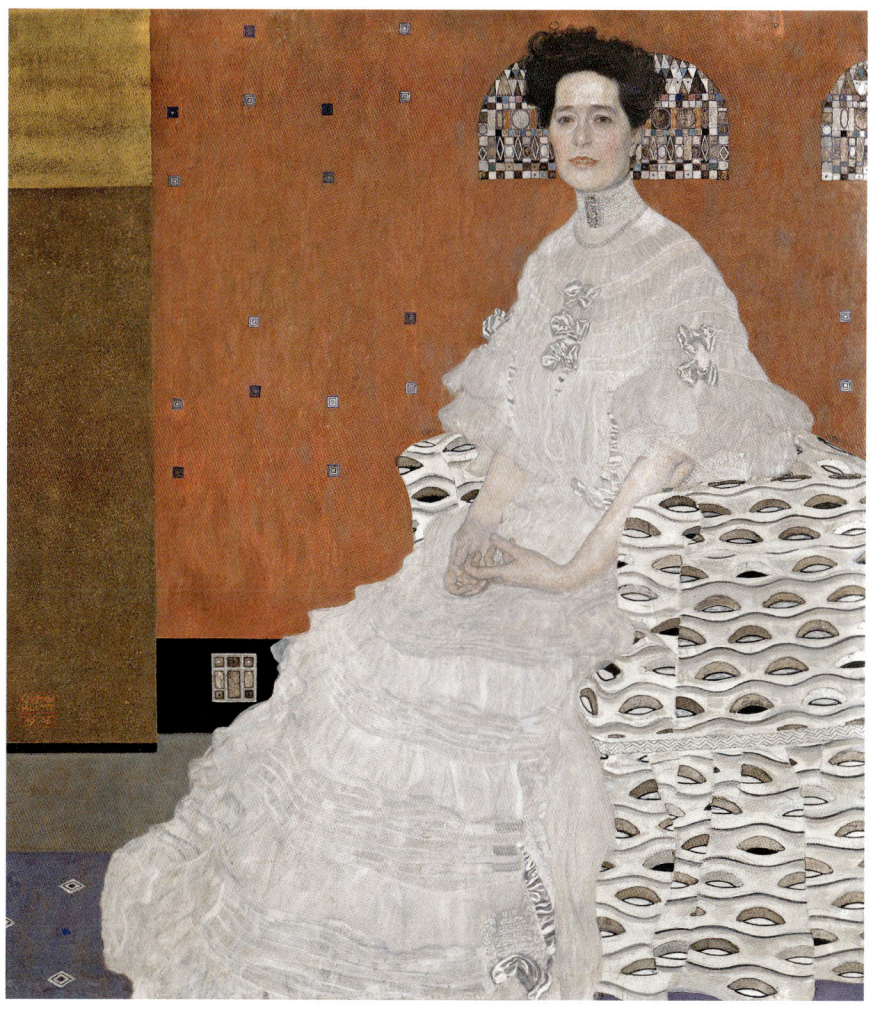

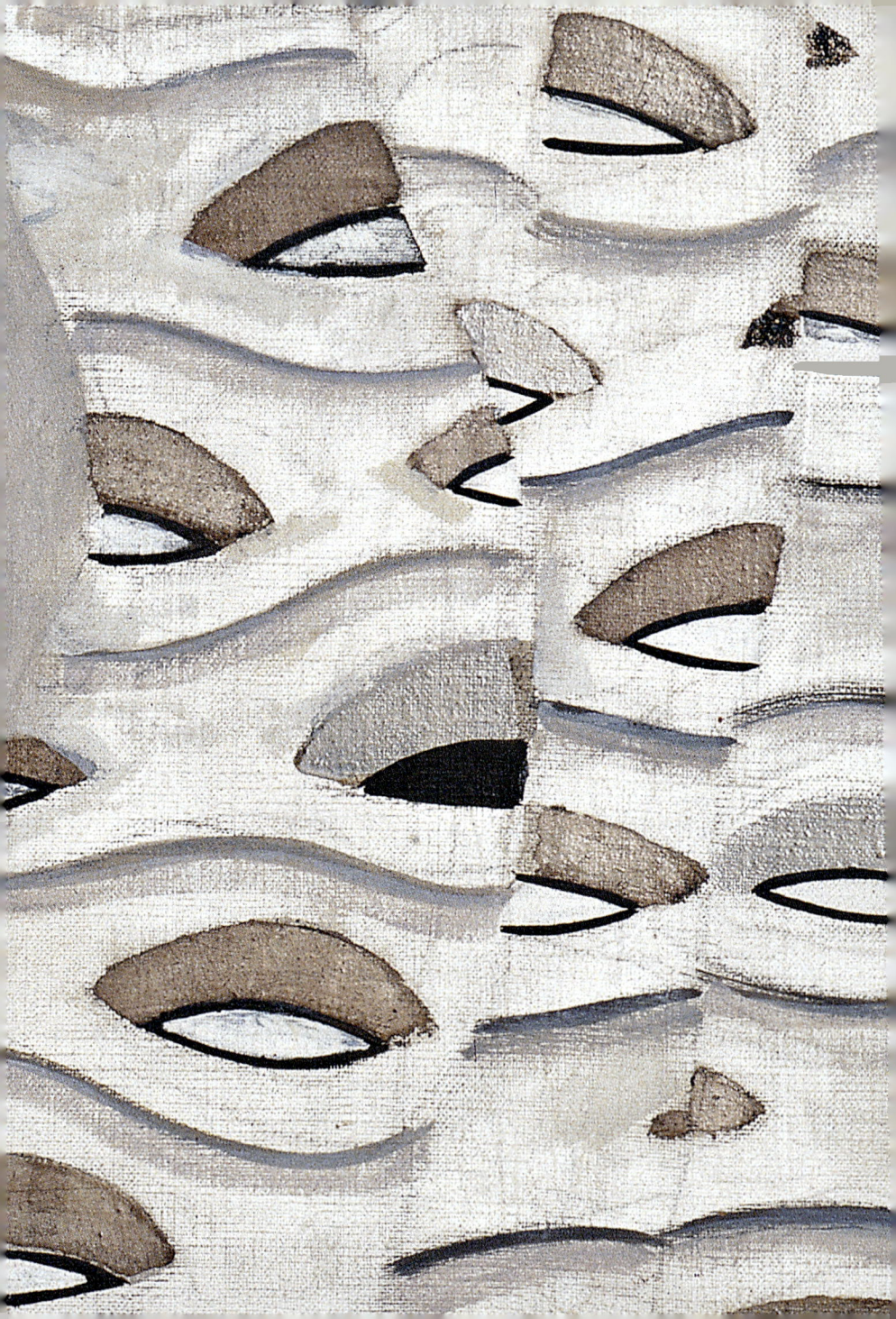

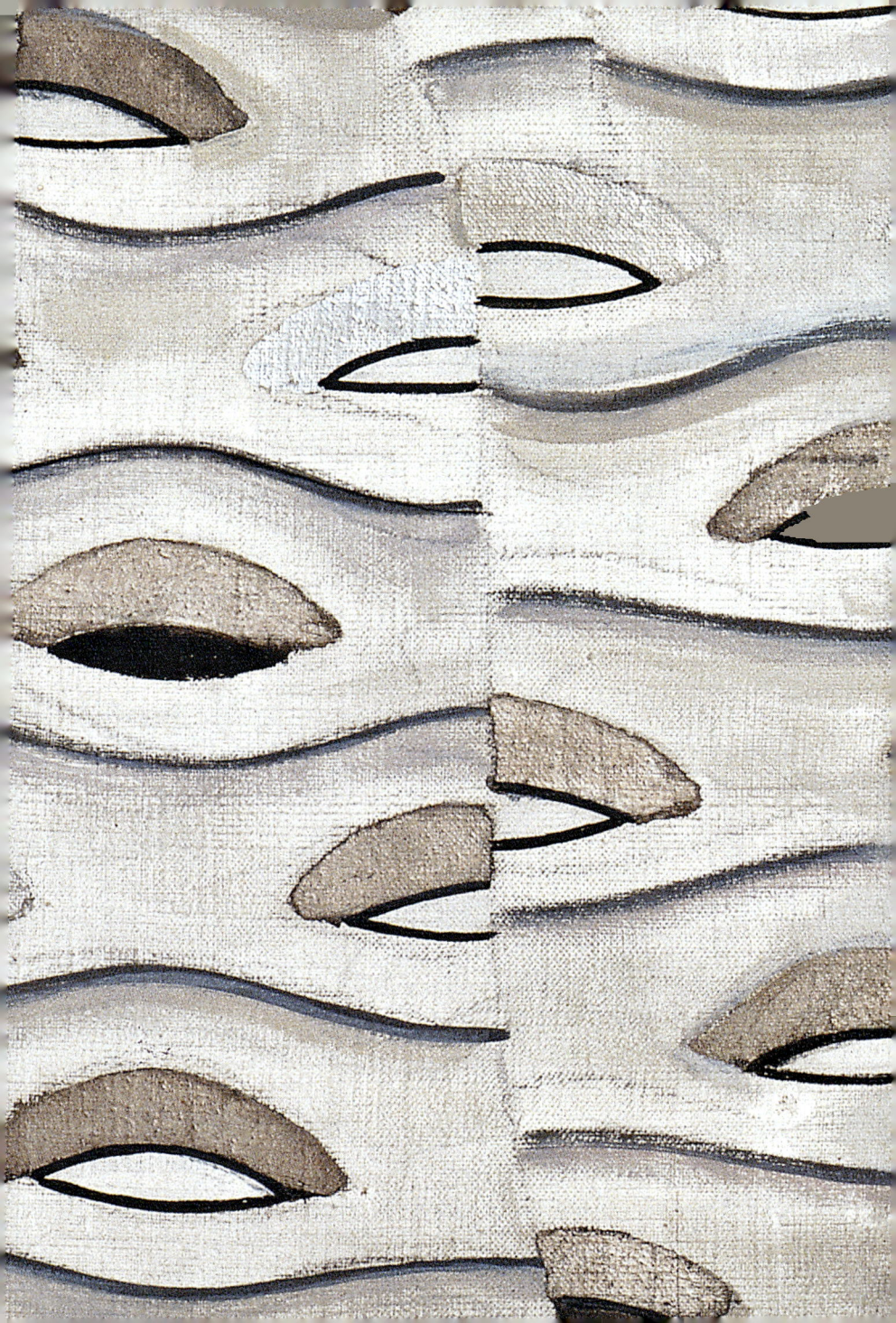

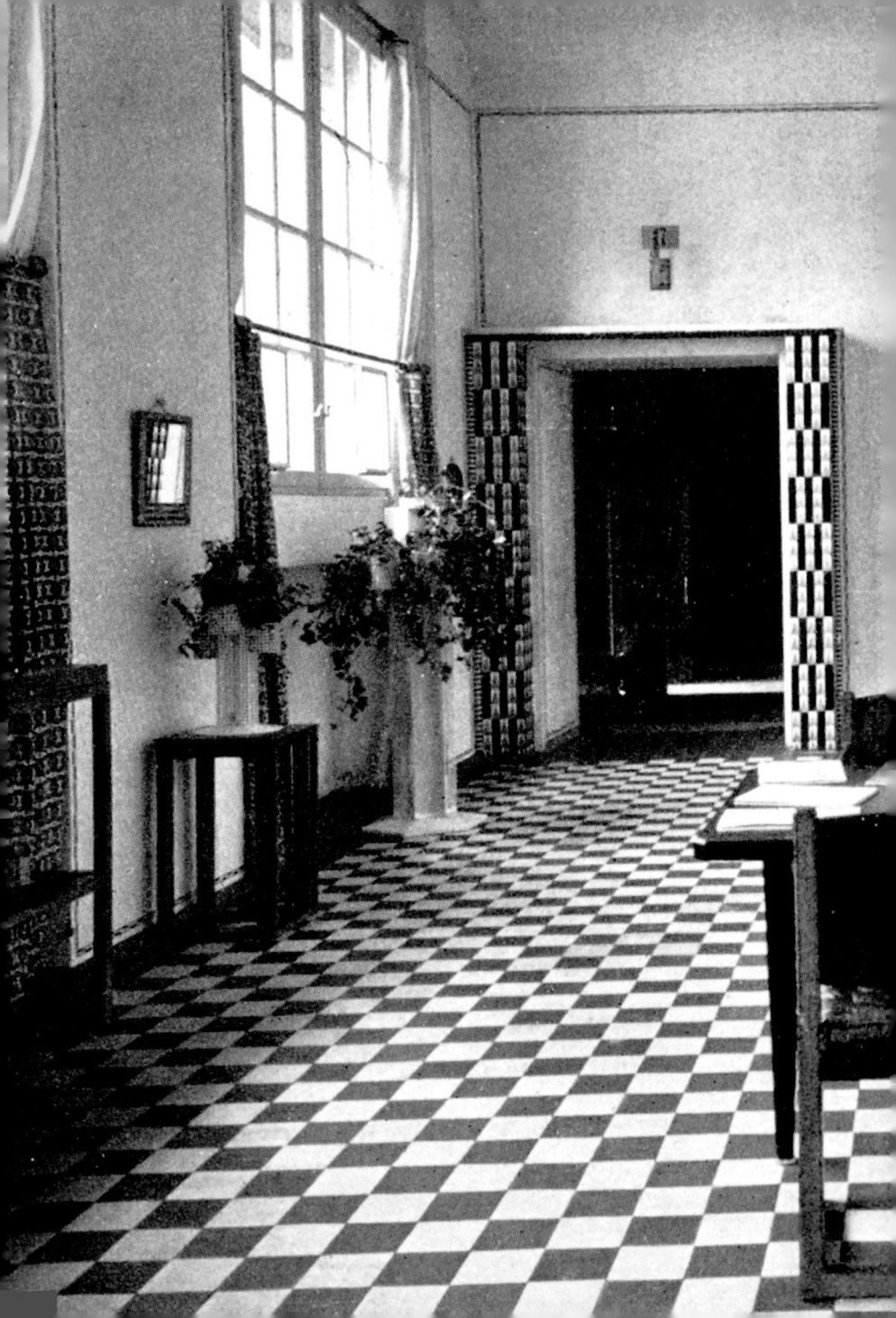

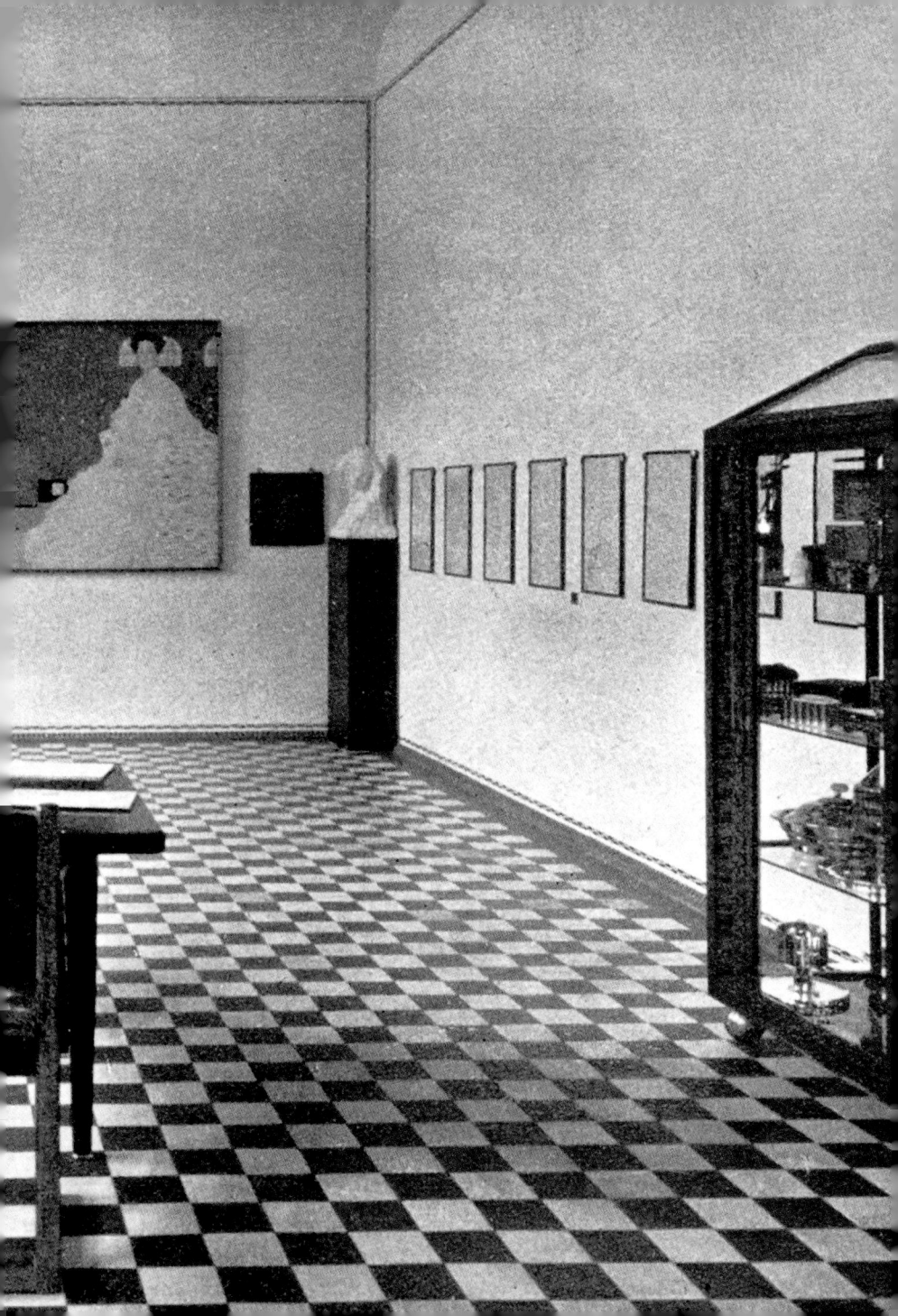

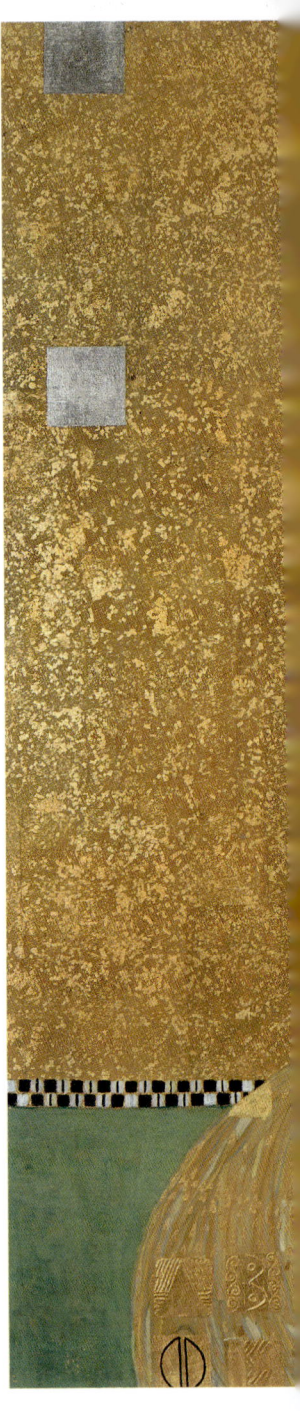

Portrait of Adele Bloch-Bauer I, 1907
Oil and gold leaf on canvas, 140 x 140 cm /
55 ⅛ x 55 ⅛ in. New York, Neue Galerie

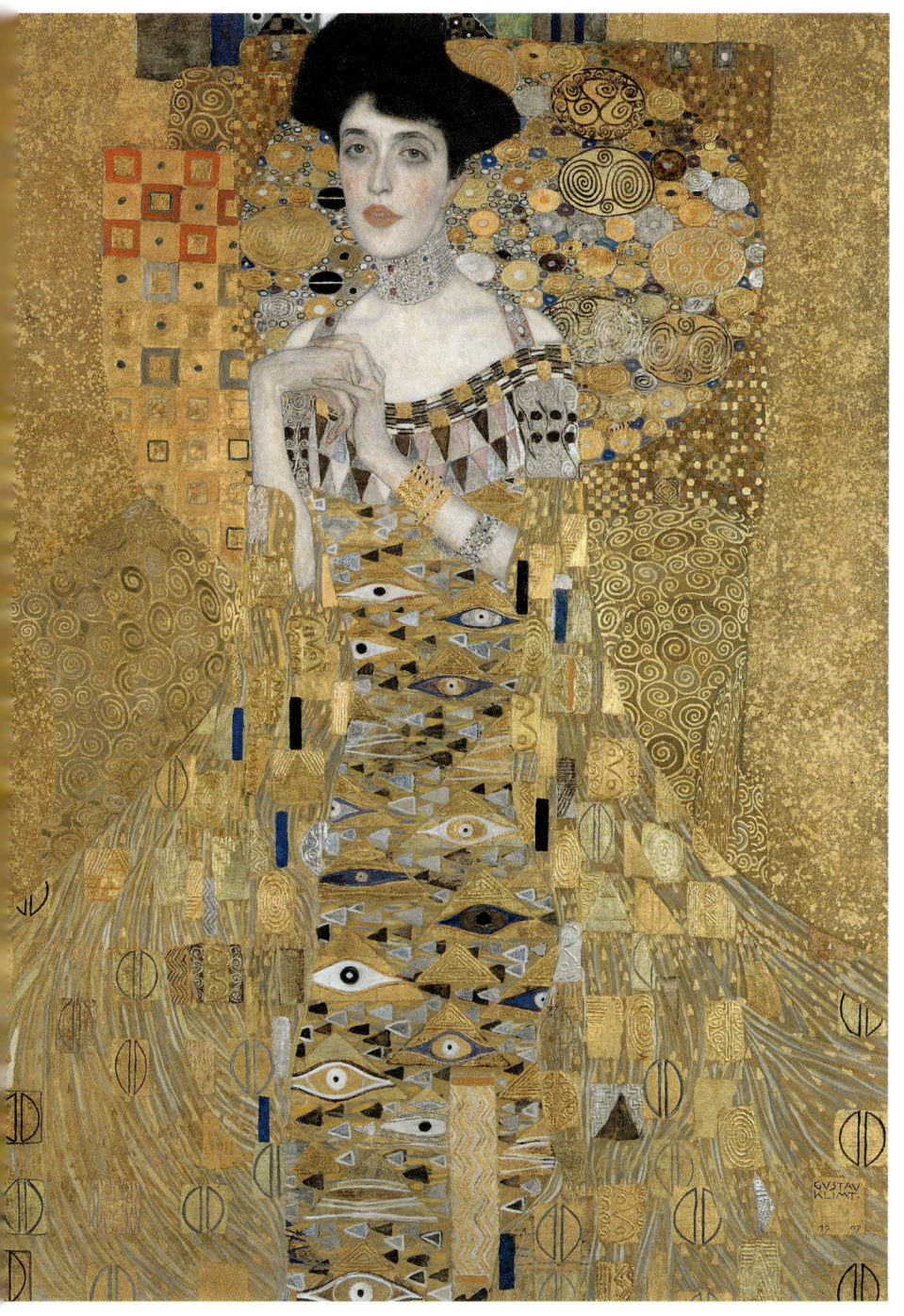

*"No Judith has yet dreamed the dream of revenge and blood
with such vehement avidity. ... With a wonderful boldness of silhouette,
with the most magnificent achievement of a dramatic physical effect,
the figure of the woman [appears] with a vitality that flows
from the most direct fount of life."*

BERTA ZUCKERKANDL, 1909

Judith II (Salome), 1909
Oil on canvas, 178 x 46 cm / 70 x 18 ⅛ in.
Venice, Ca' Pesaro, Galleria Internazionale d'Arte Moderna, Musei Civici Veneziani

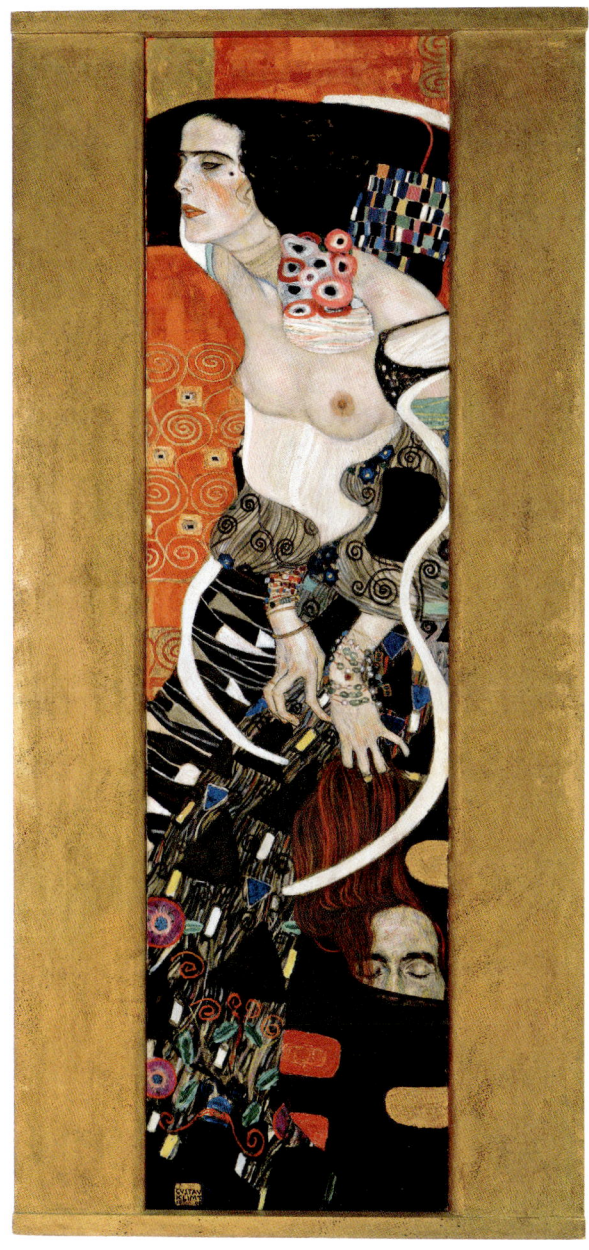

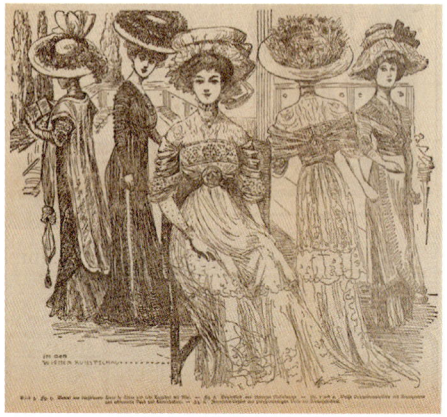

"At the Vienna Kunstschau…"
From: *Die Moden-Zeit*, Vienna, 1908

The Black Feathered Hat, 1910
Oil on canvas, 79 x 63 cm / 31 ⅛ x 24 ¾ in. New York, private collection

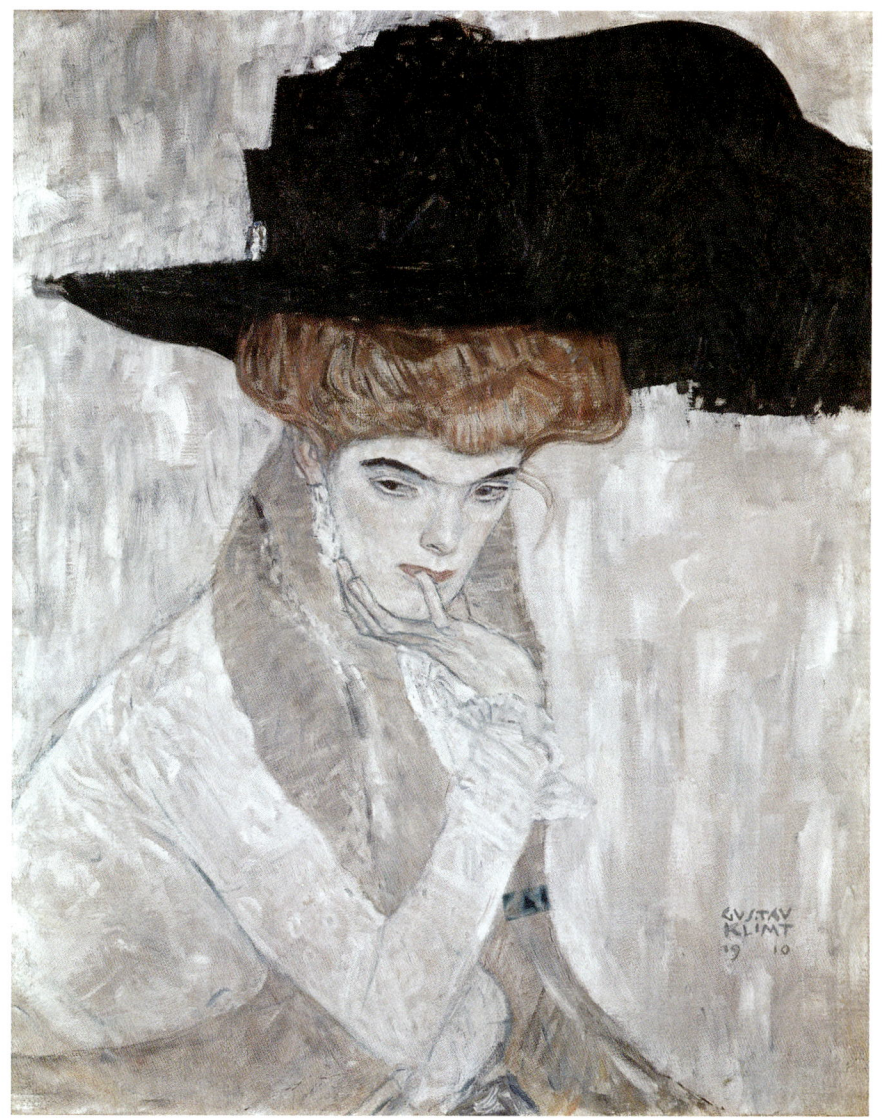

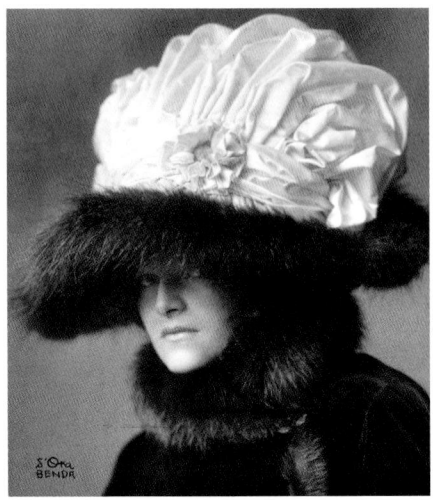

"*Klimt has discovered or invented the new Viennese woman –
a very particular type of new Viennese woman,
whose grandmamas are Judith and Salome.
She is charmingly immoral, delightfully sinful, enchantingly perverse.*"

ILLUSTRIERTES WIENER EXTRABLATT, 1909

Atelier d'Ora, **Helene Jamrich in a winter hat designed by Rudolf Krieser**, 1910
Gelatin silver print. Imagno/Austrian Archives

Lady with a Hat and Feather Boa, c. 1910
Oil on canvas, 69 x 55 cm / 27 ⅛ x 21 ⅝ in. Private collection

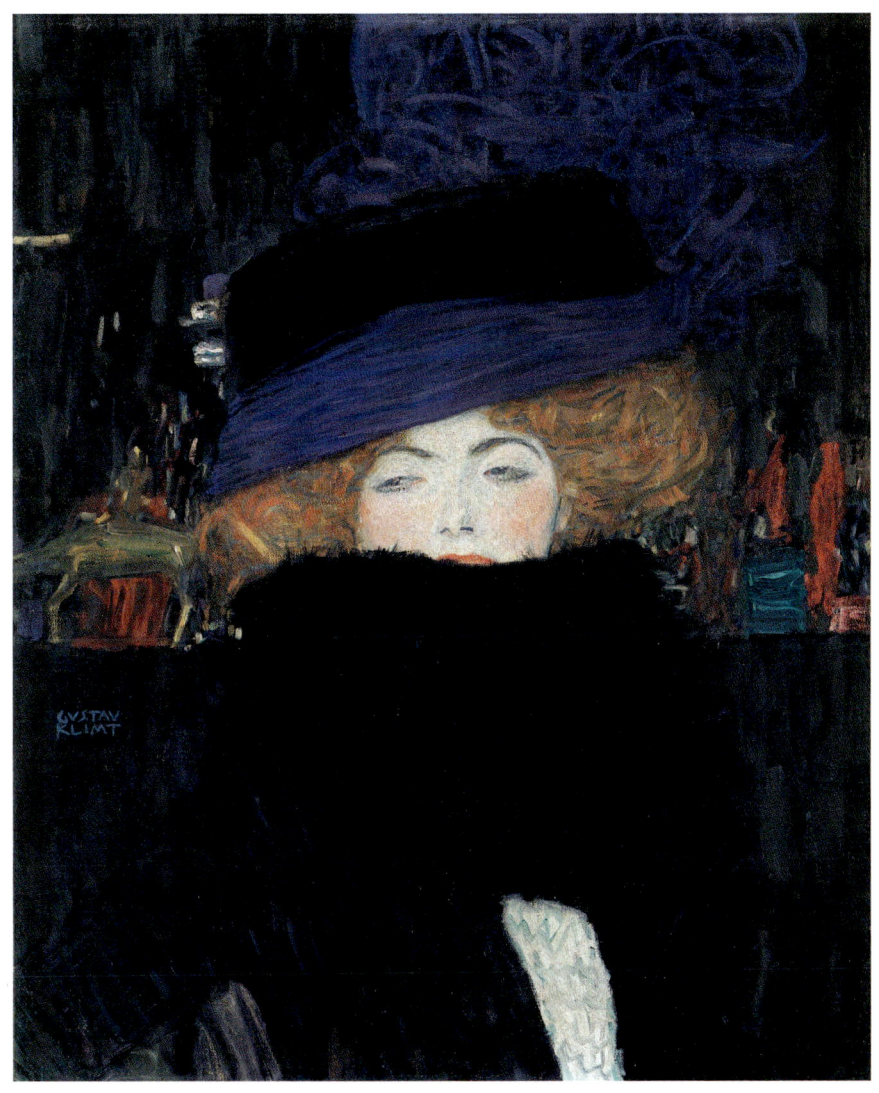

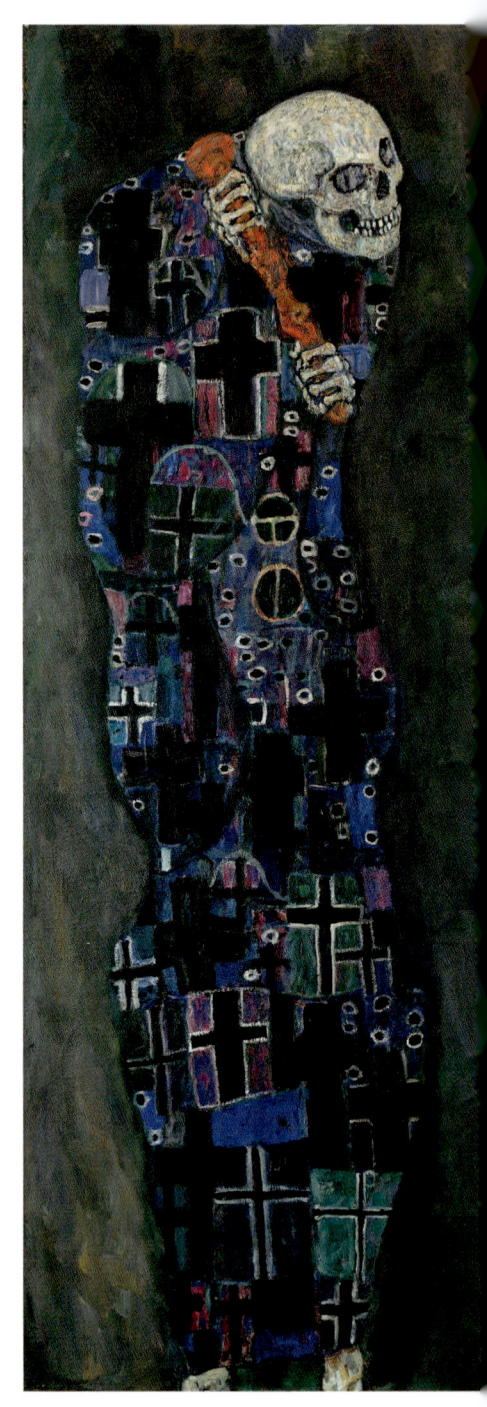

Death and Life, 1910/11, reworked 1915/16
Oil on canvas, 180.5 x 200.5 cm /
71 ⅛ x 78 ⅞ in.
Vienna, Leopold Museum

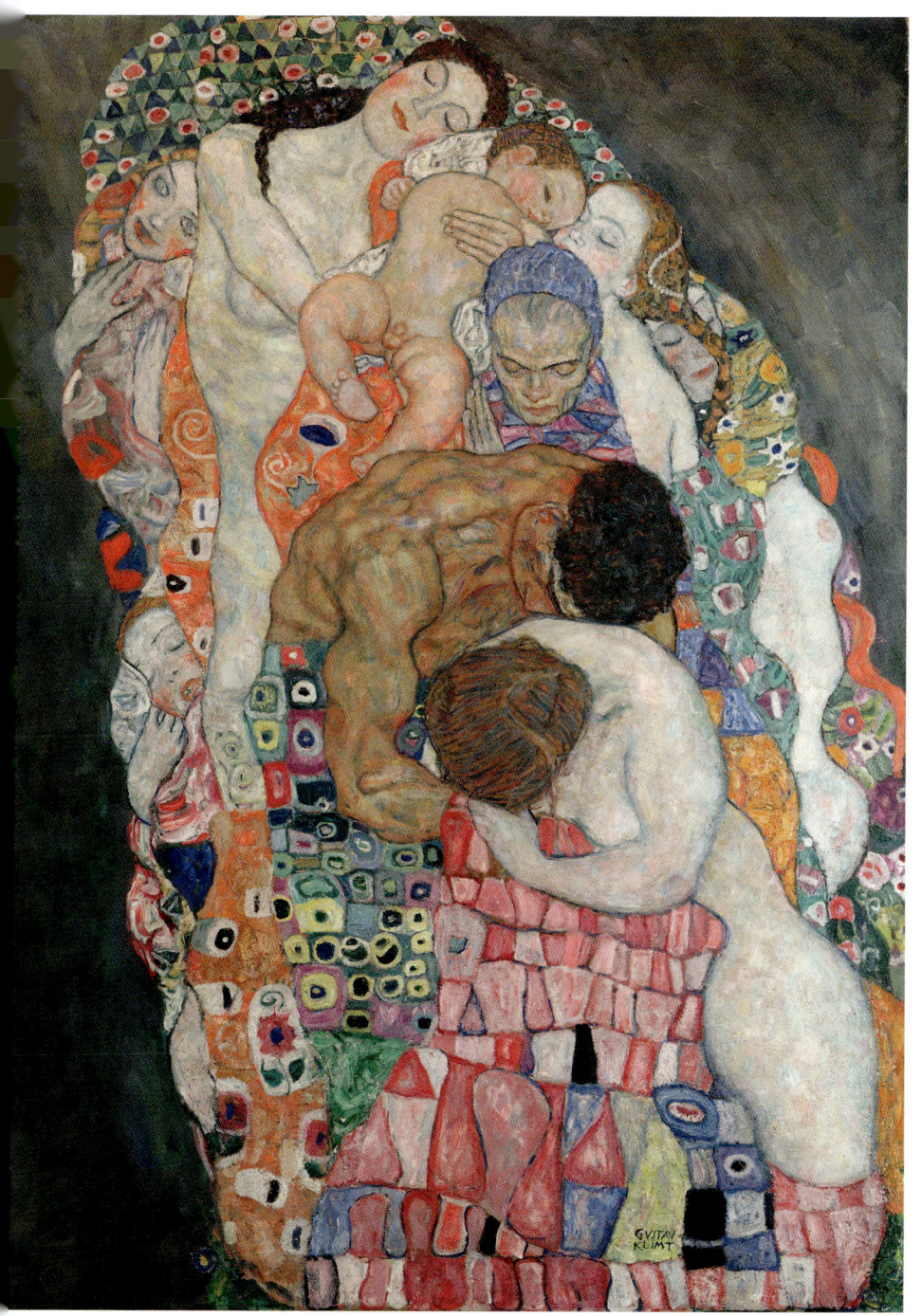

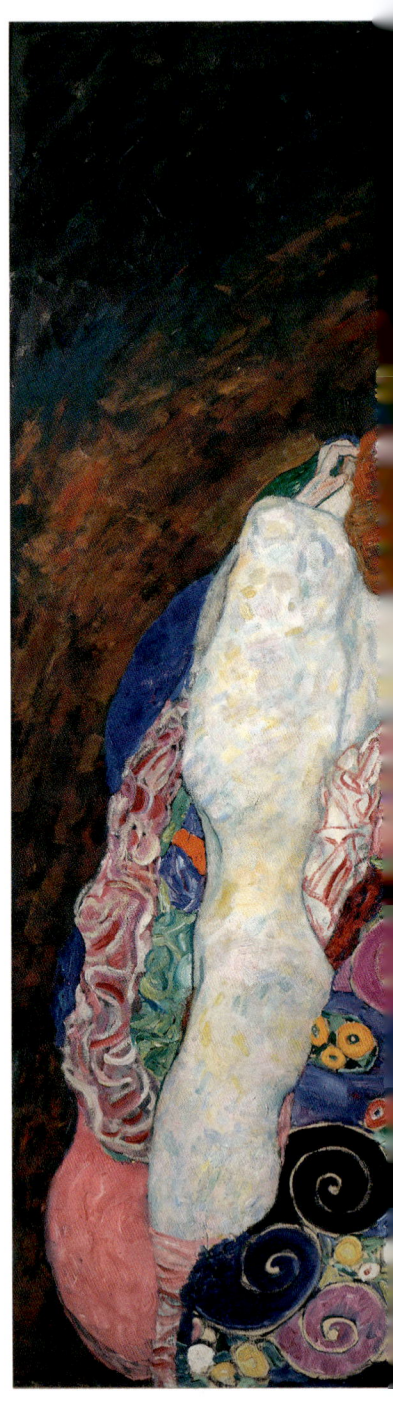

The Virgin, 1913
Oil on canvas, 190 x 200 cm / 74 ¾ x 78 ¾ in.
Prague, Národní Galerie

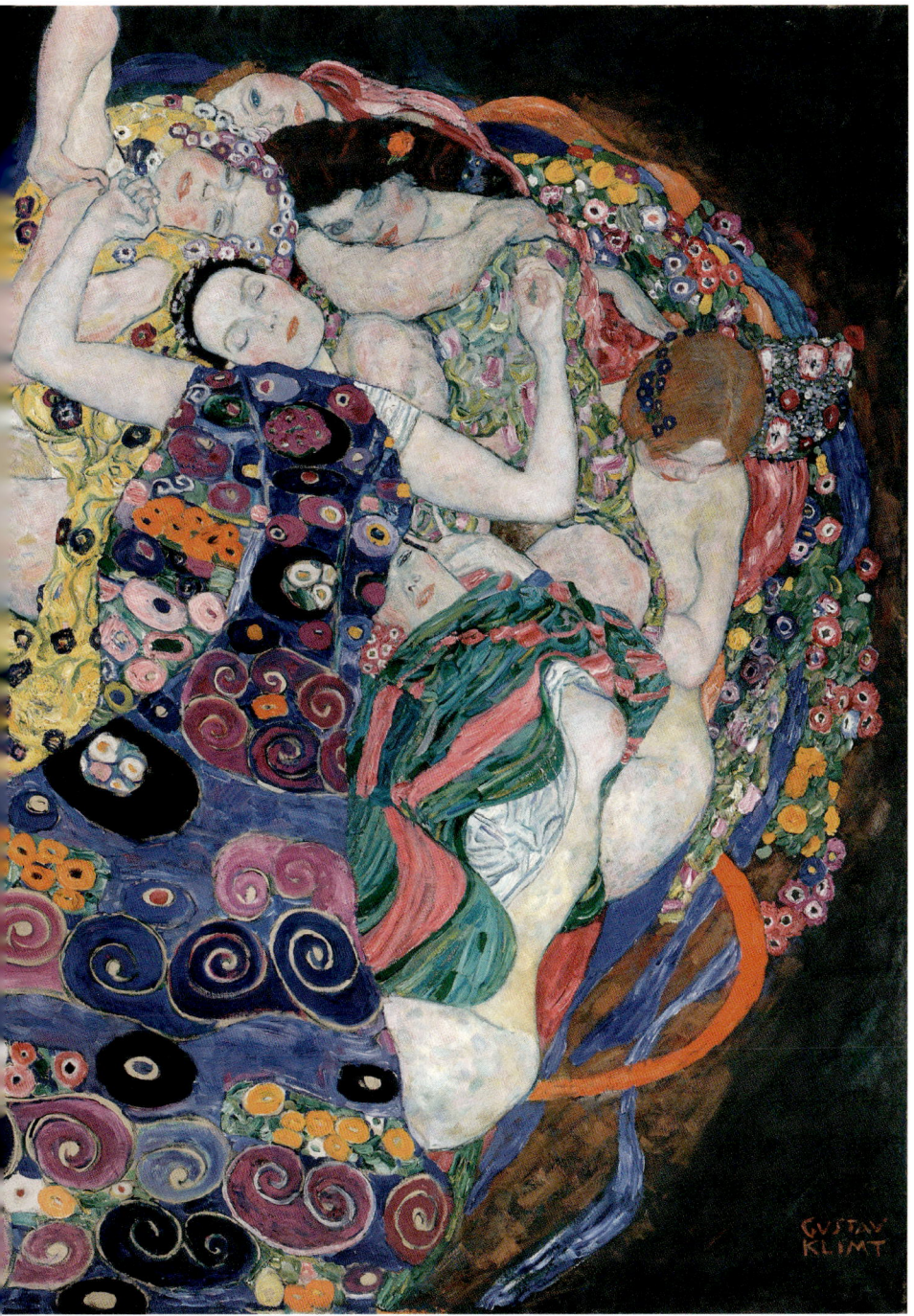

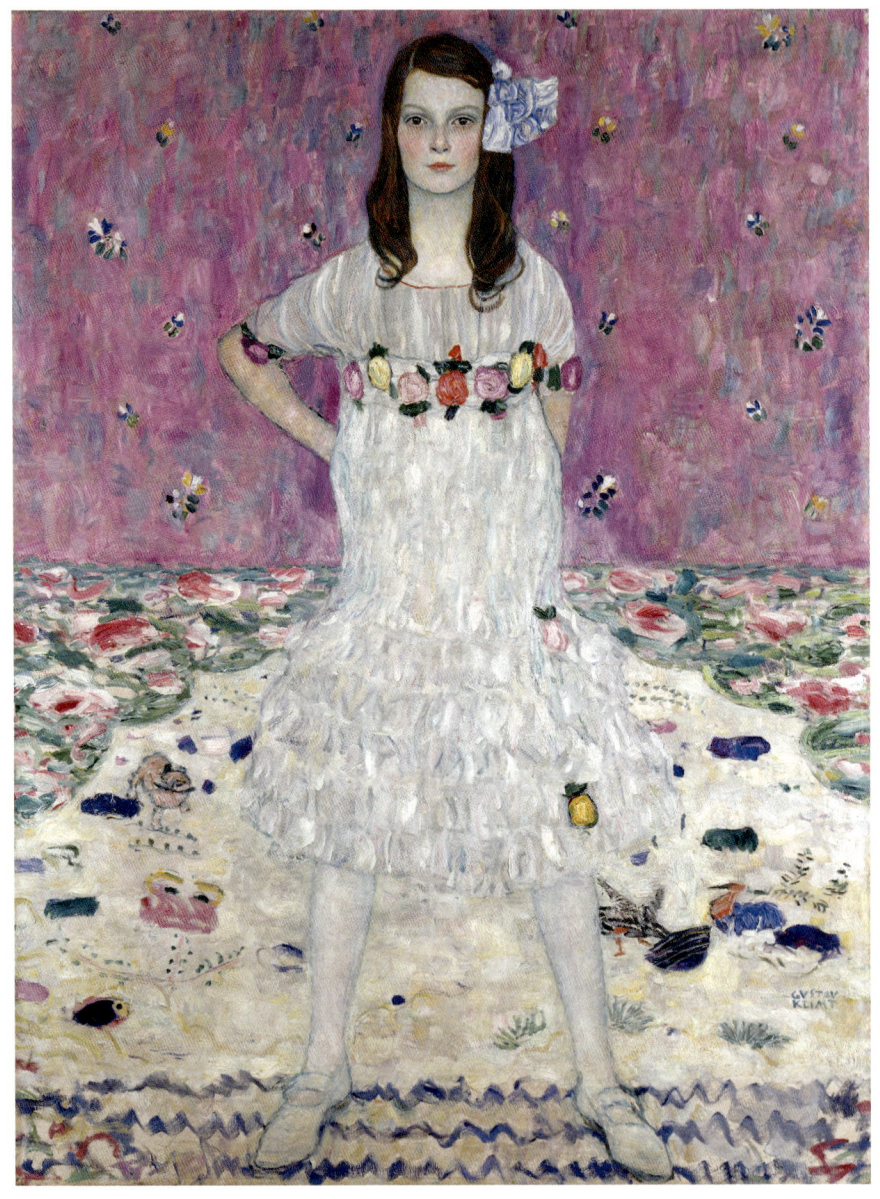

"We went every few months to Vienna and stayed about 10 days.
I was a little girl, and Professor Klimt was awfully kind.
When I became impatient, he would just say:
'Sit still for just a few minutes longer.'"

MÄDA PRIMAVESI, 1987

Portrait of Mäda Primavesi, 1913
Oil on canvas, 150 x 110 cm / 59 x 43 ½ in.
New York, The Metropolitan Museum of Art, inv. no. 64148,
Gift of André and Clara Mertens, in memory of her mother, Jenny Pulitzer Steiner, 1964

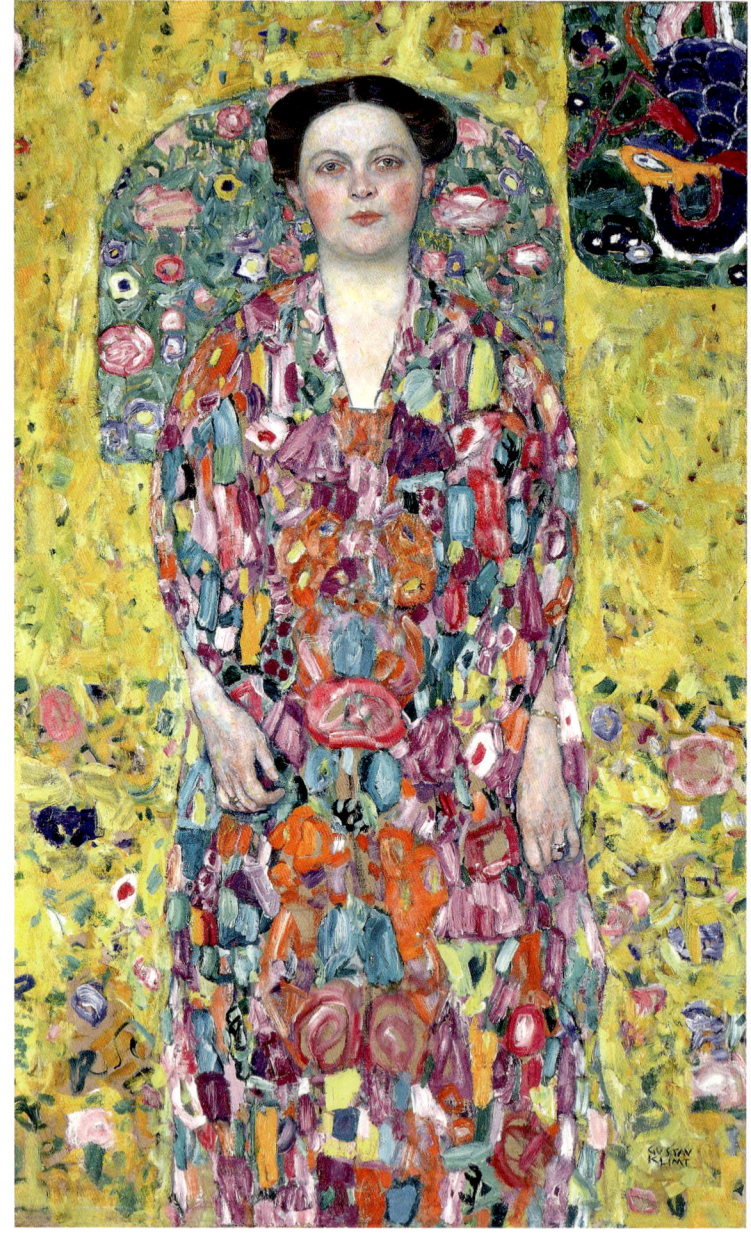

Portrait of Eugenia (Mäda) Primavesi, 1913/14
Oil on canvas, 140 x 84 cm / 55 ⅛ x 33 in.
Toyota, Municipal Museum of Art

Portrait of Adele Bloch-Bauer II, 1912
Oil on canvas, 190 x 120 cm / 74 ¾ x 47 ¼ in. Private collection

Page 346
Martin Gerlach, **Serena Lederer in her drawing room with Klimt's portrait of her daughter Elisabeth Lederer on the wall**, c. 1930
Photograph. Imagno/ÖNB

Page 347
Portrait of Elisabeth Lederer, 1914–1916
Oil on canvas, 180 x 128 cm / 70 ⅞ x 50 ⅜ in. New York, private collection

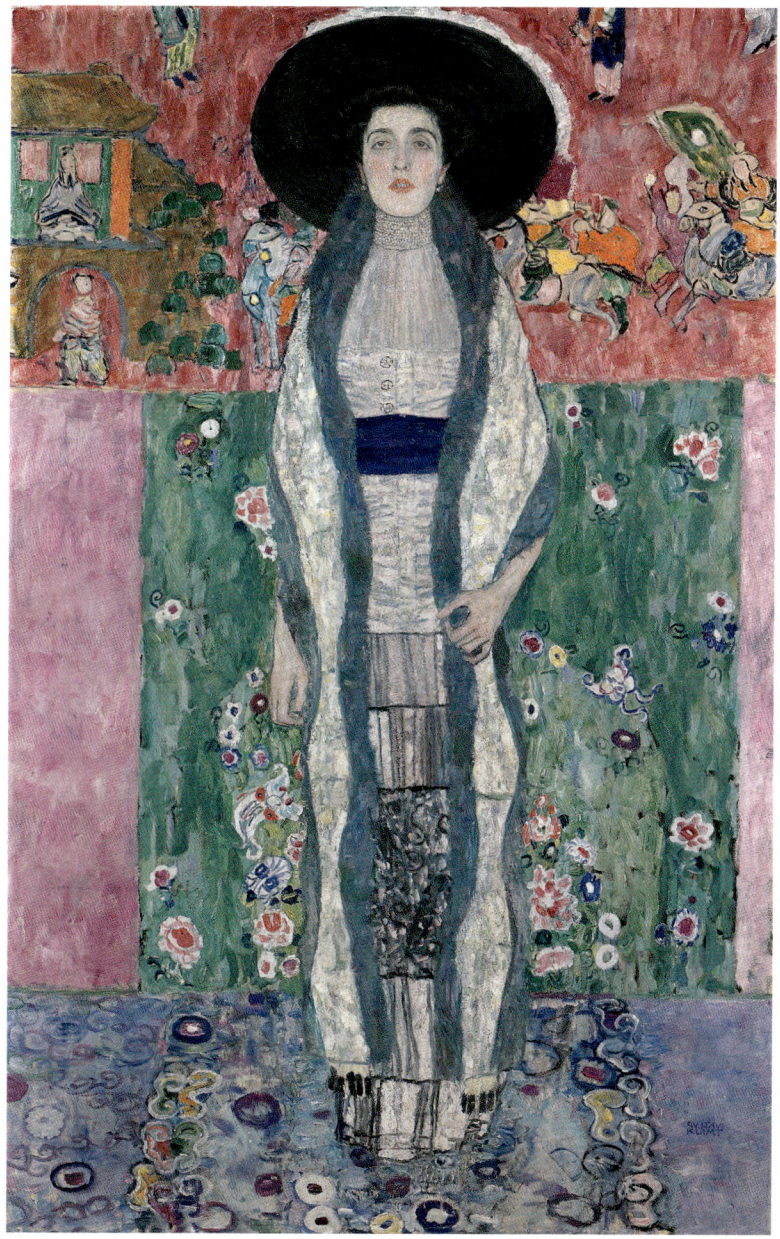

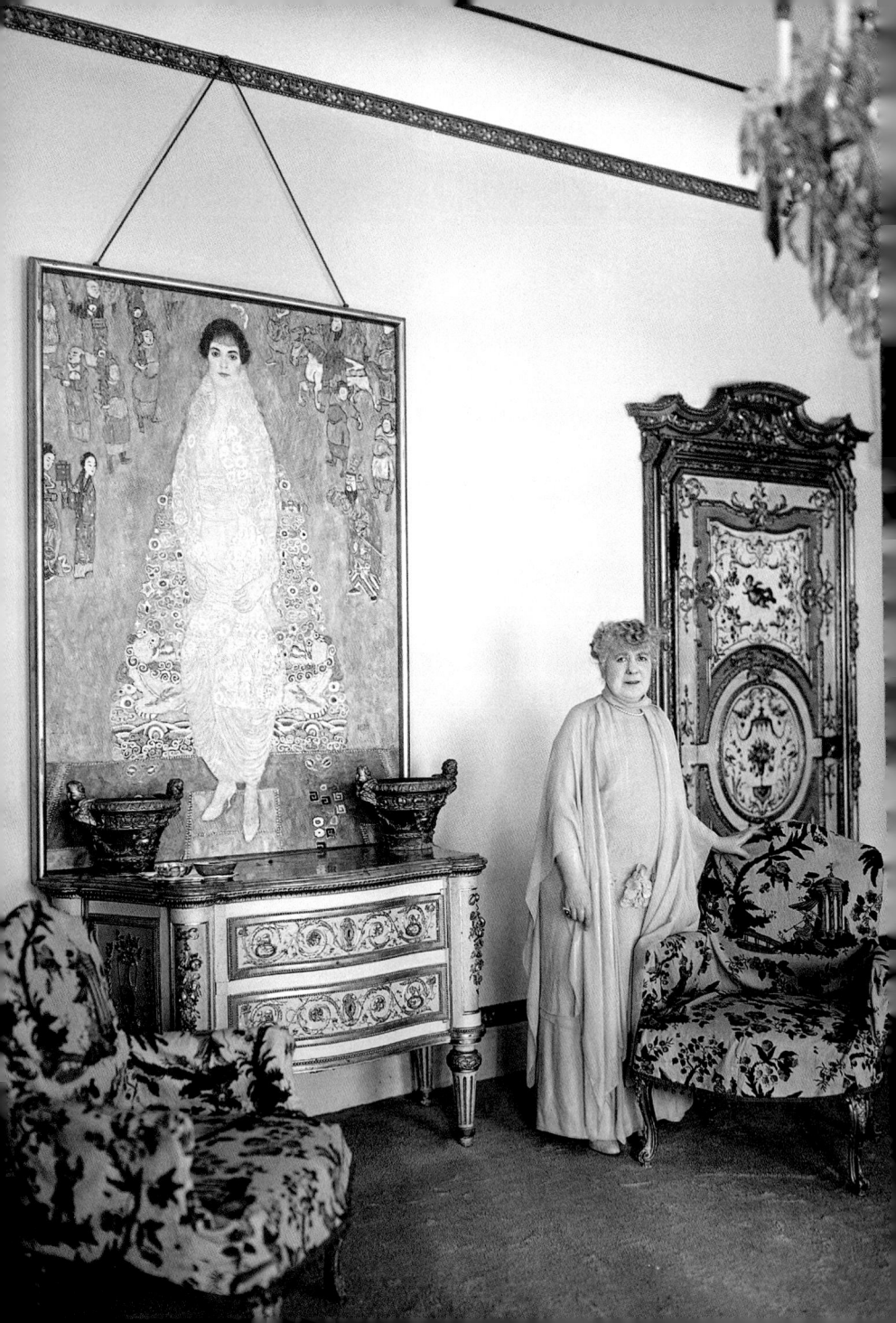

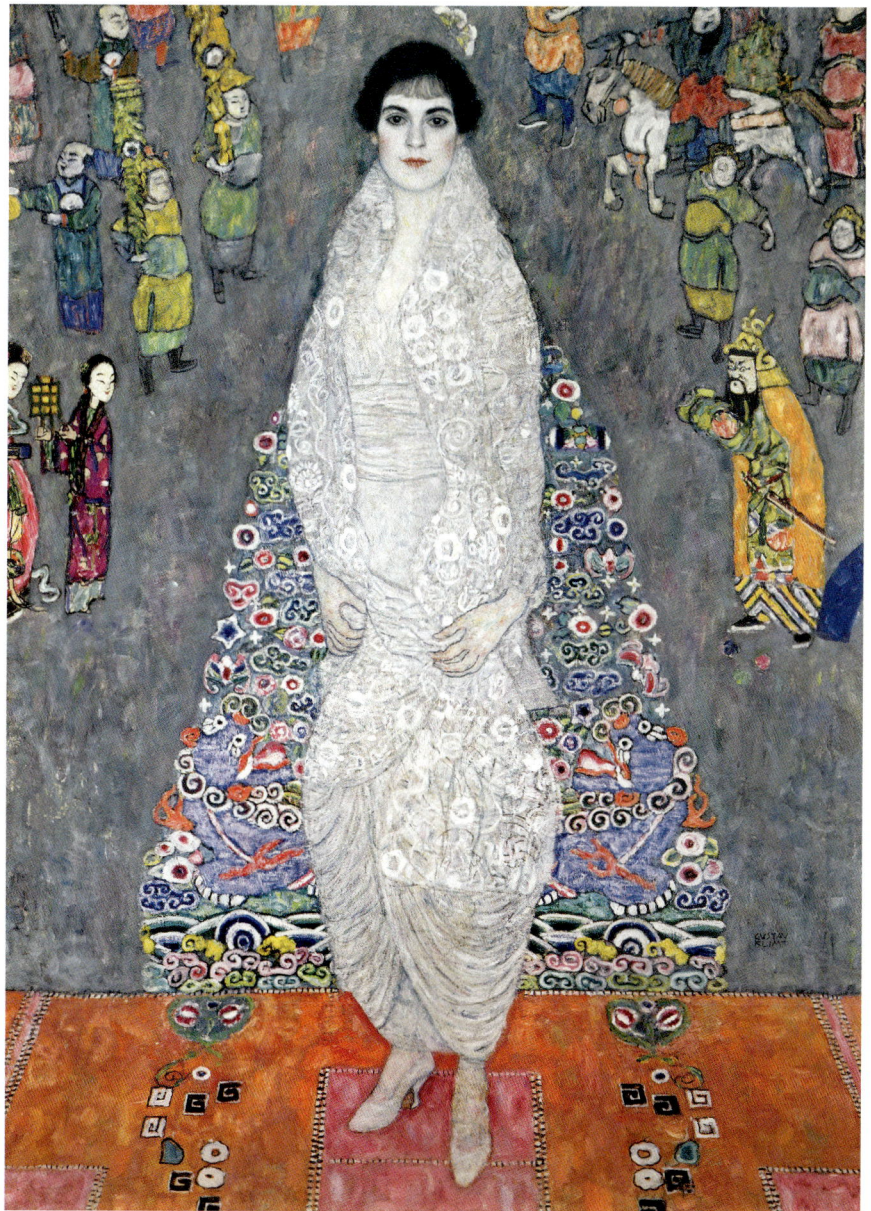

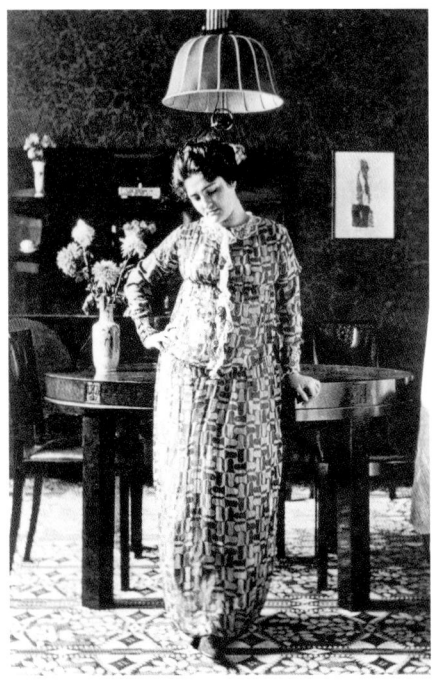

Friederike Maria Beer in a Wiener Werkstätte house dress, c. 1913
Photograph. Imagno/Austrian Archives

Portrait of Friederike Maria Beer, 1916
Oil on canvas, 168 x 130 cm / 66 ⅛ x 51 ⅛ in.
Tel Aviv, Museum of Art, Mizne-Blumenthal Collection

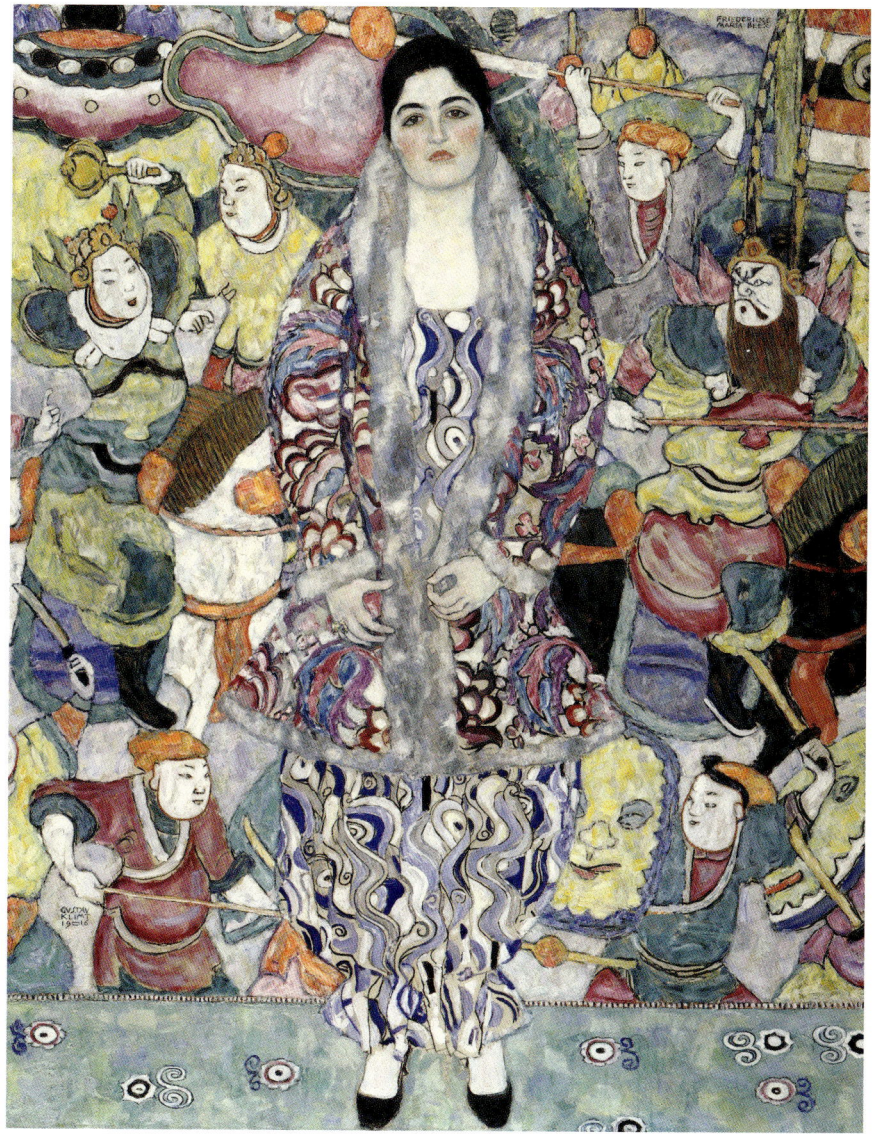

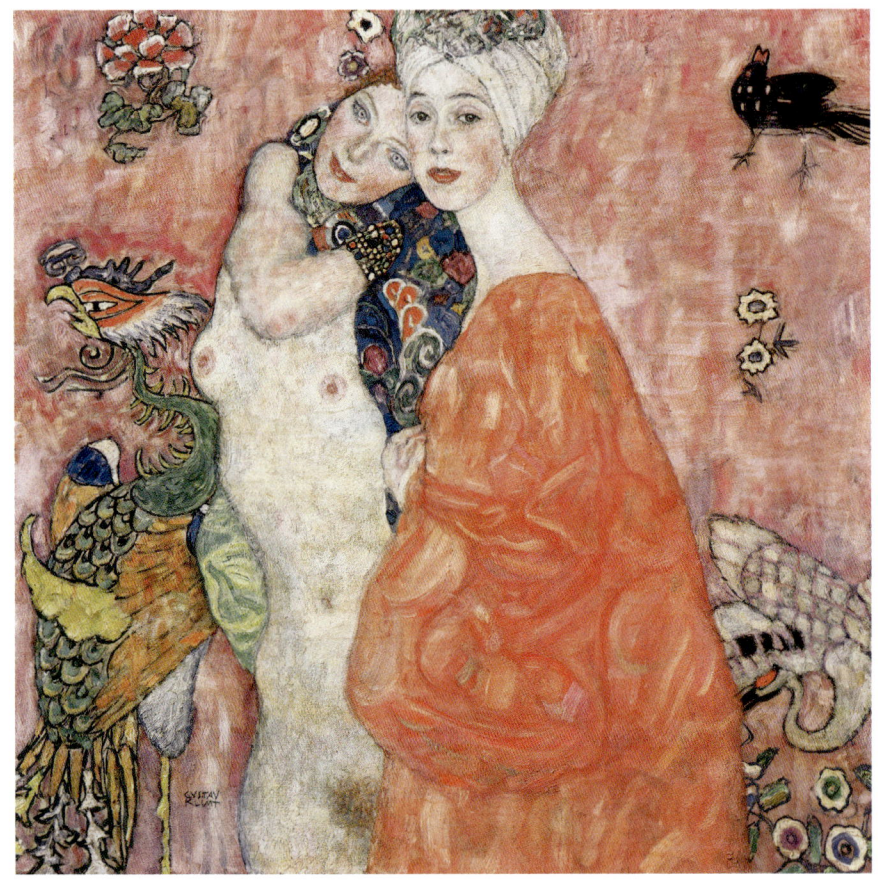

Friends II, 1916/17
Oil on canvas, 99 x 99 cm / 39 x 39 in.
Destroyed by fire in May 1945 at Immendorf Castle, Lower Austria

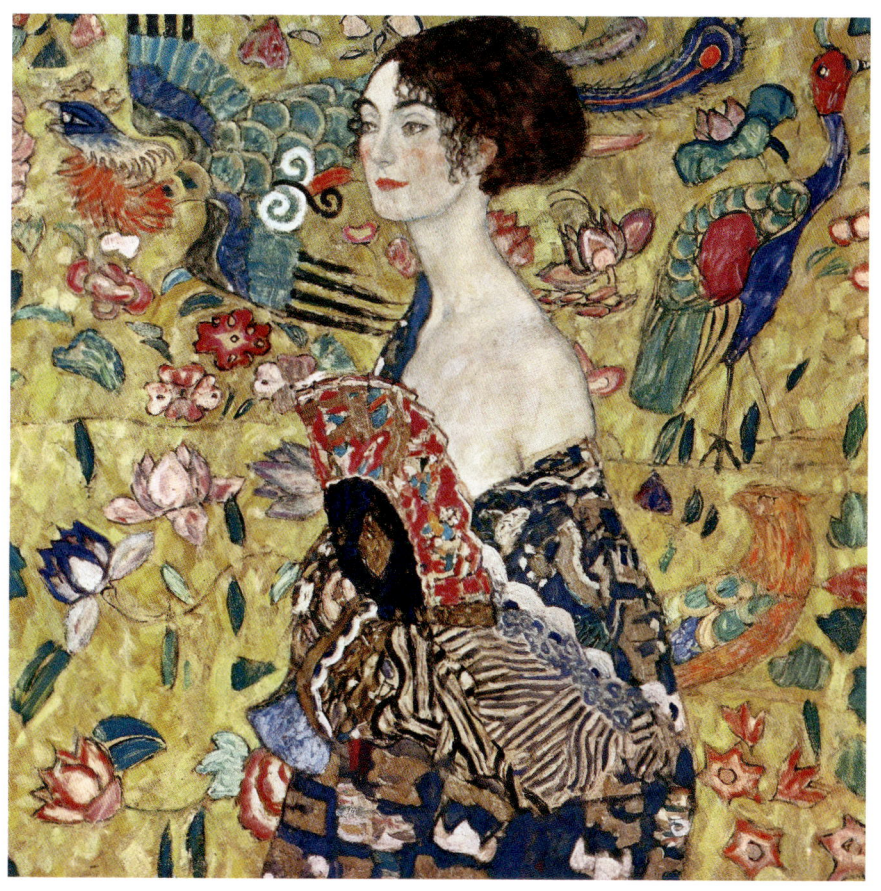

Lady with a Fan, 1917
Oil on canvas, 100 x 100 cm / 39 ⅜ x 39 ⅜ in.
Private collection

The Dancer, 1916/17
Oil on canvas, 180 x 90 cm / 70 ⅞ x 35 ½ in.
New York, private collection, courtesy Neue Galerie

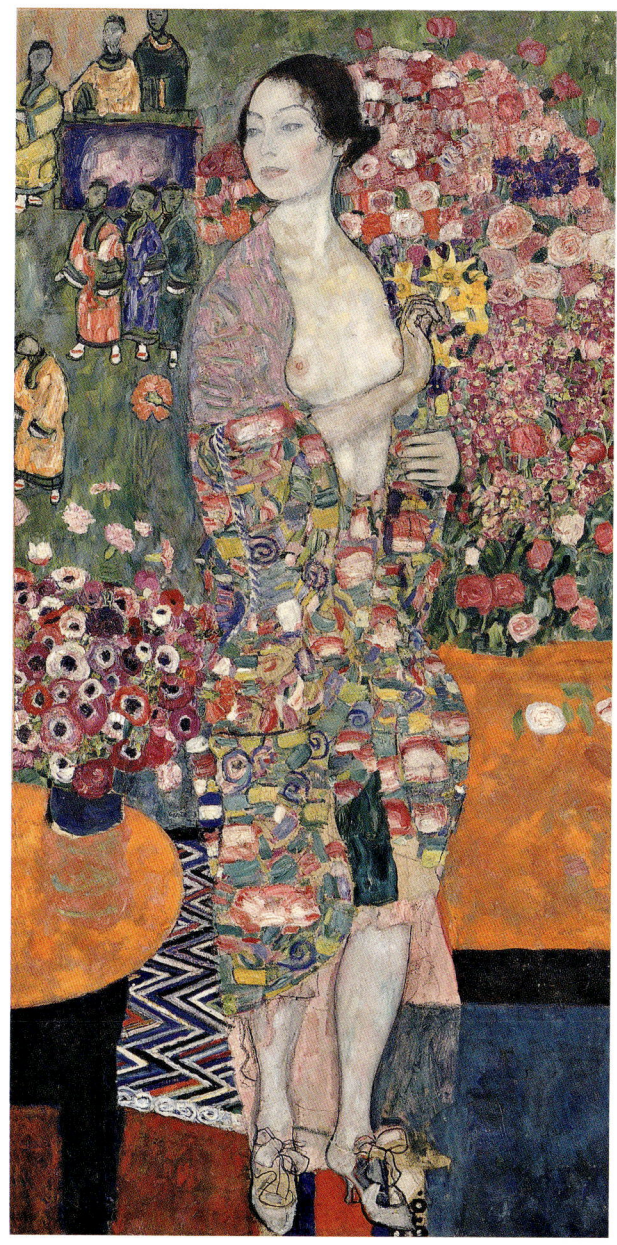

*"What initially struck the viewer as being Klimt was not him,
but something with which he was connected. Japan, China, Byzantium and
the ancient and modern Orient. Italian and modern English Pre-Raphaelitism.
French decorative and magical painting of the Moreau kind, Low Countries
mysticism from the region of Khnopff, with colonial goods and gods in between.
But if he took something from everything, it was because he was nothing less than an eclectic.
He simply used this as nourishment and transformed it into Gustav Klimt."*

FROM THE OBITUARY ON GUSTAV KLIMT, 1918

Portrait of Ria Munk III, 1917 (unfinished)
Oil on canvas, 180 x 90 cm / 70 ⅞ x 35 ½ in. The Lewis Collection

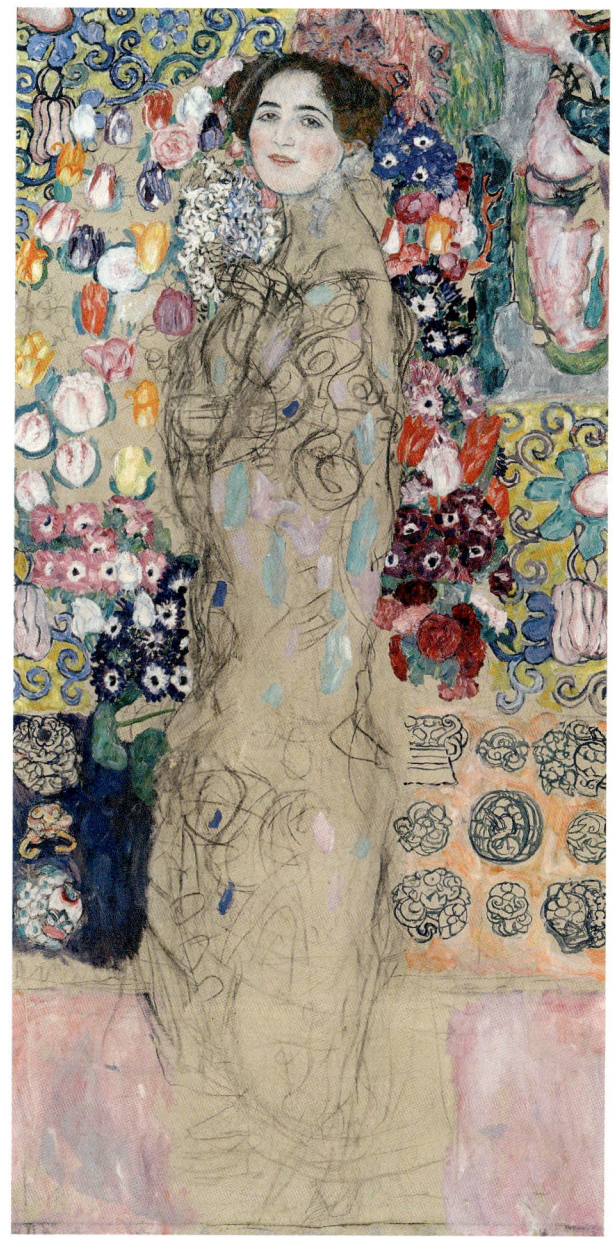

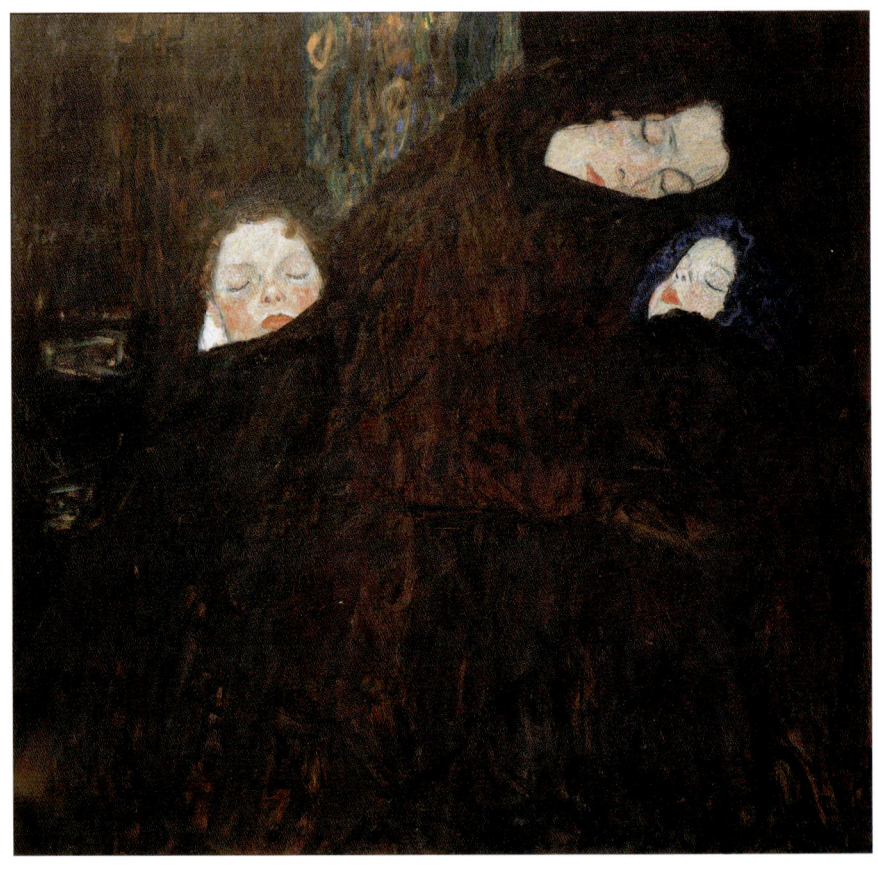

The Family (Emigrants), 1909/10
Oil on canvas, 90 x 90 cm / 35 ½ x 35 ½ in. Vienna, Belvedere

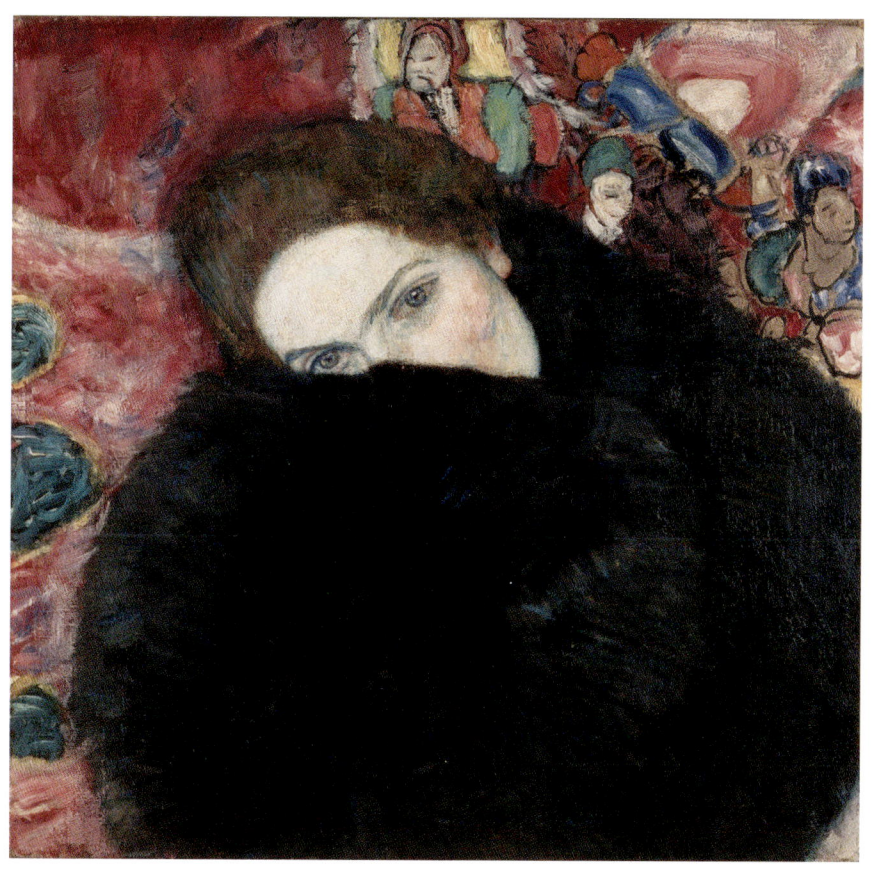

Lady with a Muff, 1916/17
Oil on canvas. Private collection

357

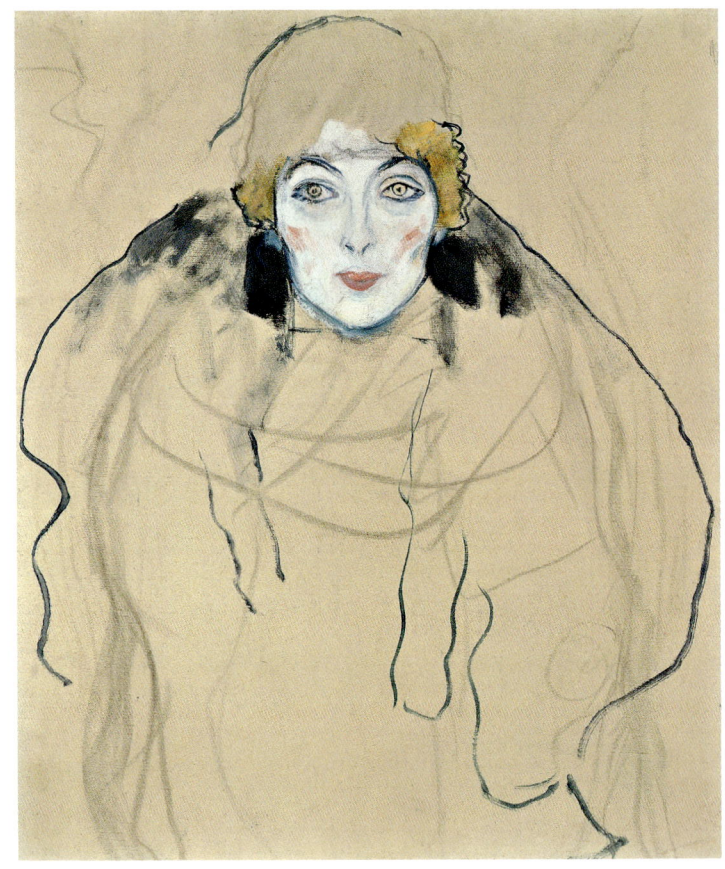

Portrait of a Lady *en face*, 1917 (unfinished)
Oil on canvas, 67 x 56 cm / 26 ⅜ x 22 in. Linz, Lentos Kunstmuseum

Portrait of Johanna Staude, 1917 (unfinished)
Oil on canvas, 70 x 50 cm / 27 ½ x 19 ⅝ in. Vienna, Belvedere

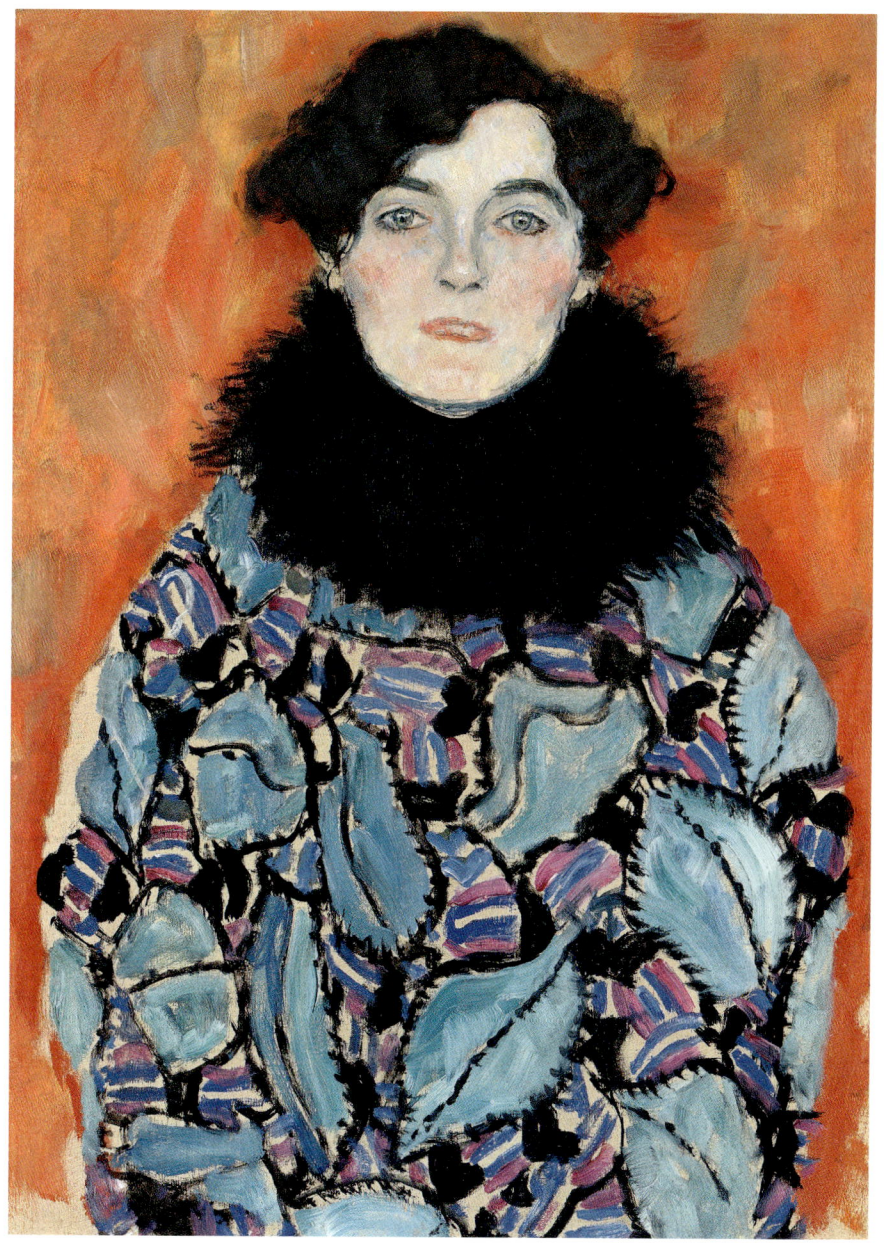

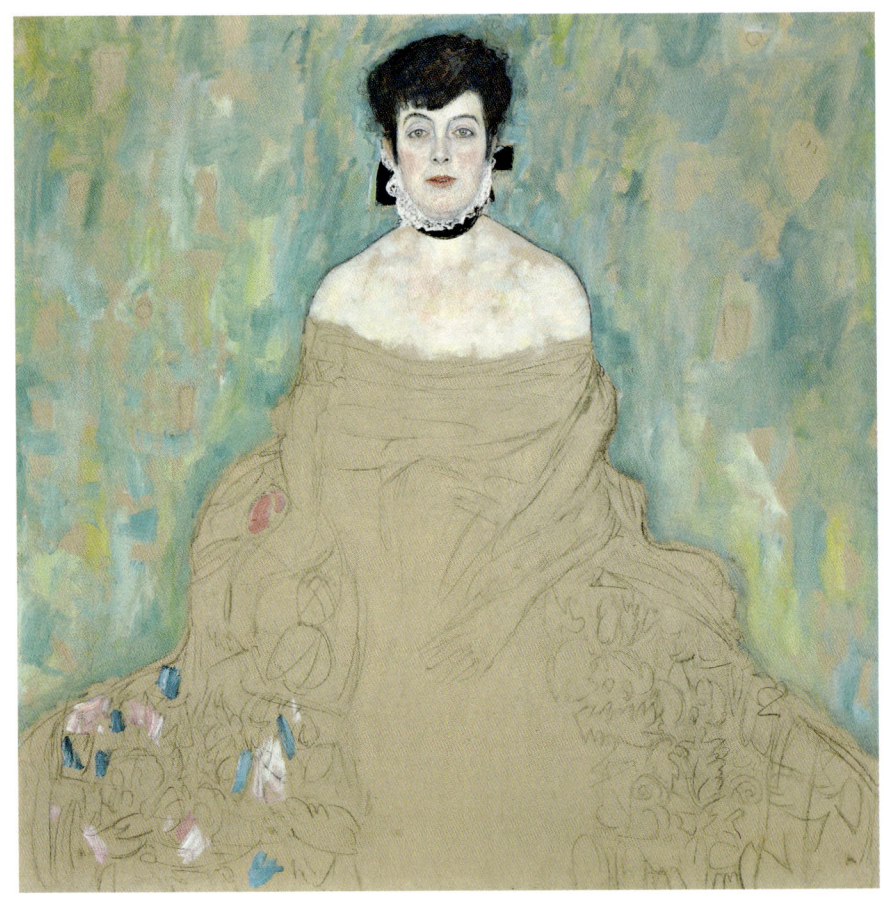

Portrait of Amalie Zuckerkandl, 1917 (unfinished)
Oil on canvas, 128 x 128 cm / 50 ⅜ x 50 ⅜ in. Vienna, Belvedere

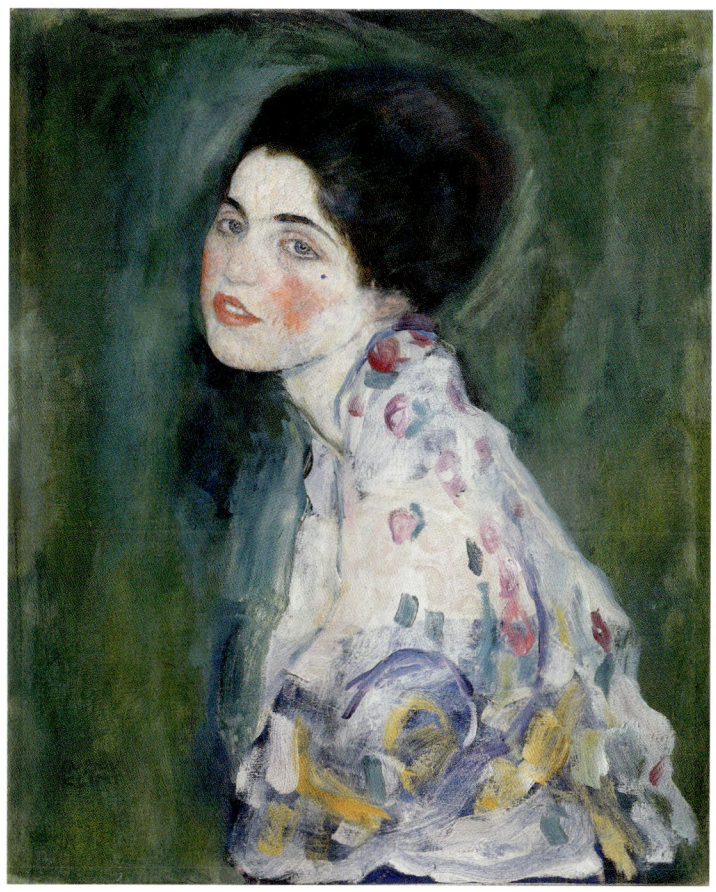

Portrait of a Young Woman, 1916/17, on the basis of a picture of 1910
Oil on canvas, 68 x 55 cm / 26 ¾ x 21 ⅝ in. Piacenza, Galleria Ricci-Oddi (stolen in 1997)

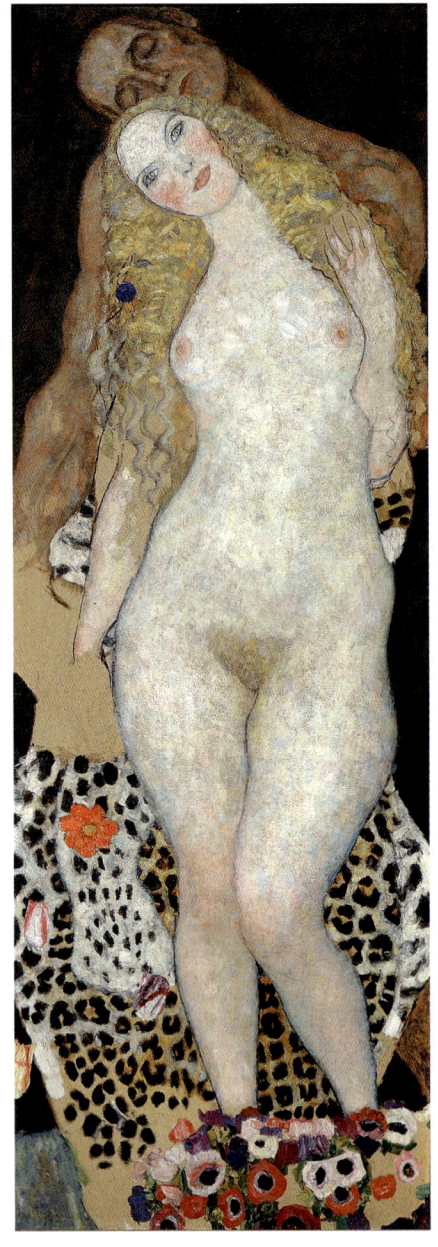

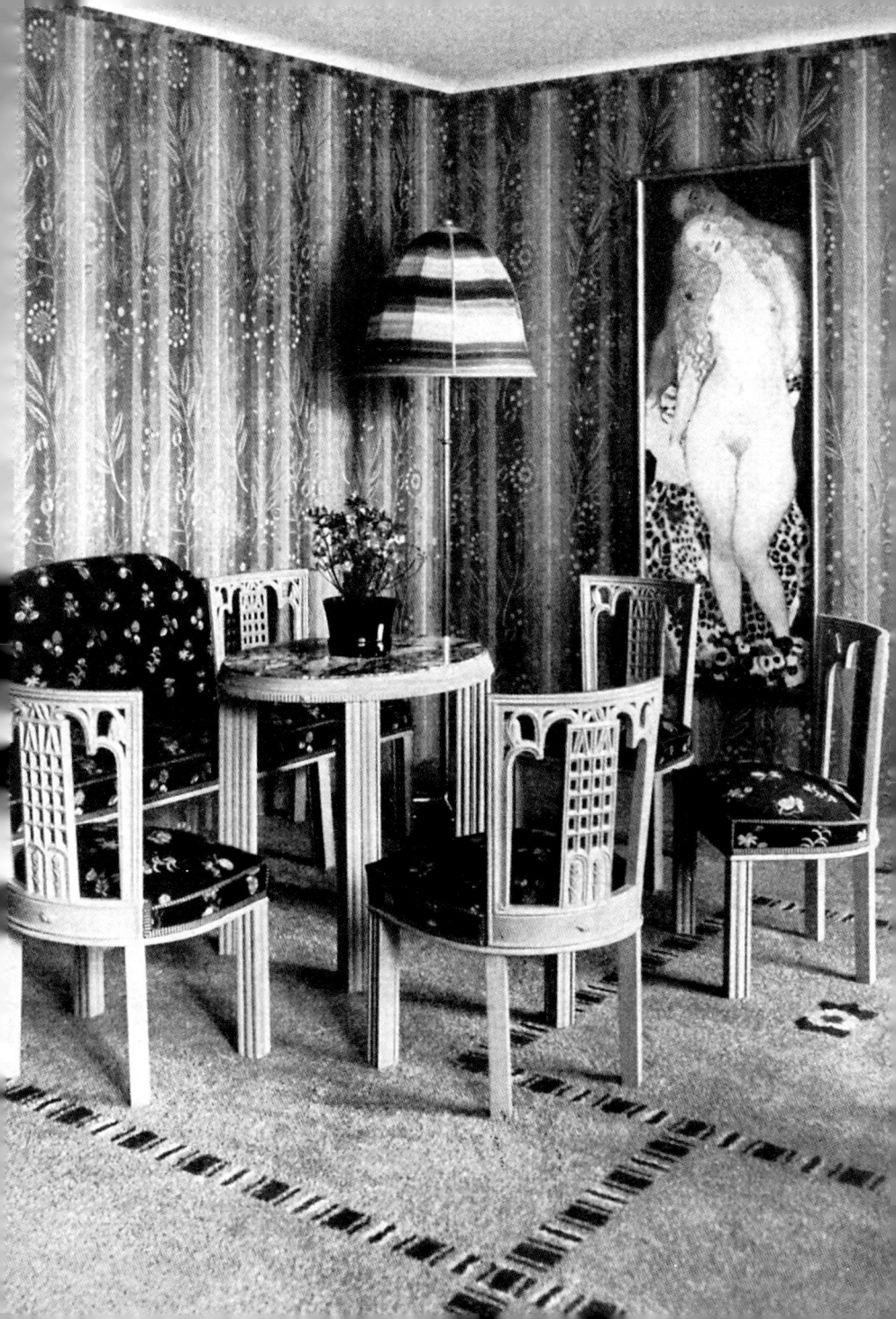

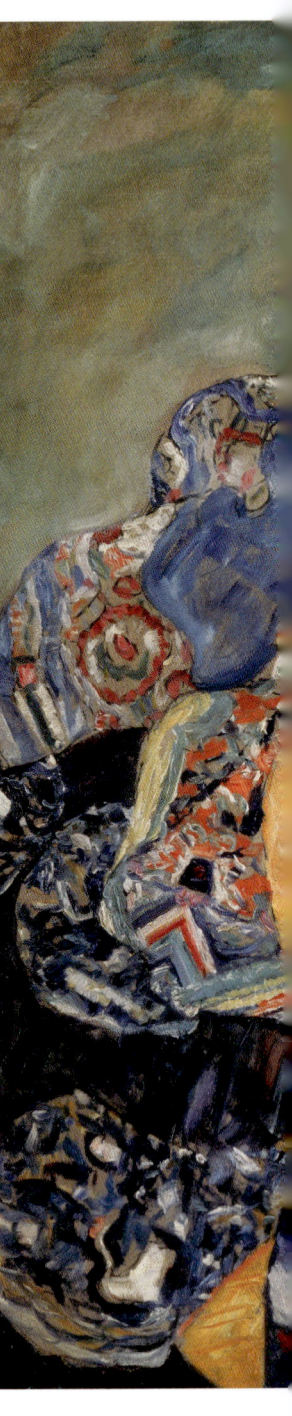

Page 362
Adam and Eve, 1917/18 (unfinished)
Oil on canvas, 173 x 60 cm / 68 ⅛ x 23 ⅝ in.
Vienna, Belvedere

Page 363
Small drawing room in the Villa Knips
With Klimt's painting *Adam and Eve* visible in the background
From: *Moderne Bauformen*, 1926, p. 361

Baby, 1917
Oil and tempera on canvas, 110 x 110 cm / 43 ¼ x 43 ¼ in.
Washington, D. C., National Gallery of Art, inv. no. 1978.41.1,
Gift of Otto and Franziska Kallir with the help of the Carol
and Edwin Gaines Fullinwider Fund 1978

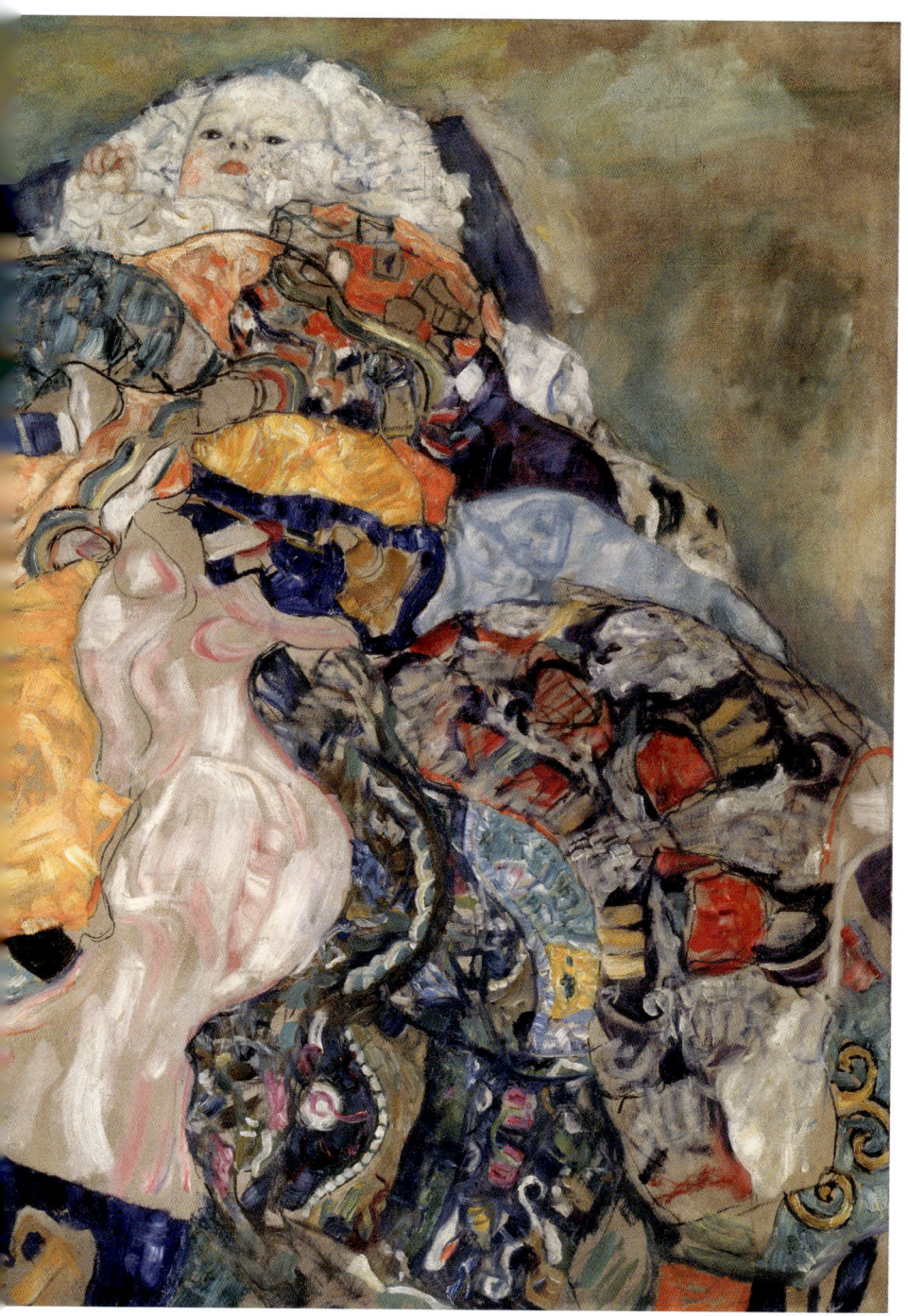

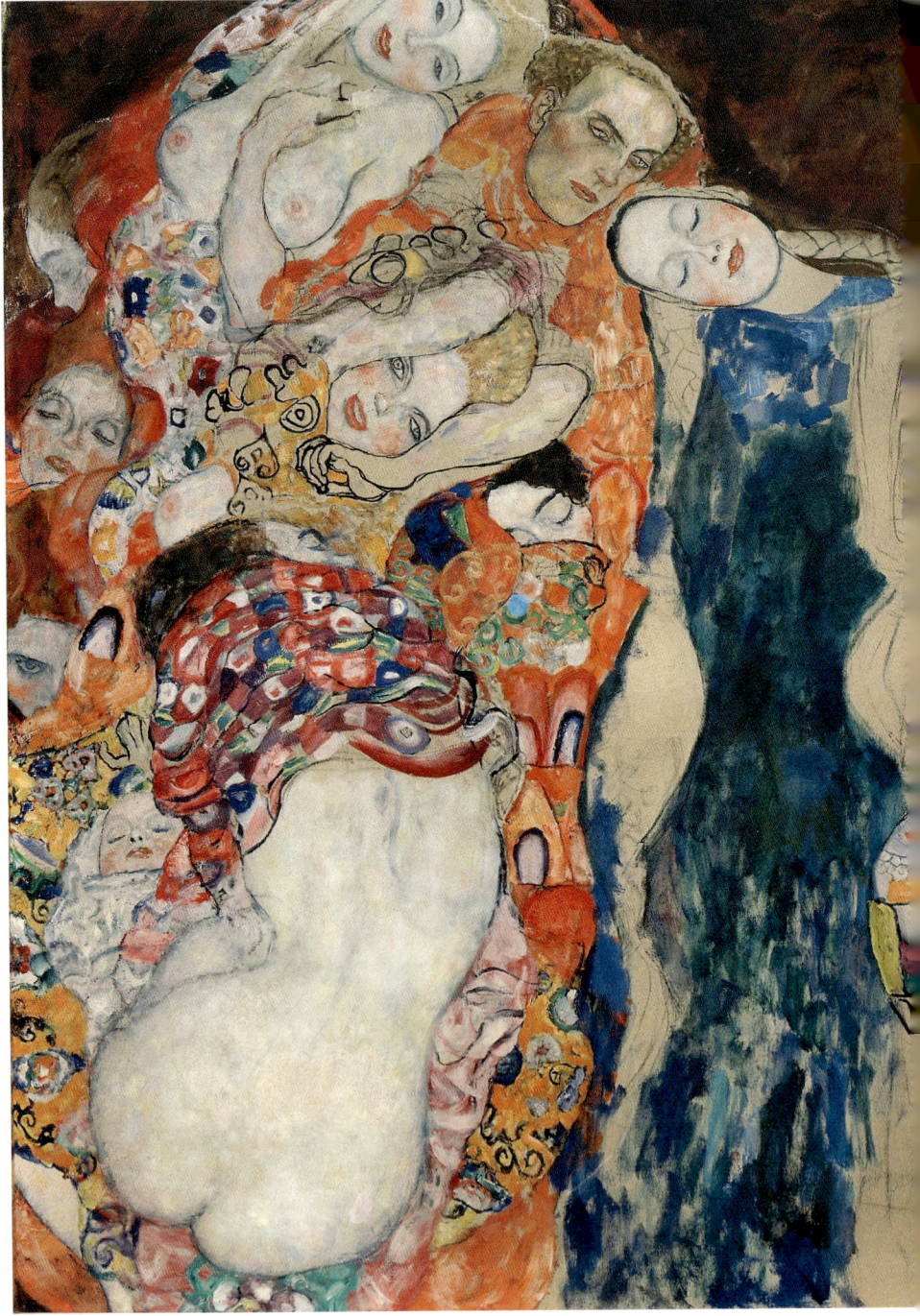

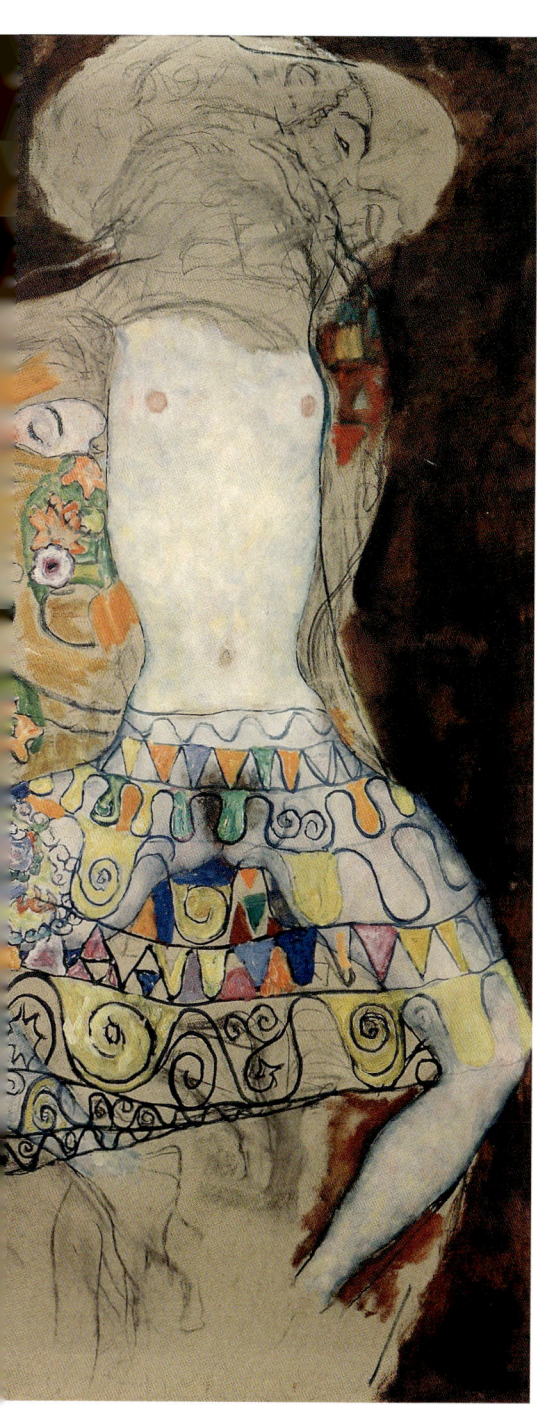

The Bride, 1917/18 (unfinished)
Oil on canvas, 165 x 191 cm / 65 x 75 in.
Vienna, Gustav Klimt | Wien 1900
Foundation, on loan to the Belvedere

Pages 368/69
Gustav Klimt and Emilie Flöge, 1909
In a rowing boat in front of the Villa
Paulick in Seewalchen on Lake Attersee
Photograph. Imagno/Austrian Archives

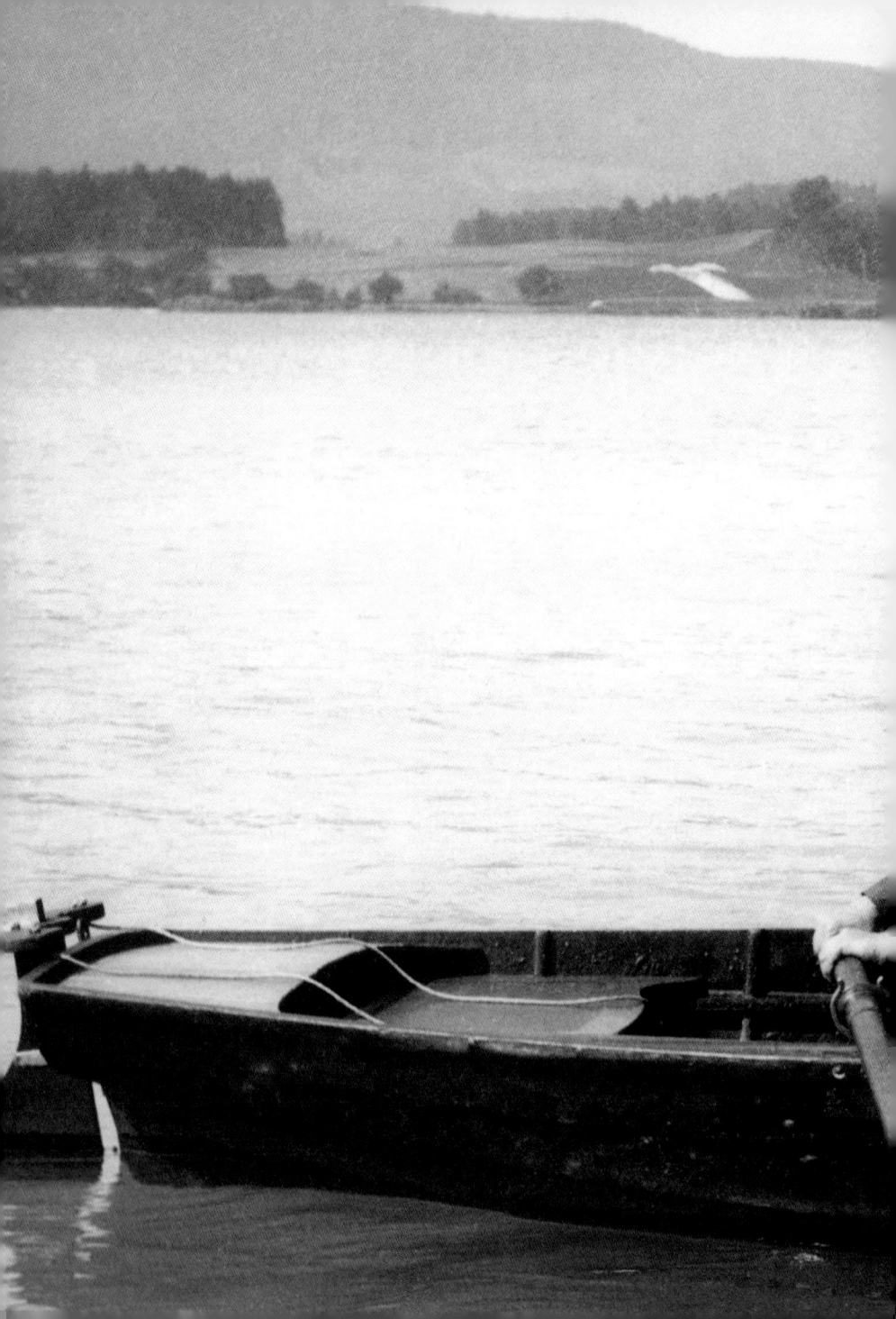

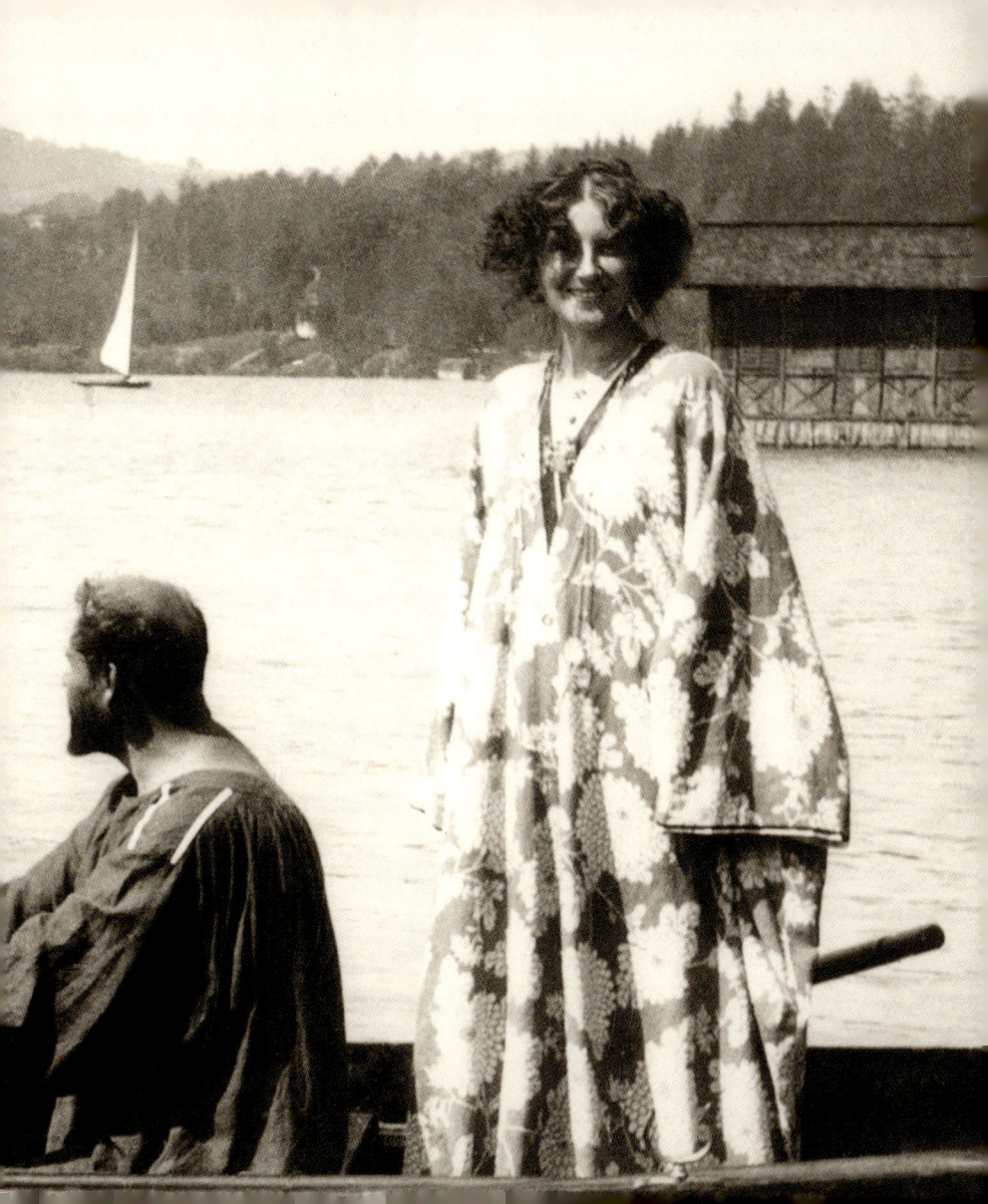

V.

The landscapes:
a reconstructed
nature

Evelyn Benesch

"I ... looked ... with my 'viewfinder',
that is, a hole cut in a cardboard lid,
for motifs for the landscapes I want to paint,
and found a great deal, or – depending
on how you see it – nothing."

GUSTAV KLIMT, 1902

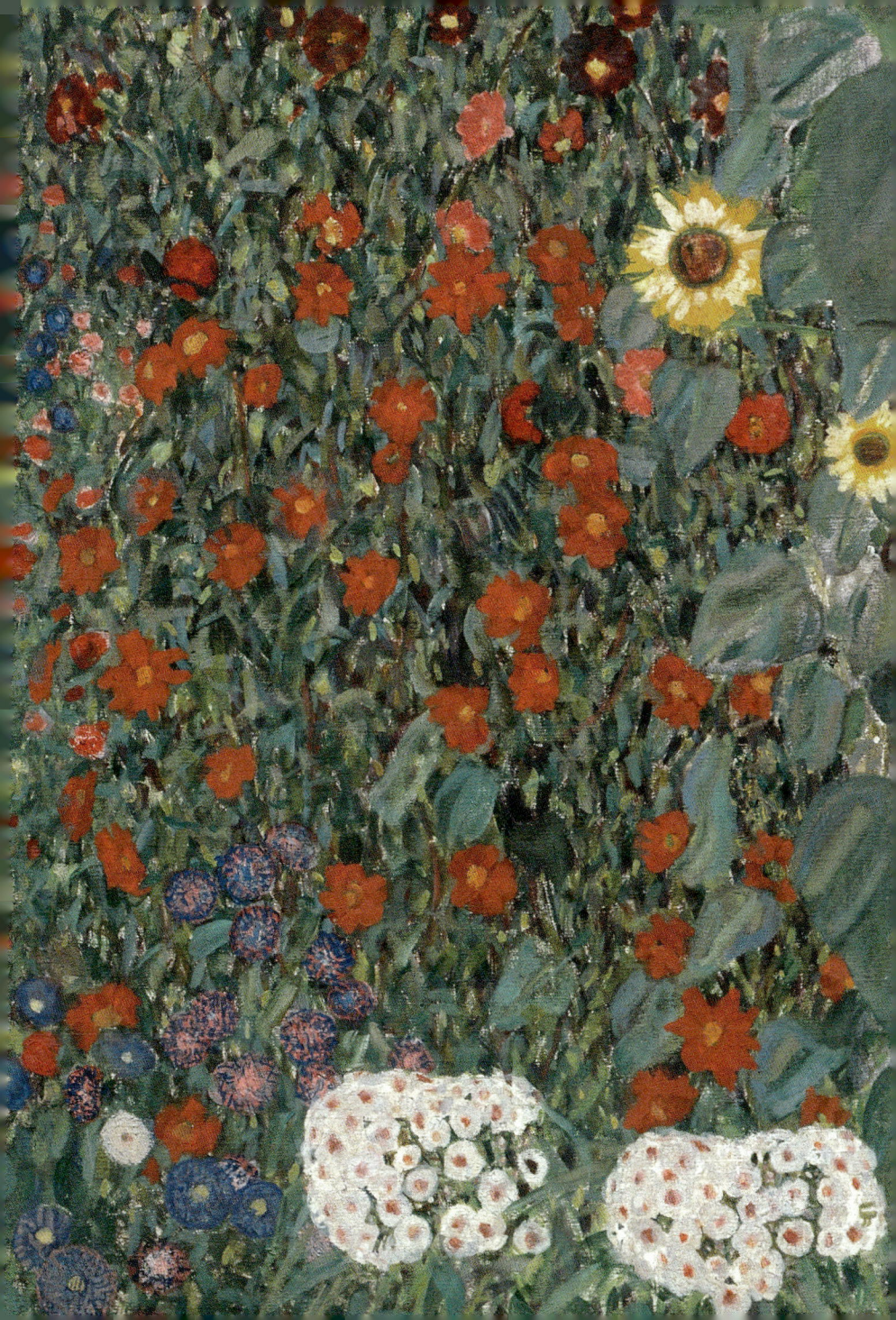

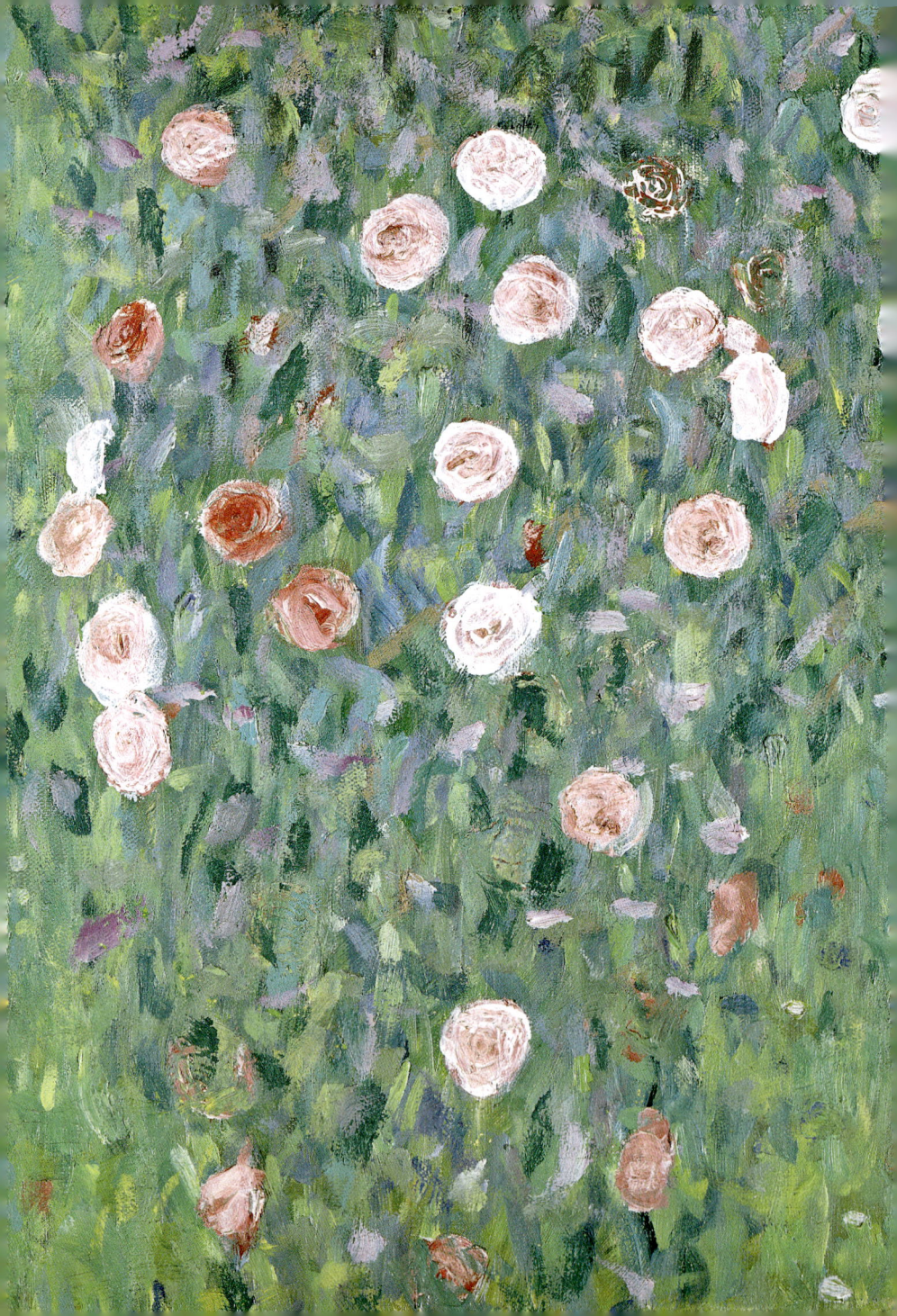

Summer holidays in the Salzkammergut

In a letter of 1903, sent from Lake Attersee during his summer break away from Vienna, Klimt described how he was taking walks through the countryside with a "view-finder" in search of suitable motifs for his landscape pictures. The artist employed this simple yet sophisticated device as a means of picturing the landscape in a square view that corresponded to his aesthetic aims. In just the same way, Klimt used a telescope to help him to filter the nature he saw before him and establish the preliminary format of his final picture. Even in his very first landscapes, produced around 1900, when he was probably not yet making use of these optical aids, Klimt reformulated nature in a characteristic fashion, insofar as he reconstructed it within the pictorial field in a composition governed by his own artistic principles.

In the second half of his life, Klimt devoted himself intensively to landscape. He painted the countryside around Lake Attersee in Upper Austria more than fifty times, in compositions showing the lake itself, the woods and forests around it, cottage gardens, solitary flowers and local buildings. Alongside large, panorama-like landscapes offering a vista of the hills and mountains ringing the lake and the small towns and villages clustered along its shore, we find close-up views of individual gardens (often assembling, in one picture, plants and trees such as the red poppy and the green apple that in real life flower and fruit in different months of the year) and depictions of particular plants. From 1899 onwards Klimt used a square support in every case: within the calm equilibrium of this classic geometric shape, he developed a spectrum of luxuriant summery nature.

Klimt's landscape themes go back to the *paysage intime* of Austrian Atmospheric Impressionism, that is, they are 'private' landscapes, personal portrayals of nature as opposed to the classical and heroic landscapes still cultivated in the first half of the 19th century. Klimt's landscape pictures have been described in the literature as "recreational pieces" (Dobai 1981, p. 13), probably because they were autonomous works, and so offered the artist an unrestricted choice of subject and an opportunity for painterly experimentation but, above all, too, because Klimt painted (almost) all of them during the summer months that he spent in the Salzkammergut region. Only a few were completed later in his Vienna studio. These unofficial landscapes are quite different from the formal portraits of Viennese society ladies that Klimt painted – as paid commissions – over the winter

Page 371
Cottage Garden with Sunflowers (detail), 1908
(see ill. pp. 440/41)

Roses beneath Trees (Roses) (detail), c. 1904
(see ill. p. 428)

months. It is astonishing to note how closely these opposite poles of 'winter painting' and 'summer painting' correspond to Klimt's seasonally different lifestyles: firmly anchored in the life of Vienna society over the winter while living with his mother and sisters, Klimt spent the summer in the private seclusion of the Salzkammergut with his chosen family, centred upon his long-standing partner and sister-in-law Emilie Flöge.

Klimt had an uncommon affinity with the natural world: he preferred to be outdoors, kept fit with gymnastics, wrestling and fencing, and regularly took long walks. It was his custom, for example, to go on foot from his apartment in Vienna's 7th district to the Meierei-Tivoli café near Schönbrunn, on the slopes of the so-called Green Mountain, to have his breakfast. As his friend, the painter Carl Moll, recalled in 1943: "Klimt was an early riser and first thing in the morning, hungry for exercise, walked from Westbahnstrasse […] just after distant Meidling, to the Café Tivoli, whose Old Vienna ambience near Schönbrunn [Palace] appealed to him, the most modern of artists, more than anywhere else. […] a sumptuous breakfast, in which a large portion of whipped cream played the main role, had to fortify him for the whole day. […] His friends were in the habit of visiting him there. Nähr, the young Schiele and others" (cit. from Nebehay 1969, p. 54). Noteworthy, too, is Klimt's interest and delight in the cycle of the seasons. As a keen observer of nature, in March 1909 he wrote somewhat less laconically than usual to Emilie Flöge about the garden in front of his studio in Josefstädterstrasse: "Passing through my garden today, the smell [was] like the scent of spring – bird song – the buds are swelling – albeit only a little – despite the winter mood – it could change in a day!" (cit. from Fischer 1987, p. 175). Egon Schiele, who visited the Hietzing studio in which Klimt worked from 1914 onwards, recalled: "Every year Klimt had the garden around the house in Feldmühlgasse planted with flower beds – it was a pleasure to arrive there amongst flowers and ancient trees" (Schiele, "Klimts Herzensgüte war echt", n.d., cit. from Roessler 1921, p. 90).

It is all the more surprising, therefore, that Klimt should have only started painting landscape, flower and garden pictures in the second half of his life, in other words, from around 1900. This seems to have been bound up with his increased desire for a sort of internal emigration and most especially for an escape from his social obligations. Klimt was at that time extremely active in the sphere of cultural politics, where his involvement included not just the founding of the Secession in 1897 but also the battle to win approval for his Faculty paintings for Vienna University (pp. 129–131; Natter 2012, Cat. 126, 127, 157; cf. *inter alia* Dobai 1981, p. 13; Koja 2002, p. 35). His search for balance found expression in his embrace of painting 'unofficial' subjects, so to speak, in pursuit of art for himself rather than for an intervening patron, and in the opportunity to embrace an unfettered painterly attitude that left conventional terms of reference behind.

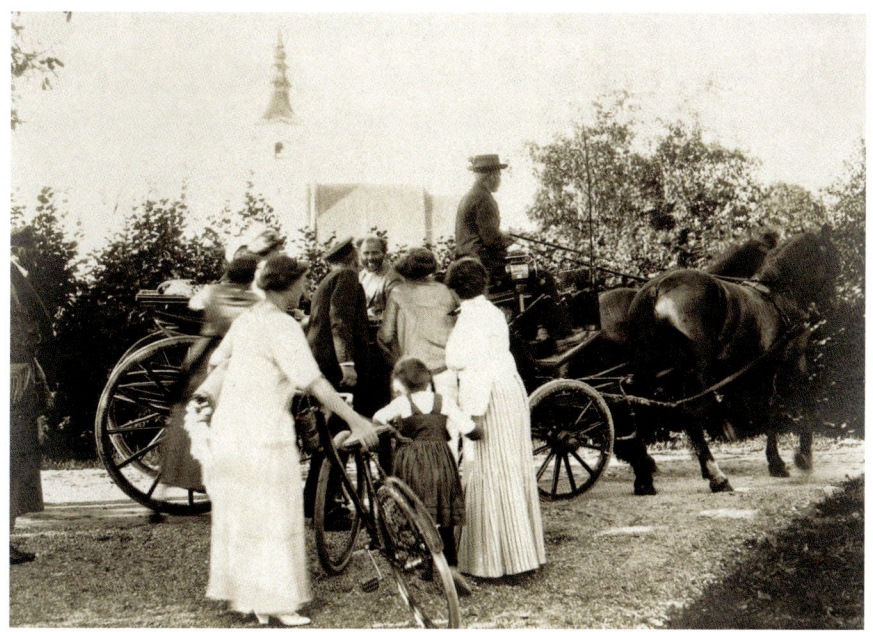

Klimt's departure from Seewalchen for the train station at Attnang-Puchheim, 1913
Photograph. Imagno/Austrian Archives

However, Klimt's landscape pictures also represented a secure source of income, a consideration that was likewise not unimportant. After the dispute over the Faculty paintings had culminated in his definitive rupture with the Ministry of Education, Klimt neither expected nor desired any further commissions from the Austrian State. He presented his landscapes to the Viennese public in Secession exhibitions and later at the Galerie Miethke. Klimt grew indignant, moreover, when other commitments got in the way of his landscape painting – as happened in 1910, when his summer was taken up by work on the frieze for the Palais Stoclet (Ch. III) in Brussels. This was also a cause of financial concern to the artist, as emerges from a letter he wrote to the textile manufacturer and founder of the Wiener Werkstätte, Fritz Waerndorfer (1868–1939): "I am returning to Vienna a bit before, or around, the middle of September – am working harder than ever – Stoclet and more Stoclet – still haven't begun a single landscape. It's costing me a fortune. Sincerely yours, GUS" (Weidinger 2007a, p. 132 and note 21).

Klimt's embrace of landscape painting as a form of 'thematic' retreat was nonetheless linked above all with the direct inspiration provided by nature herself. It is no coincidence

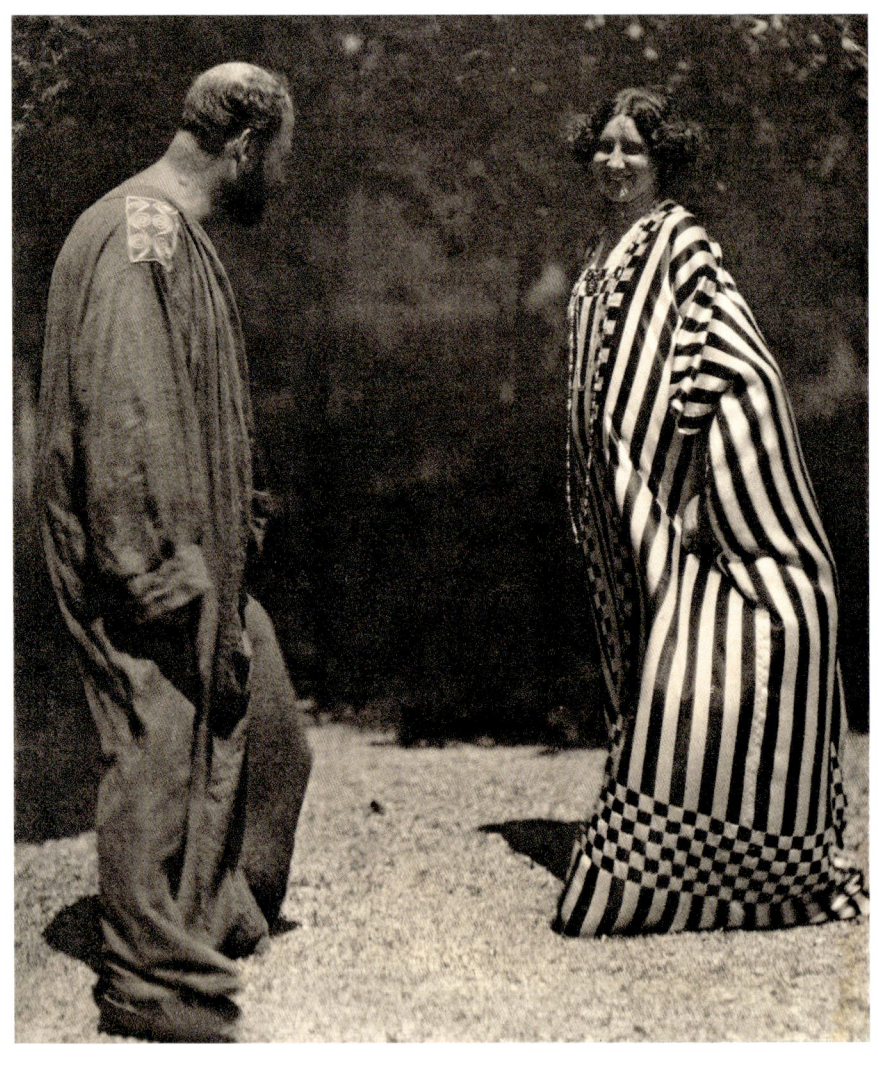

Heinrich Böhler, **Gustav Klimt and Emilie Flöge in Kammer on Lake Attersee**, c. 1909
Heliogravure. Imagno/Austrian Archives

that the artist's first forays into landscape painting commenced at the same time as his regular summer holidays in the Salzkammergut with the Flöge family – holidays that testify, moreover, to the very same desire to seek secluded privacy. Summer vacations in the fresh country air were a phenomenon of the urban bourgeoisie in the latter years of the 19th century. For the residents of Vienna, they meant 'escaping' either into the neighbouring regions of Semmering and Rax or to the lakes and mountains of the Salzkammergut, an area extending from Upper Austria to Salzburg. The Salzkammergut became all the more popular when the court around Emperor Franz Joseph also began spending the summers in Bad Ischl, at the heart of the region.

Klimt went to the Salzkammergut every summer from 1897 onwards, usually for several weeks, in the company of Emilie Flöge, her sister Helene Klimt – the widow of Gustav's brother Ernst, who had died in 1892 – Helene's young daughter, also called Helene (1892– 1980), and to whom Klimt was guardian, and the sisters' mother, Barbara Flöge (1840– 1927). It was generally the Flöges who organized the accommodation, which was arranged via friends or relatives and consisted of a suite of rooms, a whole floor or a small villa. The journey from Vienna was made by train; a carriage would be waiting at the station to take their luggage to their rented quarters (p. 375).

Klimt travelled – as was common in those days – with a large number of trunks and hampers. Painting utensils and wedged stretchers were stored in a separate chest that was sometimes sent on ahead. In numerous postcards that he wrote to Emilie, who had already departed for the Salzkammergut, his mood of happy anticipation is mingled with irritation over the irksome preparations still to be completed: "Studio trunk is packed – picture crate not yet received. Train carriage reserved. Looking forward to seeing you […]" (12 July 1907, cit. from Fischer 1987, p. 172). Elsewhere, he wrote: "Wednesday evening. After much exertion, have finished packing. Can't fit everything in. Parchment coming by post, as is paintbox. Gustav" (8 July 1908, cit. from Fischer 1987, p. 173).

St. Agatha and Golling, 1898 and 1899

Klimt and the Flöge family spent their first two joint summer holidays in the vicinity of Lake Hallstättersee and in Golling, south of Hallein, near Salzburg.

St. Agatha near Bad Goisern was the first of these holiday destinations. Easy to reach with the Westbahn railway line, this area around Lake Hallstättersee was also the summer home of the doyen of Austrian landscape painting, Rudolf von Alt (1812–1905). Emil Jakob Schindler (1842–1892) and his pupils, Carl Moll amongst them, also spent a few summers there in the early 1880s. Possibly inspired by his colleagues, Klimt, too, chose the region for a summer break. The year of his first such holiday, 1898, had brought him many responsibilities and commitments. It saw him elected president of the Secession for a second time and chairing the working committee organizing the Secession's first large-scale exhibition, staged that same year. It also witnessed the launch of the periodical *Ver Sacrum*, to which Klimt contributed several graphics. He was also greatly preoccupied during this entire period with his work on the Faculty paintings and the debate surrounding them.

A small group of Salzkammergut landscapes survive from Klimt's first stay in St. Agatha, including *After the Rain* (*Garden with Chickens in St. Agatha*; p. 410; Natter 2012, Cat. 111). This painting of a country orchard is characterized by a high horizon line and at the same time an open view of mountain slopes rising in the background. A number of fruit trees and deciduous trees seen in frontal view, their crowns extending in every case beyond the upper edge of the picture, provide the transition to the foreground, which – rather in the manner of a fold-out – is seen from above and grants generous space to the meadow with the trees and chickens. Klimt works with a limpid palette of light greens, greys and blacks, heightened and animated by the white of the chickens, the red accents of the cockscombs and the delicate, colourful flowers of the shrub in the foreground. Klimt shows us an idyllic Salzkammergut scene characterized by a fleeting effect created by the weather: damp with rain, the grass steams in the summer's warmth and a sort of 'glassy' veil lies across the landscape, causing the background to blur in the haze.

A comparison may be drawn at this point with three small landscapes that Klimt executed in the early 1880s and which offer a sort of prelude to his subsequent landscape practice: *Tranquil Pond* (Natter 2012, Cat. 9) and the two forest pictures *Forest Floor* and *Forest Interior* (Natter 2012, Cat. 10, 11). These sketch-like canvases employ the palette of browns and greens typical of these years. In their colourism and their restriction to a small, quasi-private detail of the landscape, they take up directly from Austrian Atmospheric Impressionism.

Klimt's noticeably new approach to landscape painting nearly twenty years later becomes all the more striking when set against these early, traditional works. Even if the subject of *After the Rain* ultimately derives from the tradition of the *paysage intime*, Klimt has here for the first time transformed it into a view of what he has experienced at first hand. His palette of bright colours mixed with white leaves the ochre shades of the 19th century far behind and testifies to his study of French and Belgian Impressionism. Klimt had now plainly distanced himself from the Atmospheric Impressionists not just in terms of his subject and palette, however, but also in his compositional principle of a simultan-eously frontal and perspective view – a principle that he would continue to develop over the following years. The system of double vision, of a shifting focal point, was one with

Apple Tree I (detail), c. 1912
(see ill. pp. 454/55)

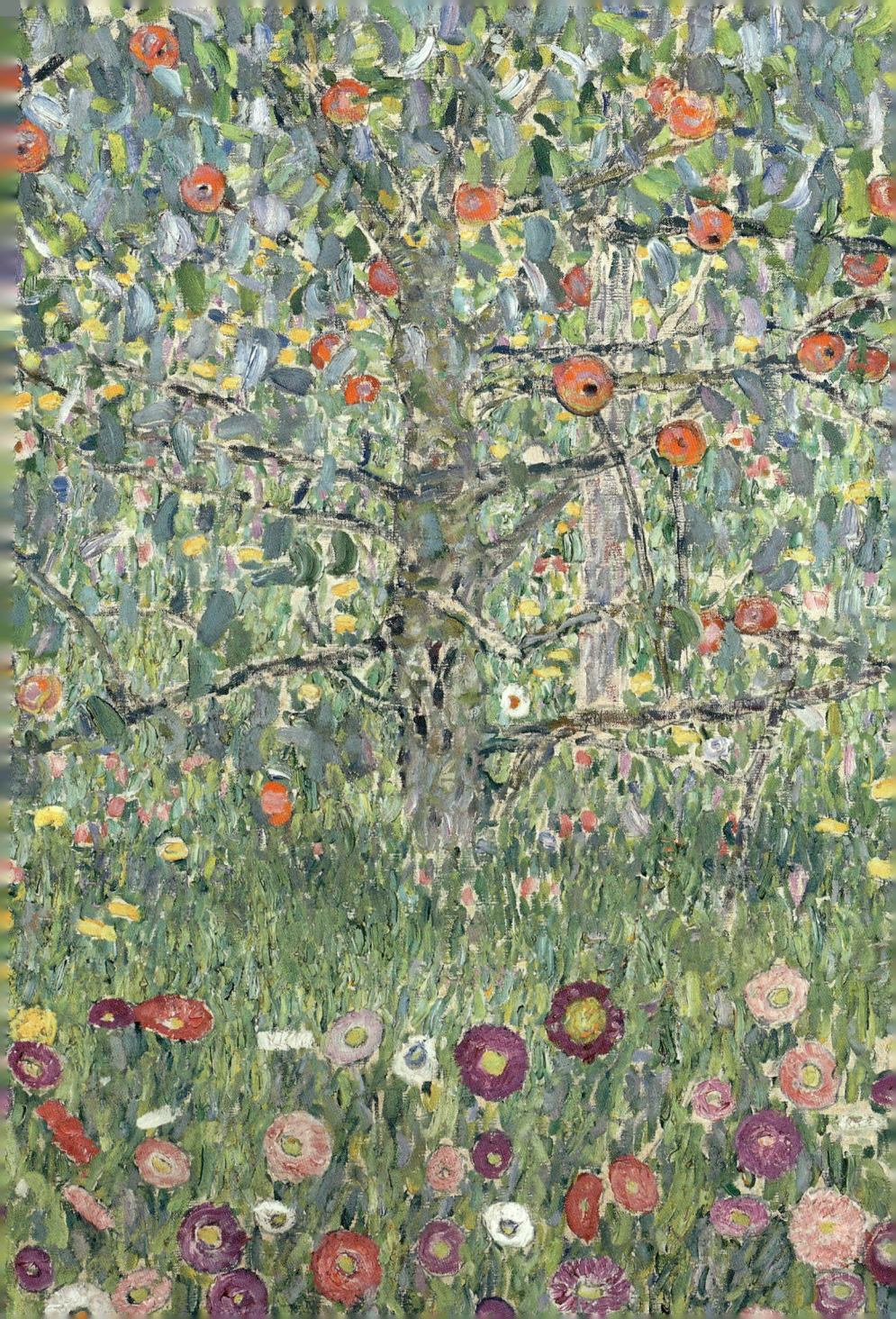

which Klimt was familiar probably first and foremost from *ukiyo-e*, Japanese woodblock prints, of which he personally owned a collection. In France, this specific feature of *ukiyo-e* was also taken up by the Nabis, above all, by Pierre Bonnard in the late 1890s. Klimt's deliberate construction of pictorial space using a high horizon and tree trunks as determining vertical elements, as employed in *After the Rain*, would likewise remain a typical feature of his landscapes. It is striking that the nature seen in Klimt's canvases from his first landscape pictures onwards, although experienced directly by the artist through the impressions of his senses, is a reconstructed one that has been artificially pieced together, so to speak.

In 1899 Klimt spent his second summer in the company of the Flöge family, this time at the spa resort of Golling, situated south of Hallein. Amongst the paintings produced during this holiday was *A Morning by the Pond* (p. 412; Natter 2012, Cat. 122), showing a view of the small Lake Egelsee. Here, for the first time, Klimt adopted the square format that he would favour for all his landscapes without exception from now on. As previously in *After the Rain*, he situates the horizon near the top of the picture and assigns a large part of the canvas to the main motif of the lake, which once again gives the impression of being a fold-out. The waters of the lake lie half in the shadow of the dark woods and half in the bright morning sun. *A Morning by the Pond* is undoubtedly the landscape picture in which Klimt comes closest to Symbolism. Devoid of all human presence and with the conifers reflected in its surface, the solitary pond shimmers in the morning sun. A mysterious atmosphere dominates the picture, issuing from the still landscape and the barely moving surface of the water. The palette is restricted to subdued tonal colours, brightened by the sunlight tinged with pink and white and the clouds mirrored in the water. Water – with its multiple connotations ranging from infinity and death to dreaming and unexpressed sensuality – dominates numerous works of Symbolist painting and literature. Within the sphere of painting, Symbolism's elusive, vague atmosphere imbued with a sense of yearning found its most potent expression in the work of Fernand Khnopff, whose portraits and landscapes were presented – *in extenso* and with great success – to the Viennese public at the 1898 Secession exhibition. Khnopff's *Still Waters*, today housed in the Österreichische Galerie Belvedere, was acquired for a Viennese private collection on that same occasion. Not least through his exploration in painting of his native Bruges, a city synonymous with water *per se*, Khnopff was strongly drawn to water, which he interpreted from a melancholy and mystical point of view. Klimt had had the opportunity to meet Khnopff in person when the "chief mystic from Brussels" – as he was described by Ludwig Hevesi, the

Forester's House in Weissenbach I (detail), 1914
(see ill. p. 463)

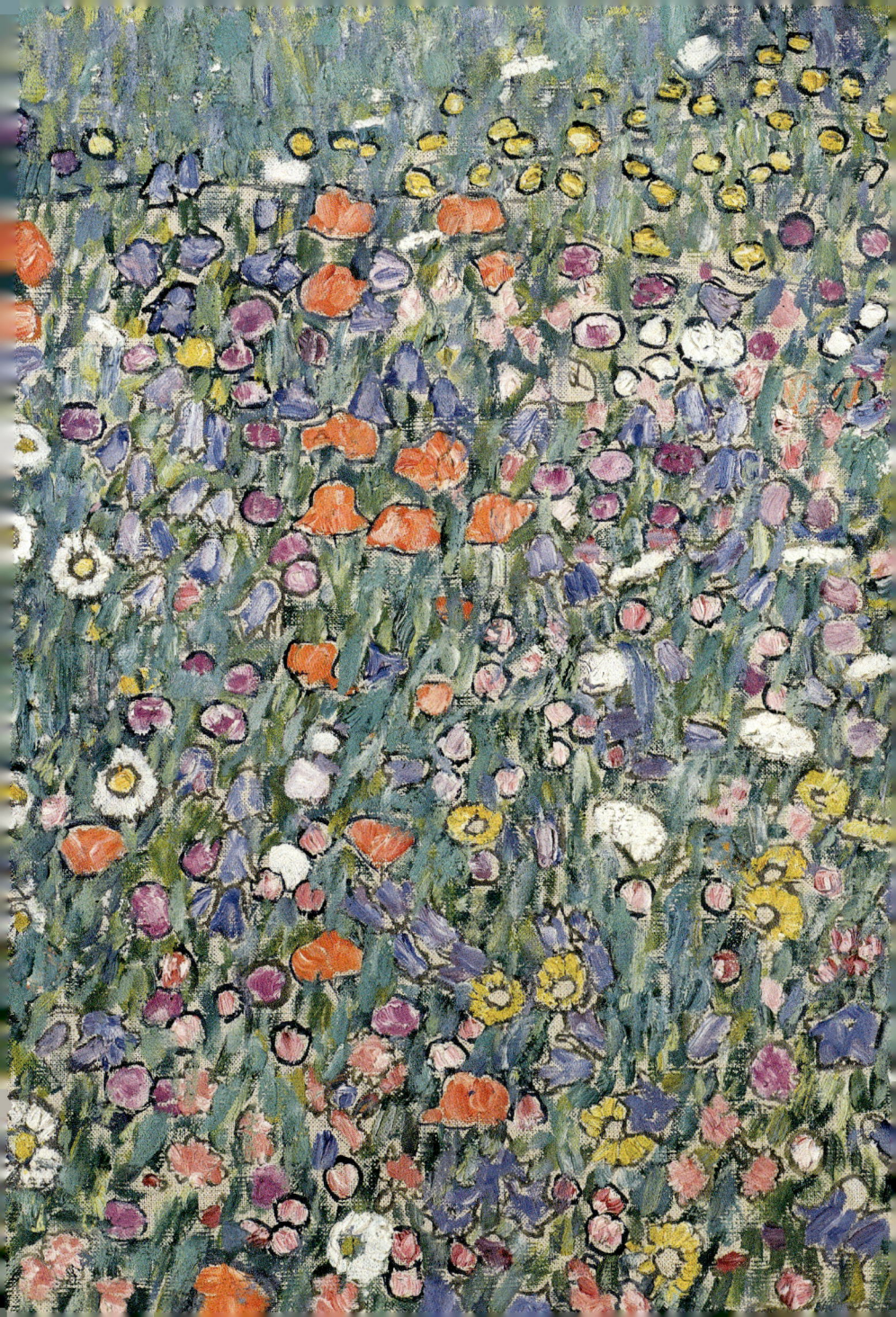

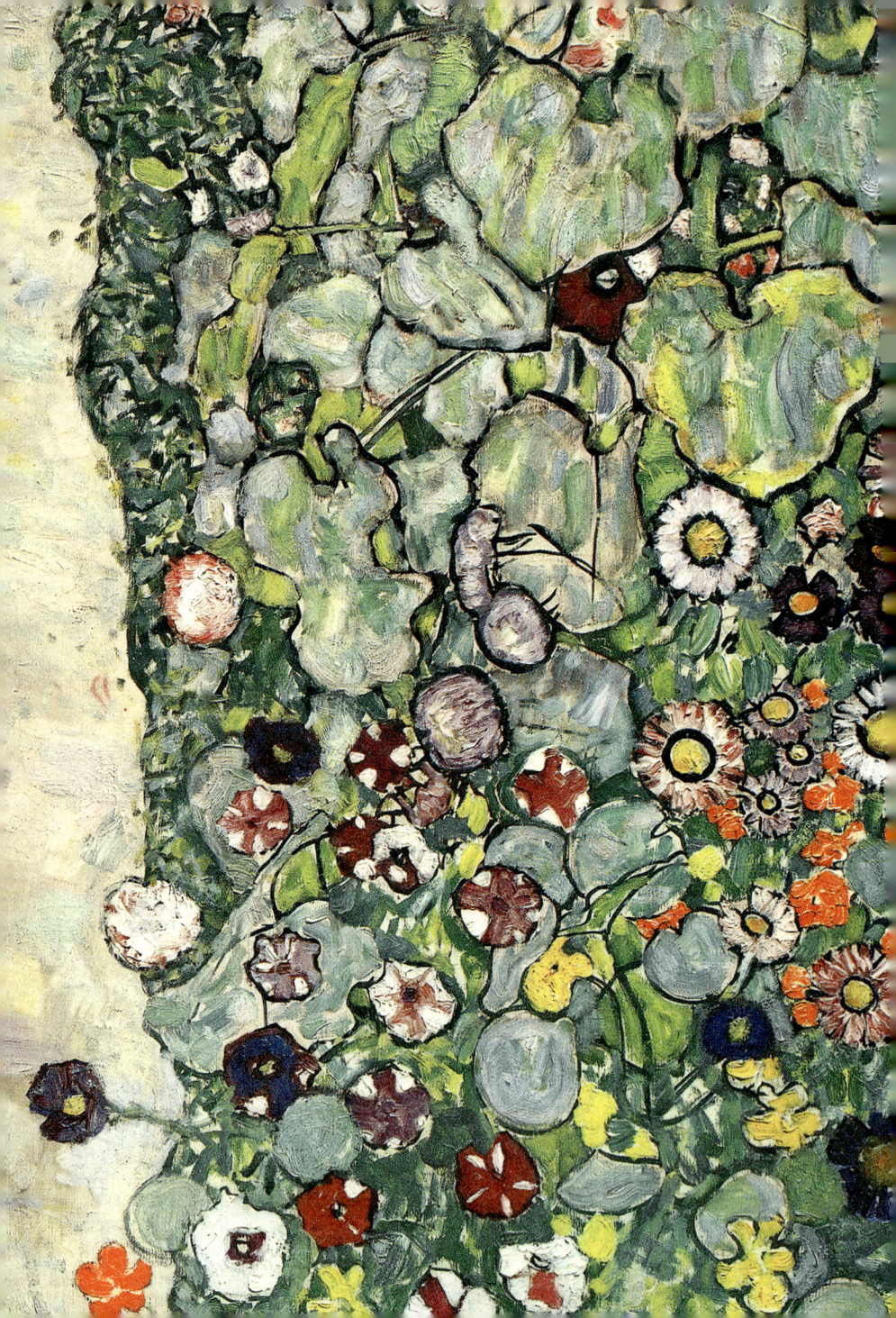

great critic of the early Secession (Hevesi 1906a, p. 30 f.) – visited Vienna for the Secession exhibition. Klimt came particularly close to Khnopff in his own, contemplative interpretation of landscape, and hence it is not surprising that his forest pictures from the period 1901–03 (pp. 422, 423, 424, 425; Natter 2012, Cat. 137, 138, 143, 160) should process the influence of Khnopff's mysterious, atmospheric pictures, removed from all sense of time.

In composition and mood, *A Morning by the Pond* is related to Claude Monet's *Morning on the Seine* series, painted in 1896/97 on the latter's studio boat on the River Seine near Giverny. These pictures by Monet, all approximately square, in each case show a view of the river in *contre-jour* and are composed around the reflection of the riverbank in waters that are still and empty of human presence.

Lake Attersee: Litzlberg, 1900–1907

From 1900 onwards Klimt and the Flöge family spent a few weeks every summer on Lake Attersee: from 1900 until 1907 in Litzlberg on the north-west shore, from 1908 until 1912 almost directly opposite, in Kammerl on the north-east side, in 1913 in Seewalchen at the northern tip and from 1914 until 1916 in Weissenbach at the south-east end of the lake. Klimt's 'classic' Lake Attersee landscapes – views of the lake, the gardens and the surrounding forests capturing the atmosphere of high summer in the Salzkammergut – were produced during his summers in Litzlberg.

In these first eight summers on Lake Attersee, Klimt and the Flöge family took lodgings at the Litzlberg brewery. This accommodation was probably arranged via relatives of Friedrich Paulick, with whom Klimt was acquainted. Paulick was a master cabinetmaker to the imperial court and the owner of a large villa in Seewalchen, where he regularly welcomed artists (Weidinger 2007a, p. 146 f.). The Flöges usually travelled to Lake Attersee ahead of Klimt, whose eagerness to hear all about life at the lake emerges from the many postcards that he wrote every year to Emilie Flöge. Even while he was still working in Vienna, he wanted to know about the weather, the quality of the water and the vegetation. It is clear in many of these postcards that he was replying to similar correspondence from Emilie: "[…] that the level of the lake is unusually low this year – bathing ought to improve later on. Apparently the hail destroyed the flowers – we'll discover some walks – your current solitude spoils the impression, I think – Imagine Litzelberg for the first time and enjoyed alone BEST GREETINGS GUS" (8 July 1908, cit. from Fischer 1987, p. 173).

Klimt was evidently inspired by his new surroundings. He enjoyed the outdoor lifestyle, swimming in the lake and taking long walks. It is possible that he even owned a

Garden Path with Chickens (detail), 1916
(see ill. p. 478)

boat, or at least that he and the Flöges always had one at their disposal for their summer holidays (pp. 468/69).

In the summer of 1900 Klimt spent a good three weeks in Litzlberg, from around 12 August to 3 September. During this time, he worked on at least five paintings, as he wrote in a letter to Vienna: "I have 5 pictures here in progress, a sixth canvas is still blank; perhaps I'll bring it home blank, too. The other 5 I think I shall be able to finish. A lake picture, a bull in a stall, a marshy pond, a large poplar and some young birches; these are the motifs of my pictures. My desire to work has, unfortunately, slackened off alarmingly as the work has progressed" (cit. from Nebehay 1978, p. 105 f.; Krug 2012a, no. 67). The landscape pictures referred to here can be confidently identified as *On Lake Attersee* (p. 415; Natter 2012, Cat. 132), *The Marshy Pond* (p. 413; Natter 2012, Cat. 128), *The Black Bull* (Natter 2012, Cat. 129), *The Large Poplar I* (p. 418; Natter 2012, Cat. 131) and *Farmhouse with Birch Trees* (p. 411; Natter 2012, Cat. 130) – works that rank among the most important examples of Klimt's landscape painting. The stylistic characteristics developed here would play a determining role in his painting of the following years, too.

In *The Marshy Pond* and *Farmhouse with Birch Trees*, Klimt takes up motifs that had already claimed his attention in previous summers. *The Marshy Pond* is thus a sort of reprise of *A Morning by the Pond* (p. 412), and *Farmhouse with Birch Trees* a further development of *After the Rain*. *Farmhouse with Birch Trees* demonstrates Klimt's progressive 're'-construction of nature on the flat surface of his picture: the horizon is situated close to the top of the painting, whereby the folded-out pictorial plane of the meadow is made even more prominent and is structured, like a system of coordinates, by the narrow verticals of the tree trunks, which are radically severed by the top of the canvas. *On Lake Attersee* (p. 415; Natter 2012, Cat. 132) represents another instance in which Klimt uses an unusual compositional angle to convey a more extreme and less familiar vision of nature. The picture – characterized by Hevesi as a "frame full of lake water" (Hevesi 1906a, p. 318) – is *de facto* a pure view of water that seems to extend boundlessly beyond the canvas. The surface of the water is interrupted only by Litzlberg Island, which projects into the picture on the high horizon like a dark patch of colour. The animated surface of the lake, seen against the light, shimmers in tiny 'sweeps' of the brush that grow increasingly smaller towards the horizon and gradually dissolve into one another. Appearing virtually colourless, almost unfinished, on the lightly and thinly primed foreground, they become green strokes before passing in the distance into a pastel-like, solid bluish violet.

Two years later Klimt returned to the same motif, in *Island in Lake Attersee* (p. 416; Natter 2012, Cat. 144). Litzlberg Island (its top here, too, sliced by the upper edge of the canvas) is now completely surrounded by the lake, which appears in a golden light. The composition – with the lake rising almost to the very top of the canvas – is bolder, the lake

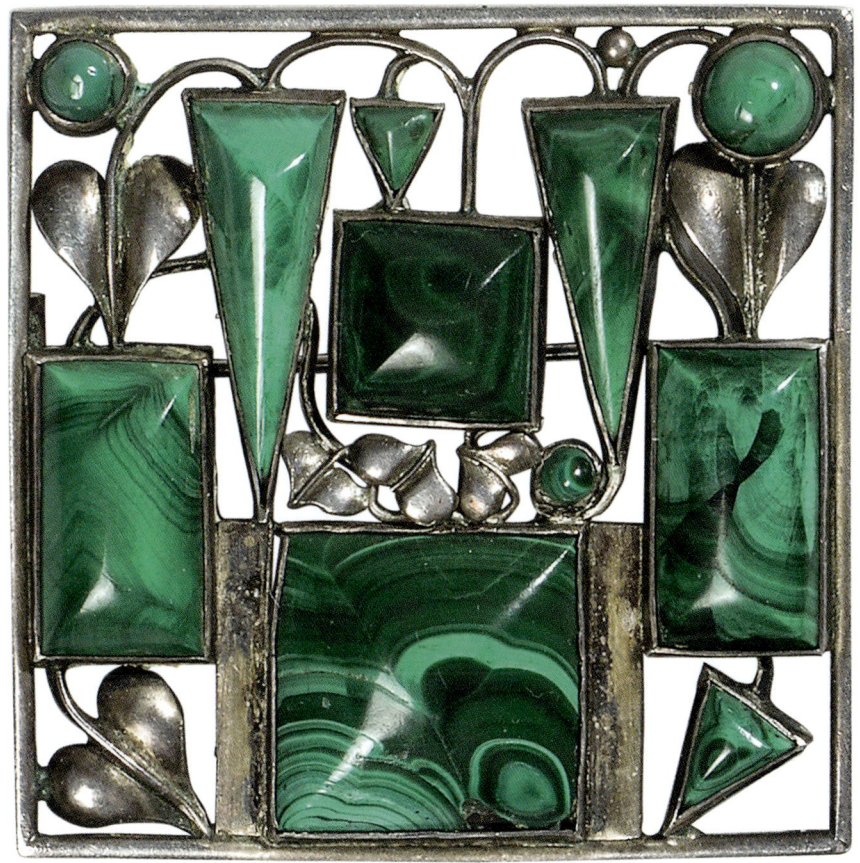

Josef Hoffmann, **Brooch owned by Emilie Flöge**, 1911
Manufacture: Wiener Werkstätte (model no. S2455)
Private collection

itsclf appears as if folded out, and the viewer is brought closer to the water. At the same time, the picture and the lake with its zones of light and shade seem to move from the background towards the foreground in even, concentric circles, in calm ripples continuing into infinity – an effect arising from the artist's representation of the small, dark island against the evening light.

Klimt uses the square pictorial format as an ideal framework within which to portray something that is happening in a static way, as it were. Thus both paintings play with the seemingly murmuring surface of the lake, whose equilibrium is barely disturbed amidst the subtle undulations of the waves but which at the same time transports a slight unease, as can be sensed in other artists' landscapes dating from this same period, such as those by Khnopff and the above-mentioned Seine pictures by Monet.

An impression of Klimt's first summer in Litzlberg – his more or less regular daily routine, his love of the lake, the pleasure he took in long walks in the surrounding countryside, but also the way in which he worked – can be gained from photographs and from the letters that the artist regularly addressed to Marie Zimmermann (1879–1975), mother of his sons Gustav and Otto. (This correspondence broke off after the summer of 1903; subsequent summers may have followed a similar pattern, but no documents relating to these later years have yet come to light.) In one such letter, probably written in August 1902, Klimt went into particular detail and set out what he called the regular way in which he spent his days, which were taken up with painting, swimming and relaxing: "I get up early in the morning – usually about 6 o'clock, sometimes a bit earlier or a bit later – if the weather is good I go into the nearby forest – there I paint a little beech wood (with the sun shining) mixed with some conifers, that takes until 8 o'clock, then breakfast, afterwards a dip in the lake, undertaken very cautiously – on top of that again a bit of painting, if the sun is shining, a lake picture, if the weather is overcast, a landscape from the window of my room – sometimes I don't paint in the morning at all and study in my Japanese books instead – outdoors. That takes me up to midday, after lunch comes a brief nap or reading – until time for tea – before or after tea a second swim in the lake, not on a regular basis, but usually. After tea comes painting again – a large poplar at dusk with a storm brewing – now and then instead of painting in the evening comes a bit of bowling in a neighbouring village – but seldom – dusk falls – the evening meal – then early to bed and again early to rise in the morning. […] The days go by in the above-mentioned way and 2 weeks have already passed, the shorter half of the holiday is over, one is then really glad to get back to Vienna" (cit. from Nebehay 1978, p. 109 f.; Krug 2012a, no. 99).

As well as providing a detailed description of Klimt's daily routine, the letter reveals that the artist painted his landscapes both outdoors directly in front of his motif – the beech wood, for example – and indoors, looking out the window. According to Klimt's niece Helene, who always spent the holidays with the family on Lake Attersee, the painter used to hide his easel under the leaves beneath the trees, so as not to have to keep carrying it back and forth between his lodgings and the woods or the garden (Nebehay 1969, p. 452 and note 6, p. 456).

The Sunflower (detail), 1907
(see ill. p. 439)

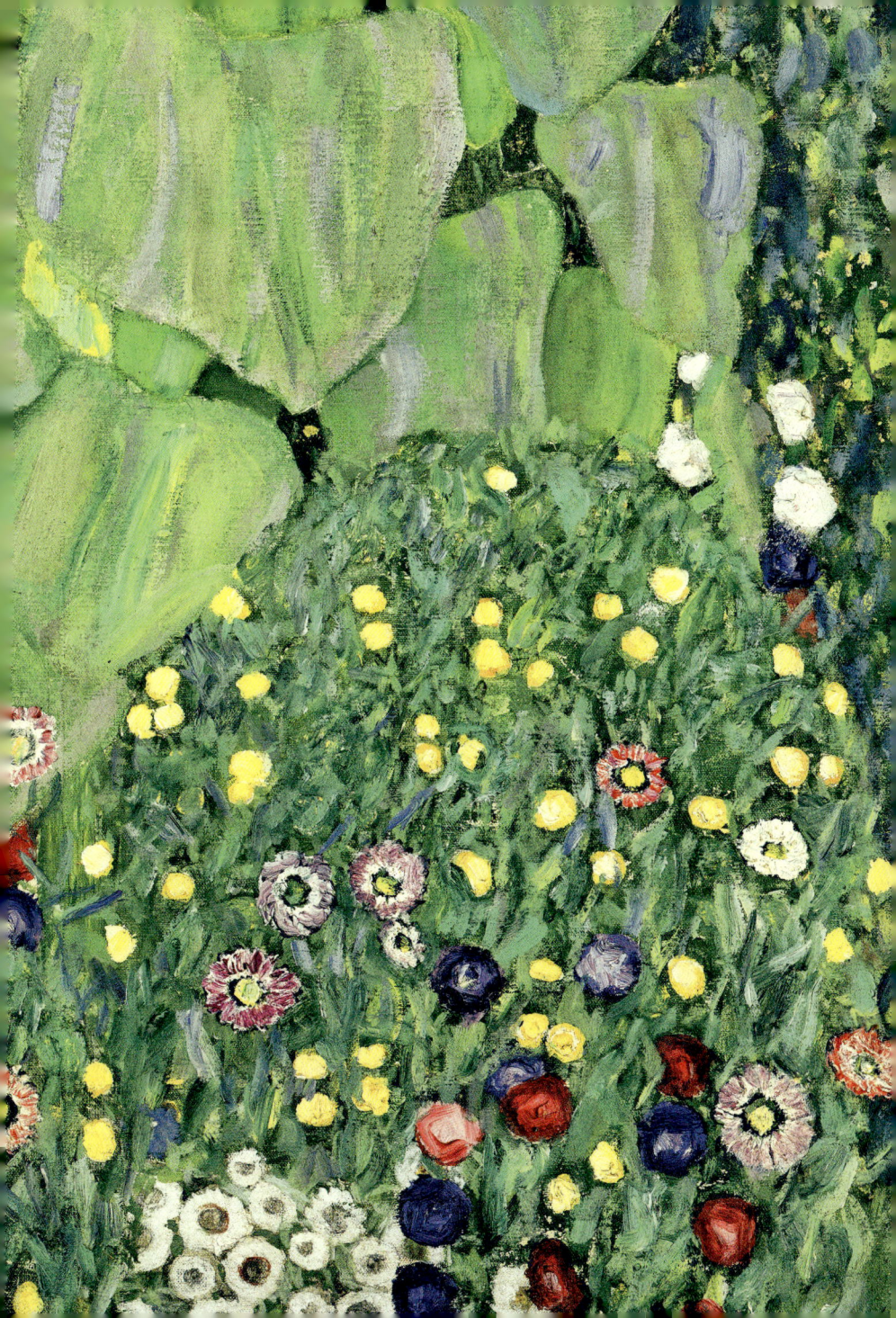

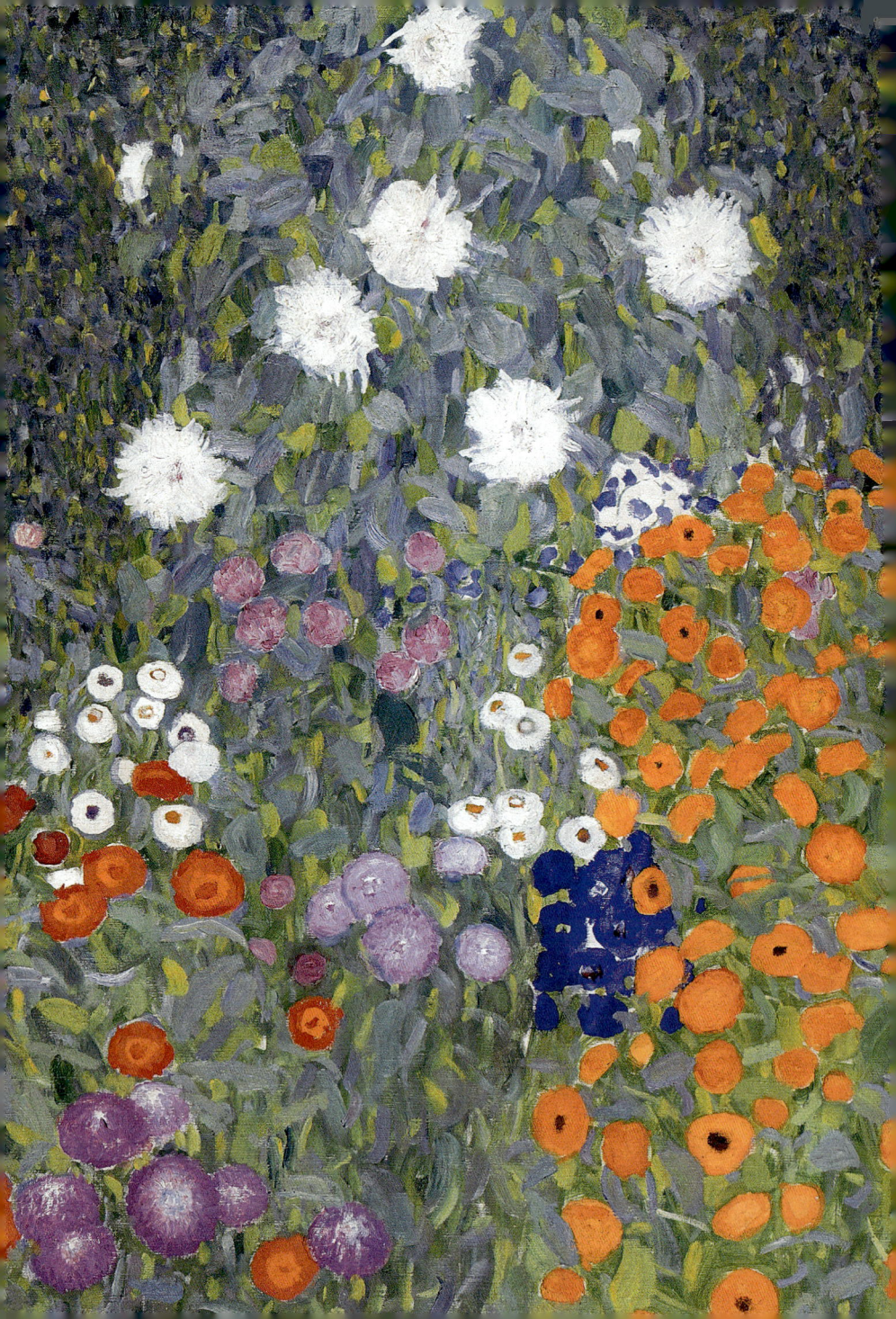

The Large Poplar II (p. 419; Natter 2012, Cat. 147), the picture mentioned in Klimt's letter, numbers amongst the few works in which he captured a turbulent meteorological mood – a gathering thunderstorm as is typical of the summer weather in the Salzkammergut. Above all, however, *The Large Poplar II* represents a major development in Klimt's exploration of post-Impressionism. In November 1903, in his review of Klimt's Secession exhibition, Hevesi characterized the massive tree as dotted with "trout spots": "[…] A very dark picture – seemingly. A massive poplar rises on the right, quite black – seemingly. On closer inspection, it is namely full of trout spots, if I may put it that way. It is speckled with yellow, blue, green and purple, but looks black. […] And the storm that is gathering from the low horizon to the high zenith is also not a black cloud, but a veritable mosaic of angular cloud fragments […] recalling asphalt, sulphur, lava, ash and the like […]" (Hevesi 1906a, p. 451). *The Large Poplar II* indeed sees Klimt for the first time employing brushstrokes that are short and close together: powerful, luminous orange is combined with purples and greens to achieve a sense of an eerie flickering in the leaves rustling in the wind of the looming storm. Klimt has here adapted the post-Impressionist technique of using dense, isolated, subtly gradated strokes of paint that appear as a solid mixture of colour in the viewer's eye. He was certainly familiar with the works of the Pointillist Théo van Rysselberghe (1862–1926), who had exhibited with the Vienna Secession in 1899, and likewise those of Paul Signac (1863–1935), featured in the Secession the following year, as well as of the Divisionist Giovanni Segantini, to whom the Secession also devoted a solo show in 1900. It is all the more striking that Klimt should appropriate from all these trends only their technique – which he would develop continuously over the following years to the point of painterly bravura. The theory underlying post-Impressionism, with its insistence upon the use of pure colours and upon the adherence to rules governing the juxtaposition of these colours on the canvas, seems to have been of no consequence to Klimt either here or later in his oeuvre.

In the letter cited above, Klimt also writes that he is painting "a little beech wood (with the sun shining)" – a forest interior lit by the morning sun, whose close-growing beech trunks are seen against the reddish-brown leaves of the forest floor rising to a high horizon and the bright strip of sky above. This painting, *Beech Forest I* (p. 422; Natter 2012, Cat. 143), belongs to a small group of views of the deciduous and coniferous forests around Litzlberg that Klimt produced between 1901 and 1903, and which also includes *Pine Forest I* (p. 424; Natter 2012, Cat. 137), *Pine Forest II* (p. 425; Natter 2012, Cat. 138) and *Birch Forest* (*Beech Forest*; p. 423; Natter 2012, Cat. 160). While Klimt comes very

Cottage Garden (detail), 1907
(see ill. pp. 436/37)

close in these atmospheric pictures to Symbolist forest views, he also reflects the eastern European tradition of lyrically melancholy depictions of deciduous woods, as found in particular in Russian Impressionism. The composition of *Beech Forest I* is once again structured by the many tree trunks cut off by the top of the canvas – a coppice of verticals that is exceptional in offering a view of the horizon.

Birch Forest of 1903 appears not unlike a detail taken from *Beech Forest I*. The birch trunks set against the dappled russet ground resemble flat cut-outs negating all sense of organic growth. We might almost ask whether this decoratively two-dimensional translation of a forest owes something to the impressions of the Ravenna mosaics that Klimt had seen in spring 1903. Although the influence of these Early Christian mosaics is more apparent in Klimt's portraiture than in his landscape painting, it can nevertheless be found here, too – in the stylized *Golden Apple Tree*, for example, likewise dating from 1903 (Natter 2012, Cat. 154), and later in individual details of the frieze for the Palais Stoclet in Brussels (Ch. III).

It is also possible to imagine Klimt selecting the composition of *Birch Forest* with the aid of the "viewfinder" mentioned in his letter of August 1902 to Marie Zimmermann, cited at the start of this chapter: "I […] looked […] with my 'viewfinder', that is, a hole cut in a cardboard lid, for motifs of the landscapes I want to paint, and found a great deal, or – depending on how you see it – nothing" (cit. from Nebehay 1978, p. 108 f.; Krug 2012a, no. 98). Klimt included a sketch of the "viewfinder" in the same letter, showing it as a square hole in a larger piece of cardboard, just as he had described it. To make the illustration clearer, he filled the imaginary pictorial field with the rough sketch of a possible landscape. Klimt probably employed a viewfinder above all in the landscapes that he painted from around 1903 onwards, in which he gradually started to isolate individual motifs from their overall context, such as a meadow, a forest or a garden. The pictorial construction of elevated horizon and fold-out foreground motif thereby remained for the moment unchanged.

At the same time, Klimt's choice of motifs can be seen tending in a new direction. His pictures no longer show Lake Attersee and the surrounding woods and forests, but nature as cultivated by human hands: orchards and cottage gardens and the individual trees and plants within them. These would subsequently be joined, too, by the man-made works of architecture around the lake. The inhabitants of the landscape continued to remain invisible, however.

Gustav Klimt and Emilie Flöge in the garden of the Villa Oleander, 1910
In Kammerl on Lake Attersee
Photograph. Imagno/Austrian Archives

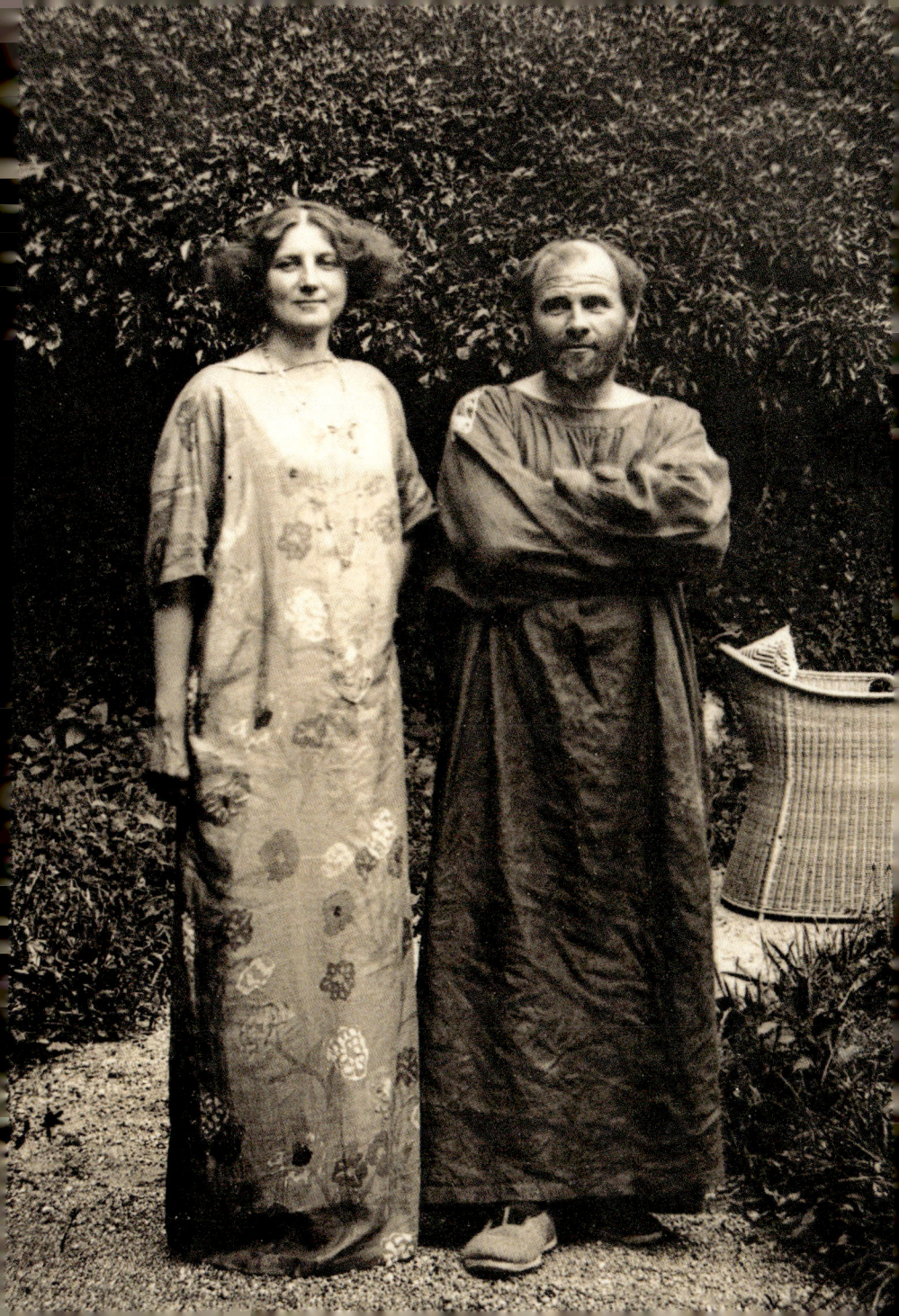

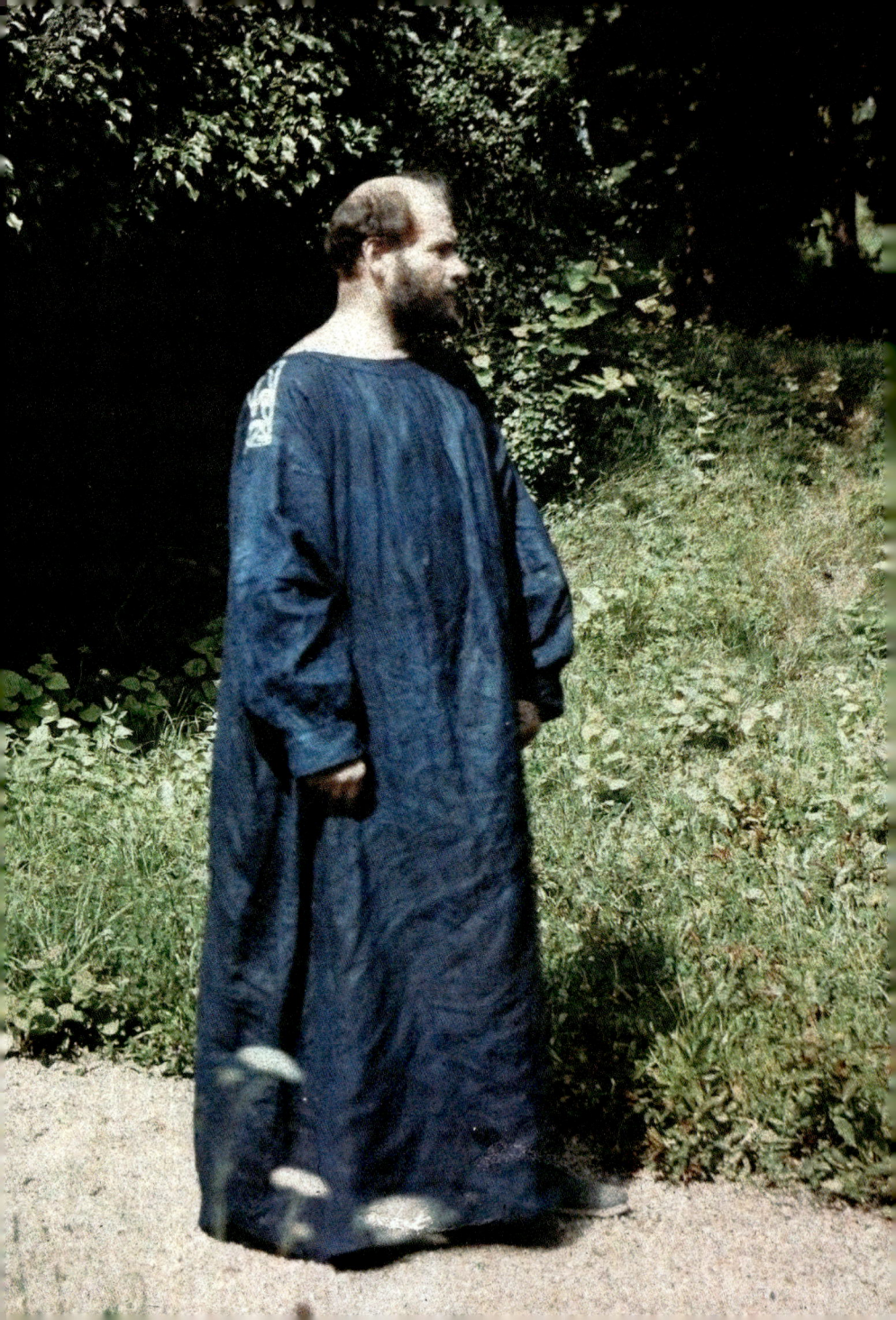

In his latter years in Litzlberg, from 1904 to 1907, Klimt produced particularly atmospheric summer landscapes in the shape of *Roses beneath Trees* (*Roses*; pp. 372, 428; Natter 2012, Cat. 165), the paintings known as *Orchard* (pp. 432/33; Natter 2012, Cat. 167) and *Flowering Meadow* (pp. 404, 430; Natter 2012, Cat. 166), and *Poppy Field* (*Poppies in Bloom*; pp. 408/09, 431; Natter 2012, Cat. 172). Employing his Pointillist-inspired technique of small, short brushstrokes, delicately laying down the paint almost like a glaze over a thin ground, he created views of luxuriant vegetation in the radiant summer heat. Meadows composed of countless colourful dots and strokes unfold across the pictorial plane like a pattern and seem to extend far beyond (and above) the pictorial field as well as into its depths. Upon closer inspection, they form different areas of the garden, as well as paths, tree crowns and individual flowers. It is a striking fact that Klimt continues to avoid directed lighting – his evenly illuminated landscapes appear timeless and seem to repose within themselves – an impression reinforced by the harmonious balance imparted by the square format.

Roses beneath Trees deserves a special mention for the fact that a pencil sketch with a rough compositional study can be associated with this painting (Vienna, Belvedere, inv. no. ÖG 8508–55). With the exception of a sketch for *Gastein* (Natter 2012, Cat. 233), this very cursorily sketched design is currently the only known preliminary drawing by Klimt that can be specifically assigned to a finished landscape. It has regularly prompted discussions over the question of whether other such sketches were perhaps destroyed in 1945 in the fire that swept the Flöge apartment (where numerous sketchbooks belonging to Klimt's estate were housed), or whether in fact Klimt did not generally make preparatory drawings for his landscapes. Only in the sketchbook of 1917, published by Alice Strobl (Strobl, vol. 3, 1984, esp. pp. 244–247), do we find – in addition to the above-mentioned drawing of Gastein – another, very summarily laid out sketch, impossible to assign to a specific painting, showing a mountainside reflected in a lake, together with a small number of drawings of individual farmhouses and a few studies of flowers. We know from Klimt's niece Helene that the artist, "pausing briefly while out for a stroll, frequently recorded rapid impressions of the landscape in a little notebook" (Nebehay 1969, pp. 38 and 452). Klimt probably laid out his pictures in rough on the canvas itself, by means of a brush and thinned paint and sometimes also in charcoal: in the case of the *Orchard* in Pittsburgh, for example, such underdrawing can be clearly made out in the path in the background and the small rosebush in front of it to the left.

Friedrich G. Walker, **Gustav Klimt in his blue painter's smock**, 1913
In the garden of the Villa Paulick in Seewalchen on Lake Attersee
Lumière autochrome plate. Imagno/Austrian Archives

In summer 1906 – during which Klimt does not seem to have commenced a single picture – the gardens around the brewery in Litzlberg served as the setting for another of Klimt's activities. It was here that the unique series of photographs of Emilie Flöge was taken, probably by Klimt, in which she poses in the wide, colourful Reform dresses that she herself had designed. Some of these photos were reproduced in the magazine *Deutsche Kunst und Dekoration* and so became very well known.

Captured as she turned on the spot and transformed into a sunflower or a cottage garden, Emilie Flöge appears in a small group of 'anthropomorphic' flower paintings from 1907/08 (pp. 387, 439; 388, 436/37; 371, 440/41; Natter 2012, Cat. 171, 173, 180). Set against a dense carpet of blossoming vegetation, *The Sunflower* (Natter 2012, Cat. 171) towers upwards from a broad plinth of wild flowers. From its position in the immediate foreground, it dominates the centre of the composition. The compact background, which is likewise brought close to the viewer, serves to monumentalize the sunflower yet further – a compositional solution and handling of space that are new and highly unusual for Klimt and which also characterize the pictures *Cottage Garden* (Natter 2012, Cat. 173) and *Cottage Garden with Sunflowers* (Natter 2012, Cat. 180). Klimt has here also adopted what, for him, is a new manner of painting, placing his colours – which are now darker in hue and composed primarily of saturated greens and reds – beside and on top of each other in a cloaking density and building up the flowers with several brushstrokes. We no longer find the light brushstroke that 'drew' a bright red poppy with a single movement of the hand, so to speak. The lightness of the Litzlberg meadow and garden pictures now seems outdated and a new phase in Klimt's painting has dawned.

Lake Attersee: Kammerl, 1908–1912

In summer 1908 the Flöge family and Gustav Klimt rented the Villa Oleander in the Kammerl district of Kammer on the north-east side of Lake Attersee, due south of Schörfling and almost directly opposite Litzlberg on the west shore. The reasons for seeking accommodation in a different part of the Attersee region were probably bound up with the growing popularity of the Litzlberg shore amongst summer holidaymakers and Klimt's equally increasing need for tranquillity and seclusion: the Klimt/Flöge party would have found the less populated area around Kammer more attractive, even if Klimt evidently somewhat missed the ambiance of Litzlberg, as emerges in a postcard of 1910 to his brother-in-law Julius Zimpel (1896–1925): "[…] Am feeling very well here – Litzlberg is more attractive – Kammer too is much prettier than on this rather 'inane' card. Best wishes. Gustav" (Koja 2002a, p. 204). From photographs and postcards dating from these Kammerl years, however, we may nevertheless conclude that the carefree 'summer life' of the Litzlberg era continued as before. Swimming, walking and taking a boat out on the water remained features of Klimt's daily routine. A letter written from Vienna to Emilie Flöge on Lake Attersee in July 1910 conveys the artist's palpable sense of happy anticipation: "[…] You should fetch the 'canoe' […] 'the best friend'. – The ship, the ship, can't you see it? [Klimt may here be quoting from Richard Wagner's *Tristan and Isolde – trans.*] Do we already have a new ship? – or don't we need it? Warmest wishes Gustav" (cit. from Fischer 1987, p. 180).

Apart from *Cottage Garden with Sunflowers,* Klimt probably produced only one other painting in 1908, *Kammer Castle on Lake Attersee I,* a view of the architectural complex – originally medieval, but remodelled in the Baroque era – of Kammer Castle, which Klimt painted from the Villa Oleander boathouse (p. 445; Natter 2012, Cat. 181). The lake façade of the squat castle with its massive hipped roof is seen parallel to the pictorial plane, as are the side wing of the castle complex, the little boathouse and the tall, flowering hedge that grows practically straight up out of the lake and ties together the additively placed components of the picture. Large, pale yellow expanses of wall alternate with elements of vegetation, such as the bushes and slender poplars, composed of many small parts. Klimt employs a reduced palette over shades of green, supplemented with ochre and a little white; the picture's only note of strong dark red is sounded by the roofs of Seewalchen church. The reflections of architecture and vegetation in the smooth surface of the lake serve above all to anchor the vertical elements – church tower, poplars and the pale sections of the castle buildings – within the composition. In *Kammer Castle on Lake Attersee I,* a change thereby manifests itself within Klimt's painting, one marked by a solidification of the composition and by structures strictly parallel to the pictorial plane.

The "viewfinder", a piece of cardboard with a square hole
From Gustav Klimt's estate. Private collection

It is probable that, in the summer of 1908, Klimt also started using a telescope as a means of arranging his compositions: he now zoomed in on his motif from a greater distance in order to record it in the square format that he preferred. In a similar fashion to the viewfinder that Klimt used for motifs closer at hand, this optical aid regulated nature and transformed her elements into building blocks that the artist would later 'reconstruct' on his canvas. Novotny was the first to propose – albeit in reference to the views of Unterach (pp. 472/73, 475, 476/77; Natter 2012, Cat. 214, 215, 223) executed several years later, in 1915/16 – that Klimt actually painted from a boat on the lake, with the additional aid of opera glasses (Novotny 1969, p. 452); Dobai reiterated this idea, but suspected that Klimt used a telescope (pp. 456/57) to coordinate his motif (Dobai 1981, p. 32); building upon these observations, Weidinger suggested that Klimt had probably used a telescope in conjunction with opera glasses as early as 1908 for the views of Kammer Castle (Weidinger 1992a, p. 55).

The structured composition parallel to the pictorial plane seen in *Kammer Castle on Lake Attersee I* can also be observed in the views of Kammer Castle painted over the following years (*Kammer Castle on Lake Attersee II, III* and *IV*; pp. 444, 445, 446; Natter 2012, Cat. 187, 190, 191) and in those of the *Park at Kammer Castle* (p. 447; Natter 2012, Cat. 186). *The Park* (pp. 434/35; Natter 2012, Cat. 185) is dominated by the vast crown of a tree, extending beyond the edges of the picture and fusing – like the sum of the canopies of all the trees – into a flat tapestry. Only in the area of the tree trunks along the bottom of the picture, which is composed in a succession of horizontal zones, does the copse open up, admitting light and, with it, a sense of space and distance. As such, *The Park* offers a clear contrast to the two Litzlberg landscapes (pp. 431, 432/33), which fan out in a broad sweep across the pictorial plane, continuing beyond the sides of the picture but nonetheless conveying a strong sense of spatial recession and offering a view into the distance above their high horizon line at the top. Alongside his tectonically built, structured landscapes with a solid foreground or an enclosed composition, Klimt would return again and again to this device of a wide, open meadow stretching like a pattern beyond the edge of the picture.

Up to this point, Klimt's stylistic development had unfolded by and large very evenly. Early influences from the Pointillism of Signac and Rysselberghe had been revitalized and reinforced by the large Impressionism exhibition mounted at the Secession in 1903, but had triggered no major changes in Klimt's approach to landscape. The same can be said of the Ravenna mosaics that Klimt also saw in 1903, and whose impact upon his landscape pictures was likewise only limited. By the same token, his introduction to the young Egon Schiele in 1907 for the time being led neither to stylistic modifications nor

Garden Landscape with Rounded Mountaintop (Parsonage Garden) (detail), 1916
(see ill. p. 479)

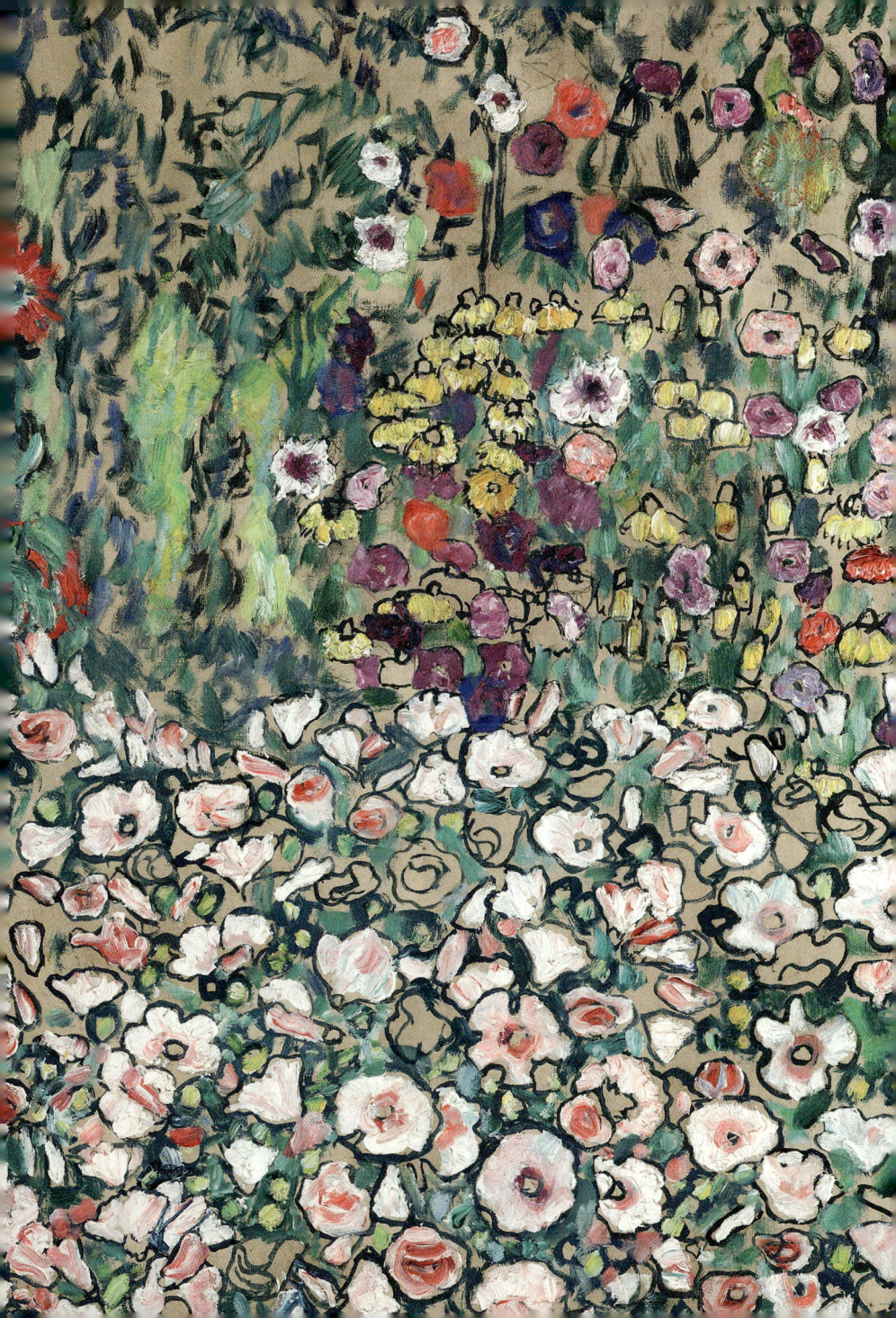

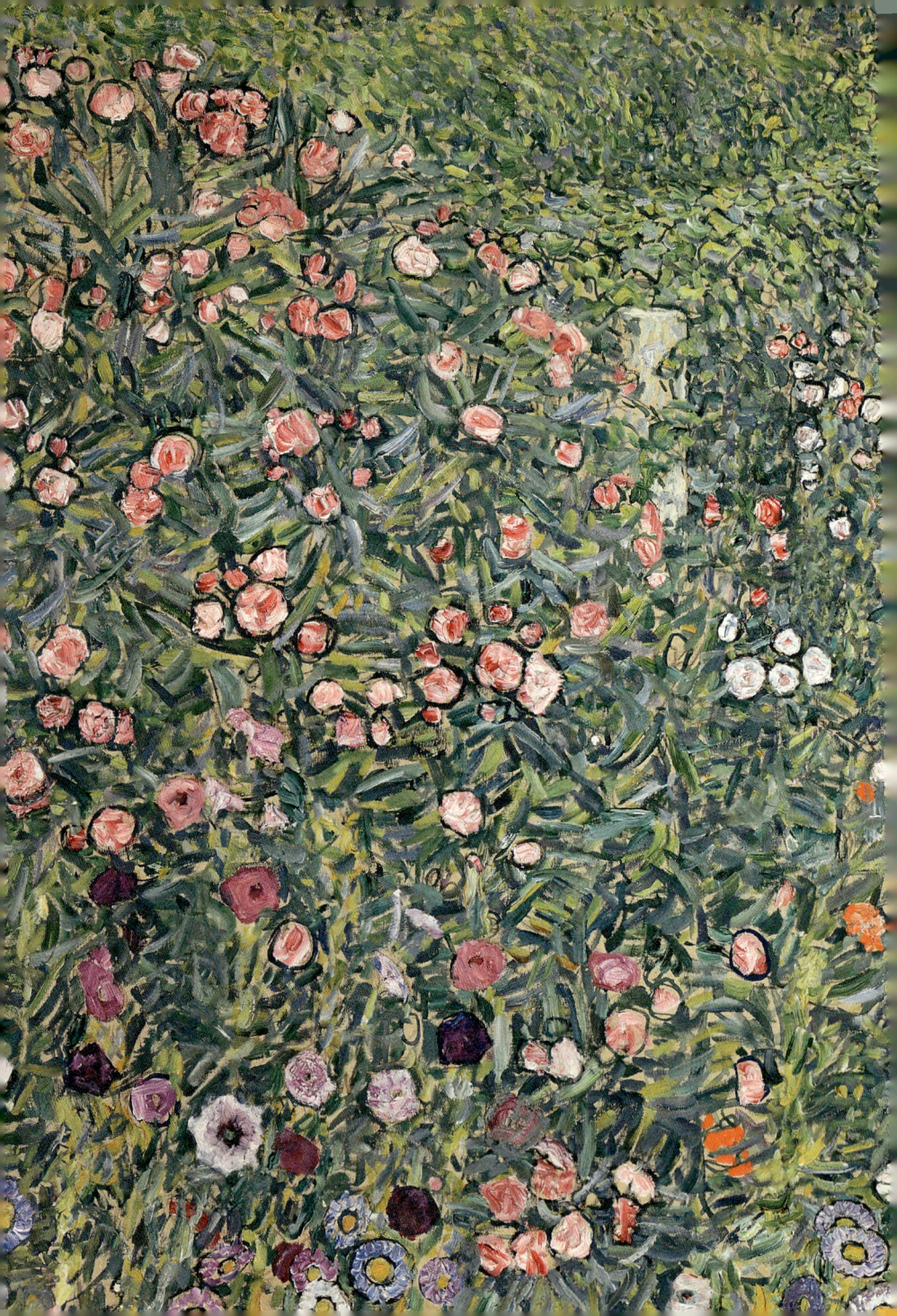

to changes in the expression of Klimt's painting, no more than did the impressions that he probably gathered on his trip to Paris and Spain with Carl Moll in 1909. It is true that, in the period after 1909, a gradual advance of colour as a design element can be observed in Klimt's painting – a development undoubtedly fuelled by his exposure to Henri Matisse and the Fauves, whose pictures – like the classically structured paintings of Paul Cézanne (1839–1906) and the more recent Cubist works of Pablo Picasso – Klimt would undoubtedly have seen. However, no written documentation exists in which Klimt shares his thoughts on these impressions and, in reply to questions from friends about this "new painting" and about how he had liked Paris, Klimt is said to have replied simply that an "awful lot of painting" went on there (Roessler 1924, p. 119, cit. from Nebehay 1969, p. 499). He was equally laconic and brief when he wrote, in his post-cards to Emilie Flöge from Madrid, that even Velázquez had proved a disappointment: "Yesterday went to Prado – very nice! – and Velasquez [sic] is really disappointing! […]" (26 October 1909; cit. from Fischer 1987, p. 178). He was impressed, on the other hand, by El Greco: "[…] Greco is also magnificent!" (28 October 1909 from Toledo; ibid.).

In summer 1911 Klimt probably spent only ten days or so at Lake Attersee. It was the year in which he completed the frieze for the Palais Stoclet in Brussels: together with Fritz Waerndorfer, he had travelled to Brussels for its installation and from there had visited London. He had also made a short trip to Rome in spring to attend the Esposizione internazionale d'arte. On Lake Attersee, Klimt worked on just one picture: *Upper Austrian Farmhouse*, a wooden farmhouse with small shuttered windows hidden behind and beneath flourishing fruit trees (pp. 448/49; Natter 2012, Cat. 194). The bluish grey of the wooden cladding, bleached by the sun, determines the overall tone of the picture, which is composed around a narrow palette of harmoniously balanced blues, greys and greens. In the foreground, densely placed brushstrokes combine to produce a summer meadow brightly dotted with red and yellow flowers. A large pear tree, functioning as a repoussoir motif, opens up the view of the house. As so often with Klimt, nature – her sap at full height – seems to grow beyond the confines of the pictorial space. But the structure and the overall composition are now denser and conceived in terms of strata lying one above the other, in a similar fashion to *The Park*.

These tendencies may be seen as an overture to the unexpectedly Expressionistic master-pieces that Klimt painted the following year, and which include *Avenue in Front of Kammer Castle* (pp. 450/51; Natter 2012, Cat. 201), *Apple Tree I* (pp. 454/55; Natter 2012, Cat. 199), *Orchard with Roses* (p. 453; Natter 2012, Cat. 198) and *Country Garden with Calvary* (p. 452;

Italian Garden Landscape (detail), 1913
(see ill. p. 462)

Natter 2012, Cat. 200), this last destroyed by fire in 1945 at Immendorf Castle. *Avenue in Front of Kammer Castle*, in particular, introduces a new approach to landscape: loading his brush with paint, Klimt all of a sudden introduces thick daubs of black, lemon yellow and purple into the picture. Thus the boughs of the trees are outlined in black, while the trunks are rendered in a bluish grey combined with shrill yellows and occasional reddish purple lights. The unusually 'radical' composition – with its strong sense of perspective conveyed by the avenue of trees leading away into the background, their dark crowns forming a peaked tunnel and so reinforcing the sense of spatial recession – is matched by Klimt's surprising choice of colour: luminous yellowish greens that stand in almost garish contrast to the energetically applied bluish greens and purples of the trees. Here, abruptly and un-announced, we see the launch of a specifically Klimtian style of Expressionism.

In this instance, too, there seem to have been no immediate triggering factors. Klimt was of course inspired, on the one hand, by Vincent van Gogh (1853–1890) and his unconventional colour combinations: these had already be seen in Vienna several years earlier in a Secession exhibition of 1903, and subsequently – and even more importantly – in a major exhibition hosted by the Galerie Miethke in 1906. But Klimt's (developmental) step may also have been a belated response to the colourful painting of the Fauves, to which Klimt was introduced at the latest in 1909 in Paris. Whatever the case, it is strik-ing to note that in this case, too, Klimt did not translate such new stimuli into his own language of form until later – a time lapse that would seem to be characteristic of his art.

In summer 1912 Klimt also produced *Apple Tree I* (pp. 454/55), one of the most power-ful, 'virile' and vibrantly colourful of all his paintings of the natural landscape. The small, bright red apples stand out clearly against the bluish-green tree, which once again bursts the bounds of the picture. The crown of the tree itself, as dictated by nature, echoes the shape of its fruits. Klimt renders the foliage in vigorous strokes of paint over a thinly primed canvas and uses his brush to draw, in dark lines, the supporting framework of branches shimmering though the leaves. The trunk, shaded greyish green, rises as a verti-cal ordering element perpendicular to the 'horizon' of the meadow. Klimt's embrace of such ordering systems, beginning with his 'retreat' into the square format, can be observed from his early landscapes onwards. Another painting from this same summer, *Orchard with Roses* (*Rose Garden*; p. 453), also employs a classically ordered arrangement: the view of the riotously flourishing and colourful garden is bordered by a 'steep' path on the left-hand edge of the picture, which directs our gaze upwards and at the same time appears as the remnant of a system of coordinates – the remnant, because the corresponding horizontal is dissolved within shaded groups of trees developing in 'unorthodox' fashion in the background. The system of composition is striking insofar as it looks back to the high horizon line of Klimt's early landscapes, while at the same time establishing – via the

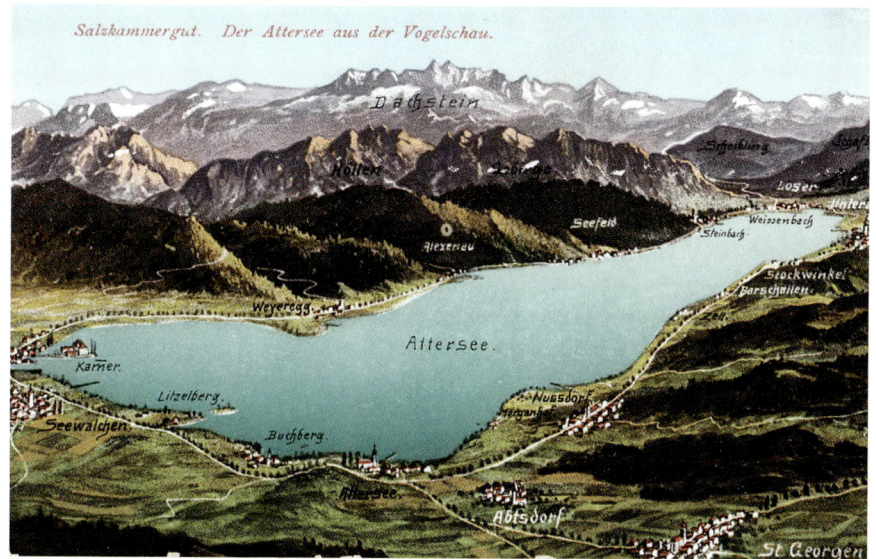

Postcard of Lake Attersee
Private collection

three-dimensional quality of the background – a kind of deep spatial box, one that can also be sensed in earlier landscapes, such as *Orchard* (pp. 432/33). *Orchard with Roses (Rose Garden)* is furthermore a prime example of the way in which Klimt 'reconstructed' nature within a picture. Thus it shows roses, poppies and apples all flowering and bearing fruit at the same point in time – something that does not correspond to the natural cycle. The decorative, aesthetic sensibility that registers nature in artistic terms inserts itself in front of a vision of nature as she truly is. Klimt does not paint nature, in other words, but allows himself to be inspired by the natural world and reconstructs it in new ways. *Orchard with Roses* was in fact Klimt's last picture of an intimate summery garden shaped by human hands, with fruit-laden apple trees, pink rose bushes and countless colourful flowers.

During this same period, small 'islands' of flowers and miniature garden landscapes reminiscent of details of Klimt's landscape paintings also made their way into some of Klimt's female portraits. This can be observed for the first time in the *Portrait of Mäda Primavesi* (pp. 278, 340; Natter 2012, Cat. 202), where the carpet on which the girl is standing mutates in the background into a garden landscape, so to speak. In the portrait of Mäda's mother, Eugenia Primavesi (pp. 285, 342; Natter 2012, Cat. 207), which Klimt produced in 1913/14, the sitter is wearing a dress that resembles a densely woven tapestry of stylized flowers. Something similar can be seen in Klimt's unfinished *Portrait of Ria Munk III* (pp. 277, 355; Natter 2012, Cat. 236) of 1917, where the background again transforms into a wallpaper of stylized flowers. It is a striking fact, nonetheless, that Klimt never crossed the boundaries between the genres – his portraits are not set in gardens or landscapes, nor are his landscapes populated with human protagonists.

Lake Garda, 1913

Klimt and the Flöges spent the summer of 1913 on Lake Garda, where the artist produced two views of the towns of Malcesine and Cassone. These compositions, unusual within his oeuvre, were evidently inspired by the terrain rising steeply above the lake and by the houses nestled closely together on its slopes. Klimt probably composed both pictures with the aid of a telescope, which he used to look for and zoom in on the architecture and landscape. He then regrouped the individual elements so that they fit harmoniously into the square format of his landscape pictures.

The cubatures of the small, greyish-blue stone houses and the church of the same colour at the top of the town in *Church in Cassone* (*Landscape with Cypresses*; pp. 458/59; Natter 2012, Cat. 205) resemble interlocking building blocks. The colouring of the architecture is accentuated by the lighter green of the deciduous trees and shrubs and by the dark, almost black cypresses, whose tall forms at the same time represent a vertical ordering element within the composition. Johannes Dobai recognized early on the parallels between Klimt's handling of architectural elements and the additive building style of Josef Hoffmann, when he observed – albeit with regard to *Kammer Castle on Lake Attersee I* (p. 443) – that "the building elements interlock […] in an intricately balanced, ornamental way, like the forms in the architecture of Josef Hoffmann" (Dobai 1978/79, p. 261). This system of building blocks stacked one on top of the other is further pursued in *Church in Cassone* and prompts a comparison – already drawn many times in the past – with the garden façade of the Palais Stoclet, which Klimt had visited in 1911 on the occasion of the building's completion (pp. 156/57). At the same time, on almost no other occasion does Klimt come closer to the structured constructions of Paul Cézanne or to the early Cubist works of Pablo Picasso and Georges Braque (1882–1963) than here – even if a direct stimulus was once again absent. Klimt's seemingly so unforeseen borrowings sooner point to a rich 'visual memory' that the artist activated when the occasion was right and whose contents he translated into his specific vocabulary of form.

In the case of *Malcesine on Lake Garda* (pp. 460/61; Natter 2012, Cat. 204), in particular, the proximity between Klimt's painting and the cityscapes produced by Egon Schiele during this same period cannot be overlooked. The houses rising in tightly packed, superimposed layers in and above their reflection in Lake Garda prompt a comparison with the houses stacked steeply above the river in Schiele's *Small Town II/III* (1912/13, Vienna, Leopold Museum). Klimt and Schiele had met for the first time in 1907. As chairman of the exhibition committee, Klimt subsequently invited the younger artist to take part in the Kunstschau of 1909. Schiele, who admired Klimt greatly, exhibited several works at the show, which earned him great success. In 1912 Schiele documented the association between the two painters – an association that ultimately brought them mutual inspiration in their art – in his monumental double portrait of *The Hermits* (Vienna, Leopold Museum).

Lake Attersee: Weissenbach, 1914–1916

From 1914 until 1916 Klimt and the Flöges spent their summer holidays in Weissenbach at the southern end of Lake Attersee. Emilie and her sisters, together with their mother and Klimt's niece Helene, took lodgings directly beside the lake, whereas Klimt – probably in greater need of tranquillity and looking for a secluded retreat – found accommodation at the entrance to the Weissenbachtal Valley about a kilometre from the lake, in a forester's house that he immortalized in two pictures (pp. 463, 465; Natter 2012, Cat. 208, 209). In particular *Forester's House in Weissenbach II*, with its intensive use of black and its contrast of the pure complementary colours red and green, bears witness to Klimt's artistic proximity to Egon Schiele. We know from contemporary accounts, however, that, despite the distance that separated them, Klimt joined the Flöges every day: he was to be found "in his kaftan-style coat with his easel and brushes in our garden or out and about, sometimes on a bicycle. He was rather dour, though not unfriendly, and had very little contact with the locals" (letter from Herta Schrey, the former owner of the Villa Sans Souci in Weissenbach, to Alfred Weidinger, 1991; cit. from Weidinger 2007a, p. 166). Joint walks and visits from friends also continued to form part of the summer routine at Lake Attersee.

The landscape pictures from Klimt's final years are characterized by a saturated palette in which the dominant note is sounded in every case by a dark green. This is accompanied by lighter shades mixed with yellow, and sometimes also with blue, and contrasted with accents of red as the complement of green. Klimt continued to compose his pictures in terms of horizontal strata. Thus *Litzlberg on Lake Attersee* (pp. 466/67; Natter 2012, Cat. 210) – a view of the artist's domicile in his first summers by the lake – lies like a narrow strip between the lapping waters of the lake, containing the blurred reflection of the houses on the shore, and the slopes rising steeply above. Klimt continued to use a tele-scope or pair of opera glasses to fix the more distant landscape in the form he desired. The views of Unterach that he painted over the next two years – *Houses in Unterach on Lake Attersee*, *Church in Unterach on Lake Attersee* and *Unterach on Lake Attersee* – are also conceived in precisely the same way.

With a picture dating from 1915/16, Klimt created a monument to the *Litzlbergkeller* (p. 471; Natter 2012, Cat. 213) just north of Litzlberg, which was one of his regular destinations in those early summers on Lake Attersee. Klimt shows us the small building with its hipped roof, surrounded by trees and directly overlooking the lake, in a frontal view as probably seen from the opposite shore. Once again, he has employed either a telescope or opera glasses to zoom in on his motif in order to represent it parallel to the pictorial plane and composed of zones lying one above the other. It was in summer 1915, certainly, that Klimt sent his sister Hermine the postcard so often cited as confirmation of his use of opera glasses: "Arrived in good shape. Forgot opera glasses – need urgently. Helene will bring them with her. Greetings Gustav" (cit. from Nebehay 1969, p. 503). In conversation with Christian Nebehay, Klimt's niece Helene had already stated that the artist used opera glasses while painting his Lake Attersee landscapes (ibid.). A striking feature of *Litzlbergkeller* is its dense, tightly woven application of paint, whereby the brushstrokes are laid down almost like the weft and warp of a tapestry. The white of the squat house stands out as an accent within the otherwise very limited palette of greens and yellows with a touch of blue.

In summer 1916 – his last on Lake Attersee – Klimt based himself in Weissenbach from the beginning of July to the beginning of September. It was a particularly productive period, during which he worked on at least seven landscape paintings, including *Houses in Unterach on Lake Attersee* (pp. 472/73; Natter 2012, Cat. 214), *Church in Unterach on Lake Attersee* (p. 475; Natter 2012, Cat. 215) and *Unterach on Lake Attersee* (pp. 476/77; Natter 2012, Cat. 223) – pictures in which he once again took up the themes and structures of preceding years. Some of these canvases remained unfinished at the artist's death – showing, in fact, that Klimt in some cases blocked out the landscape paintings of these summer holidays only in rough terms of composition and colour, in order to finish them in his Vienna studio: "From here, you entered his studio proper […]. In Hietzing, Klimt painted […] furthermore a substantial number of excellent landscapes of Lake Attersee and Lake Garda", as Egon Schiele also reported (cit. from Breicha 1978, p. 57). It is interesting in this regard to compare *Unterach on Lake Attersee*, which appears to have been left unfinished and thus illustrates the processual aspect of Klimt's method of painting, and *Orchard* (pp. 432/33; Natter 2012, Cat. 167), executed more than ten years previously. In contrast to the earlier landscape, as it were *drawn* with fine strokes and thin, almost glaze-like layers of paint, *Unterach on Lake Attersee* is vigorously modelled with a laden brush. Klimt's strokes are powerful and seemingly unmotivated and unsystematic in their placing. The picture appears to have come to a standstill at a moment of consolidation and the

Flowering Meadow (detail), c. 1904/05
(see ill. p. 430)

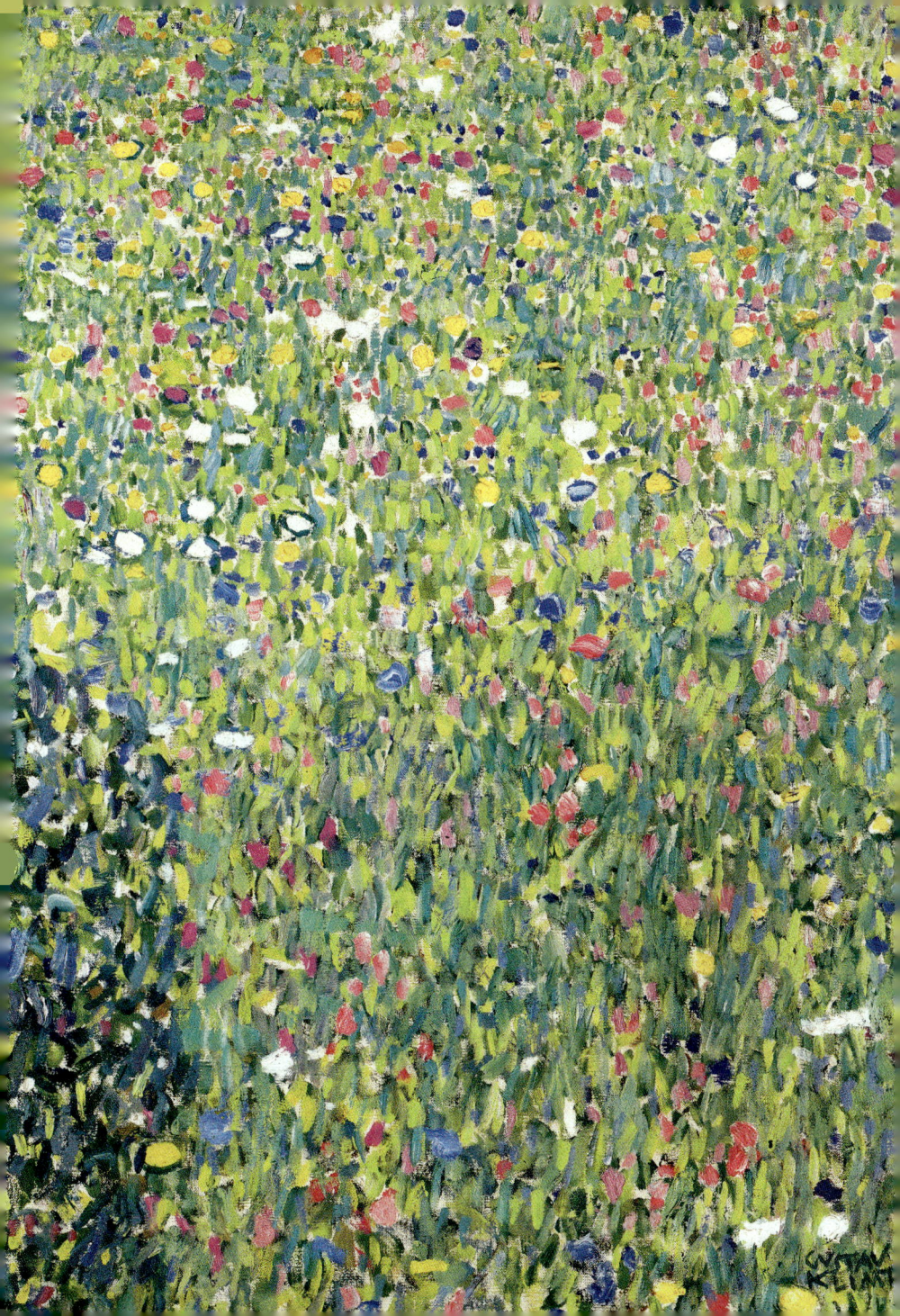

thin ground still shines through in many places on the mountainside. Unlike the ground similarly visible in the earlier *Orchard*, however, it here seems to be waiting to merge with other colours – as we can see in *Forester's House in Weissenbach I* executed two years earlier, and also in *Litzlbergkeller* completed in 1915/16. *Houses in Unterach on Lake Attersee*, meanwhile, once again serves to illustrate Klimt's proximity to Egon Schiele in these final years, namely in its colour harmony, its block-like elements and above all its use of black not just as outline but also as a vehicle of expression within the compact landscape.

The last landscapes – Vienna and Gastein, 1916 and 1917

In the very final years of his life, Klimt produced two noteworthy paintings, which have little in common with his Lake Attersee landscapes either in their subject or in their artistic execution: the fountain of Neptune in the grounds of Schönbrunn Palace in Vienna (1916) and a view of Gastein (1917), the health resort that Klimt had visited regularly with Emilie Flöge from 1912 onwards, usually prior to his obligatory holiday in the Salzkammergut. *Schönbrunn Landscape* (p. 483; Natter 2012, Cat. 216), painted in a subtly gradated palette, is Klimt's only picture with a Viennese motif. It was executed in 1916 and offers a view of the Neptune fountain in the park's lower parterre garden, which Klimt would have passed regularly as he walked to his studio in Hietzing's Feldmühlgasse after breakfasting at the Tivoli. Klimt presents the basin from an angle that effectively requires the viewer to stoop down and which draws us into the glassy surface of the water dominating the picture and reflecting the surrounding foliage in its rich palette of greens. The park in the background, with its avenues, shrubs and occasional strolling figures (the sole guests, incidentally, ever to appear in Klimt's landscapes), and the hedge leading away into the depths on the left with the tall weeping willow marking the corner, resemble the walls of a box theatre. In *Schönbrunn Park*, Klimt arrives at a spatial situation that is unusually complex for him and at the same time at a manner of painting dominated by colour planes that is not found in the rest of his oeuvre.

Klimt's very last landscape picture, *Gastein* (Natter 2012, Cat. 233), dating from 1917, is entirely different in character and is in fact his only true townscape. The canvas itself was destroyed by fire in May 1945 at Immendorf Castle in the Weinviertel region of Lower Austria, where it had been taken for safekeeping along with all the other Klimt pictures formerly in the collection of August and Serena Lederer. Even if we know it only from black-and-white illustrations, *Gastein* can be interpreted as a sombre, rather menacing picture. The residential buildings and hotels rising in dense concentration one above the other on the town's steep north-western slope are divided by a tree-lined street running like a dark chasm from the top to the bottom of the picture. Details of the buildings – window surrounds, cornices and roof ridges – seem to have been drawn with a black brush, as can be seen in the rough layout of the composition in Klimt's sketchbook of 1917. In this picture, as in the majority of his late landscapes from the Weissenbach period, Klimt places particular emphasis upon drawing in general, upon outline drawing in particular and upon the use of black – a means of expression that once again makes his proximity to Egon Schiele impossible to overlook.

Within the sphere of influence of Egon Schiele, Klimt manifested an expressive approach to landscape, a composition determined by linear structures and a powerful formal language shaped by primary colours. At the same time, however, as shown above, Klimt also engaged in a very spatial manner of painting built up out of large planes and determined by tonal colours. Both stand in contrast to the post-Impressionist means of design that informed many of Klimt's earlier landscapes, albeit personalized by his hands: a subtly gradated use of colour, placed on the canvas in small, thick strokes of paint, and above all an indeterminate mood, whereby the time of day cannot be identified, which he achieved with certain rigorously observed criteria. These included the renunciation of shadow (and hence of temporality) and of central perspective (and hence of an illusionistic spatial depth). The square format that he adopted early on furthermore provided the perfect showcase for a carefully crafted two-dimensional painting, for a nature filtered by means of anonymous light, the use of artificial vanishing points and the 'optical aids' of viewfinder, telescope and opera glasses, and then reconstructed on the pictorial plane.

Over the course of the years, Klimt moved away from a Symbolist vision of nature strongly overlaid with mythical connotations towards an independent approach to landscape coloured by Expressionist influences. The subjects of his landscape paintings thereby altered but little (essentially changing from untouched nature to a cultivated natural landscape) and, at an early stage, Klimt made the transition from the representation of anonymous landscape to that of the landscape of his personal experience. The artist's intensive exploration of nature is nevertheless just as much rooted in Symbolism as the vague, indefinable element of the atmosphere in many of his landscape pictures. One is tempted to equate it with a quality of 'elusiveness' surrounding the subject – and perhaps the painter himself, as someone seeking retreat? – that Austrian dramatist Hugo von Hofmannsthal, writing around 1907, ultimately considered characteristic of the age: "The essence of our epoch is ambiguity and vagueness. It can only rest on that which is gliding past and is conscious that what other generations believe is something solid, is something gliding past" (Hofmannsthal 1951 [posthumous], p. 272).

Pages 408/09
Poppy Field (Poppies in Bloom) (detail), 1907
(see ill. p. 431)

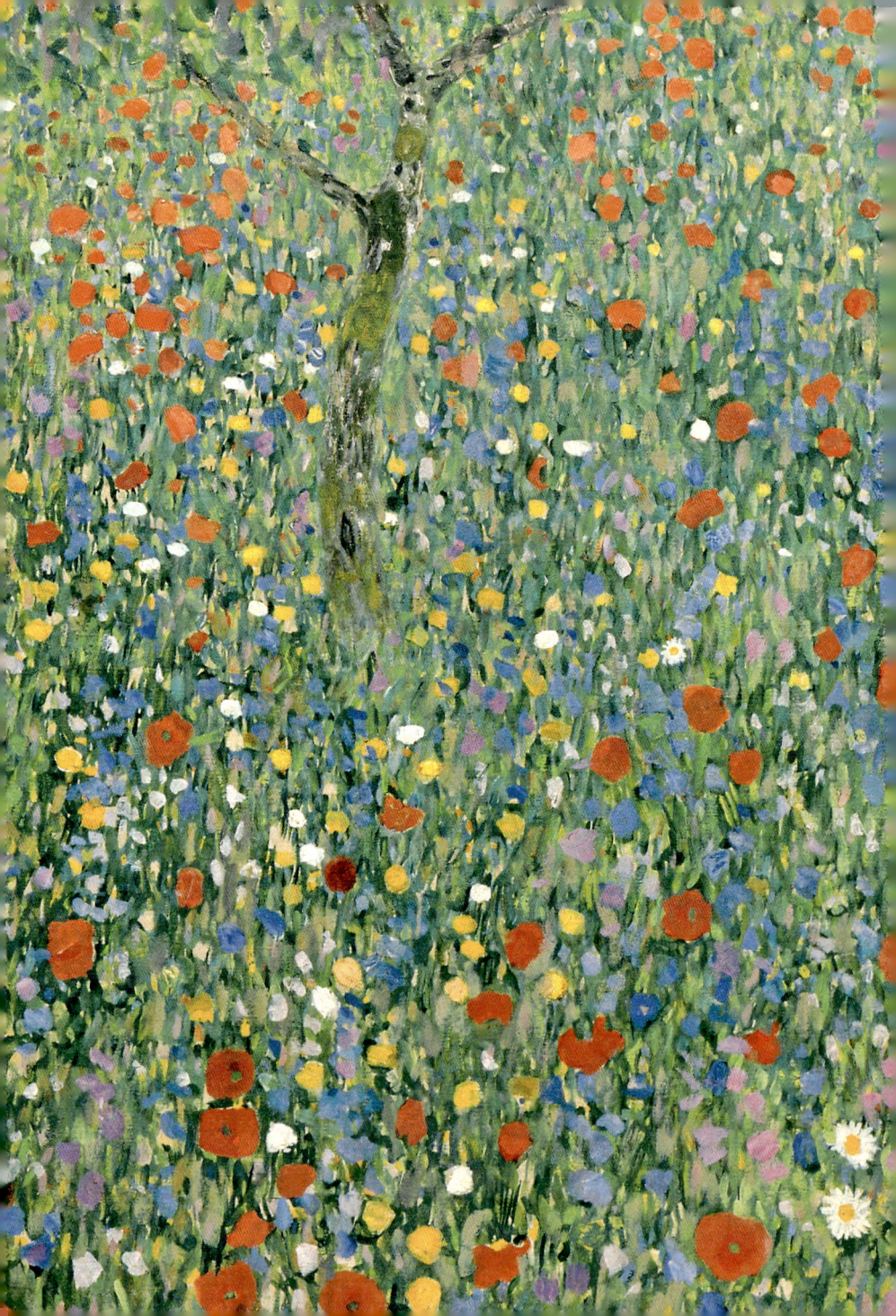

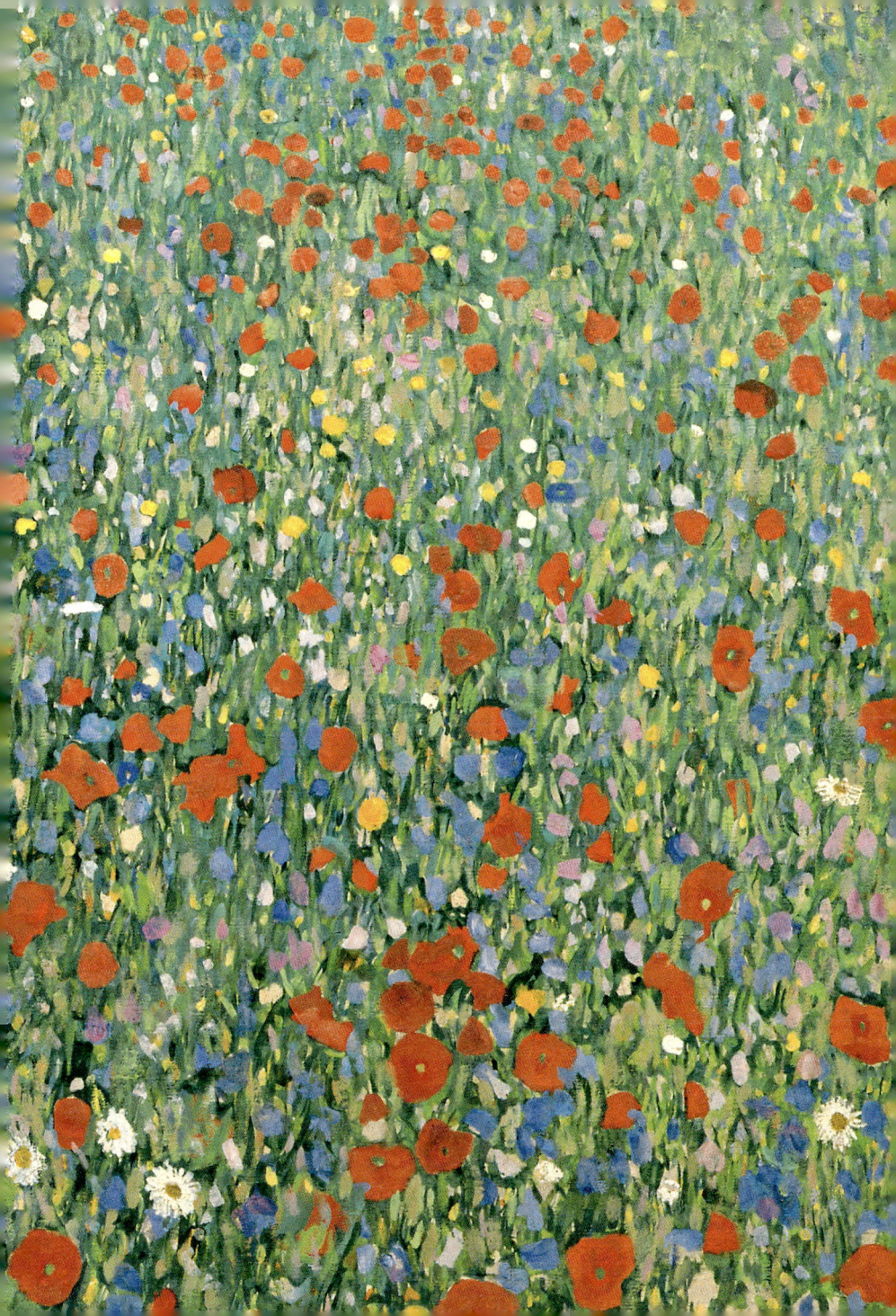

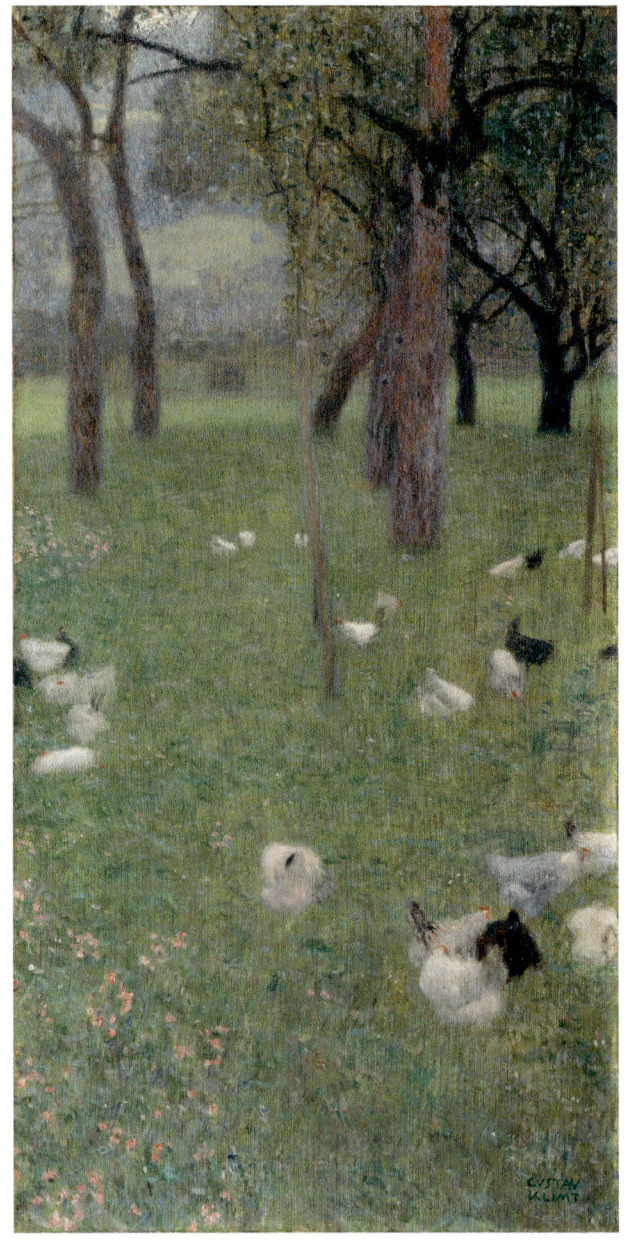

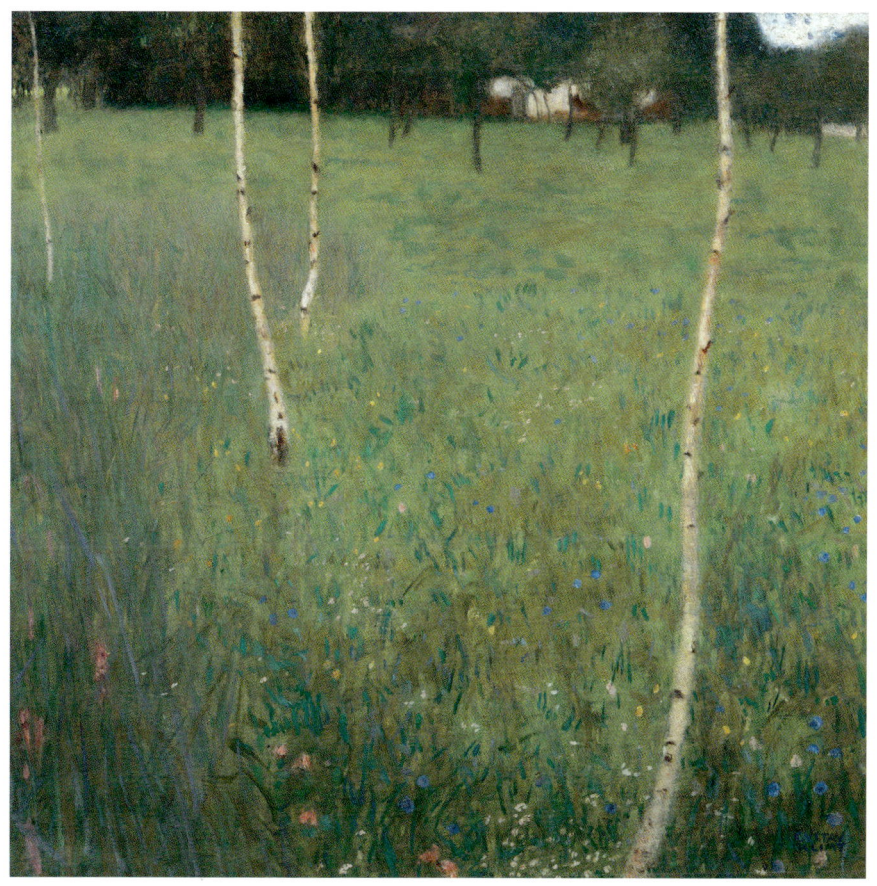

After the Rain (Garden with Chickens in St. Agatha), 1898
Oil on canvas, 80 x 40 cm / 31 ½ x 15 ¾ in. Vienna, Belvedere

Farmhouse with Birch Trees (Young Birches), 1900
Oil on canvas, 80 x 81 cm / 31 ½ x 31 ⅞ in. Private collection

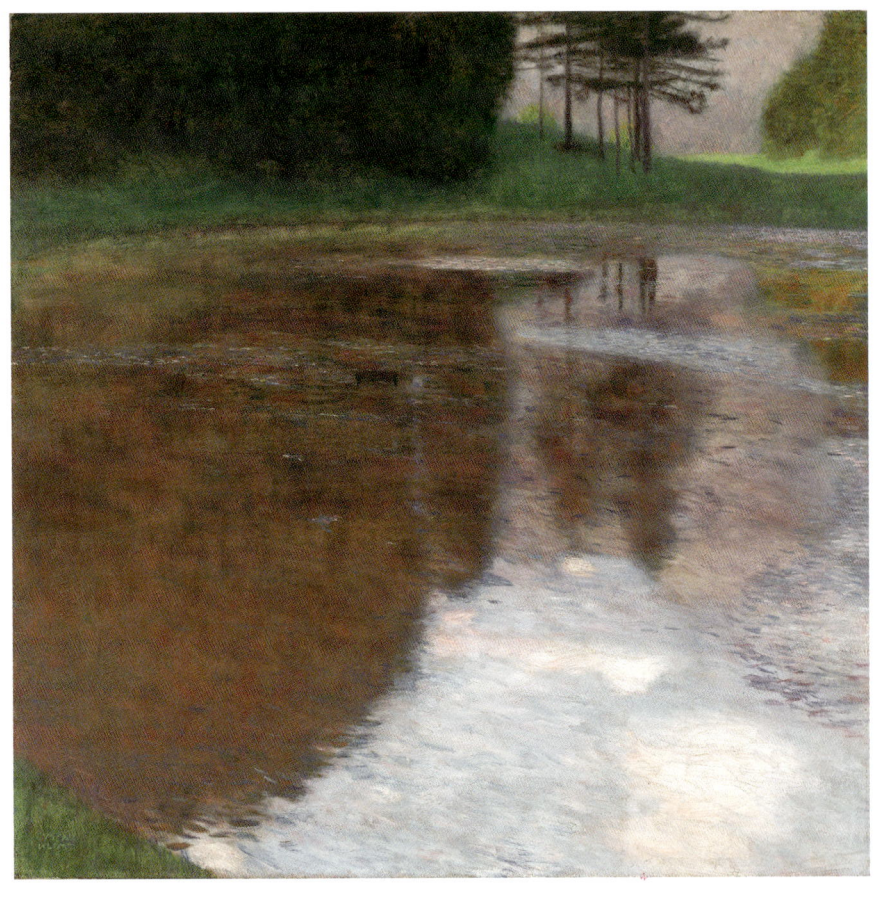

A Morning by the Pond, 1899
Oil on canvas, 75.1 x 75.1 cm / 29 ½ x 29 ½ in.
Vienna, Leopold Museum

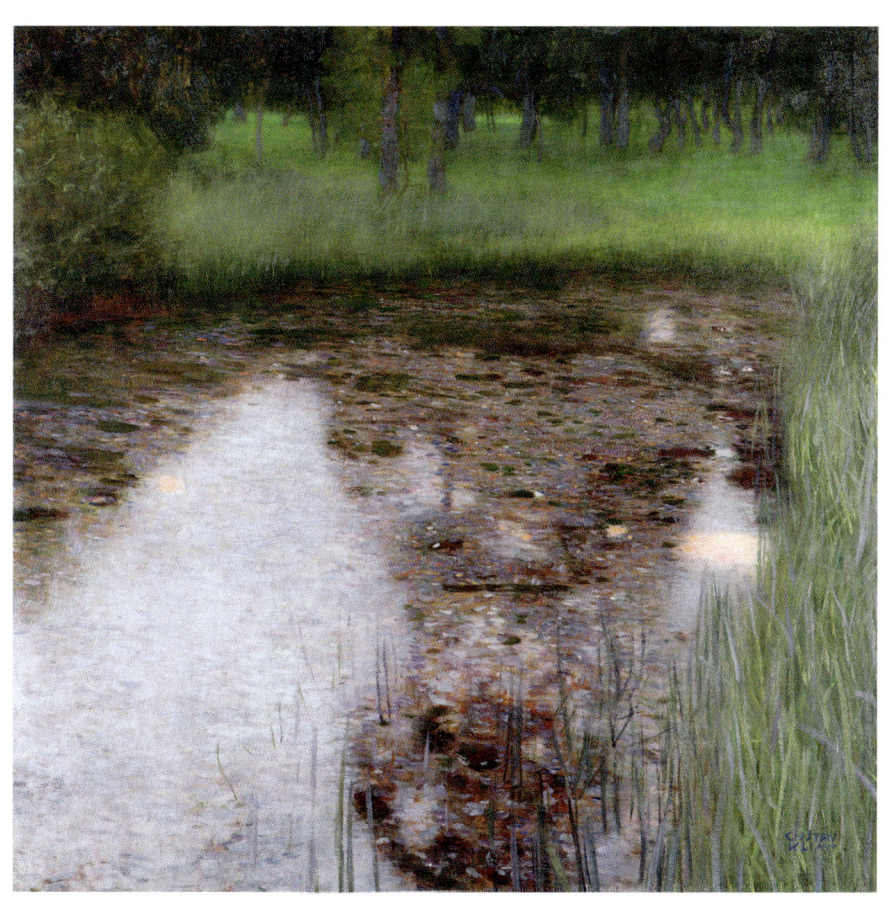

The Marshy Pond, 1900
Oil on canvas, 80 x 80 cm / 31 ½ x 31 ½ in.
Private collection

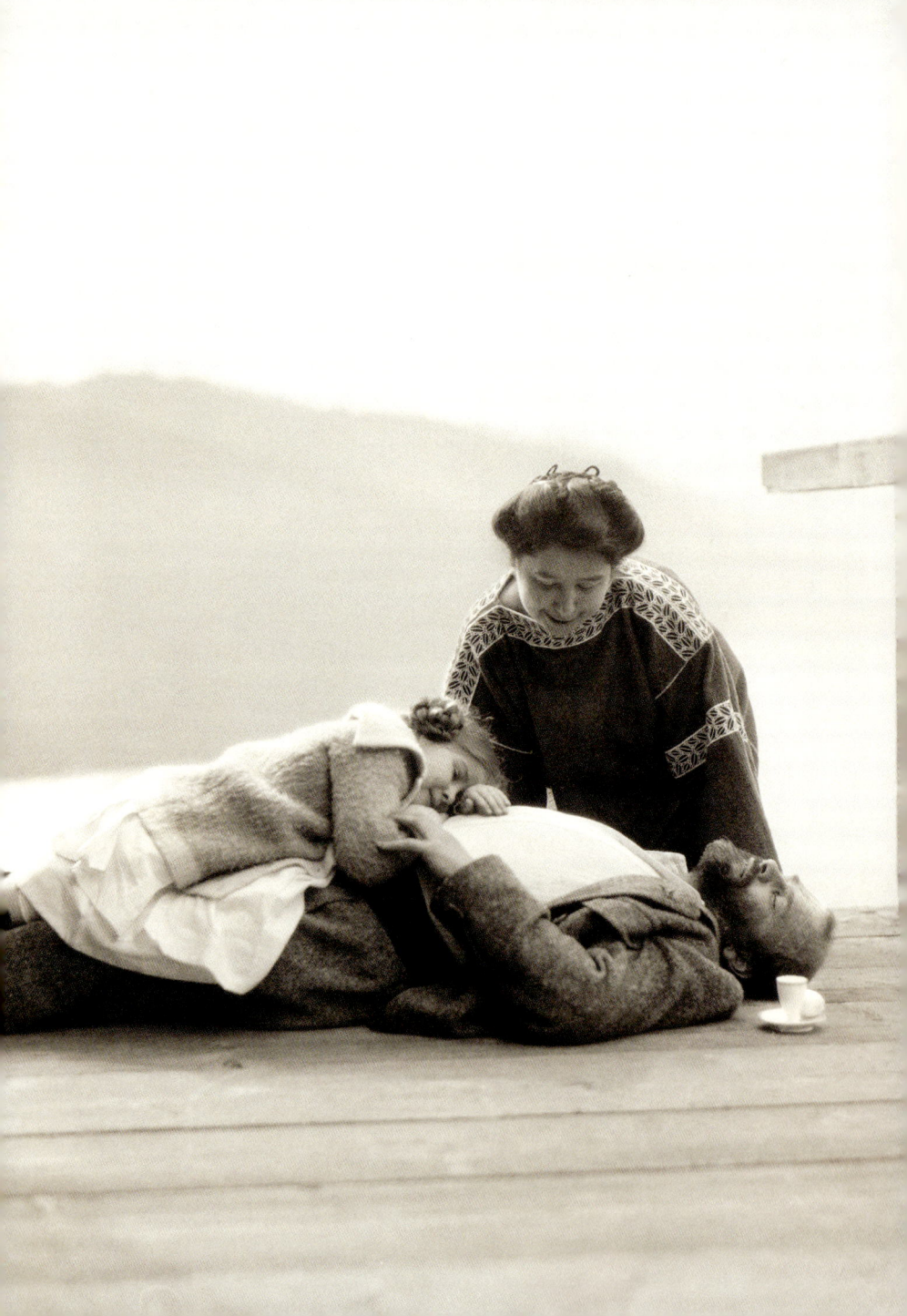

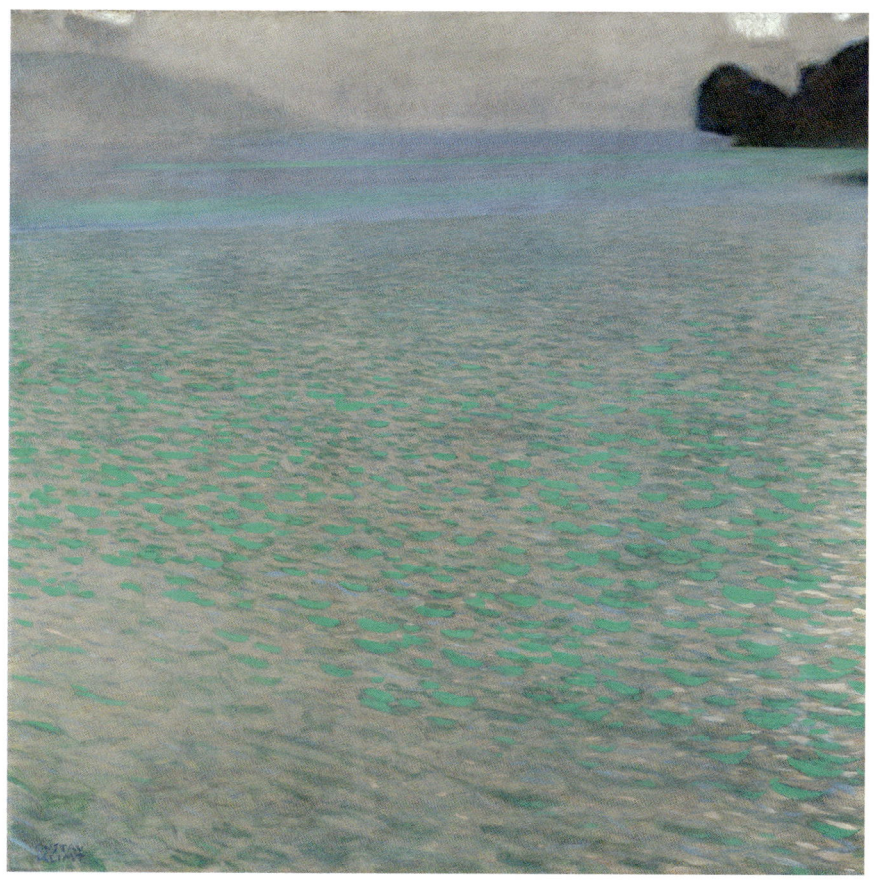

Gustav Klimt with Therese Flöge and her daughter Gertrude, 1912
On the jetty in front of the Villa Paulick in Seewalchen on Lake Attersee
Photograph. Imagno/Austrian Archives

On Lake Attersee, 1900
Oil on canvas, 80.2 x 80.2 cm / 31 ½ x 31 ½ in. Vienna, Leopold Museum

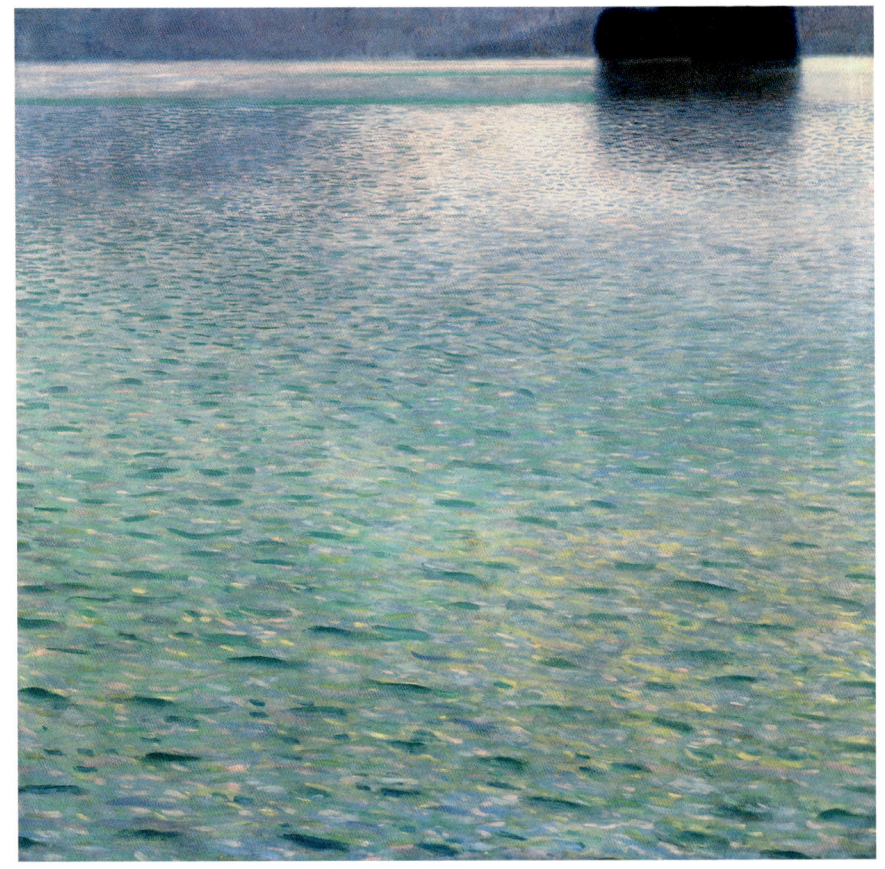

Island in Lake Attersee, 1902
Oil on canvas, 100 x 100 cm / 39 ⅜ x 39 ⅜ in.
USA, private collection, courtesy Galerie St. Etienne, New York

Gustav Klimt, Emilie and Helene Flöge on a jetty on Lake Attersee, 1906
Photograph. Imagno/Austrian Archives

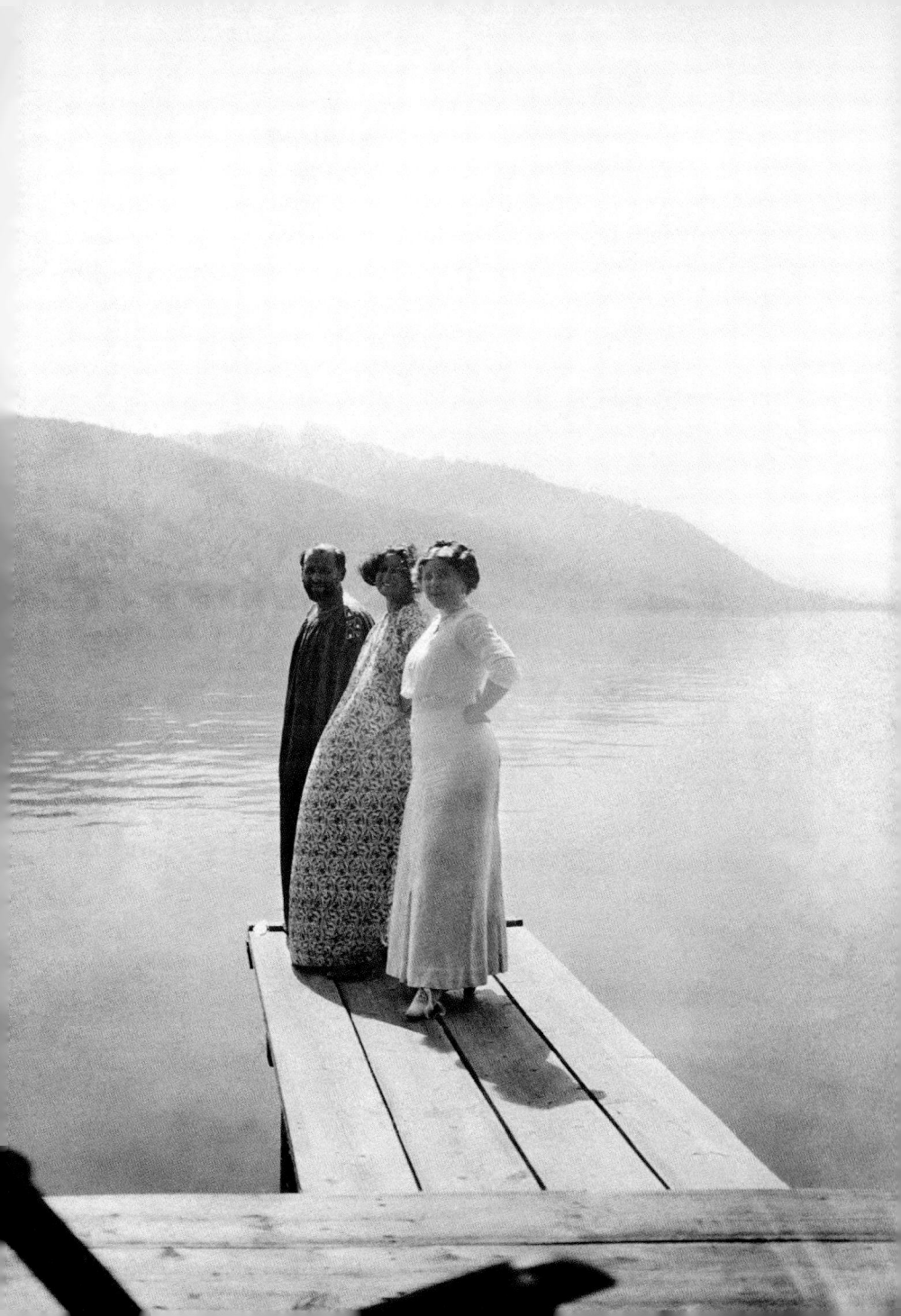

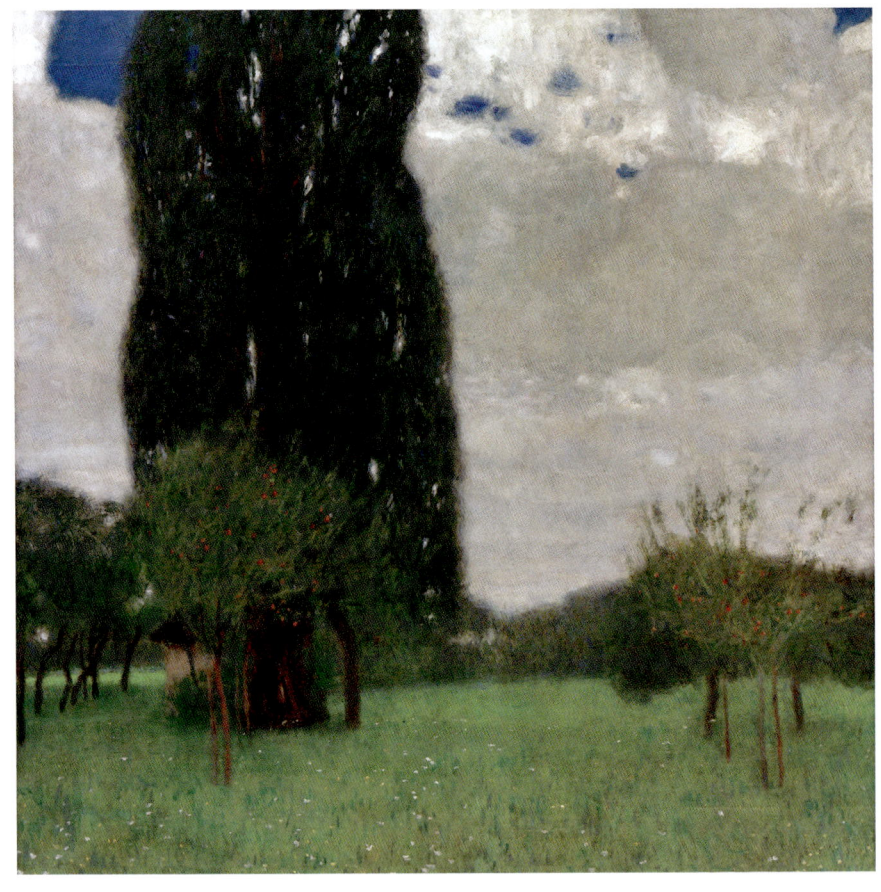

The Large Poplar I, 1900
Oil on canvas, 80 x 80 cm / 31 ½ x 31 ½ in.
New York, private collection

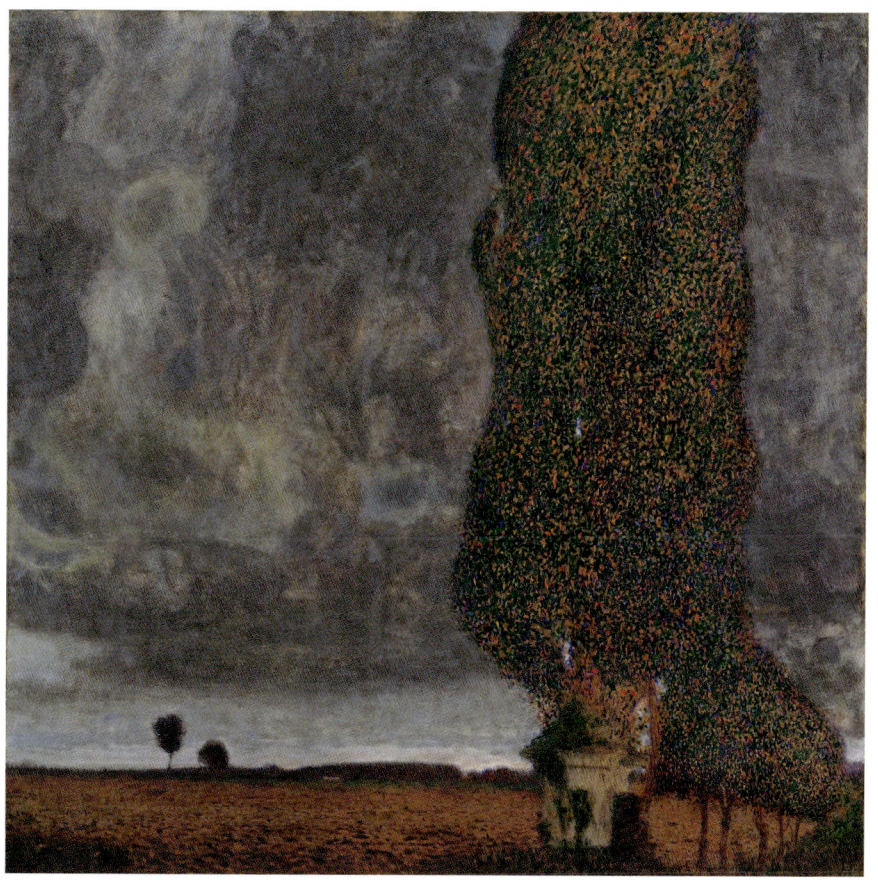

The Large Poplar II (Gathering Storm), 1902/03
Oil on canvas, 100.8 x 100.7 cm / 39 ⅝ x 39 ⅝ in.
Vienna, Leopold Museum

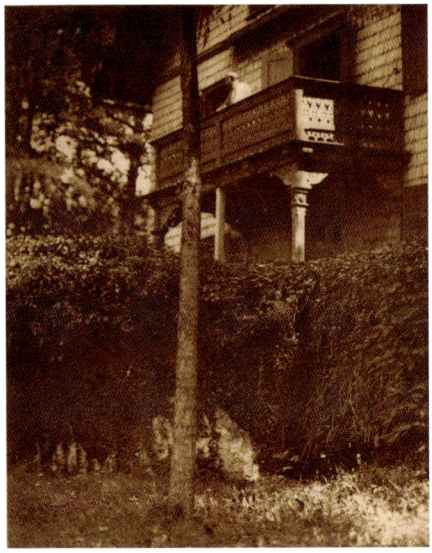

Heinrich Böhler, **The house in Kammer on Lake Attersee
where Gustav Klimt spent his summer vacation**, 1909
Heliogravure. Fondazione Gino e Gianna Macconi, Mendrisio, Switzerland

Farmhouse in Kammer on Lake Attersee (Mill), 1901
Oil on canvas, 88 x 88 cm / 34 ⅝ x 34 ⅝ in. Vienna, private collection

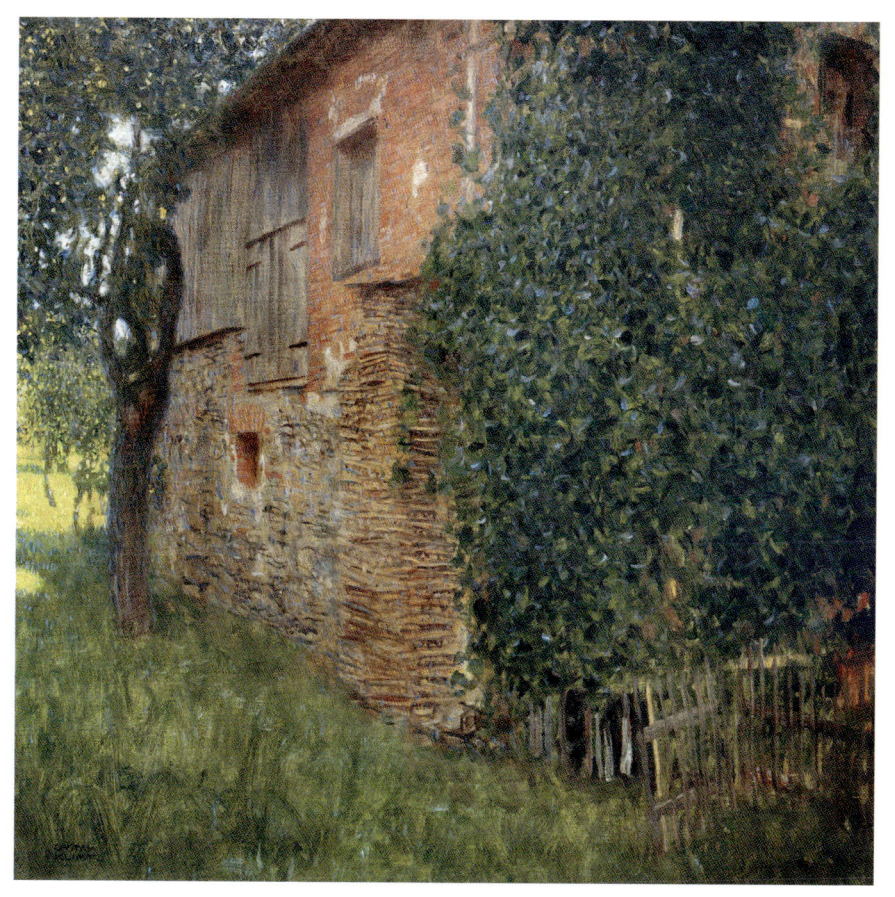

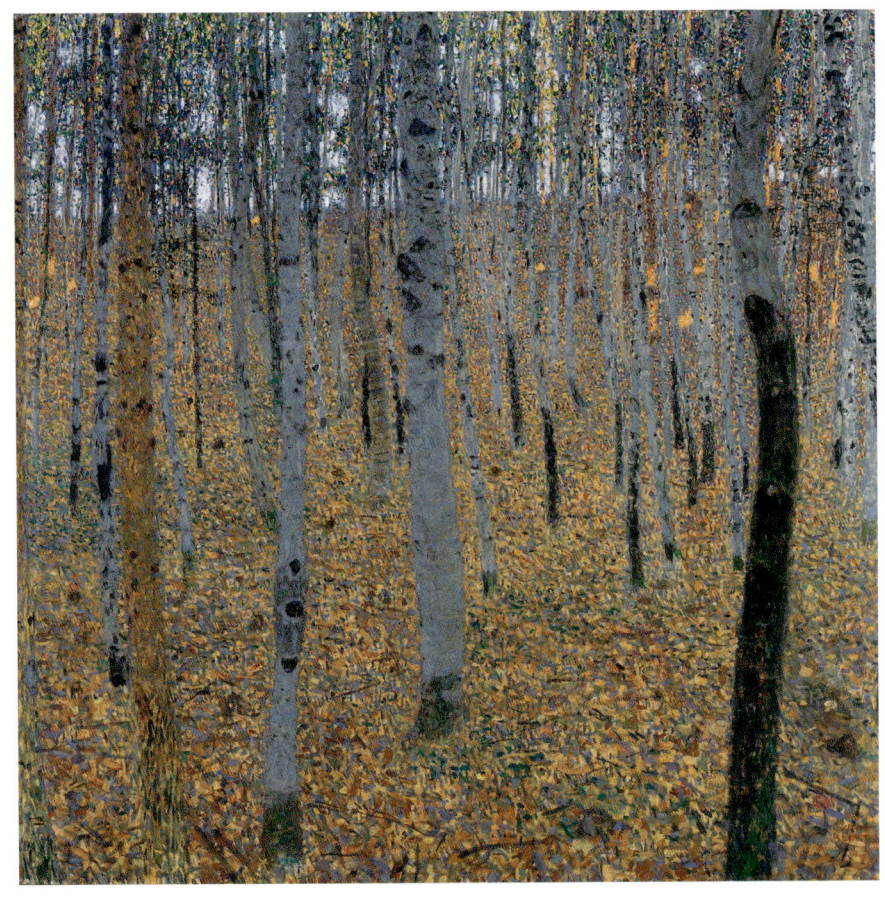

Beech Forest I, c. 1902
Oil on canvas, 100 x 100 cm /39 ⅜ x 39 ⅜ in.
Dresden, Staatliche Kunstsammlung

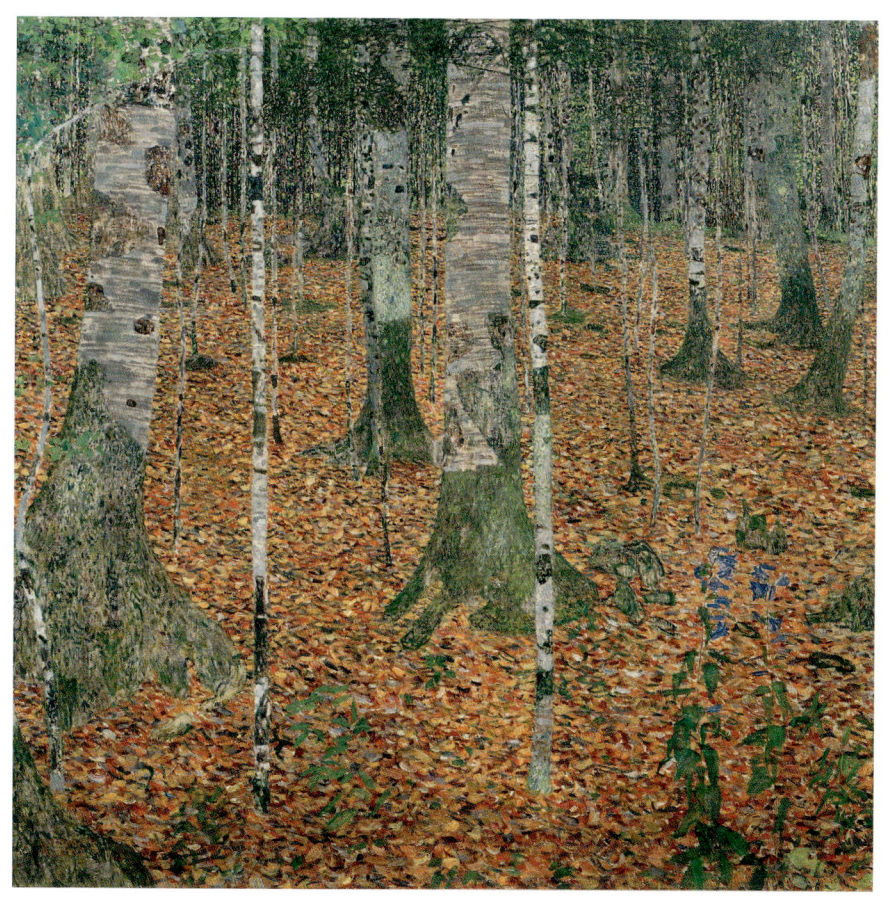

Birch Forest (Beech Forest), 1903
Oil on canvas, 110 x 110 cm / 43 ¼ x 43 ¼ in.
Private collection

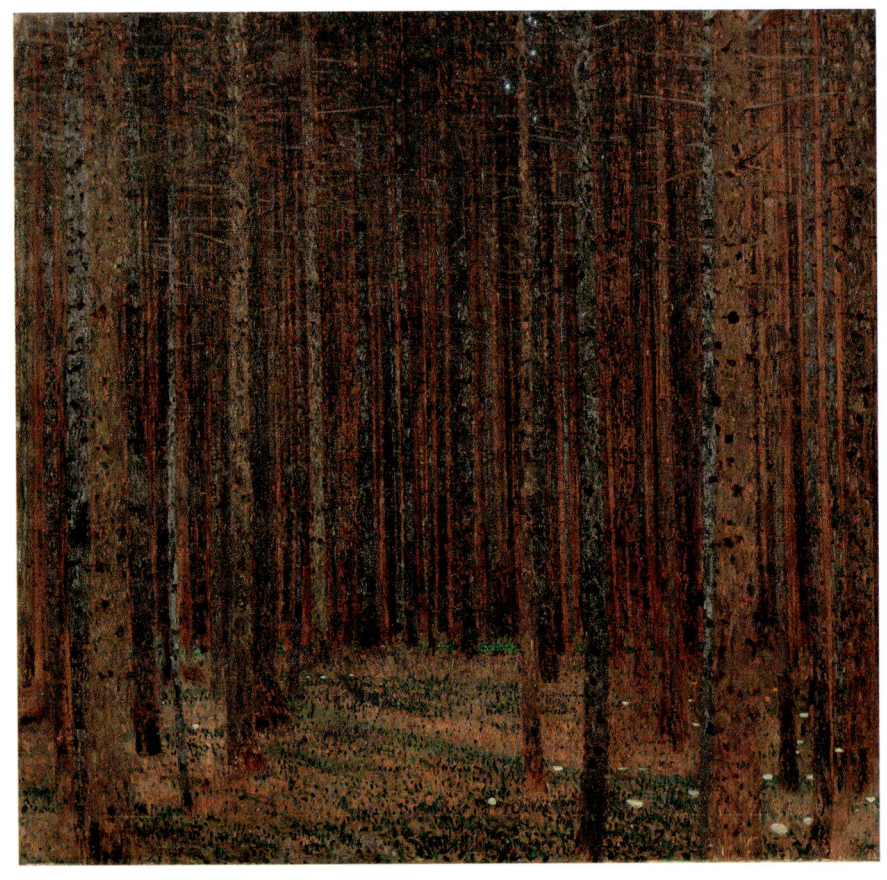

Pine Forest I, 1901
Oil on canvas, 90 x 90 cm / 35 ½ x 35 ½ in.
Kunsthaus Zug, Kamm Collection Foundation

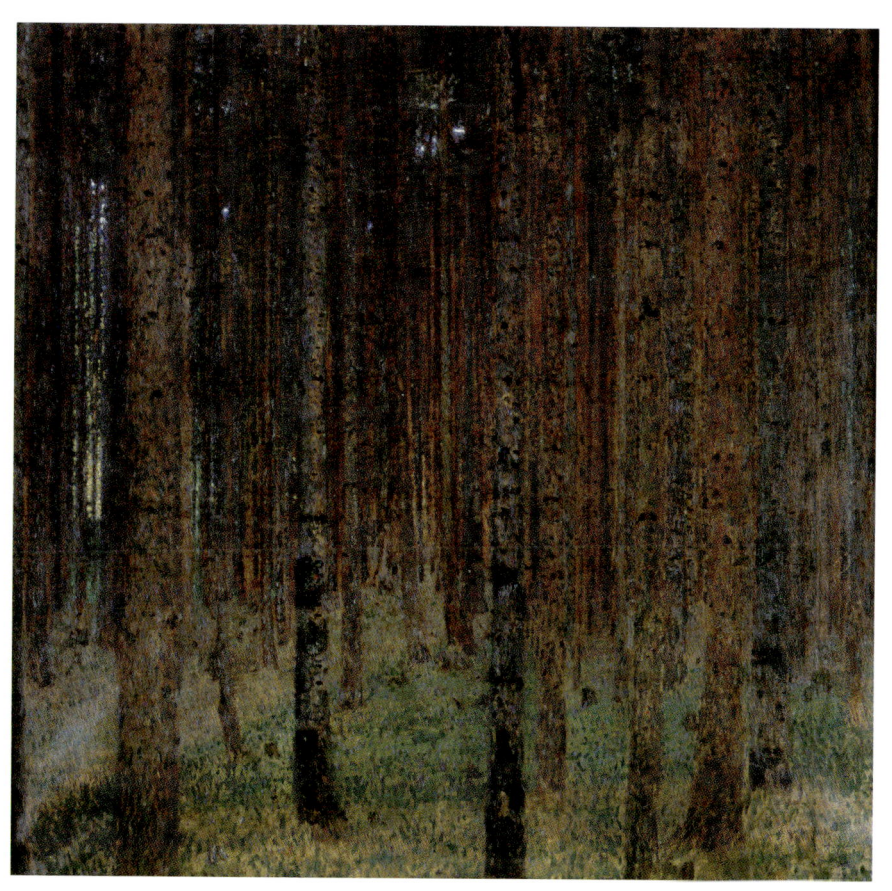

Pine Forest II, 1901
Oil on canvas, 91.5 x 89 cm / 36 x 35 in.
Private collection, courtesy Galerie St. Etienne, New York

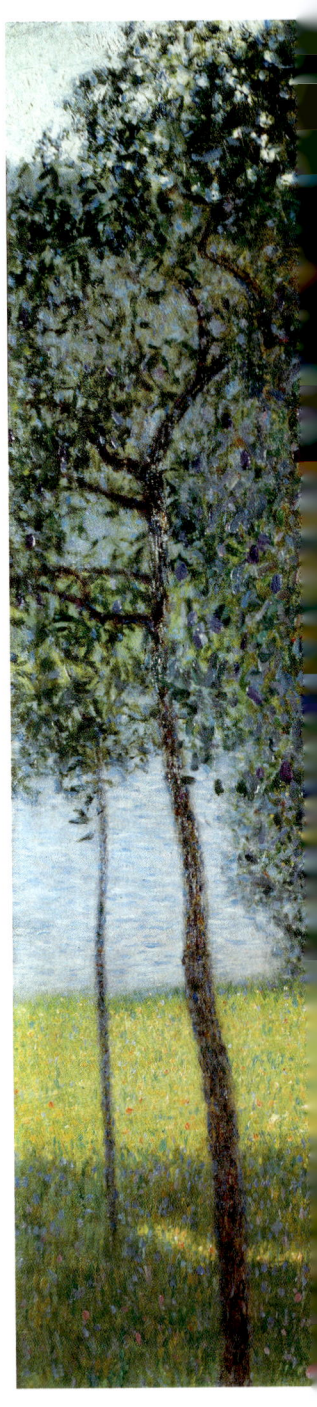

Fruit Trees, 1901
Oil on canvas, 90 x 90 cm /35 ½ x 35 ½ in.
Private collection

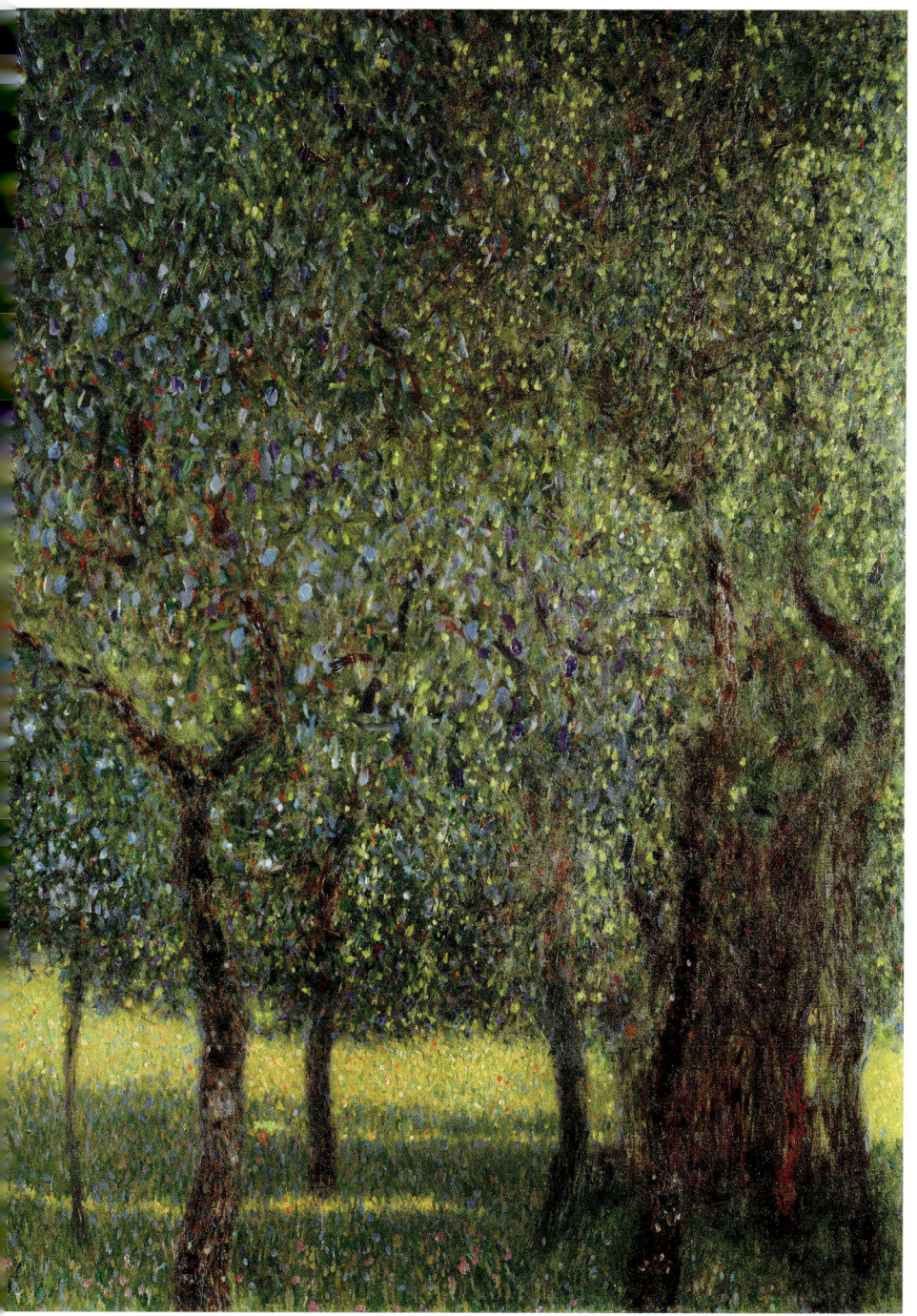

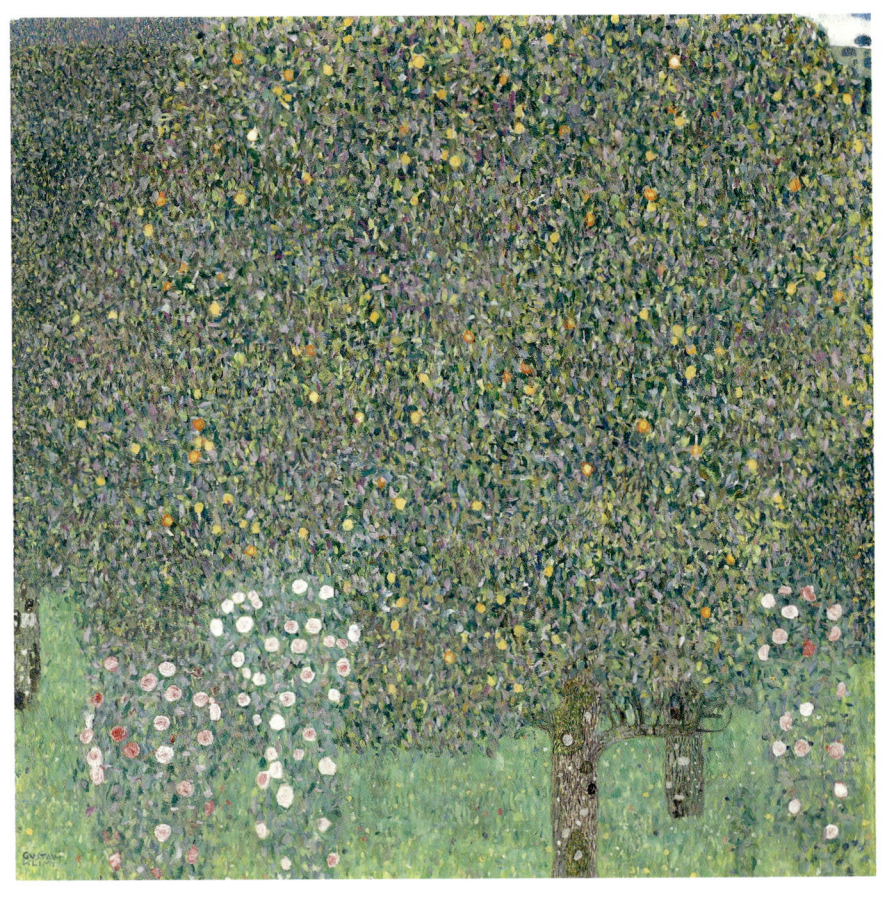

Roses beneath Trees (Roses), c. 1904
Oil on canvas, 110 x 110 cm / 43 ¼ x 43 ¼ in.
Paris, Musée d'Orsay

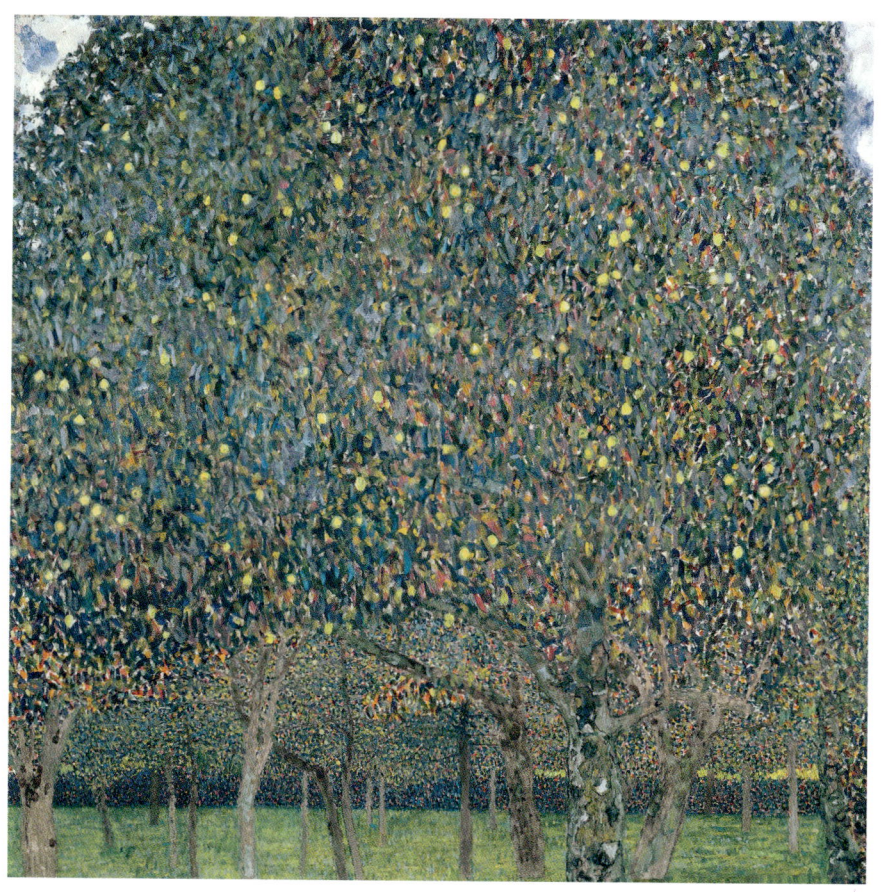

Pear Tree (Pear Trees), 1903, later reworked
Oil and casein on canvas, 101 x 101 cm / 39 ¾ x 39 ¾ in. Cambridge, Massachusetts,
Harvard Art Museums/Busch-Reisinger Museum, Gift of Otto Kallir 1956

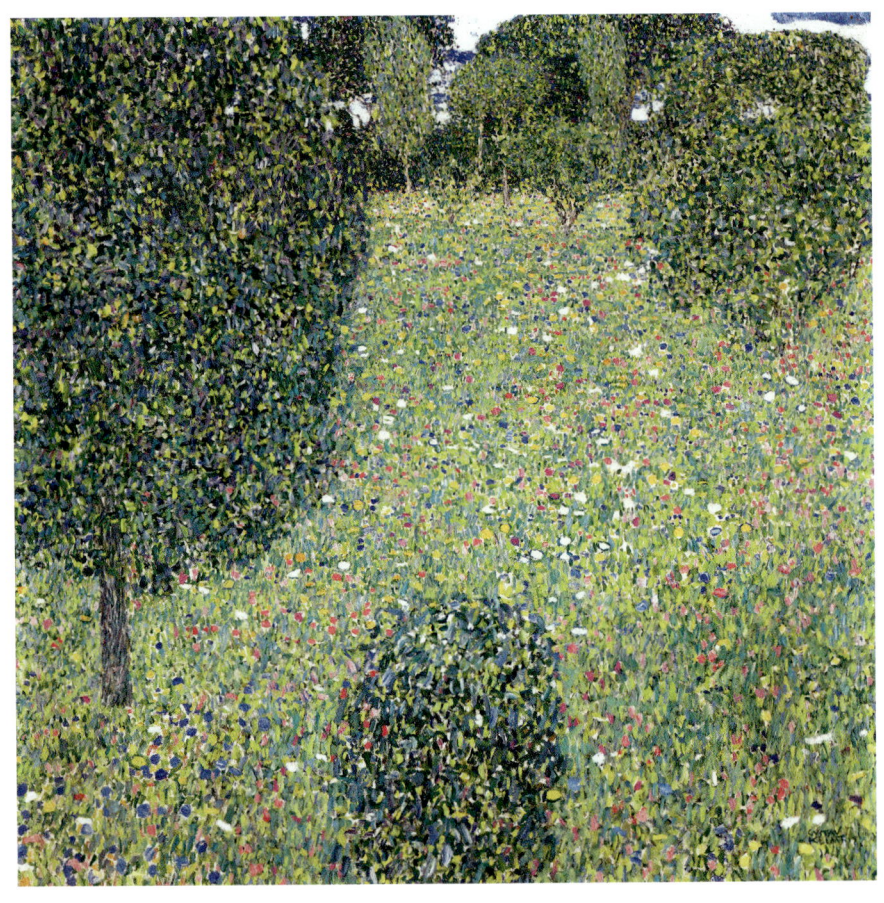

Flowering Meadow, c. 1904/05
Oil on canvas, 110 x 110 cm / 43 ¼ x 43 ¼ in.
Private collection

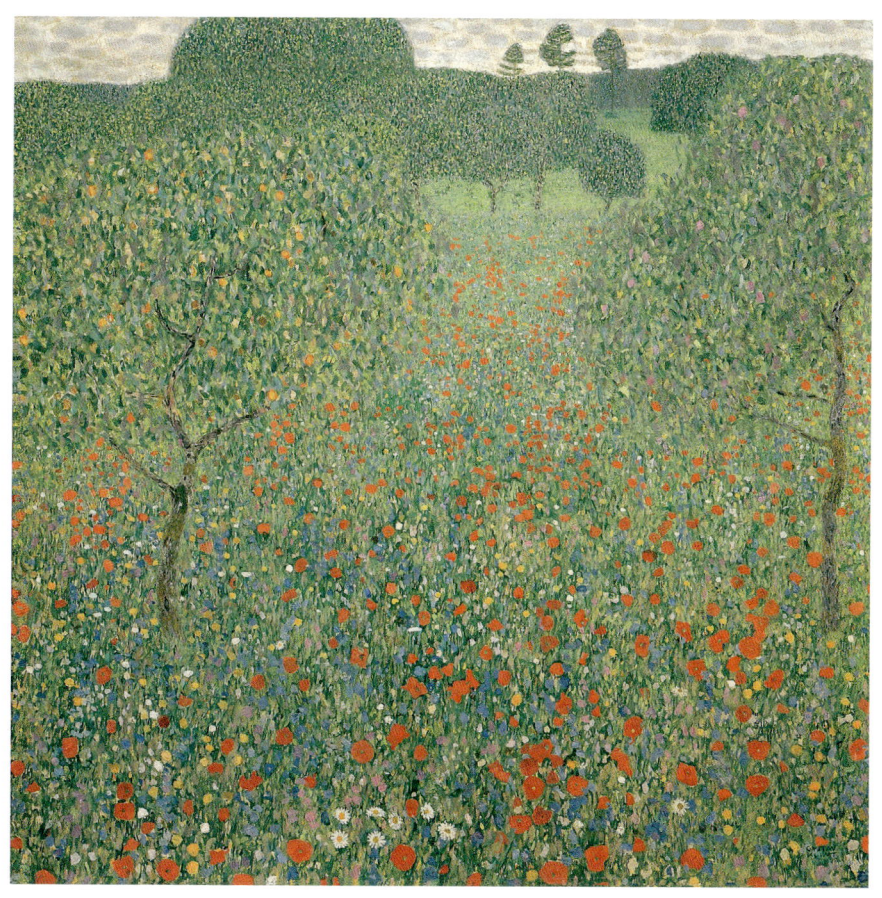

Poppy Field (Poppies in Bloom), 1907
Oil on canvas, 110 x 110 cm / 43 ¼ x 43 ¼ in.
Vienna, Belvedere

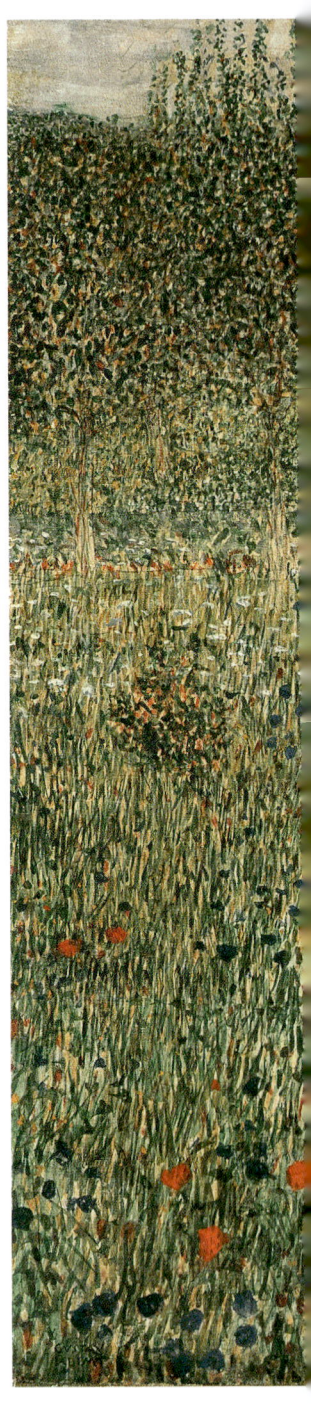

Orchard, c. 1904/05
Oil on canvas, 98.7 x 99.4 cm / 38 ⅞ x 39 ⅛ in.
Pittsburgh, Pennsylvania, purchased with The Carnegie
Museum of Art, Patrons Art Fund

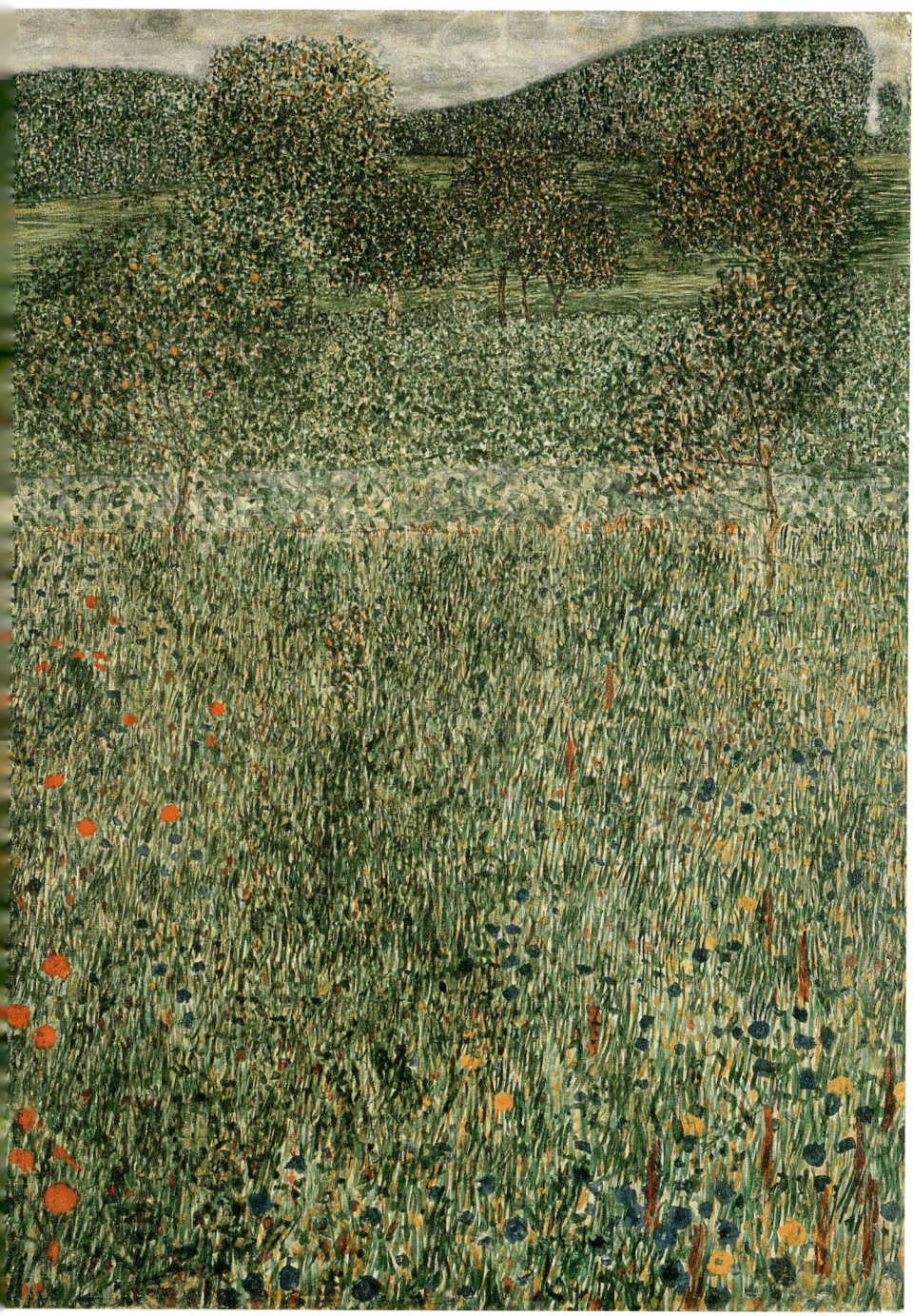

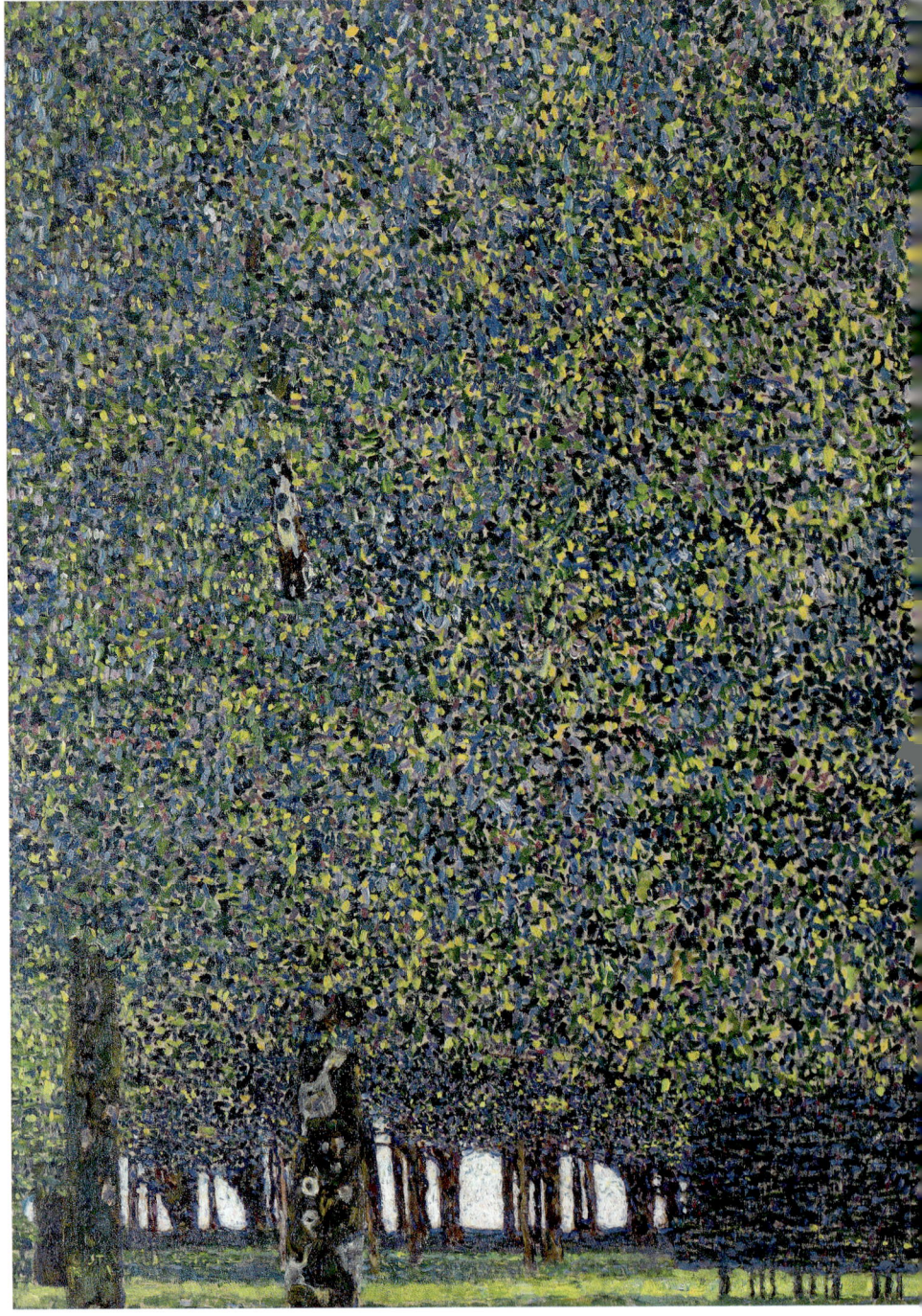

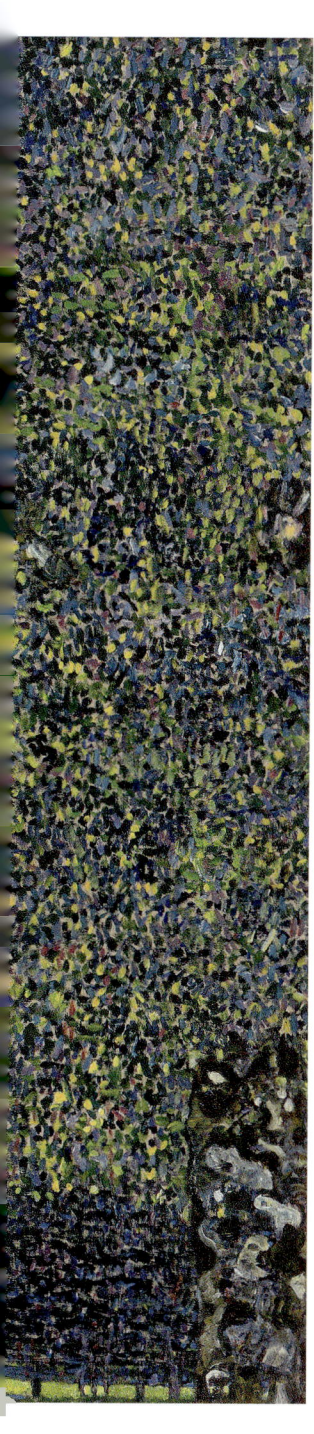

The Park, 1909
Oil on canvas, 110.4 x 110.4 cm / 43 ½ x 43 ½ in.
New York, The Museum of Modern Art,
purchased with Gertrud A. Mellon Fund

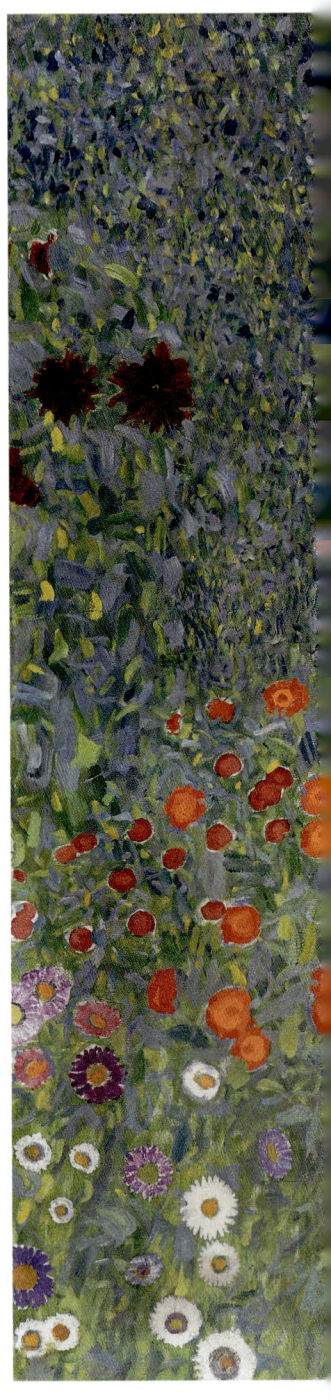

Cottage Garden, 1907
Oil on canvas, 110 x 110 cm / 43 ¼ x 43 ¼ in.
Private collection

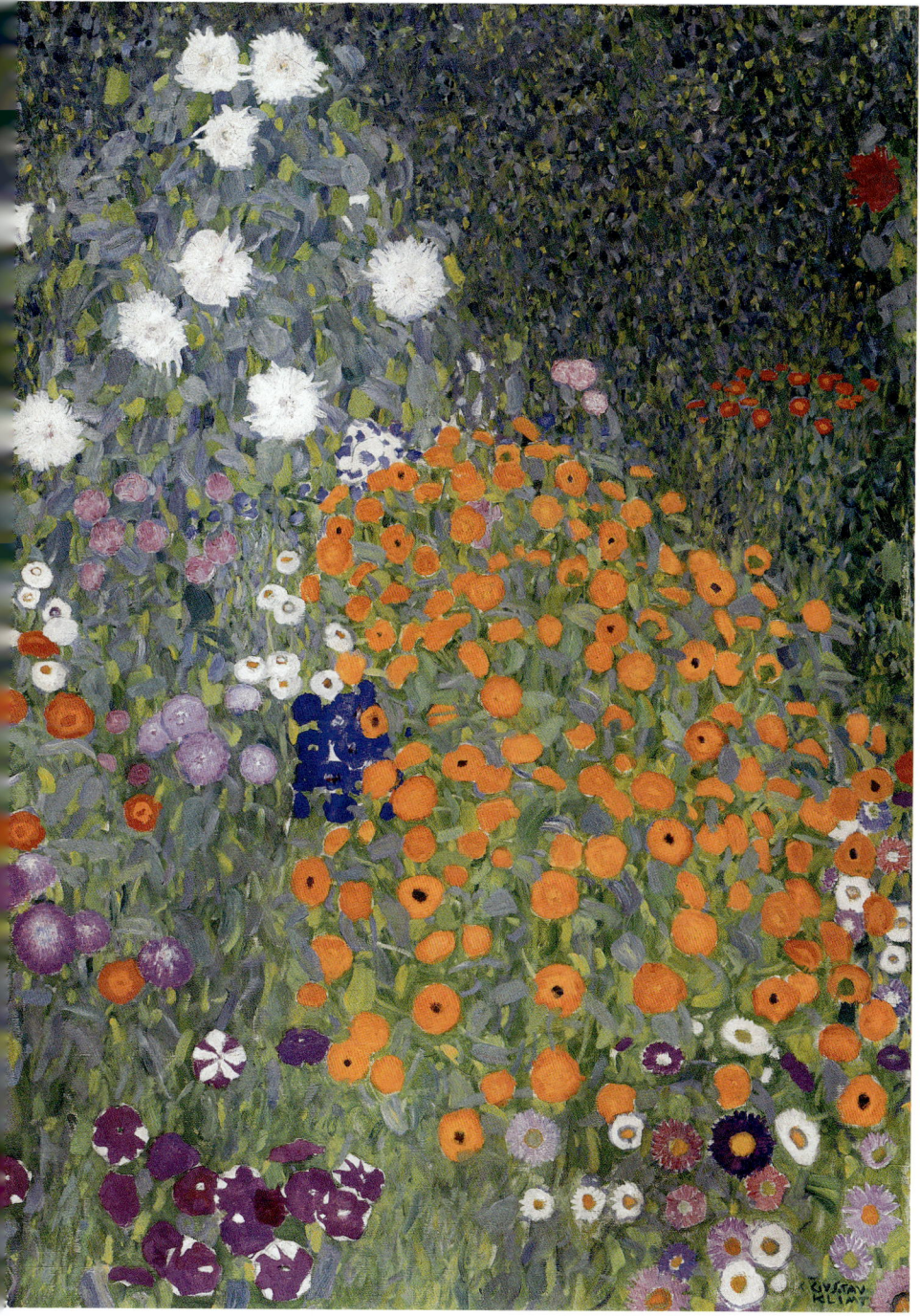

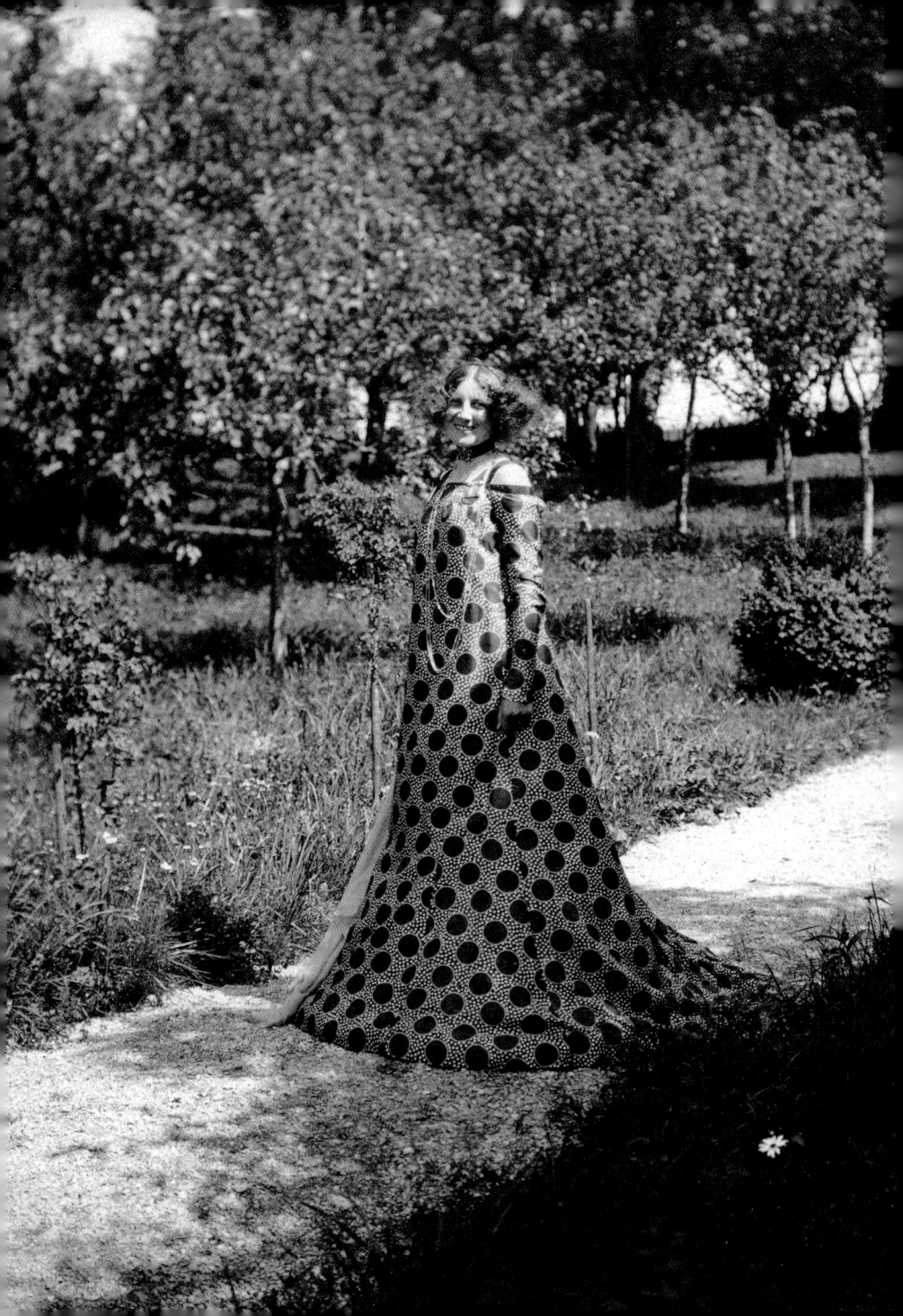

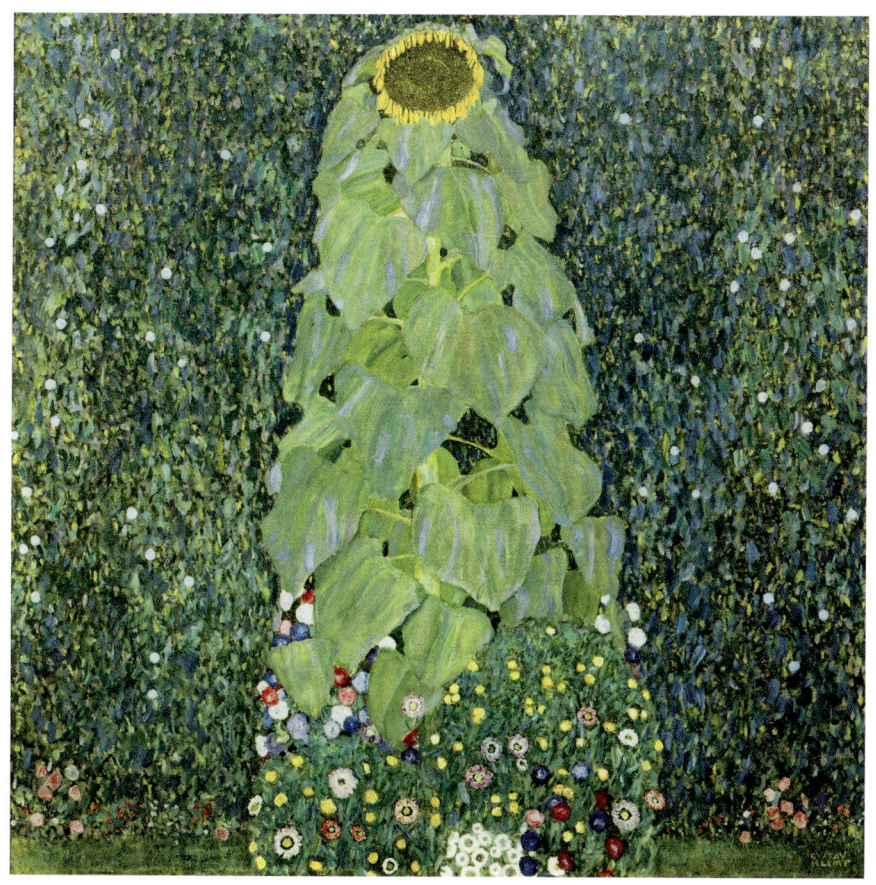

Emilie Flöge in the garden of the Litzlberg brewery on Lake Attersee, 1906
Photograph. Imagno/Austrian Archives

The Sunflower, 1907
Oil on canvas, 110 x 110 cm / 43 ¼ x 43 ¼ in.
Vienna, Belvedere

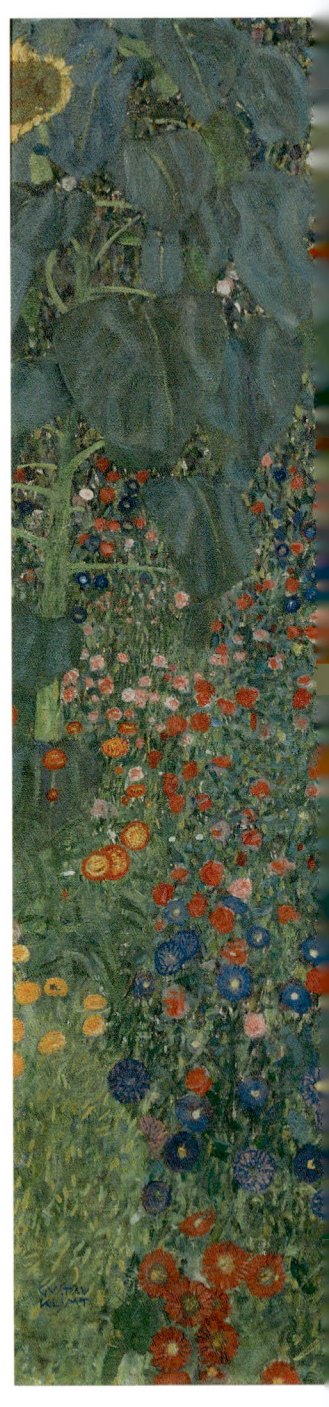

Cottage Garden with Sunflowers, 1908
Oil on canvas, 110 x 110 cm / 43 ¼ x 43 ¼ in.
Vienna, Belvedere

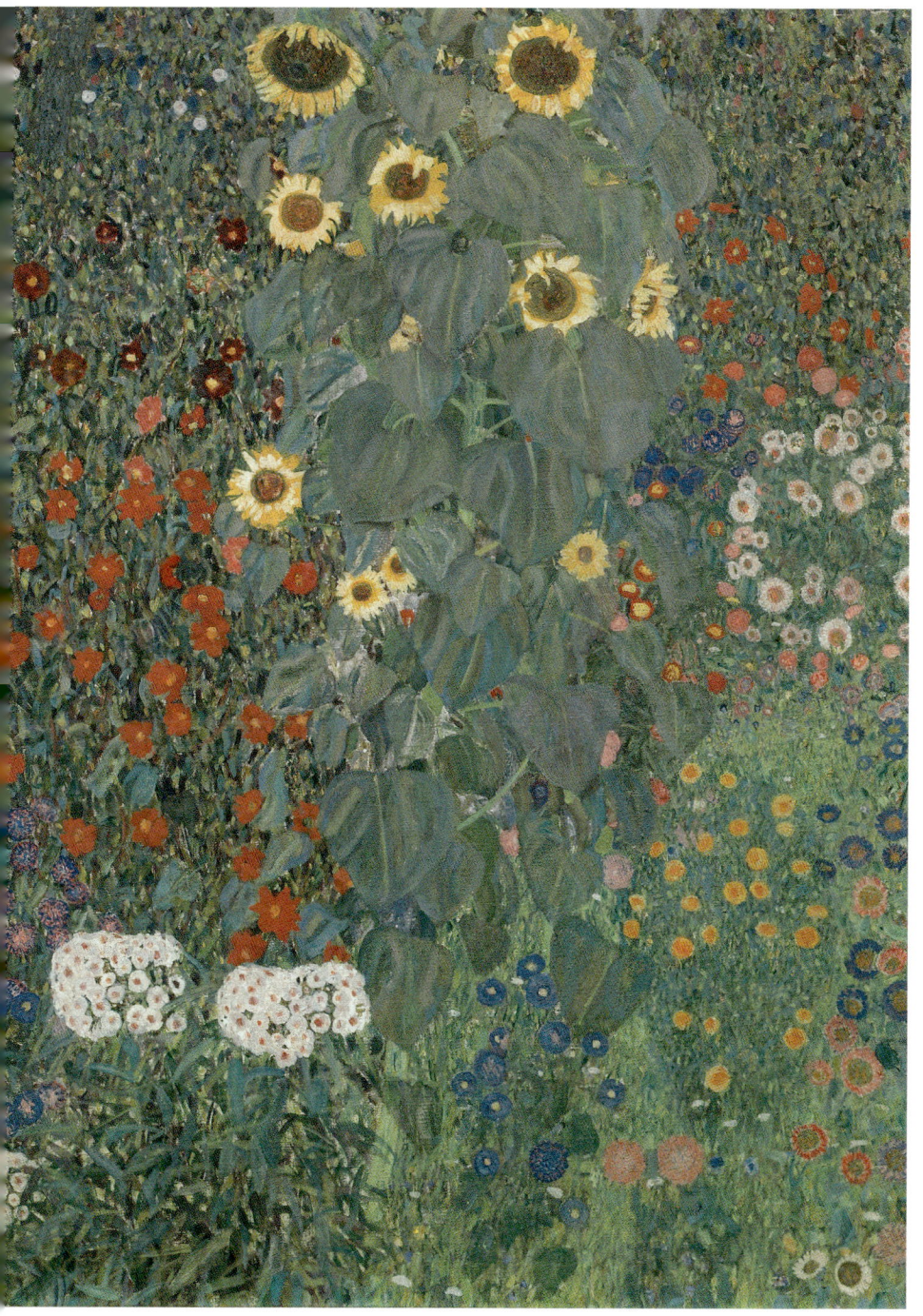

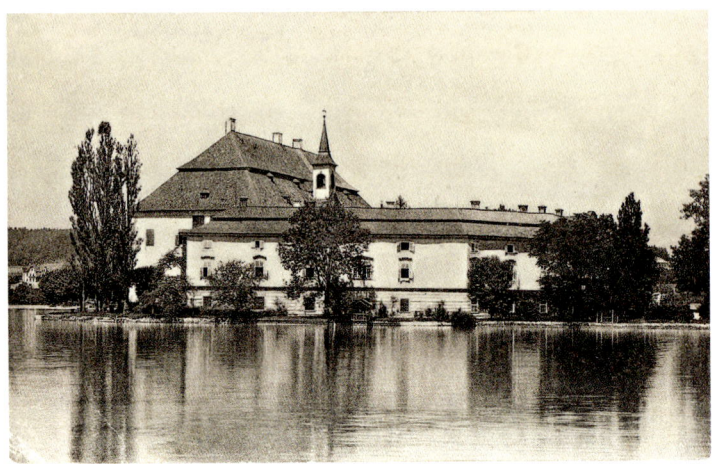

Kammer Castle, c. 1905
Postcard. Vienna, private collection

Kammer Castle on Lake Attersee I (Castle in the Lake), 1908
Oil on canvas, 110 x 110 cm / 43 ¼ x 43 ¼ in.
Prague, Národní Galerie

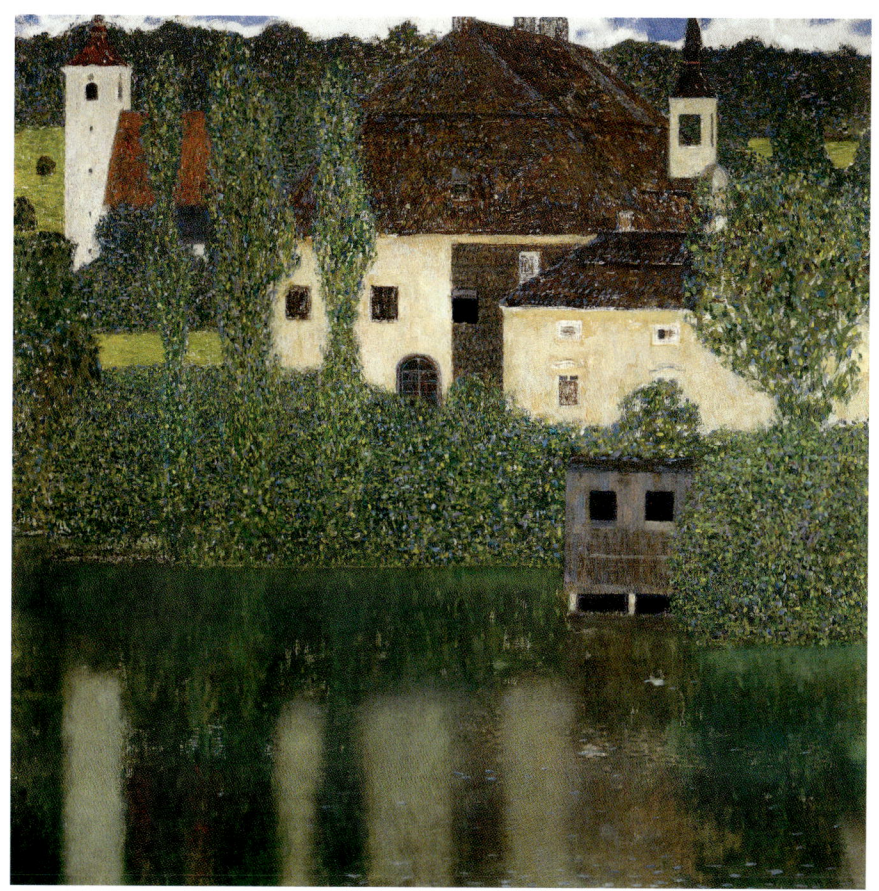

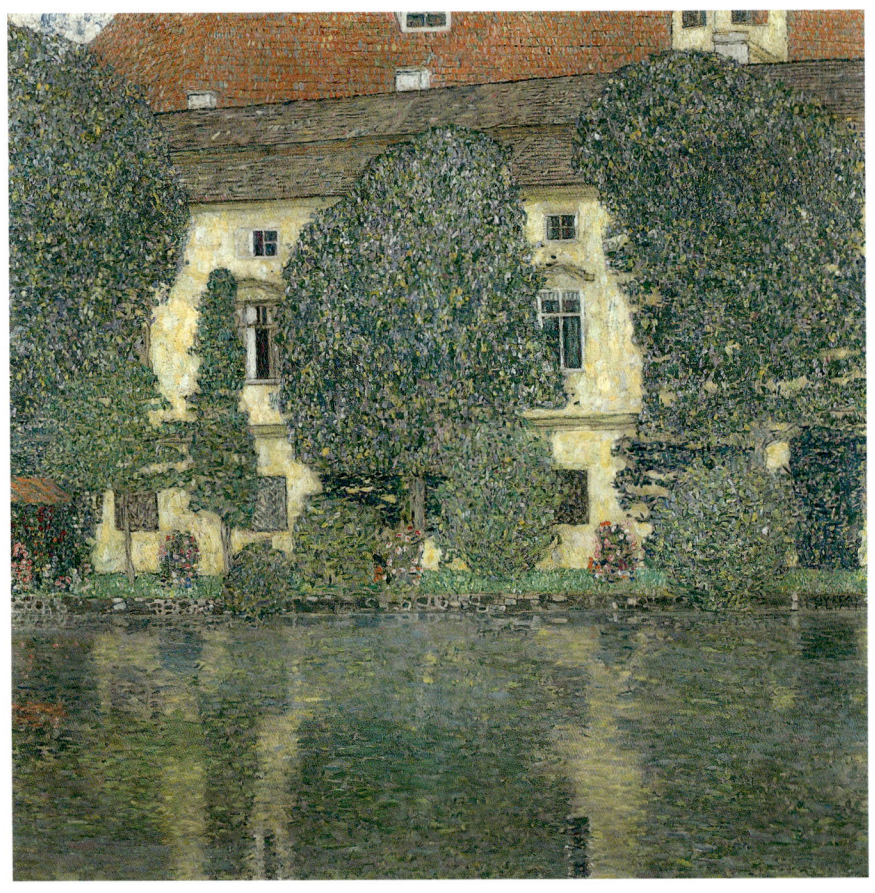

Kammer Castle on Lake Attersee III, 1910
Oil on canvas, 110 x 110 cm / 43 ¼ x 43 ¼ in.
Vienna, Belvedere

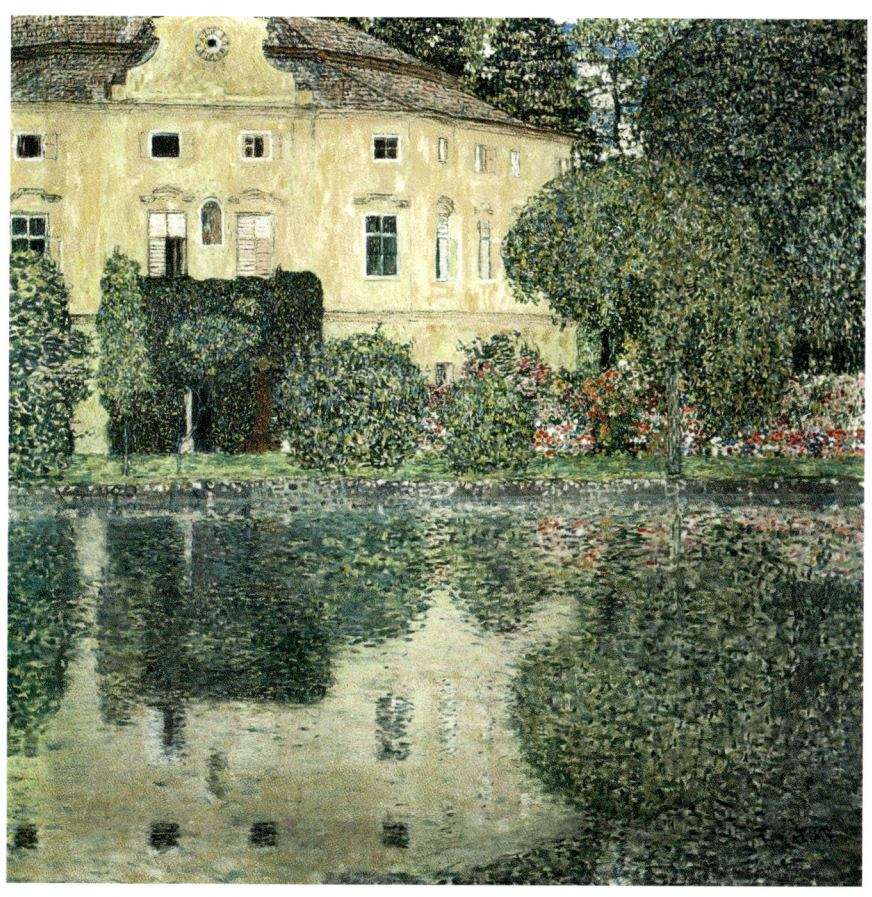

Kammer Castle on Lake Attersee IV, 1910
Oil on canvas, 110 x 110 cm / 43 ¼ x 43 ¼ in.
Vienna, private collection

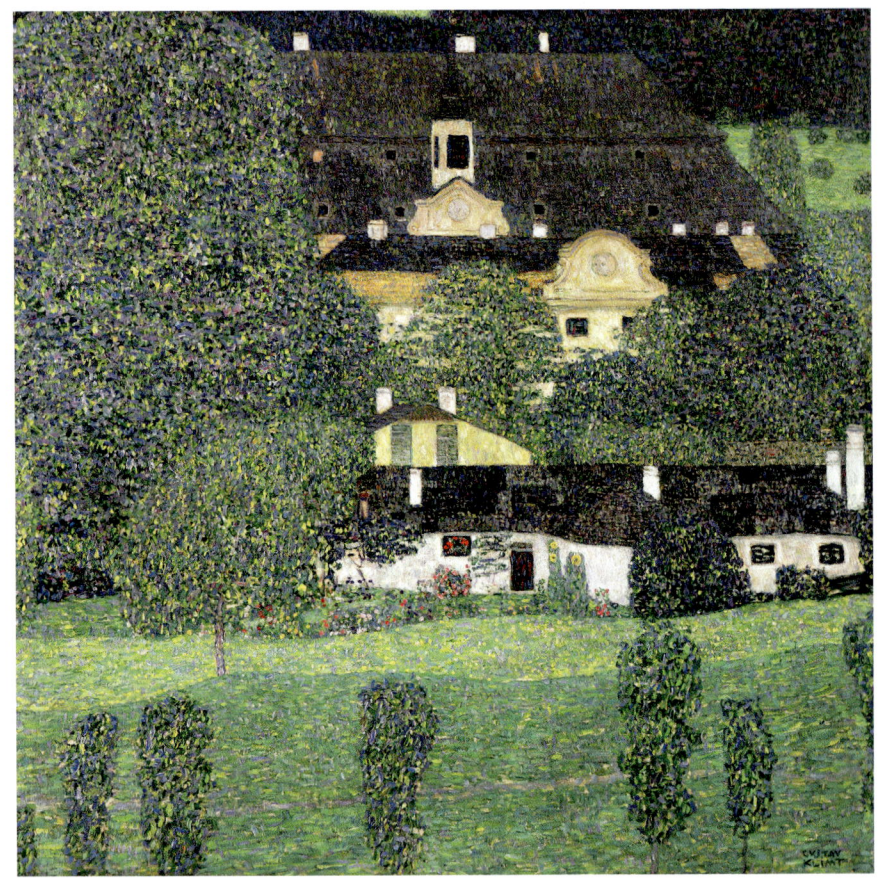

Kammer Castle on Lake Attersee II, 1909
Oil on canvas, 110 x 110 cm / 43 ¼ x 43 ¼ in.
Private collection

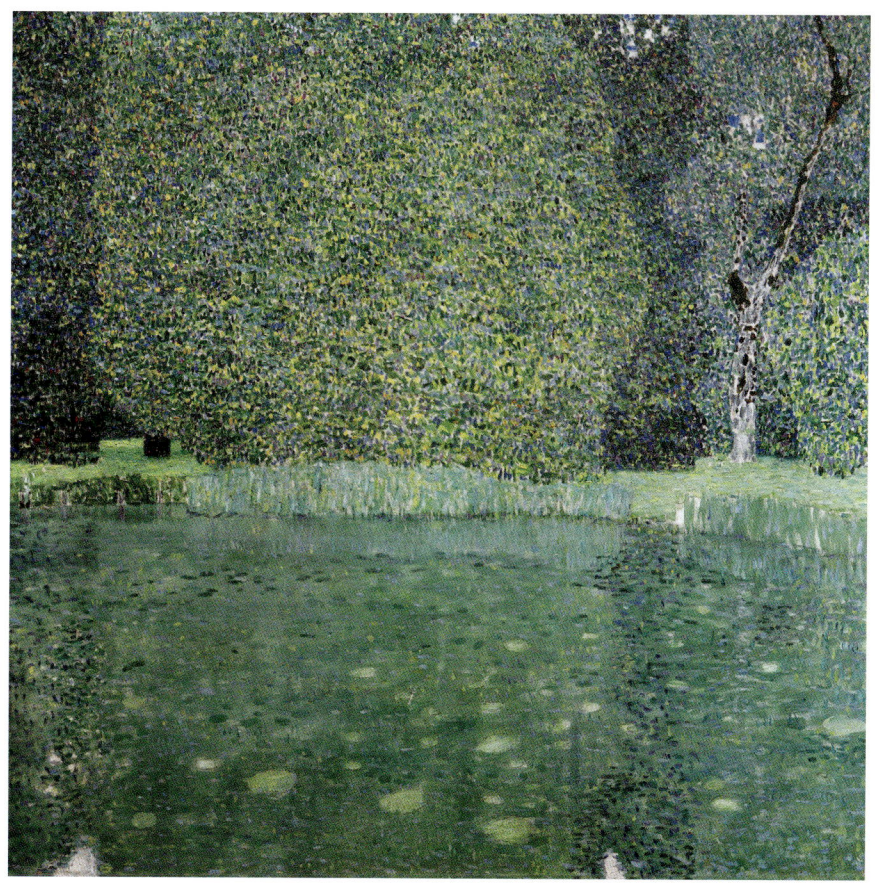

Park at Kammer Castle, 1909
Oil on canvas, 110 x 110 cm / 43 ¼ x 43 ¼ in.
New York, private collection

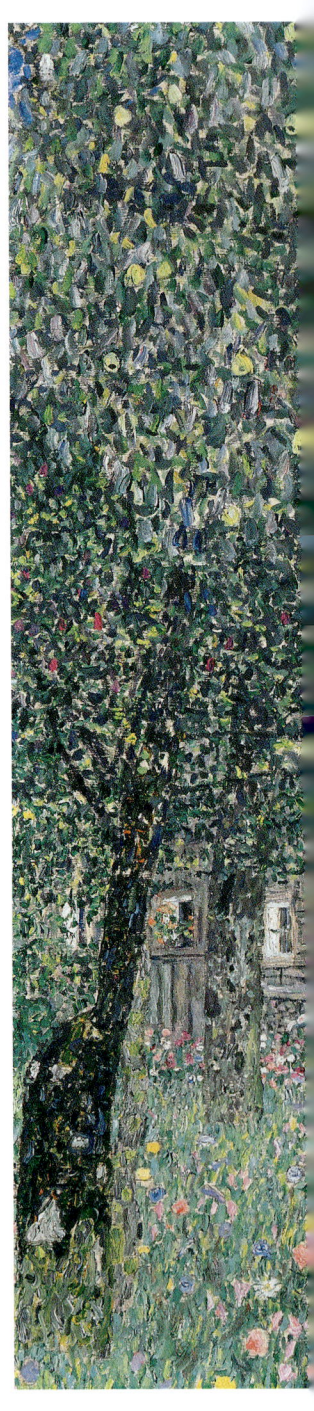

Upper Austrian Farmhouse, 1911
Oil on canvas, 110 x 110 cm / 43 ¼ x 43 ¼ in.
Vienna, Belvedere

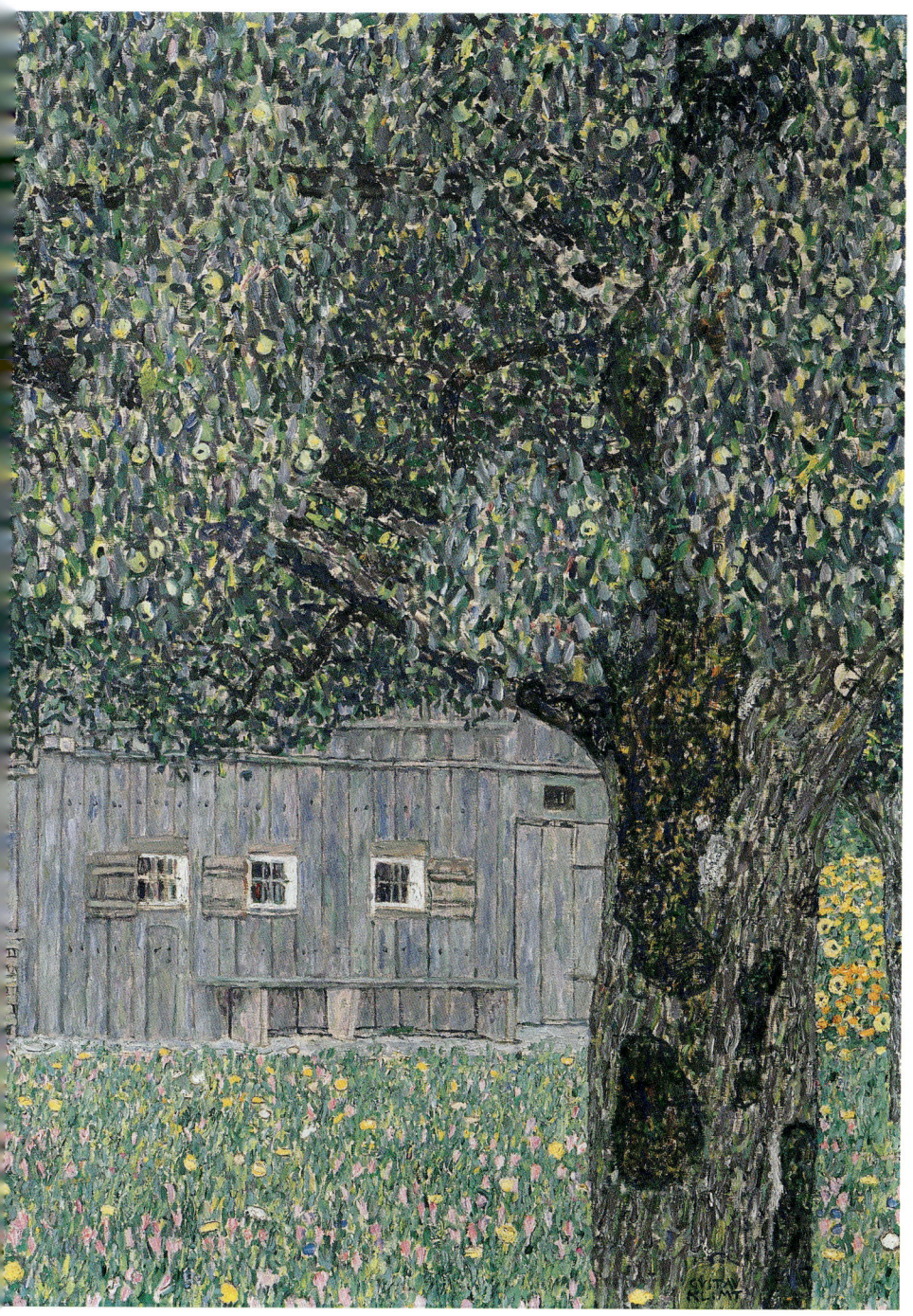

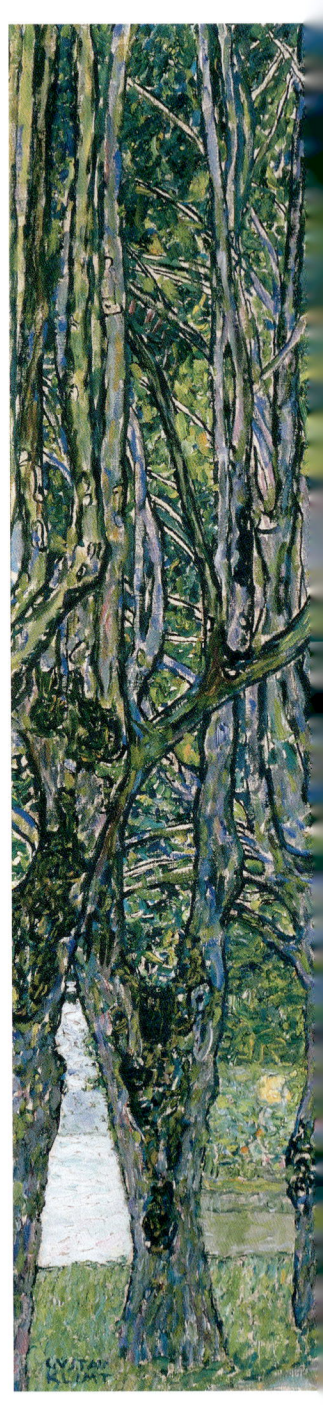

Avenue in Front of Kammer Castle, 1912
Oil on canvas, 110 x 110 cm / 43 ¼ x 43 ¼ in.
Vienna, Belvedere

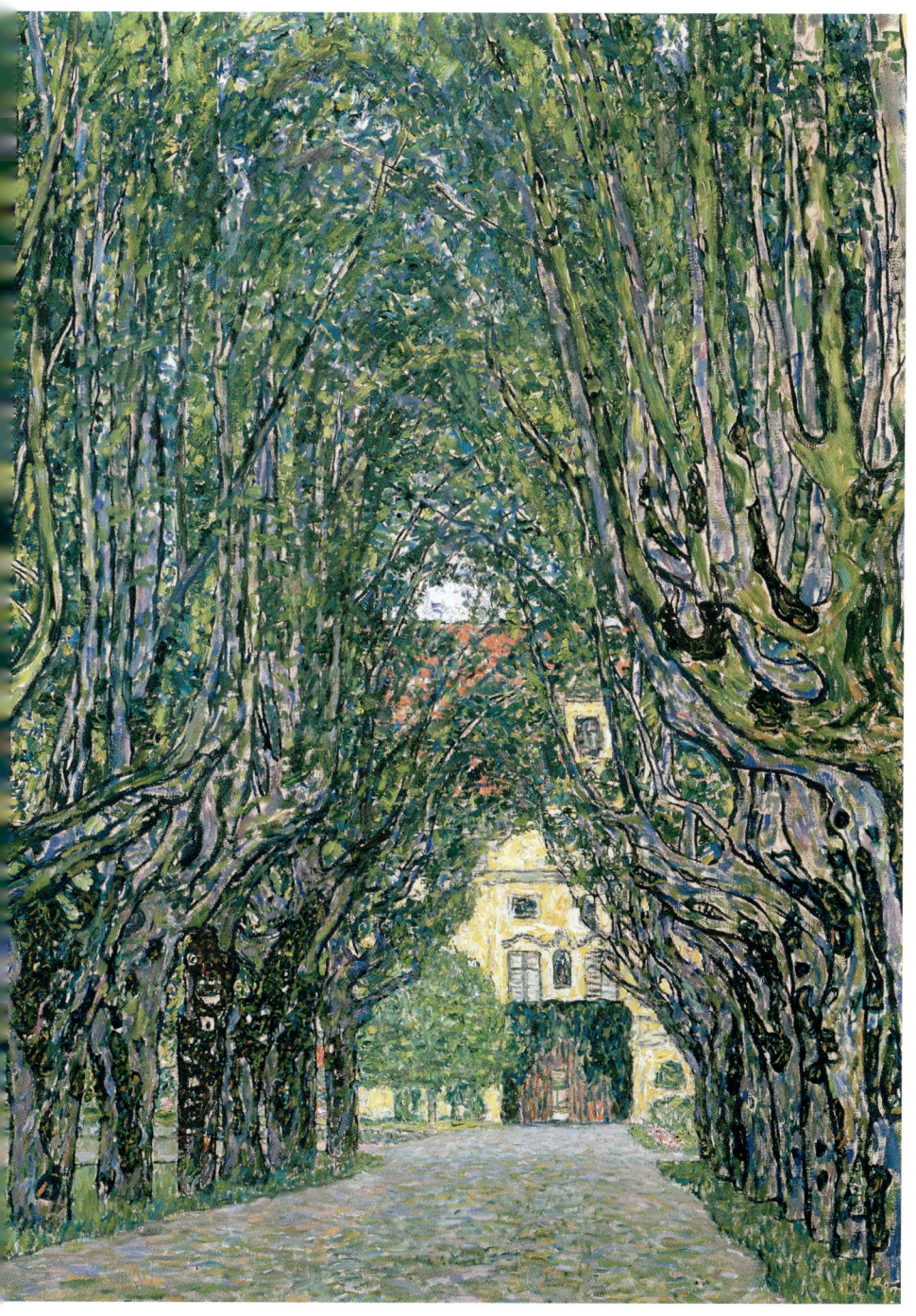

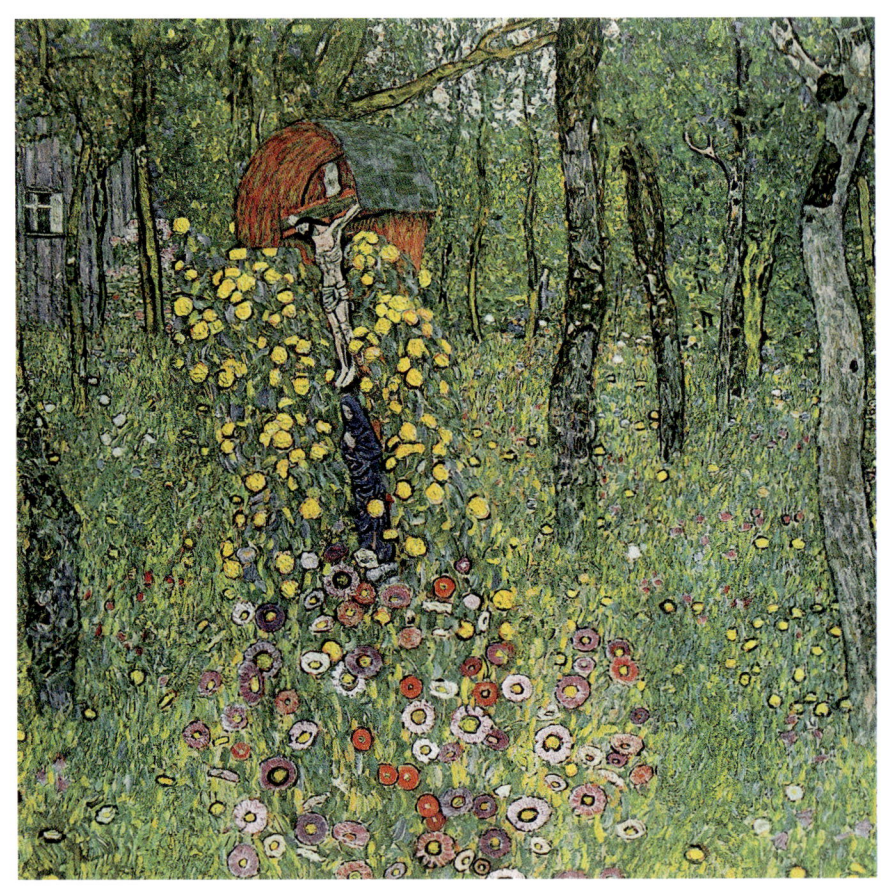

Country Garden with Calvary, 1912
Oil on canvas, 110 x 110 cm / 43 ¼ x 43 ¼ in.
Destroyed by fire in May 1945 at Immendorf Castle, Lower Austria

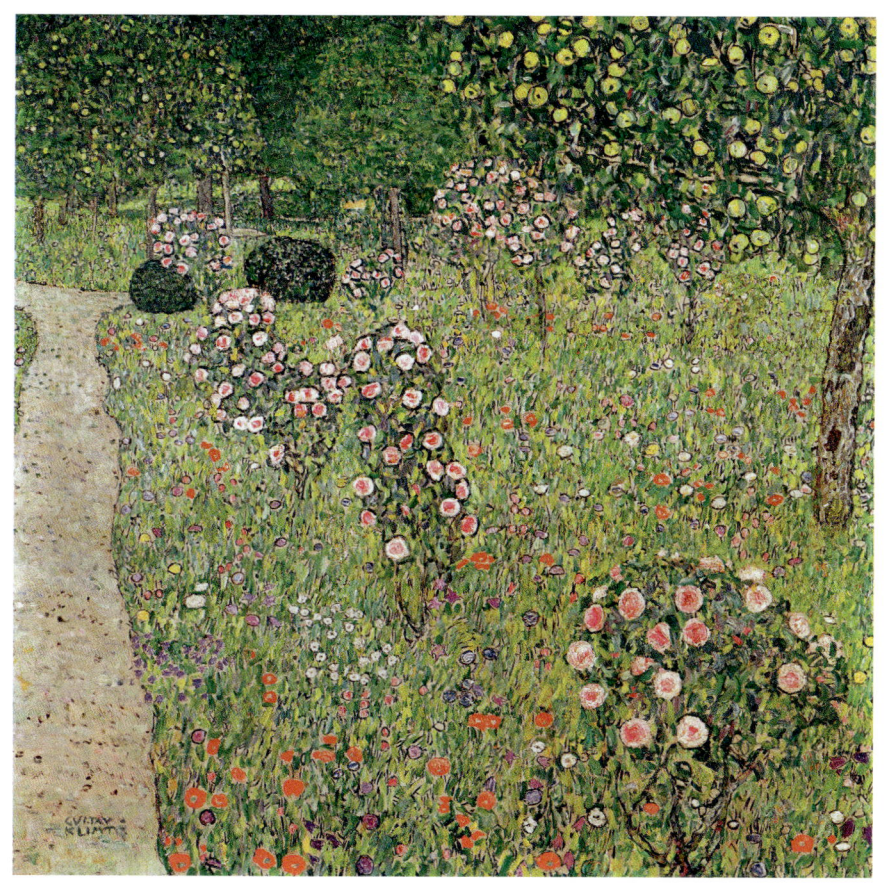

Orchard with Roses (Rose Garden), 1912
Oil on canvas, 110 x 110 cm / 43 ¼ x 43 ¼ in.
Lower Austria, private collection

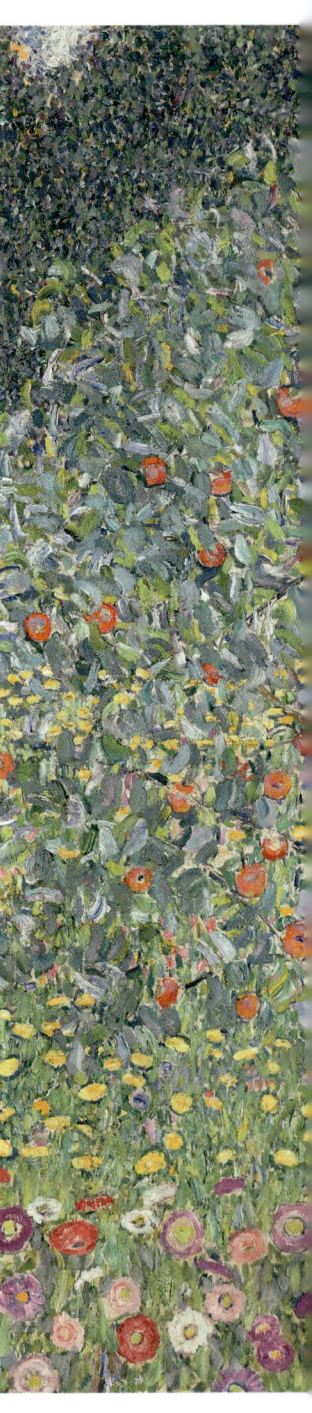

"When painting, you transform yourself quite suddenly, almost magically, into the most 'modern man', whom you might not actually be in real life on that day and at that hour!"

Apple Tree I, c. 1912
Oil on canvas, 109 x 110 cm / 42 ⅞ x 43 ¼ in.
Private collection

Pages 456/57
Gustav Klimt, 1904
On the deck of the Villa Paulick boathouse
in Seewalchen on Lake Attersee
Photograph. Imagno/Austrian Archives

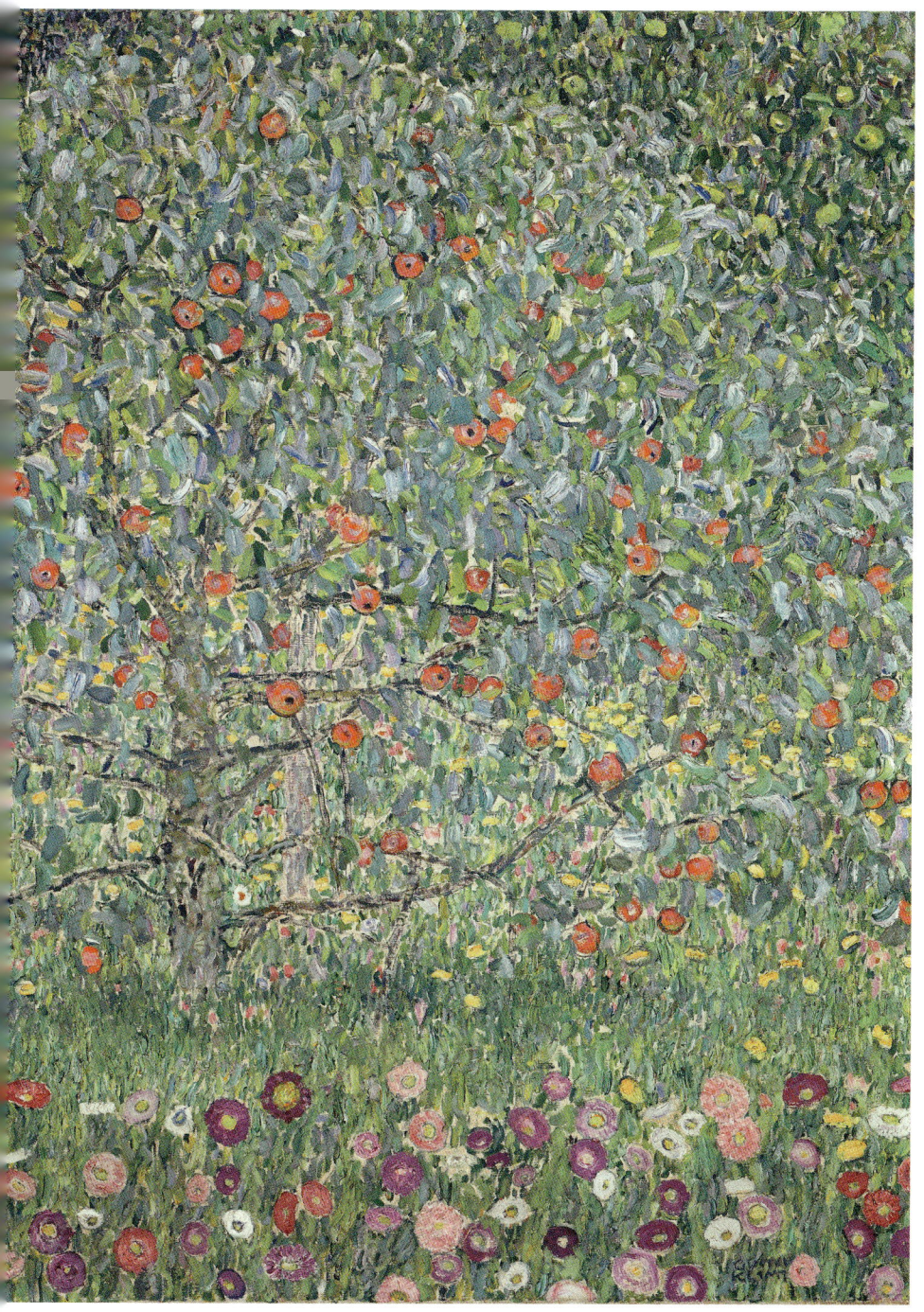

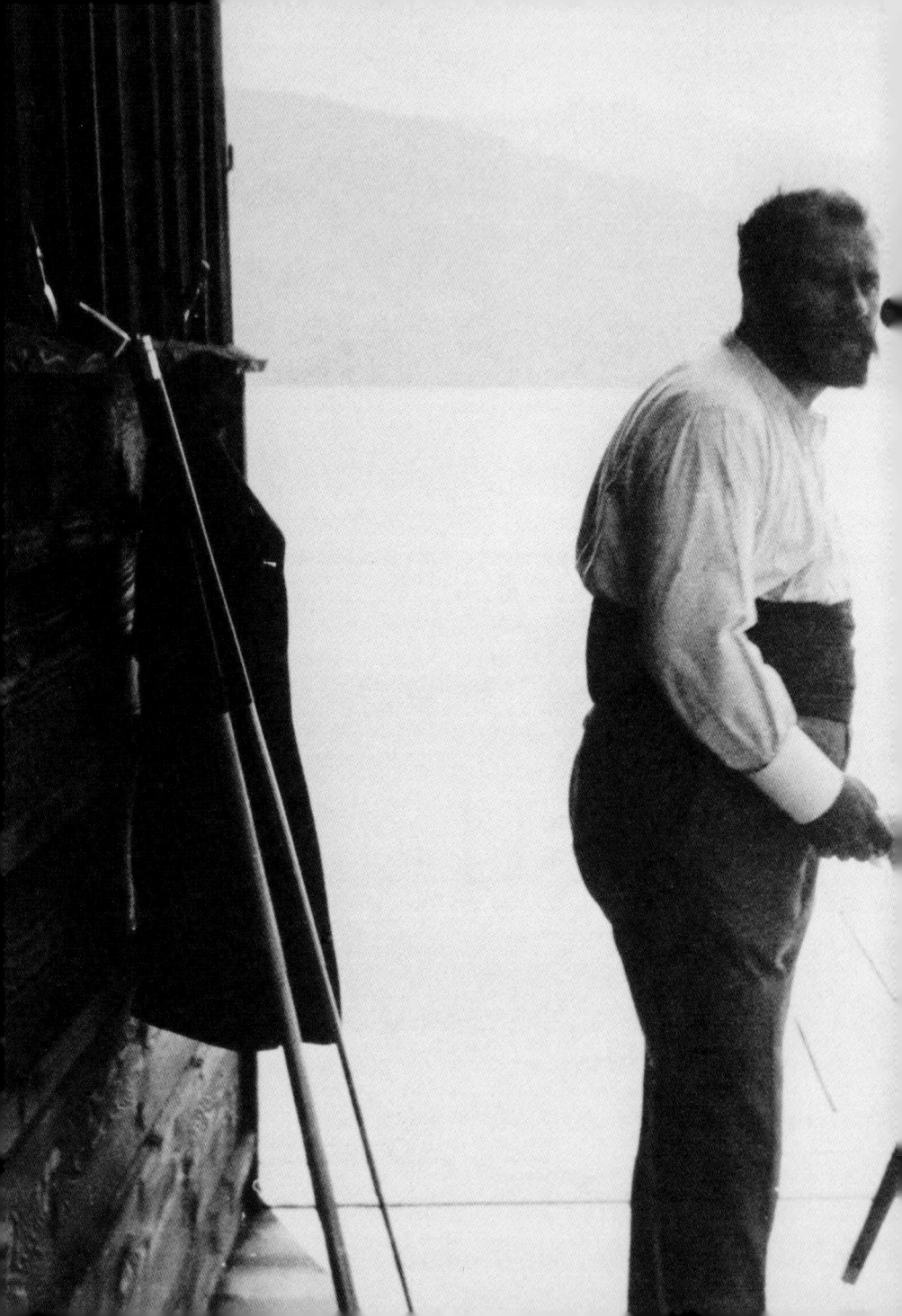

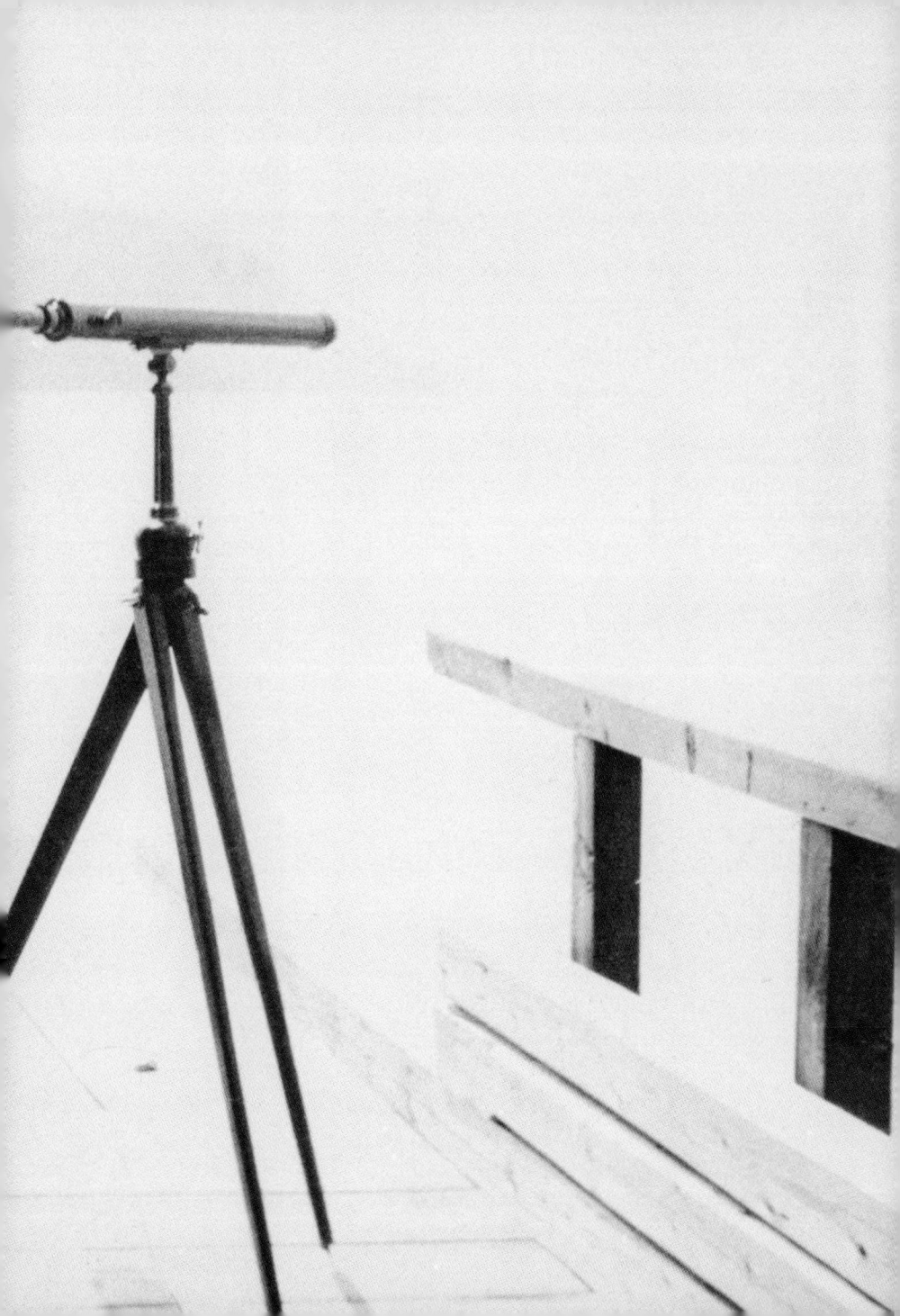

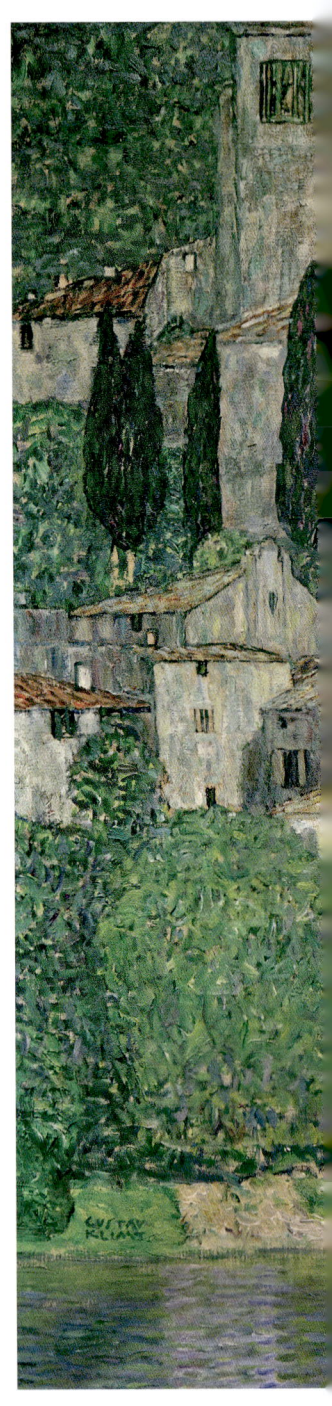

Church in Cassone (Landscape with Cypresses), 1913
Oil on canvas, 110 x 110 cm / 43 ¼ x 43 ¼ in.
Private collection

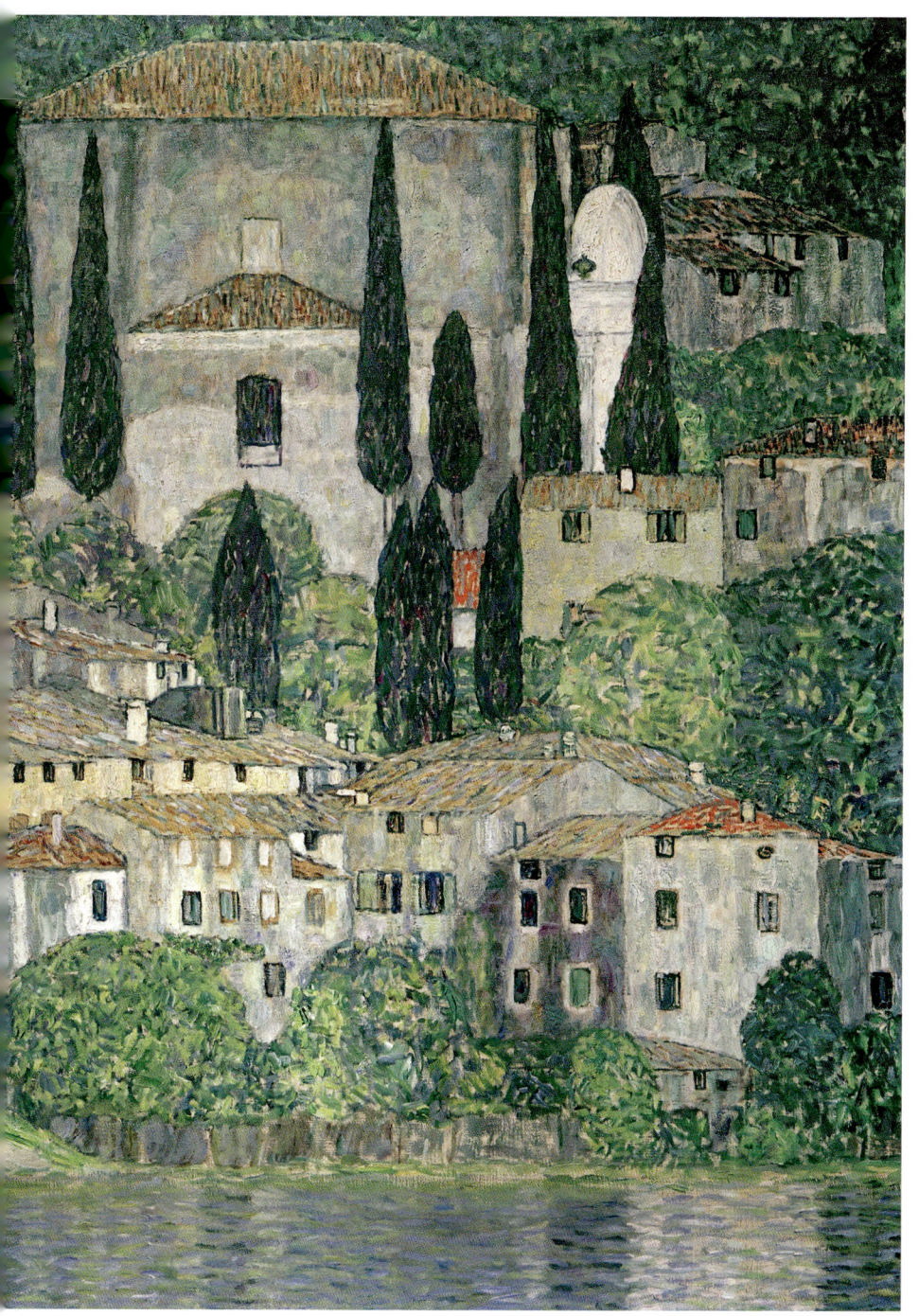

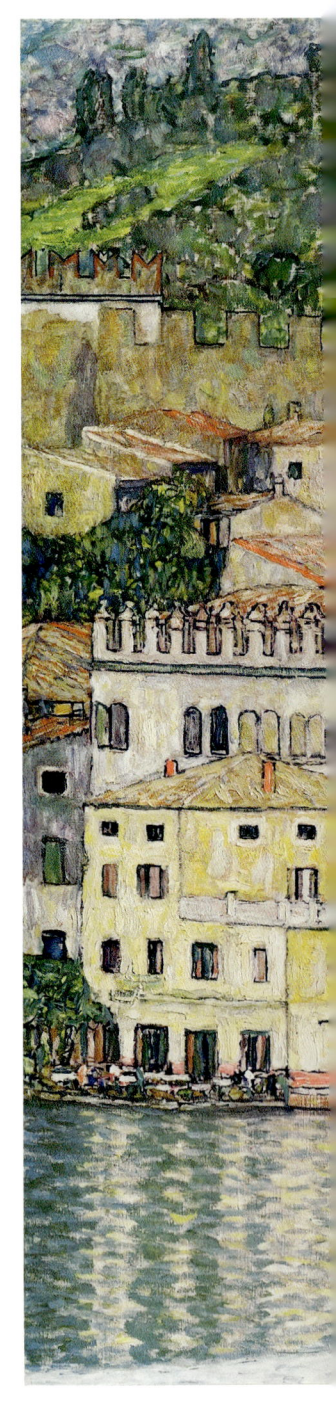

Malcesine on Lake Garda, 1913
Oil on canvas, 110 x 110 cm / 43 ¼ x 43 ¼ in.
Destroyed by fire in May 1945 at Immendorf Castle, Lower Austria

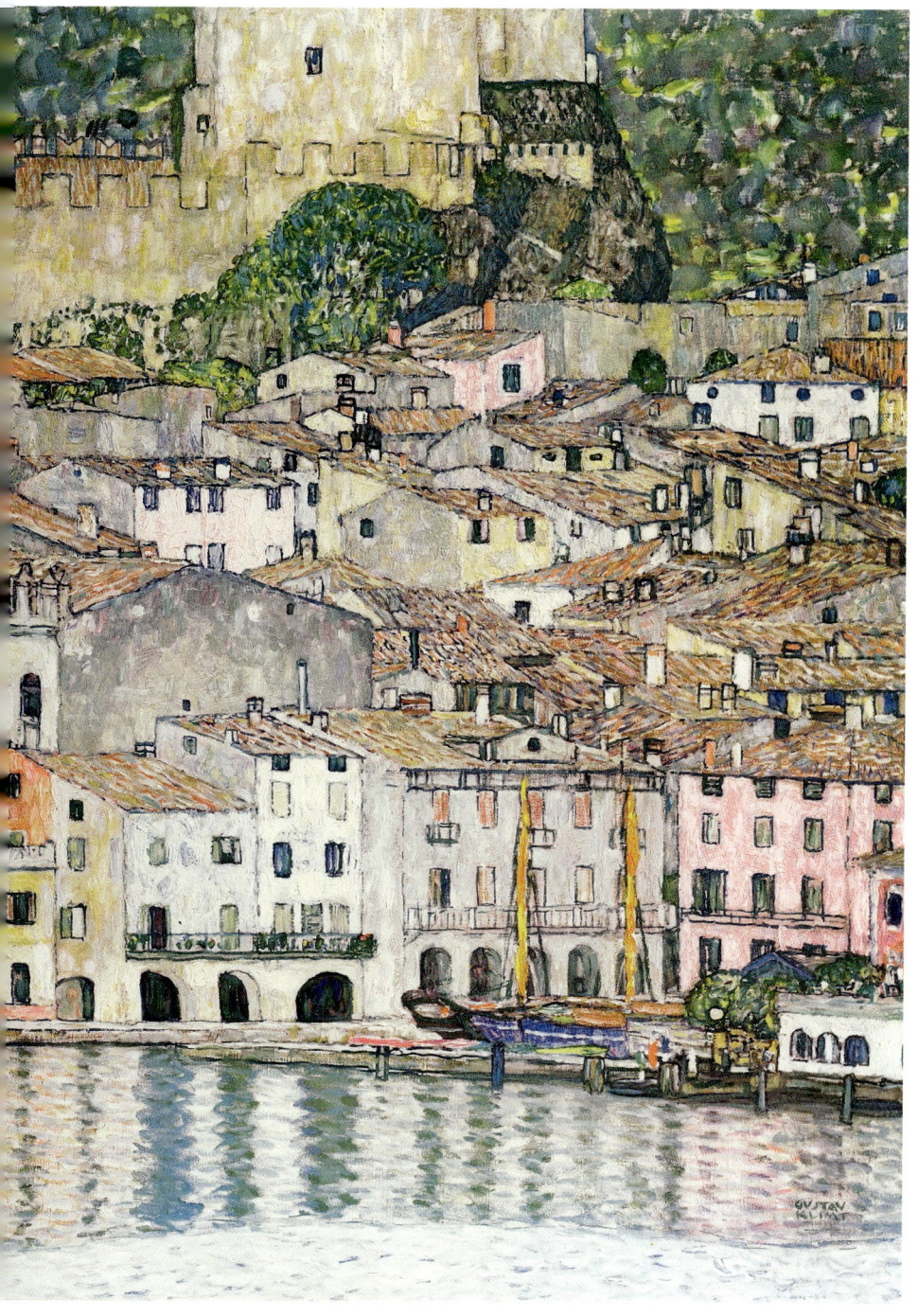

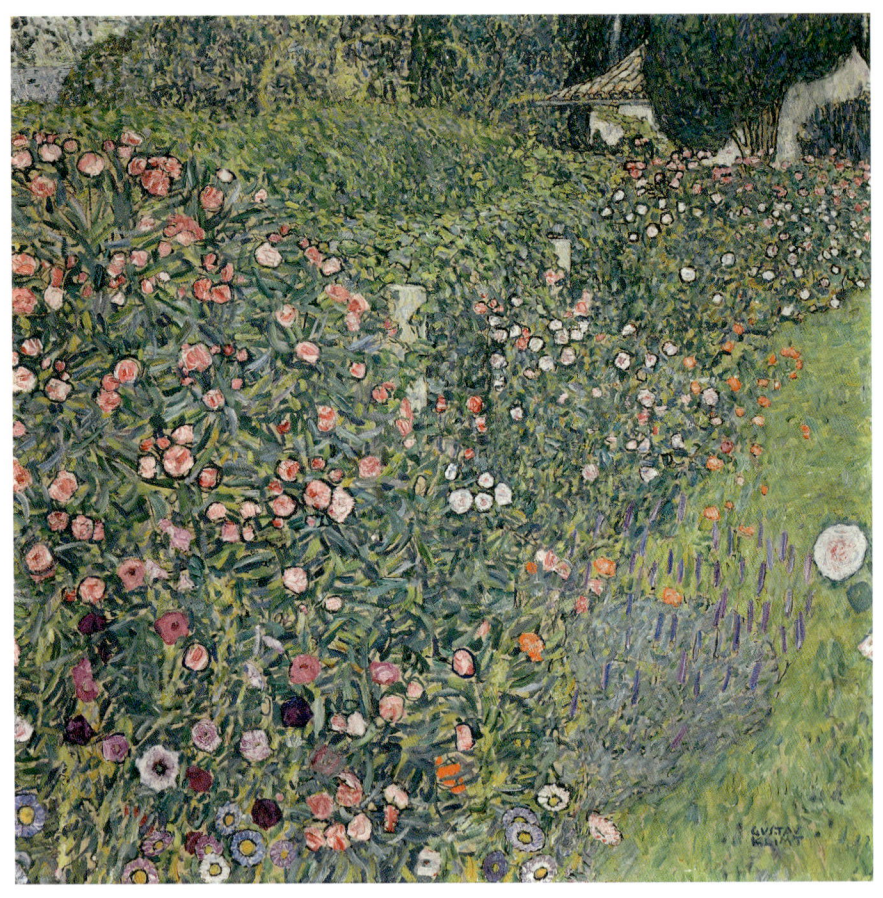

Italian Garden Landscape, 1913
Oil on canvas, 110 x 110 cm / 43 ¼ x 43 ¼ in.
Kunsthaus Zug, Kamm Collection Foundation

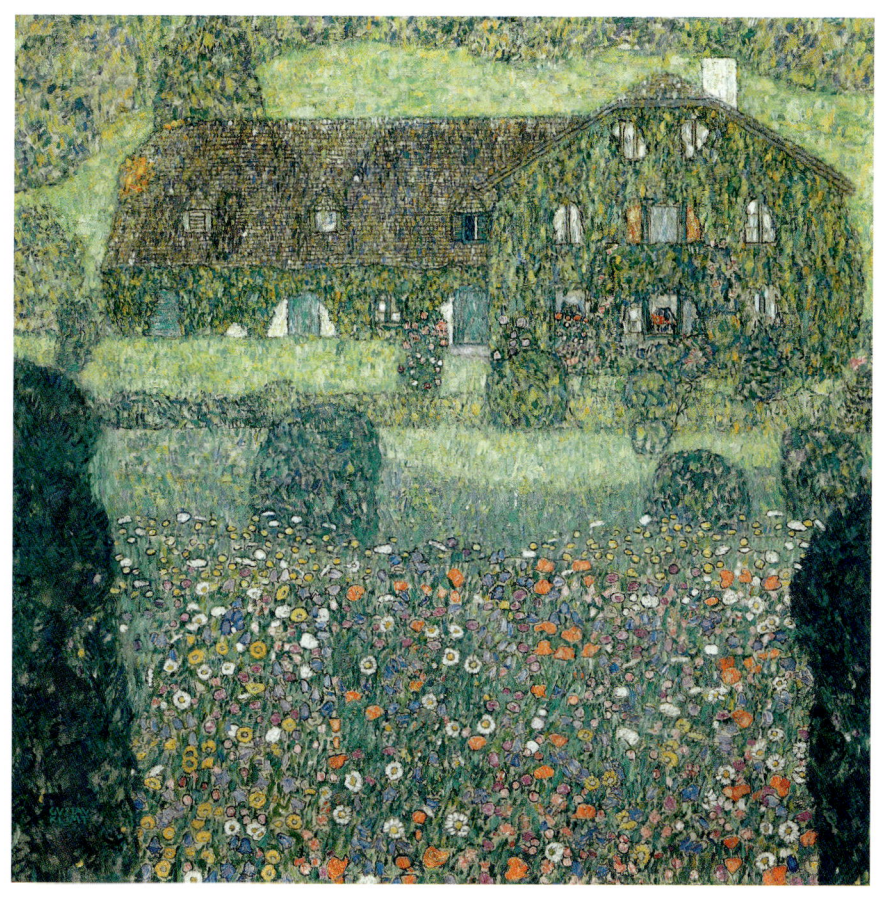

Forester's House in Weissenbach I, 1914
Oil on canvas, 110 x 110 cm / 43 ¼ x 43 ¼ in.
Private collection

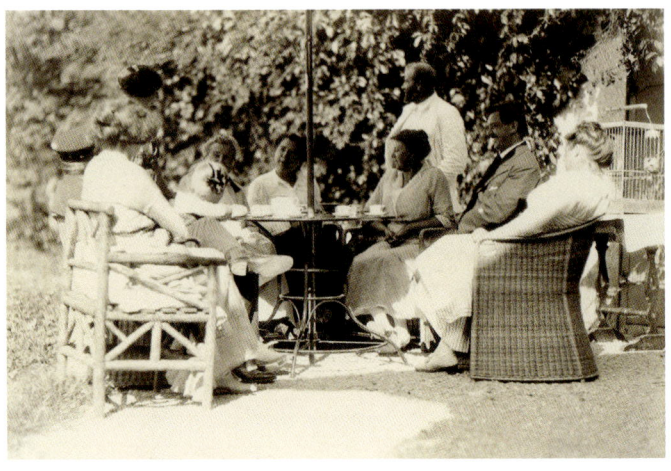

**Gustav Klimt with the Flöge family and Otto Prutscher
in Weissenbach on Lake Attersee**, 1914
Photograph. Imagno/Austrian Archives

Forester's House in Weissenbach II (Garden), 1914
Oil on canvas, 110 x 110 cm / 43 ¼ x 43 ¼ in.
New York, private collection

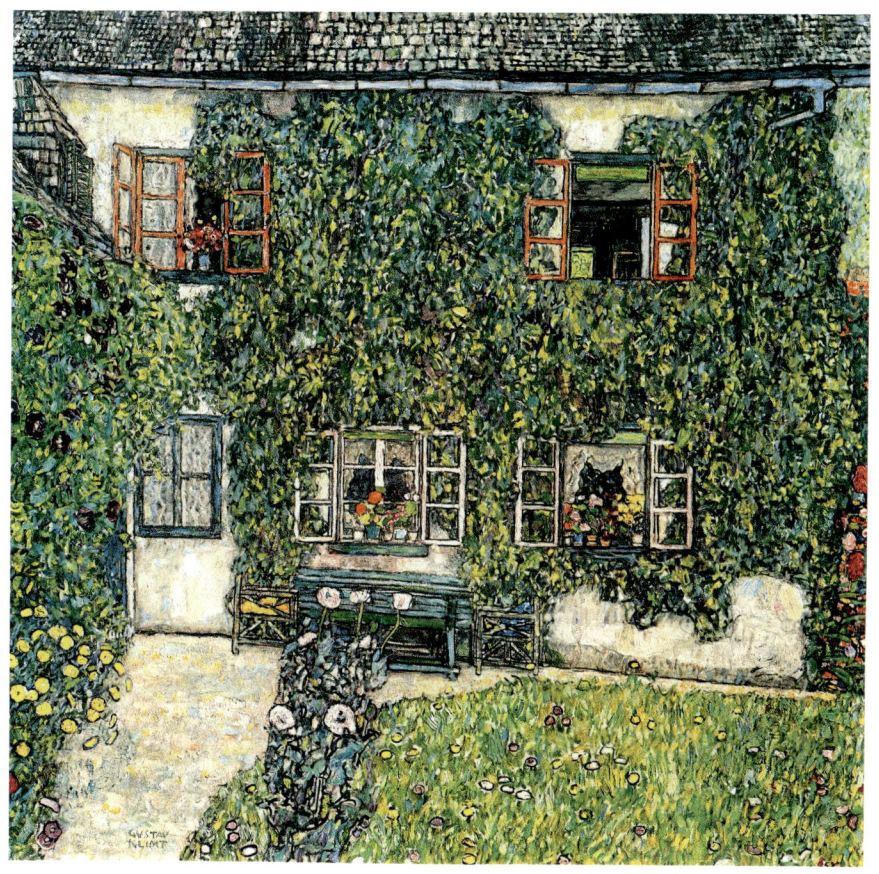

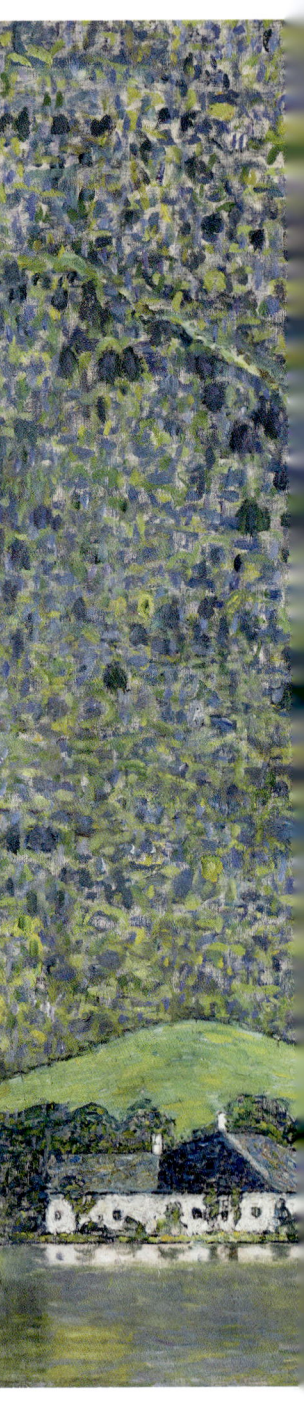

Litzlberg on Lake Attersee, c. 1915
Oil on canvas, 110 x 110 cm / 43 ¼ x 43 ¼ in.
Private collection

Pages 468/69
**Emilie Flöge, Gustav Klimt, Therese Flöge, Emma Bacher,
Rudolf Schuh and Paul Bacher**, 1904
On a jetty near the Litzlbergkeller on Lake Attersee
Photograph. Imagno/Austrian Archives

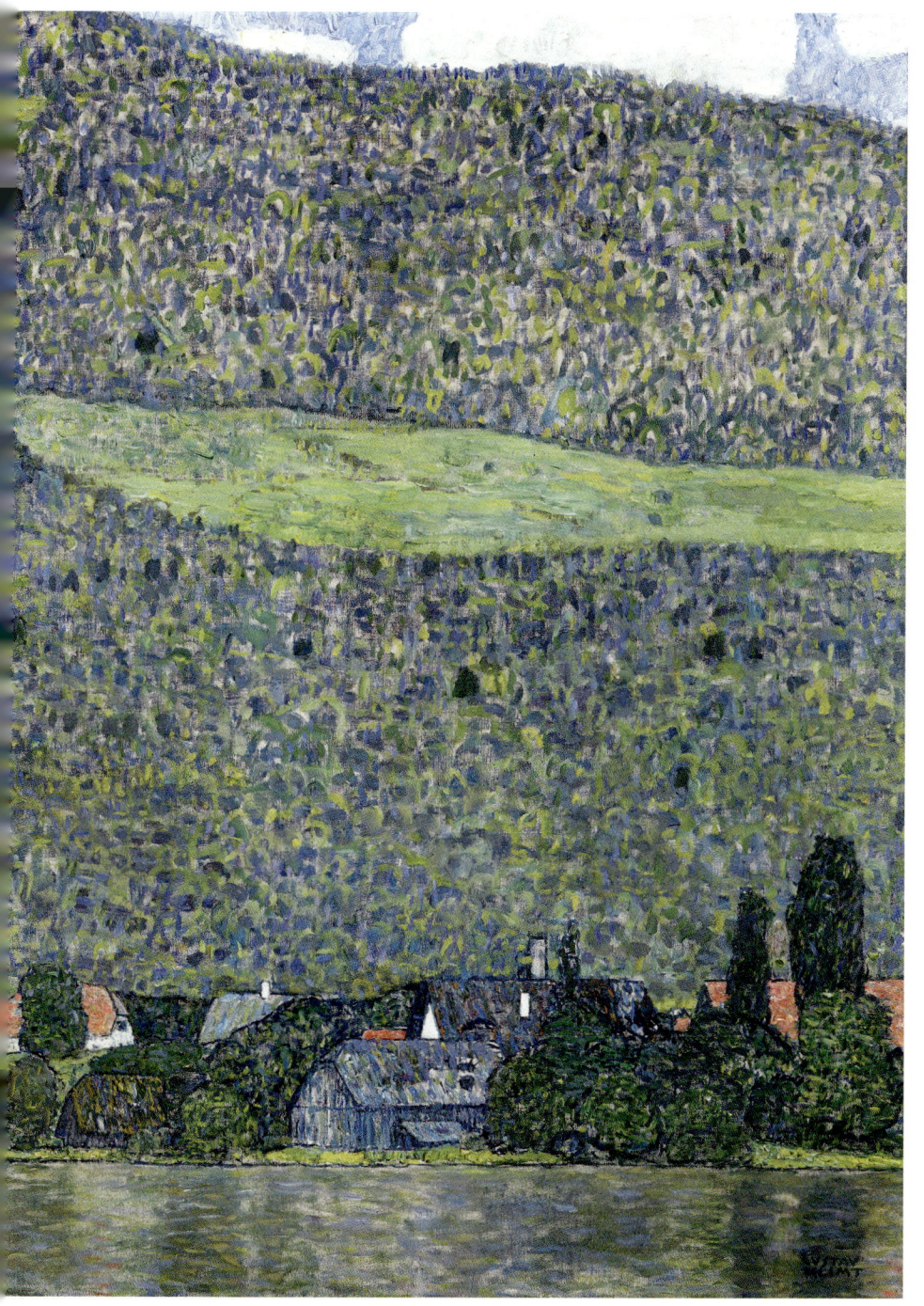

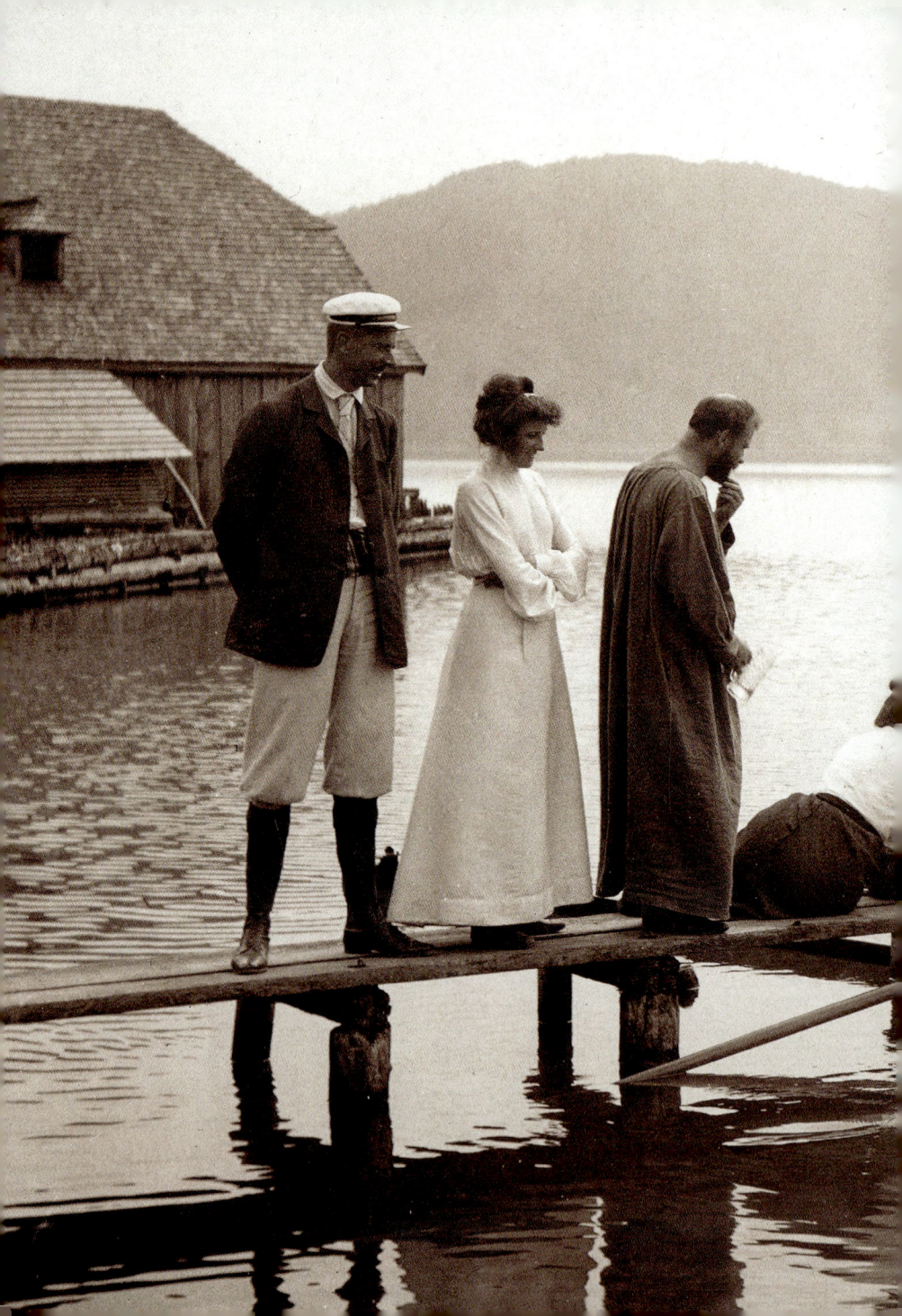

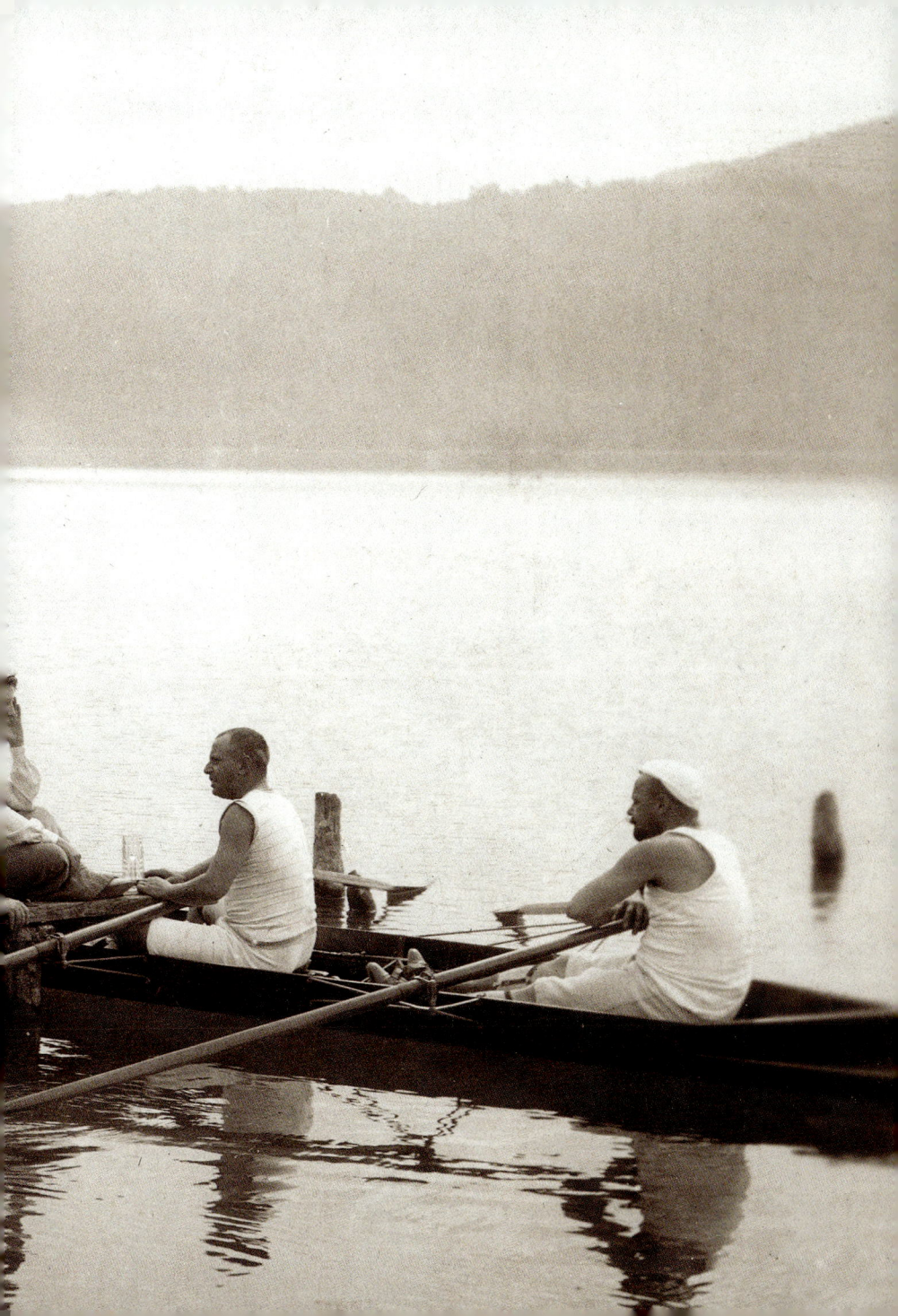

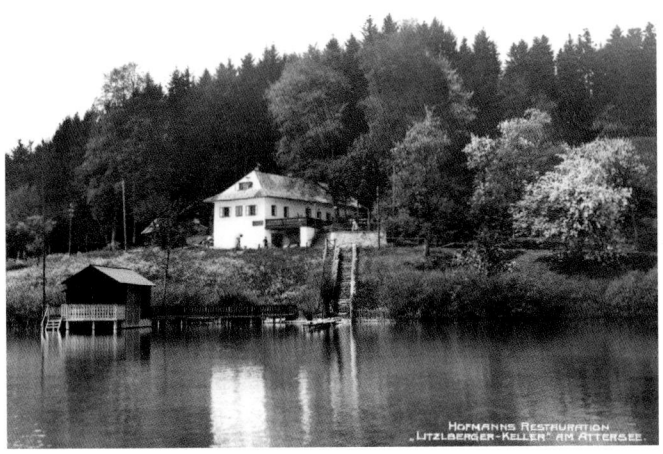

The Litzlbergkeller café-restaurant, c. 1900
Photograph. Private collection

Litzlbergkeller, 1915/16
Oil on canvas, 110 x 110 cm / 43 ¼ x 43 ¼ in.
Private collection

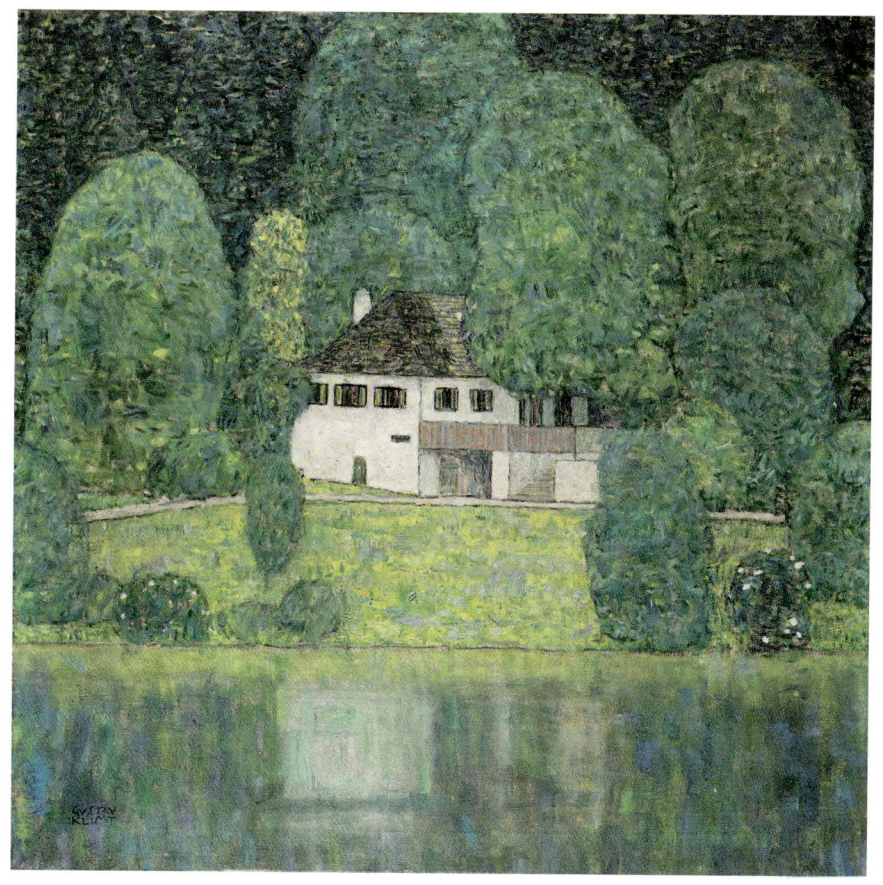

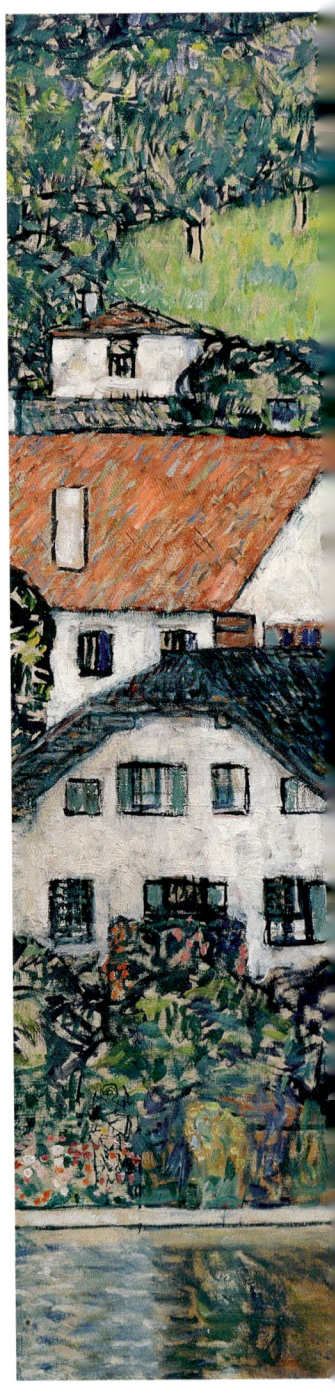

Houses in Unterach on Lake Attersee, 1915/16
Oil on canvas, 110 x 110 cm / 43 ¼ x 43 ¼ in.
Private collection

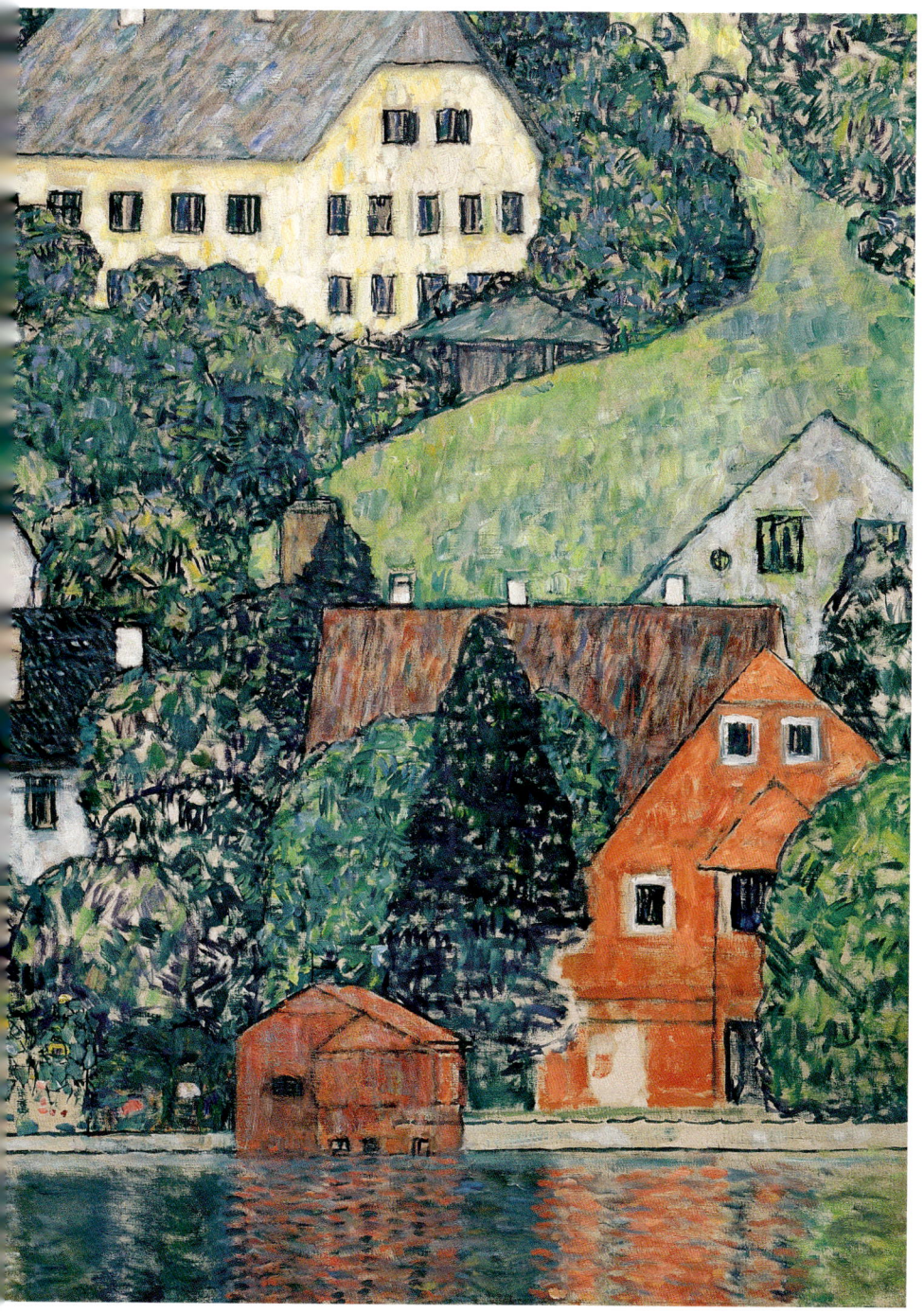

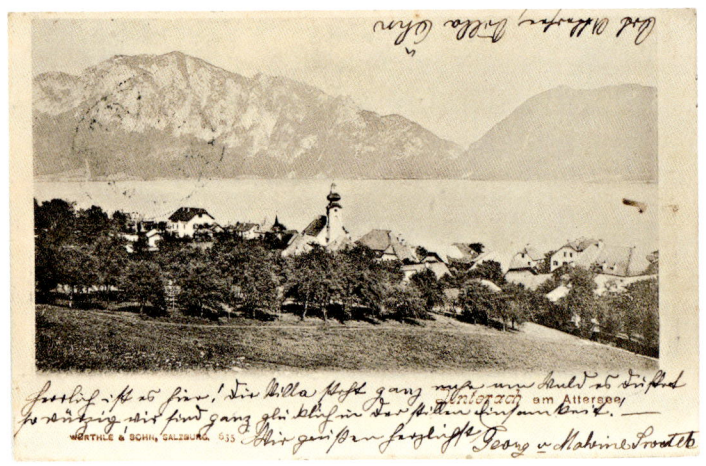

Church in Unterach on Lake Attersee
Postcard. Vienna, private collection

Church in Unterach on Lake Attersee, 1915/16
Oil on canvas, 110 x 110 cm / 43 ¼ x 43 ¼ in.
Private collection

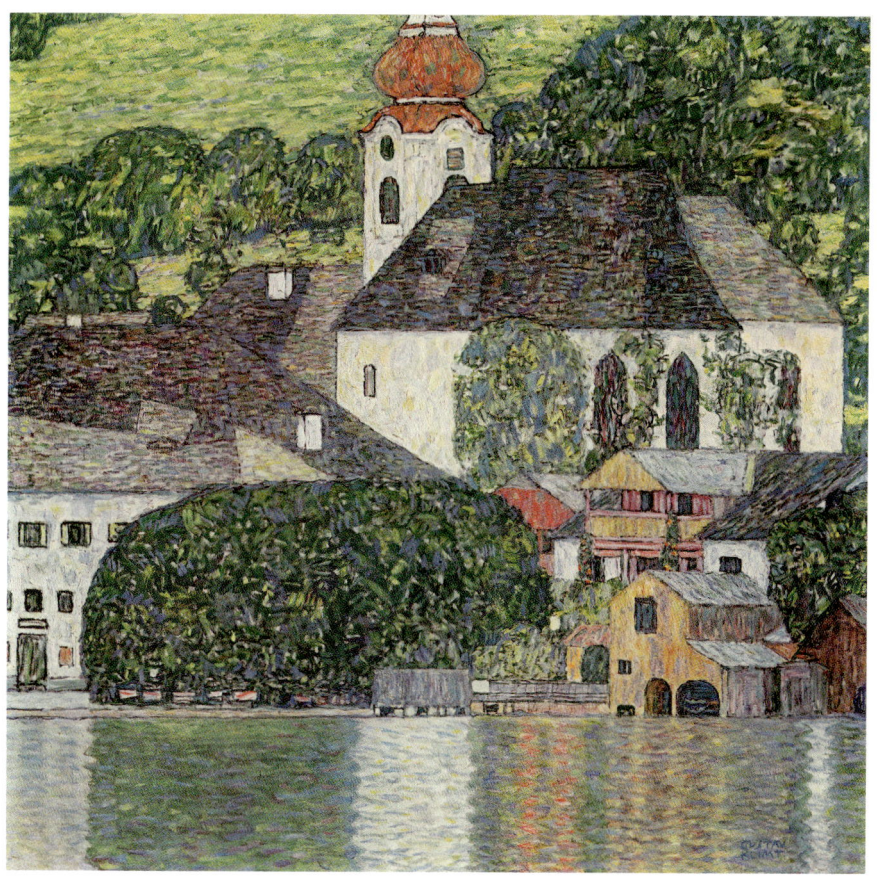

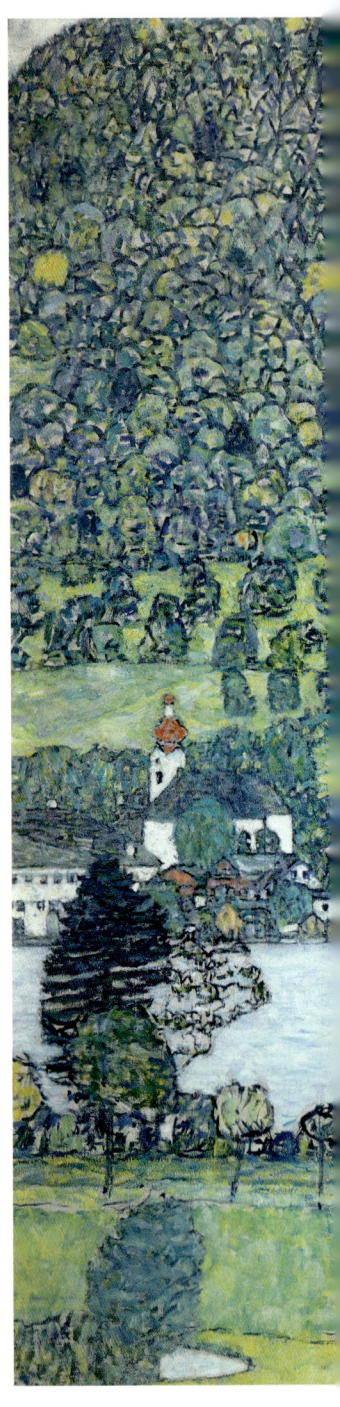

Unterach on Lake Attersee, 1916
Oil on canvas, 110 x 110 cm / 43 ¼ x 43 ¼ in.
Private collection

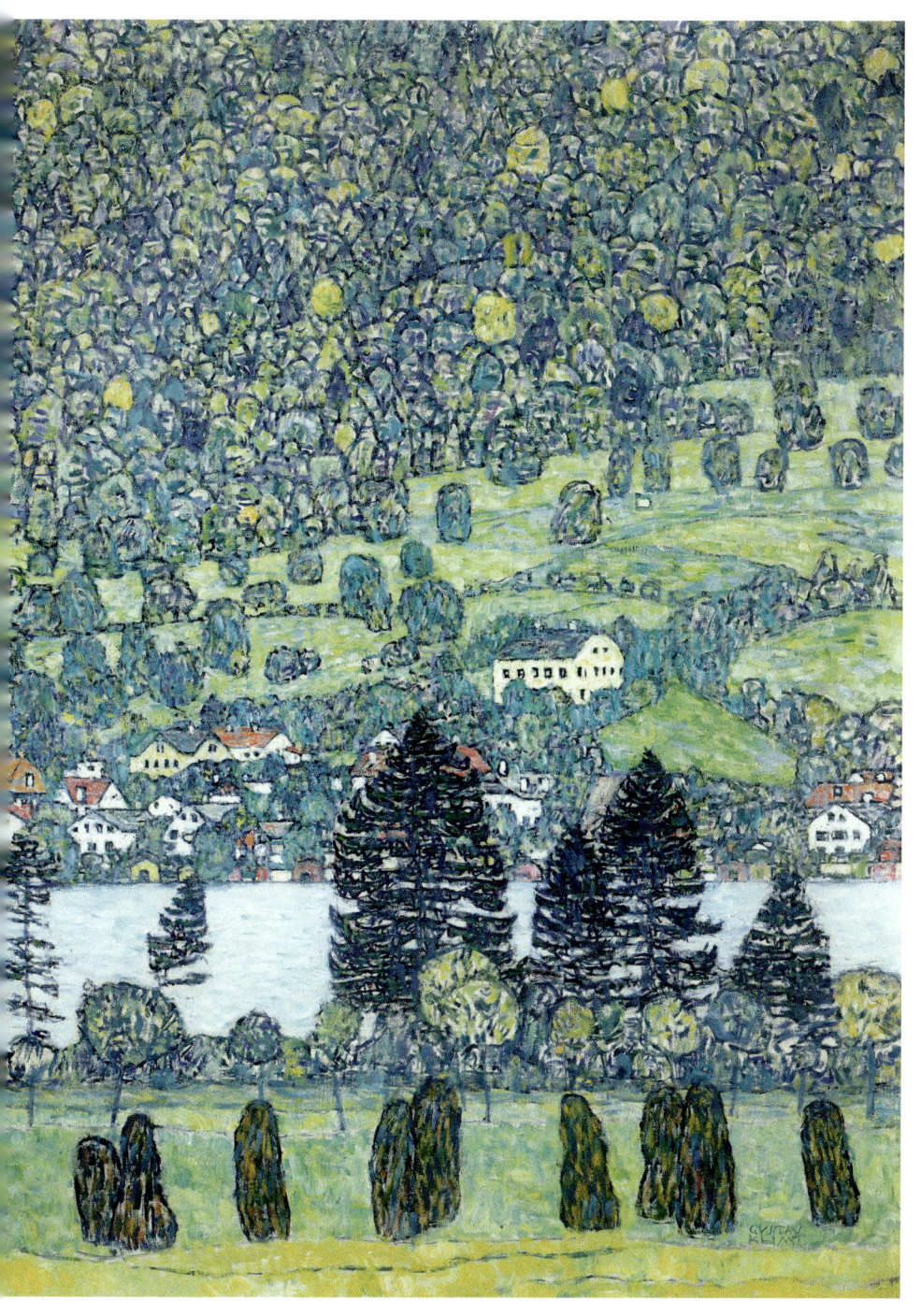

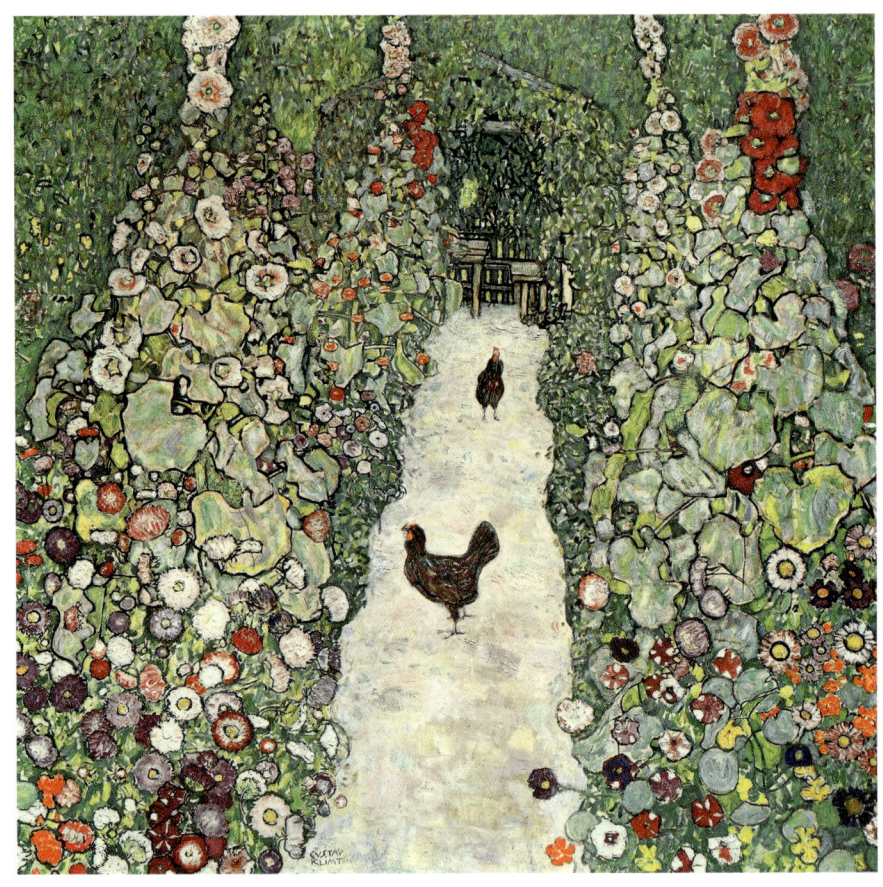

Garden Path with Chickens, 1916
Oil on canvas, 110 x 110 cm / 43 ¼ x 43 ¼ in.
Destroyed by fire in May 1945 at Immendorf Castle, Lower Austria

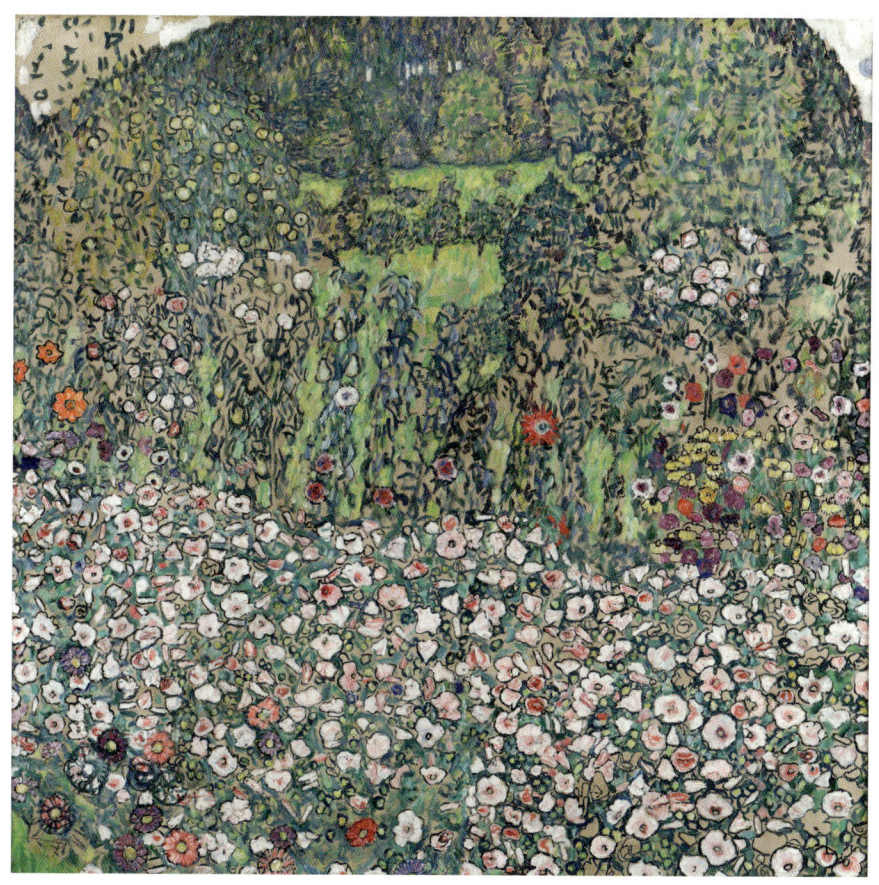

Garden Landscape with Rounded Mountaintop (Parsonage Garden), 1916
Oil on canvas, 110 x 110 cm / 43 ¼ x 43 ¼ in.
Kunsthaus Zug, Kamm Collection Foundation

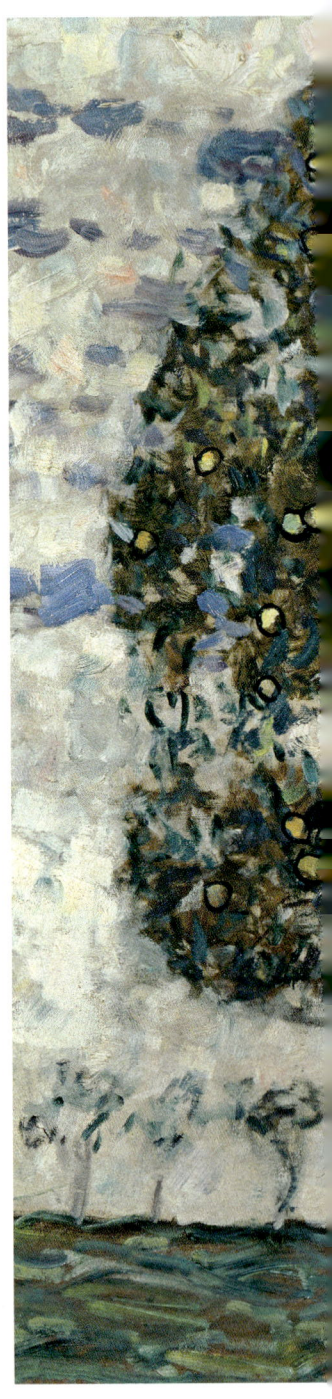

Apple Tree II, 1916
Oil on canvas, 80 x 80 cm / 31 ½ x 31 ½ in.
Private collection

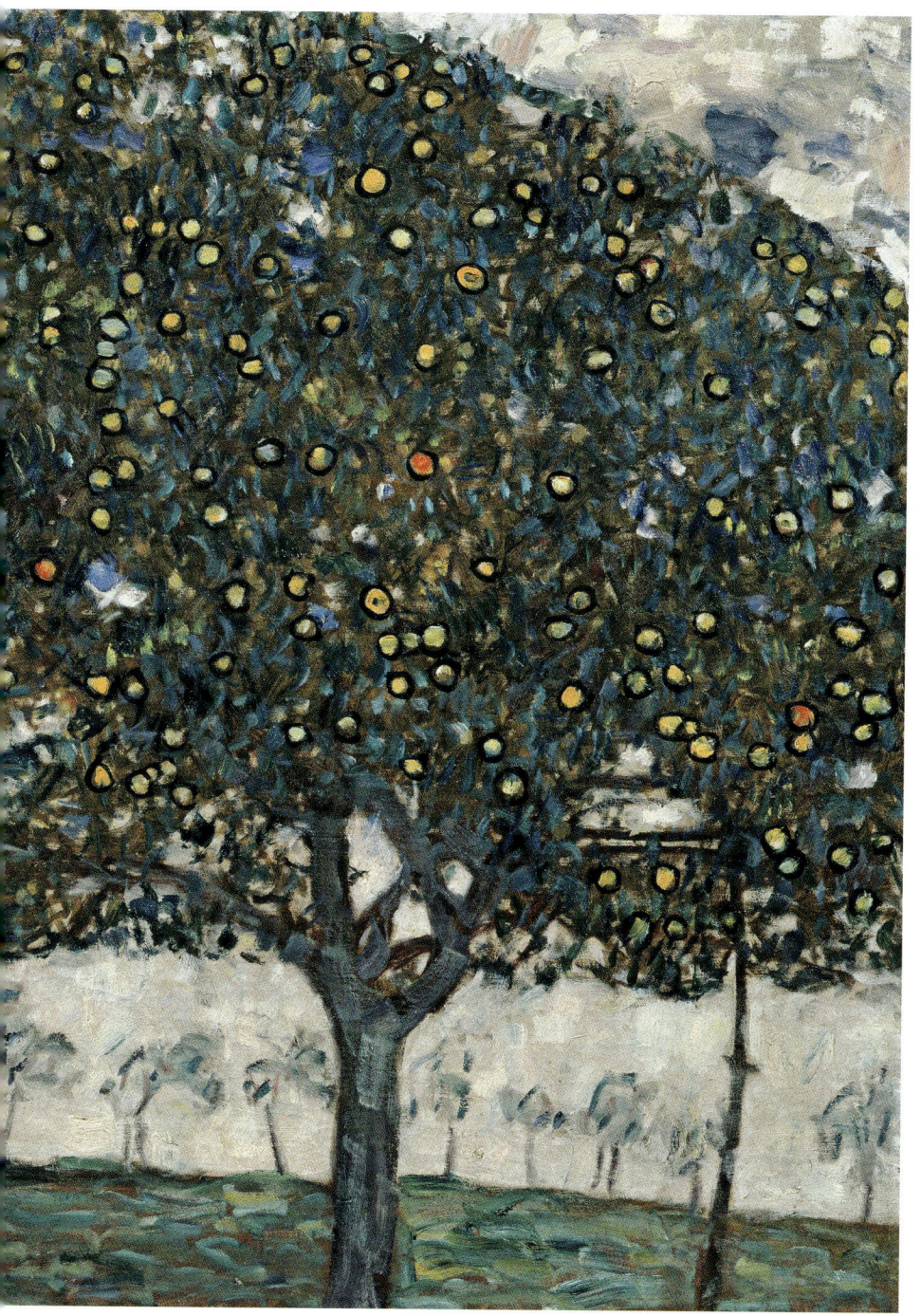

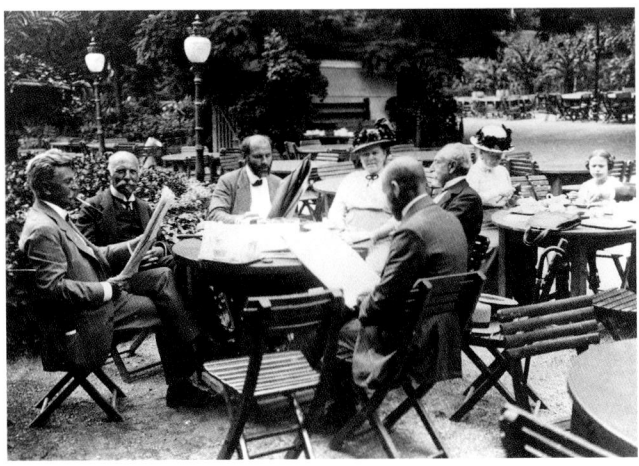

Gustav Klimt with friends at the Meierei-Tivoli café in Schönbrunn, c. 1914
Photograph. Imagno/Austrian Archives

Schönbrunn Landscape, 1916
Oil on canvas, 110 x 110 cm / 43 ¼ x 43 ¼ in. Private collection

Pages 484/85
Gustav Klimt with friends on an outing to Gahberg Mountain by Lake Attersee, 1908
From l. to r. Hannerl Grögl, unknown, Emilie Flöge, unknown, Emma Bacher,
Helene Klimt, Heinrich Böhler, Klimt standing in the background
Photograph. Imagno/Austrian Archives

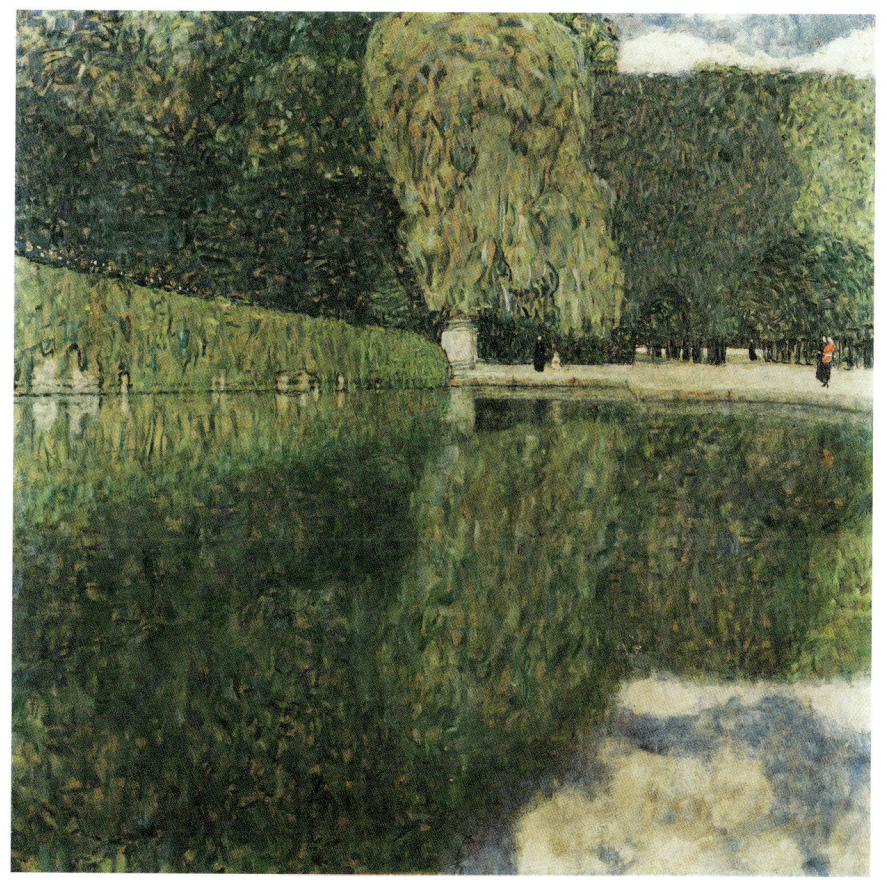

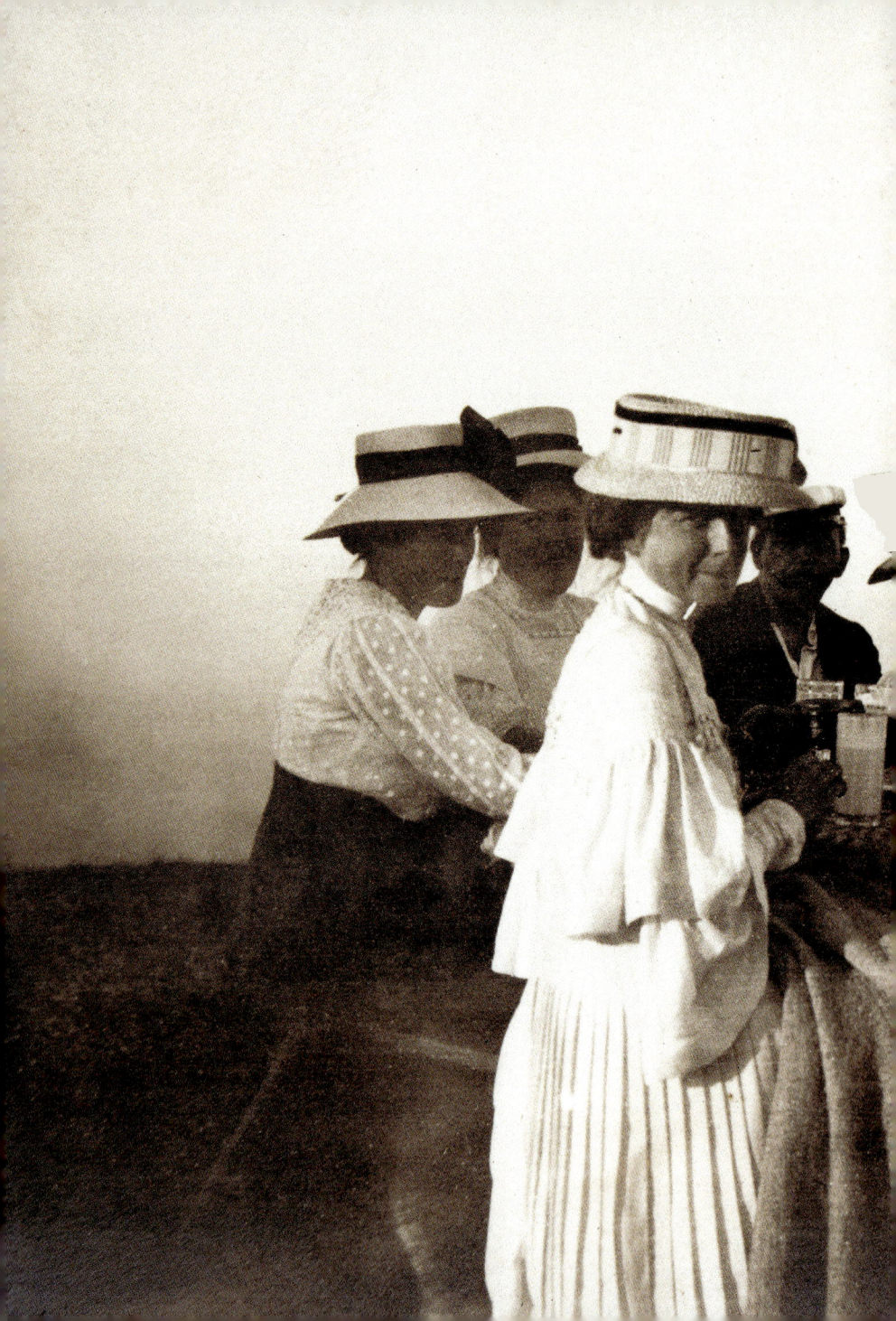

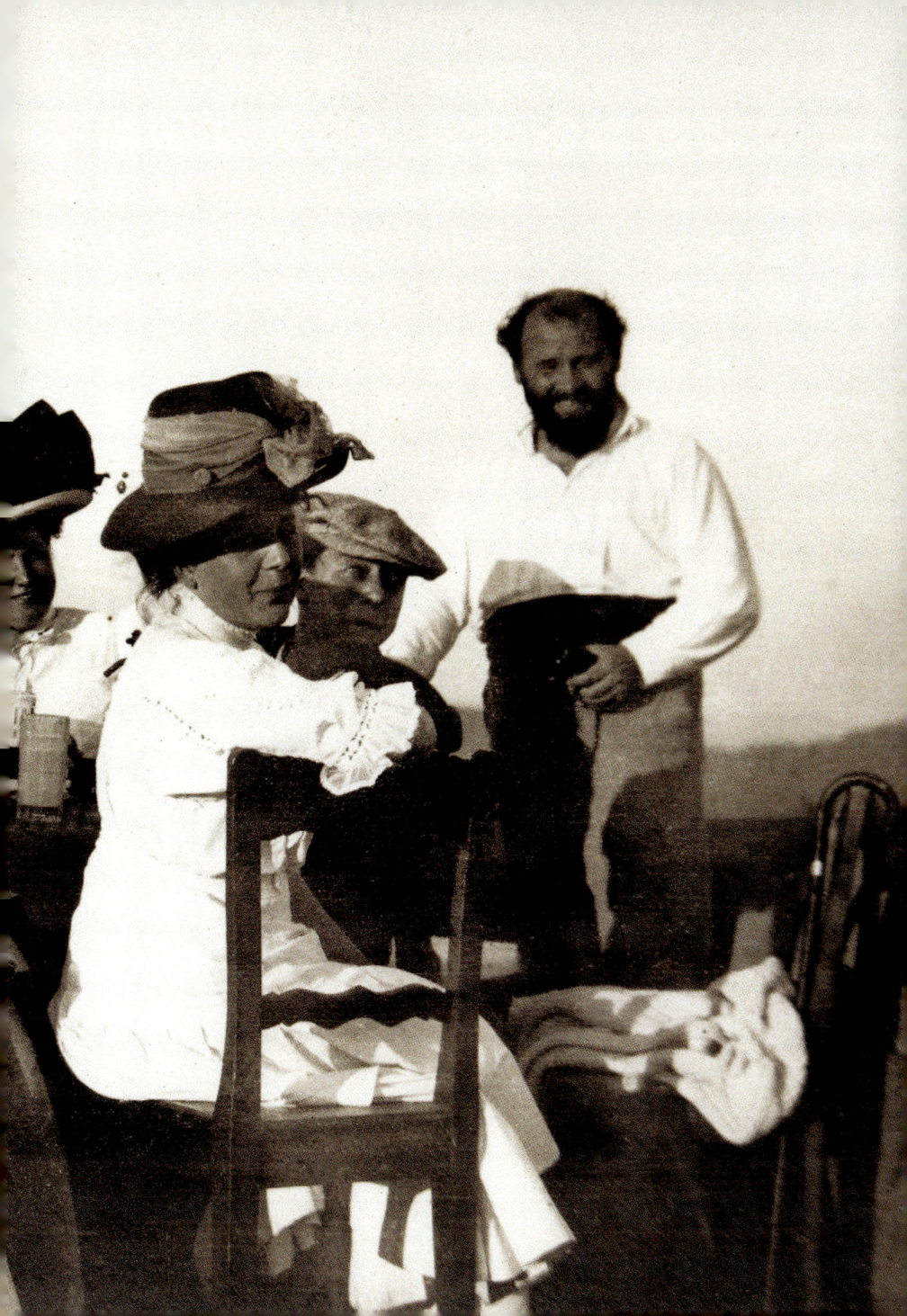

VI.

Biography

Michaela Reichel

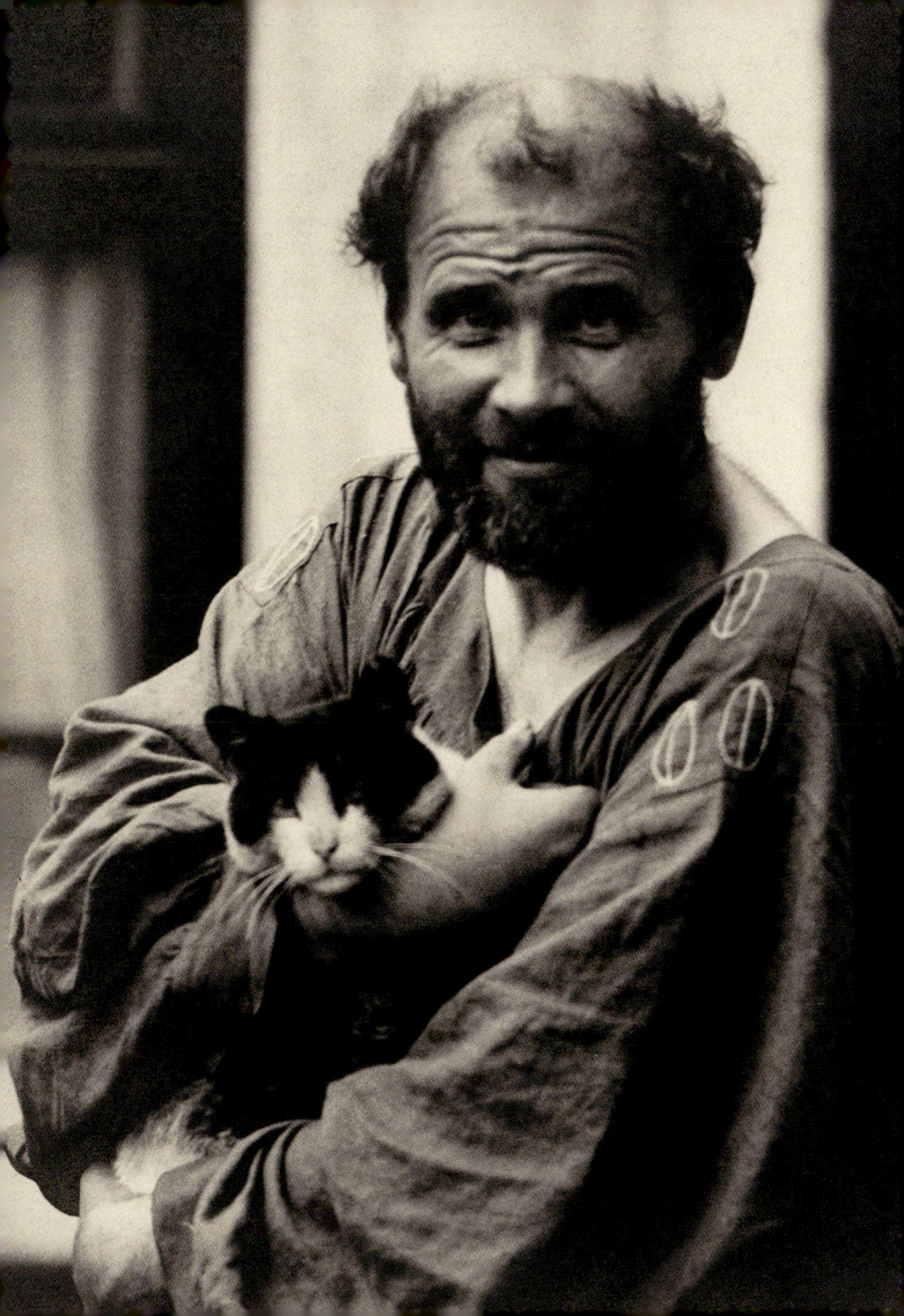

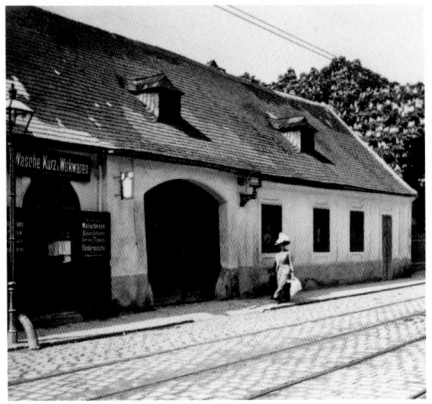

Page 487
Moritz Nähr
**Gustav Klimt with cat
outside his studio**, 1911
Photograph. Imagno/Austrian Archives

**The house at 247 Linzerstrasse, Vienna,
where Gustav Klimt was born**, 1918
Demolished in 1967
Photograph. Imagno/Austrian Archives

1860   Gold engraver Ernst Klimt marries Anna Finster.

1862   Gustav Klimt is born on 14 July as the second child – his elder sister, Klara, was born in 1860 – and first son. The family lives in impoverished circumstances in Vienna.

1864   A second son, Ernst, is born on 3 January. Four more children will follow, the last born in 1873: Hermine, Georg, Anna, Johanna.

1876   Gustav Klimt begins his training at the School of Applied Arts, which evolved out of the Imperial and Royal Austrian Museum of Art and Industry. He meets Franz Matsch, a fellow student. Klimt's initial plan is to become a drawing teacher. At the suggestion of Rudolf Eitelberger, founder of the School of Applied Arts, he continues his studies under Ferdinand Laufberger and – after the latter's death in 1881 – under Julius Victor Berger.

1878   Klimt's younger brother Ernst is also accepted into the School of Applied Arts.

1879   Together with Franz Matsch, Ernst and Gustav Klimt form the Künstler-Compagnie ('Artists' Company'). In canvassing for work, the trio promote their ability to fulfil commissions rapidly and in a style so similar that it is difficult to distinguish between their individual hands. During the course of the next two years, the young artists are engaged by Ferdinand Laufberger (Natter 2012, Cat. 1) and Julius Victor Berger (Natter 2012, Cat. 8) to assist on projects.

From 1880 on   The Künstler-Compagnie works with architects Ferdinand Fellner and Hermann Helmer on a number of the latter's new buildings, creating interior decorations for the salon of the Palais Sturany in Vienna (Natter 2012, Cat. 2), the concert hall in Carlsbad (Karlovy Vary; Natter 2012, Cat. 7) and the municipal theatre in Reichenberg (Liberec; Natter 2012, Cat. 13–15).

1883   Klimt completes his training at the School of Applied Arts. He begins work on the interior decoration of Peleş Castle in Sinaia, Romania (Natter 2012, Cat. 27–35), and continues until 1885. Klimt, his brother Ernst and Franz Matsch move into a studio at 8 Sandwirtgasse in Vienna's 6th district.

Group photo taken around the time the Secession was founded, c. 1903
On the left with hat and walking stick, Carl Moll; partly obscured by Moll, Josef Hoffmann; beside him, Gustav Klimt; to his right in the centre, Alfred Roller; in front of him with cigarette, Fritz Waerndorfer; standing at the back on the right with bowler hat, Kolo Moser
Photograph. Imagno/Austrian Archives

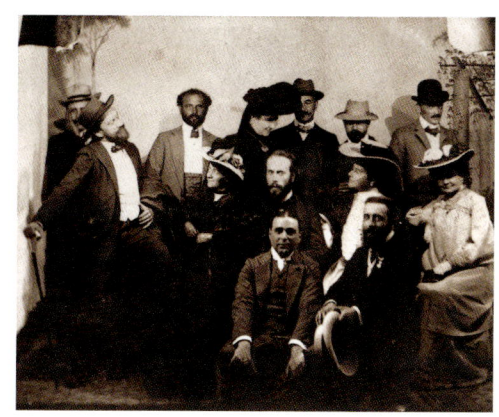

1884/85   The Künstler-Compagnie embarks on interior decorations for the municipal theatre in Fiume (Rijeka, Croatia; Natter 2012, Cat. 39–44), and one year later, upon those for the theatre in Carlsbad (Karlovy Vary; Natter 2012, Cat. 47–51) and for two rooms in the Villa Hermes built for Empress Elisabeth in the Lainz game park (Natter 2012, Cat. 36, 45, 46).

1886   The artists are commissioned to execute the paintings for the two staircases in Vienna's brand-new Burgtheater (pp. 49–51), a task that occupies them until 1888 and for which they are awarded the Gold Cross of Merit by Emperor Franz Joseph I.

1888   Klimt's friendship with Serena Lederer (p. 302) probably dates from this year. Serena and her husband later number amongst his staunchest supporters. Serena Lederer and her sisters Jenny Steiner and Aranka Munk commission Klimt to paint numerous portraits of members of their family. Over the years, the Lederers build up a collection of almost twenty oil paintings and countless drawings

by Klimt. Erich, one of Serena Lederer's sons, represents an important contemporary witness to Gustav Klimt's oeuvre. Accompanied by his Künstler-Compagnie colleagues, the artist makes his first trips, to Innsbruck, Salzburg and Lake Königssee, and in 1888/89 to Cracow, Trieste and Munich.

Around 1889   The Klimt brothers are introduced to the Flöge family and thereby come into contact with wealthy members of the Vienna bourgeoisie. Daughters Emilie and Helene Flöge subsequently play central roles in the lives of Ernst and Gustav Klimt. With his brother and Franz Matsch, Klimt visits St. Wolfgang and Munich.

1890   On 26 April Gustav Klimt wins the Emperor's Prize – awarded this year for the very first time – for his gouache *Interior View of the Old Burgtheater*. The Künstler-Compagnie accepts its last commission, the decoration of the staircase in Vienna's new Kunsthistorisches Museum (pp. 54/55), which the artists complete in April 1891. Klimt moves into an apartment at 36 Westbahnstrasse in the

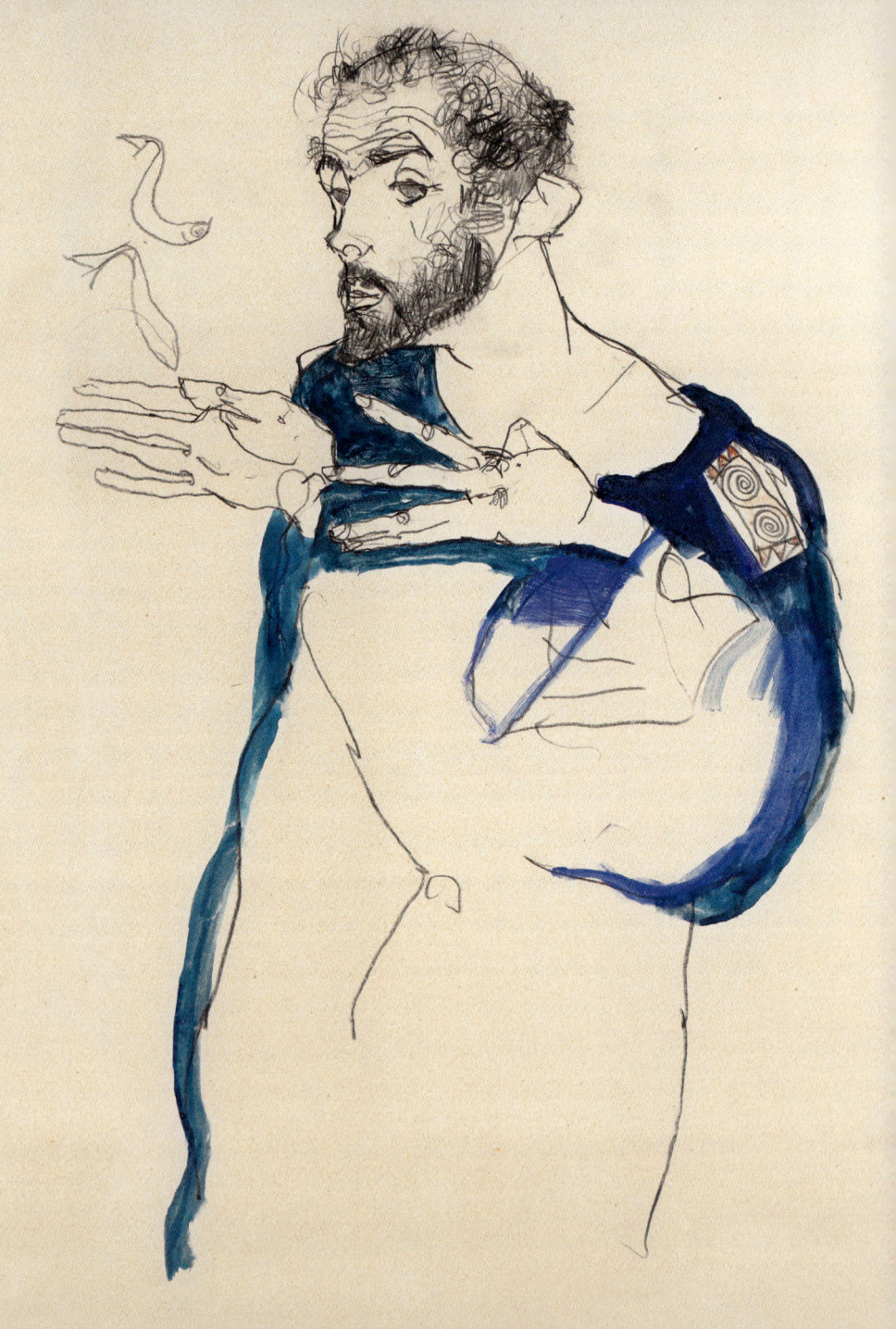

Egon Schiele
**Gustav Klimt in his blue painter's
smock**, 1913
Pencil and gouache on paper,
48.1 x 32 cm / 18 ⅞ x 12 ½ in.
Private collection

7th district with his mother and two unmarried sisters. He will live there until his death.

1891   The Klimt brothers and Franz Matsch are elected members of the Society of Vienna Artists, or Künstlerhaus. Ernst Klimt marries Helene Flöge.

1892   The three Künstler-Compagnie artists move into a studio at 21 Josefstädterstrasse in the 8th district. Klimt's father dies in July, followed unexpectedly on 9 December by his brother Ernst. Klimt becomes guardian to his young niece Helene Luise (p. 261). The death of his brother leaves a great gap in Klimt's life. Franz Matsch leaves the communal studio, which Klimt continues to use as his workspace until 1911. Klimt spends New Year 1892/93 as a guest at Totis palace in order to paint his picture *Auditorium of the Theatre in Esterházy Palace in Totis* (Natter 2012, Cat. 72).

1893   Klimt takes part for the first time in the annual Künstlerhaus exhibition in Vienna.

1893–1897/98   Alongside a number of commissioned portraits (pp. 57, 61; Natter 2012, Cat. 73, 74, 78, 90) and portrait sketches (Natter 2012, Cat. 93, 98, 99, 100, 106, 107, 108), Klimt produces paintings for the Palais Dumba in Vienna (pp. 62/63).

1894   Klimt and Matsch jointly embark on the commission for the Faculty paintings (pp. 126, 129–131; Natter 2012, Cat. 103, 105) intended for the Great Hall of Vienna University. In 1897/98 Klimt submits compositional studies that become the subject of fierce debate over the following years.

1896   In February Klimt is appointed a member of the curatorium of the Gesellschaft für vervielfältigende Kunst, a Viennese art publishing company.

1897   The conflict that has been smouldering for years within the Society of Vienna Artists comes to a head. Numerous members – including Klimt – break away and found their own Austrian Association of Visual Artists, more familiarly known as the Secession. Klimt becomes its first president. The Secession journal *Ver Sacrum* regularly reports on his work over the following period. Support for the Secessionists and thus also for Klimt is voiced in the press by art critics such as Berta Zuckerkandl, Hevesi and Hermann Bahr. The first Klimt painting to be seen by the German public (Natter 2012, Cat. 72) is shown in the International Exhibition of Art in Dresden. Klimt spends his first

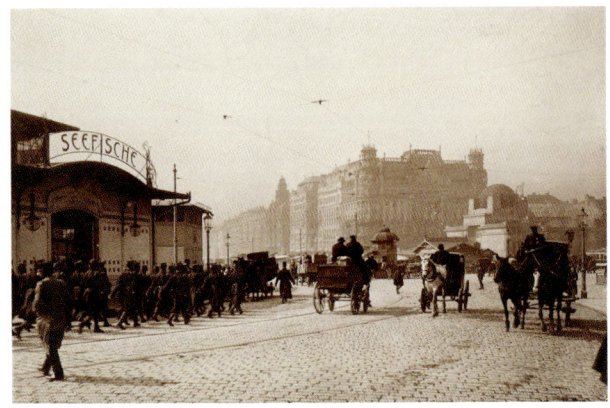

summer with the Flöge family; they stay in Fieberbrunn in the Tyrol.

1898 The Secession holds its first exhibition on the premises of the Imperial and Royal Garden Society in Vienna. Klimt becomes a member of the London-based International Society of Painters, Sculptors and Engravers and of the Munich Secession, and takes part in the Salon d'automne in Paris. He pays his first visit to the Salzkammergut, where he will paint numerous landscape pictures over the coming years. At the beginning of September he pays a visit to the spa resort of Franzensbad (Františkovy Lázně). Klimt finishes the *Portrait of Sonja Knips* (p. 301), the first of a series of large-format portraits of fashionable female members of Viennese society.

1899 Klimt completes *Nuda Veritas* (p. 111) and sends the paintings *Pallas Athene* (p. 112) and *Portrait of Sonja Knips* (p. 301) to London for inclusion in an exhibition mounted by the International Society. On 6 July his son Gustav Ucicky is born. The baby's mother, Maria Ucicka, is one of the artist's models. In

August Klimt travels to Golling, near Hallein, with the Flöge family. On 1 September Klimt's second son, Gustav Zimmermann, is born to Marie Zimmermann, another of his models.

1900 Klimt spends his summer vacation with the Flöge family in Litzlberg on Lake Attersee, where they will holiday every year from now up to 1907.

1901 In his "Speech on Klimt", Hermann Bahr takes up the artist's cause. Klimt paints *Judith I* (p. 305). The start of his friendship with Fritz Waerndorfer, who over the course of the years acquires several of Klimt's oil paintings, including the scandalous *Hope I* (p. 133).

1902 Klimt exhibits the *Beethoven Frieze* (pp. 114–117, 119–125) as part of the *Gesamtkunstwerk*, or total work of art, presented at the fourteenth Secession exhibition. He continues his series of paintings of fashionable society ladies with the portraits of Emilie Flöge (p. 311) and Gertrud Loew (p. 317). On 23 June Klimt's second son with Marie Zimmermann, Otto Zimmermann, is born. He dies less than three months later, on 11 September.

**View of the Secession building
from the Naschmarkt**, c. 1900
Postcard. Private collection

Egon Schiele
Head of the dead Gustav Klimt, 1918
Black chalk on paper,
46.9 x 30.1 cm / 18 ½ x 11 ¾ in.
Vienna, Leopold Museum

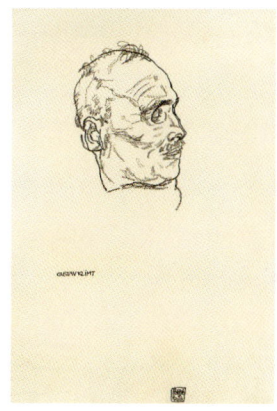

1903   On a trip to Ravenna, Klimt sees San Vitale's Byzantine mosaics. The same trip also takes him to Venice. Winter sees Klimt back in Italy, again in Venice and Ravenna, but also in Padua, Florence, Pisa, Verona and on Lake Garda, amongst other places. In Vienna, Waerndorfer, Kolo Moser and Josef Hoffmann found the Wiener Werkstätte ('Viennese Workshop').

1904   Paul Bacher, a friend of Klimt's, takes over the Galerie Miethke, which represents the artist from 1905 onwards. Klimt paints a portrait of Margaret Stonborough-Wittgenstein (p. 321) that is received with little enthusiasm by its clients, however. Karl Wittgenstein nevertheless subsequently purchases *The Golden Knight* (pp. 134/35), *Water Snakes I* (p. 137) and three of Klimt's landscape paintings (pp. 439, 440/41, 445). On 1 July the Flöge sisters open their fashion salon at 1b Mariahilferstrasse in the 6th district. "Schwestern Flöge" will remain one of Vienna's leading fashion houses right up to its closure in 1938.

1905   Divisions within the Secession lead to the resignation of Carl Moll, Klimt, Moser, Waerndorfer, Hoffmann and others. One year later, the 'Klimt Group' founds the Austrian Artists' Association, with the aim of organizing further joint exhibitions. Following an escalation in the long-running battle over the Faculty paintings (pp. 126, 129–131; Natter 2012, Cat. 103, 105), Klimt returns all the money he has been paid so far and reclaims possession of his compositional studies. Critics such as Karl Kraus and Hermann Bahr, respectively, argue vehemently for and against Klimt. In 1903 Bahr had already printed a collection of the censuring articles published in the course of the debate. Klimt himself comments on the affair in his painting *Goldfish* (p. 309), whose alternative title is "To My Critics".

1905–1910   Klimt works on the designs for the interior decoration of the dining room in the Palais Stoclet in Brussels. The Stoclet frieze is his contribution to this Wiener Werkstätte *Gesamtkunstwerk*, created for the Stoclet family.

1906   In May Klimt travels to London, Brussels, Berlin and Dresden. In December he makes a trip to Florence.

Gustav Klimt's passport, 1917
Vienna, Albertina

1907   Klimt's 'golden period' culminates in the *Portrait of Adele Bloch-Bauer I* (pp. 328/29). In summer Klimt is introduced to Egon Schiele.

1908   The group around Klimt organizes the Kunstschau art exhibition in Vienna. Amongst other paintings, Klimt shows *Friends I* (Natter 2012, Cat. 175), *The Three Ages of Woman* (pp. 140/41) and *The Kiss* (pp. 142/43). The exhibition also features works by young artists such as Oskar Kokoschka and Max Oppenheimer (1885–1954). Berta Zuckerkandl's brother-in-law Viktor buys the painting *Poppy Field* (p. 431) and thereby lays the foundation of his Klimt collection, which will total eleven paintings. Klimt spends the summer on Lake Attersee with the Flöge family, this year for the first time in the Villa Oleander in Kammer. The party will return to Kammer for the next four summers up to 1912.

1909   The Internationale Kunstschau is staged in Vienna with works by Gauguin, van Gogh, Matisse and Munch. Egon Schiele also exhibits for the first time. Klimt shows *Judith II (Salome)* (p. 331), *Hope I* (p. 133) and *Hope II* (pp. 144/45). In May Klimt travels to Prague and in October/November to Paris and Spain.

1910   Ludwig Hevesi, one of Klimt's most loyal supporters, dies. His death also signals the end of our most abundant supply of information about the artist's work from a contemporary source. Klimt's works (among others, pp. 331, 333, 356, 434/35, 446, 447) are seen for the first time in Italy, within the framework of the ninth Esposizione internazionale d'arte, held in Venice.

1911   Klimt visits Rome and Wodolka (Odolena Voda) in Bohemia (today Czech Republic), amongst other places. He moves into his last studio, at 11 Feldmühlgasse in Vienna's 13th district.

1912   Klimt becomes president of the Austrian Artists' Association and a member of the Berlin Secession. He completes his second portrait of Adele Bloch-Bauer (p. 345). Klimt's lover Consuela Huber gives birth to their first child. From this year onwards, Klimt and Emile Flöge spend not only their summers together on Lake Attersee but also pay an annual joint visit to Bad Gastein. In 1912 Klimt also makes another trip to Wodolka in Bohemia.

1913   Klimt spends time with friends on Lake Garda (pp. 458/59, 460/61, 462). From

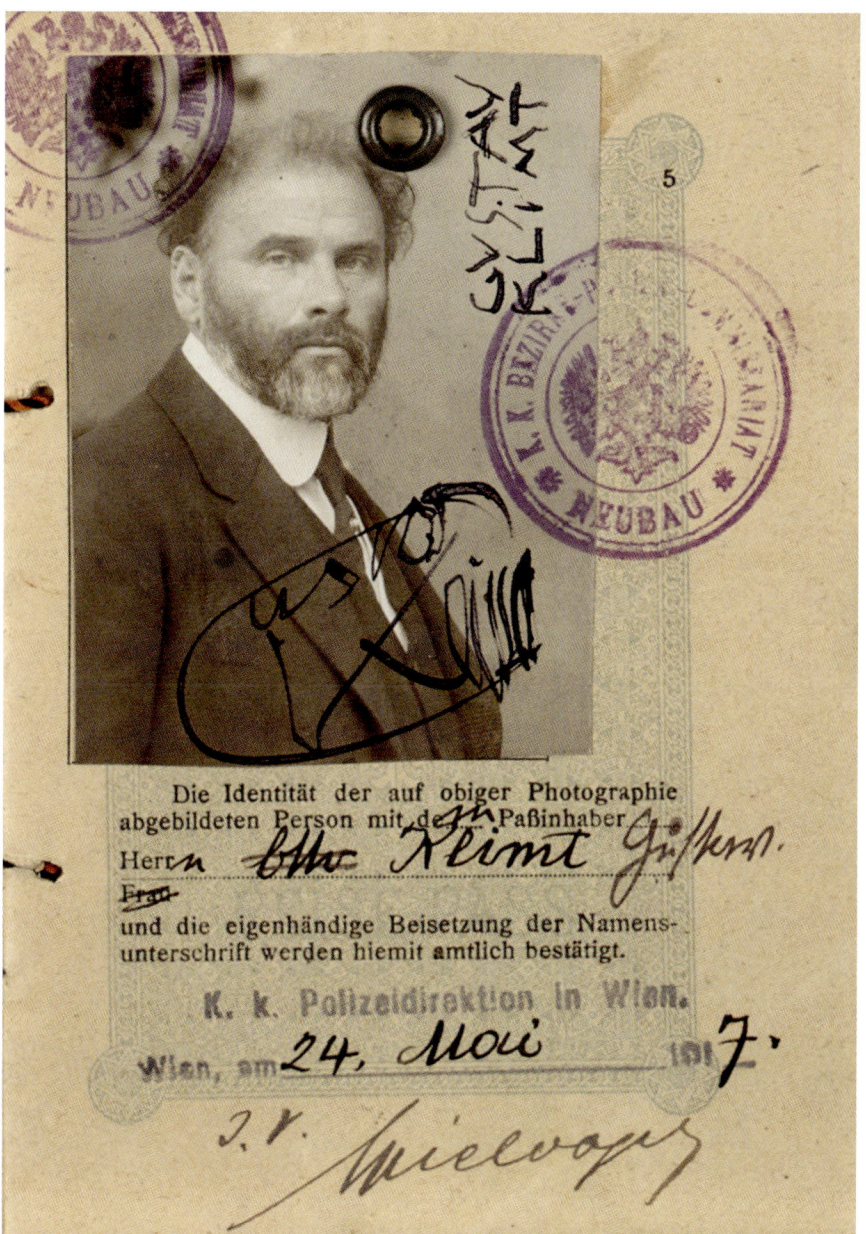

Die Identität der auf obiger Photographie abgebildeten Person mit dem Paßinhaber

Herrn ~~Otto~~ Klimt Gustav

~~Frau~~

und die eigenhändige Beisetzung der Namensunterschrift werden hiemit amtlich bestätigt.

K. k. Polizeidirektion in Wien.

Wien, am 24. Mai 1917.

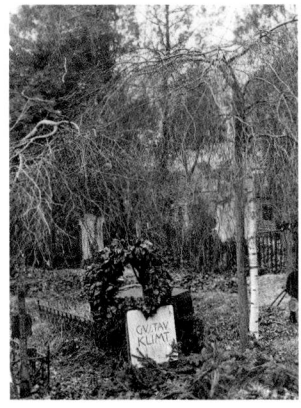

Gustav Klimt's grave in the Hietzing cemetery at 15 Maxingstrasse, Vienna, c. 1925
Photograph

Egon Schiele
Poster for the 49th Secession exhibition in Vienna, 1918
Imagno/Wien Museum

Pages 498/99
Moritz Nähr, **Gustav Klimt's last studio at 11 Feldmühlgasse, Vienna**, 1918
On the easels, the unfinished pictures *Lady with a Fan* (see p. 351) and *The Bride* (see pp. 366/67).
Photograph. Imagno/Austrian Archives

here he travels on to Seewalchen on Lake Attersee with some members of the Flöge family. In Vienna, he paints the portraits of Mäda (p. 340) and Eugenia Primavesi (p. 342). From 1912 onwards the Primavesis become avid collectors of Klimt's works, eventually owning seven of his pictures.

1914 The start of the First World War. Klimt takes no further part in foreign exhibitions in 'enemy' territory. He paints several Lake Attersee landscapes (pp. 463, 465, 466/67). Klimt's lover Consuela gives birth to their second child. Klimt spends the summer with the Flöge family in Weissenbach on Lake Attersee, as he will also do in 1915 and 1916.

1915 Klimt's mother dies. The artist makes two short trips to Moravia. Klimt's lover Consuela gives birth to their third child.

1916 Klimt again spends the summer on Lake Attersee and produces his last landscape paintings treating motifs from this region (pp. 476/77, 478, 479, 480/81).

From 1916 on He accepts a few more portrait commissions, including those of

Friederike Maria Beer (p. 349), Charlotte Pulitzer (Natter 2012, Cat. 234) and Amalie Zuckerkandl (p. 360).

1917 Klimt is made an honorary member of the Vienna Academy of Fine Arts and the Munich Academy. His last paintings, such as *Baby* (pp. 364/65), *Adam and Eve* (p. 362) and *The Bride* (pp. 366/67), remain unfinished. He takes three short breaks in Winkelsdorf in Moravia. He also holidays with Emilie Flöge in Bad Gastein and Hintertux, in the Tyrol.

1918 Gustav Klimt dies on 6 February following a stroke.

1920 Max Eisler publishes the first monograph on Klimt.

1928 The first major retrospective of the artist's work since his death, the Klimt commemorative exhibition is staged in the Vienna Secession building.

1945 A large number of works by Klimt, including the paintings confiscated from the Lederer collection, are destroyed by fire while in storage at Immendorf Castle, Lower Austria.

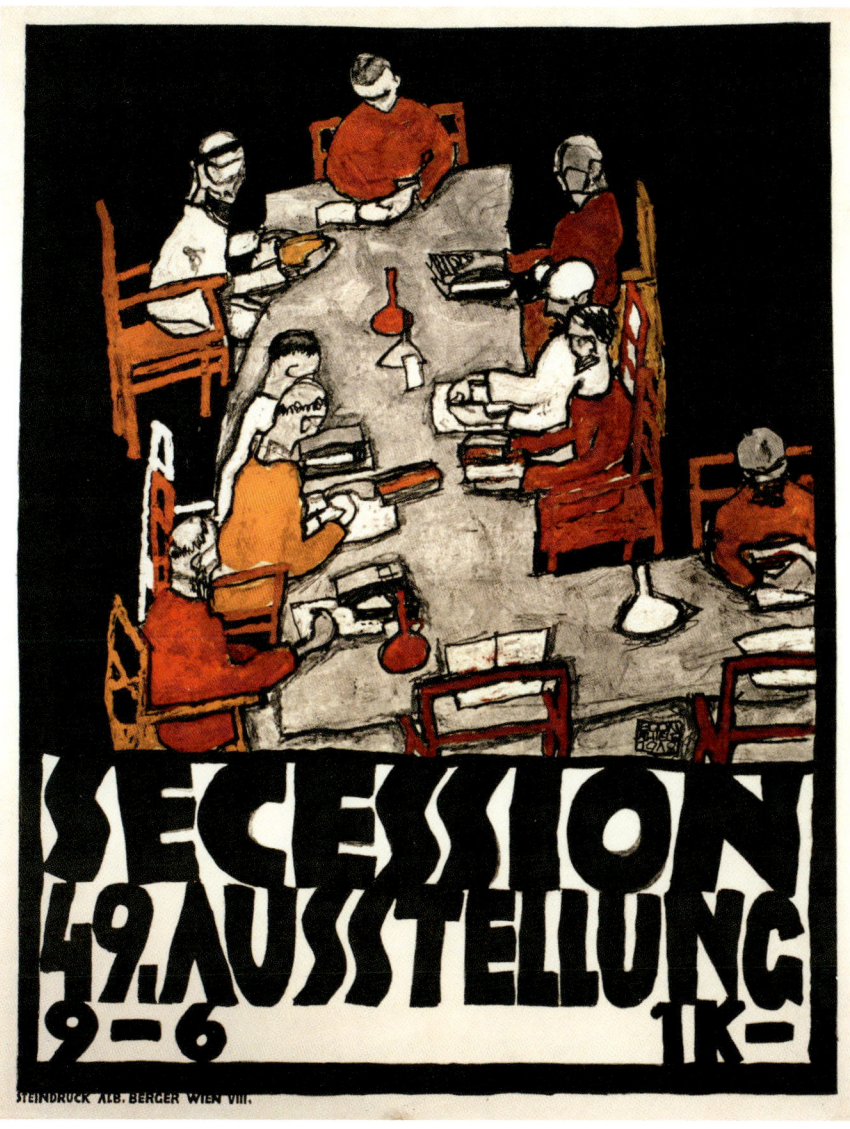

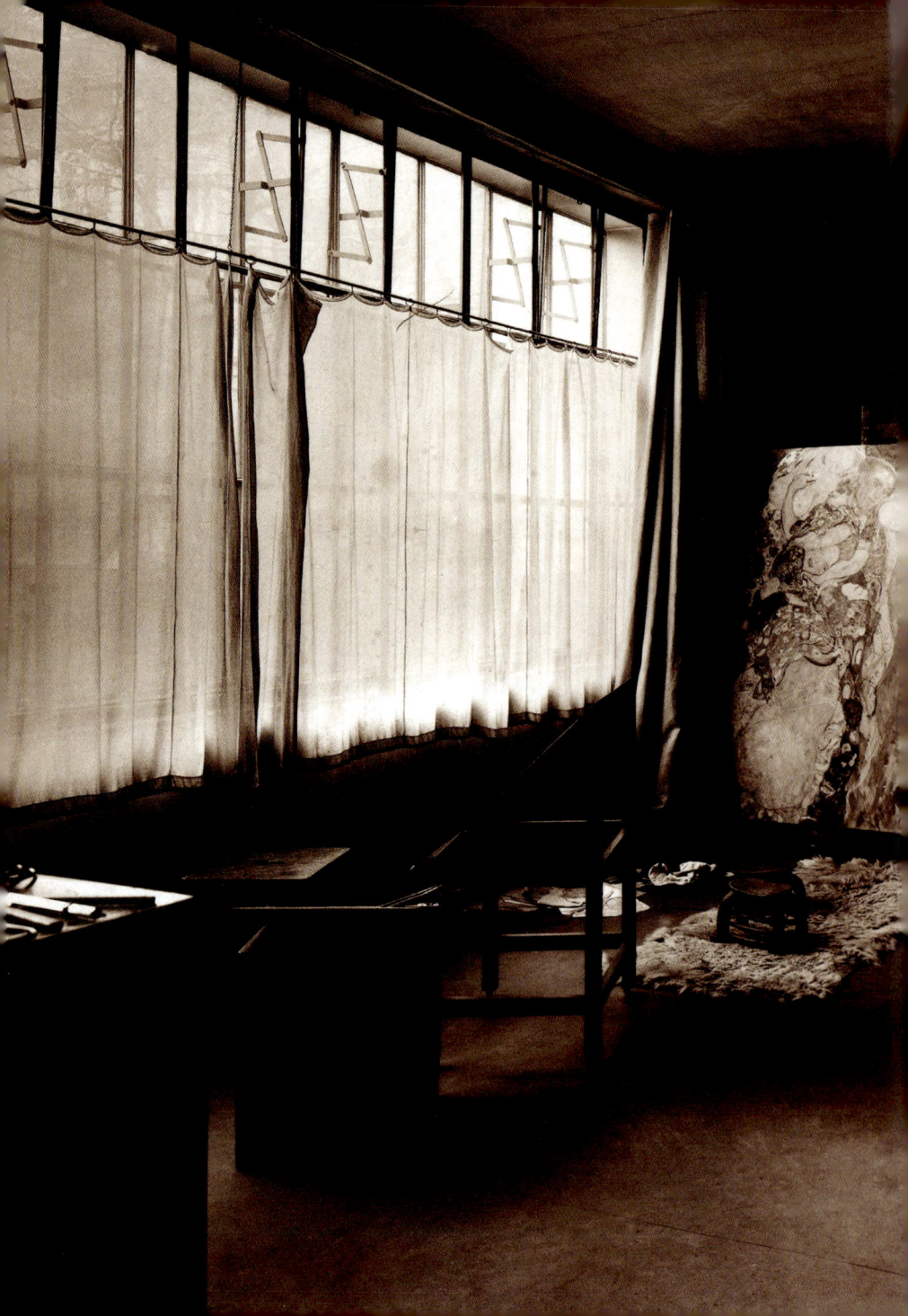

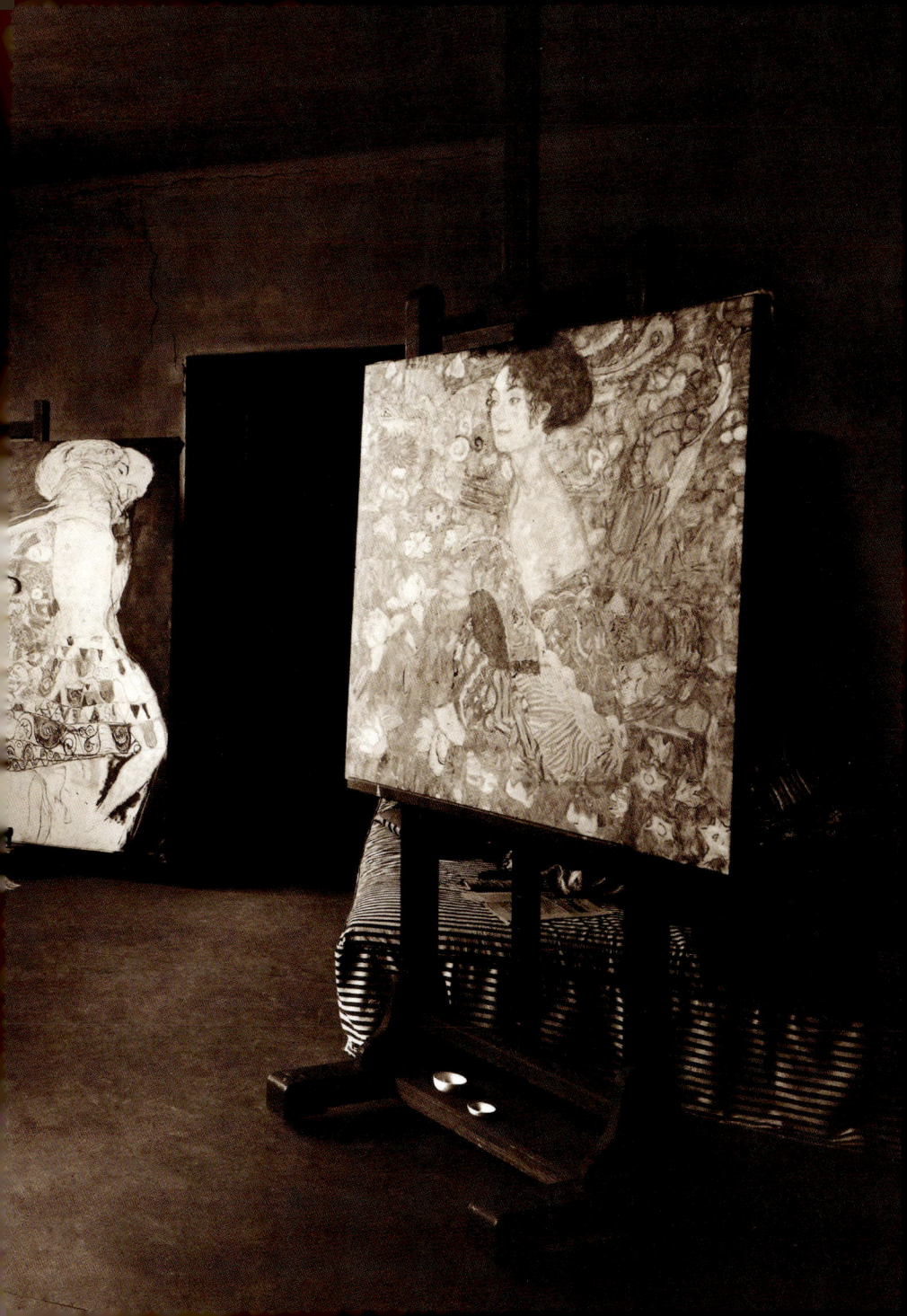

Selected Bibliography

Bahr, Hermann, *Secession*, Vienna 1900 (reprint Weimar 2007).

Bayer, Josef, "Das K. K. Hofburgtheater als Bauwerk mit seinen Sculpturen und Bilderschmuck", in *Die Theater Wiens*, vol. 3, ed. by the Gesellschaft für vervielfältigende Kunst, 1894.

Bisanz-Prakken, Marian, *Der Beethovenfries. Geschichte, Funktion und Bedeutung*, Salzburg 1977.

Bisanz-Prakken, Marian, *Heiliger Frühling. Gustav Klimt und die Anfänge der Wiener Secession 1895–1905*, Vienna/Munich 1999.

Bisanz-Prakken, Marian, "Der Beethovenfries von Gustav Klimt und die Wiener Secession", in *Gustav Klimt. Beethovenfries*, ed. by die Vereinigung Bildender Künstler-Innen Wiener Secession, Vienna 2002, pp. 19–39.

Bisanz-Prakken, Marian, *Toorop in Wenen, inspiratie voor Klimt*, catalogue accompanying the exhibition of the same name at the Gemeentemuseum, The Hague, 2006/07, Zwolle 2006.

Bisanz-Prakken, Marian, "Klimts 'Erfüllung' und ihre Replik – eine Gegenüberstellung", in *Belvedere. Zeitschrift für bildende Kunst*, Vienna (2006), special volume on Klimt, pp. 20–37.

Bisanz-Prakken, Marian, "Gustav Klimt. The Late Work. New Light on 'The Virgin' and 'The Bride'", in Price, Renée (ed.), *Gustav Klimt. The Ronald S. Lauder and Serge Sabarsky Collections, Neue Galerie New York*, Munich et al. 2007, pp. 105–129.

Bisanz-Prakken, Marian, "Der 'Beethovenfries' und Klimts 'Gabe der Empfänglichkeit'", in Weidinger 2007, pp. 93–117.

Bisanz-Prakken, Marian, "Klimts zeichnerisches Universum. Grundhaltungen - Seelenstimmungen", in: Natter 2012, pp. 362-449.

Bisanz-Prakken, Marian, supplementary 5th volume to: Strobl, Alice, *catalogue raisonné of all Klimt's drawings* (4 vols.), Salzburg 1980 ff., in preparation.

Breicha, Otto (ed.), *Gustav Klimt. Die Goldene Pforte. Werk – Wesen – Wirkung. Bilder und Schriften zu Leben und Werk*, Salzburg 1978.

Bruyn, Edmond de, "Adieu à Monsieur Adolphe Stoclet", in *Le Flambeau*, no. 6, 1949, pp. 1–5.

Dobai, Johannes, "Die Landschaft aus der Sicht von Gustav Klimt. Ein Essay", in *Mitteilungen der Österreichischen Galerie*, Vienna, vol. 22/23 (1978/79), no. 66/67: Klimt-Studien, pp. 241–272.

Fischer, Wolfgang Georg, *Gustav Klimt und Emilie Flöge. Genie und Talent, Freundschaft und Besessenheit*, Vienna 1987.

Gerlach, Martin, *Allegorien und Embleme. Originalentwürfe von den hervorragendsten modernen Künstlern, sowie Nachbildungen alter Zunftzeichen und moderner Entwürfe von Zunftwappen im Charakter der Renaissance*, with introductory text by Albert Ilg, Vienna 1882–1885.

Giese, Herbert, *Franz von Matsch. Leben und Werk 1881–1942*, unpubl. doctoral thesis, University of Vienna 1977.

Hamann, Brigitte, *Meine liebe, gute Freundin! Die Briefe Kaiser Franz Josephs an Katharina Schratt*, Vienna 1992.

Hevesi, Ludwig, *Acht Jahre Secession (März 1897–Juni 1905). Kritik – Polemik – Chronik*, re-issued and with an introduction by Otto Breicha, Klagenfurt 1984 (1st edn. Vienna 1906).

Hevesi, Ludwig, *Altkunst – Neukunst, Wien 1894–1908*, Vienna 1909 (reprint 1986).

Hevesi, Ludwig, "Internationale Kunstschau Wien 1909", in *Zeitschrift für Bildende Kunst*, Leipzig, vol. 20 (1909), pp. 221–226.

Hofmann, Werner, *Gustav Klimt und die Wiener Jahrhundertwende*, Salzburg 1970.

Hofmann, Werner, "Gesamtkunstwerk Wien", in *Der Hang zum Gesamtkunstwerk. Europäische Utopien seit 1800*, ed. by Harald Szeemann and Susanne Häni, Zurich 1983, pp. 84–92.

Hofmann, Werner, *Gustav Klimt und die Wiener Jahrhundertwende*, Hamburg 2008.

Hofmannsthal, Hugo von, "Der Dichter und diese Zeit", undated, in *Prosa II*, ed. by Herbert Steiner, Frankfurt am Main 1951.

Hofstätter, Hans H., *Symbolismus und die Kunst der Jahrhundertwende. Kunstgeschichte, Deutung, Dokumente*, Cologne 1965.

Ilg, Albert, "Das neue Hofburgtheater", in *Die Presse*, Vienna, 11 October 1888, pp. 1–3.

Ilg, Albert, *Zwickelbilder im Stiegenhaus des k. k. Kunsthistorischen Museums in Wien von*

Ernst und Gustav Klimt und Franz Matsch, Vienna 1893.

Karpfinger, Otto, "Des Kunsttempels Traumlandsherkunft", in *Secession: Die Architektur*, ed. by the Vereinigung Bildender KünstlerInnen Wiener Secession, Vienna 2003, pp. 35–60.

Kitlitschka, Werner, *Die Malerei der Wiener Ringstraße (Die Wiener Ringstraße. Bild einer Epoche. Die Erweiterung der Inneren Stadt unter Kaiser Franz Joseph*, vol. 10, ed. by Renate Wagner Rieger), Wiesbaden 1981.

Koja, Stephan (ed.), *Gustav Klimt. Landscapes*, catalogue accompanying the exhibition of the same name at the Österreichische Galerie Belvedere, Vienna, 2002/03, Munich/ Berlin/London/New York 2002.

Kriller Beatrix/Kugler Georg, *Das Kunsthistorische Museum. Die Architektur und Ausstattung. Idee und Wirklichkeit des Gesamtkunstwerkes*, Vienna 1991.

Krug, Hansjörg, "Gustav Klimt talking to and about himself", in *Gustav Klimt, The Complete Paintings*, ed. by Tobias G. Natter, pp. 458–505, Cologne 2012.

Loos, Adolf, "Von einem armen, reichen Manne", in *Neues Wiener Tagblatt*, Vienna, 26 April 1900.

Mahler-Werfel, Alma, *Diaries 1898–1902*, ed. and trans. by Antony Beaumont and Susanne Rode-Breymann, London 1999.

Max Klinger Beethoven: XIV. Ausstellung der Vereinigung Bildender Künstler Österreichs, Secession, exh. cat., Vienna 1902.

Natter, Tobias G., "Beschreibungen der Klimt-Frauenporträts", in Natter/Frodl 2000, pp. 76–147.

Natter, Tobias G., "Fürstinnen ohne Geschichte? Gustav Klimt und 'die Gemeinschaft aller Schaffenden und Genießenden'", in Natter/Frodl 2000, p. 57–74.

Natter, Tobias G., *Die Welt von Klimt, Schiele und Kokoschka. Frühe Sammler und Mäzene*, Cologne 2003.

Natter, Tobias G. (ed.), *Gustav Klimt. Sämtliche Gemälde*, Cologne 2012.

Natter, Tobias G./Frodl, Gerbert (eds.), *Klimt und die Frauen*, catalogue accompanying the millennium exhibition at the Österreichische Galerie Belvedere, Vienna, Cologne 2000.

Nebehay, Christian Michael, *Gustav Klimt. Dokumentation*, Vienna 1969.

Nebehay, Christian Michael, "Gustav Klimt schreibt an eine Liebe", in *Mitteilungen der Österreichischen Galerie*, Vienna, vol. 22/23 (1978/79), no. 66/67: Klimt-Studien, pp. 101–118.

Nossig, Alfred, "Das kunsthistorische Hofmuseum in Wien", in *Allgemeine Kunst-Chronik*, Vienna, XV, no. 21 (1891), p. 564.

Novotny, Fritz/Dobai, Johannes, *Gustav Klimt*, Salzburg 1967 (2nd revised edition 1975). English edition: *Gustav Klimt*, trans. by K. O. Philippsonn, New York 1968.

Olbrich, Joseph Maria, "Das Haus der Secession", in *Der Architekt. Wiener Monatshefte*

für Bauwesen und decorative Kunst, Vienna, vol. 5 (1899), January issue, p. 5.

Roessler, Arthur, "Erinnerungen an Egon Schiele", in *Das Egon Schiele Buch. Mit einem Beitrag von Arthur Roessler und einem Leitspruch von Gustinus Ambrosi*, ed. by Fritz Karpfen, Vienna 1921.

Roessler, Arthur, *Der Malkasten. Künstleranekdoten*, Vienna 1924.

Rychlik, Otmar, *Gustav Klimt, Franz Matsch und Ernst Klimt im Burgtheater. Mit einem Beitrag von Christoph Brenner*, Vienna 2007.

Rychlik, Otmar, "Neues Klimt-Buch unter Beschuss. Gastkommentar", in *Die Presse*, Vienna, 31 October 2007, feuilleton, p. 35.

Schnitzler, Arthur, *Komödie der Verführung*, Berlin 1924.

Schölermann, Wilhelm, "Neuere Wiener Architektur", in *Deutsche Kunst und Dekoration*, Stuttgart, vol. 3 (1898/99), pp. 197–216.

Schorske, Carl Emil, "Cultural Hothouse", in *New York Review of Books*, New York, vol. 11 (December 1975), p. 41.

Schorske, Carl Emil, *Wien. Geist und Gesellschaft im Fin de siècle*, Frankfurt am Main 1982.

Seifertová-Korecká, Hana, "Ein Frühwerk von Gustav Klimt – Der Theatervorhang in Reichenberg (Liberec)", in *Alte und moderne Kunst. Fachzeitschrift des Marktes für Antiquitäten, Bilder, Kunstgegenstände alter und moderner Kunst,*

Vienna, vol. 12 (1967), no. 94, pp. 23–28.

Sekler, Eduard F., *Josef Hoffmann. Das architektonische Werk. Monographie und Werkverzeichnis*, Salzburg/Vienna 1982.

Sternthal, Barbara, *Gustav Klimt 1862–1918. Mythos und Wahrheit*, Vienna 2006.

Strobl, Alice, "Zu den Fakultätsbildern von Gustav Klimt", in *Albertina Studien. Jahresschrift der Graphischen Sammlung Albertina*, Vienna, vol. 2 (1964), no. 4, pp. 138–169.

Strobl, Alice, catalogue raisonée of all Klimt's drawings, Salzburg 1980 ff. Vol. 1/1980, vol. 2/1982, vol. 3/1984, vol. 4/1989.

Strobl, Alice, "Klimts Fries für den Speisesaal des Palais Stoclet in Brussels", in Friedrich Kurrent/Alice Strobl, *Das Palais Stoclet in Brussels von Josef Hoffmann mit dem berühmten Fries von Gustav Klimt,* Salzburg 1991, pp. 65–90.

Tekhne, "L'Excursion des architectes belges du 22 septembre", in *Tekhne,* vol. 2 (1912), no. 79, pp. 801 f.

Tietze, Hans, "Gustav Klimts Persönlichkeit. Nach Mitteilungen seiner Freunde", in *Die Bildenden Künste. Wiener Monatshefte*, Vienna, vol. 2 (1919), no. 1–2, pp. 1–10.

Valéry, Paul, "Dance and the Soul", in *Dialogues*, trans. by W. M. Stewart, Princeton 1989 (French edition 1923), pp. 27–62.

Vergo, Peter, *Art in Vienna 1898–1918: Klimt, Kokoschka, Schiele and their contemporaries*, London 1993 (3rd revised edition).

Weidinger, Alfred, contributions to the catalogue of works, in: Weidinger 2007, pp. 232 *passim* (with corrections in the 2nd English ed., Weidinger 2008).

Weidinger, Alfred, "The Stoclet House is really very beautiful", in Weidinger, Alfred, *Gustav Klimt*, Munich/Berlin/London/New York 2007, pp. 119–136.

Weidinger, Alfred, "Symbolism in the landscape paintings", in Weidinger 2007, pp. 177–190.

Weixlgärtner, Arpad, "Gustav Klimt", in *Die graphischen Künste*, Baden, vol. 35 (1912), pp. 49–66.

Zuckerkandl, Berta, "Koloman Moser", in *Die Kunst,* 10 (1903/04), pp. 329–345.

Zuckerkandl, Berta, "Die XXIII. Ausstellung der Wiener Secession", in *Die Kunst für Alle*, Munich, vol. 20 (1905), no. 19, pp. 441–449.

Zuckerkandl, Berta, *Zeitkunst. Wien 1901–1907*, Vienna/Leipzig 1908.

Zuckerkandl, Berta, "Die Kunstschau II. Gustav Klimt", in *Wiener Allgemeine Zeitung. 6 Uhr-Blatt*, Vienna, 6 May 1909, pp. 2 f.

Zuckerkandl, Berta, "Kunst und Kultur. Der Klimt-Fries", in *Wiener Allgemeine Zeitung*, Vienna, 23 October 1911.

Sources, Chapter 1

BDA = Bundesdenkmalamt (Austrian Federal Office for the Care of Monuments), records relating to the Villa Hermes in the Lainz game park.

MAK-Archiv, Akt Zl. 1892–0582: Appointment of former pupil Franz Matsch as Professor of Painting.

MAK-Archiv, Akt Zl. 1893–0313: Appointment of Franz Matsch as Imperial and Royal Professor of Painting at the School of Applied Arts on 1 October 1893.

MAK-Archiv, Akt Zl. no. 1880–620: Four Baron von Halen-Linsberg scholarships are awarded to Franz Matsch, Gustav Klimt, Carl Füller and Emanuel Merinsky, students at the School of Applied Arts.

Restoration report by conservator Gustav Krämer, in BDA, Vienna I, Dr. Karl-Lueger-Ring 2, Burgtheater, Zl. 7268/78.

Index

Photo credits

© Peleş National Museum Sinaia, Romania. The Ministry of Culture and National Patrimony, Bucharest, Romania and Peleş National Museum-Sinaia, Romania/Luciano Romano, Naples: pp. 45, 46, 47

Photographer Luciano Romano, © Société Compagnie Immobilière SAS et consorts STOCLET, toute reproduction est interdite: pp. 188–198, 202–207, 209–223, 227–237, 239–241, 243–253

Réunion des Musées Nationaux, Paris. © RMN (Musée d'Orsay)/Thierry Le Mage: pp. 372, 428

Staatliche Galerie Moritzburg, Landeskundemuseum Sachsen-Anhalt, Halle an der Saale: p. 306

Technisches Museum Wien, Vienna: p. 13 left

© Verlag Galerie Welz, Salzburg: pp. 62/63, 138/39, 317, 347, 351, 357, 465, 466/67, 476/77

Wien Museum, Vienna: pp. 42/43, 267

Acknowledgements

The publisher would like to thank all the museums, libraries, private collections, archives and institutions named in the picture captions and the photo credits for their kind assistance in the publication of this book. A great many curators, collectors and art dealers, and likewise photographers and photo agencies, have played a vital role in ensuring the success of the project through their energetic and personal commitment. Our grateful thanks go to Raven Amiro (National Gallery of Canada, Ottawa), Angela Baillou (Christie's, Vienna), Hannah Bary (Galerie St. Etienne, New York), Christian Brandstätter, Hannah Darvin (Sotheby's Picture Library, London), Bernhard Deckenbach (Wien Museum, Vienna), Alexandru Duta (Muzeul National Peleş, Sinaia), Franz Eder (Verlag Galerie Welz, Salzburg), Holger Gehrmann (Artothek, Weilheim), Gabriele Göbl (Bayerische Staatsgemäldesammlungen, Munich), Yaffa Goldfinger (Mizne-Blumental Collection, Tel Aviv Museum of Art), Agnes Husslein-Arco (Belvedere, Vienna), Ilse Jung (Kunsthisthorisches Museum, Vienna), Jane Kallir (Galerie St. Etienne, New York), Ingrid Kastel (Grafische Sammlung Albertina, Vienna), Daniela Kumhala (Leopold Museum, Vienna), Katja Lehmann (Scala, Florence), Thomas Matyk (MAK, Vienna), Fabrice Mourlon Beernaert (Brussels), Christian Müller (Kunstmuseum Solothurn), Marco Obrist (Kunsthaus Zug), Janine Pereira Alves, Gerald Piffl (Imagno, Vienna), Marie Schuh (Wienerroither & Kohlbacher, Vienna), Renée Price (Neue Galerie, New York), Janis Staggs (Neue Galerie, New York), Christina Stehr (bpk, Berlin), Johannes Stoll (Belvedere, Vienna), Lilian Tone (Museum of Modern Art, New York), Steffen Wedepohl (Bridgeman, Berlin) and Beate Witt (Bridgeman, Berlin).

We would like to thank the lithographers Giuseppe Brisotto and Silverio Zanotto.

The magnificent photographs of Gustav Klimt's works in Peleş Castle in Sinaia, Romania, and in the Palais Stoclet in Brussels were taken for this book by Luciano Romano.

We owe a particular debt of thanks to the Stoclet family who, by granting us permission to commission brand new photography of the Stoclet frieze, enabled this book to present a comprehensive visual documentation and fresh scholarly evaluation of Gustav Klimt's Brussels masterpiece.

Imprint

EACH AND EVERY TASCHEN BOOK PLANTS A SEED!
Each year, we offset our annual carbon emissions with carbon credits at the Instituto Terra, a reforestation program in Minas Gerais, Brazil, founded by Lélia and Sebastião Salgado. To find out more about this ecological partnership, please check: www.taschen.com/institutoterra. **Inspiration: unlimited. Carbon footprint: (almost) zero.**

Want to see more? Visit taschen.com to view our current publications, browse our latest magazine, and subscribe to our newsletter.

© 2025 TASCHEN GmbH
Hohenzollernring 53, D–50672 Köln
www.taschen.com

Original edition:
© 2012 TASCHEN GmbH

Project management: Petra Lamers-Schütze
English translation: Karen Williams, Rennes-le-Château; Eva Dewes, Saarbrücken (chapter 2); Joan Clough, Penzance (chapter 6)

Printed in Bosnia-Herzegovina
ISBN 978-3-8365-6290-4

Cover
Detail of the 'Dancing Girl' ('Expectation'), 1909–1911
Mosaic frieze. Carrara marble, gold and silver mosaic, coloured mosaic pieces, ceramic, enamel, mother-of-pearl, paste gems, semi-precious stones, chased gilded and silvered sheet copper and brass, sheet brass, brass tubing, gold leaf
Long walls each 200 x 738 cm / 78 ¾ x 290 ½ in.
Brussels, Palais Stoclet, dining room

End papers
Detail of the right-hand mosaic wall, 1909–1911
Brussels, Palais Stoclet, dining room

Pages 1–7
Details of the right-hand mosaic wall, 1909–1911
Brussels, Palais Stoclet, dining room

The editor and author
Tobias G. Natter is an internationally acknowledged expert on the art in Vienna around 1900. For many years he worked at the Austrian Belvedere Gallery in Vienna, latterly as head curator. From 2011 to 2013 he was director of the Leopold Museum in Vienna. In 2014 he founded Natter Fine Arts. He is the author of TASCHEN's *Gustav Klimt. Complete Paintings, Art for All. The Colour Woodcut in Vienna around 1900,* and *Egon Schiele. The Complete Paintings 1909–1918.*

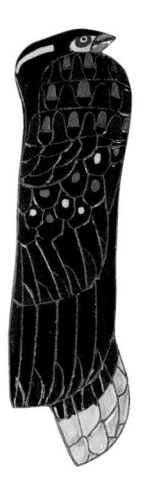